Preaching the New Lectionary:
The Word of God for the Church Today

Reginald H. Fuller

Preaching the New Lectionary:

The Word of God
for the Church Today

The Liturgical Press, Collegeville, Minnesota

International Standard Book Number: 0-8146-0847-7.

Reprinted from *Worship*, Volume 45, Number 2 (February 1971) through Volume 48, Number 2 (February 1974), and Number 8 (October 1974). Third Printing, 1975.

In Memoriam

Edward Leith Merrow
Priest, Counselor, and Friend   ✠ Easter Day 1974

Foreword

In order to make such a bulky book available at a not too exorbitant cost, it was decided to republish the commentaries exactly in the order and form in which they first appeared in *Worship*. The commentaries were begun in Lent 1971, when the Roman Communion was partway through series C, and continued until we had completed the full cycle at the end of the post-Epiphany *per annum* Sundays in 1974. This accounts for the rather odd order in which the material is presented. To rearrange it in the logical order — from Advent A through the Sundays *per annum* C — would have added considerably to the cost. It would also have disturbed a number of cross-references to earlier material.

Another apparent infelicity is that from Lent C through the *per annum* Sunday 2 A — that is, in the commentaries published in *Worship* 45/2 (February 1971) through 45/10 (December 1971) — practical suggestions for the homilist were somewhat desultory and mingled with the exegetical comment. As a result of requests from readers, however, it was decided thereafter to separate off and develop more systematically these practical suggestions. I concurred wholeheartedly with this request, because these practical suggestions correspond to an essential part of sermon preparation as technically understood: namely, what the Germans call *Predigt-meditation*. It is in these meditations that the shift is made from exegesis — which with Dean Krister Stendahl of Harvard I understand to be the method of discovering what the authors at the various levels of the tradition intended to say in their situation, or, in other words, the attempt to understand what the text *meant* — to answering the question: What does the text *mean* now, in our situation today? Simply to repeat what the text said can either reduce the living word of God to a dead record of the past or, if spoken into the contemporary situation, can result in making the text say the precise opposite of its original intention.

A word of warning. The suggestions to the homilist are just that, only suggestions. For the sermon meditation, the homilist needs to be familiar with the text on the one hand and the situation and needs of the congregation on the other. Consequently only he will have an inkling of what the text is saying to his particular church. The suggestions are no more than hints of what the text might mean, given a particular situation. Therefore in using the commentary the homilist will need to do his own sermon meditation, as well as compose the homily.

One further point. During any three-year period, a few Sundays will be replaced by special occasions, like Corpus Christi, for example, or the Transfiguration in the Roman lectionary, but will occur in later years. In "plugging the holes" left in the *Worship* articles over the past three years by such pretermissions, I have been guided by the following principles. Only those Sundays which occur in the Roman use during the whole decade 1970–1980 have been provided for. Sundays which will never occur in this decade in the Roman lectionary or Sundays which will occur only in the calendars of other churches have not been covered. I regret particularly the latter omission, but once our basic principle was abandoned, it would have led to enormous complications and would have increased even more the size of an already bulky book, to say nothing of the cost. Not infrequently (e.g., Christmas I and II) a particular reading occurring in the lectionary of another communion will be used elsewhere in the Roman lectionary, and comment upon it can be found in the appropriate place in this book by consulting the Biblical Index of the Readings. The Revised Standard Version of the Bible has been used throughout.

Writing these commentaries month by month has brought me many friends and letters of appreciation, and I hope that their republication in a more permanent form will continue to meet an obviously felt need.

Virginia Theological Seminary   *Reginald H. Fuller*
Eve of the Presentation of the Lord, 1974

Contents

PROPER OF THE SAINTS [A REFERENCE GUIDE]

APPENDIX OF MISSING SUNDAYS

Roman Table of Sundays and Holy Days: 1974–1980

Year[1]	Sunday Cycle	Baptism of the Lord	Sundays after Epiphany	Lent 1	Easter	Pentecost	Trinity Sunday	Corpus Christi	The Sunday of the Year after Corpus Christi Is Sunday ...	Advent 1
1974	C[2]	Jan. 13	7	Mar. 3	Apr. 14	June 2	June 9	June 16	12	Dec. 1
1975	A	Jan. 12	5	Feb. 16	Mar. 30	May 18	May 25	June 1	10	Nov. 30
1976	B	Jan. 11	8	Mar. 7	Apr. 18	June 6	June 13	June 20	13	Nov. 28
1977	C	Jan. 9	7	Feb. 27	Apr. 10	May 29	June 5	June 12	12	Nov. 27
1978	A	Jan. 15	4	Feb. 12	Mar. 26	May 14	May 21	May 28	9	Dec. 3
1979	B	Jan. 14	7	Mar. 4	Apr. 15	June 3	June 10	June 17	12	Dec. 2
1980	C	Jan. 13	6	Feb. 24	Apr. 6	May 25	June 1	June 8	11	Nov. 30

[1] The above Table of Sundays and Holy Days is an adaptation of the Roman calendar observed by Roman Catholics in the United States, who celebrate Epiphany and Corpus Christi on Sunday.

[2] Year C is the year whose number is evenly divisible by three.

Introduction

Reading the Bible in corporate worship is the most universal and probably the least contested of Christian liturgical customs. What is read is germinal to the themes which are amplified by other liturgical segments. Ideally, the readings also provide the preacher with his *raison d'être*. Since they form the verbal heart of the liturgy, selection of the readings is the crucial choice which determines many subsequent choices which liturgy planners must make.

The determination of such fundamental elements must not be left to whim or to the preferences of local planners. The purpose of a lectionary is to unfold the full sweep of God's revelation, not avoiding the hard words. If properly designed, a lectionary keeps the church from the ever-present danger of domesticating the Scriptures — muting the trumpet of their prophecy or dulling the edge of their judgment. The Scriptures are, of course, the church's book and they cannot be understood properly apart from the tradition and the worshiping community. But the church must continue to allow herself to be addressed by the Scriptures — by the whole design of God. The lectionary and the calendar together constitute the time-tested antidote for subjectivism in the liturgical reading of the Bible and the subsequent preaching of the word.

The *Ordo Lectionum Missae* (1969) was prepared in response to such statements in the Constitution *Sacrosanctum Concilium* of Vatican II as: "The treasures of the Bible are to be opened up more lavishly, so that richer fare may be provided for the faithful at the table of God's Word" (51), and "the ministry of preaching is to be fulfilled with exactitude and fidelity. The sermon, moreover, should draw its content mainly from scriptural and liturgical sources" (35), and in the Constitution *Dei verbum* on Divine Revelation: ". . . all the preaching of the Church must be nourished and ruled by sacred Scripture. For in the sacred books, the Father who is in heaven meets His children with great love and speaks with them" (21).

Adoption of a three-year cycle has made the new lectionary more comprehensive in its coverage of the biblical writings. It has also allowed for the inclusion of major books which the former lectionary had rather neglected, such as Mark. The provision of a complete set of readings from the Hebrew Scriptures maintains a proper balance between the testaments.

Preparation of the new lectionary provided an occasion for scripture scholars to work closely with liturgists so that the best achievements of intensive biblical scholarship in recent decades could make its proper contribution. Giving the synoptic evangelists their own integrity by assigning to each of them a year within the cycle is one obvious example. Less obvious are the scholarly principles according to which the reading from the Old Testament was coordinated with the gospel lesson. An early liturgical usage common to the churches of both East and West accounts for the reserving of Lent and Easter, in large measure, for the Fourth Gospel, which is also used to supplement the brevity of Mark.

Publication of this lectionary has had a far-reaching ecumenical impact, especially in North America. Both because of the sweep of its concept and the thoroughness of its scholarship, it commended itself to other churches. The Presbyterian *Worshipbook* (1970) and the *Services for Trial Use* (1971) of the Episcopal Church both contain lectionaries based upon it. *The Church Year — Calendar and Lectionary* (1973) of the Inter-Lutheran Commission on Worship follows a similar course. The United Church of Christ and the Christian Church (Disciples of Christ) have adopted the Presbyterian revision, and the Commission on Worship of the Consultation on Church Union prepared a revision to which the Methodist Church is committed.

In a few short years virtually all American and Canadian churches will be using lectionaries more notable for their similarities than for their differences. This common approach was achieved neither because of official pressure nor as the result of interconfessional dialogues, but simply because liturgical and scriptural leaders in the churches had become convinced of the value of such a sign. It is interesting to speculate on the impact of this consensus upon Christian unity. Already clergy of various backgrounds are gathering for common bible study in anticipation of the Sunday sermon. Study groups of lay persons could be organized along similar interchurch lines. Such ecumenical groups could provide a diversity of insight into the texts and create a beneficial climate of expectancy for the Liturgy of the Word the following Sunday.

If the new lectionaries are to achieve their full potential in parish use, however, the Sunday pericopes will require considerable study, especially on the part of preachers. Limitations upon available time and lack of exegetical expertise make aids for such study indispensable. The series of articles projected by the editors of *Worship*, beginning in 1971, was the first to meet this need. In Professor Reginald H. Fuller they had an author who not only has impeccable credentials as a biblical scholar but is sensitive to the spirit of worship and the needs of the people. His contributions have been pastoral as well as scholarly. His articles have been helpful not only to countless preachers, but even to those who undertook revisions of the Roman lectionary.

It is gratifying that the editors of *Worship* are republishing the Fuller articles. In this new format they will continue to be a useful tool for sermon preparation and bible study. Because of the ecumenical consensus in lectionary reform, this series on the Roman lectionary will be of assistance in many other churches as well. *Worship* has continually addressed itself to the ecumenical dimension of the liturgical enterprise. It may now enjoy some of the fruits of its labors through the expanded audience for this book.

Common use of the treasures of the Bible has long been cherished as a sign of fundamental unity across denominational boundaries. Formerly that commonality was insured through the use of the so-called historic pericopes. The appearance of the *Ordo Lectionum Missae* broke that common bond, but a new consensus has almost spontaneously arisen on its foundations. The churches were ripe for such a change.

I have always been thrilled by those marvelous lines from *Grosser Gott*, "And from morn to set of sun/Through the Church the song goes on." Similarly, it is thrilling to contemplate the sign of Christian unity as the churches of our Lord order their worship according to the same portions of Scripture and base their proclamation of God's Good News on the same blessed words. The thrill is intensified as one remembers the testimony of the Prophet: ". . . so shall my word be that goes forth from my mouth; it shall not return to me empty, but it shall accomplish that which I purpose, and prosper in the thing for which I sent it" (Isaiah 55:11).

Division for Parish Services   *Eugene L. Brand*
The Lutheran Church in America

Preparing the Homily

I. INTRODUCTORY CONSIDERATIONS

Since the Second Vatican Council, it has become increasingly accepted that the ministry of the word is an essential part of the liturgy. It is my understanding — and my observance of current practice bears this out — that in the Roman Catholic Communion a homily is expected at every celebration of the liturgy. The same is undoubtedly true, and probably always has been, among the Lutherans, though for them this would normally mean only on Sundays. I must confess to a sense of shame when I attend the holy communion in my own Anglican tradition and observe that Anglicans priests of all complexions, evangelical as well as high church, are content to celebrate the eucharist without preaching. They ought to have a strong sense of guilt at their dereliction of duty.

This requirement or at least this desirability that there should be proclamation of the word undoubtedly makes many demands upon the preacher, and very little help has been given in the procedure to be followed in the preparation of a homily. It was to meet this gap that, as an emergency measure, I undertook to write the commentaries which appeared in *Worship* over a space of three years and have been recently reissued in book form. In what follows I shall try to analyze the procedures which I followed. Here I must confess that I did not start out with any clear-cut methods or prior understanding. True, I had certain ideas about the function of the liturgical preaching, for I had written on the subject some fifteen years previously.[1] I had a general idea gathered

The Preface "Preparing the Homily" was published by Dr. Fuller in *Worship* (October 1974) 442–457.

[1 *What Is Liturgical Preaching?* (Studies in Ministry and Worship; London: SCM Press 1957). — Editor.]

from my German Lutheran contacts that there were basically three stages of sermon preparation, the third being the actual composition of the sermon.

First, it should begin with exegesis. Exegesis, as I understand it, poses the question: What did the text *mean* in its original situation? The disciples of Bultmann, following Karl Barth, insist that exegesis itself already poses the question: What does the text mean today? and that until one has heard it speak to the contemporary situation, one has not heard the text. But I agree with such different scholars as Dean Krister Stendahl [1a] and Bishop Stephen Neill [2] in assigning this concern to a later stage, to the stage of exposition. Users of the *Interpreter's Bible* will remember the two divisions, exegesis and exposition. I follow the arrangements of this commentary and distinguish between exegesis, which asks: What did the text mean? and exposition, which asks: What does it mean today?

If the homilist understands his own task in these terms, he will see that he is concerned with two poles, the word of God as it is attested in Scripture, and the concrete situation in which the congregation finds itself today. His task is to take what the Scripture said and make it say the same thing, but in such a way that it can address the congregation today.

The first part of the homilist's task is in theory always the same. What the Scripture *said* remains said in that situation for all time. What the Scripture *says* is in principle variable, because the new situation always slants, though it does not determine, what was once said. Here we stumble upon Bultmann's hermeneutical principle of the *Fragestellung*, the question we bring to the text. Our questions to some extent condition what Scripture says to us. Of course we should try to be as objective as possible in exegesis, recognizing that complete objectivity is never wholly possible. But at any rate we should not make a virtue of our lack of objectivity, as the Bultmannians seem to do.

The second part of the homilist's task is that for which he and he uniquely is properly equipped, an intimate knowledge of his people, of their concerns, their joys, sorrows, temptations and sins. His parish calls, his counseling sessions, his hearing of confessions should equip him for this. It is not here but in the preliminary work of exegesis that the pastor and homilist is likely to find his real difficulty. Exegesis demands certain

[1a] K. Stendahl s.v. "Exegesis" in *Interpreter's Dictionary of the Bible*.

[2] S. C. Neill, *The Interpretation of the New Testament* (London: Oxford University Press 1964) 87.

academically acquired skills, and he may well fight shy of this. My commentaries in *Worship* were designed to help particularly at this point. They were motivated by the conviction that I had developed in Germany when I studied at Tübingen in 1938–1939, that a true proclamation of the word of God depended upon a correct exegesis of the text. I will now try to lay bare some of the presuppositions of my method, and the procedures which in large part developed as I went along month by month producing my commentary.

II. EXEGESIS—SOME GENERAL CONSIDERATIONS

To do exegesis, every method of biblical criticism must be brought into play where appropriate. For the first task of exegesis is to reconstruct the situation for which the text was originally written. Especially important here is the question of the audience or addressee. As Professor Willi Marxsen has observed,[3] this is really more important than the question — so beloved of students who have just made their acquaintance with biblical criticism — of authorship. Yet authorship is also important, precisely in this connection. It makes a difference to the situation envisaged, whether one thinks, for example, that Colossians was written by Paul or by an unknown Paulinist in the subapostolic age.

Here it is important not to be afraid of critical positions. It is useful, for instance, to divide the Pauline letters between the homologoumena (those letters of which there is no reasonable doubt) and the antilegomena (those about whose Pauline authorship there are varying degrees of doubt). The antilegomena, if post-Pauline, are to be understood as witnesses to early Catholicism — that is, to the institutional consolidation of Christianity after the deaths of the original witnesses and the nonarrival of the parousia.

We need not of course dismiss early Catholicism as an aberration or degeneration, like Käsemann, who discovered or rediscovered its importance. We may regard it, as I do personally, as a natural, inevitable and justifiable development. But we cannot ignore it in our exegesis; otherwise we shall make the antilegomena more Pauline than they actually are. Texts which witness to the institutionalization of the Church in this way should not be harmonized with the genuine Paul or explained away but be allowed first to speak in their own right. But neither should their difference from the authentic Paul be so exaggerated that

[3] W. Marxsen, *Introduction to the New Testament*, tr. G. Buswell (Philadelphia: Fortress 1968) 10.

the texts concerned are dismissed as valueless for preaching. It has been said, for instance, that in Tübingen today the view is held that you cannot preach from a text in Acts because Acts is early Catholic and un-Pauline and therefore it is not gospel!

Turning to the gospels, the modern view, a view which has become widely accepted since the fifties, is that these documents consist of three strata. On the top level we have the theology of the evangelist, which is commonly known as the evangelist's redaction. Below this lies the tradition, the Jesus material as it was put constantly to use in the oral period between A.D. 30 and 65/70. Right at the bottom is the stratum of the authentic Jesus material, authentic sayings and parables spoken by him, authentic memories of his career from baptism to crucifixion. As has frequently been observed, Catholics especially should feel no discomfort at this modern understanding of the gospels as largely the product of the Church, for their high doctrine of the Church should help them to accept this view.

The arrangement of a three-year cycle of readings from Matthew, Mark-John and Luke successively has made the topmost level of the gospel tradition, the respective evangelist's redaction, particularly important to the homilist. I recently heard a parish priest complaining because the same incident came up more than once in three years in the different evangelists. He suggested therefore that the lectionary needed revision. But the fact of the duplication of a pericope directs the homilist to what is distinctive in that particular evangelist.

Above all, the homilist must avoid the temptation of harmonizing. A conspicuous instance of this occurred when the Marcan form of the temptation narrative was read for the first time on Lent 1. I heard a homilist start by saying that Mark had obviously abbreviated the story, and proceed to preach about the three temptations as recorded in Q (Matthew and Luke), which he treated on a purely historical level! He thus missed the challenge of facing up to the temptation as presented by the Marcan redaction. *Why*, if he knew the Q tradition, did Mark omit the three temptations? Where did his real interest lie? Those are the questions which the homilist should have asked.

A study of the lectionary shows that most of these duplications occur at the major feasts and holy days of the year. Not only the temptation story but particularly the passions are taken each year from a different gospel on Passion (Palm) Sunday. In his exegesis the homilist should concentrate upon what is distinctive in the particular evangelist's presentation.

It is clearly important to acquaint oneself with the methods and principles of redaction criticism. The redaction is discernible in such factors as the arrangement and order of individual pericopes in any given gospel, in touches which the evangelist has clearly added with his own hand. Where we possess the evangelist's source, this is relatively easy, for we need only compare the evangelist with that source. Thus if we accept the two document hypothesis (the priority of Mark and the common source of Matthew and Luke, commonly called Q), we can see where Matthew and Luke have altered Mark and where Matthew and Luke diverge in their presentation of the Q material. In the latter case, of course, it is more difficult to decide which of the two reproduces the original and which has made the alteration, but a knowledge of the stylistic peculiarities and theological interests of the two evangelists helps us to answer this question.

Where we do not possess the source of the evangelist's material — namely, in the case of Mark and in the case of the special material of Matthew and Luke, source criticism is of no use. Here only form and tradition criticism can help. Thus we can distinguish between the pure form of a pericope and the disturbance of this form by later comment or application. Even here we cannot be sure whether the accretion is due to the evangelist himself or had already taken place earlier in the tradition. But as we become more familiar with the style and concerns of any given evangelist, we learn to discern the sort of thing which that evangelist is likely to have added himself. The third type of material where we can pinpoint the evangelist's redaction is where he composes fresh material. A good example of this are the Marcan summaries, such as Mark 6:53-56.

This distinction between the three different levels of the tradition can be very helpful for the preacher, for it can give him three possibilities of treating a particular pericope. A good instance of this is the parable of the sower. At the Jesus level this consists of the pure parable itself (Mk 4:3-8). At a later stage in the tradition the Hellenistic missionary church added the allegorical interpretation (Mk 4:14-20). Finally, the evangelist Mark added from another tradition the passage on the interpretation of parables (Mk 4:10-13). The homilist will have to decide which of these three levels speaks most directly to the situation of his congregation, and treat the parable at that level. It would be a mistake to reject the later levels of the tradition as valueless because they do not go back to the historical Jesus. The later levels represent successive expositions of the Jesus tradition in a new situation. Tradition is a living and growing thing. In fact the homiletical use of a text is itself part of the history of its tradition.

Many of the Sunday pericopes consist of miracle stories. Here again there are, at least in principle, three levels of tradition. First, there is the miracle as it actually occurred in our Lord's ministry. Authentic sayings of Jesus show that for him exorcisms and healings were signs of the inbreaking of the eschatological reign or kingdom of God.[4] Next comes the shaping of these miracle stories in the post-Easter community. Usually this is in the interests of a particular Christology. Thus they may present Jesus as the eschatological prophet[5] or the divine man.[6]

A good example of this is the feeding of the multitude which occurs several times in the gospels and is read more than once in the three-year cycle. Personally, I do not doubt that Jesus celebrated an eschatological meal with his disciples in a tense atmosphere of crisis at the turning point of his ministry. But later, in the post-Easter community, this authentic memory was taken up and shaped by two different interests. The eschatological meal became a model for the Church's eucharistic meal, while the interest in Jesus as an eschatological prophet led to the development of an emphasis on the miraculous multiplication of the loaves, a greater feat than that of Elisha (2 Kgs 4:42-44).

Finally, there is the evangelist's redaction of the miracle tradition. Mark clearly wished to reduce the emphasis on the miraculous. The reason for this is that the Christians in his church were being tempted by false teachers (Mk 13:6, 22) to think of Jesus as a divine man, who dis-

[4] Mt 12:26 (Q) par.; Mt 11:4b-6 (Q) par. On the question of the historicity of Jesus' miracles, see R. H. Fuller, *Interpreting the Miracles* (London: SCM 1963) 18-45.

[5] See F. Hahn, *The Titles of Jesus in Christology* (London: Lutterworth 1969) 352-388; R. H. Fuller, *The Foundations of New Testament Christology* (London: Lutterworth 1965) 167-173; R. E. Brown, "Jesus and Elisha," *Perspective* 12 (1971) 85-104.

[6] H. D. Betz, "Jesus as Divine Man," *Jesus and the Historian*, ed. F. J. Trotter (E. C. Colwell Festschrift; Philadelphia: Westminster 1968) 114-133; J. M. Robinson and H. Koester, *Trajectories through Early Christianity* (Philadelphia: Fortress 1971) 216-219.

played his divine powers solely through his miracles. Mark did not altogether reject the picture of Jesus as a miracle worker, for he accepts and preserves a relatively large number of such stories. But he tones them down by the device of the messianic secret. Demons who confessed Jesus as the Son of God (apparently the title which the false teachers used in association with their Christology) were silenced. People who were healed were likewise silenced. And above all, the disciples were silenced after the transfiguration — until after the resurrection!

Mark's point seems to be that Jesus can only be rightly confessed as Son of God in the light of his crucifixion and resurrection. We must recognize that we are dealing not with history as such here, but with Mark's interpretation of history. The divine man Christology was allowed into the canon of Scripture only after it had received this Marcan correction. This would seem to forbid the homilist from exploiting the miracles of Jesus for their own sake. He can safely treat them only as prefigurations (in Austin Farrer's word) of the supreme messianic miracle, which is the death and resurrection of Jesus. Thus redaction criticism helps the homilist to use the miracle stories as a real proclamation of the gospel.

We see something similar happening in the great Johannine signs, which occur in the Lenten series of readings. Here the divine man tradition is corrected, but in a different way. The miracle stories are frequently used as a launching pad for typically Johannine dialogues and discourses. The best examples are the miracles of the feeding of the multitude, the blind man of Siloam and the raising of Lazarus in chapters 6, 9, and 11 respectively. The feeding of the multitude is explained in the ensuing discourse as a sign that Jesus is the bread which came down from heaven and gives life to the world. The healing of the blind man is a sign that he is the light of the world, and the raising of Lazarus a sign that he is the resurrection and the life. Here again the homilist would not want to treat the miracle stories as they are found in the pre-Johannine tradition, simply as signs that Jesus is a great wonder-worker, perhaps the greatest of wonder-workers. Rather, if the homilist is to preach the gospel, he will use the miracle stories as signs of what the Johannine discourse reveals Jesus to be.

The passion narratives, which are read in Holy Week, benefit the homilist greatly if critically treated. Quite early on, the form critics saw that these narratives differ from the rest of the gospel material in that they are more or less continuous, not a string of pericopes. Basic to them is genuine historical reminiscence of the end of Jesus: his arrest, the preliminary investigation before the Sanhedrin, the trial proper before Pilate which established that Jesus could without too much difficulty be disposed of as a messianic pretender, and finally his actual crucifixion and death. These bare facts, however, do not themselves contain the gospel. The gospel comes from the way these bare facts were interpreted by the post-Easter Church. We know from 1 Corinthians 15 that from the very early days the death of Jesus received a threefold interpretation.

First, it took place in *fulfillment of the Scriptures*. The cross was a scandal not only for the Jews but even for the believers themselves. They had to come to terms with it in their own minds, and the only way they could do so was to discover predictions of the passion in the Scriptures — what we now call the Old Testament. This led them first to those psalms which speak about the righteous sufferer and his vindication, notably Psalm 118:22, which speaks of the rejected stone which became the chief cornerstone. Then there were the great passion Psalms 22 and 69. Details from these psalms have undoubtedly colored the passion narratives, and it is always a moot point whether the facts led to the prophecies or the prophecies suggested the facts. Probably it was a bit of both. The basic facts of the passion (like Judas's betrayal of Jesus, Simon's denial and the disciples' forsaking of Jesus) were so scandalous that they drove the early Christians to the Scriptures, whereas peripheral details, like the casting of lots for Jesus' garments, could well have been added to fulfill the prophecy of Psalm 22.

Second, the early community asserted that Jesus had died *for our sins*. This atonement theology probably entered at a slightly later stage, perhaps after the community had hit upon Isaiah 53, and possibly in connection with its Passover celebration. Anyhow, it is clear that this motif has had little effect on the passion narrative itself, only upon the institution at the Lord's Supper, which was probably a separate pericope on its own (cf. 1 Cor 11:23-25).

The third motif was that Jesus died *as Messiah*. This is strongly attested by the title on the cross whose historicity is beyond all doubt, though in the intention of those who perpetrated it the title meant a political pretender. But this motif has colored the Marcan form of the trial scene before the Sanhedrin (note its absence from John), while the king motif is particularly stressed in the trial before Pilate.

Then comes each evangelist's own treatment of the passion. Mark was probably the first to combine the passion narrative with pericopes about the words and deeds of the earthly Jesus. This too was part of his attempt to tone down the divine man motif. Mark emphasizes the *theologia crucis* in his own distinctive way, which is different from that of Paul. Jesus is forsaken by all, finally even by God, for he dies with the words "My God, my God, why hast thou forsaken me?" on his lips. This must not be harmonized with the words from the cross in the other gospels.

Matthew basically followed Mark but played down Jesus' isolation, stressing the paradox of his royalty in the midst of humiliation, and the motif of Scripture fulfillment. Luke probably had an independent passion narrative which he has touched up with additions from Mark. It has been said that Luke transposed the passion story from the key of tragedy to the key of pathos. John, lastly, emphasizes the majesty of Jesus in his suffering. Jesus remains master of the situation throughout. The passion is the manifestation of his glory. He dies with the triumphant cry *tetelestai*, which the Revised Standard Version, following the King James Version, weakly rendered: "It is finished." The Vulgate was better: *consummatum est.*

In the Easter season the preacher has to handle among other things the resurrection narratives. We have to remember that the New Testament nowhere narrates the resurrection as such. The event in which God raised Jesus from the dead is shrouded in the mystery proper to an eschatological event, occurring at the precise point where observable history comes to an end. The two this-worldly events which *are* narrated are the discovery of the empty tomb and the appearances of the risen one to his disciples. Here the basic facts belong to the earliest tradition (1 Cor 15:3-8), but the *stories* of the empty tomb and apppearances are the product of later development. Surprisingly, it was the empty tomb pericope which first took shape (Mark 16:1-8). It was used as the vehicle for the Easter proclamation. This is uttered by an angel, *angelus interpres*, a frequent scriptural device: "He is not here, he is risen."

As 1 Corinthians 15:3-8 indicates, the appearances were first listed, not narrated. The appearance stories apparently had not yet taken shape by the time Mark was written, unless we are to suppose that episodes like the walking on the water and the transfiguration are postresurrection stories retrojected into the earthly ministry. The appearance stories as they are found in the later gospels are used as vehicles for the Church's post-Easter theology, which springs from its faith in the resurrection.

The Easter event is the foundation of the Church as the eschatological community and the inauguration of the Church's mission. The kerygma and the two sacraments of baptism and the eucharist are grounded importantly upon the Easter event, but even they have some roots in the historical Jesus. The apostolate is similarly grounded. The emphasis on the material reality of the Lord's risen body in Luke 24 and John 20, which is at variance with the more "spiritual" presentation of the earlier appearance story (Mt 28; Jn 21), guards against the interpretation of the encounters as purely subjective experiences rather than as revelatory disclosures of eschatological reality.

III. THE CHURCH YEAR

The context in which the homilist operates is that of the church year. This provides a kind of hermeneutical framework in which the liturgical use of Scripture is set. It is therefore important for the homilist to understand something of the rationale of the church year.

The church year is centered upon the reality of salvation history, focused in the Christ event. In the earliest Church there were two main celebrations: the Lord's Day or Sunday, and the period of the *Pentecostē*. The first weekly observance of the Lord's Day, was not so much a historical commemoration of the resurrection as the fulfillment of the sabbath, the proleptic participation in the rest that remaineth to the people of God (cf. Heb 4:9; Epistle of Barnabas 15.8). The second celebration was the *Pentecostē*, the annual period of fifty days which began with the (Christianized) Passover and concluded with the day of Pentecost.

It could be argued that we ought to have returned to this simple calendar with its exclusively eschatological emphasis. But for pedagogic and other reasons it was deemed advisable to retain the articulated church year as it developed in the main after the Age of Constantine. All the same, it is important that we should learn to understand the articulated church year in the light of the simpler eschatological scheme — an understanding as important for the preacher as for all participants in the liturgy. The articulated church year breaks down the total complex of the Christ event into its constitutive parts, yet does so not merely for historical commemoration but to expound a particular aspect of the total eschatological event. Each separate "mystery" — to use the language current in Roman Catholic theology — must always be seen as part of the total mystery of the Christ event.

xxvi

The church year starts at Advent 1, where the day's theme is the culmination of the future eschatology taken over from the end of the previous year. Thus one year dovetails into another. It is this prominence of future eschatology which has led in part to the dropping of the old pericope for the day—namely, the entry into Jerusalem, which however is still retained as an option by the Lutherans. Today's theme is not the first coming of Christ in humility, but his coming again in glory. It is only at Advent 2 that the thought of the first coming begins to take over in preparation for the celebration of Christ's birth. On Advent 2 and 3 the figure of John the Baptist moves into the center of the stage. This is significant. At first sight John the Baptist would seem to postdate the coming of Christ, if by that coming we have in mind his birth at Bethlehem. But the appearance of the Baptist at this point calls our attention to the fact that when we speak of the first coming of Christ, we are referring not merely to Bethlehem but to his first coming in its totality, which includes the whole ministry capped by death. It is for this total coming that John serves as the forerunner. On Advent 4 the Blessed Virgin Mary takes over the stage, thus serving as the immediate preparation for the birth of Christ.

But although Christ's first coming in humility is the primary focus during the second, third and fourth weeks of Advent, the theme of the second coming is not dropped altogether. For the two comings must always be considered together. The first is an anticipation of the second, and the second the completion and fulfillment of the first. Thus the theme of the second coming is carried through to Christmas itself, especially in the propers for the midnight mass. The word *Epiphania* is used in the Christmas lessons from Titus to signify *both* comings.

When they come to deal with the Incarnation itself, the Christmas propers are clear about the place of the nativity story in the mystery of Christ. The birth is emphatically only *Vorgeschichte*, a prelude to the Christ event proper, which really begins with the baptism of Jesus and continues through his crucifixion and subsequent vindication. In this prelude God is inserting into human history the one through whom his act of redemption will be wrought. This is the biblical way of looking at the birth stories. They are not concerned with the combination of humanity and divinity in a single person, as though humanity and divinity were abstract qualities. Thus the affirmation of the Johannine prologue, that the Word became flesh, is not merely an interpretation of Christmas but declares the inauguration of a history in which the Word will be dynamically enfleshed in the career of Jesus from Jordan to Calvary. For the flesh of Jesus, in Hoskyns' words, is his whole observable history, not abstract humanity.

Although the arrangements of the new Roman calendar at Epiphany have not gone so far in the right direction as they might have done,[7] the tendency of the reform is clearly to play down the story of the wise men and upgrade the baptism of Jesus, which was the original emphasis of this festival and which, though obscured in the West, has always remained preeminent in the East. It is in the baptism that the process of the revelation of God in the human history of Jesus properly begins; the baptism is therefore, rightly understood, the first of the epiphanies. The visit of the magi, like the rest of the infancy stories, is only a prefigurement of the revelatory event proper.

Even though the new Roman calendar has introduced the rather colorless designation of Sundays *per annum* for the period between Epiphany and Lent, the propers themselves, notably the gospels and the accompanying Old Testament readings, maintain the epiphany themes. In the stories of the early ministry Jesus is manifested as the Messiah in word and deed. In the Episcopal and Lutheran adaptations of the Roman calendar these epiphanies are fittingly climaxed on the last Sunday before Ash Wednesday in the reading of the transfiguration story — which the Roman lectionary, following its ancient but purely adventitious tradition, reads on the second Sunday of Lent.

In recent times Lent has come to be thought of almost exclusively as a season of personal penitence. (The Lutheran tradition has been an exception: as a glance at the Lutheran hymnals will show, even the earlier part of Lent was devoted to the passion.) It is not surprising that voices continue to be raised in favor of a shorter Lent. Of course there is a place for personal penitence, but to keep it up for forty days and forty nights tends to pall.

Wisely, the new calendar makes a shift in emphasis which people have not yet understood. Ash Wednesday becomes the great day of penitence in the Church, a sort of Christian *yôm kippur*. The readings of Lent 1-5 now focus upon the baptismal mystery — a theme which will be reinforced by the new rites of the catechumenate. Together, catechumens and faithful prepare to participate, or to renew their participation, in the

[7] The suppression of the Baptism of our Lord in some years in favor of the magi story is regrettable.

baptismal mystery at the paschal feast. Thus the emphasis of the readings is the new life to which the baptized are called and its ethical demands. Of course this still involves the note of penitence, but it is penitence placed in a proper evangelical perspective, rather than a pious work. The epistle readings are drawn largely from the Pauline exhortations, or parenesis, which is based on Hellenistic catechetical formulae, while the gospels in year A — which form the best series and are recommended for invariable use when the rites of the catechumenate are being celebrated — comprise the great Johannine signs, long viewed as symbols of the Christian experience of baptism.

Holy Week or Passion Week speaks for itself. On the Sunday the theme of the triumphal entry (except in the Presbyterian/United Church of Christ adaptation of the new calendar) is clearly relegated to the subordinate position it has always really had. The homily should be based upon the passion, and if it deals with the entry at all, then only as the curtain raiser to the passion.

The ancient unitary paschal feast has been split up into a group of three celebrations (Maundy Thursday, Good Friday and Easter vigil). Each of these three days has its own distinctive color expressed by the different way in which the eucharist is celebrated on it. Maundy Thursday, the thanksgiving for the institution of the Lord's Supper,[8] is a brief outburst of joy. When the service concludes with the stripping of the altar and the darkening of the church, the brevity of this outburst is dramatically emphasized. The Good Friday communion (whether it be from the reserved sacrament, as in the Roman and Episcopal provisions, or whether the eucharist itself is celebrated, as in the Lutheran tradition and in an increasing number of Anglican churches) is celebrated in the bare church in an atmosphere of extreme austerity. At the Easter vigil the great point about the eucharist is that it marks a transition — from darkness to light, sorrow to joy, bondage to freedom, death to life.

It is a pity that in modern parish life the fifty days of Easter count for so little compared with the forty days of Lent. The new rites of the catechumenate provide some hope that a more constructive use may be made of this period. It is a time when the Church should be conscious

---

[8] The Roman Catholic provisions call for the homilist to explain two further "mysteries," the institution of the priesthood and Christ's commandment of brotherly love. The late Dean Duncan Jones of Chichester used to call this day the Anglican Corpus Christi.

both of the presence of the risen Lord in its midst and of the presence of the newly baptized. The liturgical gospels reflect these two themes. We first read the appearance stories and later the farewell discourses of the Fourth Gospel. For the newly baptized are, with the rest of the faithful, now enjoying the foretaste of eternal life in the Spirit-filled community.

Ascension Day emphasizes one aspect of the Easter season. This season is the celebration not only of the victory of Christ over death but preeminently of his exaltation as Lord, or Kyrios, of the Church and the world. Ascension Day does not inaugurate a new period but is merely an incident in the fifty days. Finally, although Pentecost celebrates the gift of the Spirit, it too merely highlights a theme which to some extent is present throughout the great fifty days. Note for instance the repetition from Eastertide of John 20:19-23 as the gospel. The use of this reading on the day of Pentecost has caused some perplexity. Why read on Pentecost what happened on Easter Sunday? Such objections indicated a naive historical way of thinking. The gift of the Spirit is the outcome of the total Easter event. Probably the risen Lord conveyed his Spirit in every one of his appearances, and it was not confined to a single day in the way the Lukan schematization suggests.

If Pentecost marks a single event at all, that event is the inauguration of the kerygma. And in the church year it also marks the conclusion of the Easter season. The post-Pentecost season begins at once, and the Pentecost observance is, very rightly, no longer extended into an octave, which unduly prolonged the fifty days and obscured their unique significance.

The post-Pentecost season is bounded at each end by a solemnity, the feast of the Trinity at one end and the feast of Christ the King at the other.[9] In the post-Pentecost season the systematic reading of Scripture, begun in the post-Epiphany season, is resumed. After the excitement of Christmas-Epiphany and Lent-Holy Week-Easter it is sound to relax somewhat. Now Scripture is read in course and the reading of it is less colored by the season of the year. Here is the chance for broad themes of theology and ethics to be broached. It is important, however, to note that

[9] The Lutheran provisions call particular attention to the two boundaries of the post-Pentecost season by prescribing white as the liturgical color for each occasion. They do the same thing for the two Sundays which on their reckoning (as in the Episcopal provisions) bound the Epiphany season — that is, the Baptism of the Lord and the Transfiguration.

at the tail end of the Sundays of the year, or post-Pentecost period, a futurist-eschatological note comes in.[10] So we end where we began — with the theology of Christian hope.

IV. FROM EXEGESIS TO PREACHING

In the first section of this article we offered some general considerations about exegesis, laying considerable stress on the value for the preacher or homilist of the critical approach to the Bible. We will now briefly summarize the main steps in exegesis and then consider how one might move from exegesis to sermon composition.

Ideally, exegesis should start with a translation of the passage from the Greek (or Hebrew, in the case of the Old Testament). Very few, however, will be able to attempt this. So we must be realistic and suggest that where this is not possible, the best alternative would be to compare at least two different modern translations.[11] Any marked variations will call attention to a disputed point of exegesis and drive the homilist to commentaries for closer investigation. In the light of his findings, he must weigh the pros and cons and decide which interpretation to accept.

He should then look in the margins of the various versions to see if there are any disputed readings (text criticism). These too can be checked in commentaries, so that a decision is reached as to which text to accept.

Thirdly, the homilist should turn to points of literary criticism. What is the literary *genre* of this pericope (e.g., miracle story, parable, sayings collection)? Having ascertained this, let him look for signs of redaction which are visible; for example, through the disturbance of the original genre by additional material or through changes made in a known source. What light is thrown on the evangelist's understanding of the pericope by the place in which he locates it? In other words, the homilist must study the context of the pericope. Introductory questions are also rele-

---

[10] It is much to be desired that the last *per annum* or post-Pentecost Sundays should always feature the theme of future eschatology, regardless of how many Sundays there are to this season in any given year. In effect, this would mean prescribing a Third-Last, Second-Last and Last Sunday before Advent, as the American Book of Common Prayer office lectionary and the German Lutherans do.

[11] The English Revised Version and the American Standard Version still enjoy the advantage of being the most literal translations and therefore particularly helpful to those who have little or no Greek or Hebrew. Of the most recent translations, the Revised Standard Version is the most literal, but it occasionally substitutes a completely different idiom for the original and makes it more difficult for the student or homilist to appreciate the force of the Hebrew or Greek text.

vant here (date, authorship, addressees), for they determine the situation to which the text was addressed.

Fourth, look out for any significant theological words in the pericope and make a study of these words with the help of a concordance or theological dictionary. Be careful to look at the context of other passages; don't simply look at the word in isolation.[12]

Fifth and last, in the light of all the information thus gathered, let the homilist try to write out his own paraphrase of the passage, stating in his own words what the biblical writer was saying to those he addressed.

The next stage forms a bridge between the exegesis and the sermon. It is what the Germans call the *Predigtmeditation* or sermon meditation. The preacher has to concern himself with two poles — the original message of the pericope, as distilled from the exegesis, and the current situation of his audience or congregation as he envisages it when they are gathered for the liturgy. Here he will have to draw upon his knowledge of their concerns, as disclosed through parish calling, counseling and the confessional as mentioned above, or through the media or current literature. (I am writing these words in England on the morning after the shattering news of President Nixon's resignation. On such an occasion the homilist will want to bring the word of God to bear upon the situation: indeed it is one of the rare occasions when the homilist may feel obliged to depart from the liturgical text.) Then he must decide how the text speaks in judgment and memory, in wrath and grace to this situation. He must ask: What is the law and what is the gospel contained in the text? Finally, he should envisage the result he looks for from his hearers: repentance, renewed faith, some act of devotion or some concrete act of obedience.

These are the considerations I had in view and which I developed as I wrote my commentaries on the new readings, and it is my hope that these observations may be of help to the homilist and preacher as he continues the responsible task of declaring the word of God to the people of God.

[12] See J. Barr's provocative critique of the Kittel *Wörterbuch* method in his *Semantics of Biblical Language* (Oxford University Press 1961).

Reginald H. Fuller

Preaching the New Lectionary:
The Word of God for the Church Today

Lent of Year C ✓

In the course of centuries, Lent, like other seasons of the church year, had accumulated a good deal of debris, for example, scripture readings associated with concerns which were local to the city of Rome or are now obsolete: the preparation (both by public discipline, instruction and exorcism) of catechumens for the Easter baptisms, the papal station Masses and the restoration of penitents. In the new lectionary much of this is swept away, and in place of it there is now a series of readings which form a direct preparation of the faithful for the paschal feast. The Old Testament readings expound the Old Testament salvation history (particularly the exodus) as a type or foreshadowing of the redemptive act of God in Christ. The epistle lessons propound the believers' participation in the death and resurrection of Jesus in baptism and in the Christian life; while the gospels narrate incidents from our Lord's earthly ministry which in one way or another foreshadow and prepare for his death and resurrection, and thus prepare us to celebrate our redemption at Easter.

FIRST SUNDAY OF LENT[1] ✓

Reading I: Deuteronomy 26:4-10.
For many Christians this passage is associated with the Harvest Festival or Thanksgiving Day rather than with the beginning of Lent. Read at this time, however, it emphasizes not so much the harvest offering, but the confession of faith which accompanies it (vv.5-9). Contemporary scholars regard this confession as one of the oldest fragments of the Bible and as basic to the Old Testament as the pre-Pauline "kerygma" (or the summary of the Christian message) in 1 Cor 15:3-8 is to the New Testament. What the death and resurrection are to the New Testament, that the exodus is to the Old. Each message, that of the Old Testament and

[1] Further comments on Lent of year C will be found in the final chapter.

that of the New Testament, when heard and believed, issues in a "confession," a confessional recital. This is what liturgy is all about. It is the church's act of confessing its faith. The confession of its faith in the context of praise is one of the basic activities of the church.

Responsorial Psalm 91:1-2,10-11,14-15.

Psalm 91 is traditional to Lent I (hence the old Latin name for this Sunday, *Invocavit*). It is, of course, the psalm quoted by the devil to Jesus in what for Luke is the third temptation. In the story the devil had misapplied the promise of angelic assistance (Lk 4:10). Verses 14-15 put that promise into proper focus: only those who cleave to God in love will be delivered, and therefore Christ, who set his love upon the Father, as the Fourth Gospel repeatedly emphasizes, was delivered not from the cross but out of the cross into the resurrection.

Reading II: Romans 10:8-13.

Note how the theme of confession is taken up again in the second reading. Here we have the central New Testament message: Jesus (i.e., the earthly One who was crucified) is the heavenly Lord, for God raised him from the dead. This is the basic Christian profession of faith. This was the subject matter for the catechumens' instruction, and the profession of faith which he made at his baptism. Out of this simple but profound confession grew the church's baptismal and conciliar creeds. And, too, this confession forms the stuff of the great eucharistic prayer or canon of the Mass. Note how the phrase "confession with the lips," applied here to the baptismal confession, is taken up again in connection with the church's liturgical prayer in Heb 13:15. The unity of the church amid the pluralism of its members ("Jews and Greek"), the unity of the New Testament amid the variety of its idioms, the unity of the liturgy despite the alternative eucharistic prayers (a little hard for those who have set such store by unvariable uniformity), lies in this common, basic confession: Jesus is Lord, and God has raised him from the dead.

Gospel: Luke 4:1-13.

This is Luke's version of the temptation, replacing this year the familiar form from Matthew, which was traditionally used on this day. The combination of this story with the Old Testament lesson and the epistle lights up a new aspect of this well-known story. Jesus, thrice tempted by the devil, makes a threefold *confession*:

"Man shall not live by bread alone."
"You shall worship the Lord your God,
  and him only shall you serve."
"You shall not put the Lord your God to the test." [2]

This threefold confession, in which Jesus stands his ground against the devil, plots the future course of his ministry, which will culminate in the confession which he made before Pontius Pilate (I Tm 6:13). It was this confession, this single-minded concentration on the will of God for him, which characterized his whole ministry and which finally brought him to the cross.

SECOND SUNDAY OF LENT ✓

Reading I: Genesis 15:5-12,17-18.

Three themes are combined in this Old Testament reading: the promise to Abraham of abundant posterity, the promise of the land to Israel, and the sealing of this promise with a covenant ceremony. Genesis contains several such encounters between God and Abraham, all of them variant traditions of the same basic fact that God intervened in history to choose a people unto himself. On one side, this choice is a pure act of grace on God's part, and on the other, a sheer act of faith on Abraham's (*sola gratia, sola fide!*). But note: this grace-faith drama is set in the context not of individual salvation, but of an entire salvation *history*, and of the people of God in history. St. Paul saw the fulfillment of this promise to Abraham in the Christ event and in the Christian ecclesia (Gal 3, Rom 4). The Pauline doctrine of grace and faith must also be set not in an individual context but in the context of a salvation history and of a community.

Responsorial Psalm 27:1,7-9c,13-14.

The relation between Old Testament lesson and epistle is only of the most general kind, but a connection appears to be made by the responsorial psalm: "I believe that I shall see the goodness of the Lord in the land of the living." For Abraham, the "land of the living" was Israel, into which his descendants would enter. For the Christian believers, the land of the living in which they believe they will see the goodness of the Lord is the

[2] The translation of this member is here revised in conformity with the version of the Lord's Prayer proposed by the International Consultation on English Texts. See *Prayers We Have In Common,* a publication of the ICET (Philadelphia: Fortress Press 1970) pp. 5–8.

"commonwealth in heaven" of which the epistle speaks. (In the Book of Common Prayer, Psalm 27 is, significantly, one of the psalms provided in the office for the burial of the dead.)

Reading II: Philippians 3:17 — 4:1.

The epistle's relation to the gospel is more obvious. Both passages speak of a "change": the epistle, of the change of earthly, human existence which is promised in the final consummation; and the gospel, of the change which Jesus experienced as he prayed with the disciples on the holy mountain. The term "glorious body," like Paul's term "spiritual body" (1 Cor 15) rests on the Jewish apocalyptic hope that the life of the age to come will not be a mere prolongation of this earthly existence, but an entirely transformed, new mode of existence. Into this existence Christ entered as the first fruits at his resurrection, thus opening for his believers the possibility and hope that they, too, will at the final consummation enter into the same transformed mode of existence.

Gospel: Luke 9:28-36.

When we interpret any pericope from the gospels we may read it at three different levels: at the level of what actually happened (called by New Testament scholars the "Jesus tradition"); the shaping of the story in the oral tradition of the Christian communities; and lastly, the use to which the evangelists put the story in their written gospels. It is the task of the preacher to attempt a fourth level of understanding, to ask what the text means here and now, as it is read in the liturgical assembly.

That Jesus and some of his disciples went up the holy mount after he broke off his ministry in Galilee, and that there a change of plan — a journey to Jerusalem and something of the meaning of that journey — was communicated we need not doubt. The original meaning of the incident was that it inaugurated the final stage of the ministry.

But the story has been written up by the later community in the light of its Easter faith. That events in Jesus' life were not properly understood until after his resurrection is indicated by Jn 2:22; 12:16. The change in the appearance of Jesus' face reminds us of what happened to Moses when he went up to Mount Sinai (Ex 34:29). Moses and Elijah, the two Old Testament prophets who in the first century A.D. figured prominently in Jewish expectations of the End, talk with Jesus about his departure (the Greek word is "exodus"); the departure referred to is Christ's death, resurrection and ascension. His companions can accept the idea that Jesus is on a par with Moses and Elijah as figures of the End-time. But a voice proclaims the sole finality of Jesus: "This is my Son; listen to *him* (the last phrase echoes Moses' prediction of the prophet of the End-time in Dt 18:15). Afterwards we are told simply, "Jesus was found alone." This story is rich in symbolism, proclaiming Jesus as the Son of God and as the second Moses who accomplished the new exodus.

Since Luke lays so much stress on Jerusalem as the center toward which the ministry of Jesus moves, as the place where the mighty, saving act of man's redemption is accomplished, and as the center from which the gospel goes forth to the ends of the earth, we can be fairly certain that it was he who added the words "at Jerusalem." The gospel is not a timeless myth (cf. 2 Pt. 1:16!), but something that happened at a particular time and place in history.

The preacher can relate his own application to any of these three levels. If he takes the "Jesus level" he will concentrate on the church's preparation to follow her Lord on the last stage of his ministry. If he follows the line of the oral tradition, he will expound the redemption as the second exodus and Jesus as the second Moses. If he takes Luke's own level he may develop the centrality of Jerusalem in salvation history.

THIRD SUNDAY OF LENT ✓

Reading I: Exodus 3:1-8a,13-15.

A single thread runs through the three lections for today. This thread is indicated by the name which God reveals to Moses: I AM WHO I AM, or, as some of the best contemporary scholars interpret it, "He causes to be what comes into existence." God is the God of Abraham, Isaac and Jacob, which Pascal contrasted with the God of the philosophers. The biblical God is not abstract, impersonal reality, but the God who forcefully intervenes in history, calling Moses and sending him to bring the sons of Israel out of Egypt, leading them through the wilderness (Reading II), refreshing them with the water from the Rock and giving them the promised land. Then, finally, this biblical God sends his Son, giving his people one last chance to repent and accept his salvation (the gospel).

As on previous Sundays, we read about the exodus story as a type of redemption in Christ. God sees the affliction of his people, the whole of humanity, and "comes down" to deliver them from the slavery of sin and to bring them into the "land flowing with milk and honey," the kingdom of God. (We are here reminded of the symbolism of the baptismal ceremonies.)

Responsorial Psalm 103:1-4,6-8,11.

So in the responsorial psalm we praise the God of the Bible for showing his ways to Moses and his works to the people of Israel, for redeeming our life from the pit, and crowning us with steadfast mercy and love. A psalm sung by Israel about the exodus becomes a hymn of the Christian community about the death and resurrection of Christ.

Reading II: 1 Corinthians 10:1-6,10-12.

There are two curious features about Paul's treatment of the exodus story. First the Rock is said to follow the Israelites in the wilderness. Paul here takes up a rabbinic legend according to which the Rock which Moses smote in the wilderness to supply water for the Israelites accompanied them (an inference from the fact that it is mentioned more than once in the exodus story), and boldly identifies this Rock with Christ. Probably the basis for this is the equation of Christ with the "wisdom" of God, which according to the wisdom literature was the personified agent not only of creation but of all God's acts in salvation history. "Christ" here means: God going out of himself as he is in himself, in his actions in creation and in salvation history. For Paul, as for the New Testament generally, the going out of himself on God's part culminates in his redemptive act in the history of Jesus of Nazareth. Here is the salvation-historical basis of the doctrine of the Trinity. Note also that the food (the manna) and drink of the wilderness are portrayed as types of the Christian sacraments of baptism and eucharist. Sacraments are quite literally a "viaticum" — a nourishment of the pilgrim people of God on its way from Pentecost to the Second Coming.

Gospel: Luke 13:1-9.

Jesus refers here to two disastrous events which must have been recently in the news (though they are not otherwise known to historians), one the outrage of a tyrant, the other apparently an accident to construction workers. He draws from these disasters a warning for Israel: unless you repent (i.e., reorient your attitude to my message), you will likewise perish. The parable of the fig tree reinforces this challenge to repentance. This links the gospel with the warning in the second part of the epistle: "Let anyone who thinks he stands take heed lest he fall." Neither the old Israel nor the new dare presume upon a false sense of security. Such is the challenge of Lent: it is directed not merely to devout individuals but to the church as an established institution.

The traditional association of this Sunday with an outburst of joy in the midst of Lenten austerity, indicated by the old names Laetare or Refreshment Sunday, still characterizes the new readings and gives them their common theme: the joy when the Israelites ate the passover for the first time in the promised land, the joy of realizing that the Christians are a new creation, and the merriment over the prodigal's return. The *Responsorial Psalm 34:1-6* likewise invites us to joy as we taste the goodness of the Lord.

Reading I: Joshua 5:9a,10-12.

In last Sunday's epistle the manna was interpreted as a type of eucharistic food, the bread of the pilgrims. In today's Old Testament reading the manna of the wilderness ceases — because it finds fulfillment in the unleavened cakes and parched bread of the passover rite as the produce of the promised land. So too, the eucharist finds its fulfillment in the messianic banquet of the kingdom of God. May we also draw a parallel between the Lenten eucharists and the manna, and between the Easter eucharist and the pascha? The early Christians really believed that Christ would return at pascha, and when he did not come they celebrated the eucharist instead — so the Easter eucharist had a closer relation to the messianic banquet than any other eucharist of the church year.

Reading II: 2 Corinthians 5:17-21.

It is remarkable that Paul appeals to the very people he addresses as a new creation to be reconciled to Christ. For being a new creation is not an assured possession, it has to be renewed constantly. That renewal is the purpose of Lent, and to make this an ever available possibility is one of the important tasks of the apostolic ministry. It is a ministry of "reconciliation." God's act of salvation in Christ and the ongoing work of the apostolic ministry are not to be separated. The second is a continuation of the first, all part of the same salvation history. This salvation history is inaugurated in the event in which "for our sake he made him to be sin who knew no sin." What does this bold assertion mean? It can best be understood from the word at the cross, "My God, my God, why hast thou forsaken me?" Here the Christ enters into the direst consequences of man's sin — his alienation from God — in order that we who are sinners and therefore alienated from God might become the "righteousness" of God, i.e., reconciled to him. He crosses over to where we are to bring us to where he is. The Greek fathers were saying the same thing in their own terms when they asserted that Christ partook of our human nature in order that we might become partakers of his divine nature.

Gospel: Luke 15:1-3,11-32.

It is remarkable how the foregoing epistle provides the right context for interpreting the parable of the prodigal son. This parable is often understood as a simple illustration of God's forgiveness, without any need for Christ's atoning death on the cross: "There is no place for Jesus in the parable of the prodigal son." But the first thing to notice is that Jesus is not giving general teaching, but commenting on a very concrete situation: the Pharisees were grumbling because he was eating with the outcast (vv. 1-3: it is important that this setting is included in the gospel reading). In other words, the parable is precisely a comment on *Jesus'* action: he is not left out of the parable because the parable presupposes and interprets his action. When Jesus eats with the outcast this is not just humanitarian broad-mindedness, or a cavalier disregard for the religious laws; it is *God* breaking through his own laws in order to reach out and save those who have broken them. Already, in his ministry, he who knew no sin is "made to be sin": he takes his place alongside of sinners in the place where they are, in order that they might become the righteousness of God. The parable shows exceedingly clearly that our Lord's ministry was of a piece with his death on the cross. Our difficulties about the doctrine of atonement today are largely due to our separation of the cross from his whole life.

FIFTH SUNDAY OF LENT

In the old calendar Lent V marked the beginning of Passiontide. But in the new arrangement the Passion season begins on Palm Sunday, which is now called Passion Sunday. So Lent V continues the themes of the earlier Lenten season. At first sight, especially in Reading I and in the Responsorial Psalm, there is a surprising note of joy and refreshment, more suggestive of Lent IV. But our understanding of today's readings will be put in a proper context if we recall the ancient meaning of Lent — the preparation for the Christian pasch, the celebration of the death and resurrection of the Messiah. The refreshment and the joy are held out to the ecclesia as a promise for the Christian pascha, to those who have first participated in the passion and dying of the Savior. Only those who share his sufferings can know the power of his resurrection (Reading II).

Reading I: Isaiah 43:16-21.
In the second part of Isaiah the impending return from Babylon is depicted as a new exodus. "The former things" and "the things of old" refer to the first exodus. This is now replaced by a "new thing," the return from exile, in which the miracles of the first exodus are repeated. In Christian biblical theology the redemption wrought by Christ picks up the same imagery. The "new things" now become the death and resurrection of the Messiah and the "drink," the sacraments of the new covenant.

Responsorial Psalm 126.
The final stanza shows that we are entitled to refer the restoration celebrated in the first and third stanzas, the "great things" of the second stanza, and the joy which permeates the whole poem to the Easter event, the death and resurrection of the Messiah:

> "He that goes forth weeping,
>   bearing his seed for sowing,
>   shall come home with shouts of joy,
>   bringing his sheaves with him."

"The metaphor of sowing in the Old Testament almost demanded a Messianic application" (E. C. Hoskyns).

Reading II: Philippians 3:8-14.
Chapter 3 of Philippians is a polemic against Paul's opponents. Whether they were Judaizers (i.e., advocates of imposing the Jewish law on Gentile Christians) or some kind of syncretists or "enthusiasts" is uncertain, though at present scholarly opinion is moving in favor of the latter. Enthusiasts would suppose that through their baptism into Christ they had already attained and were already perfect. Against their position Paul opposes his theology of the cross, not simply as an abstract doctrine but as a reality to which his whole apostolic life is conformed. Only by becoming like Christ in his death, only by sharing his suffering and living under the "not yet!" ("*not* that I have *already* obtained"), can the apostle know the power of Christ's resurrection now, and eventually attain to the resurrection himself when Christ comes again. Thus the Lenten liturgy seeks to mold Christian existence to conformity with the cross.

Gospel: John 8:1-11.

The *pericope de adultera* is now agreed by most scholars to be not part of the original text of John, though of course it is part of the canonical text. The earliest MSS. either omit it or place it elsewhere. Nevertheless, despite its late attestation, it is almost certainly a very early and good tradition. The Scandinavian New Testament scholar H. Riesenfeld has given an interesting explanation why this story "went underground," as it were, for so long. This happened during the period when the church was struggling to maintain a strict discipline over its members. The story of the woman taken in adultery seemed to encourage laxity in marriage standards. But this is not actually so; after all, Jesus does say to the woman: "Go, and do not sin again." He recognizes sin as sin, and in saying "neither do I condemn you" he does not condone the sin, but pronounces the forgiveness of God. It is true, however, that the scribes and Pharisees come in for sharper condemnation, and are put to shame. For none of them could claim to be without sin. It is a pictorial illustration of the saying, "Judge not, that you may not be judged" (Mt 7:1). This does not, of course, rule out official acts of the judiciary, only personal acts of judgment. As Dorothy Sayers observed, the deadliest of the seven deadly sins is not sexual sin but the sin of pride: the scribes and Pharisees walked away and never heard Jesus say, "Neither do I condemn you."

Holy Week of Year C ✓

The origins of this most solemn season in the church year are generally known. The early church followed Jewish practice and observed a single festival of redemption (the Christian pasch, preceded by a fast of twenty-four or forty hours). The purpose was not historical commemoration but "eschatological celebration." The redemptive event was a unitary feast, embracing the passion, death, resurrection, exaltation of the Messiah, the outpouring of the Spirit and the anticipation of his coming again.

In the post-Constantinian era two things happened: the unitary feast was broken up into its constituent parts, thus producing Good Friday, Easter Day, Ascension Day, Pentecost [1] (the theme of the second coming being meanwhile absorbed by Advent); while under the influence of local historical commemorations at Jerusalem such subsidiary occasions as the Palm Sunday entry and the institution of the Lord's Supper acquired days of their own.

But along with the development there was also a somewhat older interpretation of the Sunday before Easter, namely, as an anticipation of Good Friday. This earlier association has always been retained in the West with the reading of the Matthew passion on this Sunday. But the new name (Passion Sunday) brings this aspect of the day once more into prominence, and the relegation of the traditional name Palm Sunday to a subordinate position puts that aspect into its proper focus. In the liturgy the entry figures (as indeed has always really been the case) only as a preliminary devotion.[2]

[1] As a commemoration of the gift of the Spirit, rather than as the conclusion of the fifty days.

[2] Outside the Roman obedience the triumphal entry did succeed in gaining some foothold in the liturgy itself. Various Lutheran rites either make it the gospel for

Gospel for the Procession with Palms: Luke 19:28-40.

In view of the subsidiary character of this part of the service the homilist would be advised, if he deals with the entry at all, to relate it closely to the passion. Our Lord entered Jerusalem to go to his passion. This is how it turned out. Historically speaking, his motive was probably to lay down (with full knowledge that it would almost certainly cost his life) the final challenge to his people to accept the message and coming of the kingdom of God. They refused, rejected his message and brought him to the cross. As John's Gospel reminds us (12:16), the true meaning of the entry did not dawn upon his disciples until after Easter. Then they came to see that the entry was paradoxically the procession of a king to his coronation (his crown would be of thorns and his throne a cross). Like Mark (contrast Matthew and John), Luke does not recall the prophecy of Zechariah ("Tell the daughter of Zion"), but Luke's readers who know their Greek Old Testaments are surely meant to recall that prophecy as they hear of Jesus riding on the "colt." A peculiarity of Luke's version is his translation of Hosannah: "Peace in heaven and glory in the highest." This not only explains the Hebrew word for his Greek readers; it also deliberately recalls the songs of the angels at the nativity. "Peace" and "glory" were there proclaimed as a future promise that would become a reality only through the cross. Christmas cannot be detached from Good Friday and Easter except at the cost of trivializing and sentimentalizing it.

In the Mass for Passion Sunday, as well as in those for the Easter Triduum, the readings are the same in all three series, excepting the gospels for Passion Sunday and the Easter Vigil, which this year are from series c.

Reading I: Isaiah 50:4-7.

This is the third servant song of deutero-Isaiah. The situation presupposed is that Israel in exile is rejecting the prophet's message. The people are "weary" (of his constant predictions of deliverance despite the continuation of the exile?). But the prophet is undeterred: God has given

the day or allow it as an alternative. In the Church of England 1928 Book of Common Prayer it was allowed when there was more than one celebration. Pressures were brought to bear on the Liturgical Commission of the Episcopal Church to allow the entry as an alternative to the passion but were successfully resisted in the recent Prayer Book Studies No. 19, *The Church Year* (1970).

him the word and he must deliver it, even at the cost of personal suffering. And he is confident that God will eventually prove him right. In
exactly the same way, Jesus' passion was the outcome of his obedient
delivery of the message of the kingdom in face of his people's rejection,
and his constant reliance that God would prove him right. The passion
and death of Christ are not isolated events, but of a piece with his whole
ministry. The early church was right in seeing that the servant songs
came to rest in the passion and death of its Lord.

Responsorial Psalm: 22:7-8, 16-17a, 18-19, 22-23ab.
Psalm 22 is the passion psalm *par excellence.* It was probably the first Old
Testament passage to be adopted in the "passion apologetic" (B. Linders)
of the early community. After Easter the early Christians had to reconcile (both for their own faith and for their hoped-for converts from
Judaism) their conviction that Jesus was indeed the expected deliverer
with the scandalous events of his passion. They found their earliest answer
in Psalm 22. This psalm can serve thus because it describes the sufferings
of the righteous in language which astoundingly anticipates the events of
the passion, not so much through mechanical prediction as through the
psalmist's profound insight into the nature of innocent suffering. But
more, it goes on to speak of the vindication of the righteous one: note
the fourth stanza (vv. 22–23ab) in the arrangement of the psalm here.[3]

Reading II: Philippians 2:6-11.
Modern New Testament scholars (for a recent Catholic example see the
commentary in German by J. Gnilka) are widely agreed that this is a
hymn composed prior to Paul. It is often called the *Carmen Christi* (from
Pliny's description of Christian worship). There is much dispute about
its proper division into stanzas, but the following reconstruction has much
to commend it:

[3] Psalm 22 has especially colored the way Mark and Matthew tell the passion
story (less so Luke, read this year). The question inevitably arises whether some
of the details of the narration have been taken from the psalm rather than from
historical memory. This may have happened in some of the peripheral details, e.g.,
the division of the garments, but the main facts of the passion stand because of
their scandalous nature: it was this scandalous nature that sent the early Christians
to their Old Testaments, not their reading of the Old Testament that led them
gratuitously to invent fresh scandalous events.

I.

Christ Jesus, though he was in the form of God,
did not count equality with God a thing to be grasped,
but emptied himself,
taking the form of a servant,

II.

being born in the likeness of men,
and being found in human form he humbled himself
and became obedient unto death
[even death on a cross: *added by Paul*].

III.

Therefore God highly exalted him
and bestowed on him the name
which is above every name,

IV.

that at the name of Jesus
every knee should bow [in heaven and on earth and
    under the earth: *may be a later,*
    though pre-Pauline addition]
and every tongue confess "Jesus Christ is Lord"
    [to the glory of God the Father:
    perhaps added by Paul].

Stanza I will refer to the pre-incarnate existence of the Christ: he was of equal status with the Father (see the Old Testament speculations about the divine wisdom). This status he voluntarily surrendered and became subject to man's bondage to the powers of evil ("the form of a servant": some refer this to the suffering servant, but at this point the hymn refers to what is common between Christ and all men, not to what distinguishes him). The last line of stanza II refers to what is unique: he becomes obedient unto death (Paul emphasizes that that was the scandal: the death on the cross). Stanza III marks the turning point of the Redeemer's way: his exaltation; while stanza IV speaks of his ultimate triumph over the whole created universe. The *Carmen Christi* sets the death of Christ in its total context. It is at once the nadir of the divine condescension begun in the incarnation, and the ground of his exaltation and final triumph.

Gospel: Luke 22:14 — 23:56.

The passion narratives, we are told by modern New Testament scholars, differ in form from the rest of the gospel materials. Everything prior to the passion consists of "pericopes," i.e., short units which before they were combined in our written gospels were handed down in oral tradition as isolated units. The passion story, however, was from the start a continuous narrative. And the church has always understood the difference by redividing the gospels into pericopes in her lectionary, and by reading the passion as a continuous narrative. One would hope that at least at the principal Sunday Mass the long form will be used intact. When read by three different persons, as the rubric suggests,[4] the long form can sustain interest without boredom, and accords more with the literary and pre-literary form of the material.

Each of the four evangelists has his own distinctive perspective on the passion. Mark emphasizes the isolation of the Christ: betrayed, forsaken and denied by the disciples, mocked and tortured by his enemies, railed at by the brigands crucified with him, and finally bereft of the presence of his Father. Matthew brings out the royalty of Christ, but it is a paradoxical royalty, manifesting itself precisely in humiliation. John is also concerned with the royalty, but it is a royalty visibly present (see below). Luke takes a different line. It has been well said that he transposes the passion from the key of tragedy to the key of pathos. It is the story of a martyrdom (note the parallels with Stephen's martyrdom in Acts), of one who goes out in sympathy to others: e.g., "the daughters of Jerusalem"; "Father forgive them"; "Today you will be with me." Note also the serenity of his death ("Father into thy hands . . . .") in each of the evangelists. The passion story is intended not merely to narrate what happened, but to interpret it as good news. The "brief homily" permitted by the rubric may well concentrate this year on the unique features of th Lucan portrait of the passion.

(We ignore here the provisions for Monday through Wednesday of Holy Week and the Chrism Mass of Holy Thursday. Since these meditations are designed to assist the parish pastor in the preparation of his homilies, we confine ourselves to those occasions when the congregation as a whole is expected to be present.

(Although by ancient tradition the crucifixion is anticipated on Passion

---

[4] In some Anglican churches the congregation has also been involved by taking the parts of the disciples and the crowd.

[Palm] Sunday, the nucleus of the original unitary paschal feast is spread over the last three days of Holy Week, which taken together still form a distinct unity. These days should be understood not as three different commemorations [last supper, crucifixion, resurrection] but as a three-fold celebration of the total redemptive event, each day accentuating one aspect of it without losing sight of the whole.)

HOLY THURSDAY

A rubric of the new Roman Missal suggests three subjects for the homily in the Mass of the Lord's Supper: the institution of the eucharist; the institution of the priesthood; and the commandment of brotherly love. Of these, the first is covered by *Readings I* and *II*; the second, by the *Gospel*, while the third is implicit in all of the readings.

Reading I: Exodus 12:1-8, 11-14.

Although it is much disputed whether the Last Supper was a passover (so the synoptic gospels) or a meal preceding the passover by twenty-four hours (so John), two things are certain: the original meal of Jesus and his disciples was undoubtedly surrounded by passover associations; and the accounts of the institution have been impregnated with paschal theology, both in Paul (see *Reading II*) and in the Synoptists. Preeminently, too, the Israelite passover provided the background for the annual Christian paschal feast, and therefore most especially for the Easter eucharist at the conclusion of the vigil. It is therefore doubly fitting that the triduum should begin with this reading.

Three points may be drawn out here. First, the passover is a(n annual) memorial of the great redemptive act of God which constituted his first people. "Memorial" means more than mentally recalling. The devout Jew believed that when he celebrated the passover he was actually there: coming out of Egypt with his forefathers. The same realism colors the Christian eucharist and preeminently the triduum. Second, the shedding of the blood of the lamb provided an obvious type for the death of the Lamb of God who takes away the sin of the world. For the Christian dispensation the bloodshedding is more than a ritual or cultic act, it is a moral act (Heb 10:5-9) which becomes an event of salvation history. It is the making present of this event which is one of the main meanings of the eucharist. Thirdly, the passover was eaten in great haste and expectation. In the course of centuries this sense of urgency was transformed into an expectation of the Messiah, who was to come that night. The early

Christians likewise began their passover celebration looking for the coming of Christ, and even when the second coming did not occur, they believed he came in the Easter eucharist in anticipation of his final coming (*Marana tha!*).

Responsorial Psalm 116:12-13,15,16bc-18.

This psalm underlines two aspects of the eucharist: the sacrifice of thanksgiving, and the communion among believers, a sharing of the cup. Some traditions have overemphasized the one to the exclusion of the other. The eucharist is both together.

Reading II: 1 Corinthians 11:23-26.

This is one of the earliest fragments of Christian tradition preserved in the New Testament (see also 1 Cor 15:3-7). Paul says he "received" it before he delivered it to the Corinthians c. 50 A.D., and the words for "receive" and "deliver" represent words for the handing on of tradition as in rabbinic practice. So we are dealing here not with a vision "received from the Lord," but with a tradition handed down through human witnesses but always under the supervision of the exalted Christ. It is not a complete description of the Last Supper, but a liturgically stylized account selecting and interpreting those features of the meal which were of importance for the Christian eucharist. Its mention of the supper between the bread and the cup indicates its primitive character. Only Paul and the long text of Luke mention the command to repeat and the memorial aspect of the eucharist. But the other accounts presume this by their very existence, for they were recorded precisely because the church was "doing this" as a memorial of the Lord. Paul also preserves what is more prominent in the synoptic accounts, the anticipation of the second coming. In Paul as in the Synoptists, the eucharist looks both backward and forward, backward to the redemptive event of the cross here made present, and forward to the second coming here anticipated.

Gospel: John 13:1-15.

The theme of brotherly love is met at the footwashing, as the Lord says: "I have given you an example, that you should do as I have done to you" (13:15). This example is further defined later in the discourse, after supper: "I give you a new commandment: love one another as I have loved you" (13:34, the versicle before the gospel; the Latin *mandatum* gave this day its traditional English name of Maundy Thursday). Modern exegetes

Holy Week of Year C 17

find two themes in the footwashing, the first symbolic, the second exemplary. The symbolic meaning asserts that Jesus lays aside his garments as a parable of humiliation. He stooped first to become incarnate, then to die to cleanse mankind from sin. Finally he returns in glory to the Father. The whole incident is an acted parable of the *Carmen Christi* (see above). The symbolic meaning is expressed in v. 3, "Jesus, knowing that the Father had given all things into his hands, and that he had come from God, and was going to God." The exemplary meaning is expressed in v. 15. Neither meaning must be treated in isolation from the other: the exemplary meaning is enclosed within the symbolic. For the redemptive act of God alone makes possible the following of Christ's example, while unless we follow that example and reproduce in our own human existence the pattern of his, the redemptive act becomes an abstract myth, divorced from our own existence.

The third suggested theme, the institution of the priesthood, requires very careful handling. It would be easy to move straight from the command "Do this" to the institution of Christian priesthood. But this would be an oversimplification, and for two reasons. First, Vatican II, especially in the Decree on the Ministry and Life of Priests, set the eucharistic presidency in the wider context of a total pastoral ministry of word and sacrament. Second, there is no explicit evidence in the New Testament as to who presided at the eucharist.[5] Only in the second century does it become clear that it is the bishop who presides with his presbyters; only later still does the presbyter become the normal eucharistic president; and finally, even later (Cyprian) is the title *sacerdos* accorded to the eucharistic president. The command "Do this" (plural) is addressed to the Christian church as a whole. The eucharist is an action of the whole church and the preeminent expression of its priestly character (1 Pt 2:1-10; Ap 1:6; and perhaps Heb 13:15). Thus whoever presides at the eucharist and recites the great thanksgiving is the mouthpiece of the church's priesthood. At the same time, by showing forth Christ as both victim and priest in the great eucharistic action, the eucharistic president exhibits the priesthood of Christ to the church.

GOOD FRIDAY:

Reading I: Isaiah 52:13 — 53:12.

When Philip the Evangelist discovered the Ethiopian eunuch reading

[5] See Raymond E. Brown, *Priest and Bishop: Biblical Reflections* (New York: Paulist Press 1970).

this fourth servant song passage, the eunuch asked, "About whom does the prophet say this, about himself or about someone else?" (Acts 8:34). On the technical level of Old Testament scholarship there is no consensus on the answer to that question. But for the New Testament, as for Christian faith, these words finally come to rest in the fate of Jesus of Nazareth. Echoes of Isaiah 53 occur in the earliest strata of the New Testament (Rom 5:25; 1 Cor 15:4) and have colored the Jesus tradition in the gospels (Mk 10:45b; 14:24). How far Jesus explicitly applied this chapter to his own understanding of his mission it is difficult to say, but he certainly understood his mission generally in terms of the Isaianic servant (e.g., Mt 11:5 and par.). Isaiah 53 contributed three essential points to the understanding of Christ's death: his suffering was innocent, vicarious and redemptive; it avails for all men (the rabbis equated the "many" with all men, including the Gentiles); the righteous sufferer is finally vindicated: "The will of the Lord shall prosper in his hand. . . ."

Responsorial Psalm 31:1, 5, 11-12, 14-16, 24.
This is another psalm about the suffering and vindication of the righteous one. Though it has played a less important part in coloring gospel passion accounts, it provides Luke's version with its last word from the cross. It is therefore peculiarly appropriate in this year of series c.

Reading II: Hebrews 4:14-16; 5:7-9.
The author of Hebrews is rather like a musical composer: he enunciates his theme (Christ's high priesthood) several times before he fully develops it (7:1 10:18). This is its third enunciation. In it he characterizes the high priest in three ways: he can sympathize with our temptations and infirmities because of his complete identification with man in his incarnate life; he prayed for deliverance and was heard (a clear reflection of the Gethsemane tradition, but note that "save from" does not mean "escape from" but "deliverance through"); he "learned obedience": the incarnation was so real that Jesus did not fulfill the Father's will as an automaton, but only through struggle and temptation and "learning experience." It was only after he was "made perfect," i.e., had carried his earthly mission to its completeness, that he "became" the source of salvation, viz., by his high priestly work in heaven. All else — his incarnate life and its struggles, his obedience to death — was but the prelude to the exercise of his high priestly office in heaven.

Gospel: John 18:1 — 19:42.

As we have seen, each evangelist has his own particular perspective on the passion, and John's perspective is that the kingship of Jesus constantly shines through his humiliation. All the way through, Jesus is in command of the situation. He sets the passion in motion by voluntarily coming forward for his arrest. The temple police, awed by his personality, fall back. Peter would stop the arrest, but Jesus intervenes. On the cross Jesus makes his last will, bequeathing his Mother to the disciple and the disciple to his Mother. (John may regard Mary as a symbol of the church.) Finally, it is Jesus who decides on the moment of his death: he gives up his spirit. The passion narrative is a commentary on the saying: "I lay down my life, that I may take it again. No one takes it from me, but I lay it down of my own accord" (Jn 10:18). Although the evangelist has packed most of his theology of the cross into his discourses, especially in the farewell address, at least two points of interpretation are brought out in the narrative. First, Pilate (like Caiaphas earlier, on the atoning death) bears unwitting testimony to Christ's kingship when he brings Jesus before the people and when he refuses to alter the inscription on the cross. The second point is that the Baptist had proclaimed Jesus as the true paschal Lamb of God who takes away the world's sin, and now Christ dies as such at the moment when the passover lambs were being slaughtered. Then at his death he announces the completion of his sacrifice: "It is accomplished" (Jn 19:30). (The RSV translation is weak, the Vulgate's *consummatum est* gets the point.)

EASTER VIGIL

This is the archetypal liturgy of the whole church year. It consists of four parts: 1) the service of light with the Easter proclamation; 2) the liturgy of the word; 3) liturgy of baptism; 4) liturgy of the eucharist.

The origins of the service of light are probably pagan, and their Christian meaning is uncertain though strangely moving. It is perhaps well, therefore, that it is recommended that this ceremony be performed outside of the church, and suggested that other ceremonies more adapted to the culture of a particular region may be substituted.[6]

The Easter proclamation focuses upon the three main themes of the vigil service: deliverance of Israel in the exodus ("This is the night when you first saved *our* fathers"); the baptismal deliverance of the new Israel

[6] Some Anglicans are experimenting by placing the ceremony of the new fire *after* the prophecies, so that its kindling marks the *transitus* of the Messiah.

("This is the night when Christians everywhere . . . are restored to grace"); the resurrection of Christ ("This is the night when Jesus Christ broke the chains . . .").

The nine scripture readings of the vigil service and their responsorial psalms are too many to comment upon, but we select a few of the more important.[7]

Reading I: Genesis 1:1 — 2:2.

It is appropriate to read the story of the first creation on the night which celebrates the inauguration of the new creation. The Genesis story is not to be read as historical narration. Its importance is proclamatory: God is the source of the whole creative process; it depends at each moment upon him; and man is the one species selected by God to bear his image, to have an I-thou relationship with the source of all being. The reading of this story further points towards the new creation and restoration of the divine image which had been defaced by sin.

Reading II: Genesis 22:1-18.

Special interest attaches to this lesson because already in Jewish tradition the "binding" of Isaac was associated with the passover. The story was expanded to bring out, among other things, the following points: Isaac freely consented to die as a sacrifice; his sacrifice was victorious, available for the sanctification of men. The Isaac story was therefore ready for the early Christians to use as a type of Christ's sacrifice, which is exactly what Paul does in Rom 8:32. There are even suggestions in Judaism that Isaac's reprieve was a kind of death and resurrection, thus making it eminently fitting for use in the Easter vigil.

Reading III: Exodus 14:15 — 15:1

This is the most important reading in the whole series, an importance underlined by the requirement that this passage must invariably be used. It appears that its use on this occasion goes back to the earliest days of Christianity, and was probably taken over from the Jewish paschal liturgy. The crossing of the Red Sea is the supreme type of Christ's death and resurrection, and of the Christian's dying and rising again with him in baptism (see 1 Cor 10:1-11).

Epistle: Romans 6:3-11.

This epistle marks the decisive turning point in the vigil service. Here we move from the Old Testament to the New Testament, from type and

[7] For comments on the other scripture readings, see the Easter Vigil of years A and B, below:

prophecy to fulfillment — hence the rubric requiring that the altar lights be lit at this point. The basic significance of the vigil service lies in the experience of this turning point. This is the *transitus*, the passing from darkness to light, from death to life, from bondage to freedom, from the old age to the age to come. This transition, accomplished in our baptism, is possible for us because Christ first made it. But it has to be renewed constantly. Note that the verbs which speak of our dying with Christ are in the past tense (that was accomplished once for all in baptism), while the verbs which speak of our resurrection are hypothetical and future, and depend upon our moral obedience. Our dying with Christ to sin has to be renewed constantly by a daily decision (1 Cor 15:31a). Thus this epistle prepares us for the baptismal vows in the service, a solemn annual liturgical renewal which has to be expressed morally every day.

Gospel: Luke 24:1-12.

None of the gospels relates the actual resurrection, viz., the rising (or raising by God) of Jesus from the dead. There are two reasons for this. 1) No one was present to witness it: there were witnesses of the empty tomb and of the appearances, but these are the aftermath of the event, not the event itself. 2) Resurrection is transformation into an entirely new mode of existence (not mere resuscitation to the old life as in the raisings of Jairus' daughter, the widow's son at Nain, and Lazarus). It takes place at the point of intersection between this age and the age to come, between time and eternity. Only the this-side aspect of it ("He is not here") is open to this-worldly observation. Christ can only be revealed by God to the witnesses as already risen. So the gospel of the day gives us not a narrative of the resurrection, but the witness of the empty tomb. In itself, an empty tomb is susceptible of diverse interpretations. The true meaning of it— and here lies the real *euangelion*, the Easter message — is conveyed by the two "men in dazzling apparel" (angels, i.e., communication from the beyond). "He . . . has risen."

The church which has believed this proclamation can now proceed to baptize, to renew its baptismal vows, and to celebrate the paschal eucharist, in all of which the past (Christ's death and resurrection) is "co-celebrated," i.e., brought from the past into the present, and the future (the second coming of Christ) anticipated. *Marana tha!*

Easter Season of Year C

This season no longer runs forty days to Ascension, but fifty days to Pentecost. Like the ancient fifty days in which Israel enjoyed the fruits of the land, so the church reflects in these fifty days on the fruits of Christ's redemption, the life and witness of the church, as well as on the post-Easter revelation of the risen One.

EASTER SUNDAY

Reading I: Acts 10:34a, 37-43.

New Testament scholars regard the "kerygmatic" speeches of Acts not as records of what was actually said by Peter or others on a particular occasion, but as samples of the "kerygma" or basic message of the earliest Jerusalem church. While Luke has undoubtedly had a hand in giving them their present shape, they enshrine very early Christological patterns. This sermon, for example, contains the following points:

1. The earthly ministry of Jesus culminating in his death was Israel's rejection of the proffered salvation. The word "tree" calls attention to the scandalous nature of the death of Christ: "Cursed is he who hangs on a tree" (Dt 21:23; see Gal 3:13).

2. Christ's resurrection was God's vindication of Jesus and all that he had stood for, in face of his contemporaries' rejection of it. This "No-Yes" interpretation of Golgotha and Easter is characteristic of the earliest period.

3. The apostles witness the events from the beginning of the earthly ministry through the appearances.

Note too the suggestion, present elsewhere, that the context of the resurrection appearances was, at least sometimes, a meal. The roots of the Christian eucharist lie not only in the last supper, but in the meals which the risen One celebrated with his disciples in the Easter season.

Responsorial Psalm: 118:1-2, 15-16a, 17, 22-23.

Psalm 118, with its reference to the stone rejected and made the headstone of the corner, was perhaps the earliest psalm that the primitive community applied to the death and resurrection of Christ. It was the basic Old Testament text for the "No-Yes" interpretation of the earliest kerygma.

Reading II (first alternate): Colossians 3:1-4.

"*If* you have been raised with Christ" is a common turn of phrase. It means, "If (and of course you are)." Colossians is more positive than Rom 6 (see vigil service) that baptism includes *both* the dying *and* rising with Christ. But it still maintains two reservations: the resurrection with Christ has to be implemented by constant moral effort; it is a hidden reality which is not finally revealed until Christ's second coming.

Reading II (second alternate): 1 Corinthians 5:6b-8.

As the Jewish housewife springcleaned before passover to make sure there was not a crumb of leavened bread left in the house, so Paul, in figurative language, urges the Christians at Corinth to purge out the leaven of malice and evil, so that they may celebrate the festival of Christ's sacrifice as the true paschal lamb with the unleavened bread of sincerity and truth. This is the earliest reference we have to the Christian reinterpretation of the passover. It may even indicate that 1 Corinthians was written with the feast in view.

Gospel: John 20:1-9.

This text presents many difficulties for the preacher. It is a combination of two different traditions. The one is the well-attested and reliable tradition that Mary Magdalene (other names are added in various forms of the tradition, but there is no consistency here) visited the grave of Jesus on Easter morning, found it empty and reported the fact to the disciples. The other, less attested, tradition is of Peter's visit to the grave (see Lk 24:12). (In the earliest and strongly attested tradition, Peter was the recipient of the first *appearance*.) To the less attested tradition John has added the race between Peter and the "other disciple," probably with a symbolic significance. The "other disciple" comes to faith in the resurrection through the mere sight of the empty tomb. In the earlier tradition, however, the disciples came to faith in the resurrection through seeing the risen Lord.

The caption at the head of the gospel suggests that the basic kerygma here is that Christ was raised from the dead "in accordance with the scriptures." Here is the only possibility of developing a kerygmatic message from this confused amalgam of traditions.

Reading I: Acts 5:12-16.

Here is a vignette of the apostles' ministry in the early community after Pentecost. It shows the power of the risen Christ at work in his church. The apostolic preaching is not mentioned here, but there are never signs and wonder without the proclamation of the word. The phrase "were added to the Lord" is very striking. New converts were "added," i.e., they were brought into an already existing community. They did not hear the message and get together and form a community on their own. The community was already there. And they "were added": a reverential passive denoting that it was *God* who added them. It was not the church that added new members. The new converts did not become members on their own, but God translated them into the redeemed community.

Responsorial Psalm: 118:2-4, 22-27ab.

On the importance of this psalm in the Easter season, see above under Easter Sunday.

Reading II: Revelation 1:9-11a, 12-13, 17-19.

This is the opening vision of the Apocalypse, in which John the Seer sees the risen Christ and receives the messages for the seven churches. Some have held that this vision was a continuation of the resurrection appearances. It is true that the language of vision is used about the original appearances (1 Cor 15:3-8), and that in the earliest tradition the appearances were appearances "from heaven" (Paul, Mark, Mt 28:18, Jn 21) rather than, as in the later tradition (Lk 24; Jn 20), massive apparitions of a Christ still on earth. But Paul (1 Cor 15:8) is emphatic that the appearance to himself on the Damascus road was last, not only in date, but as a matter of principle. Paul himself had later visions of the risen Christ (2 Cor 12:1-4; note that there he pictures himself as being transported to heaven, rather than the risen Christ as appearing from heaven upon earth). Moreover, the resurrection appearances were revelations which formed the church and gave it its mission in the world. Subsequent visions, like those of Paul in 2 Cor 12:1-4 and of John the Seer in our reading, only continue what was begun at Easter. The auditory element here repeats (but does not add to) the original Easter revelations: Christ reveals himself as alive out of death.

Gospel: John 20:19-31.

This, the traditional gospel for this Sunday, describes two appearances: to the disciples on Easter evening, which appears in various forms in Matthew, Luke and here; and to Thomas a week later, which is peculiar to John. The element of doubt, which characterized the appearance tradition almost from the beginning, and proves that the appearances were not merely wish fulfillment, has here been expanded for apologetic purposes, enabling the risen One to establish his identity. The earlier tradition had pictured the risen One in more spiritual terms; this later emphasis on the physical reality of the risen body preserves the truth of the identity-amid-change between the earthly Jesus and the resurrected One. But John has given this story his own twist by taking up a concern of the later church. How could a man believe in the risen One if he had not received an appearance? Answer: seeing him is no guarantee of believing. Even disciples had to come to faith when they saw him; so those who have not seen him can still have the blessedness of faith through believing the testimony of the first witnesses.

THIRD SUNDAY OF EASTER

Reading I: Acts 5:27b-32, 40b-41.

The apostles had been arrested for preaching while under orders to desist. In a tremendous gesture of defiance, which has been the inspiration of the church in all times of persecution, they replied, "We must obey God rather than men," and they start at once to preach to the Sanhedrin, enabling Luke to give us another fragment of the primitive Christian kerygma. The most striking feature here is the concept (highlighted in the caption heading in the *Lectionary*) of a double witness: the apostles and the Holy Spirit (see Jn 15:26). The Spirit and the apostolic word are both necessary: without the Spirit the word becomes a dead formula, no longer speaking meaningfully to the contemporary situation, while without the word, the Spirit becomes uncontrolled enthusiasm divorced from the original witness to the Christ event.

Responsorial Psalm: 30:1, 3-5, 10-11a, 12b.

The hope of a future resurrection is found only in some of the latest parts of the Old Testament, and is absent from the psalms. When the psalmist speaks of being brought up from Sheol and restored to life, he is using metaphorical language for deliverance from earthly troubles (in this case probably illness). But Christian apologetic, followed by liturgical piety, interpreted the psalm christologically— the "I" who speaks becomes Christ and the deliverance, his resurrection.

Reading II: Revelation 5:11-14.

This is John's vision of the heavenly liturgy, of which the liturgy of the church on earth is a reflexion (see the eucharistic preface; in the picture the four living creatures and the elders suggest the participants in the Christian liturgy of the time). Christ is addressed as "the Lamb that was slain," i.e., as the paschal lamb, a tradition going back at least to 1 Cor 5 (see Easter Sunday). Is this actually a fragment of the early Christian paschal liturgy?

Gospel: John 21:1-19.

This story, widely regarded as an appendix to John's gospel but apparently composed by members of the Johannine school, is in surprisingly close contact with early tradition. It probably goes back to the first appearance of the Lord to the twelve by the Lake of Galilee, here set in the context of a meal. But at some stage this primitive story was combined with the miraculous draft of fishes which figures in the earthly ministry at Lk 5. Some think that the story there is a retrojection of an appearance story into the earthly life, but the current trend is to regard Jn 21 as a projection of the earthly miracle in a resurrection context. The number 153 has symbolic significance, though the evangelist does not explain. Clearly it has some connection with the mission of the church, which the apostles are commissioned to inaugurate.

In verses 15-19 we encounter another story which goes back to very early tradition, namely, the first appearance to Peter, in which the first of the apostles is entrusted with the pastoral care of Christ's flock (see also Mt 16:17-19 and Lk 22:31-32). To this early tradition has been added a final paragraph containing a prediction (regarded by New Testament scholars as *ex eventu*) of Peter's martyrdom. This is the earliest reference to that event and its only mention in the New Testament.

FOURTH SUNDAY OF EASTER ✓

Reading I: Acts 13:14, 43-52.

The first reading continues to be from Acts instead of from the Old Testament. Acts shows us the Christian community in the first year after the

Easter events, and thus mirrors the impact of the resurrection experiences on the apostolic church.

This week's reading tells of the preaching of Paul and Barnabas at Pisidian Antioch during the so-called first missionary journey. The pattern of events is typical, and repeated in many cities on the missionary journeys: the apostles preach in the synagogue; a certain number of Jews and Gentile converts to Judaism believe, while others reject the message and stir up opposition against the apostles; whereupon they declare their intention of turning to the Gentiles. The proclamation of the word of God has no promise of success. But the word must be proclaimed whether men hear or whether they refuse to hear (Ez 3:5). What matters is that the word is proclaimed faithfully. This matters even more than that it should be made to seem relevant by artificial stunts and gimmicks.

Responsorial Psalm: 100:1-3, 5.

This Sunday, formerly called the Third after Easter, was traditionally known as *Jubilate*, especially among the German Lutherans, because of the old introit, Ps 66. Now, in series c, we use another *Jubilate*, Ps 100. Easter is preeminently the season of joy: note also the last sentence of *Reading I* and the joyful tone of the hymn in *Reading II*. Easter joy (*jubilate*) is not the joy of anticipation, like that of Advent (*gaudete*), nor the brief moment of relief like the joy of mid-Lent (*laetare*), but the exuberance of sorrow which has been turned into joy (Jn 16:20-22, from the old gospel of this day).

Reading II: Revelation: 7:9, 14b-17.

We normally associate this passage with All Saints Day, but it is just as appropriate for Easter. The joy of the martyrs is also the sorrow which has been turned into joy: the martyrs have come out of the great tribulation (not merely tribulation, but *the* tribulation; the Seer regards their martyrdom as part of the Messianic woes, a sharing of the cross of Christ). Paschal imagery is picked up in the phrase "the blood of the Lamb" (see last Sunday's *Reading II*, with its reference to the lamb that was slain), as also the image of the shepherd who will guide the martyrs to springs of living water, an image which will recur in the gospel.

Gospel: John 10:27-30.

This gospel is not from the shepherd discourse proper, which comes earlier in Jn 10, but an echo of it in the next section, Jesus' discourse at the feast of the dedication. It is tempting, as some commentators have done, to rearrange the text and to put these verses back in the good shepherd discourse. But it is characteristic of John to return to an earlier theme and to develop it further. The earlier explanations of the good shepherd parable had dealt with the gate and the shepherd, while this one deals with the sheep, their relation to the shepherd and their enjoyment of eternal life already in the life of discipleship (following), also the thrice repeated assurance that they shall not perish or be snatched out of the shepherd's hand (at the final judgment).

While all this is stated in typically Johannine language, its substance correctly reproduces the teaching of the earthly Jesus as recorded in the Synoptists. To hear and to respond to Jesus' word on earth is the decisive factor which will determine men's acceptance by God at the last judgment (e.g., Lk 12:8-9).

The concluding sentence about the unity of the Father and the Son gives the basis for the Nicene faith, but was meant by the evangelist not in an ontological or metaphysical sense, as in the later dogmatic formulae, but in the dynamic-historical sense of Hebraic thought.

The Father and the Son are one because of the Father's call of the Son and his response in history, resulting in a complete alignment of the words and acts of the Father and the Son. The history, of course, has an external background in the relation of the Father and the Son, as the prologue (Jn 1:1-14) makes clear.

✓ FIFTH SUNDAY OF EASTER

Reading I: Acts 14:21-27.

This is the homeward leg of the first missionary journey, where Paul and Barnabas revisited the communities they had established on their outward trip. Current scholarship tends to regard ordination of elders (presbyters) in Acts 14:23 as a Lucan anachronism. In Paul's churches, if 1 Corinthians is typical, the ministry was charismatic (1 Cor 12:4-11, 27-30). Here Luke describes an ordination service as he knew it in the church of his day. But whether it is the charismatics of the Pauline age, the elders of Luke's time, or the threefold ministry of the second century and after, the function of all these ministries is to keep the church on the foundation laid by the original apostles.

When the apostles return to the church in Syrian Antioch they report not what *they* had done, but what "God had done with them." It was he—

not their own missionary strategy — who had opened a door of faith to the Gentiles.

Responsorial Psalm: 145:8-13ab.

This is another psalm of exuberant joy. The psalmist exults in God's mighty acts in creation and in salvation history. In the earlier part of the Old Testament the kingdom of God is a timeless truth. Later it seemed that God's kingship was denied by the disasters which had befallen his people, and as a result the hope arose that God would eventually reestablish it. He was always king *de jure*, but at the end he would become king *de facto*. The New Testament message is that this has now happened — by the resurrection of Jesus Christ from the dead. So the deeds and works the church celebrates are comprised in the salvation history of Christ's death and resurrection. God's kingdom is now inaugurated *de facto* through the Easter events.

Reading II: Revelation 21:1-5a.

This is John the Seer's vision of the new heaven, the new earth and the new Jerusalem. These "new things" have been established in principle through the resurrection and they are anticipated in the life of the church. Now God does indeed dwell with men, though only in the veiled form of the word and sacraments. Here there is a foretaste, an apéritif (R. Alves) of that joy. But not until the end shall all tears be wiped away from the eyes of his people. Mourning and crying and pain are certainly not unknown in the church, but faith knows that even now all things are being made new.

Gospel: John 13:31-33a, 34-35.

It helps make sense of the opening passage with its five bewildering references to the glorification of God and the Son of man if we regard it with some recent commentators as an early Christian hymn. It celebrated the enthronement of Christ as Son of man at his exaltation and looked forward to his coming in glory. This explains the shift from the past tense to the future:

> Now is the Son of man glorified,
> and in him God is glorified [at Christ's
> exaltation];

if [*since*] God has been glorified in him
    [at the exaltation],
God will also glorify him in himself,
and glorify him at once [at the parousia,
    expected shortly].

In taking up this hymn, John has shifted the tenses backwards. The past tenses now refer to the glorifying which has taken place through the Son's revelation of the Father during his incarnate life, while the future tenses now refer to the glorification that will take place at once in the passion, death, resurrection and ascension of the Son. Thus the hymn becomes an expression of the basic themes of the Johannine theology of glory.

At his departure Jesus leaves his disciples a new "commandment" (see the covenant which Jesus bequeaths in Lk 22:29 and the institution of the last supper in the Synoptics). Some have criticized John's concept of love for being more restricted and introverted than that of the sermon on the mount. The Johannine Christ speaks of the mutual love of the Christian community, not of the love even of one's enemy. Could it be, however, that the command of love which, as we have suggested, parallels the institution of the last supper in the Synoptics is speaking explicitly to the agape meal of the early community? For the agape meal was the focal expression of love within the community.

SIXTH SUNDAY OF EASTER

Reading I: Acts 15:1-2, 22-29.

This is Acts' version of the apostolic conference at Jerusalem. Paul's account of it in Gal 2:1-12 tallies to some extent. The *dramatis personae* (Paul, Barnabas, Peter, James) and the points at issue, viz., the circumcision of Gentile converts to Christianity, are the same. But the outcome is different. In Paul the conference results in the "gentlemen's agreement": Peter will head up the mission to the Jews, Paul the mission to the Gentiles, and the law will not be imposed on the Gentile churches. In Acts the conference concludes with the adoption of a compromise solution (the apostolic decrees). The Gentiles are spared the burden of circumcision, but must observe a certain minimum of legal requirements. Acts has probably combined the results of two separate conferences. The first conference concluded as Paul said, in a gentlemen's agreement, but left unclear what was to happen where, in mixed communities, Jews and Gentiles ate together the eucharistic meal. Hence the subsequent fracas in Antioch described by Paul in Gal 2:11-14. It was to deal with this later problem that a second conference was apparently held, the results of which were communicated to Paul on his last visit to Jerusalem (Acts 21:25. If Paul has been present when the decrees were promulgated, as Acts 15 alleges, why would James have to inform Paul of them in Acts 21?). This makes sense. Compromise solutions are often necessary to preserve the unity of the church when the issues at stake can be relegated to the category of adiaphora, things indifferent.

Responsorial Psalm: 67:1-2, 4-5, 7.

Psalm 67 combines thanksgiving for harvest with prayer for continued blessings. It serves as an appropriate thanksgiving for the resurrection and for the continuation of the enjoyment of its benefits in the church and the spread of its benefits to all nations.

Reading II: Revelation 21:10-14, 22-23.

This is a continuation (in part a repetition and in part a further development) of the picture of the descent of the holy city. The descent is repeated, but a further description of the city is given: its radiance, its walls and gates, its foundations, its need of neither temple nor sun. There is a partial correspondence between the holy city and the church on earth. The church, too, has a radiance, not the splendor of a worldly power (though she has often masqueraded as such since the time of Constantine) but the radiance of the word and sacraments and the presence of the Spirit. She, too, has the continuity with the old Israel suggested by the symbolism of the twelve gates, angels and tribes. Her foundation is the twelve apostles — their witness to Jesus Christ and his resurrection, perpetuated in her scriptures and expounded in her doctrine by the successors of the apostles. But there *is* a temple in the church, a visible place where God's presence is made known in word and sacrament. This is not because he is not everywhere, but because in this age and on earth he wills to be manifested in a particular place, at a particular time, in a particular rite and a particular sacrament, this bread and this wine. Here is the scandal of the church's particularity. To seek in this age on this earth to abolish the temple, as some kinds of secular interpretations of the gospel would like to do, is to ignore the "not yet" and to suppose that we are already in heaven. That is *Schwärmerei*, fanaticism.

Gospel: John 14:23-29.

In the Easter season we tend to read the farewell discourses with their promise of the coming of the Paraclete (rsv "Counselor") as discourses given by the risen-and-not-yet-ascended Lord, given as it were during the forty days in preparation for the coming of the Spirit at Pentecost. For the evangelist they are discourses of the earthly Jesus, placed in the context of the last supper. They look through and beyond the death of Jesus to his glorification which releases the gift of the Spirit. Thus in the early church the whole of the fifty days included the celebration of the gift of the Spirit, not just the day of Pentecost. We are here listening to a promise fulfilled at Easter. In the fourth gospel the risen Christ conveys the gift of the Spirit to his disciples on Easter Sunday evening (see Pentecost Sunday, the gospel). The Spirit is (as also in Paul's letters) the gift of the risen Christ. In the gift of the Spirit the risen Christ and the Father come and make their home with the disciples. The function of the Spirit is to "teach you all things, and bring to your remembrance all that I have said unto you." It is not the work of the Spirit to convey ever new revelations, but to unfold in ever new understanding, ever new interpretation and application the once-for-all revelation of Jesus Christ ("all that I have said unto you"). "His work is more than a reminiscence of the *ipsissima verba* of the Son of God; it is a living representation of all that he had spoken to his disciples, a creative exploitation of the gospel" (Hoskyns). This on-going work of the Spirit gives the disciples peace and takes away their fear, because the Spirit is always there as their helper who stands by them in persecution and martyrdom.

ASCENSION DAY

Let us remind ourselves once more that if we are to be true to the perspectives of the New Testament and the early liturgy we should not think of the Ascension Day as a historical commemoration. In the New Testament the ascension is normally proclaimed as an integral part of the Easter event: God raised Jesus and exalted him to his right hand (so always Paul). The earlier perspective on the Easter appearances is that they were appearances from heaven of the already risen-and-ascended Christ. Hence Paul could include his Damascus experience among the appearances in 1 Cor 15.

The later appearances narratives (Luke, John) show a tendency to separate resurrection and ascension. But still they are not really regarded as two successive events. They are separated in order to contemplate the meaning of two aspects of a single indivisible event. When this separation occurs, the ascension seems variously located: in Lk 24 on Easter Sunday evening, or at the latest the next day; in Jn 20 sometime between the appearance to Mary Magdalene (who is told not to touch the risen One because he is not yet ascended), and the appearance to Thomas (who *is* invited to touch him); in Acts 1 after the forty days (which, however, are symbolic of the time of revelation, and there may be no intention to suggest the ascension actually "occurred" on the fortieth day). For several centuries the church did not, either in its writings or in its liturgy, treat the ascension as though it "occurred" on the fortieth day. With the new church calendar, we still keep it on the fortieth day as a matter of convenience (and that this is not an absolute rule is indicated by the rubrical permission to transfer the observance to the following Sunday), but simply in order to isolate for contemplation one aspect of the total Easter event.

Reading I: Acts 1:1-11.

It is curious that in his two-volume work Luke tells the story of the ascension twice over (Lk 24; Acts 1). The reason is that each narration brings out a different aspect of the truth. The Acts version looks forward to the future, to the inauguration of the church's mission and the final return of the ascending One. Luke's perspective on salvation history represents an adjustment. Salvation history, already in the Old Testament, is constantly readjusted in the light of earlier events. The earliest church only looked for a brief interval between the ascension and the parousia, an interval which would be marked by the apostles' mission to Israel and by persecution and martyrdom. Now the salvation history is greatly extended. Already Paul had modified it to include the mission to the Gentiles. Now for Luke the church is here to stay, with a mission to the whole civilized world. But the hope of the parousia is still maintained, and the church's mission is viewed as a preparation for the end.

Responsorial Psalm: 47:1-2, 5-8.

This is one of the enthronement psalms, psalms which, according to some scholars, were sung at a (hypothetical) annual feast in which the king was enthroned in order to symbolize Yahweh's kingship over his people. As the king took his seat upon his earthly throne the whole people would have chanted this psalm in celebration of the kingship of Yahweh. The church in her liturgy has associated this psalm with, and transferred it to, the ascension of Christ. Ascension Day is the feast of Christ's enthronement. Henceforth God exercises his sovereignty over the universe through his exalted Son.

Reading II: Ephesians 1:17-23.

Ephesians, whether written by Paul himself or, as now seems more likely, by a close disciple of the apostle who was steeped in the thought of his master, begins like most of Paul's letters with an opening thanksgiving and prayer. This prayer reproduces the pattern and phraseology of a liturgical hymn. The first part of our pericope prays for the church's growth in wisdom and knowledge and looks to the risen and ascended Christ for the power to foster this growth. The hymn then goes on to elaborate on the exaltation and kingship of Christ. The New Testament views Christ's kingship as exercised in two concentric circles. The inner circle embraces the church, where his kingship is known and acknowledged; the outer circle, the world, where he is *de facto* king but where his kingship is as yet unrecognized (O. Cullmann). The church's function is to extend that inner circle to cover more and more of the outer one.

Gospel: Luke 24:46-53.

This reading consists of two halves. The first half is Luke's version of the appearances to the apostles, which, like the ascension story in Acts, looks forward to the mission of the church and the empowering of the church with the Spirit for that mission. In the second half, the ascension is narrated as in Acts 2. In the gospel the ascension narrative looks backward rather than forward. The ascension is here presented not as the inauguration of the period of the church — which it also is — but as the conclusion of the earthly ministry of Christ. It is a farewell scene, as is indicated by the blessing. Henceforth Christ will be with them in a new way. "Jesus is not seen at all times by the believers in this position: even for the disciples it came to an end" (Schlatter). But unlike most partings, it leaves the disciples rejoicing — precisely because he leaves them with his blessing. Such is the outcome and conclusion of his earthly ministry.

SEVENTH SUNDAY OF EASTER

Ascension Day no longer inaugurates a fresh season, nor does it have an octave. The new name for this Sunday is yet another expression of what we have noted several times already, that the fifty days are a continuous celebration of the Easter events, with different accentuations at different times. But this Sunday still continues the theme of Ascension Day itself, namely, the enthronement of Christ at the right hand of the Father.

Reading I: Acts 7:55—8:1a.

At the moment of his death Stephen is granted a vision of heaven with the Son of man "standing at the right hand of God." There are two unusual features here. First, the use of the title Son of man, the only time it is used by anyone other than the earthly Jesus himself (Jn 12:34 is only a partial exception, for here the Jews are merely repeating Jesus' *own* words). The second unusual feature is that Christ is described as standing rather than sitting at God's right hand. There is no universally accepted explanation of either of these features. Perhaps the title Son of man is used here because it suggests that the exalted Christ is pleading the cause of his first martyr in anticipation of his function as Son of man at the last judgment (Lk 12:8-9; Mk 8:38), and is standing in order to welcome his martyr to heaven. In any case, Stephen's martyrdom is an appropriate gospel for this day, as it is a vision of the ascended Lord.

Responsorial Psalm: 97:1, 2b, 6, 7c, 9.

This is another of the enthronement psalms (see Ascension Day). It is noteworthy that the earlier parts of the Old Testament do not deny the existence of other gods, but assert that Yahweh is above them all (henotheism rather than monotheism). Similarly in the New Testament Christ at his ascension triumphs over the demonic forces of evil (Phil 2:10). Demythologizing the language, we might say that God in Christ is above all false absolutes that men choose for themselves.

Reading II: Revelation 22:12-14, 16-17, 20.

This reading might seem more appropriate for Advent, and indeed this particular Sunday has always had about it something of an Advent character (see the old epistle, I Pt 4:7-11, with its exhoration to watchfulness in view of the impending end). As we have noted earlier, the fifty days originally included the Advent hope. It is because Christ has been exalted that we can hope for his coming again:

> "What no eye has seen, nor ear heard,
>   nor the heart of man conceived,
>   what God has prepared for those
>   who love him" (1 Cor 2:9).

The experience of Easter is of such a quality that the believers know that there is more to come: the kingship of Christ, now inaugurated but hidden, must finally triumph universally. The final words, "Come, Lord Jesus," are from the earliest liturgy of the church (*Marana tha*). In the eucharist the ascended Christ comes in anticipation of his final coming, and here he offers the thirsty the water of life without price.

Gospel: John 17:20-26.

Traditionally the prayer of Jesus at the last supper has been called the high priestly prayer. It represents not only what according to the fourth gospel was the substance of Jesus' prayer at the last supper, but also the prayer he continues as the ascended high priest in heaven. It is a prayer "ut omnes unum sint." The unity for which he prays is not grounded on ecclesiastical joinery, for "It must not be supposed that the unity of the church is to be attained by a long history of human endeavour" (Hoskyns). Rather, the unity of the church is a unity based on the common sharing of word and sacraments, in which the act of God in Christ, on which the unity of the church rests, is made ever present.

The first half of this Sunday's gospel concerns the life of the church on earth. Her unity is a unity for mission, a unity whose aim is that the world may believe "that thou hast sent me." The second half of the gospel turns to the final destiny of the church — what traditionally we call the church triumphant, but what John would rather call the church glorified (*ecclesia glorificata*). Even if Bultmann were right in assigning all the passages in John which express a future eschatology to the hand of an ecclesiastical redactor (e.g., 5:28-29; 6:40), it is clear from this passage that John has not entirely eliminated the future consummation in favor of a realized eschatology. There *is* a future destiny for the church: "That they may be with me where I am, to behold my glory." This future element chimes in perfectly with the future hope of the epistle — according to tradition by the same hand as the gospel, but in any case the product of a mind from the same theological school.

PENTECOST SUNDAY[1]

Pentecost originated as a final celebration of the ingathering of the grain harvest which had begun at passover. Later Judaism transformed it into a feast of salvation history, celebrating the giving of the Law at Sinai and the establishment of Israel as God's people. All of these associations were

[1] In years A and B the readings of the vigil of Pentecost, which do not change, are commented upon for the convenience of those who wish to use them Saturday afternoon and evening.

carried over into the Christian feast that marked the conclusion of the great fifty days. The grain harvest and the Law are replaced by the gift of the Spirit, and the constitution of the old Israel, by the constitution of the new. The feast of the Law becomes the feast of the Spirit.

Reading I: Acts 2:1-11.

There is no unanimity in the New Testament about a single outpouring of the Spirit. The gospel of the day, as we shall see, places the gift of the Spirit on Easter Sunday evening, while Acts 2 puts it at Pentecost. Perhaps originally the gift of the Spirit was associated with each of the resurrection appearances, and perhaps also the Pentecost story corresponds to the otherwise unknown appearance to the five hundred (1 Cor 15:6). Historically, this appearance marks the foundation of the church as a wider community than the original twelve, and the beginning of the kerygma. Perhaps, as a later part of this story suggests (the crowd's suspicion that the apostles were full of new wine), the beginning of the kerygma was marked by an outburst of glossolalia such as Paul describes taking place at Corinth in 1 Cor 12-14. This earlier concept of glossolalia has been overlaid with a new symbolism (whether due to Luke or to his tradition, we cannot say) in which Pentecost reverses the effect of Babel.

Responsorial Psalm: 104:1ab, 24ac, 29bc-31, 34.

This is a hymn of praise to God for his works in creation. The dominant theology of the Spirit in the wisdom literature ("the Spirit of God fills the world") stresses the work of the Spirit in the created order. By contrast the New Testament concentrates almost exclusively on the eschatological work of the Spirit. The pneumatology of the New Testament is conditioned by its Christology. When the psalmist speaks of the "renewal" of creation through the Spirit he is probably thinking of no more than the renewal of nature at springtime. But in Christian use it can be reinterpreted to mean the eschatological renewal of creation, a renewal of which the church is the first fruits.

Reading II: 1 Corinthians 12:3b-7, 12-13.

Paul's Corinthians were very keen on glossolalia. But its effect on the community was questionable. It led to divisiveness: the tongue speakers treated those who did not have that particular gift as second-class citizens. In reply Paul insists on several things here: to have the Spirit means to confess that *Jesus* is Lord. Here Paul's use of the name Jesus is especially nuanced. "Jesus" means the earthly Jesus, Christ crucified. The Corinthians regarded the death of Christ as a mere episode of the past, and put all their money on the purely spiritual, ethereal Christ. Paul recalls them to the centrality of the cross, which pricks the bubble of their enthusiasm.

Second, the gifts of the Spirit take different forms, not just the one form of tongue-speaking. Each gift, however unspectacular, has to be used for the common good.

Third, the gift of the Spirit must not lead to individualism but to the building up of the corporate body of the community. The church is one body through a common baptism and a common "drinking of the one Spirit." The latter is probably a reference to the baptismal eucharist rather than to a rite analogous to the later confirmation (see "spiritual" drink in 1 Cor 10:4). Here is a further suggestion that 1 Corinthians was written for the paschal feast.

Gospel: John 20:19-23.

We have seen already that John places the giving of the Spirit on Easter Day, and have discussed the historical and theological ground for this. Here as in Acts the Spirit empowers the church for her mission ("even so I send you"). The mission is defined here, however, not as kerygma but as the forgiving and retaining of sins. The traditional Catholic and High Anglican interpretation of this has seen it as a reference to the sacrament of penance. This is probably an anachronism so far as the evangelist is concerned. In the New Testament, forgiveness of sins is baptismal language (see Lk 24:47), and what we have here is the Johannine version of the tradition which includes in the appearance stories the command to baptize. Our text speaks of the giving or withholding of baptism consequent on faith or unbelief at hearing the gospel message. Only derivatively and insofar as the sacrament of absolution is a renewal of the baptismal status can this text be stretched to cover the traditional interpretation.

If our new interpretation be sustained, it is significant that both *Reading II* and the *Gospel* speak of baptism, for in patristic times Pentecost was the day when those who for some cause had missed their baptism at Easter were baptized. Baptism was not continually administered at any time of the year because its corporate significance was paramount.

Trinity Sunday to Sunday 13 C

Feasts in honor of a doctrine rather than of an event of salvation were a late medieval introduction. Purists might argue that they be altogether abandoned, but the Spirit has spoken even in the medieval church! The *doctrine* of the Trinity is implicit, rather than explicit, in scripture. What we have in the New Testament is first a triadic structure in basic Christian experience: the Spirit brings the believers in faith to Jesus as the one in whom God is finally present in revelatory and saving action. This structure of experience issues very early in triadic formulae for blessings (2 Cor 13:13) and, at a late stage in the New Testament, in the baptismal formula (Mt 28:19). Thus the church was eventually led to define the dogma of the Trinity, which it did in terms of Greek philosophy rather than in the salvation-historical language of the Bible. Therefore the philosophical language must continually refer us back to the historical experience of the Bible. This means the whole Bible, Old Testament as well as New Testament. For Yahweh in the Old Testament is not just what later theology called the "first person," but Father, Son and Spirit. For in the Old Testament God is the God who exists in himself, who goes forth out of himself in revealing and saving action, and who brings men to respond in faith to that saving action.

Reading I: Proverbs 8:22-31.

The concept of the divine wisdom is mythological in origin, but was taken up into the Yahwistic religion to express God's self-disclosure. This self-disclosure comes to be personified or hypostatized as the divine wisdom. Wisdom means God's going forth from his "aseity" (his being-in-himself) in revelation and action. The hymn in Prv 8 is somewhat rudimentary in its understanding of wisdom as divine activity, for unlike later passages (Sir 24:1-24; Wis 7:22–8:1) it does not assign to wisdom an active role in creation: she is merely "around" when God creates. In its later development wisdom acquires a subjective role in human existence, becoming the organ of man's religious experience. In this way, "Wisdom" becomes the predecessor of both the Logos and the Holy Spirit. Thus we may read this passage as a step on the road to the doctrine of Trinity.

Responsorial Psalm: 8:3-8.

This psalm puts into verse form the theological truth of the creation story in Gn 1. God is the creator of the whole universe and man is the crown of creation, destined for glory and honor and invested with dominion over the created order. He exists in what Gn 1 calls the divine "image." God's name, whose wonder is proclaimed, is in Christian understanding a threefold name, a God who is in his own eternal being, who goes forth out of himself in creation and redemption and creates man's response to that creation and revelation. All this is latent in this psalm.

Reading II: Romans 5:1-5.

This is one of those artless passages where the apostle exhibits the triadic structure of Christian experience. God is the source of our redemption, but it is through Jesus Christ that this redemptive act is performed, and through the Holy Spirit poured into our hearts that we come to experience that redemptive action.

Gospel: John 16:12-15.

Here again the doctrine of the Trinity is implicit. The revelation which Jesus Christ brings is from the Father, and it is the function of the Spirit to take that revelation and make it meaningful to each succeeding Christian generation. The Spirit does not convey new independent revelations ("on his own authority"), but constantly updates our understanding of the once and for all revelation of God in the Christ event.

CORPUS CHRISTI

It is a little difficult for an Anglican to approach this set of readings without at least some reservations. To many of us it would seem more fitting, with the early church, to celebrate the *event* of the institution of the eucharist, and to do this on Maundy Thursday, rather than to have a special day to commemorate a doctrine.[1] But most churches of the

[1] It should be added that most contemporary Anglican theologians have little

Anglican Communion provide a eucharist in "thanksgiving for the institution of holy communion" which may be used at any suitable time. This is widely used on the Thursday after Trinity Sunday, though it would rarely be used again on the ensuing Sunday. But when one turns to the actual readings provided in the *Lectionary*, one finds that, after all, by the very genius of scripture they are concerned with saving events rather than with the later expressions of eucharistic doctrine.

Reading I: Genesis 14:18-20.

It is striking that the Epistle to the Hebrews, which elaborates on Melchizedek as a type of Christ's high priesthood, never mentions the gifts, the bread and wine, which he presented to Abraham. This is all the more surprising since these gifts were allegorically interpreted in Philo and in the rabbis, and, in the church fathers from Cyprian onwards, as a type of the eucharist, especially in its sacrificial character.

Maybe we can remain true to the New Testament and yet give the Melchizedek text a fitting interpretation for Corpus Christi. Westcott suggests that Melchizedek is presented in Hebrews as a priest not in sacrificing but in blessing, "that is, in communicating the fruits of an efficacious sacrifice already made." This we can accept, so long as we also affirm that the sacrifice made once for all becomes a present reality in the eucharist through the consecration and sharing of the bread and wine, and, because of the presence of the sacrifice, communicates its fruits.

Responsorial Psalm: 110:1-4.

This is one of the royal psalms. Its date and original reference are in dispute. There is a trend to interpret it as a reference to the early kings of Judah in the Davidic line, though earlier critics regarded it as an attempt of the priestly family of the Hasmoneans to justify their claim to kingship as well as priesthood. In either case, Melchizedek is taken as the prototype of the priest-king. The author of Hebrews takes up this psalm because it enables him to develop his own teaching on Christ's high priesthood. In the earlier church the messiahship (kingship) of Jesus was firmly established. Now Hebrews develops the further Christology (implicit in the early church's sacrificial interpretation of Jesus' death) that he is also

difficulty with the doctrine of transubstantiation itself, rightly understood. We would recognize it as a valid attempt within the terms of a given philosophy to express a doctrine which we too accept, though it is not expressed in terms of a philosophy which we would necessarily want to use today.

priest. The psalm may remind us that in the eucharist Christ is himself the true priest who presides over his eucharistic banquet and gives himself as the sacrificial victim to the faithful. He "gives himself with his own hand" (St. Thomas Aquinas). The ministerial priest who presides at the earthly altar is the instrument by which Christ's true high priesthood is externalized.

Reading II: 1 Corinthians 11:23-26.

This was the epistle for the mass of the Lord's Supper on Holy Thursday (q.v.), suggesting that the feast of Corpus Christi is an extrapolation of the earlier occasion. On Holy Thursday we contemplate the institution of the eucharist in its relation to the whole series of events of the *triduum sacrum*. On Corpus Christi the eucharist is isolated for contemplation as an ongoing rite in the church.

Gospel: Luke 9:11b-17.

Many motifs have shaped the narratives of the feeding of the multitude. On the historical level there can be little doubt that the meeting of Jesus and his followers in the desert marked the critical turning point in the Galilean ministry. (See John's note that Jesus' followers wanted to make him king, i.e., a political Messiah, and Mark's enigmatic note that Jesus sent his disciples away while he dismissed the crowd. In the light of John's account it is clear that Jesus did this to prevent the disciples from becoming infected with the crowd's dangerous political messianism.) There is no reason why this critical meeting should not have been accompanied by a meal, which like all Jesus' meals with his disciples would have eschatological associations, as foretaste of the eschatological banquet.

In earliest Christianity Jesus was interpreted as the prophet of the endtime, repeating Moses' gift of the manna (a theme which comes out most strongly in the Johannine discourse following this episode) and the miraculous multiplication of the loaves by Elisha (2 Kgs 4:42-44).

Further, the language of the eucharistic liturgy has colored the narrative: "sit down"; "taking"; "loaves"; "blessed"; "broke"; "gave"; "ate".

We generally think of the Last Supper as the institution of the eucharist. But the New Testament sees two further bases for the rite: the meals of the earthly Jesus with his followers, and the appearance meals after the resurrection. These meals emphasize an aspect that was certainly present in the Last Supper (Mk 14:25; Lk 22:16-18), namely, its eschatological character. The eucharist is not only a feeding upon a past sacrifice made a present reality, but it is also a foretaste of the Messianic banquet. The (now optional) sequence of Corpus Christi shows that this eschatological significance of the eucharist was not forgotten in the middle ages: "Grant us with your saints, though lowest/ Where the heav'nly feast you show/ Fellow heirs and guests to be."

TWELFTH SUNDAY OF THE YEAR

After the fast and festival season we return to the "green Sundays," now designated as Sundays of the Year. The epistles and gospels form a continuous reading of selected books (Luke for this year, and Galatians for the next few Sundays). The Old Testament reading is generally connected with either the epistle or the gospel, and sometimes with both. Occasionally it is hard to discern any obvious connection with either.

Reading I: Zechariah 12:10-11.

The original meaning of this passage from deutero-Isaiah (see 52:13– 53:12) is highly uncertain, but one thing is clear: the New Testament church (Jn 19:37 and Rv 1:7) took it as a Messianic prophecy, referring either to the crowd's seeing the pierced Christ on the cross at the crucifixion (Jn) or to the ungodly at the parousia (Rv). It has been argued that this text underlies all the references to the "seeing" of the Son of Man coming on the clouds of heaven (e.g., Mk 13:26). In Christian interpretation, therefore, this text refers to the remorse which will at the last judgment overtake all who have rejected Christ on earth.

It is arguable that this lesson would be more appropriate for Advent or Holy Week. At this season of the year, when we think of the Christian life in the Spirit and the pilgrimage of the church from Pentecost to the parousia, it may serve as a reassurance to the community that the cause for which it stands — the gospel of Christ crucified — is certain of ultimate vindication.

Responsorial Psalm: 63:1-5, 7-8.

Many of the psalms are intensely personal. But when they were adopted into the liturgy of the temple they acquired a corporate meaning, the "I" of the psalmist being expanded to embrace the whole people of God. In the person of Jesus Christ, who is the true Israel, the psalm is narrowed down again to a single person, the "I" of Christ himself. But then it expands once more to include the body of Christ, which in him can take these words to itself. The people of God on their pilgrimage pass through a dry and weary land where no water is. But in the sanctuary, as they assemble together to celebrate the liturgy, they have a pledge and assurance of the ultimate vindication of Christ's cause. They feast together on "marrow and fat" and praise God with joyful lips, even in the midst of the dry and weary land.

Reading II: Galatians 3:26-29.

As we continue to read Galatians we emerge from the long disputation on justification to something we feel we can really understand: the unity of the baptized in the church, transcending all barriers of nationality, race, social standing and sex. But Paul could never have written this purple passage unless he had argued through the whole question of justification. Only because baptism is the sacrament of justification are all these barriers of nature and history transcended; they are not transcended by being declared indifferent or due to misunderstanding. Only when man receives the forgiveness of justification imparted to him in baptism are these very real differences of nature, history and culture overcome. That men are one is an *eschatological* truth, a truth only "in Christ Jesus." The implementation of this truth in the common life of the church is a constant task. "Jew nor Greek" stands for racial differences, and a "white" church is a poor exhibition of catholicity. "Slave nor free" challenges us to ask ourselves whether we are, e.g., like it used to be said of the Church of England, the Tory party on its knees. "Male nor female" challenges us about the place of women in the church (second-class citizens?). But note, our text is talking about baptism, not about ordination: that is a question which has to be settled in a different context.

Gospel: Luke 9:18-24.

Peter came to his confession, "The Christ of God," not because he knew the correct doctrine of the incarnation in advance, but because of his encounter with the person of Jesus, watching him at work and hearing him speak. The doctrine of the incarnation is not the presupposition and premise of our understanding of Christ, but the conclusion of our encounter with him. That is why it is putting the cart before the horse to approach the gospels with the kind of question: If Christ is divine, why could he not do (or say, or know) this or that? We hear first what he says and see what he does, and then, as we encounter the presence of God in him who is truly man, we confess with Peter, "You are the Christ of God."

To be the Christ was not, however, for Jesus a dignity to be claimed, but a mission to be worked out, a mission that inevitably led him to the cross. And to follow him, to believe that he is the Christ, God present for us in man, is to be called likewise to take up the cross "daily," as Luke alone of the evangelists says. This "daily" task takes us back to the epistle and baptism. We have daily to die with Christ that we may rise again with him.

THIRTEENTH SUNDAY OF THE YEAR

Reading I: 1 Kings 19:16b, 19-21.

It is instructive to compare Elijah's call of Elisha with Jesus' call of his disciples as related in the gospel for this Sunday. Elisha asks: "Let me kiss my father and my mother, and then I will follow you." When Jesus called two would-be disciples, they said: "Lord, let me first go and bury my father." Elisha's call is one that could be added to already existing responsibilities. With Jesus' call it is different. All existing responsibilities have to be given up. They may be given back as part of the total call, but always as only part of it, inclosed within it, and subordinated to it.

The second difference is that Elijah's mantle falls upon Elisha. He can succeed him, become a prophet like his master when the latter finally departs (2 Kgs 2). But when Jesus ascends to heaven, his followers do not replace him. They remain followers, and he remains present as their living Lord.

Responsorial Psalm: 16:1-2a, 5, 7-11.

The early church seized upon this psalm as a prophecy of Christ's resurrection. In his Pentecost sermon as presented in Acts, St. Peter quotes vv. 9-11. Once again, the "I" of the psalms is the "I" of the living Christ. But it also includes the members of his body, and so we may take this psalm upon our own lips and make it a psalm of praise for our inheritance, for our call into the life of Christ.

Reading II: Galatians 5:1, 13-18.

Freedom is the hallmark of Christian existence. But this freedom is constantly threatened. For the Galatians it was threatened because they were succumbing to the blandishments of Paul's opponents, and falling prey to some kind of syncretism which included circumcision. For Paul this completely undermines the gospel. The Christian is free because he does not have to acquire salvation by his own works. But because he has already been given salvation as a gift, he is free to work it out in obedience. This is the positive truth behind what in the sixties gained popularity as "situation ethics." There is one obligation for Christians, and that is the law of love. "The whole law is fulfilled in one word, you shall love your neighbor as yourself." Paul does not overlook the first and greatest commandment, the love of God; he is speaking to those who have already heard the message of justification, and who have therefore been brought into the love of God. Paul is talking about how that love of God can only express itself historically as love of neighbor. Love of neighbor should provide the Christian with a set of antennae (J.A.T. Robinson), enabling him to know in each concrete situation what that love requires, without a lot of rules and regulations. The guidance he needs is provided by the "as yourself": do to others as you would have them do to you.

Flesh and Spirit in the last paragraph are not (though they are frequently thus misunderstood, even in modern translations) our so-called higher and lower natures. Flesh is our old unredeemed humanity in its totality, including what we call our higher nature. Spirit, as the capitalization suggests, is the Spirit of God, the eschatological possibility which transforms our whole human nature, lower as well as higher, so-called.

Gospel: Luke 9:51-62.

The latter part of the gospel (the call of the would-be followers) has been sufficiently treated under the Old Testament reading. Here we concentrate on the former part. The suggestion of James and John that fire should be called down from heaven to punish the Samaritans who would not receive Jesus "because his face was set toward Jerusalem" recalls their nick-name, sons of thunder (*Boanerges*). Recently attempts have been made to associate Jesus with the Zealots, the revolutionary liberationists of the day. That several of Jesus' disciples had Zealot sympathies there can be no doubt (e.g., Simon the Zealot). It seems probable that Jesus felt the constant temptation to seek an easy way out for his mission by adopting the Zealot line (O. Cullmann). But this was for him precisely that, a temptation, and one which he constantly resisted, and that brought him, humanly speaking, to the cross. This recent controversy is a warning against the "peril of modernizing Jesus" (H. J. Cadbury). Every new movement of thought seeks to enlist Jesus on its side. But he remains himself, the judge of all human causes. He turns and rebukes them!

✓ Sundays 14 C to 22 C

✓ FOURTEENTH SUNDAY OF THE YEAR

Reading I: Isaiah 66:10-14c.

Originally this prophecy from trito-Isaiah spoke of the joy following the restoration of God's people from exile. The returning exiles are received back by the holy city as a mother who consoles them at her breasts and dandles them on her lap. The metaphor is mixed, for it also speaks of Yahweh sending his "prosperity" (*shalom*, which the comment in italics at the head of the lesson inadequately renders "peace," presumably to establish a link with the gospel) like a river. (Note also the reference to peace in *Reading II*; otherwise there seems very little to link the three readings.) It is, however, an appropriate reading for the post-Pentecost season in which the church enjoys the fruits of redemption, particularly the gift of the Spirit.

Responsorial Psalm: 66:1-3a, 4-7a, 16, 20.

This is a psalm of thanksgiving for a national deliverance, pictured in imagery derived from the original exodus. "He turned the sea into dry land; men passed through the river on foot." The prophecies of deutero-Isaiah spoke of the return from exile in these terms, so the psalm forms a good response to *Reading I*. It is a thanksgiving for all the blessings of redemption and for us particularly, for the gift of the Spirit.

The latter verses of the psalm (here represented by vv. 16 and 20) take a surprisingly individualistic turn. It is reasonable to suppose that at some juncture two originally distinct psalms have been combined. The Christian sees his own personal religious experience as part of the experience of the entire body, while the experience of the entire body is reflected in the experience of the individual. The gift of the Holy Spirit is at once corporate and individual. At times in the history of the church one aspect has been emphasized at the expense of the other. Both must be held in balance.

Reading II: Galatians 6:14-18.

It was Paul's custom to dictate his letters to an amanuensis, and then to take the pen himself and add a few concluding words. In these words he summarizes and drives home the message of the whole letter. The purpose of Galatians was to dissuade his Gentile readers from lapsing into syncretism. They were probably not Judaizing in the strict sense, for Paul has to remind them that anyone who gets circumcised is obligated to keep the whole law, which would have been self-evident to a genuine Judaizer. Paul "glories," not like his opponents, in circumcision, but in the cross. What matters is that the believers have been recreated to a new existence. For Paul what matters in this new existence is not the marks of circumcision, but the marks of his apostolic sufferings, in which Christ crucified is manifested. Finally, the apostle gives his readers his blessing in a style which suggests (as the conclusions of other letters, especially 1 Corinthians, suggest even more clearly) that his letters were written to lead into the celebration of the Lord's Supper.

Gospel: Luke 10:1-12, 17-20.

All three of the synoptic gospels record a mission of the twelve during Jesus' earthly ministry. The mission of the seventy (some texts have seventy-two) is peculiar to Luke. In chapter nine Luke has already followed his Marcan source for the mission of the twelve. Here he follows Q. and his special material for the mission of the seventy. The Q. material is also used by Matthew in his mission charge to the twelve. So it is clear that the idea of mission of the seventy was created, not by Q. or Mark, but by Luke or in his special material. There can be little doubt that the number seventy is symbolic. The mission of the twelve represents the church's mission to Israel (twelve tribes); and the mission of the seventy, its mission to the nations of the world (which, according to Jewish tradition, numbered seventy or seventy-two). Some critics maintain that the whole idea of missions during the earthly ministry is a retrojection of the post-Easter mission into the earthly life of Jesus. But it is noteworthy that the disciples are charged to proclaim Jesus' own message: "The kingdom of God has come near to you," not the Christological kerygma of the post-

Easter church. The mission is to be characterized by urgency and detachment. The exact expression of this urgency and detachment is conditioned by the circumstances of the time. But in some form or other urgency and detachment must always characterize the church's mission.

Two other features are worthy of note. First, it is not the disciples (and therefore not the church) that initiate the mission. The initiative comes from the Lord of the harvest in response to the church's prayer. The disciples return from their mission elated by their success, but Jesus at once dampens their elation: "Do not rejoice in this, that the spirits are subject to you; but rejoice that your names are written in heaven." There is for the missionary an even more significant joy: prior to their mission they had been admitted to the privilege of partaking in the eschatological salvation. When they forget that, they are tempted to think that the mission is their own cause and that the success is their own achievement. Even an apostle or evangelist is a justified sinner.

✓✓ FIFTEENTH SUNDAY OF THE YEAR

Reading I: Deuteronomy 30:10-14.

This is part of Moses' farewell discourse in Deuteronomy. In fact it is a liturgical sermon urging Israel to renew the covenant, and was probably composed in the time of exile. It suggests (see Jeremiah) the concept of the law no longer written on tables of stone, but engraved on the heart, thus presaging the development of the wisdom tradition after the exile. Paul in Romans picked up this passage (v. 14) and applied it to the gospel and the righteousness that comes by faith (Rom 10:5-8). As Dodd has pointed out, Paul is not really doing violence to Deuteronomy, which is less legalistic than, say, Leviticus: "The deuteronomic code . . . bases righteousness on the love of God, to which we should be provoked by his grace towards his people."[1] Hence *Reading I* prepares us for the gospel of the day, which features the double command of love.

Responsorial Psalm: 69:13, 16, 29-30, 32-33, 35ab, 36.

Like so many other psalms, this one begins as the prayer of an individual in distress and ends on a note of assurance. These psalms reflect the pattern of Christ's death-resurrection and the Christian's experience of sin and justification. It makes a fitting response to Dt 30:10-14, interpreted in the light of Rom 10:5-8.

[1] C. H. Dodd, *The Epistle to the Romans* (New York: Harper and Brothers 1932) 165.

Reading II: Colossians 1:15-20.

This passage is a Christological hymn. The first part speaks of Christ in terms of the later Jewish concept of wisdom, the image of God personified as the agent of creation and preservation. The second part moves to the theme of redemption, but is patterned on the first part. As pre-existent wisdom, Christ was the first-born of creation. As the risen one, he is the first-born of the dead. As the agent of creation he created the cosmic powers. In his exaltation he is their victor and the head of his body, the church. The divine wisdom becomes incarnate in Jesus, and the incarnation reaches in its climax the cross, which is the source of conciliation and peace.

It was a bold step for the New Testament to identify Christ with the pre-existent "Wisdom." What led it to take this step? It was the conviction that the God who had revealed himself and acted in Jesus Christ was the same God who had created the world. Redemption is not redemption out of the world, but the restoration of the created world when it had fallen into sin. The implications of this for the Christian attitude to the world are far-reaching. Christianity says a preliminary "Yes" to the world as God's creation, and a preliminary "No" to it as subject to the powers of evil. But it says an ultimate "Yes" to the world, because that world has been reconciled through the blood of the cross.

Gospel: Luke 10:25-37.

The double commandment of love has come down in two different forms. In the Marcan/Matthean form it is Jesus who gives the command in response to a question; in the Lucan form it is elicited from the "lawyer" in response to Jesus' counter-question. The content of the commandment is not original to Jesus, for it is a combination of texts from Deuteronomy and Leviticus. Nor is it certain that the combination is original to him, for it is also found in the Testament of the Twelve Patriarchs (although some scholars think that there it is a Christian interpolation). It is arguable, however, that in Christian tradition the double argument stems from Jesus, and that Luke's form of it is a secondary adaptation to the dramatic exigencies of his pericope. Even if Jesus was not the first to combine love of God and neighbor, he understood that combination with a unique and radical seriousness (G. Bornkamm). There can be no love of God which does not express itself in love of neighbor. Yet conversely, there is no authentic love of neighbor which does not spring from love of God, for otherwise it is a refined, subtle form of self-love. In

Luke's dramatic construction Jesus' acceptance of the lawyer's reply leads to a further question on his part. He wished to "justify himself," to get the whole thing straight. He asks, "Who is my neighbor?" The dramatic exchange is the springboard for the parable of the Good Samaritan. But the parable doesn't really answer the lawyer's question. It ends by reversing it: "Which of the three *proved neighbor* to him who fell among the robbers?" It is just here that the point of the parable lies. "You shall love your neighbor" doesn't mean you may love some people but not others. Rather, it means: be a neighbor to another, not just indulging in general sentiments of benevolence, but doing concrete acts for the person in concrete need. "Neighborliness is not a quality in other people, it is simply their claim on ourselves. We have literally no time to sit down and ask ourselves whether so-and-so is our neighbor or not. We must get into action and obey; we must behave like a neighbor to him" (D. Bonhoeffer).

✓✓ SIXTEENTH SUNDAY OF THE YEAR

Reading I: Genesis 18:1-10a.

The annunciation of Isaac's birth to Abraham has no obvious connection with the thanksgiving for the Christian mystery in Colossians (*Reading II*) or with Martha and Mary in Luke (*Gospel*). Perhaps there is a thread linking the revelation of Isaac's birth to Abraham and the mystery hidden for ages and generations and now made manifest. God is a God who acts in history, his actions are constantly new, and accompanying his actions is the revelation of their meaning. Action plus revelation of its meaning equals mystery. Annunciation scenes are a device to disclose the meaning of God's acts in salvation history. A major figure in salvation history has his birth announced by an angel (often a birth out of due course, a supernatural birth). The birth of Isaac was supernatural, because both Abraham and Sarah were too old to become parents. This and other similar birth stories (e.g., Sampson, Samuel) provide the Old Testament precedent for the annunciation of the birth of Jesus to Joseph in Matthew, and to Mary in Luke. For Jesus' birth is likewise supernatural. In other words, Jesus is not merely a product of human history but an intervention, indeed, the final eschatological intervention of God in salvation history. The meaning of this history is disclosed to Joseph ("He will save his people from their sins") and to Mary ("He will be great, and will be called the Son of the Most High").

Responsorial Psalm: 15:2-4ab, 5.

This psalm is one of the "entry psalms" sung as the pilgrims entered the temple. It describes the character of the man whom God will accept as a worthy pilgrim, a man of justice, sincerity and integrity. Abraham was known for his justice, and this psalm serves as a fitting response to the first reading.

Reading II: Colossians 1:24-28.

Colossians is one of the *antilegomena,* i.e., a letter regarded, at least by more radical critics, as deutero-Pauline. If it be so, the present passage is remarkably close to what St. Paul would have written, and is the product of a mind thoroughly impregnated with the thoughts of the apostle. For it interprets the apostle's self-understanding precisely as in Galatians, 1 and 2 Corinthians and Romans. Suffering is one of the hallmarks of apostleship. The apostle fills up that which is lacking of Christ's afflictions: a bold formulation, which, however, does not mean that something is lacking in the atoning power of Christ's death. The clue lies in the undoubted letters, which present Paul's suffering as an epiphany, manifestation or proclamation of Christ's cross. What is "lacking" is not the atoning power of the cross, but its manifestation in the church as a present reality. As in the undoubted letters, Paul's gospel is a "mystery" (1 Cor 2:1), the proclamation of a new saving act, a complete *novum* unheard of before. For Paul this mystery has a particular nuance (see Rom 11:25): it involves admission of the Gentiles to the privileges of the end-time community.

There are also some differences between our passage and the undoubted letters. In the latter Paul does not speak of the church as the body of Christ *tout court,* but employs that image as a metaphor or simile to express the unity of the church amid the diversity of its members. Also, the undoubted letters either reject the notion that Christians already here in this time could be "mature" (*teleioi,* literally, "perfect"), or use it ironically. Colossians and Ephesians speak of perfection as a goal toward which the Christian should progress in his earthly pilgrimage. The differences are slight but significant. The *antilegomena* presuppose a later situation in which it is recognized that the church is here to stay, to live in history and to produce a Christian culture.

Gospel: Luke 10:38-42.

This well-known idyllic scene is placed by Luke immediately after the

Good Samaritan (see last Sunday). In this position it corrects the activistic impression that might otherwise be deduced from Jesus' answer to the lawyer's question, "Do this, and you will live." Activism must spring from hearing the word of God. Most of us would feel that we have to combine Mary and Martha, hearing the word of God and going out into the world in active service. But we must recognize that some have a primary vocation to be Mary, others to be Martha.

SEVENTEENTH SUNDAY OF THE YEAR

Reading I: Genesis 18:20-32.

Another reading from the Abraham cycle. Its context is clear: God is about to destroy Sodom and Gomorrah. The J. tradition from which this comes uses the occasion as an opportunity to reflect on the problem of divine justice, and casts its reflections in the form of a dialogue between Abraham and Yahweh. Abraham is the mouthpiece of the conviction that, as a God of justice, Yahweh would not destroy Sodom if it also meant the destruction of a few righteous men with the guilty majority. Pleading his case by a kind of Dutch auction, Abraham arrives at the point where he asks Yahweh if ten righteous men would be enough to save the city and is assured that it would. The dialogue is then broken off, but the city is not spared. So in the Genesis narrative the dialogue throws the wickedness of Sodom into even sharper relief: there weren't even ten righteous men there. The writer of this article will never forget hearing a sermon on this text from a German pastor after the collapse of the Third Reich. It was in support of the Stuttgart declaration of corporate guilt by the Evangelical Church in Germany. What has this text to say to the American nation as the Vietnam war draws to its close?

Responsorial Psalm: 138.

As the reference to the temple in v. 1 suggests, Ps 138 is a liturgical psalm of thanksgiving for deliverance. It forms a suitable response to the Genesis reading, in which God is depicted as a God of mercy as well as of justice.

Reading II: Colossians 2:12-14.

Here is another passage where Colossians differs from the undoubted letters. In Rom 6 Paul says that in baptism we share the death of Christ, but that our rising with him is conditional on our (daily) dying to sin and walking in newness of life. It awaits its final fulfilment at the final resurrection. Colossians abandons this reservation and speaks of the baptized as already risen, though a little later it emphasizes the necessity of implementing the resurrection by ethical obedience, so that it is not so far removed from the position in Romans after all.

The picture of Christ's nailing to the cross "the bond which stood against us" is intriguing. A "bond" is a kind of I.O.U. The precise background of the metaphor is uncertain. Is the writer thinking of the *titulus* on the cross, so that "The king of the Jews" means that Jesus is king of his people because he forgives them their sins? Or is it derived from the *tropaion*, the post on which a triumphant military commander would hang the spoils he had taken from his enemies? If the source of the imagery is uncertain, the meaning is clear: in the cross Christ achieved for man the forgiveness of sin. All Christian experience throughout the ages has known this, even if the various theories of the atonement are intellectually unsatisfying.

Gospel: Luke 11:1-13.
This pericope consists of two parts: the delivery of the Lord's Prayer, followed by a catena of sayings on petitionary prayer.

The Lucan text of the Lord's Prayer in RSV is shorter than the Matthean, consisting only of five petitions compared to Matthew's seven. The RSV follows the earlier Greek texts. The later text was assimilated to the Matthean form, which became traditional in the liturgy. The additional petitions of Matthew ("Thy will be done" and "But deliver us from evil") are probably liturgical expansions, each of the extra clauses being elucidations of the petition immediately preceding it. The simple address "Father" (Abba) was characteristic of Jesus. "Our Father in heaven" (Matthew) is again a formalized liturgical expansion.

A Jew of Jesus' day would have shrunk from calling God "Abba," for this was the familiar address of the child to his human father. God would be addressed as "our" or "my Father." Here lies the unique filial consciousness of Jesus, which is the foundation of his own life of obedience and of the church's later Christological interpretation of his person. "Hallowed be thy name" is usually called the first petition, but it is probably a glorifying of the name of God, which in Jewish prayer always precedes petition. Each of the succeeding petitions is patient of an eschatological interpretation. Obviously this is the case with "Thy kingdom come." But the "bread" of the third petition (literally, *tomorrow's* bread) quite likely means the Messianic banquet. These two petitions pray for a foretaste already here and now of the blessings of the end. The "forgive us our sins" refers to the last judgment, but is likewise anticipated in our justification. Our forgiveness of others does not earn God's forgiveness for us, but is the condition of our continuance in forgiveness (see the parable of the unforgiving servant, Mt 18:22-35). "Temptation" (Greek *peirasmos*) is a technical term for the Messianic woes. It is a prayer not that God would stop tempting us to sin (for God does not do this, as St. James correctly observes) but rather for our preservation in the Messianic woes, the final great tribulation, anticipated in the trials of faith during the Christian's life.

Matthew's comment on the Our Father takes up the petition for forgiveness; Luke's, the whole idea of petitionary prayer. Some modern devotional writers are squeamish about petitionary prayer, but in Jesus' teaching petition is prayer *par excellence*. Prayer in the Bible is primarily not mystical experience, but working with God in carrying out his purposes in salvation history. The supreme petition of Christian prayer is for the Holy Spirit (v. 13). It is interesting that some ancient texts of Luke read, "Let the Holy Spirit come upon us and cleanse us," instead of the petition for tomorrow's bread. This is unlikely to be the true reading, but it is a significant early interpretation which supports the eschatological interpretation of "tomorrow's bread."

The doxology to the Lord's Prayer which appears in late texts of Matthew is not part of the original text. But it was Jewish custom to add a doxology and Jesus probably expected his disciples to follow this. Here the *Missale Romanum* was more faithful to the letter of scripture, while Orthodoxy and Protestantism are truer to the probable implicit intention of it!

There are parallels in Jewish prayers to every petition of the Our Father. But this does not deprive it of its originality. The meaning of each of Jesus' petitions is formed by his proclamation of the kingdom of God, not as a purely future hope, but as a reality already proleptically present in his own person.

EIGHTEENTH SUNDAY OF THE YEAR

Reading I: Ecclesiastes 1:2; 2:21-23.

Ecclesiastes is not one of the most loved books of the Bible. In fact we may sometimes wonder why it is in the canon at all. But with that taste for shocking paradox that was characteristic of him, Sir Edwyn Hoskyns used to say that Ecclesiastes was the most Christian book in the Old Testament! What he meant was that Ecclesiastes is a ruthless exposure of what human life is apart from God, and if taken really seriously, prepares the way for a hearing of the gospel of Christ. Ecclesiastes is not so much good news, but the bad news which has to be heard before the good news becomes audible. "Vanity of vanities" — all of human life is ultimately futile and meaningless if viewed in itself, apart from God.

Responsorial Psalm: 95:1-2, 6-9.

The *Venite* consists of two parts, the first a call to worship, the second a warning against neglect of the word of God. The first part is very popular among Anglicans as the invitatory canticle to the office of Morning Prayer, but in most recent revisions the stern warnings of the second part have frequently been omitted. Yet it was this second part that the author of Hebrews (Heb 3:7—4:13) took up and expounded as especially relevant to his church. The situation of the people of this church was that they were growing stale instead of advancing in the Christian life (the medieval sin of accidie), as Israel grew tired in the wilderness.

Reading II: Colossians 3:1-5, 9-11.

As we have seen earlier in these meditations, Colossians goes further than Romans in recognizing the risen life as already a present reality in which the baptized share. But Colossians does not overlook the need for the continual reiteration of the imperative ("seek those things . . . ; put to death . . . ; do not lie . . ."). Maintenance of the baptismal state of being raised with Christ depends upon constantly and actively seeking to live out the risen life. "Seek those things which are above": i.e., a "transcendent quality of living. This transcendence is not to be understood spacially, as it were, suggesting a neo-Platonic escape from this present world, but a qualitatively transcendent existence within the world. Our relation to God is not a 'religious' relationship to the highest, most beautiful, powerful and best Being imaginable — but our relation to God is a new life in 'existence for others,' through participation in the being of Jesus . . . the 'man for others,' and therefore the crucified, the man who lives out of the transcendent" (D. Bonhoeffer). Hence the apostolic writer concludes, not with the individualistic ascetic that we might have expected from his initial prohibitions of immorality, etc., but with an affirmation about the Christian community as a community in which there is neither "Greek nor Jew, circumcised nor uncircumcised, barbarian, Scythian, slave, free man." Such distinctions belong to the penultimate, not to the ultimate. It is easy to translate these human divisions into contemporary terms.

Gospel: Luke 12:13-21.

The gospel of this day draws together the thoughts of the first two readings and gives them precision. The rich fool is a man who lived his life without reference to God and was caught in the toils of futility and meaninglessness ("vanity of vanities!"). He organized his life without reference to the transcendent; he did not "seek those things that are above." So comes the crashing judgment: "This night your soul [i.e., your life] is required of you." Because he viewed this present existence as autonomous, without reference to God, because he organized it without reference to the transcendent upon which it depends (note how he thought his own existence was under his own control), it came as a shock to learn that it was God's to give and God's to take away again. The rich fool condemns himself to an existence which is, qualitatively speaking, a life in death.

NINETEENTH SUNDAY OF THE YEAR

Reading I: Wisdom 18:6-9.

The Book of Wisdom, which, with its philosophical approach, appears to deal in timeless truths, nevertheless contains a long section which interprets the salvation history of Israel in terms of wisdom (11:2—19:22). It contains a lot of midrashic rewriting of the biblical accounts, much of it apparently emanating from the recital of the passover haggadah in a wisdom milieu. This is what we seem to have here. "That night" is a reference to the night of the first passover at the exodus (see the Easter Proclamation: "This is *the night* when first you saved our fathers"). But between the Easter Proclamation and the midrashic haggadah of the Book of Wisdom there is a shift. "Our fathers" in the Wisdom passage means the patriarchs, who are credited with having received from God the promise (here "oaths," sworn by God) of the future exodus. The author of Wisdom again reflects the paschal liturgy of his day by attributing to Israel's first passover his own contemporary practice of "singing the praises of our fathers," i.e., the Hallel psalms.

As the Christian church reads this passage it does so with further shifts. The exodus contains within it the promise of the Christian Easter, just as the revelation of the patriarchs contained in it the promise of the first exodus. The call of Israel foreshadows the call of the ecclesia. But just as the old Israel was a *communio sanctorum* of the exodus generation and the patriarchs, the church is a communion of saints which embraces all generations.

Responsorial Psalm: 33:1, 12, 18-20, 22.

This is a psalm of thanksgiving for the mighty acts of God in salvation history. Its accent on God's choosing of the people (the refrain "Happy are the people the Lord has chosen to be his own" and the verse "Blessed is . . . the people whom he has chosen as his own heritage") makes it a fitting response to the reading of Wisdom.

The doctrine of election has in our day fallen into neglect, largely because of a reaction against its distortion in Calvinistic theology. It is a thoroughly biblical doctrine. It does not (as Calvinism has often said) assert that God has picked out certain individuals for salvation and consigned the rest to damnation. Rather, it states that God has chosen *a people*, first the old Israel, then Christ as the sole bearer of Israel's privileges and prerogatives, and, by incorporation into him, the Christian ecclesia, which is ultimately to embrace in its unity (at least in principle) the whole of mankind.

"It is no formal election of a set of favorites of heaven, who were to earn rewards from which the rest of the world were excluded. It was the election of a people to know what are the rights of men, that they might be witnesses to all men of *their* rights" (F. D. Maurice).

In this sense we may agree with article seventeen of the Thirty-nine Articles of Religion that "the godly consideration of our election in Christ is full of sweet, pleasant and unspeakable comfort."

Reading II: Hebrews 11:1-2, 8-19.

Hebrews 11 is often called "the roll call of the heroes of faith." Yet strictly speaking, the Bible knows no heroes, for heroes are witnesses to their own achievements, whereas in Heb 11 the great figures of salvation history from Abraham to the prophets and martyrs of the old covenant are adduced not for their heroism but precisely for their "faith," which is in the author's thought closely linked to hope. Faith is taking God at his word when he makes promises for the future. Thus the Old Testament figures become examples for the new Israel, the new wandering people of God. The new people has also in each succeeding generation had to imitate

Abraham, who "went out, not knowing where he was to go," and his family, "who lived in tents because they had no abiding city here, but looked forward to the city which has foundations."

Gospel: Luke 12:32-48.

The core of this section of Luke is the parable of the waiting servants (vv. 35-38) and on this our meditation will concentrate. It was probably not realized by those who drew up these lessons, but there is a remarkable convergence between the first reading and this gospel. For in its Lucan form the original parable of the doorkeeper (see Mk 13) has been expanded with elements taken from the Christian paschal feast: "Let your loins be girded [see Ex 12:11] and your lamps burning and be like men who are waiting for their master to come home." The early Christians literally believed that the return of their Lord would take place at the passover, as the first Israel believed that Messiah would come that night. When the Christ did not return literally at midnight, then the church celebrated the eucharist-agape in which he came in advance of his final coming. So the promise was fulfilled: "He will gird himself and have them sit at table and he will come and serve them." Every eucharist, especially every Sunday eucharist, is a reflection of the paschal eucharist, and so the same promise is fulfilled here, too.

At the same time, the essential attitude enjoined upon the disciples, "Watch," is a counterpart of the attitude inculcated in *Reading II*, the attitude of a faith which is prepared to go out not knowing where it is to go. Both speak in different ways of that readiness to be on the move, not to get bogged down in false securities on the assumption that here we have an abiding city.

ASSUMPTION OF THE BLESSED VIRGIN MARY: AUGUST 15[2]

The continued observance of the assumption on a Sunday when August 15 falls on that day would seem to contradict the new general principle that only dominical feasts should displace the regular Sunday propers. Perhaps the significance of this is that Mariology rightly understood is an aspect of Christology. The Blessed Virgin Mary is nothing in herself, but of great importance in salvation history as the chosen instrument of the incarnation.

For an Anglican, who is not committed to the dogma of 1950, the assumption of Mary belongs to the poetry of the Christian religion, some-

[2] Comments on Sunday 20 C will be found in the Appendix, below.

thing we sing about in hymns, but only a pictorial expression of the scriptural truth: "All generations will call me blessed." This is how the assumption is treated in a well-known Anglican hymn:

> O higher than the cherubim,
> More glorious than the seraphim,
>   Lead their praises,
>   Alleluia.
> Thou bearer of the eternal Word
> Most gracious, magnify the Lord,
>   Alleluia.
>
>   (Athelstan Riley)

It was in the same spirit that in the seventeenth century a statue of the crowned madonna and child was placed over the porch of St. Mary the Virgin, the university church at Oxford.

Reading I: Revelation 11:19a; 12:1-6a, 10ab.
The meaning of this mysterious passage is obscure, and many interpretations have been suggested. The child who is born is clearly the Messiah. This is shown by the application of the Messianic Ps 2:9 to the child in v. 5, and by the proclamation that follows his exaltation to the throne of God (v. 10). But who is the woman? There are three possibilities: 1) She is the old Israel, the nation from whom the Messiah came. Much in this passage suggests the old Israel waiting for the birth of the Messiah. The Old Testament background suggests this (see Is 66:7). On this view the seer is taking up and partly Christianizing earlier pictures of Israel waiting for the coming of the Messiah. 2) The woman is the church, the new Israel, the mother of the faithful. This is supported by 12:17, which speaks of other children belonging to the woman who "keep the commandments of God and bear testimony to Jesus." 3) An interpretation popular among medieval expositors, and revived in a somewhat more sophisticated form in recent Catholic exegesis (and clearly accepted by the choice of this passage for Assumption), equates the woman with the Blessed Virgin Mary.

Probably there is no need to choose between these three interpretations. For Mary is the daughter of Zion, the quintessential expression of the old Israel as the community of faith and obedience awaiting the coming of the Messiah, the community in which the Messiah is born. But she is also the quintessential expression of the new Israel, of those who "believe" and are justified on the ground of their faith, of those who obey his word and who suffer for the testimony of Jesus.

Responsorial Psalm: 45:9b-11, 15.

In its original intention this psalm celebrates the marriage of an Israelite king to a foreign princess. In order to fit it to its liturgical use here an allegorical interpretation has to be given. The king in the psalm has to be equated with the Messiah (there is New Testament precedent for this, Heb 1:8-9); the queen, with Israel, his bride. This provides an indirect connection with the Blessed Virgin Mary as the personification of Israel. But the allegory must not be pressed. Not only does it do violence to the original meaning, but it does not fit the desired application. For Mary is the mother, rather than the bride of Christ, and his bride only insofar as she is the personification of the true Israel, one who believed in him (Acts 1:14).

Reading II: 1 Corinthians 15:20-27.

This is the passage to which the Protestants appeal against the dogma of the bodily assumption. It asserts that all men are in bondage to death, and that they can only attain to immortality through the resurrection of the dead. Christ, however, has broken the bondage of death and become the first fruits of the dead. Meanwhile, all in Christ await their resurrection until the parousia. There is therefore no place in the "order" for a prior resurrection of the Blessed Virgin Mary: Christ the first fruits, then at his coming those who belong to Christ. It must be left to Catholic exegetes to square the dogma of the bodily assumption of Mary with this scripture. As an Anglican the present writer would simply claim that the life which all believers have is inalienable by death, that therefore the Blessed Virgin Mary, like all the saints, has some kind of continuing existence in Christ (see Rev 6:9), and that we express the high honor due her by picturing her as exalted to the very throne of God.

Gospel: Luke 1:39-56.

This gospel falls into two parts, the visitation narrative and the Magnificat. There is an interesting textual problem in v. 46. Some MSS. read "Elisabeth said," a reading which would fit the typology: Hannah-Samuel/ Elisabeth-John the Baptist. It is arguable, however, that in the structure of the Lucan infancy narratives, the purpose of which is to bring out the relation of John to Jesus as that of the forerunner to the Messiah, of inferior to superior, the Magnificat must be assigned to Mary. Perhaps the pre-Lucan source, which quite likely came from "Baptist" circles, had attributed the song (modeled on the song of Hannah) to Elisabeth, and Luke himself transferred it to Mary.

The Magnificat should be read not as an individual utterance of Mary, but as the utterance of the representative of the true Israel. This is indicated by the switch from the first person singular to the third plural at v. 50. It is the true Israel personified by Mary who rejoices in the Lord at the coming of the Messiah, whose humiliation ("low estate") the Lord regards, and who henceforth will be called "blessed" as the people to whom the Messiah has come. This is not to downgrade Mary, but to exalt her role as the key-pin of salvation history.

TWENTY-FIRST SUNDAY OF THE YEAR

Reading I: Isaiah 66:18-21.

The gathering together of all peoples of the world at Zion at the beginning of the Messianic age is a frequent picture of the Isaianic and other Old Testament prophecies. Christian faith sees the fulfillment of these prophecies partly in the bringing of people from all nations into the catholic church, and partly in the future coming of the Son of Man to gather all the nations of the world into his kingdom.

John Mason Neale's translation of an early Eastern Orthodox hymn expresses this typology and this faith:

> Rise, Sion, rise, and looking forth
>   behold thy children round thee!
> From east and west, from south and north,
>   thy scattered sons have found thee:
> And in thy bosom Christ adore
> For ever and for ever more.

Responsorial Psalm: 117.

This psalm, which calls upon all nations to praise the name of Yahweh, is cited by St. Paul (Rom 15:11) in a catena of Old Testament texts to illustrate the universal scope of God's redemptive purpose in Christ. It is therefore an appropriate response to the Old Testament reading with its picture of the movement of all peoples to Zion.

Reading II: Hebrews 12:5-7, 11-13.

This reading is at first sight curiously divergent in theme from the other readings of this Sunday. Elsewhere the theme is the universality of the gospel; here it is the divine disciplining of the faithful.

Hebrews alternates between ethical exhortation and doctrinal-exegetical exposition. The exposition, which reaches its culmination in the long section on the high-priestly office in Christ (7:1—10:18), is intended to undergird the exhortation. This exhortation reflects the situation of the author's readers. They have been Christian for a long time, and are yielding to discouragement and frustration. The "discipline" to which they are being subjected is probably not acute persecution, but the petty pin-pricks of their non-Christian neighbors.

We can connect this reading with the other readings about the universality of the church in a way similar to the procedure of Hebrews itself. Christians today are not in most places suffering acute persecution, but they are troubled by the drift from the churches and by the prevailing contempt for the gospel. This reading tells us that we have to face this "painful rather than pleasant" period, because the Lord is disciplining his people. This discipline is, however, a sign of his love for his church. And then the other readings undergird this exhortation with the reassurance that the gospel is indeed "catholic," for all men and for all times, and that all nations *are* destined to come into God's kingdom.

Gospel: Luke 13:22-30.

This lesson, which culminates in the great proclamation that many shall come from east and west and take their place in the kingdom of God, begins somewhat unpromisingly with the assertion (in response to the question whether many or only a few shall be saved) that one can only enter that kindom by a narrow door. The universalism of the Christian gospel is no easy-going thing. It is intended for all men, but is offered through Christ alone. The universality goes hand in hand with the "scandal of particularity." The Messianic banquet is for those who are prepared to "eat the flesh" of the Messiah and to "drink his blood."

✓ TWENTY-SECOND SUNDAY OF THE YEAR

Reading I: Sirach 3:17-18, 20, 28-29.

This is a lesson on humility, chosen to fit the gospel of the day. Pride is the deadliest of the seven deadly sins, while humility is perhaps the most characteristic of Christian virtues. The humble man finds "favor" in the sight of the Lord not because that favor is a reward for his humility, but because humility like faith, to which it is akin, means abandoning self-assertion, all trust in one's own righteousness, and allowing God to act where we can do nothing.

Responsorial Psalm: 68:3-4a, 4c-6b, 9-10.

Psalm 68 is a confused melee of themes, thought by some scholars to be not a unitary psalm, but a series of headings to a number of different liturgical pieces. To read it is rather like reading the chapter headings of a book. But it contains passages of considerable beauty and it is possible, as is done here, to combine excerpts from it into a meaningful hymn. This selection is a hymn of praise to God for granting his favor to the poor (the "humble" of *Reading I*).

Reading II: Hebrews 12:18-19, 22-24a.

This reading from Hebrews would have fitted far better the theme of the previous week, the movement to Zion. It presents a contrast between the law and the gospel, between Mount Sinai and Mount Zion. Coming to this mountain is the favor which the Lord grants to the "humble."

Gospel: Luke 14:1, 7-14.

The parables read here (vv. 7-11) and the ensuing exhortation are connected by their common context in a meal of Jesus. The parable looks like a piece of prudential advice, how to behave at a dinner party so as to avoid an embarrassment. But since it is precisely a parable it must not be interpreted as a piece of worldly wisdom, or even as a lesson in humility as usually understood. It deals rather with an aspect of man's relationship with God. God in the person of Jesus (see v. 8) is inviting men to the Messianic feast. The only way to respond to this invitation is by the renunciation of any claim or merit of one's own. The Pharisees expected the best seats as a reward for keeping the Torah, but like the outcast they have to learn that salvation has to be accepted as an unmerited gift — exactly as we interpreted humility in *Reading I*. The ensuing exhortation is likewise not a piece of worldly advice, but also a kind of parable, its point being that men's final acceptance in the Messianic banquet depends on their acceptance of others now. In other words, forgive and God will forgive you. Thus humility in the Christian sense is not purely a passive virtue; like faith, to which it is so closely akin, it is highly active.

√ Sundays 23 C to 31 C

The three readings to be commented upon here have very different themes: the discernment of God's will possible only through the Spirit of God; the transformation of personal relations in Christ; and the renunciation of possessions as the prerequisite for true discipleship. It would tax our utmost ingenuity to discover a common theme between them. The only discernible connection of thought is between *Reading I* and the *Responsorial Psalm.*

Reading I: Wisdom 9:13-18.

This is part of the prayer which the Book of Wisdom puts into the mouth of Solomon. The earliest version of Solomon's prayer is in 1 Kgs 3:6-9, where he prays for "understanding." Then comes 2 Chr 1:9-10, where Solomon prays for "wisdom" to help him in performing the duties of kingship. The author of Wisdom expands on this point and enunciates the doctrine that the will of God can only be discerned by the help of wisdom and the Spirit of God — the parallelism suggesting that the two concepts are synonymous.

While v. 15 recalls Plato's *Phaedo,* the author does not teach a non-biblical dualism of body/soul. The body is a hindrance to the knowledge of God's will, not the seat of evil. It is its finite, not its evil, character that is its drawback. Only God's Spirit, or wisdom, enables a man to transcend that finitude.

Responsorial Psalm: 90:3-6, 12-14, 17.

Verses 3-6, from part one of the psalm, point up the contrast between

God's eternity and man's mortality. With this compare the first part of *Reading I*. Verses 12-14, 17 come from the second half of the psalm, which is a prayer for God's favor as a compensation for man's fleeting life, so that despite his transitoriness his work may prosper. The prayer for wisdom in v. 12 recalls Solomon's prayer.

Reading II: Philemon 9b-10, 12-17.

The letter to Philemon is the only personal letter of Paul which has survived. Onesimus, a slave who had run away from his master Philemon, a Christian of Colossae, had joined Paul where the latter was in prison. (Rome as the locale is the traditional view; Ephesus is popular today because of the distances involved: Colossae-Ephesus rather than Colossae-Rome.) Under Paul's influence Onesimus had become a Christian. In sending him back to his master, Paul commends him as "no longer a slave, but a brother." Paul did not thereby abolish slavery (that would have been impossible for the ancient world), but transformed the relationship. Not until the nineteenth century did the Christian conscience come to realize that slavery as an institution was wrong. Paul drew what consequences he could from his principle that in Christ there is neither slave nor free. Future generations have to give their own implementation to that principle in the light of their situation.

Gospel: Luke 14:25-33.

This gospel consists of a string of sayings on the cost of discipleship, followed by two parables to illustrate the necessity of facing that cost (the tower builder and the king going to war).

"Hate" (v. 26) is harsh. It has been suggested that the original Aramaic meant simply "love less than." But this in turn is probably too weak. The real meaning is that following Jesus means the surrender of the whole of a man's life. Then, as we have already noted in an earlier passage, the disciple receives back from Christ those aspects of the old life that are now needed to provide the context in which the claims of discipleship have to be worked out.

The saying in v. 27 does not mean that all true disciples must be martyrs in the literal sense. Yet martyrdom is discipleship carried to its ultimate conclusion. Hence the honor the church has always paid to its martyrs.

Reading I: Exodus 32:7-11, 13-14.

The heading calls attention to Yahweh's abandonment of his intention to punish Israel for making the golden calf and worshiping it. But the really significant feature of the text is Moses' action as a mediator. He makes intercession for them by pleading the promise of God to the patriarchs. This picture caught the attention of the psalmist (106:23). In this respect, as in others, Moses foreshadows the Messianic work of Christ. There is no New Testament passage which directly recalls this incident, but the same mediatorial function is ascribed to Jesus as is performed here by Moses. On the cross Jesus prays, "Father, forgive them." He now lives in heaven as the high priest to make intercession for his people (though in Hebrews this is Aaronic rather than Mosaic typology); and he is given the title of "mediator" between God and man (1 Tm 2:5, read next week) as Moses had been mediator between Yahweh and Israel.

Responsorial Psalm: 51:1-2, 10-11, 15, 17.

It will help us to relate this psalm to the foregoing reading if we think of it as uttered by Christ in his capacity as mediator. He takes men's sin upon himself, even to the extent of confessing their sin on their behalf. In his work *Atonement and Personality* (1917), R. C. Moberly, an Anglican, built up an impressive interpretation of the atonement as a perfect act of repentance on man's behalf.

Reading II: 1 Timothy 1:12-17.

If, as many modern scholars think, the pastoral letters are the work of a later author who was a member of the Pauline school, this passage is nevertheless thoroughly impregnated with the mind of the apostle. It speaks of the understanding of the atonement Paul acquired in the miracle of his apostolic call. That was a sheer act of "overflowing grace" to one who acknowledged himself to be the "chief of sinners" because he had persecuted the church.

Gospel: Luke 15:1-32.

The gospel consists of three parables: the twin parables of the lost sheep and lost coin, and the parable of the prodigal son. (The short form gives only the twin parables.) The prodigal son already occurred by itself on Lent IV (q.v.). Prefaced by the twin parables, the prodigal son acquires an accent it does not have when it stands alone. Taken alone, the emphasis is on the prodigal son's initiative in returning home. The twin parables emphasize the prevenient action of God in seeking and saving the lost, a thought that is then carried over into understanding the action of the father in the third parable: while the returning prodigal was still at a distance, he "ran" and welcomed him home.

Thus understood, all three parables are linked with the atonement, which, as we have seen, runs like a thread through all the readings of the day. While the earlier readings had employed the Christ-to-God aspect of the atonement, the gospel balances this aspect with the movement of God through Christ to man. The atonement is not the human act of the son appeasing an angry deity, but God's gift to man in which he undertakes to do for man what man could not do for himself. Christ is the presence of God in man for us, seeking and saving the lost.

TWENTY-FIFTH SUNDAY OF THE YEAR

All the readings of this Sunday have some bearing on Christian responsibilities in relation to social justice, politics and wealth, though, as we shall see, proper interpretation of the gospel is problematical.

Reading I: Amos 8:4-7.

Amos, the prophet of social justice par excellence, denounces the rich who just can't wait for the new moon festival or the sabbath day to be over, so that they may engage in business and make profits, cheating and exploiting the poor in the process. He threatens them with divine judgment. Many contemporary applications should suggest themselves.

Responsorial Psalm: 113:1-2, 4-8.

This is one of the first hallel psalms (113–118), so called because they begin with "Alleluia" and celebrate the mighty acts of Yahweh. Verses 7-8 provide a striking contrast to vv. 4-6, between the majesty of Yahweh and his condescension to the "poor." It is doubtless because of these final verses, with their reference to God's vindication of the poor, that this psalm has been chosen as a response to the Amos reading.

Reading II: 1 Timothy 2:1-8.

Much of 1 Timothy consists of a church order, setting out the duties of the church's ministry and (so here) describing the liturgical activities of the Christian assembly. It represents an attempt on the part of the Pauline churches to consolidate their life after the pioneering missionary work of the apostle.

Since the time of Cyrus the Jewish community had prayed even for its pagan rulers, and the church continues the practice. Such prayer recognizes the function of the state in relation to the gospel. If the state functions properly, it creates those outward conditions of tranquillity under which the gospel may be preached and the life of the community flourish. This positive view of the function of the state is found in most places in the New Testament (cf. esp. Rom 13). But there is another side to the state, its potentially demonic side (Rv 13). Yet even the demonic state continues to fulfil some of its God-given functions of maintaining domestic peace and justice (there were police even in Nazi Germany and they weren't all brutal). To that extent it still merits the prayers and obedience of the Christian community, even if at other points some kind of resistance is the order of the day.

Gospel: Luke 16:1-13.

The gospel consists of the parable of the unjust steward, followed by a string of sayings on the right use of wealth. These sayings probably did not belong originally to the parable, for the parable itself hardly intends to hold up the unjust steward as an example of the right use of wealth! Taken by itself, the parable is a challenge of Jesus to his contemporaries to a drastic decision for the coming kingdom of God before it is too late (cf. the parable of the wise and foolish virgins). The string of sayings gives a new application to the parable: the disciples are to show as much intelligence in the use of wealth as the unjust steward used in his own interests.

TWENTY-SIXTH SUNDAY OF THE YEAR

Reading I: Amos 6:1a, 4-7.

Last week's Old Testament reading dealt with the question of social injustice. This lesson is a denunciation of private luxury. It forms a fitting companion reading for the parable of Dives and Lazarus, which is the gospel of the day.

Responsorial Psalm: 146:6c-10.

This psalm initiates the last group of Alleluia psalms in the psalter, all of them hymns of praise to Yahweh for his mighty acts. Again this psalm is highly fitting for this Sunday. Verses 9-10 echo the denunciation of the rich in *Reading I* and God's concern for the poor, the hungry and the oppressed. It thus looks forward to the *Gospel*.

Reading II: 1 Timothy 6:11-16.

This section from 1 Tm 6 has been interpreted as an ordination charge (E. Käsemann). In this charge the ordinand is reminded of the confession of faith he made at his baptism. As an ordained minister he now has to teach this faith to others. This suggests an important relation between ordination and baptism. Ordination is the form that the fulfilment of their baptismal vocation takes for some. The "commandment" may be the actual ordination charge (cf. Moses' charge to Joshua at his ordination in Nm 27:19), an Old Testament type which provided both the synagogue and the early church (cf. Hippolytus' ordinal) with the model for their ordination practices.

Gospel: Luke 16:19-31.

The first part of the parable of Dives and Lazarus is a well-known folk-tale relating the reversal of fortunes in the next world. It is a conventional piece of moralizing. As so often with the gospel parables, however, there is a surprise at the end — the dialogue between Dives and Abraham. This is where the real point of the parable lies. The rich man asks that Lazarus be allowed to convey a special warning to his five brothers who are still alive. The answer is that they have the word of scripture and that is sufficient. Those who are unmoved by the message of scripture will not be convinced by a miracle either, even by a resurrection. Such, presumably, was Jesus' point in telling the parable.

By placing it after the string of sayings on the right use of wealth which follows the parable of the unjust steward, Luke — and evidently the compilers of this lectionary — calls attention to the conventional part of the story, the reversal of the fortune of rich and poor in the next world.

Since the first part of the parable is conventional, it would be wrong to build up a doctrine of the next life on the reference to Abraham's bosom.

TWENTY-SEVENTH SUNDAY OF THE YEAR ✓

Reading I: Habakkuk 1:2-3; 2:2-4.

These verses give the gist of the three parts of Habakkuk. First the prophet cries out against the injustices that he and his people are suffering from the hand of foreign conquerors. How long will Yahweh let this go on happening and not intervene? Then comes the answer: Yahweh *will* intervene, but in his own good time. It may seem slow, but come it will. Meanwhile the attitude required of Yahweh's servants is what the prophet calls "faith": "the righteous shall live by his faith." The meaning of the word translated "faith" here (*'emunah*) is steadfast loyalty, holding on in obedience to Yahweh's law, even when it apparently pays no dividends. This word becomes very important both for the Qumran covenanters and for the New Testament. In the Qumran commentary on Habakkuk we read: "This [i.e., our saying] refers to all in Jewry who carry out the Law [i.e., to the Quamraners]. On account of their labor and of their faith in him who expounded the Law aright [i.e., the sect's founder, the Teacher of Righteousness] God will deliver them from the house of judgment." Here faith has already acquired its New Testament sense of personal trust. Compare Rom 1:17 and Gal 3:11, which develop the notion of personal trust adumbrated at Qumran to mean trust in the justifying act of God in Christ toward the ungodly. Hab 2:4 thus becomes the key text for Paul's doctrine of justification—a considerable development from the original meaning in Habakkuk. Heb 10:38 reverts closer to the original sense. For this author faith recovers its meaning of holding on in the midst of adversity. The preacher has two options: either he can expound the text in the original sense of Habakkuk and relate it to contemporary society (violence!), or he can develop it in the Pauline sense and relate it to the justification of the ungodly—in which case the lament of the first half will have to be related to the situation of the sinner in bondage to sin (inauthentic existence).

Responsorial Psalm: 95:1-2, 6-9.
The *Venite* has already been used on the Eighteenth Sunday of the year.

Reading II: 2 Timothy 1:6-8, 13-14.
Although belonging to the Pauline corpus, the pastoral epistles are widely regarded today as deutero-Pauline, written within the Pauline school, but reflecting the conditions of the next generation after the apostle himself, and seeking to preserve his teaching in the new situation.

Two features in this passage may reflect the sub-apostolic situation: 1) the channeling of the ministerial charismata through the laying on of hands instead of by direct inspiration as in 1 Corinthians ("the gift that is within you through the laying on of my hands"); 2) the consolidation of the apostolic message into a "pattern of sound words." E. Käsemann has characterized these developments as "early catholicism," which for him is a loaded term implying degeneration and corruption. But they can be recognized as legitimate and necessary adaptions in the changed situation, following the decease of the apostles and their consequent inability to exercise the kind of personal control over the charismata as Paul did in 1 Corinthians. For "Timothy" — and therefore all successors to the ministry of the apostles — has not merely to preserve the tradition, but to give living testimony to it, i.e., to unpackage it and make it relevant address to the contemporary world. Such testimony, the text warns us, will involve a "share of suffering for the gospel." Newman in his Anglican days once startled the comfortable bishops of the established church by saying: "We could not wish them a more blessed termination of their course than the spoiling of their goods and martyrdom" (Tract I, 1833). Very unrealistic in the situation, no doubt, but soundly based on our text.

Again the preacher has two options: he can relate this directly to the Habakkuk saying about faith, and exhort the congregation to witness, suffering and endurance, applying it to their concrete situation. Alternatively, he could develop the New Testament concept of apostolic succession, as involving the guardianship of the apostolic faith, but also living testimony and preparedness for suffering. The elder Archbishop Temple inscribed over an archway at Lambeth Palace: "Apostolorum nobis vindicamus non honores sed labores."

Gospel: Luke 17:5-10.

The request "Increase our faith" comes immediately after a warning to beware of temptations to faith (*skandala*). The parable, which forms the second half of our gospel lesson, is connected with the saying about faith, because it warns the disciples against supposing that faith, and the obedient service of the Lord in which faith is expressed, establishes a claim for reward. "When you have done all that is commanded you, say, 'We are unprofitable servants; we have only done what was our duty.'"

The preacher could take up the first part of this gospel lesson, the request for an increase of faith, and relate it to the Habakkuk saying taken in its original sense. He can then take the saying about the sycamore tree as a vivid though deliberately absurd illustration of the power of faith. If he decides instead to concentrate upon the parable of the unprofitable servants he can link it with the Pauline doctrine of justification by faith and not by works, stated more concretely in Jesus' aphorism about the unprofitable servants. Or again, the preacher can note that this parable is explicitly addressed to the apostles (v.5), and relate it to Paul's call to Timothy to witness to his faith even at the cost of martyrdom. The parable will then contain the warning that even martyrdom is not a "good work" in the sense that it entitles the martyr to a reward for individual achievement.

√ TWENTY-EIGHTH SUNDAY OF THE YEAR

Reading I: 2 Kings 5:14-17.

The most significant feature in the story of Naaman the Syrian occurs prior to our pericope. Naaman expected a spectacular cure and was annoyed when Elisha told him to go and wash in the Jordan: That puny little ditch, when there were far greater rivers back home! Reluctantly, Naaman was persuaded to try it. Jordan stands for the "scandal of particularity." There is no other name under heaven by which we must be saved. The gate is narrow, and the way is hard, that leads to life. Unless you eat the flesh of the Son of man, and drink his blood, you have no life in you.

In antiquity leprosy was regarded as the worst of diseases, and its cure an impossibility. Thus it became a parable of man's plight, from which he would only be delivered by the Messiah, i.e., by a miracle at the end of time.

Another aspect of this story, which is taken up by the New Testament in Jesus' sermon in the synagogue at Nazareth (Lk 4:16-30), is the fact that Naaman was a Syrian and therefore excluded from the community of Israel. Thus his healing foreshadows the universality of the Messianic salvation. Rejected by Israel, that salvation would be opened up to the Gentiles: "There were many lepers in Israel in the time of the prophet Elisha; none of them was cleansed, but only Naaman the Syrian" (Lk 4:27).

This theme of universality is also picked up in the gospel of the day, in which the nine lepers from the chosen people did not return to give thanks, but only the tenth, and he was the Samaritan.

The preacher, therefore, could develop either theme from the story of Naaman — the scandal of particularity or the universality of the Messianic salvation. Both themes can be related to the gospel, the second also to the *Responsorial Psalm.*

If he takes the scandal of particularity it gives an opportunity to answer the "blue domers" who ask, "Why go to church when I can worship God in the open air?" God has chosen *this* way for salvation — Christ alone — the word and sacrament alone — here on this Sunday morning. If he takes the universality of the Messianic salvation he can counter the idea that salvation is a monopoly of the WASPS — including Catholic WASPS!

Responsorial Psalm: 98:1-4.

Psalm 98 is from a collection of magnificent enthronement psalms (93, 96–100). (See our comments on the *Responsorial Psalm* of Ascension Day.) They are full of exuberent joy at the saving power of Yahweh, visibly expressed (according to scholarly theory) in the enthronement of the king at the new year festival.

The antiphon underlines the fact that the *nations* see God's saving power. If, as some think, the psalm originally celebrated Israel's return from exile in Babylon — it is certainly imbued with the theology of Deutero-Isaiah, as the words, "saving power," "victory" and "vindication" show — the nations are passive witnesses, rather than active participants in the divine salvation. As spectators they watch Israel's returning from exile and see in it an act of Yahweh's self-vindication. But in the Christian liturgical community, for which the saving power of God is manifested in the Christ event, this must be reinterpreted to mean that the nations actually participate in the salvation. It is in this sense that *Cantate Domino* is provided at Evensong in the Book of Common Prayer as an alternative to the Magnificat.

Thus the preacher can treat this psalm as a response to the universality of the Messianic salvation prefigured in the healing of Naaman the Syrian.

Reading II: 2 Timothy 2:8-13.

Even if the modern critical view of the pastorals as deutero-Pauline is correct (see the previous Sunday), the first paragraph of this reading may well be part of Paul's genuine farewell letter to Timothy, onto which the passages directed against Gnosticism and towards setting up a church order were grafted by the deutero-Pauline author. In any case this passage fittingly reflects Paul's situation in prison at Rome just before his martyrdom. There is a poignant contrast between the apostle's own condition — wearing fetters like a criminal — and his confident assertion that the word of God is not bound. (I heard this as a sermon text more than once in Germany during the church struggle, when Pastor Niemöller and others were imprisoned by the Gestapo.) Paul is also confident that his suffering will contribute to the forward movement of salvation history: "I endure everything for the sake of the elect, that they also may obtain the salvation. . . ." This notion is fairly common in the Pauline writings (cf. the catalogues of Paul's sufferings in 2 Corinthians and also Col 1:24). Here would be the basis for developing a scriptural understanding of the doctrine of the "merits" of the saints: suffering offered obediently to God is like prayer in that it contributes to the furthering of God's saving purpose.

The final part of the reading consists of an early Christian hymn, based on the Pauline conception of dying/rising with Christ (Rom 6), the dominical saying about confessing/denying Jesus now, and the Son of man confessing/denying the disciple accordingly at the parousia (Mt 10:33 and par.). Very striking is the twist that is given in the last two lines: even if we are faithless, God still remains faithful. This is quite contrary to the parallelisms of the three succeeding pairs. The hymn is quoted here because its opening part illustrates the preceding verse, but then, like so many similar quotations, continues after it ceases to be relevant to its context, thereby proving that we do have a quotation here.

There is a wealth of material in this for the preacher. He could relate Paul's imprisonment, and his confidence that his sufferings contribute to the advancement of God's purpose, to the imprisonment of Christians for their faith in various parts of the world today. He could seek to provide an authentically scriptural understanding of the doctrine of the merits of the saints. Or he could take the hymn and expound the faithfulness of God, even when his Christians deny him. What seems difficult, however, is to relate this reading to any of the other readings of the day, and it probably should not be attempted.

Gospel: Luke 17:11-19.

We have already suggested how this lesson may be linked with the first reading, and how cleansing from leprosy is a type of Messianic salvation. Also, we have called attention to another link between this gospel and the Old Testament reading — the universality of the Messianic salvation.

But there is yet another theme in the gospel which could be developed. This is the theme of gratitude. It is striking that all ten lepers were healed. The grateful one got no more than the others did — except the assurance from the Lord, "Your faith has made you well." Nor did the other lepers lose what they had. There was no punitive miracle returning them to their leprous state. There is much to meditate upon here. The gifts of God are without repentance, gratitude has no ulterior motivation, e.g., to secure further blessings. Ingratitude is perhaps the most common of all human failings, as Shakespeare has so often observed: "Blow, blow thou winter wind, thou art not so unkind as man's ingratitude."

If the preacher wishes to develop this theme, we would recommend that he read Albert Schweitzer's sermons on gratitude in *Reverence for Life* (New York: Harper and Row 1969).

TWENTY-NINTH SUNDAY OF THE YEAR ✓

Reading I: Exodus 17:8-13.

It is puzzling to find this reading appointed for today. It does not have any apparent connection with any of the other readings except on one questionable interpretation (see below). It does not follow in sequence the first reading of the previous Sunday, nor does it appear to be particularly edifying. Despite the assurance in the second reading that "*all* scripture is inspired by God and profitable for teaching," the New Testament writers never made use of this incident. Their use of the Old Testament was definitely à la carte (see C. H. Dodd, *According to the Scriptures* [London: Nisbet 1952] and B. Lindars, *New Testament Apologetic* [Philadelphia: Westminster 1961]). It could be given a typological interpretation of Moses holding up his hands in intercessory prayer (so *Jerome Biblical Commentary*). But this interpretation is uncertain. It is probably meant as a symbolic action like those of the prophets, which were thought to have potent influence on the course of events (so *Peake's Commentary*).

If the preacher's exegetical conscience will permit him to accept the *Jerome Commentary* interpretation, he could expound the text typologically of Christ the heavenly priest interceding for his church militant on earth. Otherwise, he had better leave it alone.

Responsorial Psalm: 121:1-8.

This beautiful psalm of trust in the divine protection needs little comment. If we have accepted the intercessory interpretation of *Reading I*, it forms an excellent response to God's protection of his church militant on earth. In any case it suggests a reflection on the biblical truth behind the dogma of the "infallibility" of the church, namely, that God will never finally forsake his church, however severe his judgment upon her may be from time to time. His care and protection of her is exactly like that shown to the first Israel, never finally abandoning her, restoring her even after exile.

Reading II: 2 Timothy 3:14—4:2.

This reading is taken from those parts of the pastoral epistles which register the concern of the sub-apostolic age to preserve apostolic truth (see above, on the Twenty-Seventh Sunday of the year). Of the whole body of the church's tradition, scripture is the most important part. "The New Testament canon appears not as separate from, or opposed to, the Christian tradition, but rather as an expression of it" (*Principles of Church Union*, 1966). One cannot be sure that the "Pastor" (i.e., the author or redactor of these letters) meant by sacred writings or scripture our New Testament as well as the Old Testament. Most likely not, for there is no indication elsewhere in these letters that an embryonic canon of New Testament writings was already in formation. But certainly, as we read this passage today, it can be legitimately extended to cover both the Old Testament and the New Testament.

While the pastoral epistles are in some sense directed to the church at large, their primary aim is to instruct the church's ministers in apostolic succession. Hence one of the most important duties of the "man of God" (N.B.: this is a term accorded to Moses in the Old Testament tradition, suggesting a possible link with the first reading) is the study of scripture. This was nowhere put so well as by Cranmer in the ordinal of the Book of Common Prayer, in the bishop's exhortation to those about to be ordained to the priesthood:

"And seeing ye cannot by any other means compass the doing of so weighty a work, pertaining to the salvation of man, but with doctrine and exhortation taken out of the Holy Scriptures, and with a life agreeable to the same; consider how studious ye ought to be in reading and learning the same Scriptures . . . and for this self same cause, how ye ought to forsake and set aside, as much as ye may, all worldly cares and studies." And a little later in the same exhortation: ". . . that by daily reading and weighing the Scriptures, ye may wax riper and stronger in your ministry."

But as we observed, the pastorals are also in some sense directed to the church at large, and this knowledge of the scriptures, though especially the business of the clergy, is not exclusively confined to them. It is to be shared with the whole people of God. Exegesis is the especial function of the priest, but it is to lead his people also to the exegesis of scripture, an exegesis which is accomplished not merely in the understanding, but in the living of the Christian life.

The preacher has here an opportunity to explain to his people his own particular responsibility for exegesis, and the need to enlist the whole *laos* in this enterprise. In one of his sermons preached nearly half a century ago in the chapel of Corpus Christi College, Cambridge, Sir Edwyn Hoskyns aptly said: "Whether the Church of England can present the truth of the Christian religion to our generation will depend very largely upon the extent to which well-disposed clergy and laity can cooperate in wrestling with the truth of the Church" — and that meant for him preeminently the truth of the Bible.

Gospel: Luke 18:1-8.

The unjust judge belongs to a class of parables which features not a typical everyday event with a surprising element in it, but a unique occurrence of a striking kind. Such parables are common to, though not confined to, the special Lucan material. As in the story of the unjust steward, to which it is akin (Lk 16:1-9), the central figure is an unsympathetic character. Not every aspect of his behavior is held up for emulation, but only one particular aspect of it. Having refused to listen to the woman's case, the judge eventually yields in face of her continuous pestering, and agrees to hear it. Jesus' hearers are meant to infer from this aspect of the judge's behavior to God: God will indeed intervene and help his church, even though he seems to forsake it.

By his editorial introduction (v.1) Luke has shifted our attention away from the judge to the woman, and made her the example of persistent prayer. The Lord's question at the end, however, makes it clear that the judge is meant to be the central figure.

If we take the intercessory interpretation of *Reading I* and the *Responsorial Psalm*, we can build up a picture of the church in tribulation, and the assurance that God will not forsake her — again a question in the true biblical understanding of the church's infallibility. God will never abandon his church utterly and completely.

THIRTIETH SUNDAY OF THE YEAR ✓✓

Reading I: Sirach 35:12c-14, 16-18b.

This reading from Sirach (Ecclesiastes) is obviously chosen to go with the parable of the pharisee and the publican, as the heading ("The prayer of the humble man will penetrate the heavens") indicates.

During the heyday of Biblical Theology the wisdom literature was rather under a cloud. This was because it seemed hard to fit in with the salvation-historical perspective which Biblical Theology had recovered. This wisdom literature appears to deal with general religious and ethical truths and problems, quite detached from the concrete heres and nows of salvation history. Typical of this attitude is the legend that Professor G. Ernest Wright has constantly told his classes at McCormick and Harvard that he could not defend the place of Proverbs in the canon! Now, however, there has been a reaction. The wisdom literature has a place in the canon which is as central as that of the salvation-historical and apocalyptic writings. And Jesus understood himself quite as much as the bearer of the heavenly wisdom (thus holding an implicit wisdom Christology, such as came to flower in the prologue of the Fourth Gospel) as he understood himself as the eschatological prophet, the announcer and bringer of the kingdom of God. He *does* deal in what we have recently somewhat despised as "general truths of religion and ethics," and this passage from Sirach is a worthy accompaniment to the illustrative story of the gospel reading, which also deals with a "general truth of religion and ethics."

The preacher, therefore, need not shrink from dealing with such timeless truths as the statement that the prayer of the humble pierces the heavens, as well as with the events of salvation history.

Responsorial Psalm: 34:1-2, 16-18, 22.

Very appropriately this psalm is one of the wisdom psalms. So *Peake's Commentary, ad loc.*: "In [verses] 11–22 he [the psalmist] offers instruction very much in the style of the wisdom teachers, about the nature and rewards of the good life." Similarly, the *Jerome Commentary* states: "A wisdom psalm, though it is widely classified as a psalm of thanksgiving" (*ad loc.*). The author of 1 Peter takes up this psalm as a commentary on the qualities of the good life as it should be lived by the newly baptized, thus giving his stamp to its Christian application.

Reading II: 2 Timothy 4:6-8, 16-18.

This reading has no direct connection with the other sections for this Sunday but is the conclusion of the reading in course of 2 Timothy. Like the reading for the Twenty-Eighth Sunday of the year, it is part of the (possibly genuine) farewell letter of Paul to Timothy, into which the "Pastor" has inserted his church order and defense against Gnosticism.

Paul has apparently been before the court once (the *prima actio*). It went favorably, but as he poignantly laments, "All [i.e., the Roman Christians] deserted me." Yet Paul anticipated only death for himself. Nothing here about the hope of release which marked his former imprisonments.

Why did the Roman Christians desert him? The Letter to the Romans suggests that they may not have been very keen on his version of the gospel anyhow, and they would hardly want to expose themselves unnecessarily in Nero's court. Before very long, a dire persecution was to break out over the whole community. (The present writer's chronology would place Paul's trial and execution c. 60, and the Neronian persecution in which Peter fell in 64, though other chronologies are possible.)

Despite the gloomy prospects, however, Paul is full of ultimate confidence: "Henceforth there is laid up for me the crown of righteousness."

If the preacher opts for this reading as the basis for his homily, he will want to depict the circumstances of Paul's final trial and martyrdom, so far as these can be reconstructed from the text, and meditate upon the courage and faith of Christ's martyrs, and the place of that martyrdom in salvation history. On this note, three points: Paul can speak of his martyrdom as a sacrifice (cf. Phil 2:17); he prays for the forgiveness of the deserters; and he can use the language of the passion psalm (22): "rescued from the lion's mouth." The apostle's martyrdom is a reproduction of the passion and sacrificial death of the Lord himself, not in the sense that the apostle's martyrdom is in itself an atoning sacrifice, but in the sense that it will contribute to the accomplishment of God's purpose in salvation history by bringing the Gentiles into the Messianic salvation. Paul, with his near-perspective, thought that this was to be accomplished shortly. Things turned out differently: his martyrdom and that of Peter actually led to the firm establishment of the Church of Rome, which became the mother church of the West. Thus indeed the Gentile world was brought into the redeemed community, and the blood of the martyrs became the seed of the church.

Gospel: Luke 18:9-14.
This parable is of a type peculiar to Luke. There is no pictorial aspect which points to an eschatological interpretation, as in the normal parable. The story gives its example directly. The disciples are meant to pray not

like the pharisee, but like the publican. Other illustrative stories are: the good Samaritan, the rich fool, and Dives and Lazarus. They inculcate religious and moral examples of a timeless kind, and have no direct rela- tion to Jesus' eschatological message. If, however, we allow that Jesus understood himself to be not only the announcer of the inbreaking of the kingdom of God, but also the embodiment and spokesman of the divine wisdom (see above), then such parables as these fall naturally into their place as part of his teaching. The pharisee was quite right in per- forming his religious and moral duties. He was not like other men, extortioners, unjust, adulterers. Clearly, Jesus' hearers would say of the pharisee, he was a righteous man.

The tax collector, on the other hand, had nothing to commend him. He was no better than the rest of his kind. There was no question but that he was the "bad guy." Yet Jesus pronounces him to be the "good guy." How can Jesus give a verdict which to his hearers would be nothing less than "outrageous" (Eta Linnemann)? He does not mean that the pharisee was wrong in his deeds of morality and his piety, or that the tax collector was right for being a swindler and extortioner. What was wrong about the pharisee was his approach to God: he prayed with himself; he set before God all his merits, compared himself with the publican and said with Little Jack Horner, "What a good boy am I!" — thereby smashing his goodness at one blow. He came before God trusting in his own, really genuine, righteousness. The tax collector, on the other hand, knew he was a bad lot. He would not lift up his eyes to heaven but smote his breast and cried, "*Kyrie eleison*." He was accepted by God, because he threw himself on God's mercy.

This pericope offers a magnificent opportunity to proclaim the Pauline gospel of justification by faith apart from the works of the Law in the concrete, untechnical, pictorial language of Jesus, rather than in the com- plicated midrashic exposition of Paul.

THIRTY-FIRST SUNDAY OF THE YEAR

Reading I: Wisdom 11:22—12:2.

This passage from the Book of Wisdom is a fine pre-Christian exposition of the universality of the divine mercy. It begins by asserting the utter insignificance of man in language reminiscent of Deutero-Isaiah. With "speck that tips the scales" compare "drop in the bucket" in Is 45:15. The thought of God's transcendence serves to magnify the condescension of his mercy. The mercy or love (the passage uses "love" as a verb, but not as noun, the latter being almost unique to the New Testament) of God manifests itself in two categories of action: in creation and preservation, and in the forgiveness of sin. The striking and unique phrase "hast loathing for none of the things which thou hast made" was taken up in the Sarum form for the blessing of ashes on Ash Wednesday: "nihil odisti eorum quae fecisti." It so impressed Cranmer that he inserted it not only into his new collect for Ash Wednesday, but also in the penitential office for that day and in the third of his Good Friday collects. The thought is that though man has made such an awful mess of God's creation, yet it still is God's creation. His immortal spirit still dwells in all things (12:1), and man can therefore plead to God not to allow his handiwork to be destroyed, any more than a painter or sculptor could bear to see the product of his genius devoured by fire or smashed to pieces.

It is not clear whether the author, a Hellenistic Jew, is thinking in Hebraic or Greek terms when he speaks of the indwelling of God's immortal spirit in all things. (Cf. the Pentecost antiphon, "The Spirit of the Lord fills the whole world.") The spirit could be, as in Greek thought, *sophia*, the agent of the divine immanence; or, more biblically, it could be *ruach*, the creative power of the transcendent God at work in created things. Probably the author thinks fundamentally in biblical terms, but easily slips into the Hellenistic language to express authentically biblical thoughts. The point is so incidental to his main concern (pleading to God that creation is his handiwork) that we should not use this passage to build up any particular cosmological or anthropological doctrine. In the New Testament the dominant conception of the Spirit is not universal-immanentist, but eschatological. It does not dwell in all things and all men by creation but is a gift to those who believe in Christ Jesus.

The preacher will find plenty of material for a homily from this reading: the paradox of the transcendence of God, on the one hand, and his infinite mercy, on the other; or the truth that man and the world are still God's creation, despite human sin, and therefore basically salvable.

Responsorial Psalm: 145:1-2, 8-11, 13cd-14.
In the original Hebrew this fine psalm of praise is constructed on an acrostic pattern. Each verse begins with a letter of the Hebrew alphabet in order, from aleph through teth. It is a fitting response to the reading on the universal scope of the divine love and mercy. Note especially the last two lines of v. 9:

> The Lord is good *to all*
> and his compassion is over *all that*
> *he has made.*

Reading II: 2 Thessalonians 1:11—2:2.

In the latter part of the post-Pentecost season the readings from the New Testament become progressively eschatological, thus leading up to the climax in the new solemnity of Christ the King and the first Sunday of Advent. Like a musical composer, the lectionary enunciates the theme which it will develop later on.

In German scholarship, 2 Thessalonians is often classed among the deutero-Pauline letters. But the ground for this is not very strong. Most English-speaking scholars assume that it was written by Paul himself after 1 Thessalonians, in order to correct certain mistaken deductions which have been made either from the earlier letter or from the apostle's teaching on his foundation visit. It appears that a false letter, purporting to be from Paul, has been circulated in the community at Thessalonica, asserting that the day of the Lord has already come. False prophets (spirit and word) are making the same claim. Probably this points to some early gnosticizing tendencies similar to those appearing a little later at Corinth (1 Corinthians) and Philippi (Phil 3). In the gnostic systems men were divided into various categories in virtue of their creation, e.g., some were pneumatics, who belonged to the upper realm of light, and some were psychics or "hylics," who belonged only to this world. The Christian gospel, as the false teachers understood it, revealed to a privileged elite their true nature. You either had it or you hadn't. The gospel came not to make you what you were not, but to restore the memory of your lost origin. Once a person had recovered the knowledge of his true nature, there was no need for anything else, so the day of the Lord had really come. The elite already enjoyed immortality. The resurrection for them was passed already (cf. 2 Tm 2:18). For Paul this was a corruption of the gospel all along the line, and his letters, when they are not directed against Judaizers (like the first part of Galatians, and Romans), are directed against the early Gnostics at one point or another of their teaching. Here, in 2 Thessalonians, Paul's answer is that the day of the Lord has not yet come, and there is much of a highly apocalyptic nature that must happen first (see 2:3-12).

It is regrettable that this reading leaves us somewhat up in the air. We get a statement only of the false position, not Paul's reply. (The

Episcopal Church, which has in principle adopted the new Roman lectionary for trial use, has changed this lesson to 2 Thes 1:1-5, 11-12, for this very reason.) Perhaps the preacher would be advised, therefore, to confine himself to the first paragraph, which is the conclusion of the apostle's thanksgiving and prayer, with which his letters normally begin. It presents the Christian life as growth in grace, a theme characteristic of the earlier post-Pentecost season, prior to the development of the futurist-eschatological emphasis of the later Sundays.

Gospel: Luke 19:1-10.

This story has been added to his Marcan source by Luke from his special material. It illustrates a theme common in the Synoptists, Jesus' eating with the outcasts of society. This type of behavior is attested in a remarkable number of different gospel forms (parable, aphorism, pronouncement story — so here — and miracle story). This multiple attestation, as C. H. Dodd has argued, is strong proof of its historical character. Thus one of the most certain facts we know about Jesus is that he ate with the outcast.

Whether the story of Zacchaeus is based on a real occurrence, or is a late composition, we have no means of knowing. By his occupation, Zacchaeus had excluded himself, in the popular estimation, from his people. He was a quisling who had thrown in his lot with the hated occupying power for the sake of pecuniary gain. But for Jesus this does not disqualify the tax collector from the Messianic salvation: he also is a son of Abraham (and for Luke this implies — since now it is not the Law which ultimately determines a man's relation to God, but a man's attitude to Jesus — that so also are Gentiles, as Paul had argued). Zacchaeus' determination to see Jesus and his climbing up into the sycamore tree are taken as a sign of genuine faith, which could break through the barriers between God and man set up by the Law.

By entering into Zacchaeus' house Jesus dramatizes the coming of the divine salvation. Zacchaeus' promise to restore what he had extorted from his fellow Jews is a measure of his repentance. It goes far beyond the legal requirements of restitution (e.g., Lv 6:1-7). Now he hears the word: "Salvation is come to this house," i.e., to him and his whole household or family. As in Acts, the conversion of the head of the household carries with it all the other members of the family, a circumstance which has led J. Jeremias to argue that the early church practiced infant baptism in conversion situations. This suggests that the story, even if based on a genuine incident in Jesus' ministry, had been shaped for the Gentile mission. Now comes the pronouncement in which the whole story culminates: "The Son of man came to seek and to save the lost."

Critical scholars today are divided on whether Jesus actually used the term "Son of man." But they are generally agreed that even if he did, he did not directly identify himself with that figure, since the Son of man was to appear in heaven at the end as a transcendental figure, while Jesus was a lowly figure on earth. It was the post-Easter church that identified Jesus first with the coming Son of man and later in his ministry. But this identification was already implicit in Jesus' claim to be already dispensing on earth the eschatological salvation. In this saying it is the church speaking as it looks back on the whole earthly ministry of Jesus as an accomplished work ("he came"); it is the church confessing that in that history the Son of man came to seek and save the lost. Such a claim was already implicit in the historical Jesus' conduct in eating with the outcast and in his interpreting that conduct by the parables of the lost sheep and lost coin.

In his homily the preacher would obviously turn to the punchline of the Zaccahaeus story and expound the earthly life of Jesus as God's seeking and saving the lost — a seeking and saving which is a present reality in the eucharist, when the Son of man (Jn 6:53!) comes under the forms of the bread and wine to seek and save the lost.

Last Sundays of Year C

All Saints' Day is one of the most loved feasts in the church year. At least this is so for Anglicans and I suspect the same is true for the Roman Catholic Church, too.

In its setting in the new calendar the feast takes on added significance, for it marks the transition from the earlier part of the post-Pentecost season, with its emphasis on growth in grace, to the last Sundays of the church year, when the emphasis shifts to the "last things," the final consummation of history.

It is not entirely clear whom we are to include in this celebration. Originally, it was a commemoration of martyrs in the early persecutions whose names were unrecorded, and who therefore were not, and could not be, included by name on the day of their martyrdoms. They were not, in the language of the later West, officially "canonized," although they may have qualified if anything had been known about them. Yet, the New Testament calls all baptized Christians "saints," *hagioi*, holy ones. Even in writing to the Corinthians, whom he has to castigate for the worst possible moral offenses, Paul can call them saints (1 Cor 1:2; the Greek means called as saints, not just called to be saints as the R.S.V. translates it). Their sanctity is not a moral achievement, not even the complete triumph of grace in their lives, but rests upon their having been made objectively holy by baptism (see 1 Cor 6:11). Yet it was a natural development that the term saint should have come to be reserved for those in whom grace had its most signal triumph, for those who had achieved the Pauline imperative, "become what you are."

In the light of this New Testament doctrine, All Saints' Day could be interpreted as a commemoration of all the faithful departed. But the church has traditionally separated this wider commemoration from All Saints' Day and observed it on the day following. Thus she has drawn a distinction between those for whom she finds it natural to thank God for the victory they have achieved by his grace, and those for whom she finds it more fitting to pray that God have mercy on them in "that day" (cf. 2 Tm 1:18).

Reading I: Revelation 7:2-4, 9-12.

The Book of Revelation or the Apocalypse is not meant to be a timeless description of what it is like in heaven. Like all apocalyptic literature, it is written to encourage the faithful in a time of great distress. Writing about 96 A.D., John the Seer expects a great persecution to break out on the church in Asia Minor. Many Christians will die a martyr's death. He seeks to assure them that this outburst of hostility against the Christian community (by the emperor Domitian?) is the prelude of the End, when God will vindicate his martyrs. So the seer describes the triumphant state which awaits them in this symbolic language of white robes, palms, etc., and pictures them as singing the song of triumph which was probably sung in the church on earth (perhaps a paschal hymn), "Salvation belongs to our God. . . . Amen! Blessing and Glory. . . ."

If we take the seer's words literally, he was mistaken in thinking that his crisis was the last of the crises before the End. But that is the literary method of all apocalypses. Each succeeding crisis in the church's history confronts us with the eternal issues of life and death. History is a struggle between good and evil in which, through the victory of Christ, the victory of the faithful is assured. Meanwhile, in the very midst of her tribulations on earth, the martyr church already sings the songs of victory in her liturgy.

In another way, too, the church is an anticipation of the kingdom of heaven. For she, too, is a pluralistic fellowship consisting of "people from every nation, race, tribe and language."

For the homily there are several themes which could be developed. In a situation of crisis the preacher could draw out the promise of ultimate victory for God's cause. He could develop the theme of the church's liturgy on earth as an anticipation of the victory song of heaven. Or he could speak of the church catholic as transcending all nations, races, tribes and languages, and perhaps relate this quite concretely to local tensions within his congregation and parish, with a plea that the church should be a model community where these differences, though not denied, are transcended.

Responsorial Psalm: 24:1-6.

This psalm is of a liturgical type, not like many of the psalms an expression of personal piety. It was probably used in early days to accompany a procession of the ark to the temple. Two choirs sing antiphonally. One asks, who is worthy to ascend the hill of the Lord? The other choir replies, Those who have the necessary moral qualities. When Ps 24 is used as a responsorial psalm to Rev 7 on All Saints' Day, the temple becomes a figure for the consummated kingdom of heaven. Those deemed worthy to enter are the Christian saints.

Reading II: 1 John 3:1-3.

The first Epistle of John was written to condemn the false teachings that were afflicting the churches around 100 A.D. This heresy involved a denial of the true humanity of Christ and a wrong understanding of Christian existence. Our passage is concerned with the second aspect. The false teachers represented some kind of gnostic movement. They based their system of beliefs on what they claimed to be a revealed "gnosis" or knowledge. They claimed that they were already perfected, and therefore had no need to make any moral effort. Against this our author insists on the element of the "not yet" in the Christian life. It does *not yet* appear what it shall be. To be a child of God already here and now is only an advance installment of our final salvation. The writer is making the same point as Paul was making when he called the gift of the Spirit a "down payment." The final consummated state is for the Christian still a matter of hope. Meanwhile his present task should be to purify himself from sin as Christ is pure.

Note also the element of healthy agnosticism in this author's description of the future state. He cannot describe it, except to say that "we shall be like him." That warns us not to take the language of the apocalypse as a literal description, but as valuable hints that suggest a truth to be grasped intuitively, though incapable of definition. It is enough to know that we, and all the saints, will be "like him."

Are we to suppose that the saints are already "like him?" Or do they, too, have to wait until he appears? Holy scripture gives no clear answer. We are told all that we need to know for our present existence. We have been made God's children; we have a hope of achieving the ultimate destiny for which we were created, and meanwhile our task is to strive for purity of life.

Again, there are many themes for a homily. Perhaps the most suitable theme for All Saints' would be a reflection on the purity of life manifested in the saints. In this way the epistle could be linked with the sixth beatitude, which will be read for the gospel. Blessed are the pure in heart, for they shall see God.

Gospel: Matthew 5:1-12a.

The beatitudes form the opening of the Great Sermon. In Matthew it is the sermon on the mount, in Luke the sermon on the plain. Matthew's purpose in choosing this location is because he understands the teaching of the sermon as the new law, corresponding to the old law which was given on Mount Sinai, and for him Jesus is the second Moses, the giver of the new law. Each of the beatitudes falls into two parts. The first part describes the humiliation of the present, the second the glory to come. The beatitudes are addressed not to all men indiscriminately, but to the disciples, to those who have left all to follow Jesus. Note that in Luke the beatitudes are all in the second person plural. Here Luke is probably original, for the 'you' style has survived in the last of Matthew's beatitudes. So Jesus is addressing those who have left all to follow him. *They* are the poor — in spirit, as Matthew correctly explains. They are the ones who realize that they are spiritually the have-nots, who have no righteousness of their own, and therefore they hunger and thirst for (God's) righteousness. The second group of beatitudes is more activistic. It is the merciful, the pure in heart, and the peacemakers who are pronounced blessed. Faith, if it is genuine, works through love, as Paul put it. It is those who combine both the passive and active sides of a true relation to God who are pronounced already here and now to be blessed, and promised future participation in the kingdom of God.

It has often been observed that the beatitudes describe the life of Christ himself. He was all the things and did all the things the beatitudes numerate. And that brought him to the cross, and beyond that to his resurrection. All Saints' suggests the further thought that the saints are those who most perfectly manifested the Christ-like character described by the first part of the beatitudes, and who therefore now partake of the promises in the second part: *Theirs* is the kingdom of God, *they* are now comforted, *they* have inherited the "land," *ha-aretz*, the promised land of the kingdom of God; *they* are filled with the delights of the messianic banquet, *they* have obtained mercy, *they* have achieved the full potentialities of divine sonship.

Once again, there is a whole wealth of material here for the preacher. Perhaps the best way of going about a homily for All Saints' Day would be to take the beatitudes first as description of the life of Christ, and then the lives of the saints as a reflection of that life. From that we can move to an exhortation to the congregation to strive to follow Christ's life as exemplified in the lives of the saints, so that we, too, may become partakers of the inheritance of the saints in light.

THIRTY-SECOND SUNDAY OF THE YEAR

Reading I: 2 Maccabees 7:1-2, 9-14.

This reading is part of the story of the martyrdom of the seven brothers and their mother during the persecution of the Jews who remained faithful to the law under Antiochus Epiphanes. The resistance was later organized into a successful revolt against the Syrian occupying power under the leadership of the Maccabees. This passage provides evidence for the later development in Judaism of the hope for the resurrection from the dead: "The King of the universe will raise us up to an everlasting renewal of life. . . . One cannot but choose to die at the hands of men and to cherish the hope of being raised again by him" (cf. Dan 12:2). This later Jewish hope was not merely for the resuscitation of the earthly body and a prolongation of this present earthly existence, but of translation into an entirely new mode of existence (note particularly the word *renewal* of life). This existence so transcends this present life that it can only be spoken of by means of inadequate symbols (white robes, shining like stars, being like angels) or, in Paul, as existence in a "spiritual body."

The homilist has two options. He can take the seven brethren as examples of those who chose to "obey God rather than man" and relate this demand to the requirements of the Christian life today in some quite concrete way, e.g., perhaps with reference to the Berrigan brothers. Or he can develop the theme of the resurrection hope, which for the Christian has been made a sure hope by the resurrection of Jesus Christ from the dead and by our union with him in baptism and eucharist. The latter theme suits better the gospel reading and the theme of the year.

Responsorial Psalm: 17:1, 5-6, 8 and 15.

This psalm, like so many in the psalter, is a personal lament. The psalmist is in distress; he cries out for vindication, and ends on a note of confidence:

"When I awake I shall be satisfied." It is doubtful whether this psalmist was thinking of the resurrection when he spoke of "awaking." He probably meant no more than the confidence that he would come through his present distress. But when juxtaposed with the first reading, the psalm acquires a greater depth of meaning. The earlier part becomes the prayer of the martyrs for vindication, and the confident ending and expression of the resurrection hope.

Reading II: 2 Thessalonians 2:16-3:5.

This selection straddles the two major halves of 2 Thes. The first part, after the opening thanksgiving, wrestles with the doctrinal problem of the delay in the second coming, and concludes with a thanksgiving and exhortation. Verses 2:16-18, the first two verses in our reading, form a concluding benediction to this section. Chapter 3 then begins a second major section, consisting of ethical exhortations (see the following Sunday). This hortatory section is introduced with the apostle's appeal for the prayers of the congregation (3:1-2) and an expression of confidence that God will enable the Thessalonians to grow in grace (3:3-5). These verses form the second part of our reading.

If the preacher wishes to relate this text to the eschatological note of the season, he should emphasize the apostle's description of God as the giver of "eternal comfort and good hope." In expounding this theme he may want to draw on some of the insights of the recent theology of hope (J. Moltmann, Johannes Metz).

An alternative, less attuned to the dominant note of the season, would be to speak of intercessory prayer. The Thessalonians are invited to cooperate with the labors of the apostle. Through their prayers they have the privilege of contributing to the "speeding on" and triumph of the word of God. Our intercessions tend to be mostly for the health and safety of the people for whom we pray. Not that this is wrong, so long as it is included within the overall purpose and will of God — health and safety to enable the person prayed for to do the will of God more effectively. But the apostle's overriding concern — and it should be the overriding concern of our intercession, too — is that the word may speed on and triumph. That is a model of what prayer in the Christian community should be concerned about even today.

Gospel: Luke 20:27-38 (long form); 20:27-28a, 34-38 (short form).

This is the pericope known as the "Sadducees' question." The long form of the gospel reading spells out their question in full. It is framed in terms of the Jewish law, and was an attempt of the Sadducees, who denied the resurrection, to reduce that hope to an absurdity by a fictitious and improbable case arising from the so-called levirite law (Dt 25:5; compare Gn 38:8). As that law is no longer relevant in the Christian church, the option is given of omitting the question.

Jesus' answer makes two points about the resurrection. First (see our comments on *Reading I*), resurrection is not a prolongation of our present earthly life, but an entirely new mode of existence, where marriage and giving in marriage are unknown. Since in the new life there is no more death, there is no need for provision to perpetuate the human race (this explanation is peculiar to Luke). The second point in Jesus' answer is that the Pentateuch, so far from rendering the resurrection an absurdity, has an understanding of God which is fully consistent with such a hope. This conclusion is reached by an argument which would be convincing to Jesus' contemporaries, but which seems artificial to us. The Bible goes on talking about God as the God of Abraham, Isaac and Jacob even after their deaths — therefore they must be still alive. The alert reader will note that the first answer was dealing with the problem of resurrection, a Palestinian-Jewish problem, whereas the second part really answers an entirely different question, viz. one about immortality — a more Hellenistic concept. One suspects that two different traditions have been combined somewhere along the line. The essential point, that of the second part of Jesus' answer, is that the Christian future hope depends not upon wishful thinking, but upon the very nature of the God we believe in. God has revealed himself in biblical experience as essentially the God of the living. In biblical history, in both Old and New Testaments, he enters into a personal relationship with men, and that relationship — God being the kind of God that he is, in fact being God and not anything else — cannot be destroyed, even by death. "Neither death nor life . . . can separate us from the love of God which is Christ Jesus."

Once again this suggests to the preacher a certain agnosticism about the nature of the future life: one can think of it in Hebraic terms as resurrection, or in Hellenistic terms as immortality. What matters is the kind of God we believe in, and the faith that, if God is God, the relationship into which he has entered with us in Christ is inalienable.

Reading I: Malachi 4:1-2a.

Nothing is known of the prophet Malachi. Even his name, which means in Hebrew "my messenger," may simply be a deduction from Mal 3:1. Nor is it known when he wrote, though he probably came after the exile. It is therefore impossible to place his prophecies in a concrete historical situation as they should be, like all Hebrew prophecy. But this does not matter very much for our present reading, since it has a timeless quality about it: the warning that the day of the Lord is coming and that it will spell doom to all the arrogant and evildoers. But for those who fear the name of God, that day will mean vindication and salvation which is beautifully described as the rising of the sun of righteousness with healing in its wings. In his well-known Christmas hymn Charles Wesley applied these words to the birth of Christ:

> Risen with healing in his wings
> Light and life to all he brings,
> Hail, the Sun of Righteousness!
> Hail, the heaven-born Prince of Peace!

Thus interpreted, our reading strikes two notes. One which will be dominant for the next two Sundays, that of the last judgment, and the other the coming of Christ in his nativity, which will be developed in the latter Sundays of Advent. The end of the old church year dovetails with the beginning of the new.

In the perspective of Malachi, however, the positive part, the rising of the sun with healing in its wings, refers to the last judgment just as much as does the negative part, the warning to the arrogant and evildoers. Karl Barth once protested that for many Christians the last judgment had become a dire expectation of doom (think of the *Dies irae!*), whereas the New Testament Christians looked forward to "that day" with joy, waiting for and earnestly desiring the coming of the day of the Lord (2 Pt 3:12 R.S.V. marg.).

Clearly, the preacher would be attracted by the passage about the rising of the sun of righteousness. He has two options. Either he can expound it in reference to the first coming of Christ as a preparation for Advent and Christmas, or he can speak of the joy which Christians should associate with the last judgment.

Responsorial Psalm: 98:5-9.

This is another of the enthronement psalms which celebrate the kingship of Yahweh. It has already been used earlier in the church year. Today the eschatological note should be stressed. He *comes* to judge the earth. He *will judge* the world in righteousness. If the homilist has chosen to speak about the joyfulness of the last judgment in the Malachi text, he would be able to bring the psalm in to support this point.

Reading II: 2 Thessalonians 3:7-12.

Here we are in the substantive exhortation of the second major part of 2 Thes (see previous week). This idleness was apparently occasioned by a highly concrete situation. There were members in the church at Thessalonica who, perhaps misled by some early form of gnosticism, believed that the day of the Lord had already come. Since they thought they were in heaven already, the curse of having to work (Gn 3) had been removed. They could therefore eat, drink and be merry

Idleness today is hardly likely to be due to an over-realized eschatology. It is no longer true that those who do not work are not allowed to eat, as it was the case in the subsistence level economy of New Testament times. For this very reason this passage points up an interesting problem of what is called hermeneutics. This is the problem of getting the text to say the same thing in a completely altered situation. You can no longer get the same meaning if you just report what it says *verbatim*. Its expressions have to be changed in order to put across the same idea. In a society whose economic injustices condemn a large segment of the population to unemployment, it is no good just lifting the Thessalonian text about those who refuse to work not being allowed to eat, and to use it as an argument against welfare payments. This is what fundamentalist middle America may be sometimes tempted to do. Of course there are shirkers in all societies, and they need the warning of this text. But they are just as likely to be found among the affluent as among the poor. After all, our text was directed precisely against the "strong," those who were already "there," already in the kingdom of God. It was not directed against the weak who were conscious that they were spiritually the have-nots of this world. The hermeneutical task is therefore a really delicate one, demanding of the preacher the utmost sensitivity. If he remembers that in Christian behavior the paramount criterion is the law of love, he will be able to avoid a false hermeneutic as he seeks to translate the New Testament injunctions into an entirely changed situation.

Gospel: Luke 21:5-19.

Once more we must remember that the literary style of apocalyptic is a peculiar one. The authors do not conceive themselves to be predicting, in an abstract, uninvolved way, the "last things" that are to happen centuries hence. Rather, they are interpreting the present crisis in which they are involved as the last crisis of human history, to be followed very soon by its consummation. Also, apocalyptic literature tends to expand in transmission. Material is added as commentary to what is already there and this is then adapted in the light of unfolding events. As history proceeds the original crisis may get worse, or it may be temporarily lifted. A good example of this process is the transmission of the so-called apocalypse of Enoch, which suffered additions and alterations over a period of some 150 years. So, too, is it with our Lord's apocalyptic words. There can be no doubt that he predicted the destruction of the temple. In fact, that was one of the charges brought against him at his trial, although his accusers could not make it stick (Mk 14:58; 15:29; Jn 2:19; cf. Acts 6:14). With the series of crises in Judean history that mounted to a crescendo during the sixties of the first century A.D., this nuclear saying of Jesus was expanded into a "little apocalypse." Traditional apocalyptic material with its predictions of cosmic disasters preceding the end, plus allusions to the events which were already unfolding, were combined with genuine sayings of Jesus. One cannot always be sure where the genuine sayings of Jesus end, and the apocalyptic material and descriptions of actual events begin. But in our present passage we may reasonably conclude that the predictions of historical disasters — war, earthquake, pestilence and famine — reflect the events of the sixties, although some of it is described in conventional apocalyptic language. The predictions of persecutions are genuine warnings of Jesus, addressed to his disciples (12a, 16-19), but elaborated in the light of what actually happened to Peter, Paul, James the Just and others during that decade (v.12b). The promise of divine assistance to his disciples in the time of trial reflect an original promise of Jesus of the gift of the Holy Spirit.

This gospel reading confronts the preacher with two problems, one arising from its highly complex character, the other from the fact that it refers to a first century crisis which no longer obtains today. The best thing to do with such literature is to treat it as an inspired insight into the meaning of history. History is a constant struggle between the forces of good and evil. The Christian has no right to expect that everything is going to get better and better, or that Christ's cause will progress without hindrance. All he knows for sure is that God will eventually bring good out of evil, that the right will triumph in the end and that the Christian's task in the present is to show patience and endurance: "By your endurance you will gain your lives."

It was a happy inspiration when Pope Pius XI made the last day of October the feast of Christ the King. Although in some ways it duplicated certain themes of Ascension Day, it provided for a distinctive emphasis on Catholic social action, the counterpart of the social gospel in American Protestantism. It also provided liturgical support for the social teachings of the great papal encyclicals from Leo XIII on.

Now the time has come for a review of Pope Pius XI's action. Feasts governed by the secular calendar, like the "last Sunday in October," lack sound precedent in liturgical history. The Feast of Christ the King, if it is to be observed at all, ought to be integrated into the church year. Moreover, there was a danger of isolating the kingship of Christ from its proper biblical context, which is eschatological. His enthronement at the Ascension is the opening act of his final eschatological reign, and his continued heavenly rule between the Ascension and his return mark the progressive defeat of the powers of evil. For he must reign until he has subjected all his enemies under his feet.

These needs were met by another happy inspiration, the transference of the feast to the last Sunday of the church year. This Sunday has always had a strong eschatological tone, even with the traditional readings. Johann Sebastian Bach composed a setting of *Wachet Auf* (Sleepers, Awake) for this Sunday, which in German Lutheranism is known as *Ewigkeitssonntag* (Eternity Sunday).

Reading I: 2 Samuel 5:1-3.
David was always regarded as the ideal king, and when the messianic hope developed, it was natural that the Messiah should be thought of as a Son of David. He would be not only a descendant of David but also the type of king which David was.

There are two attitudes to kingship in the Old Testament. One, representing the royal ideology of the Davidic court, pictures the king as the sacramental expression of Yahweh's kingship. Our passage is an expression of this line of thinking. It stresses the humane sides of kingship — the solidarity of the king with his people ("We are your bone and your flesh") and the king as shepherd. These traits were taken up on a higher level in the christology and ecclesiology of the New Testament. Christ is one with his body the church, and he is the Good Shepherd, who lays down his life for the sheep. He knows his sheep by name.

But there is also another attitude to kingship in the Old Testament. All human kingship risks a denial of the ultimate sovereignty of Yahweh, who alone is king. This other ideology is conscious that kingship can easily degenerate into tyranny. Chapter 8 of 1 Sam is the classical formulation of this view.

The first attitude is expressed in the English coronation service, the second in the American constitution, with its elaborate system of checks and balances. The dialectical tension between these two views is maintained in the New Testament. In Rom 13 the state is the minister of God (the Greek word is *leitourgos*, a liturgical functionary: the English monarch is vested at his/her coronation in quasi-priestly vestments), whereas in Rev 13 the state is the beast from the abyss. This dialectic must be maintained in any doctrine of the state, and not even the American constitution should be interpreted undialectically! Liturgical minister and great beast — all states can be either of these and even both at the same time.

In preaching on the present text it is possible to speak either of the Christian doctrine of the state and to bring out its dialectical character, or — which would fit better with the theme of the Sunday — of King David as a type of Christ the King, who is at one with his people and is their shepherd.

Responsorial Psalm: 122:1-5.

This psalm was sung by the pilgrims as they went up to Jerusalem for the festivals. The first part, which forms our reading, expresses the pilgrim's excitement as he arrives within the sacred precincts. He exults in the unity which Jerusalem symbolizes as the festal crowds, representing all the tribes, flow together to the temple of Yahweh.

In some strands of post-exilic Judaism it became part of the eschatological hope to envisage a day when the nations would flow togther to Jerusalem (e.g., Is 25:6). The New Testament sees this hope partially fulfilled in the admission of the Gentiles to the church and completely realized in the final coming of Christ. See especially Romans 9-11, where the Apostle Paul develops the thought that in bringing of the collection from the Gentile churches to Jerusalem he is symbolizing the partial fulfillment of this hope, and propounds the conviction that his mission will contribute decisively to the final fulfillment, when the fulness of the Gentiles will be gathered in and all Israel will be saved (Rom 11:25-26). In contemporary preaching we may interpret the liturgy as a pilgrimage to Jerusalem. Here is our Jerusalem, the anticipation of the heavenly city where Christ's kingship will be finally realized.

Reading II: Colossians 1:12-20.

Verses 15–20 form one of the great christological hymns of the New Testament, comparable to Phil 2:6-11 and Jn 1:1-14. Some scholars regard it as a baptismal hymn. Verses 12-15, which precede it, certainly fit such a baptismal context very well when it speaks of "our" (i.e., the Christian community's) being qualified to participate in the inheritance of the saints, and of our translation from darkness into the kingdom of the Son of God, for this is precisely what happens in baptism. But the hymn itself is purely christological and has a cosmic sweep. It speaks about two different works of the Son of God. His first work in his pre-existent state is his agency in creation and preservation. It describes this pre-existent state and work in terms derived from the wisdom concept as it had been developed especially in Hellenistic Judaism. In the second part of the hymn (from v.18) it speaks about his redeeming work. This work is stated not in chronological order, but it does refer to the incarnation ("in him all the fulness of God was pleased to dwell"), to the cross[1] and its cosmic, reconciling effects, to his resurrection as the first-born from the dead, and to his establishment of the church as his body.

It was a bold step when the Greek speaking Christians identified Jesus of Nazareth as the incarnation of the heavenly wisdom, and claimed for him all the theology of wisdom which had been worked out in Hellenistic Judaism. It seems at first sight a far cry from his simple message of the in-breaking of the kingdom of God. Yet Jesus himself had claimed to be the mouthpiece of the divine wisdom (e.g., Lk 11:49). It was a natural development of this that the Greek speaking Christians identified him as the incarnation of the personified wisdom of later Jewish tradition. This enabled them to oppose the gnosticism which denied the salvability of

[1] This is probably a Pauline or Paulinist addition to the hymn.

creation and interpreted redemption to mean redemption *from* creation, by asserting that the redemption effected by Christ was the redemption *of* creation. If the wisdom of God means God going forth out of being in himself in creative and redemptive activity, then this early Christian hymn proclaims that it is the same God who creates and redeems.

What has all this to do with the kingship of Christ? The preface of the hymn gives the answer. It is precisely the acts of God in Christ celebrated in the hymn that have transferred us into the kingdom of his beloved son. The kingship of Christ means that the eternal Son of God who became incarnate in Jesus is the "cosmocrator" — the ruler of the universe. The church, his body, is the sphere in which that kingship, though still hidden, is acknowledged and proclaimed. The world is the universe over which Christ's kingship is destined to prevail.

This text offers the preacher the opportunity to be quite specific about the kingship of Christ. It is not just an abstract idea: it involves the doctrines of the creation, redemption and reconciliation of the universe and of the church as the sphere where his universal reign is already acknowledged and proclaimed.

Gospel: Luke 23:35-43.

It must be admitted that the story of the penitent thief comes as an anti-climax after the tremendous cosmic sweep of the Colossians hymn. The kingship of Christ is certainly one of the themes of this gospel. First the taunt of the crowds and the inscription on the cross, the one ironical, the other intended as a false charge but true for the eyes of faith. Then there is the penitent thief's request that Jesus should remember him when he came to his kingly power and the assurance that the thief would be today with him in paradise. The first two texts domesticate the idea of kingdom. He is king of the Jews, not of the cosmos. The third text individualizes it, and, one is almost tempted to say in the context of this Sunday, trivializes it. Of course, Christ's kingdom has its domestic and individualistic aspects. It *is* the kingdom of the Jews, of the religious of the church as well as of the universe. And he is the king of the believer who is brought to penitence by the contemplation of the cross.

The preacher could draw out the domestic and personal aspects of Christ's kingship, if he so desires, but if he wants to do justice to the cosmic breadth of this Sunday's celebration of the kingship of Christ he will find more adequate material in the first two readings.

Advent of Year A

There is some uncertainty what should be the dominant theme of Advent. Is it focused upon the traditional "last things" — the end of the world, the general resurrection, the last judgment and the new heaven and new earth? Or is it a period of preparation for the feast of the incarnation? Does it place us back in the period of salvation history prior to the coming of the Messiah?

The new lectionary has tidied up this confusion by developing the future-eschatological themes in the last Sundays *per annum* of the old year, and by bringing these themes to a climax on the first Sunday of Advent. It then allows other themes, the preparation for the incarnation, to take over increasingly from the second Sunday of Advent on. Thus the successive church years dovetail into one another.

FIRST SUNDAY OF ADVENT

Reading I: Isaiah 2:1-5.

This is a vision of the pilgrimage of all the nations to Zion to be taught the ways of Yahweh. He will arbitrate international disputes and a universal peace will follow. The prophecy is almost reproduced verbatim in Micah 4. It is uncertain whether Micah lifted it from Isaiah or Isaiah from Micah, or whether both derived it from a common source. Scholars seem to favor the third possibility. It certainly looks like an ancient liturgical fragment.

It is important to notice two things about this vision. It is speaking about what will happen at the end of history — in other words, it is eschatological. It is not envisaged as a possibility within history. Holy scripture does not permit us to indulge in the illusion that a time will come within history when there will be no more wars. This does not, of course, mean that we should not work to eliminate the causes of war or to avert or bring to an end particular wars. It only means that we should not cherish extravagant hopes which are doomed to inevitable disappointment. The final abolition of war is possible only when God's purpose has triumphed in the consummation of history. The second point to notice about it is that it is only when the nations have been taught God's ways and walk in his paths that they will beat their swords into plowshares, etc. "It is a beautiful vision; but, be it noted, peace rests in no human program, but in obedience to the divine law" (J. Bright in *Peake's Commentary on the Bible*).

Responsorial Psalm: 122:1-9.

The responsorial psalm takes up certain points from the Old Testament lesson — the pilgrimage to Zion and the ensuing peace. For a commentary see the previous Sunday, Christ the King, series C.

Reading II: Romans 13:11-14.

This is the traditional epistle for the first Sunday of Advent. It is full of great New Testament eschatological words: night/day, darkness/light, sleep/wake, hour and "full time." This language presupposes the early Christian scheme of the two ages, this present evil age and the new age which is soon to dawn. It interprets Christian existence as a life of tension. It is lived within this present old age but is already determined by the new age which is soon to come. The Christian stands in the dark with his face lit by the coming dawn. He can therefore already cast off the works of darkness, and put on the armor of light. He can live "as in the day," although actually he is still in the night.

Note that it is not by his own unaided effort that the believer is to conduct himself as becomingly as in the day, but rather "by putting on the Lord Jesus." In Gal 3:27 the same phrase is associated with baptism: "As many of you as were baptized into Christ have *put on* Christ." Hence in our present passage Paul is exhorting the Christians to live out the implications of their baptism, in the power that their baptismal status gives.

One final problem. Paul tells his readers that "our salvation" is nearer than when we first believed, i.e., nearer than it was when we first became Christians. By "our salvation" Paul is not thinking of salvation in an individualist, pietistic sense as though we were now nearer to our death and therefore to heaven. He means the great day of salvation, the consummation at the end of history. Like all the early Christians the apostle believed that this end was to come very shortly — so soon, in fact, that it was now appreciably nearer than when the Romans first became Christians. Paul was clearly mistaken as to the date, for we are still here today and the consummation has not come yet. Perhaps an answer can be sought along these lines: the Christian has always to live as though the final consummation were just around the corner, in the certainty of it, a certainty so strong that already the light of the new age is casting its ray upon the Christian's present existence.

Several possibilities open themselves up to the homilist. He may characterize Christian existence as an "advent situation" — the Christian as living in the present age, but decisively conditioned by the age to come. He may exhort the congregation to live out the implications of their baptism, in which they were translated into the advent situation, or he may wrestle with the problem of the non-fulfilment of the imminent end-expectation of the earliest church and how that end-expectation can become an existential reality for the contemporary believer.

Gospel: Matthew 24:37-44.

This passage is from Matthew's version of the so-called synoptic apocalypse (Mt 24 / Mk 13 / Lk 21). Like other contemporary Jewish apocalypses the synoptic apocalypse relates a series of catastrophes identifiable with historical events which preceded the Jewish revolt of 66–70. These events are to usher in the final consummation — the return of the Son of man, the last judgment, and the new heaven and the new earth. Such an apocalyptic scheme creates an overall impression which conflicts with the general tenor of Jesus' teaching elsewhere, including this present passage, which Matthew has inserted from his sayings source into the synoptic apocalypse. Here, in sayings which have the freshness of authentic Jesus material, the end is depicted not as something which is preceded by a carefully planned apocalyptic timetable, but as something which is to come suddenly, like Noah's flood: "They did not know until the flood came: watch, for you do not know the day when your Lord is coming . . . for the Son of man is coming at an hour you do not expect." This coming of the Son of man will be accompanied by the ultimate separation of the saved and the lost. Two men will be in the field, one taken and the other left, two women grinding at the mill, the one taken and the other left: one will be saved, the other rejected. Therefore watch, as a householder must watch for the thief. There can be no doubt that sayings like this, rather than the synoptic apocalypse as a whole, correctly reproduces the eschatological message of Jesus.

But this brings us face to face with the same problem as in the Pauline passage, though here it is Jesus rather than the early church who was apparently mistaken about the date of the end. It did not come soon. Once again we can take the apocalyptic perspective as an expression of the eternal consequences of the choice with which Jesus confronts his hearers. They must certainly react as though the end were just around the corner. Professor Joachim Jeremias has recently made a further suggestion. It is bold but exciting: Jesus does not regard the will of God as fixed and immutable. God can shorten the days for the sake of the elect (Lk 18:7-8) and he can also lengthen the period of grace (Lk 13:6-9) as a free act of mercy.

The homilist has two possibilities before him. Either he can exhort his hearers to eschatological alertness: watch — at any moment you have to make an eternal choice. Or he may want to wrestle with Jesus' as well as the early church's near expectation of the end, and try to make sense of it for present Christian existence. The eternal import of the choice Jesus presses upon us means, to say the least, that we must live alert "as though" the end were coming at any moment. Or — taking up the suggestion of Jeremias — the homilist can lead his hearers to see how it is the grace and mercy of God that the end did not come when Jesus said it would, but that God has given mankind longer time to prepare for the great day.

SECOND SUNDAY OF ADVENT

Reading I: Isaiah 11:1-10.

As we have indicated above, the second Sunday of Advent marks the shift from future eschatology to the preparation for the incarnation. This shift appears in all the readings of this Sunday, though as we shall see, the epistles of Advent II and III contain echoes of the earlier theme.

First we have today one of the great messianic prophecies of Isaiah. It pictures the ideal king from the family of David. He is to be endowed with the spirit of Yahweh and with charismatic gifts. Note the three pairs; the first two are powers of intellect, the second pair practical ability and the third gifts of piety. The benefits of his reign are described in idyllic terms.

This picture is much older than the messianic hope proper. It probably expresses what each succeeding generation hoped for from its Davidic king. Yet the ideal was never realized, and the poem was shelved for messianic fulfilment. Christian faith naturally found its fulfilment in the coming of Jesus, and that is the sense in which we read it in the liturgy today.

Responsorial Psalm: 72:1-2, 7-8, 12-13, 17.

This psalm is remarkably similar to the prophecy we have just read, and suits it admirably as a responsive reading. It is a prayer that the monarch (presumably again a king of David's line, for much of the prosperity of his kingdom recalls the reign of Solomon) may have used in prosperity and peace. Again, like the Isaianic prophecy, this psalm was later interpreted messianically both in Judaism and in Christianity.

Reading II: Romans 15:4-9.

This is the traditional epistle for this Sunday, and, because Cranmer constructed a new collect on the basis of this lesson, Anglicans have long called Advent II Bible Sunday. Unfortunately this had the effect of distracting attention from the main Advent theme of this reading. Two things are to be noted. First, the "scriptures" and the "things written" in former days refer to what we should now call the Old Testament. There was as yet of course no New Testament in the early church; in fact when Paul wrote Romans he was actually taking a hand in producing what would later become the New Testament. During these Advent Sundays, there is, as we have seen, a particular emphasis on the Old Testament as the book of promise. This theme is taken up in our present passage with its reference to hope: Paul prays that by the encouragement of the scriptures we might have hope. The Old Testament is precisely the book of hope and of promise. It is an incomplete book which points forward to an event which had not yet taken place, viz., the final act of God. Jew and Christian ought to be able to agree about this. But then comes the point of divergence. Christians believe that the event toward which the Old Testament points has, in principle at least, already occurred with the coming of Jesus Christ. Jews of course are bound to continue to believe that the event has not yet taken place.

But the Christian belief that the promises of the Old Testament have already in principle been fulfilled does not mean that there is no further room for hope. Paul says that the Old Testament scriptures are written in order that the *Christians* may still have hope. The current theology of hope (Jürgen Moltmann and Johannes Metz) stresses that the acts of God are always such that they contain within them the hope for more. This is a pattern which reproduces itself again and again throughout salvation history. When the Christian faith that God has fulfilled his promise in the sending of his son Jesus Christ is kindled, it at once also raises the hope of the second coming. So Christian existence remains, like that under the Old Testament, an existence geared to the future. That is why the Old Testament does not become irrelevant now that the event to which it points has taken place. We still read the Old Testament to orient ourselves in hope to the future, to the final event toward which the Old Testament points, the consummation of the kingdom of God.

Clearly, this reading requires of the homilist an exposition of the great theme of Christian hope. To prepare himself to handle it, he would do well to read something of the works of Moltmann and Metz.

Gospel: Matthew 3:1-12.

If the lessons of this season are preparatory to the incarnation, it seems a little odd that John the Baptist should figure so prominently on these Sundays. John the Baptist does not — like the Old Testament prophets or like the annunciation story which we shall read on the last Sunday of Advent — point toward the nativity, but rather to the ministry, life and death of Jesus: "He who is coming after me is mightier than I . . . he will baptize you with the Holy Spirit and with fire"; "Behold the lamb of God, who takes away the sin of the world."

When New Testament scholars speak about the incarnation, however, they tend to think of it in somewhat wider terms than popular piety — or even dogmatic theology — does. The incarnation, from the biblical perspective, is the whole "Christ event," the total coming of the Son of God in the flesh, which includes not only his nativity, but also his whole ministry, his death, resurrection and ascension. In fact, most of the New Testament, aside from the infancy narratives of Matthew and Luke, can proclaim the Christ event without speaking of the nativity at all. So when the Advent season prepares for the "advent" of Christ this is not just his nativity, but rather his total coming. The nativity is merely one way of speaking of the advent of Christ, and not the central one at that. Hence it is wholly appropriate that John the Baptist should figure prominently in the Advent season as a herald of the Messiah's coming.

Reading I: Isaiah 35:1-6a, 10.

Although this chapter comes from the earlier part of Isaiah (1-39), its theme and mood are far more reminiscent of the unknown prophet of the exile whom we call the second Isaiah (Is 40-55). Like the second Isaiah, the writer of this chapter speaks of the return from Babylonian exile in terms of the exodus: in the return to Jerusalem the miracles of the first exodus will be repeated (cf. Is 40), the wilderness will rejoice and blossom as it did in the exodus, and the ransomed of the Lord shall return and come to Zion. There will also be accompanying miracles: the eyes of the blind will be opened, and the ears of the deaf unstopped, the lame will walk, and the tongue of the dumb shall sing.

This passage is very important for the New Testament. Jesus' healing miracles for instance are recounted in language derived from this passage. Thus, the story of the deaf-mute in Mark 7 actually uses the unusual word *mogilalos* for "dumb" which the Septuagint (Greek Old Testament) uses for this passage. Again, in the answer to John in prison (see the gospel of this day) there are further echoes of this passage.

The New Testament took up such prophecies as Is 35 and found their fulfilment in the Christ event. It is in the coming of Christ that the wilderness blossoms as the crocus, it is in him that the *glory* of the Lord is made manifest (cf. Is 35:2 and 40:5 with Jn 1:14), it is in Christ that God comes to save his people and in Christ that the exiles return to Zion with great joy.

There is nothing unusual in this shift of application. It is a procedure that took place constantly throughout the Old Testament and Judaism, and it is simply continued in the New Testament. Each successive event in salvation history discloses a new meaning in previous prophecies. In this way the word of the Lord, once uttered, continues to be an effective force in salvation history.

Responsorial Psalm: 146:6c-10.

This is the first of the final group of Hallel (Hallelujah) psalms in the psalter. It is a psalm of praise to Yahweh for his mighty acts of salvation, and it takes up some of the themes we have already found in this day's Old Testament reading. The Lord opens the eyes of the blind. "The way of the wicked he brings to ruin" in the psalm recalls the verse "your God will come with vengeance." Once again, Christian faith can see the fulfilment of all these blessings in the coming of Christ. It is he who executes justice to the oppressed, who feeds the hungry (Mk 6:37-44 and parallels), who upholds the widow (Mk 12:41-44). And above all, it is in him that the reign of God is established to all generations.

Reading II: James 5:7-10.

This reading is "odd man out" among the lessons appointed for this Sunday. It is the only reading which does not take up the theme of the healing miracles which accompany the advent of the Messiah. And when it speaks of the "coming" of the Lord it is thinking not of his first advent but of the last judgment: "The judge is standing at the doors." This is not an oversight on the part of those who drew up the new lectionary. Here we have a lingering echo of the futurist eschatology which was dominant on the last Sundays of the old church year, and continued through the first Sunday of Advent. Even when we concentrate on the first coming, we must not lose sight of the second. Even as we rejoice with exuberant joy at the first coming, we must also listen to the warning of the impending judgment, and to the challenge to be patient. The use of the farmer as an example of patience seems to be suggested by our Lord's parable of the seed growing secretly (Mk 4:26-29), where it was applied to the coming of the kingdom.

A second illustration of patience (and of suffering as well) is taken from the Old Testament prophets. This, too, is especially apt for the Advent season. The Old Testament prophets believed that the word they uttered would be fulfilled very shortly, but they had to learn that God fulfils his word in his own good time, even the word which he had promised through the prophet to fulfil very shortly. Does God therefore deceive the prophets? Not if Jesus is right (see First Sunday above) in maintaining that God can rescind his holy will as a free act of mercy. When that happens the lesson of patience is especially pertinent.

Gospel: Matthew 11:2-11.

The casual reader of the gospels is often puzzled by this story. How is it that John came to wonder whether Jesus was the Coming One? After all, had not John already greeted Jesus as the Coming One (Mt 3:14)? Was he now perhaps having second thoughts? Had Jesus turned out to be a different kind of Messiah from the kind John had expected — one meek and lowly of heart, rather than one who purged the threshing floor with the winnowing fan of judgment?

These are interesting questions, but they are irrelevant to a proper understanding of our text. The real question is the one addressed to us: Can *we* believe that he is the Coming One, or must *we* look for another?

In answer to John's question (which is our question, too) Jesus does not give a straight Yes or No, but points to what is happening in his ministry: the blind receive their sight, etc. Note the oblique way in which Jesus speaks of his mighty works. He does not say that *he* is healing the blind, etc. The blind are given their sight by God! Thus Jesus indirectly affirms that his miracles are works of God wrought through him. But he never says so directly. The hearer has to work this out for himself, and to make a decision of faith.

Traditional apologetics used to cite the miracles of Jesus as "proofs" of his "divinity." This is not the way the Bible uses them. They are not proofs but signs — signs for those who have eyes to see and ears to hear. And they are not signs of Jesus' divinity (a Greek rather than biblical term) but signs that God is present and at work in Jesus. Note that Jesus' answer echoes the language of Is 35 and other prophecies (Is 29 and 61). So the reader is confronted with a decision: Either these works are signs of the eschatological presence of God in Jesus — or they are ultimately trivial episodes with no claim to our faith. But: "Blessed is he who takes no offense (i.e., does not stumble) at me," that is to say, the man who sees that God is eschatologically active in Jesus' word and work, is already a partaker in the blessings of the messianic age.

The second part of the gospel reading deals with the place of John the Baptist in salvation history. He is the messenger who prepares the way of the Messiah, he is the expected Elijah returned to herald the end. Yet he who is least in the kingdom of heaven is greater than he. For John stands at the threshold of the new age. He is the last of the prophets, and, like them, still points forward to the kingdom of heaven and the coming of the Messiah. He still stands on the Old Testament side of the great divide between the two ages. He is the "sentinel at the frontier between the aeons" (Bornkamm).

Two basic possibilities are open to the preacher today. The more obvious choice is to expound the Old Testament lesson, responsorial psalm and gospel as a promise and fulfilment of the first advent of the Messiah, with emphasis either on the accompanying signs or on the work of John the Baptist (the latter is the primary theme of the Sunday). Alternatively, the homilist may choose to expound the epistle, in which case he would have to concern himself with the second coming of the Messiah and the consequent need for patience. Should he opt for the latter, it is important for him to see that the epistle of James does not stand alone, but is part of the New Testament canon. Its one-sidedness (all the New Testament writings are in some way one-sided) needs to be balanced by the witness of the other books in the New Testament canon. So today the one-sided concentration of the James passage on the second coming needs to be balanced by the emphasis on the first coming in the other readings. The Christ who is to come again is the same Christ who has already come in the incarnation. His work will then be the consummated work initiated in his first coming. Only so can we give an authentically Christian exposition of James.

✓   FOURTH SUNDAY OF ADVENT

The rhythm of Advent differs from that of Lent. Lent descends from Ash Wednesday through the penitential season to the abyss of passion week and Good Friday — and then Easter bursts suddenly upon us. Advent on the other hand rises in a steady crescendo toward the full light of Christmas. This rhythm is aptly symbolized by the German custom of the Advent wreath, which is becoming popular in this country also. The crescendo of Advent is reflected in the liturgical readings, which, beginning with the prophecies of Isaiah and John the Baptist, find their culmination on Advent IV in a series of readings which focus on the Blessed Virgin and the annunciation of Jesus' birth.

Reading I: Isaiah 7:10-14.

This text may be interpreted at two quite different levels (though, as we shall see, there is a real connection and continuity between these two levels).

First, there is the meaning of the text in its original historical situation. This situation is described in 2 Kings 16:5-9. Syria has entered into an alliance with the northern kingdom of Israel against the southern kingdom of Judah of which Ahaz is king. Together they have laid siege to Jerusalem. Isaiah offers Ahaz a sign that everything will eventually turn out successfully, but Ahaz piously refuses such a sign, doubtless because he wants to have no truck with Isaiah's advice. But Isaiah goes on and gives the sign anyhow: "A young woman shall conceive and bear a son, and shall call his name Emmanuel." It is probable that the young woman in question is the wife of the king, and the son to be born Hezekiah. The sign will then concern the continuation of the Davidic dynasty, a sign that God is with his people. This is the first level of meaning.

At the second level, the text is taken up by the Evangelist Matthew and applied to the birth of Jesus. The Lucan infancy narrative also echoes it (see Lk 1:31), thus indicating that this application represents a tradition earlier than the two evangelists. In the Septuagint translation used by the evangelists 'young woman' is rendered *parthenos* (virgin). In a sense the resultant application of Is 7:14 is far removed from what the prophet originally intended: he was thinking only of the immediate political situation and of the certainty that God would shortly intervene on the side of Judah. But in linking this assurance with the continuance of the Davidic line, Isaiah had expressed a hope that continued in Israel, and which for the Christian church found its final fulfilment in the birth of Christ from the virgin Mary. He is the true Emmanuel, God with us.

Responsorial Psalm: 24:1-6.

In the Anglican liturgical tradition this psalm is associated with Ascension Day, for which it is one of the proper psalms for the second evensong of that feast. It is equally suitable, however, for Advent, for it is one of the entrance psalms, composed for the processional entry of the king into the temple. In Christian usage it can be applied either to the ascension, Christ's entry into heaven, or to the incarnation, his entry into the tabernacle of the flesh.

Reading II: Romans 1:1-7.

This is the opening greeting of Paul to the Romans. Nearly all of his letters were written to churches he himself had founded, but Romans was an exception. It is written to a church already founded by others to prepare the way for a later visit there by himself (Rom 15:22). Part of its purpose is to acquaint the Christians in Rome with the Pauline version of the gospel. He begins by sketching the gospel in a traditional form in which there are a whole series of expressions not otherwise used in his letters:

> descended from the seed of David
>> according to the flesh
> designated (enthroned) as Son of God in power
>> according to the Spirit of holiness.

Paul can safely assume that the Romans had heard of this or similar creedal statements, and will see at once that he preaches the same faith they have received from others before him. Later on Paul will give another formulation of the gospel: "For I am not ashamed of the gospel: it is the power of God for salvation to everyone who has faith." (1:16). This is not a different gospel but the same gospel stated in Paul's own language.

Jesus himself had not called particular attention to his Davidic descent. That would have suggested to his contemporaries a political conception of messiahship, from which he was at pains to disassociate himself. But the post-Easter community found it necessary in preaching to Israel to stress Jesus' Davidic descent as a vital qualification for messiahship. Thus it passed into the general stock of christological concepts. Here it is used to stress the earthly side of Jesus' history ("descended from David according to the flesh"), as contrasted with his exalted status after the resurrection ("enthroned as Son of God . . . by his resurrection from the dead"). Thus the Davidic descent of Jesus stresses not his exalted majesty, but his terrestrial lowliness.

Gospel: Matthew 1:18-25.

In the New Testament the supernatural conception of Jesus figures only in the two annunciation stories in Matthew and Luke. Apart from these two stories (with the possible exception of an editorial adjustment at the end of the Matthean geneology, Mt 1:16, though the text here is uncertain) Jesus is represented as the son of Mary and Joseph (which is what he legally was).

It is remarkable that both Matthew and Luke, whose infancy stories are in most aspects poles apart from one another, agree that Jesus was conceived by the power of the Holy Spirit, his mother remaining a virgin. Clearly the tradition is much earlier than either Matthew or Luke. But as to its ultimate origin the historian can only conjecture. The real question is what the evangelists intended to convey in this story. These stories are an affirmation of faith in the transcendental origin of Jesus' history. He is not a product of human evolution, the highest achievement of humanity, but the intervention of the transcendent God in human history from outside. "The incarnation is like a dagger thrust into the weft of human history" (Hoskyns). To affirm the Virgin Birth is not merely to affirm a theological miracle (though that, no doubt, is presupposed by the evangelists) but to affirm the faith which the evangelists were affirming in narrating the annunciations.

Christmas Season of Year A

The feast of the nativity of our Lord has become one of the chief feasts of the church year, second only to Easter, and like it the center of a cycle of other feasts dependent upon it. This was not always so: Christmas Day is a comparatively latecomer to the calendar, first testified at Rome in the year 336. Unlike Easter, it was not taken over from the Jewish calendar, nor was it determined by an exact knowledge of the date of Christ's birth, for which the New Testament gives no precise information. Nor does it appear that, as in the case of the "historical" feasts that later grew up around Easter, like Palm Sunday, Maundy Thursday, etc., its celebration was due to the exploitation of the local possibilities at Bethlehem, despite the fact that the building of the Church of the Nativity almost coincides with the earliest evidence of the feast (330). Rather, it appears to have been determined by the widespread pagan festivals of the winter solstice, celebrating the beginning of the return of light after the shortest day. Thus in origin the feast of Christmas does not have an exclusively historical motivation. It is not *merely* a commemoration of Christ's birth, but the celebration of the dawn of the light of God's eschatological self-disclosure, the coming of his kingdom. Thus Advent has been a fitting preparation for the celebration of the nativity.

It is interesting to recall that during the Cromwellian period (1649–1660) in England, efforts were made to abolish Christmas on the ground that it had no sanction in scripture. This proved to be one of the most unpopular measures taken at the time, and in the end did more than anything else to alienate the majority of Englishmen from the Puritan experiment. Actually they opposed it for the mainly pagan customs that had gathered around the feast. In view of the social accretions and commercial exploitation now, more than there was in the seventeenth century, perhaps the Puritans had more justification for their case than we would like to admit. Yet, *abusus non tollit usum,* and our aim must be to work for a proper understanding of Christmas among church people. This can best be done by deemphasizing the historical aspect of it and laying stress upon its theological (or eschatological) aspect. For that we have been prepared by the Advent readings, which serve to set the feast in its proper theological and eschatological perspective. Such an emphasis will be our endeavor as we meditate and comment upon the readings which follow.

MASS AT MIDNIGHT.
Reading I: Isaiah 9:2-7.
This is the most famous of all the messianic prophecies of Isaiah. But its original meaning was very different from the associations which have grown up around it in Christian use at this season. It may have been composed originally as a liturgical anthem to be sung on the occasion of the coronation of the Davidic kings of Judah. Every time a new descendant of David ascended the throne it was hoped (note the irrepressible hope of Old Testament religion!) that *this* king would in fact prove to be the ideal king. The joy of the occasion is expressed by two comparisons: the joy of harvest and the joy of victory on the battlefield (v. 3). The new reign ushers in freedom from want and freedom from oppression (for the allusion to Midian see Judges 6-8) and of peace (the burning of the bloody debris of the battlefield). The "birth" of the child (v. 6) was actually the enthronement of the king, which in the royal theology was conceived as God's adoption of the king as his son (cf. Ps 2:7). The king is hailed by a series of royal titles. This is one of the few places (cf. Ps 45:7) in which the king is actually called "God." Usually this was anathema for Israelite religion, even in the royal theology, to go as far as that, though it was common enough in the surrounding nations. Probably we should understand the king's divinity in a modified sense. He is the embodiment of God's own kingship, his representative on earth.

Christian faith reinterprets this passage. The joy is the joy of the advent of Christ, which ushers in deliverance for the oppressed (Lk 4:8) and peace between God and man (Jn 14:27). The words "to us a child is born" now suggest the birth at Bethlehem, rather than the enthronement of a king. This reminds us that the birth of Jesus is only the beginning of the Christ event, that the nativity stands really for the total advent of Christ, the whole saving act of God in him. Finally, it seems more appropriate to hail Jesus as "God," rather than the king of Judah. Yet, even here we must be careful. The New Testament never does so without qualification. Jesus is not *Deus in se* (such a notion would compromise the unity of God), but *Deus pro nobis*, God turned to us in his grace and salvation.

The homilist has several possibilities here. He may speak, for instance, of Christ as our peace, and link this thought with the song of the angels (see gospel). Or he may speak of the paradox of Christ's lowly birth and his universal reign. Bethlehem is part of the paradox of Calvary.

Responsorial Psalm: 96:1-3, 11-13.

This is probably the most magnificent of all the enthronement psalms which celebrate the kingship of Yahweh. Much of its content also appears in another place in the Old Testament, namely in 1 Chr 16, a cento of psalms put together by the Chronicler to mark the bringing of the ark into the temple by David.

The theme of a "new song" can be traced all through the Bible. The old song was sung by Moses and Israel at the Red Sea (Ex 15). One might say that the whole liturgy of the Old Israel was a continuation of this old song. But it lost its zest with the passage of time and especially in the exile: "How shall we sing the Lord's song in a strange land?" So Deutero-Isaiah looks for a new song to be sung after the return (Is 51:11). This hope for a new song was disappointed at that time, and the new song becomes part of Israel's eschatological expectation. In the book of Revelation (Apocalypse) the new song's promise is fulfilled at last in the celebration of the victory of the Lamb. Christmas marks the first step toward that victory, so the church can already here and now take up the new song (as she always does in her liturgy). In the birth at Bethlehem Yahweh truly comes to judge and save the world.

Reading II: Titus 2:11-14.

This epistle reading speaks of the two comings of Christ: 1) "the grace of God has appeared," i.e., in the Christ event (and Bethlehem marks the inception of its appearance); 2) "awaiting our blessed hope, the appearance of the glory. . . ." The second coming, which had been the dominant theme at the beginning of Advent, but which had fallen into the background as the season progressed and the expectation of the birth of Christ took over, is not completely forgotten even now that Christmas has come. For it is only in the light of the second coming that we can celebrate the first coming. People who forget this sentimentalize Christmas into a "baby Jesus" cult. In the nativity Christ comes first in great humility in anticipation of his coming again in majesty and great glory. It is especially fitting that this note should be struck at the midnight mass of Christmas, for much of our traditional imagery speaks of the Lord's second coming as taking place at midnight. This imagery goes back to the parable of the ten virgins: "At midnight there was a cry, 'Behold the bridegroom!'" (Mt 25:6).

Gospel: Luke 2:1-14.

The infancy narratives in Matthew and Luke pose very difficult problems for those who would use them to reconstruct actual history. The two narratives agree on the following points: the names of Mary and Joseph as the parents of Jesus, his supernatural conception and Bethlehem as the place of his birth, and its dating in the reign of King Herod. Clearly these items go back to earlier tradition, prior to the evangelists (80–90). Is the location of his birth at Bethlehem simply an expression of faith in his Davidic Messiahship (cf. Micah 5)? Probably this question will never be answered. Then there is the unsolved problem of the census. Luke dates it during the period when Quirinius was legate of Syria. This we know from Josephus to have been A.D. 6–9, a dating which appears to be confirmed by the fact that Josephus places the first census in Judea (cf. Acts 5:37) at about A.D. 6. This is immediately after Judea came under Roman rule — a more plausible reason for a Roman census than at the time Judea was still a quasi-independent kingdom. But this dating for the census clashes with Luke's other statement, supported by Matthew, that Jesus was born in the reign of Herod, i.e., not later than 4 B.C.

Many attempts have been made to vindicate Luke's account of the nativity census. For instance it has been suggested on the basis of remarks by Josephus that Quirinius had already been in Syria as early as 10–7 B.C. with a legatine commission. But the neatest solution, recently proposed, is a different though perfectly plausible translation of Luke 2:2, "This census took place before the one that was made when Quirinius was legate of Syria." Another problem is that we have no evidence for people returning for a census from their normal domicile to their ancestral abode. These historical problems should warn us that, in the words of the *Jerome Commentary*, "the details of the narrative are symbolic and biblical; they communicate the mystery of redemption, not a diary of early events." That is certainly how the narrative should be heard at the first mass of Christmas.

Probably we should not romanticize the shepherds. They had a bad reputation as thieves, and in any case they were poor. In fact, as Joachim Jeremias has shown, they were classed with tax collectors, prostitutes and the like as members of despised trades. This fits in perfectly with the emphasis of Luke's gospel.

The angelic announcement (cf. the annunciation stories) is the biblical way of bringing out the meaning of an event in salvation history. This is the birth of One who is to be the Saviour, the Christ (Messiah) and Lord. In the second proclamation, made by the "multitude of the heavenly host" not his titles, but the effect of the Christ event are announced: glory to God, and peace (with the full meaning of Shalom) among men. The words "with whom he is well pleased" vary in the Greek texts. The King James Version favored a text which gave the sense: good will (i.e., God's good will or favor) toward men. The Vulgate preferred a reading which yielded, literally, the sense "to men of good will." This is probably the right text, but the literal meaning is badly misleading. "Men of good will" is a Semitic idiom which means, men who are the objects of *God's* favor. So actually the Vulgate reading comes to very much the same thing as the King James'. This is a warning against much of the loose talk about men 'of good will' that goes on at Christmas time, especially in the secular world.

What should the homilist try to do with this gospel? The numerous historical problems that the story presents should keep him from taking it in a naive, historical way, as a "diary of early events." Two lines may be suggested: He might explain how shepherds were members of a despised trade, and show how the incarnation is meant especially for the poor, the despised and the oppressed. Alternatively, he can take up the angelic pronouncements as a proclamation of the meaning of the nativity, that with the birth of Jesus the divine salvation has entered the world.

MASS AT DAWN.

Reading I: Isaiah 62:11-12.

This passage is from what is now commonly called the Third (or Trito-) Isaiah. These chapters take up the themes of Is 40–55, which announced the impending return of the exiles from Babylon to their homeland (Is 40). But it reapplies these themes to a new situation. It is no longer the exiles returning to their homeland, but the pilgrims going up to the temple at Jerusalem for the feast (tabernacles?). When read at the second mass of

Christmas these themes are reapplied to the birth of Christ. The passage now speaks of the joy of the new Israel at the advent of its salvation.

If the homilist chose to take this text, he might fix upon the pregnant phrase "sought out." The incarnation is God's search for man (K. Barth), the answer to all religion, which is man's search for God. The church is the result of this search, not an institution founded by men for the cultivation of religion.

Responsorial Psalm: 97:1 and 6, 11-12.

Like the other enthronement psalms, Ps 97 is appropriate for any Christian festival. A different selection of verses from it was already used in series c during the Easter season. The present selection includes verses 11-12, with reference to the dawning of the light, imagery which has passed into the lore of the season and is expressed in so many Christmas carols.

Reading II: Titus 3:4-7.

This passage is very similar to the second reading at the midnight mass (Ti 2:11-14). Both passages speak of the "appearance" of the divine salvation, and can therefore be related fittingly to the nativity. But there is a difference, too. The earlier passage, as we saw, went on to speak of the second coming, and made it the basis of an ethical exhortation. This passage takes a different direction. The appearance of "our God and Saviour" in the Christ event leads to our regeneration and renewal, our rebirth as sons of God (cf. Gal. 4:5-7). Christ is Son of God by right, man has forfeited his divine sonship by the fall. But Christ has appeared to give us rebirth as sons of God. This thought is succinctly expressed in the collect which Cranmer composed in 1549 for the second mass of Christmas: "Almighty God, who hast given us thy only begotten Son to take our nature upon him . . . Grant that we, being regenerate and made thy children by adoption and grace, may daily be renewed by thy Holy Spirit. . . ." And an Anglican poet (Christopher Wordsworth) taking up the great patristic paradoxes on the incarnation, expressed it thus:

> God comes down that man may rise,
> Lifted by him to the skies;
> Christ is Son of Man that we
> Sons of God in him may be.

Should the homilist choose to base his sermon upon this epistle reading, he could speak of the contrast between Christ's divine sonship, which is his by right and nature, and ours which comes only by adoption and grace. There is far too much talk nowadays about all men being sons of God. In biblical perspective they are only potentially so until they are incorporated into Christ.

Gospel: Luke 2:15-20.

This reading completes the narrative begun in the gospel for the midnight mass, the pilgrimage of the shepherds to Bethlehem, their visit to Mary, Joseph, and the babe in the manger. The angelic message had told them that the things they would see would be a "sign" (Lk 2:12). What they see has a meaning beyond what is visible to the eye, which can only see a baby, his mother and her husband, a common enough sight. But this sight is a "thing that has happened." The word translated 'thing' can also mean in the Greek 'word,' i.e., a significant, meaningful communication. So the sight of the child is a sign communicating to them the significance of what the angelic message had proclaimed, that God's salvation had come to earth. The shepherds do not see the salvation itself, but only its outward sign, the birth of the child, wrapped in swaddling clothes.

This reading again is a protest against the sentimentalizing of Christmas. We are not just celebrating the birthday of "baby Jesus," but rather the dawn of the messianic salvation, of God's peace and favor toward mankind. The homilist can thus use this gospel to explain the true, Christian meaning of Christmas. Only in this way can "Christ be put back into Christmas."

MASS DURING THE DAY.

Reading I: Isaiah 52:7-10.

This magnificent passage from Deutero-Isaiah is rather similar to the Old Testament reading for the second mass (see above), and even closer to the enthronement psalms which form the responsorial reading for all three masses. The prophet announces the return in words identical with those which scholars think were used at the new year enthronement festival: "Your God reigns." This proclamation is described as bringing "good tidings." The Hebrew word for good tidings lies at the root of the New Testament term *euangelion* or gospel. Paul took up this very text and applied it to his own apostolic work of preaching the gospel in Rom 10:15, and it probably influenced Jesus' own formulation of his message of the kingdom or reign of God.

The use of this passage in the liturgy today suggests yet another application. It can be referred to the angelic proclamation at the nativity. This is indeed a proclamation of good tidings, a publication of salvation, an announcement of the beginning of the dawn of God's reign. It is in the incarnation that the church sees the return of Yahweh to Zion to comfort his people (Is 40:1) and to Jerusalem. Here the Lord bares his arm and men see his salvation.

The angel at the nativity, Paul in his apostleship, and the church today all make the same proclamation: "Your God reigns"—through the sending of Jesus Christ into the world. The incarnation as the good news of God's reign—this should be the theme of the homilist if he chooses to preach on this text.

Responsorial Psalm: 98:1-6.

Selections from this psalm have already appeared in series c, twenty-eighth and thirty-third Sundays of the year. It is also very similar to the psalms used in the first and second masses of this day and to the first reading of this mass. Its applicability to Christmas is obvious.

Reading II: Hebrews 1:1-6.

Hebrews is unique among the letters of the New Testament. Although it clearly ends like a letter (Heb 13:22-25), it does not begin like one. The author does not start with his own name nor greet the people as was customary. There is no statement of the author's name nor whom he is writing to. Instead he plunges immediately into his theological exposition: "In many and various ways God. . . ." Actually Hebrews looks like a series of liturgical sermons on a collection of Old Testament texts. In fact, the author himself or the editor calls the work a "word of exhortation" (Heb 13:22). The first of these sermons, whose exordium we have here, uses a row of texts to establish Christ's superiority over the angels. It is probable that the readers, presumably Jewish Christians with syncretistic leanings, wanted to range Christ among a whole hierarchy of angelic mediators (cf. the later gnostic aeons, also Col 2:18) and thus deny the uniqueness and the finality of the revelation he brought.

The author prefaces his texts with what looks like an early Christian hymn to Christ, similar in theme to the Johannine prologue which follows as the gospel for this mass. The hymn in Hebrews seems to be based on an earlier Jewish hymn to wisdom. Wisdom existed with God from all eternity and was the agent of creation and preservation. She manifests herself to men on earth and then returns to heaven. In its Christian adaptation the hymn identifies Christ with wisdom as the agent of creation and preservation. He appears on earth. Note that the whole Christ event is covered by the words, "when he had made purification for our sins." There is no explicit mention of the incarnation or the earthly life as in most of the other hymns, though the author himself does add an allusion to his entry into the world in v. 6. After his sojourn on earth he returns to heaven and is exalted to the right hand of the majesty on high, triumphant over the angels who are here conceived, as so often in early Christian mythology, as hostile powers. A further point to be noted about this hymn is that it sets Christ's revelation of God in Israel's salvation history. The same God who has now spoken "in the last days" (i.e., eschatologically) in his Son, had spoken previously in "many and various ways." In the Greek the word for 'many' brings out the fragmentary, partial character of the previous revelations.

This is a very important passage, for it relates the final revelation of God in Christ to the Jewish religion, and by analogy to other religions, too. All religions contain fragmentary and partial disclosures of God, and each religion has its own distinctive insight. But what was fragmentary and partial is now finally and fully disclosed in Christ. Here is the New Testament and biblical approach to the question of the non-Christian religions, which has exercised Christian thought so much since Vatican II: the claim that the final revelation is given in Jesus Christ. Of course our apprehensions of it are never final. The finality of the revelation must not be confused with any particular Christian theology or expression of the Christian religion, for all these are still fragmentary in character. Our claim is for Christ, not of our understanding of him. This is not a piece of religious imperialism, or triumphalism. It follows directly from the eschatological character of Christ's revelation: God has spoken "in these last days." He has spoken not merely by the prophets but by his Son, the unique and final embodiment of his total self-disclosure.

This prologue to the Epistle to the Hebrews provides the preacher with a magnificent opportunity to expound the fragmentary and partial character of God's self-disclosure in the other religions and the finality of his revelation in Christ.

Gospel: John 1:1-18 (long form); 1:1-5, 9-14 (short form).

It is fairly certain that John the evangelist did not himself compose the hymn to the Logos, but that it already existed prior to his use of it. But its origin is much in dispute. Some think that it came from gnostic sources, some regard it as a Hellenistic Jewish hymn to wisdom. It has even been suggested that it was a hymn to John the Baptist, celebrated in the "baptist" circles as the bearer of the final revelation of God. It would then have been adapted by the evangelist for Christian use by adding a series of "footnotes" to the hymn: "he — the Baptist — was not that light," etc. It is interesting that the shorter form of the gospel drops precisely these parenthetical notes.

Whatever its origin, the Johannine prologue sketches in the eternal background of what happened in the ministry, life, and death of Jesus. This whole ministry was the revelation of the Word made flesh, the embodiment in a human life of the totality of God's self-communication to man. This self-communication did not begin with the Christ event, it began with creation (cf. Heb 1:1-4), God created the universe in order to communicate himself to it in love. He communicated himself to man throughout history. This he did especially though not exclusively in Israel's salvation history recorded in the Old Testament. As the prologue puts it: "the life was the light of man . . . that was the true light that lightens every man coming into the world." The reception of this revelation — here the evangelist has in mind the consequence of the incarnation — restores man to the divine sonship. It gives them power to become children of God.

It is often debated where John moves from the preexistent Christ to the incarnation. Clearly he has done so by verse 14. Yet the parentheses about the Baptist have the effect of changing the earlier statements about the Logos into statements about the Word made flesh. Thus the whole Johannine prologue is a commentary on the rest of John's gospel. The entire life of Christ is the story of the Word made flesh.

The most obvious course for the homilist to take would be to combine Hebrews 1:1-3 and John 1:1-14. Both speak of the Christ event as the culmination of God's revelation or self-communication to the world in creation, to mankind in general (John 1), and to Israel in particular (Heb 1).

HOLY FAMILY (SUNDAY AFTER CHRISTMAS)

The popular devotions which had in the Latin rite gathered around the Sunday in the Octave of the Epiphany as a result of its old gospel, Luke 2:42-52, have now been officially recognized and transferred to this Sunday. Incidentally, the Episcopal Church has not gone along with this, but observes the Octave of Christmas as a continuation of the celebration of the nativity, with especial emphasis on its theological aspects. (The readings are: Is 60:13-21; Gal 4:4-7 and Jn 1:1-18.) There is of course no question that the place of the family in Christian life needs emphasis now more than ever before, when the stability and integrity of family life are threatened on every side. Equally it is true that the life of the Holy Family provides the model for all Christian family life. Yet a word of warning against sentimentalizing the occasion: it will best be avoided if the homily sticks closely to the scripture lesson of the day.

Reading I: Sirach 3:2-6, 12-14.

This passage is obviously a commentary on the fifth (fourth) commandment: Honor thy father and thy mother. It adds the point that obedience to this commandment atones for sins (vv. 3, 14), an ideal typical of later Judaism. This latter point should not be taken with full theological seriousness. The central message of the New Testament is of course that atonement for sin is through Christ alone. The point should be taken merely as an incentive or inducement to obedience to this commandment, for in a loose, nontheological sense it may well be said that love of one's parents makes up for many other sins.

Sirach of course takes for granted the simple subordinationist ethic of the Hellenistic world. In our days the nuclear family and the consequent segregation of the sexes (a former seminarian of mine observed that in his suburban parish there were no grandparents resident) raise quite serious hermeneutical problems. How does one make the simple ethic of biblical times relevant to contemporary society? What does the commandment say to a society which banishes its parents to an old people's home thousands of miles away? Or leaves them to the care of social workers and the welfare state? How can we restore the personal relationships which were the strength of the old three or four generation family in a society so structured that it is impossible to return to the models of the past? The homilist can hardly be expected to offer answers to these problems, but the text does at least suggest that people ought to be made aware of the questions.

Responsorial Psalm: 128:1-5.

This wisdom psalm, with its introductory beatitude ("Blessed is everyone . . .") presents the fear of the Lord as the basis of family, social and economic prosperity. On a superficial level it seems to express a naive,

Deuteronomic confidence that obedience to the law will be an insurance against disaster, and a conviction that disaster can always be explained as punishment for disobedience, views which are seriously questioned already in the Book of Job. Yet there is something to it. Where there is a wholesome respect for God and his will, man's relationships with his fellow men do stand a better chance of being well ordered and harmonious. The man who fears the Lord is not tempted to put himself in the place of God, to boast in himself and his own achievements. He is therefore freed to love his neighbor and makes it easier for the neighbor to love him.

Reading II: Colossians 3:12-21.

This is part of the "parenesis" or ethical section of Colossians. Such exhortations follow a regular pattern, which is widely believed to reproduce the structure of a primitive Christian catechism.

It begins with a list of virtues, introduced by the imperative "put on." This language reflects the vesting of the candidate as he comes up out of the baptismal font. This imperative may be preceded by another, namely "put off," followed by a list of vices. This records the stripping of the candidate prior to his baptism. Following these general exhortations there is often, especially in the later New Testament letters, a "Haustafel" or household code, listing the various members of family and society and their respective duties. Such codes were apparently derived from Stoic teaching via Hellenistic Judaism, whence they passed into Greek-speaking Christianity. That is why they reflect the subordinationist ethic of contemporary society (wives, be subject — not an idea which is likely to appeal to "women's lib!"). But this subjectionist element, derived as it is from Stoicism, is not the distinctively Christian element in the code. That is found in the words "in the Lord," in the injunction to the husbands to *love* their wives, in the earlier definition of love as forgiveness and in its motivation in Christ's forgiveness of the sinner. Here we should be able to find the raw materials for the formulation of a Christian ethic for a society which is not organized on a hierarchical, subordinationist pattern.

The homilist is faced here, as in the first reading, with a delicate hermeneutical problem which he cannot avoid if he is to make the text speak relevantly to the contemporary believer. We must distinguish between the essence of the Christian ethic and the temporal garb in which it is clothed.

Gospel: Matthew 2:13-15, 19-23.

Only by a questionable extrapolation from the text, involving an illegitimate historicization, would it be possible to relate this gospel to the theme of the Holy Family. Matthew's concern is rather to present Jesus as recapitulating in his life the history of Israel. The Hosea quotation, "Out of Egypt have I called my son," originally applied to the calling of Israel in the Exodus. For Matthew, Jesus is the second Moses and the true Israel, ideas which he expresses by means of a midrashic narrative based on the Hosea text.

Matthew next has to bring Jesus from Bethlehem to Nazareth. This is achieved differently by Luke, who represents the Holy Family as permanently domiciled in Nazareth and as only temporarily visitors to Bethlehem for the census. Matthew does it by means of an otherwise unknown text, said to be from scripture. It is commonly thought that whatever its immediate origin (some lost apocryphal work?) it is ultimately based on Is 11:1 where the Davidic Messiah is described as branch (Hebrew *neser*, suggesting Nazarene and Nazareth) from Jesse. Once again Matthew sees the movements of the Holy Family as the fulfillment of scripture.

Because of the historical problems involved in this passage and because of its theology (fulfillment of scripture, Christ as the new Israel), and also because it is difficult to relate it to the day's theme, we venture to suggest that the homilist avoid it, and instead preach on either the Old Testament or the epistle reading.

SOLEMNITY OF MARY, THE MOTHER OF GOD: JANUARY I

The new title of this feast is apparently suggested by two sentences from the day's reading. One is from the epistle: "God sent forth his Son . . . born of a woman." The other is from the gospel: "Mary kept all these things and pondered them in her heart." Only the former sentence has relevance to the *Theotokos*, for it speaks of Mary's *giving birth* to the Son of God. The latter sentence treats Mary rather as the paradigm of faith, and therefore of the Christian believer and the true Israel. The new Calendar of the Episcopal Church uses the same gospel, which is traditional for this day, but has a different title for the feast, "The Holy Name of our Lord Jesus Christ." This takes its cue from the last verse of the gospel, as did the old title, the Circumcision. Whatever the precise title of the day, its major concern is still the birth of Christ as the beginning of the saving act of God.

Reading I: Numbers 6:22-27.

This lesson comprises the Aaronic blessing, which, like the *ter sanctus* of Is 6 with its threefold form, is a remarkable anticipation of the trinitarian faith of the church. Special attention is called in the caption at the top to the last verse, "They will call down my name on the sons of Israel and I will bless them," which suggests an emphasis on the Holy Name.

People often ask glibly, "What's in a name?" In biblical thought the answer is — everything. The name stands for the whole person, his character and the power of his personality. The name of God is the Being of God himself, all that he has mainfested himself to be in his revelation in salvation history, culminating in the Christ event. To "bless" means to invoke upon the faithful all that God is and all he has done for his people. The name of Jesus is the name of the tri-une God made manifest and present in saving power. This is surely an appropriate blessing for the new (civil) year.

Responsorial Psalm: 67:1-2, 4-5, 7.

This psalm is also used on the Sixth Sunday of Easter in series C, above. Here, as the response shows, the emphasis is on prayer for God's blessing, which fits in perfectly with reading 1.

Reading II: Galatians 4:4-7.

This is the traditional lesson for the First Sunday after Christmas Day, where it has been retained in the new Episcopal Lectionary.

According to recent scholarly investigation this passage is a pre-Pauline credal formula which Paul has expanded. The words "born under the law to redeem those under the law" suggest the particular preoccupations of the apostle, and therefore were probably insertions by him. This leaves us with the formula:

> God sent forth his Son
> (born of a woman)
> that we might receive adoption as sons.

One can see from this that the purpose clause follows immediately upon the sending clause: the Son was sent that we might become sons. This purpose clause is very important, for it indicates that the nativity is not just a beautiful story devoid of connection with our own existence. Modern man asks: "What has the birth of Christ got to do with me?" The answer is that on it depends my whole status before God as his adopted son. He became human through a human birth precisely in order that we might be elevated to divine sonship in him. For further comment on this profound theological theme see above, Christmas, mass at dawn, reading II.

But we cannot dismiss Paul's addition about the law as of no relevance. It points toward the event mentioned at the end of the gospel, Christ's circumcision. In this he is shown to be "born under the law." In his incarnation and earthly life he places himself under human limitations and enters into human culture, including all the restrictions of human freedom which characterize the life of man. The law was for Paul precisely such a restriction. It told man what to do, but left him powerless to do it. Only by complete submission to human bondage could the Son of God liberate man from it. For only he remained truly free, and only he is therefore able, in Van Buren's suggestive metaphor, to pass on the contagion of that freedom to others.

There is much concern about freedom today, both individual and social. It is therefore most important that the Christian understanding of freedom should be made clear. It is that Christ has liberated man from the powers that hold human life in thrall, thus opening up for him freedom to love God and neighbor. This text offers the homilist an opportunity to expound the nature of true human freedom which God gives through Christ. This would be an appropriate theme for New Year's Day, as we are conscious that we move from the past into the future.

Gospel: Luke 2:16–21.

This gospel is almost identical with that of the second mass of Christmas Day. The only differences are that it starts at v. 16 instead of v. 15, and that it goes on to include v. 21, the circumcision and naming of Christ. This is clearly meant to be the climactic verse of today's reading, and therefore it is to this verse that the homilist should draw particular attention. He has two alternatives. Either he can speak of the circumcision and link it up with Paul's "born under the law," along the lines suggested in our comments on the second reading, or he may link up the name of Jesus with the reflections about the "name" in the first reading.

EPIPHANY

As the reader will know, the feast of the Epiphany originated in the East, where it was primarily a commemoration of the Lord's baptism. This was the first of his "epiphanies" or manifestations. Further epiphanies, such as the Cana water miracle, came later. When this festival spread to the West, it drew off some of the associations of the Western Christmas, and became primarily a commemoration of the visit of the magi. This interpretation of the Epiphany remained however peculiar to the West. In turn the visit of the magi came to be regarded as a manifestation to the Gentiles, as in the collect of the Roman Missal and the Book of Common Prayer, *Deus qui hodierna die unigenitum tuum* gentibus *revelasti*, and in the choice of the epistle for the day from Ephesians. Later still, especially in Lutheranism, Epiphany became the day to emphasize the church's missionary work. The new lectionary shows an attempt to restore the primary emphasis to the revelation of God in Christ and to relate all those secondary features to this primary theme.

Reading I: Isaiah 60:1-6.

In its original context the first part of this reading hailed the fulfillment of Is 40ff — the return of the exiles to Jerusalem. The light has now come and the glory of the Lord has been revealed. The second part predicts the eschatological pilgrimage of the Gentiles to Jerusalem that will follow the rebuilding of the city.

This lesson is doubly suited to Epiphany when given a Christian interpretation. First, the incarnation replaces the return from Babylon as God's great act of salvation. In the revelation of God in Christ the light has indeed shone in the darkness, and the glory of the Lord has risen upon the world. And as the Gentiles respond to that revelation, a response symbolically prefigured in the journey of the magi, the eschatological pilgrimage of the Gentiles to Zion is fulfilled. These two themes should provide adequate material for the homilist.

This Old Testament passage has clearly colored the narrative of the magi in Mt 2 (gold and frankincense!). It also continued to influence the development of popular legend by adding details from the Old Testament ignored by Matthew (kings and camels, e.g.)

Responsorial Psalm: 72:1-2, 7-8, 10-13.

This psalm was probably composed as a coronation hymn for a Davidic king. Expressive of the genius of Hebrew monarchy at its best, and in marked contrast to the brutal tyrannies of many oriental potentates, the hymn depicts the king as the source of justice and compassion for the poor. In all fairness, however, it should be noted that a similar portrait of monarchy characterizes the Code of Hammurabi.

The exaggerated language of the third stanza, with its picture of kings coming from afar, in fact *all* kings and nations coming to do homage to the Davidic king of Judah, is simply a poetic expression of Judah's hope that under the new king she will become the top nation as she was in the reign of David.

Christian faith sees this picture fulfilled in Christ and the universality of his gospel. Again, this fulfillment is symbolically expressed in the visit of the magi (who "bring gifts" and "fall down before him"). The psalm complements the Old Testament reading, adding what was missing there, namely the messianic King. The homilist will therefore find it appropriate to enlarge the imagery of the Old Testament reading by bringing in the figure of the king from the psalm.

Reading II: Ephesians 3:2-3a, 5-6.

The present writer is intrigued at the choice of this new epistle (the old Roman Missal had Is 60, but no epistle), for it is the same passage as Cranmer appointed for the Epiphany in the 1549 Book of Common Prayer (though in longer form, vv. 1-12) where it has remained ever since. The reading combines the same two themes we found in the Old Testament reading, the revelation or epiphany of God in Christ ("the mystery . . . made known to me by revelation") and the participation of the Gentiles in the messianic salvation ("how the Gentiles are fellow heirs, members of the same body and partakers of the promise").

Ephesians was written (whether by Paul himself or by one of his closest disciples and successors) at a time when the apostle's work was complete and the unity of Jew and Gentile in the church, for which he had striven throughout his apostolic career, was an accomplished fact. Matthew, too, was a beneficiary of this achievement (even if his view of the law is very different), and it is precisely because of Paul's success that this evangelist can use the story of the magi to symbolize the universality of the gospel.

The homilist should have no difficulty in drawing together the themes of the revelation of God in Christ and the universality of that revelation, and in combining the first two readings and the responsorial psalm for this purpose.

Gospel: Matthew 2:1-12.

Many different elements have gone into the shaping of this familiar story. First, there is the primitive Christian *kerygma* of Jesus' birth from Davidic descent, which would qualify him in Jewish eyes for the Messiahship. This *kerygma* is further expressed in the tradition that Jesus was born in Bethlehem, the city of David (a tradition about which, as we have already noted, Matthew and Luke agree). Second, there is the tradition, also common to Mark and Luke, that Jesus' birth took place near the end of the reign of Herod the Great. Third, there is a folk memory of Herod's character and of his psychopathic fear of usurpation which marked the closing years of his reign. Fourth, there is the widespread Hellenistic belief in the East as the source of wisdom. Fifth, there is the motif of the star as symbol of the Messiah. It is surprising in this connection that Matthew makes no use of Num 24:17. This text played a prominent role at Qumran and it must have shaped the magi story before it reached Matthew. Sixth, the same failure to cite obvious Old Testament texts applies to the mention of the presentation of frankincense and myrrh, which as we have seen is based on our first reading and the responsorial psalm. Again we must suppose that these Old Testament passages influenced the formation of the story, and that Matthew for some reason did not see fit to quote the passages in question. Only the formula quotation of Micah can with any degree of certainty be attributed to the evangelist, though it is unusual for such quotations to be placed in the mouth of the *dramatis personae*. The thought that the magi were Gentiles, underscored at least as early as the Gregorian sacramentary (see the collect in the Roman Missal of the day quoted above), is not at all emphasized in the narrative itself, though it is certainly present in the Old Testament scriptures that lie behind it.

It would seem faithful to the evangelist's intention if the homilist avoided laying too much stress on the Gentile origin of the magi. The point of the story as read today seems to be that by a series of signs (star, fear of Herod, the quest of discovery, and adoration of the Christ child by the magi), that child is manifested as the epiphany or revelation of God in the world.

BAPTISM OF THE LORD

In the Eastern church the primary emphasis of the Epiphany was theological, rather than historical: the epiphany of God in the humanity of the incarnate One. Indeed, the whole life of Christ was a series of epiphanies of which the baptism was the first and most important. The original prominence of the baptismal epiphany was never completely forgotten in the West, but it was relegated into a corner in the liturgy — in the Roman Missal to the gospel for the Octave, in the Book of Common Prayer to an office lesson. The revisers of the Calendar could hardly be expected to restore the baptism to its Eastern prominence by putting it on the actual day of

Epiphany. The story of the magi is too popular in Western Christian lore for that. But they have done the next best thing by featuring it on the following Sunday, and for this we may be glad. It helps to reinforce the theological as opposed to the purely historical emphasis of our Western Christmas cycle of feasts.

Reading I: Isaiah 42:1-4, 6-7.

This passage, the first of the servant songs in Second Isaiah, has deeply impregnated the gospel narratives of our Lord's baptism. The heavenly voice at the baptism is, in part at least, an echo of the words "in whom my soul delights," and a paraphrase of "with whom I am well pleased." The word for "beloved" may be an alternative rendering of "chosen one." And it is held by some that the word "son" is based on an ambiguous rendering of the original Aramaic word "servant." Note that Mt 12:18 has a formula quotation of Is 42:1-4 as an explanation of Jesus' command to the healed not to make him known, the emphasis here being on vv. 2-3 in the Isaianic prophecy. The original identity of the servant is a much controverted question. Some think he represents the whole nation of Israel, others a faithful remnant, still others an individual figure — the prophet himself, or some prophet or king from the past — or perhaps a messianic figure of the future. What the original meaning was need not concern us here. In the liturgy today, as in the evangelists, the servant is identified with Jesus, who is manifested as such in his baptism.

The latter part of the song speaks of the work of the servant. This is to establish justice on earth, to be a covenant to Israel and a revelation to the nations, to open the eyes of the blind and to proclaim the liberation of the captives. This forms a suitable introduction to the stories from the earthly ministry of Jesus which will be read between now and the beginning of Lent. Jesus' words and deeds are an epiphany of the servant of the Lord.

Probably the homilist would be best advised not to treat the Old Testament reading separately but to take it together with the baptism story, with which it is so closely associated.

Responsorial Psalm: 29:1-4, 9b-10.

In some ways this psalm is like the other enthronement psalms which we have encountered, for it celebrates the kingship of Yahweh (third stanza, last line: "the Lord sits enthroned as king for ever"). But there are differences. The second stanza suggests that the psalm had its origin in a pagan hymn to Baal Hadad, the storm God of Canaan. Its meter also recalls

Canaanite poetry as known from Ugaritic texts. But if that was its origin the hymn has been thoroughly baptized: the storm has become an epiphany of Yahweh, the Creator God.

In its present liturgical context, however, the hymn acquires yet another meaning. "The voice of the Lord upon the waters" suggests a voice from heaven at the baptism of Jesus. So the psalm becomes a celebration of the epiphany of God which takes place at the baptism of Jesus.

Should the homilist choose to comment on this psalm, it is its Christian reinterpretation that he would want to bring out. He would not, of course, suggest that this is the original meaning. Rather he would bring out the new meaning which scripture acquires in the light of the Christ event.

Reading II: Acts 10:34-38.

This passage comes from one of the kerygmatic speeches of Acts (i.e., formulations of the *kerygma* or preaching of the early church). It and Acts 1:21 are the only references to Jesus' baptism outside the gospels. Like Mark and John it presents that event as the beginning of Jesus' story. In his baptism he is anointed with the Holy Spirit and so equipped for his ministry of healing and exorcism. Note how the history of Jesus is told as a series of acts of God. It is *God* who preaches the good news of peace in Jesus Christ, *God* who anoints him, and *God* who is with him in the performance of his miracles. It is often held that there is a radical difference between the message of Jesus and the proclamation of the early church. Jesus preached the kingdom, but the church preached Jesus! There is certainly a formal difference here. But it is not a material one. In proclaiming the kingdom, in the performing of exorcisms and healings, Jesus was witnessing to the presence of God acting eschatologically in his own words and works. And in proclaiming Jesus, the church, as we can see from the present reading, was proclaiming that God had been present in Jesus' word and work. She proclaimed Jesus precisely as the act of God, the epiphany of his saving presence. This epiphany is activated at the baptism. This reading would therefore enable the homilist to expound epiphany as saving presence, a saving presence which is shown forth in Christ from his baptism and through his proclamation and works, which will engage our attention in the liturgy during the coming weeks.

Gospel: Matthew 3:13-17.

Matthew's account of the baptism differs from that of Mark, which he was probably using as his basic source, in two points. First, there is the little dialogue between Jesus and John. Matthew has inserted this because in some way he felt that Jesus' baptism at the hands of John created difficulties. It is often thought that Matthew's problem was the sinlessness of Jesus: How could the sinless One submit to a baptism of repentance for the remission of sin? But there is not a trace of concern about Jesus' sinlessness in the narrative. All the stress is on the *persons* of John and Jesus: "*I* have need to be baptized by *you*, and do *you* come to *me*?" As we saw from our discussion of the Johannine prologue (Christmas, mass during the day), there was a "baptist" sect which held that John was the bearer of God's final revelation, in competition with the Christian church. This made the story of Jesus' baptism (whose historicity, precisely for that very reason, is beyond all reasonable doubt) embarrassing for the Christians. It would seem that by submitting to John's baptism, Jesus had tacitly admitted John's superiority to himself, and therefore sided with the "baptists" against the Christians. Matthew explains it by inserting this little dialogue in which Jesus gives the reason: "Thus it is fitting to fulfill all *righteousness*." This word recalls Is 42:6 (reading 1): "I have called you in righteousness," i.e., in order to fulfill my purpose in salvation history. Thus Jesus' reply to John underlines the servant history. Thus Jesus' reply to John underlines the servant Christology of the baptism narrative. Jesus' submission to John's baptism was part of God's plan, so that Jesus should be manifested as the servant of Yahweh, now about to embark upon his mission.

Matthew's second change compared with Mark is in the wording of the voice from heaven. Mark has "Thou art my beloved Son," thus making it a direct address to Jesus only. This suggests that originally the baptism was pictured as a personal experience of Jesus, his call from God to begin his mission. Mark may already have intended this, for by including it in his gospel he tells it for the benefit of the reader, to explain to him who Jesus is, not as part of Jesus' biography. But Matthew wants to make it quite clear that the baptism is rather an epiphany, declaring to the church the true identity of Jesus: he is the servant of Yahweh, fulfilling in his person the mission of the servant as depicted in Second Isaiah.

Obviously, the homilist's task is to proclaim Jesus as servant. In doing so he may well draw together the Old Testament reading from the first servant song, Matthew's treatment of the baptism as brought out in the dialogue between Jesus and the Baptist, and the change Matthew made in the voice from heaven.

Christmas Season of Year A 133

Reading I: Isaiah 49:3, 5-6.

The readings for this Sunday continue the theme of Jesus' servanthood and its manifestation in the baptism. This accounts for the selection of reading 1, the second of the servant songs in Second Isaiah.

When we compare the second servant song with the first which we read last week, we note two points of difference. First point, the second song states that God formed his servant *from the womb*. This consciousness of predestination is characteristic of the Hebrew prophets (Jer 1:5), and recurs in Paul (Gal 1:15). Such an idea of predestination must not be allowed to harden into an abstract dogma, but be allowed to remain what it is in the Bible, a doxological expression of faith in a concrete situation. It is this fact that expresses itself in the annunciation and the infancy narratives of the gospels.

The second point to notice is the enhanced emphasis on the universal scope of the servant's mission. The first song simply included the phrase "a light to the nations." The second expands on this. "It is too light a thing" for the servant's mission to be confined to Israel: "I will give you as a light to the nations, that my salvation may reach to the end of the earth."

If this reading is selected for the homily, it would be best to develop the universal scope of the servant's work, a work which is continued in the world wide mission of the church.

Responsorial Psalm: 40:1, 3ab, 6-9.

This is a personal psalm of thanksgiving for deliverance out of tribulation. The psalmist is determined to give thanks not only with his lips but also in his life. He offers his will in obedience to the will of God. This, he says, is what God desires, not sacrifice and burnt offerings or sin offerings. While this looks like a total repudiation of all cultic sacrifice, we have to remember that this psalm was recited precisely as an accompaniment to the offering of just that, a cultic sacrifice. What the author must mean is that self-oblation must accompany the cultic sacrifice, not that the latter must be abandoned in favor of the former.

Yet, as the author of Hebrews perceived (Heb 10:5-10), this critique of cultic sacrifices points forward to their abolition by Christ's own sacrifice of himself in perfect obedience to the Father. The sacrifices of the Old Covenant were permitted to last for several centuries as a witness not only to their own inadequacy but also to the impossibility of man's offering the perfect oblation of his will. It would have been all too Pelagian for him to suppose that he could. So the sacrifices and the prophetic critique of them had to carry on until the appearance of the one true sacrifice.

The use of this psalm in Hebrews sanctions its christological interpretation, and it is in that sense that it is used in the liturgy today. This is a song of Christ, the servant, offering himself in his baptism to a life of total obedience to the Father's will, a life which will lead him to a ministry to the poor and outcast, to the sick and the suffering, and which will culminate on Calvary. All this will be the subject of the gospel readings in the coming months.

Reading II: 1 Corinthians 1:1-3.

We begin today the reading of extracts from 1 Corinthians in course. Here we have the introductory greeting which is in the conventional style of all ancient letters: "A to B, greeting." But as usual, Paul christianizes the epistolary convention. He is Paul, "called by the will of God to be an apostle of Jesus Christ." His addressees are the church of God, those sanctified in Christ Jesus, called to be saints. And his greeting is a Christian blessing: grace and peace.

The most striking feature, however, in this heading is Paul's emphasis on the universality of the church. He reminds the Corinthians that they are the church of God, *which is in Corinth.* They are the local embodiment of the universal *ecclesia.* There can be only one people of God, and each congregation is nothing by itself, but is only a manifestation of that one people. He reminds the Corinthians that they are not alone: they are called to be saints together with all those who in every place call on the name of the Lord Jesus Christ, and that that Lord is the Lord of those other churches as well as their own. The Corinthians were engrossed in their own spiritual progress and their own problems. They were congregational in a bad sense, in that they thought they were the whole people of God, living on their own. A local church can of course be congregational in a good sense if it realizes the supreme dignity of its vocation to be the representative and embodiment of the universal church. Again and again, as Paul takes up point by point the practical and theological problems that beset the Corinthian church, he will trace back their faults to the supreme mistake of identifying their own congregation with the church catholic, of isolating themselves from the whole body.

Congregationalism in the bad sense is not confined to the denomination that bears that name. In fact, Congregationalists often exhibit congregationalism in the positive sense. But it is a disease which appears to be endemic in the American religious scene. It has been attributed to the frontier situation, in which a group of pioneers get together and start a church on their own. In such an atmosphere it is difficult to foster a sense of the givenness and universality of the church. Church seems something you get together and start on your own. Hence it is of great importance to proclaim the true, biblical, Pauline view of the congregation. "It is not that the *ekklesia* divides up into *ekklesiai*. Nor does the sum of the *ekklesiai* produce the *ekklesia*. The one *ekklesia* is present in the places mentioned" (K. L. Schmidt).

Gospel: John 1:29-34.

This gospel departs from the normal rule of reading Matthew during year A, presumably because of the importance of Jesus' baptism to the Epiphany season, and is taken from St. John. The fourth evangelist avoids a direct narrative of the baptism of Jesus — probably because of claims of the "baptist" sect, which led Matthew to insert the dialogue between Jesus and John, as we saw in last week's gospel. To narrate Jesus' baptism would have made him appear too much like the subordinate of John. This impression the evangelist is at pains to correct from the prologue on through the early chapters of the gospel, and not least in the present passage ("a man who ranks before me because he was before me"). Instead, the Baptist bears witness to the theological meaning of the baptism as it was expressed in the voice from heaven and in the descent of the dove. The latter is explicitly mentioned (v. 33). The voice from heaven is clearly alluded to in the words: "This is the Son of God,"[1] and perhaps also in the reference to the Lamb who takes away the sin of the world. This too may be an allusion to the identification of Jesus with the servant of Yahweh of Second Isaiah.

If we ask what this Johannine account of the meaning of baptism adds to the synoptic accounts, two points spring to mind. One is that John makes even clearer than the synoptists (especially if we follow the variant, "elect," in v. 34) that the theological meaning of the baptism is to be sought exclusively in the manifestation of Jesus as the servant of Yahweh. The second point is that Jesus' mission as servant will include his bearing (or taking away) the sin of the world (Is 53). In this way the epiphany season begins to point beyond itself to passiontide. A homily might well seek to prepare the congregation to look further than the manifestation of God through the words and works of Christ to his suffering.

[1] Some ancient manuscripts have "elect of God" — this would strengthen the allusion to the Isaianic servant.

Sundays 3 A to 6 A

Reading I: Isaiah 8:23–9:3.

This reading overlaps with reading 1 of the midnight mass at Christmas. The verses about the birth of the Davidic king are dropped at the end, but the reading starts with the reference to the land of Zebulun and Naphtali and Galilee of the nations (or Gentiles). This passage will be taken up in the gospel of the day, where Matthew introduces it as a formula quotation to mark the beginning of the Galilean ministry. This shows how the same passage is capable of different applications. Read on Christmas night it relates to the nativity of Christ: it was then that light dawned in the darkness. Read now, it refers to the beginning of Jesus' ministry. It is with his coming to Galilee and the launching of his proclamation that the light begins to shine. Yet, as we have already remarked, nativity and ministry cannot really be separated, because both are aspects of the single Christ event, the coming of light into the darkness of the world. If the homilist likes, he can point up the different uses made of the same passage of scripture on Christmas night and on this third Sunday of the year. Or, he may prefer to take the Isaiah passage in conjunction with the gospel and expound Jesus as the servant of the Lord as he begins his ministry.

Responsorial Psalm: 27:1, 4, 13-14.

An arrangement of this psalm was used for the responsorial reading on Lent II, series c. Here its use is more apt, for it is more suggestive of epiphany themes. "The Lord is my light" picks up the light/darkness motif of reading I, while the "beauty and goodness" of the Lord of which the last two

137

stanzas speak may naturally be referred to the manifestation of God in Christ.

Reading II: 1 Corinthians 1:10-13, 17.

In the first part of 1 Corinthians Paul takes up several points which had been reported to him orally by Chloe's people. He is writing from Ephesus, and it appears that these emissaries of Chloe (one is tempted to speculate that she was a wealthy Christian woman in whose house the Corinthian Christians used to meet) have given the apostle a verbal report of what was happening at Corinth. Other reports came in through a letter sent by the congregation and brought by Stephanas, Fortunatus, and Achaicus (1 Cor 7:1; 16:17). So it is interesting to note that some of the more painful questions were passed over in the Corinthians' letter in silence, and Paul got to know of them only by the oral report of Chloe's people.

The most damaging feature at Corinth was the dissension in the community. There is no indication that this was caused by doctrinal differences, for Paul does not take issue with them on that score. Rather, the Corinthians appear to have split off into cliques, each claiming the patronage of one of the great leaders of the church. It is not clear whether the "I am of Christ" represents a fourth clique (a sort of non-party party!) or whether this is Paul's own rejoinder: "I will have no truck with any of your parties, I am Christ's." Paul meets their dissensions head-on by pointing out that they deny the baptismal reality. One is baptized into the name of Christ, not in the name of any human leader, however exalted.

Although this passage comes in course on this Sunday, it occurs providentially in the week of Prayer for Christian Unity (January 18–25). This gives the homilist a magnificent opportunity to speak about the unity of the church and the great dangers of our unhappy divisions, dangerous because they are a denial of the christological and baptismal reality.

Gospel: Matthew 4:12-23.

Matthew begins the ministry of Jesus by summarizing Mark's "Day in Capernaum." This is an epitome of the ministry: Jesus proclaimed the coming of the kingdom, he called disciples and worked miracles of healing. All of this is placed under the rubric of the formula quotation from Is 9 (see reading 1). By means of this quotation Matthew, who despite some exclusivistic sayings like 10:5, is not himself exclusivist, underlines the universality of the gospel: it begins not on Judean territory, but in Galilee of the Gentiles, and is therefore intended for all men. If the homilist does not wish to connect the epistle reading with the week of prayer for unity, he has the alternative of relating this gospel to the universality of the church's mission: the preaching of the gospel, the calling of all men to discipleship and ministry, the healing of the sick. These form the universal mission of the church today — or rather they are the continuance of the universal mission which Christ began in Galilee.

FOURTH SUNDAY OF THE YEAR

Note: We intend to follow from now on a slightly different arrangement in these meditations. First will come comments on each of the scripture passages. Then at the end we shall consider what the homilist should aim at and what alternatives are open to him in the light of all four readings.

Reading I: Zephaniah 2:3; 3:12-13.

In the Christian church Zephaniah (Sophonias) has always been one of the least known and least used Old Testament prophets. This was so from the beginning, for he is only once cited in the New Testament (Mt 13:41). He prophesied during the reign of the reforming king Josiah, and was therefore roughly contemporary with Jeremiah. But he does not seem to have been interested in Josiah's reformation. He was filled with a sense of impending doom — he had much to say about the day of the Lord, and for him as for Amos this day would be a day of darkness and not light, a day of judgment for Israel. In view of this impending judgment, Zephaniah in our present passage urges Israel to "seek righteousness, seek humility," for only righteous and humble people will escape that day. Zephaniah's single contribution to Old Testament religious thought was his emphasis on God's concern for the *Anawim*, or poor, an idea which will be taken up in the first beatitude in today's gospel.

Note that the reading is a composite one, bringing together two passages separated by more than a whole chapter. This combination of texts is wholly justified since both passages advocate humility as the only ground of security on the day of the Lord.

Responsorial Psalm: 146:6-10.

A slightly different selection from this psalm was used on Sunday 26 C. There it was meant to reinforce the theme of social justice; here it emphasizes the kindred theme of Yahweh's — and therefore the church's — concern for the poor. (Note the refrain from the first beatitude.)

Reading II: 1 Corinthians 1:26-31.

Last week we saw how Paul wrote to the Corinthians in reply (among other things) to the verbal information brought to him by Chloe's people about the divisions among the congregation. As usual, Paul goes to the theological root of the matter. The trouble with the Corinthians was that they were too sure of themselves. They boasted about their wisdom. They believed, like the later gnostics, that through their initiation into Christ they had been made partakers of a heavenly wisdom. They were already on cloud nine! They thought themselves superior to other people who had not had this experience, and hence their cliquishness which Paul was so concerned about in last week's reading.

In today's section Paul seeks to "take them down a peg or two." They think themselves wise and strong whereas actually they belong to what the outside world would regard as the dregs of society: "not many wise according to worldly standards, not many powerful, not many of noble birth." They have nothing to boast about in themselves before God. It is not their own spiritual endowments, achievements or experiences that are the ground of their salvation, but only God's saving act in Jesus Christ, a fact which should humble them. If they must "glory," all they can glory about is the Lord — the saving act of God in Christ.

There is a remarkable parallel here to the way in which Paul dealt with the Judaizers in Galatians. The Judaizers sought salvation through the Jewish law, while the Corinthians believed that they were saved through their own wisdom. In each instance Paul sees the same basic fault. Each party tries to find something in themselves to boast about, some endowment or qualification to give them security *vis à vis* God. Being a Christian, however, means surrendering all this boasting, of whatever kind. For Paul boasting is the supreme expression of man's sinfulness. Thus the gospel gets under the skin both of the Jew and Greek, the religious man and the irreligious — for both are equally exposed to the same temptation.

Gospel: Matthew 5:1-12a.

The beatitudes have already occurred as the gospel for All Saints' Day last year, with comment. There the emphasis was on the second half of each beatitude: the saints now possess the kingdom of heaven, they now are comforted, etc. Here, read in course, and combined with the lesson from Zephaniah and 1 Corinthians, the accent lies on the first half: it is the *poor*, etc., who will enjoy the blessings of the age to come.

The Homily

There is a clear theme running through all the readings of this Sunday, and that is the theme of the poor: "In your midst I will place a humble and lowly people" (caption, reading 1); "Happy are the poor in spirit" (refrain, responsorial psalm); "God chose what is foolish . . . weak . . . low and despised" (reading 11); "Blessed are the poor in spirit" (gospel). These quotations, however, only go to show what a complicated question is the place of the poor in Christian thinking. Are they the economically and materially handicapped (the stanzas of the psalm)? Or should the whole notion be spiritualized (first beatitude)?

This is a very acute question today. The church is challenged on all sides — by James Forman, by black theology, by the speeches at the Synod of Bishops in Rome last fall, by the pronouncements and decisions of the World Council committee meeting at Addis Ababa last spring, by the recent trial of Dean ffrench-Beytagh in Johannesburg — to identify with the economically underprivileged. Yet the caption and quotations just cited give us ground to pause. Dare we listen to some words of Hoskyns on this question? In a Cambridge sermon of 1932/3 he said:

"I fear lest we Christians have gone materialist and that we are nowhere in so grave a danger of materialism as at the moment when we utter the word 'poor' or 'weak,' and that we are in this danger despite the phrase which meets us at the beginning of the Sermon on the Mount, the 'poor in spirit,' a phrase introduced for the express purpose of preventing us from thinking of the poor or of the weak *merely* [my italics! Hoskyns doesn't say we should *not* think of them in those terms] in terms of lack of money, or lack of robust physical health."

He goes on to suggest that the poor might also be found in the most unlikely quarters which are hardly calculated to evoke much sympathy today any more than they were in 1932: the Tory landowner striving to preserve his estate not merely for his own family, but for the good of the whole village which is economically dependent on the estate, the French statesman of the thirties who was responsible for the security of his country against another 1914, the officials of the British War office who, remembering the horrors of Flanders, "dare not behave as though peace were assured." So Hoskyns challenges his hearers: "Are you quite certain that those whom you call the strong are not in fact the weak? Human life is strangely kaleidoscopic. The strong at one moment are the weak at another. The poor (in the biblical sense) are not a fixed, easily recognisable quantity of men and women."

But here we must be careful. We must not so spiritualize the notion of the poor, that we turn our back on the physically poor. It is precisely because the poor are the poor in an economic sense that we are to see in them especially the poor in spirit whom the Lord pronounces blessed. For to be poor in the gospel sense is to be a have-not, a have-not standing before God, dependent on him alone for deliverance. Yet we have to see the poor also in many whom the world, which sees only on the outside, sees as the rich: there is as much poverty in the biblical sense in Westchester County, Main Line Philadelphia or Chicago's North Shore as there is in Harlem, Roxbury or Watts. *All* men have to be brought into the presence of God and see themselves as the weak and the poor. The church should indeed identify herself with the economically poor because she sees in them a parable of the plight of all men before God. And the church should engage in humanitarian action on behalf of the poor because such action is a parable of the love of God in Christ who "for our sakes became poor, that we through his poverty might become rich" (2 Cor 8:9).

FIFTH SUNDAY OF THE YEAR

Reading I: Isaiah 58:7-10.

This passage is more familiar as a Lenten reading. The verses which immediately precede our reading pose the question of true fasting. Today's verses give the answer: true fasting is sharing our bread with the hungry. But the preceding question is omitted today since we are not in the Lenten fast. The effect is to throw the emphasis upon the *consequence* of sharing one's bread: "Then shall your light break forth like the dawn. . . . Then shall your light rise in the darkness." This makes the reading appropriate for the post-Epiphany season, which is concerned not only with the epiphany of God in Christ, but also with the Christian life as an epiphany of God's love for man. The theme of the Christian man as a light in the world's darkness is then taken up in the refrain to the responsorial psalm and in the gospel of the day.

Responsorial Psalm: 112:4-9.

Psalm 112 sets out the characteristics of the just or righteous man in the style of the wisdom literature. It is to be noted that the refrain, though based on verse 4a of the psalm, does not say quite the same thing. When the psalm itself speaks of light, this means the reward the upright receives for his well-doing, a state of general well-being as contrasted with "darkness," i.e., affliction. The refrain by contrast distinguishes between the just and the upright man in a way the psalm does not, and makes the former a light — i.e., a source of well-being — for the latter. When analyzed, the thought of the refrain is really far from clear, though its intention is obvious, viz. to relate the psalm to the Old Testament reading and the gospel, both of which speak of the righteous as a source of light. One may hope in the interests of clarity and of faithfulness to the text of scripture that this refrain will be reconsidered when the new lectionary comes up for review.

Reading II: 1 Corinthians 2:1-5.

It has often been thought that Paul changed his preaching at Corinth because of his failure at Athens (Acts 17). In preaching there to the Stoics and Epicureans he had tried to use sophisticated philosophical arguments replete with literary allusions. So when he got to Corinth he abandoned this style and concentrated on the message of the cross. This is unlikely, because in writing up Paul's visit to Athens the author of Acts probably followed the custom of ancient historians, composed the Areopagus speech himself and put it into Paul's mouth. It is a sample of the Christian apologetic customary at the time Acts was written. Accordingly we must suppose that at Athens as at Corinth Paul followed his usual practice of preaching Christ crucified. At Athens his message was refused because the cross was a stumbling block to the Jews. Intellectuals did not (and still do not) want to hear about man's sin and God's salvation through the cross of Jesus Christ — that is both the folly and the stumbling block. The Corinthians' present behavior — their cliquishness, their pride in wisdom — is wholly inconsistent with the gospel of the cross as they had received it through Paul's preaching. The cross of Christ was the *Umwertung aller Werte*, the denial of all human wisdom and its accompanying pride. The way the Corinthians are now behaving one would think that Paul had not preached the message of the cross, but lofty and plausible words of human wisdom like the wandering preachers and charlatans so common in the Hellenistic world. Paul has only his weak words, yet God made these words the vehicle of his "spirit and power," and after all they did bring the Corinthians to faith.

Gospel: Matthew 5:13-16.

The band of disciples, the nucleus of the future church, is described under three metaphors: salt, a city on a hill, and a light in the world. The pericope concludes with the well known exhortation especially familiar to Anglicans as the first of Cranmer's invariable offertory sentences and so constantly heard Sunday by Sunday for three centuries: "Let your light shine before men. . . ."

The Sermon on the Mount does not say that the disciples are to *become* the salt, that they are to be like a city on a hill or make themselves a light amid the darkness of the world. They *are* all those things, and that because Jesus has called them and they have responded to his call. Rather, they are expected to manifest what they are: "Let your light so shine before men." How is this done? By good works. Our text does not specify what these good works are. It is more concerned to insist that good works are not the meritorious deeds of the disciples themselves. For the world which sees them does not praise the disciples for them, but the heavenly Father. The good works of the disciples point away from themselves to the grace of God through which they were wrought.

The Homily

For this Sunday the homilist would seem to have two possibilities. The dominant theme of the readings (reading 1, the psalm and the gospel) is the Christian community as the light of the world. The homilist should start from the gospel, which shows that the Christians *are* the light of the world. They do not have to become that light through their own good works, but rather show what they are by the good works which are the fruits of God's grace. Then reading 1 and the psalm can be used to illustrate what these good works might be, especially in a Christian concern for the poor.

This theme can in turn be related to the epiphany motif. Not only is Christ the epiphany of God, but the Christian community has to be the epiphany of Christ in the world.

SIXTH SUNDAY OF THE YEAR

Reading I: Sirach 15:15-20.

This is the clearest statement in all of the canonical and deutero-canonical Old Testament writings on the subject of man's free will. It is even clearer than Dt 30:15, whose teaching it echoes. Taken by itself, this passage would seem to be unadulterated Pelegianism. It does not recognize the bias toward sin which characterizes man in his fallen state. Man appears simply as a *tabula rasa*. He has complete freedom to choose either good or evil (fire and water), and there is no apparent recognition of his need for grace. But the author's main thrust is to exonerate God from all responsibility for the evil in the world: God never told any one to be godless or gave him license to sin. The caption rightly picks this out as the point of the whole passage. If we want a complete doctrine of man's free will and the limitations imposed upon him by his fallen nature, we must take into consideration not only this passage, but also passages like Rom 7:7-25.

Responsorial Psalm: 119:1-2, 4-5, 17-18, 33-34.

Psalm 119, the longest psalm in the psalter, is a skillfully constructed acrostic poem in praise of the Torah. Every verse in the 22 eight-verse sections begins with the same letter of the Hebrew alphabet, in order throughout the alphabet. Today's responsorial psalm is constructed from the first (aleph), third (gimmel) and fifth (he) letters of the alphabet. The psalm often sounds highly legalistic in its understanding of piety, but we have to remember that Torah meant all that we mean by God's revelation of himself to man. We may therefore say that Psalm 119 represents the Torah as an epiphany of God to man and a passage from it is therefore appropriate for use during this season.

Reading II: 1 Corinthians 2:6-10.

In the immediately foregoing passage, read last week, Paul repudiated "wisdom," and claimed to preach only Christ crucified. Now he appears to take back much of what he had said. He does not entirely repudiate wisdom after all. There *is* a legitimate sense in which it can be used in Christian theology. In making this point, the apostle picks up the "gnostic" language which the Corinthians (wrongly) used about themselves: "wisdom," "mature," "mystery" (the word which the rsv translates "secret" as an adjective), "depth of God." He even quotes an apocryphal verse which would have especially appealed to them (v. 9). But there is a profound difference between Paul's use of these words and the Corinthians' use of them. The Corinthians were talking about a spiritual revelation into which they claimed to have been initiated when they became Christians. They thought that their very reception of it made them "mature." Paul, on the other hand, is talking about the meaning of the cross in salvation history (v. 8). The "mystery" is that the crucified One, precisely as the crucified, is the Lord of glory, or, to put it in our modern theological jargon, the cross is the eschatological act of God. The

Corinthians thought otherwise. For them the cross was an unfortunate episode of past history, about which least said the better. All that mattered now was that Christ was risen. He was now spirit, and as such had conveyed to them the esoteric gnosis or wisdom by means of which they were "in." They thought they were mature, but in fact, by displaying their ignorance of the cross, they were showing their immaturity.

One further point calls for comment. Paul says it was "the rulers of this world" who crucified the Lord of glory. Who were these rulers? Pontius Pilate and Herod, or the demonic powers? Perhaps, as so often, it is not a question of either/or, for the political rulers who executed Jesus may well, in Paul's thought, have been acting as the earthly agents of the powers of evil. These powers would then have blinded the rulers and prevented them from realizing that they were crucifying the Lord of glory. They of course thought that he was a mere messianic pretender. Perhaps this is also a sly dig at the Corinthians. By refusing to recognize in the crucified (as opposed to the risen) One the Lord of glory, they were aligning themselves with Pontius Pilate and Herod and so acting as agents of the powers of evil.

Gospel: Matthew 5:17-37 (long form); 5:20-22a, 27-28, 33-34a, 37 (short form).

The shorter form helps us to see more clearly the structure of the longer form. In the Sermon on the Mount Jesus enunciates the new law of the kingdom of God, or, better, the new interpretation of the old law which is to prevail in the kingdom. This new interpretation is illustrated by a series of antitheses, as they are commonly called. These antitheses follow a common pattern. First comes the formula, "You have heard that it was said (i.e., that God said) to the men of old." This formula introduces a verbatim quotation of one of the commandments from the old law. Then comes Jesus' reinterpretation, introduced with the formula. "But I say unto you." Both shorter and longer versions reproduce the first three antitheses. The prohibition of murder is enlarged to embrace anger, the prohibition of adultery to cover lustful thoughts, and the prohibition of false oaths extended to the total prohibition of swearing, since a simple Yes or No should be just as binding. The longer version includes further illustrative material and adds to the prohibition of adultery the prohibition of divorce. (Since the latter is attested elsewhere in the gospel tradition it has clearly been added to the antithesis at some point in the transmission of the tradition.) The continuation of chapter 5, not included here, gives two more antitheses, one on revenge and the other on love of the enemy.

The better righteousness which the kingdom of God requires covers not only overt behavior, but also inner motive. God's claim for obedience is an absolute, total demand, claiming the whole man in the entirety of his relations.

It has been said that the Sermon on the Mount by itself is bad news, a sharpening of the demands of the law to the point of the impossible. Thus enunciated, it throws man back on the need for grace (and so advertises the Pelagian suggestions of reading 1 taken by itself). But in the kingdom grace is given to enable a man to advance toward the goal of absolute obedience.

The Homily.

For today we offer three suggestions. First, one could take reading 1 and the gospel together. The Sirach passage offers an either/or choice: good or evil, life or death. But it appears to assume too easily that man can choose and pursue the good of his own unaided power. The antithesis puts before us the "better righteousness," which is beyond the unaided powers of man to attain, and therefore points to his need of grace.

Secondly, the homilist might wish to try his hand at applying one of the antitheses to a current ethical problem. The three antitheses included in today's gospel touch upon acute contemporary problems such as war and pacifism, sexual morality and marriage (the latter only in the longer form), and the "credibility gap" of public institutions. But the relation of the absolute demand of God to the relativities of human life is a tricky business. The preacher will need some sort of ethical methodology like that of the "middle axioms" — just as the voltage of a high power line has to be transformed downwards for ordinary consumption.

The third homiletical possibility is even more difficult. It is to relate the second reading to the contemporary theological situation. Here the homilist would have to penetrate into the basic theological stance of the Corinthian gnostics and seek to discern an analogous stance in the church and in the world today, then confront it, as Paul does, with the "mystery" of the cross. He would have to show that the supposed contemporary theological maturity (man come of age?) is, in fact, immaturity, that the cross provides a radical critique of this supposed maturity, and leads the believer on to a very different, God-centered kind of security.

Lent of Year A

As we explained in last year's introduction to the Lenten readings, their purpose is to prepare the people of God for participation in the paschal feast. The Old Testament readings focus upon salvation history as the presupposition, preparation for, and in some respects a prefiguring of the redemptive act of God in Christ. The epistle lessons set forth our participation in the death and resurrection of Christ through baptism and in the Christian life. The gospel readings of year A, after the temptation and transfiguration which are traditional on the first two Sundays, take up the great Johannine signs, which are prefigurements both of the saving events of Christ's death and resurrection and of our participation in these saving events through baptism.

FIRST SUNDAY OF LENT
Reading I: Genesis 2:7-9; 3:1-7.
If we are to understand the saving significance of Christ's death and resurrection, the most important presupposition is: man is God's creation, yet a fallen creature. Something has gone wrong with man. He is not what God intended him to be.

These two great theological truths, creation and fall, are expressed in Gn 2 and 3 in the terms of the then current mythology: the story of Adam and Eve in the garden of Eden and their eating the forbidden fruit at the serpent's behest. There is another, equally mythological, but less primitive account of the creation in chapter 1. This account states in more theological terms that God created man in his own image and likeness. There man is the culmination of creation. Chapter 2 depicts man more at its center: God makes man, puts him in the garden, and then surrounds him with all the things he needs. But in either case the theological meaning is the same: man occupies a distinctive place in God's creation.

The Hebrew word for man is "adam." Even if this is intended by the author as proper name for an individual first man, "Adam" stands for Everyman. Today, of course, it is difficult to take Adam as an actual historical individual, and easier for us to understand him as the personification of Everyman. Adam's story is the story of us all. Nor should we press the role of Eve too much, as has often happened in the past (e.g., 1 Tm 2:13-14) and make woman more responsible than man for the entry of sin into the world. After all, in Rom 5 Paul says nothing about Eve and blames it all on Adam. Man and woman are really jointly responsible for their fallen condition, even if here, as in everything else, each has a distinctive part to play. The ancient story in Genesis shows profound theological insight. Its basic message is that man cannot blame God or an evil fate for his plight — he is directly responsible for it himself. Man has made wrong choices, choices which conflict with his destiny as God created him. These choices cumulatively weigh against man's chance to make right choices, but that does not deprive him of his responsibility.

Responsorial Psalm 51:1-4, 10-12, 15.

This psalm was used on Sunday 24 of the year, series C. We suggested there that, since it was read as a response to the reading from Ex 32 (Moses as mediator) it should be interpreted christologically. It expresses the truth that Christ is the Mediator, who, though sinless, bears the sins of the world. On this occasion we may suggest a different interpretation. Here it is man, taking upon himself the responsibility for his own sinful condition which is the result of the fall. The Genesis story is not about a specific sin or sins, but about man's underlying sinfulness, his basic primary choice, of which specific sins are the fruit.

Psalm 51 is the classic treatment of repentance. It passes beyond mere shame at the consequences of sin (attrition) to an acknowledgement of guilt before God (contrition): "Against thee, thee only have I sinned." It sees forgiveness not only as the removal of guilt, but as the restoration of the right relationship to God: "Cast me not away from thy presence . . . restore me to the joy of thy salvation and amendment of life in grace for the future. Put a new and right spirit within me." For a classical treatment of repentance in the New Testament see 2 Cor 7:9-11.

Romans 5:12-19 (long form); 5:12, 17-19 (short form).

As has been the case on earlier occasions, the shorter version is very instructive for the understanding of the full text. First, it simplifies Paul's argument by removing the curious digression about the period between Adam and Moses, when man lived not under the Law and therefore could not be held accountable. This is hardly a burning issue for us today, and it also interrupts the flow of the argument and even the grammatical structure of the opening sentence. The opening "as" needs a "so" clause to complement it, but instead we get "and so" which denotes the result of the opening clause.

The shortened form has neatly dropped the "and" before the "so," thus enabling Paul to complete his analogy. The sin of Adam and his consequent death is analogous to the sin of all men and the consequent spread of death to all. But is that the analogy Paul intended to draw? Was it not rather an analogy between Adam and Christ? Paul's parenthesis makes him lose the thread of his argument, but the concluding clause of the paragraph "Adam was the type of the one who was to come" and the two "as" sentences of the concluding paragraph suggest that this was his original intention. As Adam began a history of fallen mankind, characterized by sin and death, so Christ began a new history of mankind characterized by acquittal, life and righteousness. Yet it is not an analogy in which both sides are of equal weight, and so we get the middle paragraph, "If Adam . . . , how much more (Christ)." Christ's achievement is far greater than Adam's, for Adam only introduced sin and death, whereas Christ introduced acquittal, life and righteousness. Death was negative, life is positive. Death's dominion enslaved man, Christ's dominion sets him free.

Notice how fittingly this epistle reading complements the reading from Genesis. It takes up Adam's fall, and balances it with man's restoration in Christ.

Gospel: Matthew 4:1-11.

Series A preserves the traditional reading of the Matthean temptation stories; series C substituted the account given in Luke's Gospel. The two versions are practically identical in wording, and the commonly held view today is that both evangelists took the story from the lost common source usually known as Q. There is only one major difference between the two versions, viz., the order of the temptations. Matthew has bread-temple-mountain and Luke bread-mountain-temple. Since Matthew is more given to rearranging his sources than Luke, it seems more likely that it is Matthew who has altered Q. Why did he do so? Probably because he wants to bring the two questions relating to Jesus as Son of God together. This emphasizes that for Matthew Jesus' temptations are messianic in character. The order of Q-Lk on the other hand emphasizes that Jesus is the new Adam, the antitype of the first Adam who fell when tempted in paradise (A. Feuillet). Despite the fact that we read the Matthean version of the temptation today, by reading it with Rom 5 and Gn 2-3 we are almost bound to take it in the Q-Lk sense, viz., as the temptations of the new Adam.

The Homily.

Despite the complications of Rom 5 even in the shorter version (obtained as we saw by only slightly reinterpreting Paul's argument), the homilist has a magnificent opportunity to relate the Genesis story to the gospel by means of the analogy in Romans between Adam and Christ, fall and obedience, death and life, fallen humanity and redeemed humanity. His theme will be that of Newman's hymn:

> O loving wisdom of our God!
>   When all was sin and shame,
> A second Adam to the fight
>   And to the rescue came.
>
> O wisest love! that flesh and blood,
>   Which did in Adam fail,
> Should strive afresh against the foe
>   Should strive and should prevail.

Perhaps at the moment it is easier to believe in Gn 3 than in Rom 5, to accept the fallenness of man rather than his redemption through Christ. The effects of the fall are so obvious all around us — racism, drugs, crime in the streets, war, pollution and so on. That Christ's coming has really made any difference is hard to see. The church? But even she is so mixed up with the fallenness of man. The influence of Christianity on civilization? A very ambiguous influence at best. The lives of the saints? Yes, there is something there, yet the real life of the saints, like our own, is in the last resort hid with Christ in God and discernible as grace rather than as achievement only to the eye of faith. It seems that here, as in other matters, we have to walk by faith and not by sight. Is faith then a cop-out? To the non-believer it must inevitably seem so. To the believer, however, it is the only clue for a sane understanding of man and his world, capable of explaining both the shadow side of man's existence as the effect of the fall, and the brighter side as the effect of the coming and the achievement of the second Adam.

Reading I: Genesis 12:1-4a.

Since the rise of modern biblical criticism the question has often been asked, Did Jesus intend to found a church? If we mean by that, Did Jesus foresee and intend that the outcome of his work should be an ecclesiastical organization such as emerged in the second century, or the fourth, thirteenth and sixteenth, the answer is pretty certainly No. But if by church we mean (as biblically we should) the people of God, then the answer is that the question is wrongly put. For the people of God was founded with the call of Abraham (as the caption puts it, he is the father of God's people, see Rom 5:16-18). This makes it clear that he is the father of Christian believers no less than of his physical descendants.

Some years ago, there was a revival of biblical theology centered on the notion of the "God who acts." During that period the Bible came to be known as the "Book of the Acts of God." Theologians were constantly speaking of the mighty acts of God in history. But then the question was raised, how can we really conceive today a God who acts in history? How can the nexus of cause and effect be broken by God, which this notion seems to imply? Part of the answer is suggested by this passage. God acts by calling key individuals like Abraham, and it is by these human responses that a channel for the execution of God's will is carved out in the world. It is because Abraham left his country that God was able to create of him a great nation, a blessing to all the nations of the world. Christian faith since the time of Paul has seen that promise fulfilled not only in Israel's salvation history as recorded in the Old Testament, but still more in the coming of Christ and in the history of the Christian church. This whole history can be understood as a response to the call of God, a call going out to a whole series of key men, beginning with Abraham, and culminating with Jesus Christ and his apostles.

That is why Paul can use Abraham as the paradigm of faith, even of Christian faith. Faith is obedient response to the call of God, and therefore it opens up channels for the redemptive action of God in history and in the world.

Responsorial Psalm 33:4-5, 18-19, 20, 22.

This psalm is fully consonant with our interpretation of the call of Abraham. God works in history through his word (stanza 1). It is man's response in faith, hope and obedience, that paves the way for the effective working of God in history (stanzas 2 and 3).

Reading II: 2 Timothy 1:8b-10.

It is somewhat surprising to find a reading from 2 Tm interrupting a series of readings in course from Romans. The reading about Abraham in Genesis might have suggested an excerpt from Rom 4, and we hope this possibility will be considered when the new lectionary is reviewed.

Yet the passage from 2 Tm is not inappropriate. It picks up the theme of calling from Gn 12, and speaks of the call to be a Christian. It emphasizes that this call is based not on our own merits, but upon God's purpose which he purposed long ago — when he called (e.g.) Abraham. This long established purpose has now been manifested in Jesus Christ, who has brought life and immortality to light. This last point then serves to introduce the theme of the transfiguration, in which Jesus is manifested as the Saviour who brings life and immortality to light.

Gospel: Matthew 17:1-9.

The transfiguration looks forward to the passion and the subsequent glorification of Jesus in his resurrection. Luke's version, read in series C on Lent II and commented upon above, brings out more clearly the episode's connection with the passion: in Luke Moses and Elijah talk with Jesus about his "exodus [so the Greek] which he was to accomplish at Jerusalem." Matthew follows Mark quite closely, except for the addition of verses 6 and 7, the "fear" of the disciples (so the Greek: RSV has "awe") and Jesus' attempt to quiet their fear by his reassuring touch and the words, "Fear not." Fear is always biblical man's reaction to a theophany (cf. Rv. 1:17). It is overcome, not by saying that confrontation with the presence of God is a casual, everyday experience which there is no reason to fear, but only by the encouraging word of Christ (cf. Mt 14:27; 28:5, 10).

The Homily.

A theme common to the first two readings is God's call to men to participate in salvation history (Abraham, the Christians). There have been times when the idea of vocation or calling was too narrowly restricted to the priesthood or the religious life. It would of course be unbiblical to deny that there are special forms of vocation or call which involve a special task in salvation history. Thus God called Abraham, the earthly Jesus called the Twelve, and the risen Christ called the apostles, including Paul. But this special call rests upon the general call, which is basic and common to all Christians, the call to participate in God's salvation. Jesus, in Mark, chooses the Twelve from a larger number of disciples who had already been called. The homily could clarify the difference between the general and special calls.

Should the homilist wish to take the transfiguration story, it would be natural this year to stress that element which, as we have seen, is of special concern to Matthew, the fear of the three disciples and Jesus' word of reassurance. One of the less fortunate effects of liturgical renewal has been a loss of wholesome awe in the presence of the holy realities of the liturgy. In an Anglican context Archbishop Michael Ramsey has written as follows: "The awe in the individual's approach to Holy Communion which characterized both the Tractarians and the Evangelicals of old, stands in contrast with the ease with which our congregations come tripping to the altar week by week."

I suspect that, *mutatis mutandis*, the same warning would also be relevant in the Roman communion since Vatican II. Lent, and particularly Lent II, when Matthew's story of the transfiguration is read, would be a suitable time to emphasize this now frequently forgotten theme, that the *mysterium* of the liturgy is *tremendum* as well as *fascinans*.

THIRD SUNDAY OF LENT

Reading I: Exodus 17:3-7.
This lesson is clearly chosen to fit with the gospel. The Johannine Christ promises the woman of Samaria that he will give her the water of life. In the dry climate of Palestine, water is an obvious symbol of salvation, and the allusion to the sacraments is not far below the surface in this Johannine discourse. In 1 Cor 10 Paul uses the episode of the rock from Ex 17, etc., as a type of the Christian sacraments (specifically there with reference to the eucharistic cup).

But a different emphasis in reading I is suggested by the responsorial psalm. This psalm picks up the theme of Israel's hardening of their hearts during the wanderings through the wilderness: "Harden not your hearts as in Meribah, as on the day at Massah in the wilderness," which recalls Ex 17:7, "(Moses) called the name of the place Massah and Meribah, because of the fault finding of the children of Israel."

It is worth noting that the letter to the Hebrews takes up the theme of Ps 95 and uses it as the basis for an exhortation to the Jewish Christians at Rome (?) (Heb 3:7-4:11). They had been Christians for more than a generation. The first flush of their enthusiasm had worn off, and they were finding life wearisome. The author of Hebrews compares their situation to that of the children of Israel in the wilderness, who were also finding the going tough and getting tired.

Responsorial Psalm 95:1-2, 6-7abc, 7d-9.
This psalm was used on Sunday 18 in series C. The emphasis today rests clearly on the third stanza (see reading I).

Reading II: Romans 5:1-2, 5-8.
In Romans 3:21 through chapter 4 Paul has expounded the redeeming act of God in Christ in terms of man's justification. He now sums up his argument ("seeing we are justified") and unfolds its consequences: we have peace with God, we have access to grace and we have a joyful hope of sharing the glory of God. The ground of all this is that the Holy Spirit has been given us. For justification and the gift of the indwelling Spirit are really one and the same thing. When a man receives the gift of the indwelling Spirit he is justified, when a man is justified he receives the gift of the indwelling Spirit.

In a course of lectures on justification delivered in his Anglican days (and reissued many years later after he had been a Roman Catholic) John Henry Newman sought to find a *via media* between the Reformation and the Council of Trent on the doctrine of justification, a way which would do justice to the legitimate concerns of both sides and yet transcend the antithesis. The interesting thing for us is that he sought it precisely in this understanding of justification as the gift of the indwelling Spirit. On the one hand this avoided the notion suggested by much Reformation theology that justification was no more than the external imputation of righteousness, leaving a man just as much a sinner as he was before, and on the other hand the Tridentine suggestion that justification means what it means etymologically, namely to *make* just, implying that the justified man is already become righteous in a moral sense. The Reformation was right in protesting that the justified man was still a sinner, and the Tridentine doctrine was right in asserting that justification made a real difference. The way out of this dilemma was suggested by Rom 5:2. Justification is the gift of the indwelling Spirit which initiates a transformation of man into the risen state.

Justification and the gift of the Spirit are the outcome of God's love. That love is not an abstract idea, but something that happened — on the cross. The love of God in Christ on the cross was pure love, love uncaused by the attractiveness of its object: while we were yet sinners and while we were yet helpless Christ died for us. God through the cross accepts sinners, and his acceptance of them is manifested by his sending his Spirit to dwell in them and gradually transform them so that eventually they will become in reality what they are in theory, namely righteous.

Gospel: John 4:5–42 (long form);
4:5–15, 19b–26, 39a, 40–42 (short form).

A multiplicity of themes jostle one another in this dialogue between Jesus and the Samaritan woman: 1) Jesus' request for water, leading to the declaration that he is the giver of life; 2) Jesus' suggestion that the woman call her husband, leading to an exposure of her matrimonial past (which some take as an allegorical reference to the Samaritan bible which has only the first five books of the Old Testament); 3) the woman's shift of the conversation to the basic dispute of the Jews and Samaritans — the proper place to worship Yahweh — leading into Jesus' pronouncement that the old Jewish-Samaritan debate is about to be transcended by worship in spirit and truth; 4) the woman's assurance that the dispute will be cleared up in the messianic age, leading to Jesus' declaration that he *is* the Messiah; 5) the woman's departure to fetch her friends to see Jesus, interrupted by 6 and picked up later again in the conversion of many Samaritans; 6) — sandwiched between the two parts of 5 — the disciples' return to Jesus and their perplexity over his refusal to eat, leading to the declaration that his food is to do his father's will and followed by sayings about the harvest, the latter preparing the way for the Samaritan conversions. The shorter form simplifies by omitting 2 and 6.

There are many reasons why modern scholars do not regard the Johannine discourses and dialogues as transcript of what the earthly Jesus actually said. There may be an original nucleus to the story, in which Jesus encountered a Samaritan woman and asked her for some water to drink, leading to some pronouncement by Jesus about the imminence of the kingdom of God. But the original point has been lost, and the story as it now stands has been expanded to cover various topics of interest in John's church, topics which came up largely as a result of the Samaritan mission, but partly also expressive of the evangelist's interpretation of Jesus as the bringer of the final revelation of God. In this interpretation the evangelist appropriates a gnostic (?) style and categories. On the whole we must take the dialogue as a Christian meditation on the meaning of Jesus for faith: he is the bringer of salvation, he exposes man's sin, he inaugurates the true worship of God which transcends all human approaches from man to God and is a worship in spirit and truth, a worship based upon the gospel. It is because Jesus is the bringer of the final revelation of God that he draws all men to himself as the Saviour of the world.

The Homily.

This Sunday confronts the homilist with an *embarras de richesses*, and he must obviously be selective. For Lent, and for the current situation of the church, perhaps an attack on the problem of "accidie" (the couldn't care less attitude), starting from a consideration of the "murmuring" of the Israelites in the wilderness, would be most appropriate. In the unlikely event of its being accessible, we would recommend a copy of "An Introductory Essay concerning Accidy" in *The Spirit of Discipline* by Francis Paget (published at London in 1902 by Longmans, Green and Co). This is a notable treatment of this subject, and an Anglican classic of spiritual life.

Of course, there are other possibilities for the homily, and at another season of the year rather than Lent, one would be drawn to the concept of worship in spirit and truth. This is often, at least in Protestantism, thought to refer to inner sincerity and to the fellowship of the heart, and is sometimes contrasted with formal prayer "out of a book." But worship in spirit means worship prompted by the Holy Spirit, and worship in truth means worship based on the revelation of God in Jesus Christ who is the truth. Bultmann's comment is apt: "The cultic worship of God is contrasted not with a spiritual, inward form of worship, but with the eschatological worship."

A third possibility, which however broaches the theme traditionally associated with Lent IV, would be to combine the water from the rock in reading I and the promise of Christ to give the water of life in the gospel. Again, Bultmann is helpful: "The revelation brought by Jesus gives life, and thus stills the desire which no earthly water can satisfy."

FOURTH SUNDAY OF LENT

Reading I: 1 Samuel 16:1b, 6–7, 10–13a.

The Old Testament lesson for today is somewhat of a puzzle, and what the selectors had in mind in placing it with the two lessons (reading II and the gospel) on the theme of Christ as the light is not clear. Could it be that the anointing of David to be the king (=shepherd in the psalm) is the type of the baptism of Christ which is his call to take up his mission as light of the world, and of the baptism of the believer who there receives the illumination of the Spirit?

Responsorial Psalm 23:1–3a, 3b–4, 5, 6.

It is not clear whether the psalm was chosen to go with reading I, or whether it was first suggested by the traditional (though originally fortuitous) association of this Sunday with the idea of refreshment. In Christian usage the "Lord" can of course be interpreted to mean Christ. The third stanza, which speaks of the Lord's anointing the psalmist's head with oil, suggests some link with the anointing of David in reading I, but the typology is too complicated to develop profitably in a homily. Here is another case where those responsible should either explain their intentions or revise their proposals.

Reading II: Ephesians 5:8–14.

This reading overlaps with the old epistle of the Roman Missal for Lent III. In the Book of Common Prayer that epistle was lengthened to run through v. 14 as here. It seems to have had a fortuitous connection with the station mass of St. Lawrence, anciently celebrated that day, at Rome. But its baptismal associations (a catechesis based on the contrasts once/ now, darkness/light and the concluding quotation from an early baptismal hymn) have always made this passage highly suitable for Lent. Now it becomes even more appropriate as a complement to the gospel, with its message of Jesus as the light of the world.

Gospel: John 9:1–41 (long form); 9:1, 6–9, 13–17, 34–38 (short form).

The most likely explanation of the seven miracles (signs) in the fourth gospel is that they existed together in a Book of Signs, and that the evangelist has used them as the basis for his discourses or dialogues.

The original story must have simply told how a man was born blind and was healed by Jesus. This was later expanded by a trial scene, in which the man was charged with having become an adherent of Jesus. This stage of development reflects the expulsion of Jewish converts to Christianity from the synagogue. The evangelist will then have added the christological elements, such as verses 4–5, which declare Jesus to be the light of the world, and the discussion about his origins (29–34). Thus[1]

---

[1] Bultmann's Commentary, which is notorious for its wholesale rearrangement of the text, would include within this discourse passages in other chapters which deal with Jesus as the light of the world (8:12; 12:44–50; 8:21–29; 12:34–36; 10:21).

the healing of the blind man is for the evangelist a christological sign: it shows that Christ is the light which has come into the darkness of the world. In other words, he is the revelation of God. It is easy to see how the healing of a blind man would lend itself to such christological treatment. Moreover, the mode of healing — washing in the Pool of Siloam — suggests a further connection to baptism, which in the early church was known as "illumination" (*photismos*).

The shorter form reduces the story more or less to its original narrative form, omitting most of the features derived from the church-synagogue relations and the evangelist's christological insertions. Inadvertently, however, this has the effect of removing what for the evangelist was the main point of the story (Jesus as the light of the world) and its connection with reading II ("Christ shall give you light"). Fortunately the versicle before the gospel preserves the theme of light. It is thus imperative that v. 5 should be restored to the short form.

The Homily.

The clearest choice before the homilist is to take reading II and the gospel together, proclaiming Christ as the light who has illuminated us in baptism by bringing us to the revelation of God. The homilist would naturally refer to Lent as the season in which our baptism is renewed, and in which we prepare to renew our baptismal vows at the Easter vigil. He would also speak of the ethical obligations that this involves (Eph 5:11–12). He could, if he wishes to, bring in David's anointing as a type of the Christian illumination in baptism, with a further allusion to the third stanza of the psalm.

FIFTH SUNDAY OF LENT

Reading I: Ezekiel 37:12–14.

The three readings of this Sunday fit beautifully together, for all concern the resurrection to newness of life. The passage from Ezekiel concludes and interprets the vision of the valley of dry bones (obviously a battle field) which are gradually restored to life. The interpretation identifies the bones with Israel in exile, and their resurrection to Israel's restoration from the Babylonian exile to their homeland. But it is interesting how the text shifts from the dry bones to graves: "I will open your *graves*, and raise you from your *graves*." This shift suggests that already by Ezekiel's time (cf. Is 26:19) the expectation of a general resurrection at the last day was beginning to emerge, an expectation which was to be developed in the later apocalyptic literature. But that is not the point here. Rather, the language of this future hope is transferred to Israel's return from exile. It will be like resurrection from the grave. In this figurative resurrection God will bring his people to newness of life and put his Spirit within them. This two-level theme — the restoration of God's people and the eschatological resurrection of the dead — thus start hand-in-hand as they will continue through apocalyptic literature to the New Testament.

Responsorial Psalm 130:1-2, 3-4, 5-7a, 7bc-8.

The juxtaposition of two passages of scripture often brings out new meanings in the scriptures thus drawn together. This is what has happened here. Usually one thinks of the *De profundis* as a penitential psalm. But when placed side by side with the Ezekiel vision it acquires a new emphasis: it is both the cry of the individual in the depths of sin and death and also the cry of the people of God (note the shift at the end of the third and through the fourth stanza from the individual to the community) for restoration from exile in the land of darkness and the shadow of death.

This hoped-for corporate redemption occurred in the restoration from exile. It is still the hope of the Christian community in which the Spirit dwells and it is to be finally fulfilled in the general resurrection from the dead.

Reading II: Romans 8:8-11.

The same two-level use of language is continued in this second reading. The first level, that of resurrection from the dead, is now applied to Christ. God raised Jesus from the dead by his Spirit (cf. Rom 1:4). Now the Christians through their baptism have received the indwelling of the Spirit which raised Jesus from the dead: "Your spirits are alive because of righteousness." This is the second level: the restoration of the people of God to newness of life (note also the words "because of righteousness"; as we saw on Lent III, the new life created by the indwelling Spirit is the effect of justification). Finally, the first level of resurrection is still expected for the Christians, too: "he who raised up Christ Jesus from the dead will give life to your mortal bodies." The risen life of the church in the Spirit is an anticipation of the general resurrection at the last day.

The biblical hope is not a belief in the intrinsic immortality of man (as though there were some part of us such as the soul or the spirit) which is in and by itself immortal. The whole man, body, soul and spirit, is subject to decay and death. But Christ has broken this subjection: he has burst the bonds of decay and death by his resurrection from the dead, in which he is raised to a totally transformed existence. Through baptism the believers received the indwelling Spirit, as a result of which resurrection and renewal of the whole person, body and soul, is initiated. True, even the bodies of Christians are still subject to sickness, decay and death. But the indwelling Spirit is a sign in our mortal bodies which betokens the beginning of a new life which cannot be destroyed by death. This, as Oscar Cullmann has suggested, is manifested in two ways: in the daily renewal of our inward man (2 Cor 4:16; cf. Eph 3:16) and in the occurrence of miracles of healing in the bodies of Christians. The present indwelling of the Spirit is an anticipation of the complete renewal of life which comes at the general resurrection.

Gospel: John 11:1–45 (long form);
11:3–7, 17, 20–27, 33b–45 (short form).

Here again the evangelist has combined a narrative from his source, which consisted of seven miracle stories, with a body of discourse material. In the original source the raising of Lazarus would have been a straightforward story of a resuscitation. Similar stories are Jairus' daughter and the widow's son of Naim. But note also the progression of the miraculous. Jairus' daughter has just died. The widow's son was being carried to the grave (so he must have died earlier that day as the Jewish laws require interment within 24 hours). But Lazarus has been dead for four days already.

The evangelist has placed the raising of Lazarus at a crucial position in the career of Jesus. It occasions Jesus' final journey to Judea and Jerusalem, and the sensation created by Lazarus' resuscitation sets in train the events which will lead to the crucifixion. Contrast with this the synoptic accounts, where the cleansing of the temple leads to the Sanhedrin's decision to get rid of Jesus. One should not try to harmonize the accounts. The synoptic account looks closer to history, and in John's source the cleansing of the temple, now transferred for programmatic reasons to chapter 2, was probably in a similar position. The evangelist will also have placed the Lazarus story here for theological reasons. Jesus goes to his death as the one who is the resurrection and the life, and who will die to inaugurate the resurrection of man. The theological interpretation is brought out by the dialogue and discourse material with which the evangelist farced the story itself. Therefore the high point of this gospel is the great pronouncement of verses 25-26: "I am the resurrection and the life; he who believes in me, though he die, yet shall he live, and whoever lives and believes in me shall never die." This serves the same function as "I am the light of the world" in the healing of the blind man in chapter 9. The shorter form of the gospel prunes away some of the dialogue material, the preliminary discussion between Jesus and his disciples (vv. 8–16) and some of the narrative detail (18–19, 28-32a), and in so doing throws the central pronouncement into sharper relief.

The Homily.

Once again, the homilist's choices are clear. All three lessons revolve around the same theme, death–resurrection: Christ going to his death and beyond it to resurrection, and our death and resurrection in him. If the preacher bases his homily primarily on reading I, he will emphasize God's power constantly to renew his church within history. If he opts for the gospel he may combine it with reading II and draw out the present reality of the resurrection of life in the believer through the indwelling Spirit, a present reality which, however, does not exclude but anticipates the final resurrection of the whole man at the final consummation.

Holy Week to Easter 4 A

The Procession with Palms: Matthew 21:1-11.
The triumphal entry (as we explained last year) is a subsidiary motif to today's liturgy, and if the homilist deals with it at all it should be treated as a curtain raiser to the passion story. For the passion has, in fact, if not in popular estimation, always been the major theme of this day.

In year A we read Matthew's version of the entry. It has three special features. First, unlike Mark and Luke, though like John, it explicitly cites the prophecy of Zechariah (v. 5). These fulfillment quotations are characteristic of Matthew. Sometimes the citations are applied rather mechanically, as in the present case. Matthew seems to imply that Jesus was seated upon *both* animals, the ass and the foal (v. 7)! RSV's "thereon" obscures this: the Greek means "on them." Actually, in Zechariah, the "ass" and "colt, the foal of an ass" are synonymous parallelism. It says the same thing twice over but in different words, in a way characteristic of Hebrew poetry. Behind Matthew's fulfillment quotations, some of them almost trivial, rests the genuine insight of Christian faith that the events of Jesus' earthly life were the execution of God's saving purpose, fulfilling the promises contained in the Old Testament history of his mighty acts toward Israel.

The second notable feature about Matthew's version of the entry is his change in the cry of the crowd. Mark wrote "Blessed is the kingdom of our father David that is coming." Matthew has made it christological: "Hosanna to the *Son of David*. Blessed is *he who comes* in the name of the Lord" (v. 9). This reflects the way the tradition developed: Jesus preached the kingdom of God, the early church preached Jesus as the

Christ. Yet the one really implies the other. Jesus did not announce the coming of the kingdom as an abstract idea detached from his own person, or as something purely future, even if imminent. Rather, he announced it as the inbreaking of the saving power of God in his own presence, his own words and works. The Hosanna and Benedictus, placed in this position in Matthew's narrative, and read on this Sunday, tell us that the event of the cross is the culmination of the inbreaking of the saving act of God in Jesus Christ. The cross is not a meaningless or tragic episode attached to the end of an otherwise glorious life, it is the culmination of that movement of God to man which is the whole history of Jesus.

The third feature is the response of the crowd after Jesus had entered into the city: "This is the prophet Jesus from Nazareth of Galilee." To call Jesus a prophet may seem to us a minimizing Christology. But to the earliest church this was not so. Jesus was not merely one of the long line of Old Testament prophets. Nor does it mean that he came as a social reformer. He was the last emissary from God, bringing with him God's final and decisive word to his people.

Some modern New Testament scholars consider that the entry story would have been more appropriate to Tabernacles (cf. Jn 7:2). Indeed, historically speaking, it may well have occurred there. Jesus visited Jerusalem to lay down his last challenge to his people at the heart of their religious center. By bringing it into close relation to the passion, however, Mark and the evangelists who follow him, make it clear what the meaning of the cross is, that it is God's final coming in judgment and salvation.

Reading I: Isaiah 50:4-7.
Responsorial Psalm: 22:7-8, 16-19, 22-23.
Reading II: Philippians 2:6-11.

All these readings are the same as last year's. This year they go with the reading of Matthew's passion. Psalm 22, with its response "My God, my God, why have you abandoned me?" especially highlights the climax of Matthew's passion, the word from the cross, which we will discuss below.

Gospel: Matthew 26:14-27:66.

In last year's commentary we sought to bring out the overall characteristics of the four passion stories in the gospels. The Matthew-passion, we observed, "brings out the royalty of Christ, but it is a paradoxical royalty manifesting itself precisely in humiliation."

The royal note was struck by the triumphal entry. It is strongly underlined in the trial scene between Pilate and Jesus (Mt 27:11-26), in the scene of the mocking by the Roman soldiers (27:27-31), in the title on the cross (v. 37) and in the mockery by the bystanders (v. 42).

On the other hand the humiliation of Jesus is most emphasized by the cry from the cross (v. 46). Of all the words attributed to Jesus on the cross in all four gospels, this has the highest claim to authenticity. It is preserved in the oldest tradition (Mk-Mt). It was offensive to the later evangelists who substituted more harmless words for it (Lk-Jn). It lent itself to later heretical rewriting (*Gospel of Peter*, which has "My power, my power. . . ," expressive of that writing's docetic Christology, according to which the Christ [or divinity] left the man Jesus before his death. It is given in Aramaic by Mark. And it certainly expresses the meaning of the cross more profoundly than anything else in the passion narrative. Unlike the other Old Testament citations, which were designed to relieve the events of the passion of their scandalous character, the cry from the cross actually enhances the scandal. It states what Paul in more theological vein expressed when he said that "He (God) made him (Christ) to be sin, who knew no sin, so that in him we might become the righteousness of God" (2 Cor 5:21). When he ate with the riff-raff, Jesus crossed over from God's side and put himself on the side of sinners, in order that he might seek and save them. On the cross he carries this action to its lowest point. Man as sinner is under what the Bible calls the "wrath" of God — that is to say, man's alienation from God, the sense of God's absence that springs not only from man's finitude but from his willful rebellion. It is this word from the cross that gives Jesus' death its theological meaning. It is not just the ordinary dying of any man, a biological event. It is Jesus not against God but for God, enduring the bitterest consequences of man's sin. Only by this identification does Jesus liberate man from sin and death, both understood as here in their theological sense. This saying is not only *one* of the words from the cross, it is *the* word of the cross, the interpretive word which gives the cross its whole meaning as redemptive event.

Other peculiar features of the Matthew-passion are of less moment. They include Jesus' words to Peter at the arrest (26:52-53); the suicide of Judas (27:24-25); a slight but very moving expansion of the crowd's mockery (27:43) — Bach's treatment of the phrase "for he said he was the Son of God" is one of the most impressive parts of the *Matthäuspassion*; the opening of the graves of the saints at the death of Jesus and their appearance after the resurrection, an event which is made to serve as one of the contributory factors in the centurion's confession (27:54). Some of these additions are pious and devotional, some legendary and symbolic, some apologetic. Otherwise, Matthew follows his Marcan source very closely.

If the homilist wishes to get at the heart of the message of the cross this day, he will choose as his text the cry from the cross (27:46).

As we did last year, we again remind our readers that the revised Roman Missal specifies three principal mysteries which are commemorated in this mass and which should be explained in the homily: the institution of the eucharist, the institution of the priesthood, and Christ's commandment of brotherly love. The readings are the same as in year C (Ex 12:1-8, 11-14; Ps 116:12-13, 15, 16-18; 1 Cor 11:23-26 and Jn 13:1-15). The reader is referred to our comments on these passages last year. For this year we will offer some further comments on the three themes.

1 The Institution of the Eucharist. Although we habitually speak of the *institution* of the eucharist, our Lord did not institute it in the sense of inventing an entirely new rite. Whether John or the synoptists are correct in their dating of the Last Supper — i.e., whether the Last Supper was a passover or an ordinary Jewish religious meal — it is clear that the actions at the supper, the taking of the bread and wine, the giving of thanks, the breaking of the bread and the sharing of the food and drink, were all well-known and quite regular Jewish observances. What was new was the significance with which Jesus invested the familiar actions. We have of course to allow for a certain development in the interpretive words over the bread and the cup as a comparison of the various accounts show. These expansions should be attributed to the presence of the living Christ in his church, rather than to what the earthly Jesus said at the Last Supper. In our comments last year we extracted as the meaning of the interpretive words the fact that the eucharist has both a forward and a backward looking significance. It looks backward to the redemptive event of the cross which it makes a present reality, and forward to the second coming which it anticipates.

The German Catholic New Testament scholar Heinz Schürmann also suggests one novel feature in the action of Jesus at the supper. Instead of allowing each one present to drink of his own individual cup, Jesus passes *his* cup around to all present. In Jewish meals, according to Schürmann, it was customary for the president at the meal to pass his own cup to someone whom he wished to single out for special honor, thus allowing him to share in the blessing he had said over the cup — a custom rather like our drinking of a toast. Jesus shares his cup with *all* of his disciples because he is making them all partakers in the benefits of his passion. This is an attractive suggestion which, if correct, offers a notable enrichment to our understanding of what happened at the Last Supper and what happens at the eucharist.

2 *The Institution of the Priesthood.* Last year we pointed out that this second theme requires careful handling. It is too simplistic an interpretation to say that by commanding the Twelve to celebrate the eucharist, Jesus made them priests, and that this commandment subsequently devolved in succession upon bishops and presbyters of the church. The command "do this" is given to the whole church, and the eucharist is the action in which the whole church expresses its priesthood (1 Pt 2:1-10). The eucharistic president acts as the representative and mouthpiece of the priesthood of the whole church. Both the priesthood of the church and the ministerial priesthood are derived from the very nature of the eucharist. Understand the eucharist aright, and we shall understand the priesthood both of the church and of the ministry.

3 *Christ's Commandment of Brotherly Love.* This is expressed in the footwashing and the accompanying words as given in the gospel. In our various traditions we have overemphasized the vertical relationship in the eucharist — the communion of the soul with its Lord, and underemphasized what the early church expressed in making the eucharist proper a part of a fellowship meal (called the agape or love feast), thus underscoring the horizontal dimension. The restoration of the exchange of the peace by the whole congregation is one current attempt to recover this horizontal dimension. This restored practice, at least in some Episcopal churches, has disturbed not a few of the devout, while on the other hand those who have found a new understanding of the horizontal dimension have in some places been driven underground in the so-called underground churches. This group has deprived the "established" churches of their enriched understanding of the social dimension of the eucharist. They have fallen themselves into the danger of detaching the horizontal fellowship from its roots in the vertical dimension of Christ's love for his people, a love exhibited in his sacrificial death, of which the footwashing was the symbol.

The homilist will clearly have to choose between one of these three subjects for exposition. He will obviously be guided not only by his own interests and predilection, but by his familiarity with the concrete needs of the people committed to his charge.

The readings for this day are unchanged from year to year. We will summarize last year's commentary on each of the readings and add one or two points of further interest.

Reading I: Isaiah 52:13-53:12.
The fourth servant song contributed three essential points to the early church's understanding of Jesus' crucifixion: Christ's suffering was innocent, vicarious and redemptive; it avails for all men; and the righteous sufferer will be finally vindicated.

New Testament scholars are divided on whether Jesus himself made use of this chapter for the understanding of his mission, for sayings in which references to Isaiah occur — the ransom saying in Mk 10:45 and the words "for many" in the cup-word in the institution narrative at Mk 14:24 — are probably later additions. Moreover, while some of the passion predictions may echo the language of Is 53 (see esp. Mk 9:12) they may well be in their present form *vaticinia ex eventu*.

It is important that we should see the cross not as the mechanical fulfillment of a preconceived dogmatic scheme, but as the culmination of the intensely personal mission of Jesus as a whole. He identified himself completely in his ministry with sinners, and in so doing broke through the barrier which sin set up between God and man. He stood for God on the side of sinners. It was because they saw the cross in the light of his whole ministry that the early church found in Is 53 an almost perfect prophecy of the passion and used it as a quarry for its own theological statements about the passion. But these statements are not abstract theologoumena. They are the attempt to capture into words, and to pass on to those who did not have the direct experience of the crucifixion the meaning of a real flesh-and-blood history as the action of God *pro nobis*, for us men and for our salvation.

Responsorial Psalm: 31:1, 5, 11-12, 14-16, 24.
Verse 5 of this compline psalm provided for Luke the last word of the crucified One which he substituted for the Mk-Mt word from Ps 22:1. This word misses the profound theological depth of that other saying, yet

it has a point to make. "Into thy hands I commend my spirit" ("put my life into your hands," as the refrain has it) suggests the man-to-God aspect of the cross. As well as being God's act of salvation for man, the cross is also man's offering of perfect obedience to God. This thought can be linked with the high priesthood of Christ, which the second reading will bring before us.

Reading II: Hebrews 4:14-16; 5:7-9.

As we mentioned last year, this is the third enunciation of the theme of Hebrews, the high priesthood of Christ. His high priesthood is characterized in three ways: sympathy for human weakness as the result of his own earthly experiences; the answer of his prayer for deliverance; and his learning of obedience.

As we suggested above in commenting on the responsorial psalm, the high priesthood of Christ is an expression of the man-to-God direction of the cross: as well as being God's act of salvation in identifying perfectly with sinners, it is man's perfect offering of obedience to the will of God. This in fact is the quintessential expression of Christ's high priesthood in Hebrews (see the citation of Ps 40:6-8 in Heb 10:5-10). The real sacrifice which God demands of man is the perfect offering of himself in obedience. Because of his sin, man was unable to offer this sacrifice. The Levitical sacrifices of the old Covenant could not take away sin, for they were not that perfect sacrifice, but a permanent witness to their inadequacy, as the writers of Psalms 40 and 51 knew. They were destined to last until God should provide this perfect sacrifice, which he did in sending his Son. So in man he does for us what man cannot do — the offering of the perfect sacrifice required by himself. But this does not mean that we are let off scot-free and have nothing to do for our part. Rather, it means that we are caught up into Christ's self-sacrifice, and enabled in him to offer ourselves, our souls and our bodies in union with his sacrifice, so that the imperfection of our sacrifice is transformed by the perfection of his.

Gospel: John 18:1-19:42.

We noted last year that John packs his theology in his discourses, and that, when he comes to the passion, he more or less leaves the events to speak for themselves. Two points of theological import are made in this passion narrative, however. One is, Christ's definition of his kingship as witness to the truth (Jn 18:37). The other is John's last word from the cross, which announces the completion of the sacrifice of the Lamb of God foretold by the Baptist at the beginning of the gospel. These two points may be seen as again pointing to the two-way significance of the cross — God's saving act for man, and man's offering to God.

The Homily.

We have stressed in our comments this year the two-way significance of the cross, God-to-man, man-to-God. This corresponds to the traditional dogmatic formula of the twofold office of Christ (*duplex munus*) as King and Priest, which in turn corresponds to the yet older dogmatic formula of the two natures, divine and human. As King he comes from God's side, and exercises his saving power among sinful men, identifying himself completely with them, standing where they are and bringing the saving compassion of God to them. The crucifixion, historically speaking, is the outcome precisely of this earlier activity of Jesus among men: his preaching of the kingdom, his teaching in parables, his eating with outcasts, and his calling of men to follow him. "For this I was born, and for this I have come into the world, to bear witness to the truth" (Jn 18:37). The cross is therefore the nadir of Jesus' kingly service of God toward man.

Christ is also the Priest. At the moment of his baptism Jesus says Yes to the call of God, and at each moment of his ministry he offers himself to the Father in perfect obedience, so that the Father's words become his words and the Father's works his own works. His cross is not a meaningless, tragic end to a life which had quite different meaning (like, say, the death of Camus), but the culmination of a whole real life of moment-by-moment surrender to the will of God.

I suggest that this year the homilist might bring out these two aspects of the cross — Christ as King and Christ as Priest. He will find the reading from Hebrews and the passage about Christ's kingship in the Johannine passion helpful for this.

EASTER VIGIL

As we pointed out last year, this is the archetypal liturgy of the church year. It has four parts: the service of light with the Easter proclamation, the reading of the scriptures, the baptism and the Easter eucharist. There are nine scripture lessons, the first seven from the Old Testament, the last two from the new (epistle and gospel). The homily is directed to follow the gospel and to precede the baptisms.

Last year we selected for comment readings I, II, and III, and the epistle and gospel. This year we will comment on readings IV-VII.

Reading IV: Isaiah 54:5-14.

The historical situation in which Deutero-Isaiah delivered his prophecies was Israel's impending return from exile in Babylon. Much of the language in which he described this return was drawn from the language in which the earlier event of the exodus has been narrated (see esp. Is 40:1-5). Since the exodus came to be regarded as a type for and a quarry of language for the description of the Christ event, it is natural also that the language of the return from exile should be similarly used. Christ's death and resurrection are the church's return from Babylonian captivity, as well as her exodus from Egyptian bondage. In this passage the image of Yahweh's marriage with Israel is picked up from the Book of Exodus and reapplied to the exile. In the exodus God had first taken Israel as a young bride. In the exile he had cast her off like a wife of youth. But this was only for a brief moment. Now in his great compassion Yahweh is taking her back. Note the frequency of the word "compassion," a key word which is in the gospel record and deeds of Jesus.

Another image taken up into this passage is that of the flood. The exile is like the flood, with Israel as a storm-tossed ark. Again, the flood and its abatement provide an image for speaking about the Christ event (cf. 1 Pt 3:20-21).

A third picture is that of the restoration of the city of Jerusalem, rebuilt with precious jewels. This imagery is also taken up in the New Testament and applied to the consummated kingdom, and therefore already mirrored in the life of the earthly church.

Responsorial Psalm: 30:1 and 3, 4-5, 10-11a and 12b.

In origin this psalm is the thanksgiving of an individual for his deliverance from death (see stanza I and the refrain). Already in Israel, when it was taken up into the hymn book of the temple, this psalm would have acquired a more corporate meaning, and in Christian usage it celebrates the paschal *transitus* from sorrow to joy: "Weeping may tarry for a night, but joy comes in the morning" (stanza II), and "Thou hast turned my mourning into dancing" (stanza III).

Reading V: Isaiah 55:1-11.

This reading is an invitation to the eschatological banquet, which is anticipated in the paschal eucharist: "Come, buy and eat! Come, buy wine and milk" (v. 1). It is the feast of the new covenant (v. 3) with the messianic king ("my sure love for David," v. 3). In this banquet the presence of Yahweh is near (v. 6) and available for participation. But on one condition: penitence and the reception of pardon for sin (vv. 6-7). For this moment the whole of our Lenten devotions, our going to confession and receiving absolution, has been preparatory; all these exercises are gathered up into this reading. God's ways transcend all human ways (v. 8). He calls things that do not exist into existence, and he gives life to the dead (Rom 4:17). He has raised Jesus from the dead and raised us from the death of sin to the life of righteousness (cf. the epistle). In the mission of Christ, God's word did not return to him empty, but truly accomplished that which he had purposed in sending it (v. 11).

Responsorial Psalm: Isaiah 12:2-3, 4bcde, 5-6.
Although this passage (the first song of Isaiah, *Ecce, Deus*) occurs in Proto-Isaiah, its spirit is more akin to Deutero-Isaiah. It celebrates the return from exile as a second exodus, and is a new song patterned on the original song of Moses, as the close verbal parallelism between stanza III and Ex 15:1 shows. As in reading V we have here the same fourfold pattern: exodus/return from exile/Christ's death and the resurrection/the foundation of the church and our initiation into it through baptism and eucharist.

Reading VI: Baruch 3:9-15, 32-4:4.
This passage is typical of the way which the later Jewish wisdom literature adapted the earlier prophetic teaching about salvation history. The old language of salvation history survives: "Why is it, O Israel, why is it that you are in the land of your enemies" — language which is reminiscent of the exile and of the hymns of Deutero-Isaiah. But the exile is no longer located in a geographical Babylon. It has become man's exile from the true knowledge of heavenly wisdom. Wisdom is here both equated with the Torah or Jewish law, and at the same time hypostatized or personified. The phrase "She appeared upon earth and lived among men" (Bar 2:37) is especially interesting for the student of the New Testament, for it shows how the wisdom speculations of pre-Christian Judaism provided the language and patterns of thought in which the New Testament formulated its faith in the incarnation (cf. Jn 1:14).

The inclusion of such wisdom literature among the readings for the Easter vigil is a salutary reminder that the images of Egyptian bondage and Babylonian exile are now to be taken figuratively. They are descriptions especially applicable to modern man, for they speak of his alienation from God, his sense of God's absence. This was one of the elements of truth behind the "death of God" theology which was in vogue a few years ago.

Responsorial Psalm: 19:7-10.

Psalm 19 falls into two distinct halves, perhaps indicating the combination of two different psalms. The first half is a nature psalm, praising God for his gift of the sunlight. The second half, beginning at v. 7, praises God for the gift of the light of his law. Our selection is taken from the second half. It follows appropriately upon the lesson from Baruch, since wisdom and law (Torah) are closely akin, if not identical. The refrain highlights the truth that the Lord has the words of everlasting life. The word of God is his self-communication. This self-communication was present in creation, in Israel's Torah, but above all in the life, death and resurrection of Jesus Christ (the Word made flesh, as the Johannine prologue puts it, thereby meaning the whole history of Jesus). The words of everlasting life are therefore spoken supremely in the death and resurrection of Christ. This is God's final word to man, his final act of self-communication, which is for man the source of "everlasting life," authentic existence.

Reading VII: Ezekiel 36:16-28.

This is another lesson which speaks of the return from exile in Babylon (and other countries, see Ez 36:24). Ezekiel, like the earlier prophets before him, understands the exile as a punishment for Israel's sin (v. 19). The return therefore must be accompanied by an act of purification: "I will sprinkle clean water upon you . . ." (v. 25), the gift of a new heart (i.e., one which is sensitive to the demands of God's law) and a new spirit. Christian faith sees all these purposes fulfilled not in the return but in the death and resurrection of Christ, whose benefits are made available by baptism with its accompanying ceremonies (the sprinkling of water, and the gift of the Spirit).

In the old, atomized understanding of the church year it was customary to think of Pentecost as the birthday of the church. Our renewed understanding of the unitary character of the Christ event, celebrated in this paschal vigil, should remove any sense of incongruity in the celebration of the birth of the church on this night.

Responsorial Psalm: 42:2, 4bc; 43:3, 4.

The use of this psalm (Psalms 42 and 43 are really one psalm) at the

Easter vigil is a very ancient tradition. It was originally an individual lament. The psalmist is staying by the springs of the Jordan at the foot of Mt. Hermon, lamenting his absence from Jerusalem and from the worship at the temple. Taken in its liturgical context here (cf. the former use of Ps 43 in the priest's preparation before mass) expresses the worshiper's sense of God's absence and his longing to participate in the liturgy and to be restored to the presence of God.

Responsorial Psalm (alternative): 51:10-11, 12-13, 16-17.

A different selection from this responsorial psalm was used on the First Sunday of Lent, series A. Here stanza I picks up the reference to the new heart from Ez 36:26, and the psalm forms a fitting conclusion to our Lenten devotions. Participation in the eucharist is the supreme moment when we partake in the forgiveness of sins which has been made available by the Christ event.

EASTER SUNDAY

The Easter Sunday mass is not itself the paschal liturgy. That took place at the culmination of the vigil. Rather, it is the first of a series of masses which belong to the great fifty days. In them we reflect upon the post-Easter revelations of the risen Christ and the fruits of our redemption in him.

The readings are the same for series A, B, and C. We commented on them at length last year. Here are a few hints for the homilist.

The readings suggest three different aspects of the Easter message. Reading I, taken from one of the kerygmatic speeches in Acts, is a proclamation of the death and resurrection of Christ as the final, redemptive act of God. This kerygma is at a primitive stage of development, before the full redemptive significance of the cross had been worked out. The whole life-story of Jesus is interpreted as "word" — i.e., an act of God's self-communication. The crucifixion was the radical calling into question of the validity of that word by Jesus' contemporaries. The resurrection in turn is God's vindication of the validity of that word. God set his seal on all that Jesus had said and done in his earthly ministry.

The resurrection does not mean that the earthly ministry becomes a thing of the past, a phase now finished with. Rather, it is through the resurrection that all that Christ had stood for in his earthly life: his word, or self-communication of God, his bringing healing and liberation to those in bondage to the devil — all this can now continue in the church. It is not the continued influence of a figure in past history, his teaching and example (as for instance in the case of Socrates), but it is the continuation of that same word and work. Part of the meaning of Easter is "What Jesus stood for continues" (*die Sache Jesu geht weiter*) as Willi Marxsen has put it. That is of course not the whole message, but it is an important part of it.

The two alternative epistle readings (Col 3:1-4, 1 Cor 5:6b-8) suggest another aspect of Easter. Easter is not simply the recollection of a past event, or even its representation in word and sacrament. It also celebrates our own participation in the risen life, initiated in baptism, and nourished in the holy communion. This carries with it a present imperative.

Colossians 3:1-4
1 The Easter Baptisms
You have died
You have been raised

2 The Imperative
Seek the things above
Set your mind on the things above

1 Corinthians 5:6b-8
1 The Easter Eucharist
Christ our paschal lamb has been sacrificed
Let us celebrate the festival

2 The Imperative
Cleanse out the old leaven
With sincerity and truth

The story of the empty tomb from Jn 20:1-9 treats that pericope quite differently from the earliest tradition. It is clear that for the earliest church the resurrection faith was grounded not on the discovery of the empty tomb but in the appearance: "To faith the empty tomb will be a sign of what has taken place. It will not, however, fight for the empty tomb as for an article of faith, because the truth of Easter does not in fact depend on the empty tomb" (E. Schweizer).

John's gospel, however, following a late tradition, allows the "other disciple" to come to faith in the resurrection through the sight of the empty tomb, without an angelic proclamation as in the other gospels. Before that, Peter had seen but had not yet come to faith, while Mary Magdalene had seen the stone rolled away, but concluded that the body had been removed by human hands. The empty tomb functions as a sign. But a sign is equivocal. It leaves open possibilities: *either* the body was removed, *or* Jesus has risen from the dead.

The homilist must distinguish between a sign and proof. Even the arrangement of the linen clothes (v. 7) was not a proof for Peter. Only the other disciple came to faith, because he perceived the significance of the sign. A proof coerces, only a sign can produce the free decision of faith.

SECOND SUNDAY OF EASTER

Reading I: Acts 2:42-47.

Readings from the Acts of the Apostles take the place of Old Testament readings during the Easter season in each of series A, B, and C. Such readings are appropriate because they show the continued work of the risen Christ in his church. By defining his first volume as a record of all that Jesus *began* to do and to teach (Acts 1:1), Luke implies that his second volume covers what Jesus *continued* to do and to teach.

Verse 42 is a succinct characterization of the life of the apostolic church. Here we see the necessary signs of the presence of the church: where these signs are, there the church is.

1 Apostles' Teaching. The sharp distinction between *didache* (teaching) and *kerygma* (preaching) was probably overdrawn. Certainly, the gospel has to be proclaimed in a different way to outsiders (cf. the kerygmatic speeches of Acts) from the way in which it is proclaimed in the ongoing life of the church. But the teaching here must include the continued preaching of the gospel to the already existing church, a function which is necessary to keep the church in being as a church. In the interest of such teaching, the sayings of Jesus and incidents from his life would have to be remembered, and to be given shape, and so the gospel tradition would gradually have evolved.

2 Fellowship. Koinonia means common life, a shared life. In the Christian community this is based on the sharing of the risen Christ's life with his people (what Paul in 2 Cor 13:14 calls the *koinonia* of the Spirit, and what the Johannine writer means when he speaks of his readers as having fellowship "with us," i.e., with those who have seen the risen Christ. But this vertical dimension of *koinonia* produces a horizontal dimension. The early Christians, we are told, had all things in common, the so-called early Christian communism described in the ensuing verses. Of course, such communism was not based on any economic doctrine but a spontaneous expression of Christian *agape*, necessitated in any case by the removal of the Galilean fisherfolk to the capital. Nor can it have been so general ("*all* who believed") as Luke suggests in his idealized picture; for when he speaks of Barnabas in 4:36-37, he seems to imply that there was something exceptional in what he did. This shows that the so-called communism was not meant as law for the church for all time. In Paul's churches it took the form of the collection for the Jerusalem church. But there must be some concrete expression of the horizontal dimension of *koinonia* as an essential mark of the church.

3 The Breaking of the Bread. Scholars have debated whether this is a reference to the eucharist or not. If we mean the eucharist as it later developed (e.g., by the time of Paul when the backward and forward looking elements combined), it would be an anachronism to call it such. But 2:46 expands on the brief summary of verse 4 to show that this daily meal had a distinctly sacral character. There we read that they took their food "with glad and generous hands." The Greek word represented by the English adjective "glad" is a noun meaning exuberant joy at the coming of the Messiah (so Bultmann). This shows that the daily meal was an anticipation of the messianic banquet, a partial fulfillment of the Lord's promise at the Last Supper that he would eat and drink with his disciples in the consummated kingdom of God.

4 The Prayers. This rather unspecific statement probably refers to participation in the hours of prayer of Jewish devotion. It is curious to find the earliest Christian participating in the prayers of the Jewish temple. Stephen would later have something to say about that, and then the breach between Christianity and Judaism would be widened. The observance of daily hours of prayer, originally a devout practice of individuals, was eventually developed into the monastic office. A private prayer life is clearly one of the marks of the Christian community.

One more comment. This summary does not mention baptism as one of the signs of the church's presence. But there is an oblique allusion to it in the final sentence of our reading: "And the Lord added to the number day by day those who were being saved" (v. 47). Baptism was the means by which this "addition" was effected. The phraseology tells us much about early Christian thinking on baptism. Baptism is an act through which God works, bringing the convert into an already existing community, a community of those who are on the way to final salvation. One does not become a member of the church as a result of individual decisions to get together after an individual experience of salvation.

Responsorial Psalm: 118:2-4, 13-15ab, 22-24.

This is a slightly different selection from the same psalm as was used for the mass for Easter Sunday.

Reading II: 1 Peter 1:3-9.

It is widely believed among contemporary New Testament scholars that 1 Peter is based on an Easter-baptismal homily. Some even think it is a baptismal liturgy, but that is probably going a little too far. Through their baptismal identification with Christ's death and resurrection the Christians have experienced a new birth. But the author warns his readers that this new life is not yet completely realized. They are being guarded for a salvation first to be revealed in the last time, and meanwhile they may have to face various trials, and have their faith tested in the fire of persecution.

Speaking with apostolic authority (i.e., as one whose faith is grounded on his having "seen" the risen Lord), the author distinguishes himself from his hearers, who depend for their faith on the eyewitness of others because they have "not seen." This adumbrates a theme which is to be developed in the gospel reading, the story of Thomas.

Gospel: John 20:19-31.

This is the traditional gospel of Low Sunday, and was used last year in series C. As we have pointed out, the author is here wrestling with what became a real problem in the post-apostolic church. How could one believe in the risen Lord without the benefit of a resurrection appearance? The answer is, that even seeing, as in the case of Thomas, is no guarantee of faith. Faith, for Thomas, came by hearing the word of the risen One addressing him personally. For those who come after, faith comes through hearing the word of God, through hearing the risen One speak through his apostolic messengers.

The Homily.

Two themes seem to be suggested this day. One is the essential marks of the life of a Christian community: the apostles' teaching, sacraments, prayer and common life. These marks must be applied quite concretely to the life of the local congregation. The other is the theme of seeing/not seeing and believing. This should be related existentially to the doubts of the modern Christian. Perhaps we tend to regard having doubts as somethings to be ashamed of, and it would be a good thing to bring it all out into the open, and to deal pastorally with the problem of doubt.

THIRD SUNDAY OF EASTER ✓

Reading I: Acts 2:14, 22-28.

This is part of the first kerygmatic speech in Acts, put into the mouth of Peter on the day of Pentecost. It prefaces the central events of the death and resurrection of Jesus with a brief summary of Jesus' earthly ministry, and concludes with a proof text for the resurrection. As the caption suggests, it is on this proof text that the emphasis should lie. It was not possible for Christ to be held by the powers of death. Why not? Did his divinity give him an unfair advantage over us? That is to ask the question the wrong way round. The divinity of Christ is never a presupposition for his fate in the gospels. The divinity of Christ is rather a confession of faith that we make after being confronted with the story of his fate. Christ could not be held by the power of death because in his cross he had overcome it. Death, understood at the theological rather than the biological level, means man's ultimate separation from God as the result of his rebellion and consequent alienation. Jesus had faced final separation from God in full obedience to his will right up to the end, and thereby overcame man's separation from God. Jesus could not be held by the pangs of death because he was what he was — but what he was did not involve some abstract quality of divinity that gave him unfair advantages over us, but his complete obedience to the will of God, which none of us has ever achieved. The resurrection did not snatch victory from the jaws of defeat, or reverse the tragedy of the cross like a *deus ex machina*. The resurrection made manifest what was true of the cross in itself — that it was in fact the victory over man's alienation and separation from God, over all that the New Testament means when it speaks of sin, the wrath of God and death.

Responsorial Psalm: 16:1-2, 5, 7-11.

Quite fittingly, the responsorial psalm is the psalm from which the proof text in Peter's sermon in reading I was taken. Originally, this psalm probably contained no hope of life after death, but was a thanksgiving for delivery from a plight near death. But as it passed into Christian usage it acquired a much deeper meaning in the light of Christ's death and resurrection. It is not really a *proof* text. For us it does not prove the resurrection of Christ, but it does show that the God of the Old Testament is the same God who is finally revealed in the resurrection of Jesus Christ, a God who rescues men from the power of death and opens up the path of life.

Reading II: 1 Peter 1:17-21.

In this passage the paschal-baptismal associations of 1 Peter again come out clearly. In the Christ event we were "ransomed by the blood of the lamb." This primitive Christian language interprets the death of Christ in terms of the passover. The passover lamb was not originally interpreted as a ransom for sin, or a means of expiation, but it did acquire that meaning in later Judaism. It was this later interpretation of the passover which gave the early Christians some of the language with which to speak of the significance of the death of Christ. The language may be crude and cultic, but "ransom" does speak of the liberation which Christian experience has always known to be the consequence of Christ's death (though we mustn't press it and ask to whom was the ransom paid: it must be left at the level of poetry and liturgy). Again, "blood" speaks of the event of the cross, of Jesus' total surrender of his will and life to the Father which was the means of that liberation.

This faith has two consequences which are spelled out for present behavior. At the beginning of our passage the readers are told that they must "conduct themselves with fear" throughout the time of their exile. By shifting the metaphor from redemption from Egyptian bondage to a present existence in Babylonian exile the writer damps down over-enthusiastic claims about the consequences of our participation in Christ's resurrection, and insists on the "not yet" aspect of it. We do belong to heaven, but we still have to live meanwhile on earth. Therefore "fear" — circumspection, must characterize the Christian life.

But there is a positive side of this not-yet-ness, too, which is picked up in the final verse of our reading: it is an existence characterized by confidence and hope. Not hope that everything will turn out all right (the readers were due for the fiery trial of persecution, anyhow), but the hope of final participation in the glory of Christ.

Gospel: Luke 24:13-35.

This is the most beautiful of all the appearance stories, and it seems almost blasphemy for the critical scholar to lay hands upon it. Nevertheless, modern New Testament study shows that this story has grown up through the years from an original nucleus and become the repository for theological ideas at various stages of development. Finally, Luke, with consummate literary skill, has made it into a vivid narrative.

In its present form, the story reflects the pattern of early Christian worship. The self-manifestation of the risen One takes place through the two events of the exposition of the scriptures and the breaking of the bread. The preacher has a good opportunity to relate these two events that happen in every liturgy to the appearance of the risen Christ, and to explain how word and sacrament are integral parts of a single coming of Christ to his own.

Over thirty years ago, Karl Barth wrote in his Gifford Lectures the following words: "What we know today as the church service in Roman Catholicism *and* in Protestantism is a torso. The Roman Catholic church has a sacramental service without preaching. But I wish to speak at the moment not for or against her, but about our own Protestant church. We have a service with a sermon but without sacraments. Both types of service are impossible." Barth would have to revise what he said then about Roman Catholicism today. But I wonder parenthetically whether Protestants have paid sufficient heed to his word!

The Homily.

There can be no question that today the liturgical preacher will want to expound the Emmaus story as a pattern of what happens in the liturgy. People are often puzzled by the various modes of Christ's presence. In what way is he present in his word, and is he differently present in his sacrament? Here is a chance to explain how both word and sacrament are integral parts of a single coming of the risen Christ to his people and to every Christian assembly.

FOURTH SUNDAY OF EASTER

Reading I: Acts 2:14a, 36-41.

This reading gives the tail end of Peter's kerygmatic sermon at Pentecost (of which a substantial part was read last Sunday), and goes on to indicate the response of his hearers.

The conclusion of the sermon sums up the whole kerygma in a single christological formula: God made this Jesus whom men crucified, to be both Lord and Christ. Such a statement puzzles those who approach the New Testament with the presuppositions of later dogmatics. It looks like "adoptionism" — the view that Jesus was a man who was made divine at his resurrection, the later heresy which a colleague of mine once wittily defined as the theory that Jesus was a man but graduated in divinity with honors. This, however, is to read back the later ontological Christology of the patristic church into the Hebraic parts of the New Testament. Hebrew thought viewed matters in functional rather than ontological categories (cf. Gregory Dix's book, *Jew and Greek*). Lord and Christ are functional terms, meaning that from the resurrection onwards the risen and exalted One exercised the functions of Messiah and Kyrios. Henceforth he rules over his people, forgives them, nourishes them with his word and sacraments, and commands their obedience. All that God does toward his people is done through Christ. All God's acts bring along with them, as it were, the salvation which Jesus wrought out in his earthly history. It is as important to say that *Jesus* is Lord and Christ as it is to say that Jesus is *Lord and Christ*.

The response that preaching invokes is "What shall we do?" The answer is, repent and be baptized. Repentance in this context means not merely sorrow for past individual sins. It meant a radical reassessment of Jesus and his significance. By crucifying him, Jesus' contemporaries rejected him. He was for them not the emissary from God, the bringer of man's salvation, but either an impostor or a deluded fanatic. Now they must reassess him: he *is* the emissary of God, and bringer of man's salvation. Baptism is the event in and through which the converts are brought into the sphere of his salvation. They receive forgiveness of sins, which again has a far richer meaning than the remission of individual peccadilloes: it means God's eschatological salvation in its wholeness. And they receive the gift of the Holy Spirit, for baptism "adds" them to the spirit-bearing community (see reading I, Easter II).

Responsorial Psalm: 23:1-6.

The theme of Christ as Good Shepherd, which used to belong to old Easter II, has in the new lectionary been transferred to new Easter IV. This, the most familiar of all psalms, introduces the shepherd passages in reading II and the gospel.

In the original psalm it was Yahweh who was the shepherd. When the Greek speaking Christians adopted the title *Kyrios* for the exalted Christ as a translation of the Aramaic *mari* (cf. Marana tha), the consequence was that many of the passages in the Greek New Testament which spoke about Yahweh-Kyrios were transferred to Christ-Kyrios. This did not involve any compromise of Old Testament Jewish monotheism. It meant that henceforth the exalted Christ is that aspect of the being of God which is turned toward us in saving action. Ultimately, of course, this would lead to the formation of the doctrine of the Trinity. Meanwhile, even the earliest church believed that God acts in us through the exalted Christ. Through him God exercises his Lordship, which includes his work as Shepherd, the one who nourishes and defends his people.

Reading II: 1 Peter 2:20b-25.

This is the traditional epistle for Good Shepherd Sunday. We recall that the materials used in this letter were taken from a baptismal homily. The author is exhorting his readers to patience. He holds up Christ in his passion as an example, quoting an early hymn which draws upon the suffering servant song in Is 53. But as so often happened when things are quoted, the author continues to quote when he gets beyond the point he wished to make, and speaks of Christ's passion not merely as an example of patience but as redemptive: "he bore our sins in his own body on the tree." "Tree" was an early Christian designation of the cross, recalling with defiant apologetic the Deuteronomic curse on all who hanged upon a tree. Christ's wounds bring healing, and by his redemptive death we are enabled to die to sin and live to righteousness. At this point the writer turns from the hymn to his readers. He recalls their conversion, and tells them that having strayed they have now returned to the Shepherd and Guardian (the Greek word is *episcopos*, bishop) of their souls. This last phrase throws an interesting sidelight on the development of the church's ministry by the time 1 Peter was written. While formally it was the ministerial designations (shepherd-pastor, and bishop) that provided christological titles, it was really the other way round. The church's ministers are bishops and shepherd because it is through them that the risen Christ exercises his shepherding and overseeing.

Gospel: John 10:1-10.

There is a long and complicated history behind the discourse of the Good Shepherd. It begins with a fusion of two parables, vv.1-3a and 3b-5. In the first parable the picture is of a sheepfold into which two parties seek to enter, a prowler and the shepherd himself.

The second parable concerns the relationship between the sheep and the shepherd on the one hand, and the stranger on the other. The combined parables are followed by an allegorical interpretation in which the Johannine Christ successively identifies himself with the gate and the shepherd. Today New Testament scholars would regard the two parables as originally separate and possibly authentic parables of Jesus. The fusion must have happened in aural transmission while the allegorical interpretation will be the work of the evangelist himself.

The first parable is a challenge to Israel's religious authorities. Will they accept Jesus' message? This challenge must belong to the final part of Jesus' ministry in Jerusalem.

In the second parable, the situation is earlier in Jesus' ministry. He can offer no external credentials for his authority, but there are those who respond in faith to his message because they hear in it the authentic voice of God.

In the last analysis both identifications of Jesus, gate and shepherd, make the same point. The risen Christ is the One who nourishes his people in his word and sacraments, giving them life and enabling them to have it abundantly.

The Homily.

The theme of Christ the shepherd binds the psalm, reading II and the gospel together. As shepherd, Christ feeds his church through the apostolic ministry. This should be the subject for today's homily. In expounding it, the homilist may also draw upon reading I, which speaks about baptism. The ostensibly adoptionist Christology of that reading can be used to draw out the fact that it is the risen Christ who is the Good Shepherd. It is not just that Jesus was a good shepherd during his earthly ministry. Through the resurrection "Jesus' cause continues."

Easter 5 to Ascension of Year A

Reading I: Acts 6:1-7.

For the New Testament scholar several problems are raised by this story. The main one is that although we are told that the seven were appointed to "serve tables" in order to permit the apostles to give their undivided attention to the ministry of the word, nevertheless the only members of the seven of whom we hear after their appointment turn out to be themselves notable ministers of the word — i.e., Stephen and Philip the Evangelist. Probably this confusion is due to the author of Luke-Acts, who sees in the appointment of the seven the institution of a subordinate ministry (deacons? — he uses the verb *diakonein* = serve, but doesn't actually call them deacons).

In actual fact, however, they must have been more than that — in a real sense leaders of the growing Greek-speaking part of the community. In that case the real concern of the apostles in recognizing the seven would have been to prevent a split between the Greek and the Aramaic speaking Christians (Hellenists and Hebrews). Perhaps even the act of ordination — laying on of hands with prayer — reflects the practice at the time Luke wrote, rather than that of the earliest church (cf. also Acts 13:3 and 14:23, which are probably equally anachronistic). Nevertheless, ordination by the laying on of hands with prayer must have been introduced in a Palestinian-Jewish environment, for it reflects the synagogue practice of ordaining elders — a fact which has even led some modern scholars to suppose that the seven were appointed presbyters (elders) rather than deacons. But this is improbable. The truth more likely is that we have here two levels of interpretation: (1) the original historical situation, i.e., the tensions mentioned above, (2) the recognition of the leaders of the Greek-speaking group by the Twelve, thus averting a breach between the two parties.

A homily on this passage would have to be based either on the one level or the other. If we opt for the historical level, the point at issue would be the unity of the church and the concern of the apostles to reconcile the differences between the conflicting parties. It is the bishop's function, in succession to the apostles, to bridge over the differences and to hold together in dialogue the conflicting groups (e.g., conservatives and radicals, ecclesiastical or political) in the one community. It is no easy task, but it is a truly apostolic one.

If the homilist opts for the Lucan level of interpretation, the impressive point which this passage makes for us today is the ability of the early church to adapt its ministry to changing needs. While there is basically one apostolic ministry in the church, namely the ministry of the risen Christ energized by the Holy Spirit, this ministry has in the course of history adapted itself to changing needs, and must continue to do so if it is to remain the ministry of the risen Christ.

Responsorial Psalm: 33:1-2, 4-5, 18-19.

On Sunday 19 C, when a different selection from this psalm was used, we suggested emphasis on the doctrine of election from verse 12. This verse, however, is not part of the selection for today. As a psalm of thanksgiving for the mighty acts of God in salvation history it is appropriate for the Easter season, particularly as the last stanza refers to deliverance from death. Originally, of course, this was a reference to deliverance in some natural calamity, probably famine, which is mentioned in the last line of the stanza. But in the context of this Easter liturgy it can be given a full Christian sense. In his resurrection Christ has indeed delivered the souls (lives) of his people from death.

Reading II: 1 Peter 2:4-9.

We recall that 1 Peter is full of baptismal references. Originally perhaps this passage was an instruction for baptismal candidates. It tells them the nature of the community into which they are being admitted. It is a temple (the place of God's presence) made up of living stones (i.e., men and women). It is, like the people of the old covenant (Ex 19:6), a holy or royal priesthood, a distinct race and nation. Special stress is laid upon the priestly aspect of the community, for only this aspect is spelt out in terms of implied functions. The community expresses its priestly character by offering up spiritual sacrifices acceptable to God through Jesus

Christ, and declares the wonderful deeds of him who calls it out of darkness into light.

Between this exposition of the nature of the church there is inserted a string of Old Testament quotations, connected by the theme of the stone (Is 28:16; Ps 118:22; Is 8:14-15) and applied to the person and work of Christ. These quotations were evidently suggested by the reference to the composition of the church out of living stones. This reminds the author that as living stones they are joined together by Christ who is the corner stone. Remove the prosaic quotations, and we have what may be an early (baptismal?) hymn about the church.

This is the *locus classicus* in the New Testament on the theme of the church's priesthood. It was of course the passage which inspired the Reformers to reassert the doctrine of the priesthood of all believers. Though it was understandable, it was a pity that they had to assert it polemically against the late medieval doctrines of ministerial priesthood and therefore obscured the priestly understanding of the ministry.

A recent book by an American Lutheran scholar (John H. Elliott) has sought to cut the ground from under this polemic by insisting (1) that there is a basic difference between the priesthood of the church as predicated in Ex 19:6, and the cultic priesthood of Leviticus, (2) the sacrifice offered by the Christian community is not cultic, but ethical — the living of a Christian life in the world.

It is a helpful insight that the priesthood of the church is based on Exodus rather than Leviticus. This protects the teaching of Hebrews that Christ has once for all replaced the sacrifices of the Levitical priesthood by his redemptive act, and that any priesthood we predicate of the church or its ministry can never abrogate the once-for-allness of his sacrifice and the uniqueness of his priesthood. Nor can it be denied that the author of 1 Peter sees the Exodus-type sacrifice of the church as being actualized and made visible to the world in the quality of its ethical life.

Nevertheless, I wonder whether we can exclude cultic ideas altogether from this passage. The "spiritual sacrifices" offered by the church do not exclude the "declaring" (or recital) of the wonderful deeds of God in salvation history. Here is the primary focus of the church's priesthood and this is what she does in the liturgy. Of course this issues or should issue in a life style in the world. But its cultic basis must be preserved, otherwise the whole conception of sacrifice will evaporate. The great eucharistic prayer (traditionally called the canon in the West and the anaphora in the East) is the occasion *par excellence* when we "show forth," "declare" or recite before God in thanksgiving his mighty acts of salvation. This is the primary work of the church. For this we were baptized, and for this renew our baptismal vows at Easter.

Gospel: John 14:1-12.

What C. H. Dodd wrote some years ago about the First Epistle of John is equally applicable to the discourses in the Fourth Gospel: "The argument is not closely articulated. There is little direct progression. The writer 'thinks around' a succession of related topics. The movement of thought has not inaptly been described as 'spiral,' for the development of a theme often brings us back almost to the starting point — almost, but not quite, for there is a slight shift which provides the transition to a fresh theme."

This special pattern makes an analysis of a passage like today's gospel very difficult. A number of themes arise in succession:

1 Jesus' impending departure, i.e., his death and exaltation.

2 (linked by the key word "way") Jesus as the revelation and the *way* to the Father.

3 Following this, a dialogue with Philip unfolding this christological affirmation: Jesus as the revelation of the Father, a reference to the words and works of Jesus as the words and works of the Father, words and works which make him the revelation of the Father.

4 A challenge to believe Jesus, preferably because of encounter with his whole person, or if not that, at least because of his works.

5 The promise that believers will do even greater works, because of Jesus' departure — which brings us back almost to where we started.

Obviously there is much here that we could develop for a homily. The liturgical season (the approach of Ascension Day) suggests that we read it because of what it says about Jesus' departure to the Father. No doubt when the farewell discourse was first chosen in the traditional lectionary for the lessons of the old "great forty days" our forefathers equated this departure with the ascension as a separate event, and thought of the discourses almost as though they were delivered by the risen Christ during the great forty days.

Our understanding of the Easter event today as well as of the farewell discourses is more sophisticated. For us the "going of Jesus" to the Father is the whole complex event, celebrated throughout the great *fifty* days, his resurrection, exaltation, appearances and the gift of the Spirit. And the farewell discourses themselves, while doubtless enshrining traditional sayings of Jesus, are meditations of the Johannine community upon the meaning of this total complex of events.

For us, the important message of today's pericope is that the risen, exalted Christ continues in his church his words and works. Are these greater works, the word and sacrament, greater because they will actually mediate the divine salvation whereas in the earthly Jesus his words and works only pointed forward to and prepared the central saving acts? His departure from earth was preparatory for his continual coming to his church.

The Homily.

It seems artificial to try and detect any single theme running through today's lessons. Each theme is of course related to the others because of the Easter season. Here are various lines which could be developed, depending on the homilist's knowledge of the local situation in his congregation:

1 The bridging of tensions between conflicting views or groups within the church.

2 The need for adapting the apostolic ministry to the challenges of a new world.

3 The priesthood of the church in liturgy and life.

4 The true meaning of Christ's "departure" — in order to be ever present with his community at all times in all places, through the "greater works" that his church performs.

SIXTH SUNDAY OF EASTER

Reading 1: Acts 8:5-8, 14-17.

Acts is planned to trace the expansion of the church's mission from Jerusalem, Judea and Samaria to the end of the earth (Acts 1:18). The campaign undertaken by Philip, one of the seven, after the martyrdom of Stephen, marks for Luke a decisive stage in the execution of this plan (Samaria). Equally important for Luke is the concern that each successive stage should receive the imprimatur of the original Jerusalem community and its apostles. Hence the curious anomaly that in this story baptism does not convey the gift of the Spirit, as is normally the case in Acts, but has to await the arrival of Peter and John to lay hands on the Samaritan converts.

In later times, especially in Anglican thought during the past century, and in revisions of the Book of Common Prayer produced in the 1920's, this passage was taken as the *Magna Charta* for the episcopal confirmation of children baptized in infancy. This exegesis has thus passed into the theology of the average Anglican parish priest without question. Let it be said with all emphasis that such an interpretation has no foundation in this passage, in the rest of the New Testament or in the early fathers. The author of Luke-Acts knows nothing of "confirmation" as a separate rite performed by apostles or their successors distinct from baptism (however justifiable such a development may have been in later times, granted the practice of infant baptism). Rather, he is concerned with one of his major theological themes, the maintenance of the ties between the expanding mission of the church and the mother church at Jerusalem as the center of salvation history.

Responsorial Psalm: 66:1-3a, 4-5, 6-7a, 16 and 20.

Precisely the same selection of Ps 66 was used on Sunday 14 in year C, and was commented on there. The only variation here is the optional substitution of the Easter alleluia for the refrain. However, this is an excellent example of the way in which the liturgical use of scripture is itself an exegetical act. The psalm originally celebrated some historical deliverance of the nation. It picks up the traditional language of the exodus: "He turned the sea into dry land; men passed through the river on foot" (stanza 3). Now, in this season, the mighty acts thus described as an exodus become the resurrection of Christ and our participation in it through baptism.

Reading II: 1 Peter 3:15-18.

The baptismal material in the first part of 1 Peter, which runs through 4:12, includes warnings of possible persecution (after 4:12 the tone changes and the persecution becomes actual). The reference to persecution in the present pericope are contingent in character: always prepared — *when* you are abused — *if* that should be God's will." The newly baptized, thrilled at their admission to all the privileges of the people of God as detailed in last week's epistle lesson, are here reminded that it will not be smooth going all the time. They must know what they are let in for. Indeed, how could it be otherwise, since the Christian life is a following in the footsteps of Christ? That is why the passage ends with a quotation from an early Christian hymn about the death and resurrection of Christ. (The hymn continues beyond the present reading through verse 22.) The words "the righteous for the unrighteous" are thought to have been added to the hymn so as to adapt it to its present position (cf. vv. 14, 16) in which the passion of Christ is treated as an example for the persecuted Christians to imitate. In this way we see how a hymn receives new applications by being taken up successively into new contexts: (1) into a baptism homily; (2) into a letter warning Christians for whom persecution is an impending reality; (3) as used in today's liturgy the whole passage receives yet another interpretation, and it is the homilist's task to draw out the third of these successive applications, each one built upon the earlier ones.

Gospel: John 14:15-21.

We see here the same kind of spiral thought that characterizes the farewell discourse throughout, and of which we spoke in our comments on the gospel of the previous Sunday. The points made are:

1 Love of Christ means obedience to his commandments.

2 The promise of the Paraclete (RSV Counselor) sent by the Father in response to the prayer of the Son.

3 The Spirit, which the world cannot receive, will dwell in the community.

4 The coming of the Spirit is equivalent to the return of the Son, and almost completely fulfills the primitive expectation of the parousia.

5 That the world will no longer see the Christ, but the community will (a) see him, (b) live because he lives, (c) know the mutual indwelling of Christ with the Father and of Christ with the community.

6 This indwelling is a relationship of mutual love which includes obedience to Christ's commandments.

It will again be noted how point 6 brings us full circle to where we were at point 1. Yet the spiral leads to an enrichment of understanding. The Christian life is not an external observance of Christ's commandments, but an intense relationship of the community to the three persons of the Trinity, each with a specific role to play in this relationship. The Spirit conveys the presence of the Son, who reveals the Father. But this intense personal relationship is not dissolved into mere emotion: it is concretely and soberly manifested in a life of obedience to Christ's commandments.

The departure of Jesus does not mean that he is now absent. It means his ever renewed presence through the coming of the Spirit to the community. That is the Easter message of this pericope.

The Homily.

In the latter part of the Easter season we move from the contemplation of the resurrection appearances to meditation upon the continued presence of the exalted Christ with his church through the Spirit. Thus the first reading and the gospel can be linked together. The church is a community in which the Spirit is given and shared. But this means: (a) a unity with the apostolic community and the Jerusalem church, which was the center of salvation history; (b) communion with the risen Christ and through him with the Father — a trinitarian experience; (c) not an ecstatic experience, necessarily (though such experiences may be granted *ubi et quando visum est Deo*), but keeping the commandments is the touchstone of the love of Christ and the indwelling of the Spirit. These themes could be related to the charismatic movement and/or the phenomenon of the underground church, where these are relevant to local conditions.

ASCENSION

The readings for Ascension Day are the same as those in series C, except that Matthew's story of the final appearance of the risen Lord replaces the Lucan ascension narrative.

First, let us remind ourselves that Ascension day should not be thought of as a historical commemoration. As we observed last year, the New Testament treats the ascension as an integral part of the Easter event. In fact, the earlier Easter narratives depict the appearances as manifestations of the already risen and ascended One.

This is still the situation in Matthew's story of the final appearance (Mt 28:16-20). It is the ascended One who says "All authority in heaven and earth is given to me." It is the ascended One who commissions his apostles and sends them out into the world in the great missionary charge (cf. Eph 4:8-13, where the apostolate appears as the gift of the ascended Christ).

The appearance takes place on a mountain. This, for Matthew, has theological significance. The great sermon had been preached on a mountain. The transfiguration, as in the other synoptics, took place on a mountain. And now, too, does the great appearance. This is in fact the only appearance Matthew records (apart from the personal and private one to the women, Mt 28:9-10). All the meaning of the resurrection appearances is for Matthew compressed into this single story. Such a device was probably suggested to him by the angel's charge to the women in Mark 16:7 to tell the disciples to go to Galilee, where they would see him. The primary significance of the appearances is that they are *revelations* of the risen One. Because they are revelations they can be doubted as well as believed. But those who do believe respond in adoration (v. 17).

In his opening words about his authority the risen One echoes the language about the Son of man in Dn 7:14 in the wording of the Greek Old Testament, a fact which suggests that this story must have crystallized in the Greek speaking church.

The declaration of authority is followed by a missionary charge in three parts:

1 To "make disciples" of all nations. This is typically Matthean phraseology (cf. Mt 13:52; 27:57). The longer ending in Mark, which has "preach the gospel" (16:16), probably represents the earlier tradition, which Matthew has reworded to suit his own interests. The association of the appearances with the command to mission goes back to the earliest tradition, as the word "apostle" itself shows, as do the terms in which Paul speaks of his own call on the Damascus road (Gal 1:16).

2 As in Mk 16:16, the call to mission includes the charge to baptize. All our evidence agrees that baptism was practiced by the church right from the outset, and this despite the fact that baptism had not been a feature of the Lord's public ministry. This remains true even if there was an earlier period when Jesus was working side by side with John the Baptist and during which he too baptized. There can be no doubt that it was the impact of the post-resurrection appearances which led to the revival of baptism by the earliest Christians. Baptism became the way in which those who had not had a firsthand encounter with the Christ event were brought into its sphere. The command to baptize given by the risen One in Mark and Matthew (cf. also the allusions to the forgiveness of sin in the appearance stories in Luke and John) is a verbalization of this experience.

In the earliest community and for some time (cf. Paul) baptism was administered in the name of Jesus. It is only in this passage of Matthew and in the *Didache*, a Christian writing probably dating back to the end of the first century, that we hear of the threefold formula. One may say, however, that the use of Jesus' name alone as a baptismal formula implies the threefold name. For baptism in the name of Jesus implies the confession of him as the Messiah (Jesus is Lord, was probably the earliest baptism confession), and in Jewish context Messiah means the agent of God's final salvation, while the bestowal of the Spirit is a consequence of messianic salvation. Hence we may say that from the earliest date the Jewish Christians would have understood baptism in an implicitly Trinitarian sense. The development of the threefold formula would have become necessary in Gentile communities, where the implications of the primitive confession of Jesus as Lord was no longer understood, and had to be spelled out. This does not mean that we should now go back to the earliest single formula. That would now have quite a different meaning — the repudiation of what was implicit in the earliest use of the single formula.

3 The command to baptize is followed by a charge to teach. It is not clear whether this teaching means post-baptismal instruction. "Baptizing" is a present participle in the Greek as in the English translation, and this could suggest teaching accompanying baptism, i.e., catechetical instruction.

After the charge comes a final promise of the permanent presence of the ascended Christ from now until the parousia. This is a far cry from the perspective of the earliest community, which thought of the interval between the ascension and the second coming as a period of his temporary absence. The wording of this promise thus verbalizes the experience of Christ's presence, an experience made possible for the church through the gift of the Spirit and in the cultus during the intervening period.

The Homily.

There is a wealth of material here for the preacher, and in his selection he must be guided by local conditions.

Perhaps the strongest point of emphasis this year, as one compares this Matthean story with the Lucan story of the ascension read last year, is the great missionary charge. We live in a period when Christians are ready to bend over backwards to be nice to people of other religions. Dialogue rather than evangelism and conversion is the contemporary watchword. There is a biblical justification for this in so far as we should see the truth which is in other religions as the revelatory work of the Logos which became incarnate in Christ. But Christian faith cannot remain content merely with dialogue. Somehow or other that dialogue must be steered to the confession before men of other religions that "what they ignorantly worship that we declare" to them. The same word which has spoken in their own religious experience has finally spoken in the flesh of Jesus. The mode of following the imperative to go into all the world may change. For Matthew it had already come to mean make disciples rather than evangelize, i.e., the emphasis was on catechesis. But the imperative must, one way or another, be obeyed.

Easter 7 A to Sunday 14 A

SEVENTH SUNDAY OF EASTER

Reading 1: Acts 1:12-14.

These verses form a link between the ascension story and the election of Matthias. They presuppose the Lucan scheme in which the ascension is depicted as a distinct event from the resurrection, and the coming of the Spirit as yet another distinct event, forty and fifty days respectively after Easter. The upper room was certainly historical (cf. the Last Supper and Peter's return to the house of John Mark's mother in Acts 12:12). There are four lists of the Twelve in the New Testament (Mk 3:16-19; Mt 10:2-4; Lk 6:14-16 and the present passage). They contain slight variations both in the names themselves and in the order of the names. Even between the list in Luke's gospel and that in Acts there is one variation. In Acts John is placed before James, probably because he is to appear later in Acts as Peter's right hand man.

By adding "and children" after women, the Western text took "women" to mean "wives." Some think that the Western text was correct in its understanding of "women." We know from Paul that Peter and other apostles were married. This is the last appearance of Mary the mother of Jesus in the New Testament. It is striking that our last picture of her should be as a member of the believing community engaged in waiting and in prayer.

Granted the Lucan schematization, which separates the resurrection, exaltation and coming of the Spirit, today's lesson is eminently suitable for the period between the liturgical observance of Ascension and Pentecost. That period Karl Barth once designated a "significant pause." It is a pause between the actions of God, a pause in which all the community can do is to wait and pray. It may seem paradoxical, but although the Spirit came, in Johannine language, "to abide with you [the community] for ever," the church has nevertheless to pray constantly, *Veni, Creator*

Spiritus. The gift of the Spirit is never an assured possession, but has constantly to be sought anew in prayer.

Responsorial Psalm: 27:1, 4, 7-8a.

A somewhat different selection of Ps 27 was appointed for Lent II, series C, and was commented upon last year. The same first and third stanzas were used then, but the second stanza is new and the refrain is different (with alleluia also as an alternative as always in the Easter season). These changes throw the emphasis on the idea of waiting for God to act (the refrain), and the notion of life in a praying community in the pause between ascension and Pentecost.

Reading II: 1 Peter 4:13-16.

The theme of waiting for the Spirit, which used to be expressed in the old epistle for this Sunday (1 Pt 4:7-11 in the Roman Missal and the Anglican and Lutheran books) is unfortunately lost in the new selection. One wonders what is gained by the change.

This lesson, unlike the old one, takes us into the second half of 1 Peter, which appends to the baptismal homily a warning of imminent persecution. It comes from a period (under Nero? Domitian? Trajan?) when it was beginning to be considered a crime to be Christian. Christianity was by now recognized as a religion distinct from Judaism but was not classified as a *religio licita.* Consequently Christians now had to suffer "for the name" at the hands of the state.

Gospel: John 17:1-11a.

This reading is taken from the so-called high priestly prayer attributed to the Johannine Christ at the Last Supper. Some commentators, including Westcott and Hoskyns, have preferred to call it the prayer of consecration, because in this prayer the Johannine Christ is consecrating himself for his redemptive death. He is offering himself to the Father as an obedient sacrifice, for in John "hour" means the hour of the passion. Also he prays that through his death the Father and the Son may be glorified, in other words that the Father's redemptive purpose may be accomplished in the Son. This redemptive purpose is defined as the giving of eternal life to those whom the Father has "given" to the Son. A parenthesis or a sort of footnote by the evangelist himself further defines eternal life as knowledge of the Father and the Son. In the Johannine concept of eternal life the emphasis lies not on that life's duration, but on its quality — a life of communion with the Father and the Son.

After the parenthesis the prayer resumes with the theme of glorification, in the typically Johannine spiral fashion. But the idea is enlarged to include the earlier life of Jesus, prior to the cross, and the further thought that the glory Christ receives at his exaltation is a resumption of the glory of his preexistent state. Thus the glory of the cross cannot be seen in isolation, but must be held together with the whole incarnate life, of which it is the ultimate expression, and with the preexistent life, which was a continuous act of God's self-communication and revelation.

In its second paragraph the prayer continues to look back on that earthly work, especially upon the revelation which Jesus had given to his disciples. In the Johannine scheme this must specifically refer to the farewell discourse at the Last Supper, since it is here that John gives Christ's teaching to the disciples — though it may also to some extent include the signs in which the disciples saw his glory (John 2:11; 6:68-69). But it is the words of Jesus that constitute the main content of his revelation. These words are the words which the Father had given previously to him. In receiving these words as the words of the Father, the disciples have come to believe that Jesus is sent from the Father — i.e., their response to the revelation which they have received takes the form of a christological affirmation.

All this is couched in Johannine language, yet it accurately reproduces what is true of the synoptic tradition, and indeed of the historical Jesus. Historically speaking, Jesus proclaimed the kingdom of God. This was the message he had received from his Father in his baptismal call. And when men responded to it in faith they "confessed" him, i.e., acknowledged his divine mission.

The last part of our excerpt turns from Jesus' ministry to the fate of the disciples after Jesus' departure. Having received Christ's revelation, they no longer belong to this world, but they still have to live in it. This expressed in Johannine language the same idea as the synoptic Jesus' eschatological saying at the Supper: "I will no longer drink of the fruit of the vine (implying that he was to leave them and that they would stay behind) until I drink it new in the kingdom of God (i.e., his glorification)." In that saying he consecrated himself in his departure from them as the effective means of their participation in the kingdom of God. Then, exactly following the pattern of the Johannine discourses, the prayer comes full circle, ending as it began. The opening words spoke of the hour of passion, the conclusion speaks of Jesus' coming to his Father.

The Homily.

It would seem most appropriate on this Sunday before Pentecost to take the picture of the disciples waiting in the upper room for the outpouring of the Spirit which is the result of Jesus' departure to the Father and his ensuing glorification. This departure and the outpouring of the Spirit enable his disciples to be at once *in* the world, not *of* the world, yet *for* the world, as Jesus had been during his earthly life. This picture should then be related to the life of the contemporary church, and the prayer, *Veni, Creator Spiritus*, made our prayer today.

PENTECOST

We have been informed that many parishes will in effect keep Pentecost on the Saturday evening before the feast and use the vigil readings. Hence our comments here.

SATURDAY EVENING

The new lectionary provides four alternative Old Testament passages for reading I — viz.: Gen 11:1-9, The Tower of Babel; Ex 19:3-8a, 16-20a, The Theophany at Mt. Sinai; Ez 37:1-14, Ezekiel's Vision of the Dry Bones; Jl 2:28-32, Joel's Prophecy of the Outpouring of the Spirit.

The first two passages were undoubtedly in the mind of the author of Luke-Acts when he wrote up the Pentecost story. He sees the preaching with tongues, which he interprets as the gift of foreign languages, as a sign of the gospel's transcendence of the divisions of mankind that resulted from the building of the tower of Babel. The gospel speaks to all men in their own language, and so restores the unity which had been broken by human sin. The catholic church is the advanced guard of reunited humanity. The exodus theophany is probably alluded to in the symbolism of the tongues of fire and the rushing wind. As we observed in our comments last year, the feast of Pentecost was interpreted in later Judaism as the celebration of the giving of the Law. The early church sees a contrast between the giving of the Law and the outpouring of the Spirit — a contrast already suggested by Jeremiah and Ezekiel, and expounded systematically in the Pauline writings.

The Joel prophecy is expressly cited in Peter's speech at Pentecost (Acts 2:17-21-Joel 2:28-32). In the prophet's vision the descent of the

Spirit was probably conceived in somewhat narrow, nationalistic terms. "All flesh" meant for Joel all of Israel. His point is that in the renewed, eschatological community the Spirit will not merely descend occasionally on charismatic leaders, like the judges, kings and prophets of old, but will be shared by all members of the community.

It is surprising that the Ezekiel passage is never expressly utilized in the New Testament, though it seems to underlie much of New Testament thought on the Spirit. Paul in particular associates the Spirit with resurrection, both Christ's resurrection (Rom 1:4) and the future resurrection of the faithful (Rom 8:11). But nowhere does the New Testament speak explicitly of the resurrection of the community as an event within history effected by the gift of the Spirit. Yet there can be no doubt the New Testament does understand the Christian community as the people of God, eschatologically renewed. This is evidenced by its appropriation of the titles and prerogatives used in the Old Testament for the community of the Old Covenant. The vision of Ezekiel has a special appeal today when there is so much concern for the church's renewal.

Responsorial Psalm: 104:1-2a, 24 and 35c, 27-28, 29c-30.
The same psalm is appointed for the Pentecost Sunday mass, and was commented upon last year. We could call special attention to the cosmic dimension of the Spirit's work which is emphasized in the refrain.

Reading II: Romans 8:22-27.
The first paragraph of this reading picks up the suggestion of the cosmic dimensions of the Spirit's work which, as we have just noted, is suggested by the refrain of the responsorial psalm. The Christian community is described as those who have the first fruits of the Spirit which seems to indicate that the whole cosmos is destined ultimately to be renewed by the same Spirit. Because, however, the Christians still exist in the body, they are still part of this creation, and as such they share its groanings, its longing for redemption. The epistle does not explicitly say so, but it would be consistent with Paul's apocalyptic expectations elsewhere, to infer that the redemption of our bodies means being clothed upon (2 Cor 5) with the spiritual body (1 Cor 15) and will coincide with the renewal of the whole cosmos, the new heaven and earth.

It is surprising to find Paul here equating "sonship" with the final redeemed state instead of thinking of it as a status already granted in baptism (contrast Gal 4:5-7). At first sight this looks like a flat contradiction. But Paul probably means that the final redemption will make plain what is true of the believers though in a hidden way already here and now. Cf. 1 John 3:2.

The second paragraph turns to the work of the Spirit within the community here and now. The Spirit helps the infirmity of our prayers by making intercession for us. What does he mean by "sighs too deep for words?" Some see here a reference to speaking with tongues, glossolalia, like that at Corinth. Another, more plausible interpretation is that the Spirit takes our inarticulate petitions, translates them into the divine language and presents them to God as prayer which is in his name and according to his will.

Gospel: John 7:37-39.
On the last day of Tabernacles there was a ceremony of drawing the water accompanied by the reading of Is 12:3. Some commentators think that this provides the background for Jesus' invitation to men to come to him to quench their thirst.

Two other interrelated questions are much discussed in connection with this passage. 1 What is the source of the quotation in v. 38? 2 Whose heart is referred to in the quotation, the believers of Christ? It seems best, with Fr. Raymond Brown, to take the "his" as Christ's and to see in the scripture an allusion to Moses striking the rock to produce water in the wilderness (cf. Paul's "That rock was Christ"). This brings the whole pronouncement into line with John's doctrine of the Spirit. The farewell discourses tell us that Jesus dies to make the Spirit available for his own. When his side is pierced after the crucifixion, water as well as blood comes out in symbolic fulfillment of this promise, while his conferral of the Spirit upon the eleven after his glorification on Easter Sunday night is its actual fulfillment. This gospel reading reminds us that the gift of the Spirit at Pentecost is the outcome of Christ's redemptive work. Easter and Pentecost are inseparable.

The Homily.
There is obviously a wealth of material for the homilist's use, all of it connected with the Spirit. Here are some of the possibilities, depending to some extent on the option followed for reading II.

1 The gift of the Spirit as the reversal of Babel suggests the universality of the Spirit-filled community. In a day of great international ten-

sions the church of Jesus Christ (even in Northern Ireland!) is the one fellowship which *can* transcend all human divisions — yet that affirmation comes as a judgment as well as a promise.

2 Spirit *versus* law. This topic can be highly relevant to our current discussion of situation ethics.

3 The Spirit as the power of the church's renewal (Ezekiel's vision).

4 The "democracy" of the Spirit. Not a gift for occasional leaders or outstanding persons in the community. Not confined to the hierarchy, but for "all flesh" — sons and daughters, old men and young men, manservants and maidservants, the simple believer as well as the most exalted churchman (Joel). (Remember the title of Newman's pamphlet, "On Consulting the Laity in Matters of Doctrine.")

5 The natural and cosmic dimensions of the Spirit's work (responsorial psalm and the first paragraph of reading II).

6 The Spirit as the organ of Christian prayer (Reading II, second paragraph).

7 The Spirit as the outcome of Christ's whole redeeming work, symbolized as the provision of living water (gospel).

The homilist will have to judge which of these suggested themes is relevant to local needs.

SUNDAY

The readings for Pentecost Sunday are the same every year and were commented on last year. Let us remind ourselves that, despite the narrative in Acts 2, we are not commemorating today a single definable event. The reading from Acts places the giving of the Spirit on the day of Pentecost, while the gospel puts it on Easter Day.

It is curious that the earliest account that we have of the events after Easter (1 Cor 15) does not mention the giving of the Spirit at all, despite the fact that doctrinally Paul clearly associates the gifts of the Spirit with the risen Lord. We suggested last year that the gift of the Spirit was not originally associated with a single occasion, but, even where not explicitly mentioned, was a regular feature of the resurrection appearances. We should, perhaps, not separate too sharply the events as the author of Luke-Acts tends to do in the interests of his schematization. We further suggested that perhaps the Pentecost story originated with the appearance to the more than five hundred brethren (1 Cor 15:5), since it is this appearance that marks the emergence of the church as a wider community than the original Twelve. Also Pentecost, historically speaking, marks the beginning of the kerygma. The epistle is the opening of Paul's discussion of glossolalia in the Corinthian community, and makes three points:

1 Jesus, the earthly, crucified one, is Lord. This is affirmed against the Corinthians' view that the cross was a transient and perhaps rather regrettable incident of the past.

2 There is a multiplicity of gifts of the Spirit: tongue-speaking is not even the most important, and all gifts have to be used for the common good.

3 This is because Christian faith involves community: the sacraments of baptism and the eucharist initiate into, and nourish, the life of the community, not just individual spiritual lives.

The Homily.

First Corinthians was written expressly to deal with the problems of a local congregation, and the kinds of problems that arose there constantly recur in one form or another. Consequently points 2 and 3 above should provide ample opportunity for the homilist to relate the teaching of the Apostle to the contemporary situation of church and congregation.

TRINITY SUNDAY

Last year we suggested that the doctrine of the Trinity (as distinct from triadic formulas and the triadic structure of the biblical experience of God) is implicit rather than explicit in scripture. What we observed then of the New Testament, viz., that the Spirit brings believers to faith in Jesus as the one in whom God has acted, is also true (*mutatis mutandis*) of the Old Testament. We see this in the theophany which is the subject of the first reading of this day.

Reading I: Exodus 34:4b-6, 8-9.

The first paragraph speaks of the theophany itself (Yahweh's proclamation of his name), while the second paragraph relates Moses' response to this theophany.

Later Judaism would have boggled somewhat at the suggestion that Yahweh himself "descended" and "passed by" in making this proclamation. Such crudely anthropomorphic ideas seemed inconsistent with his transcendence. Accordingly, various intermediaries were proposed as the agencies of the divine revelation, angels, the memra (word) or the Logos, the wisdom or the Spirit of Yahweh. These intermediaries paved the way for the Christian understanding of the incarnation and the Trinity. In revelation — whether the revelation of Sinai or the revelation in the Christ event — the transcendent deity goes forth out of the depths of his own being, in self-communication. He also creates the response to his self-revelation. This is the pattern of events that we find in the story of the theophany of Moses on Mount Sinai. It is a triadic pattern:

1 Yahweh in his own essential Being.
2 Yahweh going out of himself in self-communication.
3 Yahweh creating within the heart of Moses the response to this self-communication.

This triadic pattern corresponds to the New Testament formulation of God as Father, Son and Spirit. It is important for the Christian understanding of the Old Testament that Yahweh is not to be equated with the first person of the Trinity in Christian doctrine, but with all three persons. Or in the words of the so-called Athanasian creed (note that Yahweh-Lord!):

> The Father is Lord, the Son Lord: the Holy Ghost Lord.
> And yet there are not three Lords: but one Lord.

Responsorial Psalm: Daniel 3:29-30, 31, 32, 33, 34 (RSV); 3:52, 53, 54, 55, 56 (NAB).

This canticle, taken from the deutero-canonical portions of the Book of Daniel (and familiar to Episcopalians as the *Benedictus es*) is part of the Song of the Three Young Men, put into the mouths of Shadrach, Meshach and Abednego (=Ananias, Azarias and Misael) as they moved unscathed through Nebuchadnezzar's burning fiery furnace. The second half of the song is the *Benedicite, omnia opera*, also familiar as a canticle. It survives only in Greek, and it is impossible to say for certain whether it is of Hebrew or Aramaic origin. But in any case both parts of the song are impregnated with the liturgical language of the Old Testament psalms. The first stanza picks up the theme of the "name of God" from reading I. As we sing this song today we must remember that for us that name is the threefold name of Father, Son and Holy Spirit. This could be brought out by adding as a final couplet:

> Blessed art thou, O Father, Son and Holy Spirit,
> to be praised and highly exalted for ever.

Reading II: 2 Corinthians 13:11-13.

The Pauline letters were written to be read out at the Christian assembly. Here, as at the end of 1 Corinthians, this intention becomes perfectly clear: The conclusion of the letter leads into the celebration of the eucharist. Hence the exhortation to be at peace with one another and to express this by exchanging the holy kiss (which, in earlier times, as in some recent revisions of the liturgy, preceded the offertory rather than followed the canon). The triadic benediction would therefore fall naturally into place as the introduction to the eucharistic prayer (like the salutation before the *sursum corda* in later times).

There are several places in Paul's letters where a triadic understanding of Christian experience is presupposed (e.g., 1 Cor 12:4-6), but only here does he deliberately use a triadic formula. Elsewhere (*Anglican Theological Review*, April 1961) I suggested that this triadic formula has its roots in the so-called "apocalyptic trinity." Jewish apocalyptic writings sometimes speak of God, the Son of man and the angels, and this formula is carried into Christian usage as the Father, the Son (of man) and the angels (see Mk 13:32). Note, however, that the Pauline formula is not a bald dogmatic statement, but keeps close to the Christian experience: the *grace* of Christ, the *love* of God, and the *fellowship* (*koinonia*) of the Holy Spirit. It speaks of the experience of grace, love and koinonia. The order, Son, Father and Spirit, is striking, and again reflects the order of Christian experience. It is in Jesus Christ and his gracious life and death that we encounter the love of God, and this encounter leads to our incorporation into the redeemed community in which we participate in the common life of the Spirit.

Gospel: John 3:16-18.

This lesson was traditionally associated with the Pentecost season, having been used (including vv. 19-25) in the old lectionaries on Monday in Whitsun Week. It is a welcome reform to have this important pericope on a Sunday at least once every three years. For 3:16 is a succinct summary of the whole gospel in characteristic Johannine idiom.

Some may feel its use on Trinity Sunday implies a "binitarian" rather than trinitarian conception, for it mentions only Father and Son. A similar objection could have been raised against its traditional use on Whit Monday. But it is impossible to dissociate the gift of eternal life, which is the outcome of the sending of the Son, from the Spirit which is the Giver of life.

As a concluding comment on this passage let us cite some words from an essay on the "Liturgical Sermon," written by Canon M. R. Newbolt in the influential volume of Anglican essays called *The Parish Communion* in 1937:

"On a spring evening, as I passed through the Abbey gate at Chester, a street evangelist was declaiming his gospel in stentorian tones. 'God so loved the world that he gave us His Son; His only Son. That is what I have to say to you people of Chester. I do not know what you are going to do about it. God gave His Son! His only Son! Eternal Life!'— words hammered by the speaker into his audience with rhythmic, persistent repetition. 'Why,' I thought, 'can we not get this kind of simple gospel appeal inside the Cathedral? Must this message be given in the street, with an implied challenge to the official Church, outside the House of God, under its very walls?'

"Two days afterwards, while we were singing the solemn eucharist in the choir on Whit Monday, the nave of the Cathedral was packed with tourists, casual sight-seers, taking in the Cathedral as part of their day's outing. It happened that I remembered the street preacher; his words were still running in my head, but I had forgotten the opening of the Gospel for the day. It came with a shock of surprise when the Deacon from the chancel steps intoned 'God so loved the world that He gave His only begotten Son.' These very words, surrounded by what may have been unusual pageantry of lights and coloured vestments, may well have rung in the ears of some excursionist from the Potteries on that very Bank Holiday, as the street missioner's had done in mine."

The Homily.

All three of the lessons suggest that the homilist should expound the triune name, not as an abstract formula but as the basis of the biblical experience of God, both in the Old Testament and in the New Testament. Archbishop William Temple once remarked how the conclusion of the *Veni Creator* suggested at first sight that the end all and be all of Christian experience was the apprehension of a dogmatic formula:

> Teach us to know the Father, Son,
> And thee of both to be but one.
> That through the ages all along,
> This may be our endless song:
> Praise to thy eternal merit,
> Father, Son, and Holy Spirit.

But then, as he meditated on the Christian experience as expounded in St. John's gospel, he came to discover that the *Veni Creator* was talking about our participation in a rich life, the life in which God, as he is himself, discloses himself in Jesus Christ and enables those who accept him to participate in the koinonia of the Holy Spirit. This is the kind of thought the homilist will wish to impress upon the congregation today.

CORPUS CHRISTI

Last year we indicated certain Anglican reservations about this Sunday's provisions. Many Anglicans would use a set of propers provided for the Thanksgiving for the Institution of the Holy Communion on the previous Thursday, but few would want its propers to replace those of this Sunday. We also expressed some reservation about doctrinal feasts (but cf. also Trinity Sunday!) as opposed to the anamnesis of events in salvation history. Nevertheless, as we noted last year, the very genius of scripture ensures that the lessons set forth saving events rather than doctrines. And whatever the final disposition of *An Agreed Statement on Eucharistic Doctrine*, published by the Anglican-Roman Catholic International Commission may be,[1] one can at least go forward with the confidence that many of us talk what is very largely a common language about this subject.

Reading I: Deuteronomy 8:2-3, 14b-16a.

This passage comes from a recital of the events of the exodus and of the wanderings of the Israelites in the desert. It recalls especially the trials to which the people were exposed: hunger, thirst, fiery serpents and scorpions, and the provisions which Yahweh made to relieve them: the water from the rock and the manna. Paul himself treated the water from the rock and the manna as types of the two great Christian sacraments of baptism and the holy communion (1 Cor 10:1-4), and in the discourse of the bread from heaven in John 6, part of which will be read as the gospel of this day, the manna is likewise treated as the type of the eucharistic bread.

Responsorial Psalm: 147:12-13, 14-15, 19-20.

The same selection from Ps 147 is provided for the Second Sunday after Christmas, but was not used this year as there was only one Sunday between Christmas and Epiphany. It is appropriate for any festal occa-

[1] *Worship* 46 (January 1972) 2-5.

sion; but its particular relevance to Corpus Christi is the second line of stanza II: "He fills you with the finest of wheat."

Reading II: 1 Corinthians 10:16-17.

One might have expected that the epistle reading for this solemnity would be 1 Cor 10:1-4, in which Paul interprets the manna of Dt 8 typologically of the eucharist. Instead we have a eucharistic passage from a later point in the same chapter.

It is becoming the commonly accepted view that in v. 16 Paul is quoting a traditional eucharistic formula. This is indicated by the quite Jewish expression, "the cup of blessing." The verb "we bless" is also Jewish (*berakah*), and contrasts with Paul's usual preference for the Greek equivalent, "to give thanks" (*eucharistein*). The idea of "participation (*koinonia*) in the body/blood is probably also pre-Pauline though Hellenistic, and represents an exegesis of the bread and cup words. Koinonia has not merely a symbolic, but a strong realistic sense. "Body and blood" refer not to things in themselves, but to an event and a person, to Christ giving himself in his redemptive death. In the holy communion he offers real participation in himself as he gives himself to his sacrificial death. This language draws out explicitly the meaning of his words and actions at the Last Supper.

People have often wondered why the usual order, bread-cup, is reversed here, and have sometimes speculated that there were early communities which celebrated the eucharist in this order, cup-bread. This is hardly likely, for Paul himself cites another traditional formula in chapter 11 which has the normal order. Rather, the reversal must be explained from the fact that Paul wishes to give further comment of his own upon the bread-body word, and drops the cup-blood word out of the picture. For v. 17 has to be seen as Pauline comment. And it involves a remarkable shift of sense. The word body, used christologically and sacramentally in the traditional formula, is now taken up in an ecclesiological sense. The body is now not the bread but "we," the community which participates in Christ's sacramental body in the Supper. "Participation in Jesus and his (sacramental) body" becomes identical with incorporation into the Church as the Body of Christ" (Ernst Käsemann). Doubtless Paul is led to this exegetical step because of the difficulties at Corinth, which he will elaborate upon in the next chapter. The Corinthians held an all too individualistic attitude toward the eucharist. For them it was a guarantee of personal salvation. For Paul, however, it binds a man not only to Christ but also to his neighbors, to the Christian community, with all the obligations that entails. The eucharist has a horizontal as well as a vertical direction.

It was this passage that inspired St. Augustine to write his well-known words: "If you wish to understand the body of Christ, hear the Apostle speaking to the faithful, 'Now ye are the body and members of Christ.' If you then are the body and members of Christ, your mystery is laid on the Table of the Lord, your mystery you receive" (Letter 272).

Gospel: John 6:51-58.

The bread discourse from John 6 has been much discussed in recent years. The problems are:

1 Is the whole discourse eucharistic?
2 Are only vv. 51c-58 eucharistic?
3 Are vv. 51c-58 a later addition to the text?

It is clear that v. 51c represents a turning point in the discourse. The first part speaks throughout of the bread from heaven as typified by the manna. "Eating" will then be a metaphor for faith. The word "flesh," introduced for the first time in v. 51c *could* also refer to the incarnation rather than to the eucharist, though the words "shall give for the life of the world" extend the thought beyond the incarnation itself to the atoning death. But when we get to v. 53, which speaks not only of eating the flesh but also of drinking the blood of the Son of man, the eucharistic reference is beyond all doubt. This has led Bultmann to regard vv. 51c-58 as an interpolation by an ecclesiastical redactor.

In the view of the present writer the discourse is to be viewed as an integrated whole, without resort to the interpolation hypothesis. The background of the whole chapter is the early church's celebration of the eucharist proper in the context of a meal. The first part of the discourse, down through v. 51b, which focusses on the bread from heaven, is, we would suggest, a meditation on the agape. The second half, 51c-58, is a meditation on the eucharist proper, and is based on a Johannine tradition of the institution narrative.

Regarded from another perspective, the whole discourse outlines the events of salvation history, the coming of the Christ as the bread from heaven into the world in the incarnation (vv. 26-51b), the surrender of himself in his atoning death (51c), the availability of his surrendered life as the nourishment of the faithful in the holy communion (vv. 53-58). John does not regard the sacrament as a thing in itself, detached from the total saving event of Christ, but as the means by which this saving event is constantly made available for present participation in the life of the church. We note, too, how in Johannine idiom the double aspect of the eucharist expressed in the earlier institution narratives (Paul and the synoptists) is preserved. The eucharist makes the past present for participation ("flesh and blood" referring back to Christ's death on Calvary), and it makes the future ("I will raise him up at the last day," "will live because of me," and "will live forever") equally present: "*has* eternal life." Note also that the eucharistic part of the discourse does not lose sight of the manna typology: "not such as the fathers ate and died."

The Homily.

Two possibilities suggest themselves. The theme of manna runs like a thread through the Old Testament lesson, the psalm and the gospel. This can be related to the idea of the church as the pilgrim people of God, for whom the holy communion is indeed a *viaticum* as the manna was for the Israelites.

Alternatively, the homilist could address himself to the Pauline passage, and speak of the Lord's Supper as creative of community. Post-medieval western piety, whether Reformation, Counter-Reformation or pietistic, had in various ways individualized the eucharist in theology and practice. In one tradition the mass became the occasion for individual recitation of the rosary. In another, the "quiet early service" was the occasion when the devout individually "tanked up" with grace. In yet another tradition the Lord's Supper became a duplicate of penance and absolution. Much of the resistance to the liturgical changes we are experiencing today is due to the fact that these changes seek to express the corporate dimension of the Lord's Supper. Our participation in the sacramental body of Christ means we must express ourselves as his ecclesial body. We who are many become one body in him. The Pauline teaching on the corporate nature of the eucharist — the two senses of Corpus Christi — needs to be brought out in many places today, just as it has been overworked in other places at the expense of personal devotion.

TENTH SUNDAY OF THE YEAR[2]

Let us first remind ourselves that in the Sundays of the year the New Testament readings are arranged in course. Just now we are reading Romans and Matthew. The Old Testament readings usually connect either with the epistle or with the gospel.

[2] Comments on Sunday 9 A will be found in the Appendix, below.

Reading I: Hosea 6:3-6.

As the caption shows, this passage is chosen for the sake of the final couplet: "I desired steadfast love and not sacrifice," which is cited in the gospel.

The prophets denounced the practice of sacrifice unaccompanied by obedience. But they did not denounce sacrifice as such. "I desire A and not B" is the Hebraic way of saying what the priorities should be: "I desire love more than sacrifice." It is noteworthy that despite the prophetic protest sacrifices still went on — in fact, they were actually elaborated after exile. Both the prophetic protest and the sacrifices were necessary, and the continuance of both side by side witnessed to important elements of the truth. What God really wants is obvious — the total commitment of man's life to him. But it is less obvious that man can achieve this of himself. The continuance of the sacrifices was a witness to the need for the provision of the perfect sacrifice which would make possible for man the obedience which the prophets demanded. It pointed forward to the justifying deed of God of which reading II speaks.

Responsorial Psalm: Ps. 50:1, and 8, 12-13, 14-15.

Psalm 50, like Psalms 40 and 51, reflects the prophetic protest against sacrifices divorced from moral obedience. But as with Hos 6, it is very easy to misconstrue its meaning. At first glance it looks as though God does not want any cultic sacrifice at all, but only heartfelt thanksgiving, as Hosea seemed to imply when he said that God only wanted steadfast love. But again we are confronted with a Hebraic manner of speech. The protest is not against sacrifice as such, but against crude ideas of sacrifice — as though sacrifices could somehow secure the favor of God, as though, even more crudely, God needed sacrifices for his physical sustenance. In place of this the psalmist proposes that what God really looks for is the "sacrifice of thanksgiving." This is the Old Testament peace offering (Lv 3:1-16, etc.) accompanied by heartfelt thanks.

Reading II: Romans 4:18-25.

In this section Paul is offering scriptural support for his doctrine of justification by faith (shorthand for justification by the grace of God manifested in Jesus Christ and apprehended by faith). He does this by taking the story of Abraham as an example. When God promised Abraham that he would become the father of many nations, he was 100 years old and his wife Sarah 90 years. But Abraham took God at his word, being "fully convinced that God was able to do what he had promised." Similarly, faith in the gospel means faith in God's ability to do for us what we cannot do for ourselves, i.e., put us right with him, make us justified in his sight. This justifying faith accepts the fact that in the death and resurrection of Jesus Christ God has done for us what we could not do for ourselves.

Gospel: Matthew 9:9-13.

There are two unique features in Matthew's version of this story as contrasted with that of Mark. (It is usually in these unique features, the evangelist's "redaction" as it is referred to nowadays, that the evangelist's distinctive message is found, and it is to such points that the preacher will want to turn his attention.) The first is, his alteration of the name Levi to Matthew. Of course, to the precritical approach, this occasions no problem: Levi and Matthew were both names of the same person, and the author was simply referring to his own call. But the modern critical approach sees the Gospel of Matthew as the outcome of a long process of oral tradition and as a combination of earlier documents, not as direct eye-witness. So Matthew must have had some theological reason for changing the name. Now the name Matthew occurs in Mark's list of the Twelve (Mk 3:18). It seems therefore that Matthew wishes to interpret this story as the call of one who subsequently became a member of the Twelve, and one of the Twelve was a social outcast. To be an apostle is a matter of *sola gratia*.

The second change which Matthew makes to his Marcan source is the addition of the citation of Hos 6:6 in 9:13. Commonly this is taken here to mean that God wants us to keep the moral law, but does not care about the ritual. However, not only does that do violence to the original Hosea (see above: in any case the New Testament sometimes does not scruple to do violence to the original meaning). More than that, "the inferior assessment of the ceremonial law is foreign to Judaism" (G. Barth). What then is the meaning? It is surely that Jesus' action in eating with the outcast is an actualization of God's mercy (Hebrew *chesed*). It is the ultimate answer to all that the Jewish law of sacrifices had stood for: man's utter helplessness before God, his inability to achieve his own salvation. Thus the three readings and the responsorial psalm all fit together in a remarkable way.

The Homily.

It is clear that this Sunday's preaching text should be "I desire steadfast love (mercy), not sacrifice." The homilist should guard against the anti-cultic interpretation of the prophetic protest against sacrifice, showing that God did intend the sacrifices of the old law to continue, but accompanied by obedience and true devotion. Yet man was unable fully to offer the sacrifice of obedience which God really required. So Christ offered this sacrifice by enacting the mercy of God in his eating with the outcast and by dying for our sins and rising for our justification.

When these ideas have been gathered from all three readings, they can be applied as a critique of that kind of Pelagianism which recurs in one form or another in every generation, and which is so common today: that God does not particularly care whether we go to church or not so long as we live a decent life. It is not so much a matter of going to church, but of receiving the justifying mercy of God which alone renders it possible for us to offer that mercy (steadfast love) to others.

ELEVENTH SUNDAY OF THE YEAR

Reading I: Exodus 19:2-6a.

We have noted previously that during the Sundays of the year the Old Testament reading is selected to go either with reading II or with the gospel. All three lessons today contain interesting and significant material, but there does not seem to be any common theme running through them. The nearest one can get to such a theme is that the people of God is presented under a series of images: a kingdom of priests and a holy nation (reading I), the sheep of his flock (responsorial psalm; for a comment of this see the Easter IV notes, series C), a people reconciled to God through the death of his Son (reading II) and a people established by the mission of the Twelve.

The passage from Ex 19 provides the Old Testament background of the hymn about the church which is embedded in 1 Pt 2:1-10, which was used on Easter 5 A and commented upon in the previous chapter. Taken together these two passages form a classical treatment of the priestly nature of the whole church, about which the New Testament has more to say than about the priestly character of the church's ministry.

Reading II: Romans 5:6-11.

The opening verses of this reading were very important for Nygren's *Agape and Eros.* This was a one-sided book, but it had a real point. It contrasted the two concepts of love denoted by the two Greek words in the title, *agape* being biblical and *eros* pagan. *Agape* means the love entirely uncaused by the attractiveness of its object, whereas *eros* is essentially a love evoked precisely by the object's attractiveness. The one is completely selfless, the other essentially self-regarding. Although we would not, with Nygren, exclude *eros* from the man-God relationship (it is surely capable of being redeemed), what he says about the love of God in the light of our pericope is profoundly true: God sent his Son to die for the ungodly, while we were yet sinners.

Another point, which Bultmann has emphasized in connection with this passage, is the event-character of God's love. It is not just a vague idea or a benevolent sentiment, not just a vague conviction that God will keep us free from harm. It happened quite concretely in the event of the cross. It is not an inference about the universe. In fact, what we observe about the universe may very well appear entirely to contradict the love of God. Only through the cross, only through our justification and reconciliation by his blood, by the event of his self-giving death, do we know that God is love. Charles Wesley's well-known hymn "Jesus, lover of my soul" is about Christ's self-giving on the cross as the event of our justification and reconciliation.

The passage finishes with a double *a fortiori* argument. First, since we have already been justified and reconciled, how much more shall we be saved (at the day of judgment) from the wrath of God. "Wrath of God" does not mean capricious anger, but the alienation from a holy God, which is the consequence of sin, a process which reaches its culmination at the day of judgment. The fact that we are already justified and reconciled gives us confidence that we shall not be finally and eternally alienated from God. The second *a fortiori* argument concerns life between now and the last judgment — we may continue to rejoice in God who has reconciled us through Christ.

Gospel: Matthew 9:36-10:8.

The historicity of the mission of the disciples during Jesus' lifetime has been recently questioned, on the supposition that it involves reading back into the lifetime of Jesus the missions of the post-Easter church. Certainly the church's interest in this story and its preservation must have been due to the fact that she continued such missions after Easter. But their historicity to the early ministry of Jesus is clinched by the fact that the message the disciples are given to preach is the message of the earthly

Jesus ("The kingdom of heaven is at hand"), not the church's post-Easter message of Christ's death and resurrection. Yet the restriction of the mission to Israel *may* reflect the hesitations of the post-Easter Jerusalem church over the extension of the mission to the Samaritans and Gentiles (cf. Acts). But for Matthew this restriction was only temporary and limited to Jesus' earthly life, as Matthew ends his gospel with the great missionary charge, "Go and make disciples of *all* nations" (28:19). Thus he has the same perspective as the fourth gospel, which has the saying, "I, *if I be lifted up*, will draw all men to myself" (12:32), and of Ephesians, which says that it is only through the cross that the barrier between Jew and non-Jew is broken down (Eph 2:14-16). Historically speaking, this was in fact so: Jesus' earthly mission was confined almost exclusively to his own people as even Paul admits (Rom 15:8). Only after the death of the Messiah did the mission become universal in its scope.

The Homily.

The lack of any clear, consistent theme running through today's reading makes the homilist's choice a difficult one. Here are some suggestions.

If on Easter V this year the homilist did not develop the theme of the priesthood of the whole church, he might do this today. This would provide him with an opportunity to relate the ministerial priesthood to the priesthood of all believers.

The epistle reading offers an opportunity to clear up some popular confusion about what Christianity means when it speaks of the love of God. This is not a deduction about the way the universe is ordered, but a confession of faith arising from our confrontation with the death of Christ on the cross as the ground of our justification and reconciliation. Sir Edwyn Hoskyns used to say that the first letter of John was able to make the great affirmation that God is love only at the end of the New Testament period, only after what he (Hoskyns) loved to call "the turmoil" of the Epistle to the Romans. It is not a self-evident truth or a premise of the faith.

The gospel would offer an opportunity to speak of the mission of the church. A church which claims to be apostolic is a church "sent out" to preach and to bring men and women liberation from their ills. The homilist would have a chance to identify what the mission of the church should be on the local scene — precisely at what points men and women and children locally cry out for liberation.

TWELFTH SUNDAY OF THE YEAR

Reading I: Jeremiah 20:10-13.

This reading is clearly chosen to match the gospel, which speaks of the persecution which the apostles will encounter on their mission. Jeremiah was pre-eminently the prophet who suffered persecution because of his prophetic activity. His fate influenced the development of the later Jewish view that rejection, persecution and martyrdom were inseparable to the prophetic vocation, a view echoed in a number of dominical sayings (Lk 11:51, 13:33-34; Mk 12:1-9). To be a bearer of the word of God means to suffer because that word inevitably encounters hostility and rejection. It is illuminating that apparently, according to the sayings just referred to, Jesus regarded his own fate as the culmination of the rejection of the prophets and their message. But perhaps it was Paul who, more than any other New Testament figure, regarded Jeremiah as a model for his own apostleship. Certainly Paul regarded suffering as the supreme manifestation of the cross in his own apostolic ministry (cf. esp. the catalogues of his sufferings in 2 Cor 4:7-12, 6:3-10, 11:22-33).

Responsorial Psalm: 69:7-9, 13 and 16, 32-34.

Psalm 69 is one of the great passion psalms of the Old Testament, second only to Ps 22 in its influence upon the passion narratives of the gospels. Of the present selection, the final couplet of stanza I is cited by the fourth gospel in connection with the cleansing of the temple (Jn 2:17). If the church applied it to the Lord's passion, it is equally applicable in today's liturgy to the fate of Jeremiah.

Reading II: Romans 5:12-15.

In Rom 5–8 Paul is expounding the liberating effect of Christ's redemptive deed — it brings freedom from wrath, from sin, from the law as a means of salvation, and from death. Here the Apostle enunciates our liberation from sin and death by a comparison of Christ and Adam. Each wrought a deed with momentous consequences:

Adam	*Christ*
disobedience (=trespass)	obedience (death of the cross)
sin ⎫	⎧ free gift, grace
death ⎭ spreading to the many	⎨ life

Although there is an antithetical correspondence (Adam is called the "type" of Christ), the correspondence is transcended in a "much more."

The caption at the head of the lesson is unfortunately ambiguous: "nothing like" could suggest that our sin is much greater than God's grace. But Paul means it the other way round: God's grace is much greater than our sin. It was easy enough to introduce sin and death upon the *tabula rasa* of human life, but much more difficult to eradicate them after they had been introduced.

We have to guard against reading later theological ideas into Paul's statement about the fall. He does not say that Adam introduced a hereditary taint into human life which is henceforth transmitted biologically. Death, we are told, spread to all men not because Adam sinned, or because we sinned "in Adam," but because all men sinned like Adam. Adam, as it were, opened the door to sin and death: ever since they have been prowling around, and every man has fallen under their clutches because he has succumbed to sin. Adam created the environment in which all would sin and would therefore come under the dominion of death. Nor must we interpret the passage so as to mean that physical death is in a crude and mechanical sort of way a punishment for sin, even for actual sin. (If it is punishment for "original sin" such a view is even more deterministic, and ultimately gnostic.) Rather, "death" is to be understood theologically, as the *theological consequence* of sin. Death means separation from God, and separation is the consequence of sin. Physical death is not a punishment but a biological inevitability. For man, however, it is existentially the final revelation of his utter aloneness in a world in which he has cut himself off from God by sin.

Gospel: Matthew 10:26-33.

This is a continuation of the Matthean missionary charge to the Twelve, the beginning of which we read last week. As already indicated, this is a challenge to fearless proclamation in face of persecution and an assurance of God's care for his witnesses and of their ultimate vindication.

The first saying ("there is nothing covered") occurs in various contexts in the synoptists. Here it is applied to the apostolic preaching. Its original application (cf. Mk) was probably eschatological: the kingdom of God, which is operative in a hidden way in Jesus' ministry, will at the end be made visible to all who see.

Matthew is rather fond of the body/soul contrast, which is not typical of scripture. It represents popular Hellenistic language, not a systematically thought out anthropology. Who is the one who can cast into

Gehenna (RSV hell)? The Father? Christ? Satan? All three interpretations have found their advocates. The context, however, suggests that Matthew refers it to the Father — for it is the Father who is able to let the sparrows fall to the ground. The protection of the witnesses is contingent upon their faithful testimony. "You are of more value" is not a general statement about the value of human personality, it is an assurance for the messengers: while they are on duty delivering their message, they will be guarded — but even this does not exclude martyrdom. One way or another, the message will be delivered. That is what is important.

In other synoptic versions of the final saying (v. 33) a distinction is drawn between Jesus and the Son of man — though the relation between the two figures is one of functional identity. For the earlier tradition, Jesus was a figure on earth, the Son of man a transcendent figure in heaven. The resurrection revealed their identity, and Matthew carries this to its logical conclusion by substituting "I" for the Son of man on the transcendent side. The apostle's testimony on earth, whether given or shirked, will determine his fate at the end. The whole section is an exhortation to faithful and courageous testimony even in the face of suffering and persecution, presumably a very revelant message for Matthew's church.

The Homily.

Two possibilities for homiletical treatment appear to present themselves. One is the integral relation between witness and suffering (Jeremiah in the first reading, the apostles in the gospel). A church built upon the foundation of the prophets and apostles must be a witnessing and, if necessary, suffering church. This could be brought down to the level of the local congregation in a quite concrete manner.

The second possibility is much more theological. It would be an exposition of what Paul really says about the sin of Adam and its consequences for us, an attempt to disabuse people from crude notions of physically transmitted taint which leave little room for individual responsibility for sin, and on the other side a Pelagian denial that man is seriously tainted by a fallen nature. To prepare himself for this subject the preacher would have to study some modern systematic theology. Among Protestant authors in this field we would recommend Brunner's *Man in Revolt* or Niebuhr's Gifford Lectures, *The Nature and Destiny of Man.*

Reading I: 2 Kings 4:8-11, 14-16a.

The provision of hospitality by the Shunammite woman for the prophet Elisha is one of the more engaging episodes of the Old Testament. The caption fails to indicate the evident reason for its selection for this Sunday. Clearly it was chosen because it illustrated the dominical saying in the gospel: "He who receives a prophet because he is a prophet shall receive a prophet's reward."

What the historian of the Book of Kings means when he speaks of a holy man of God is shown by the other woman's reaction to Elisha's predecessor Elijah after he had restored her son to life: "Now I know that you are a man of God, and that the word of the Lord in your mouth is truth." (1 Kgs 17:24). In other words, to be a holy man of God in the Old Testament does not signalize mystical achievement but means to be the bearer of God's word — a word which is "truth," i.e., not that it passes the test of doctrinal orthodoxy, but that it effects what it says on the plane of history. Similarly, Elisha is a holy man of God not because of the achievements of his piety, but because he, like his predecessor, was entrusted with the effective word of Yahweh, to proclaim to his generation.

Responsorial Psalm: 89:1-2, 15-16, 17-18.

These verses come from one of the great messianic psalms of the Old Testament which portray the coming of the ideal davidic king. Understandably, it is a psalm which the Christian tradition has associated with the Christmas season. (It provided the offertory for the third mass of Christmas in the Roman Missal, and in the Book of Common Prayer has always been the proper psalm at one of the offices of Christmas Day.) The last stanza of this selection alludes to the messianic king. But this aspect is not stressed today. It is simply a hymn of praise for the steadfast love and faithfulness (*chesed w^emeth*, very important Hebrew words characterizing Yahweh's being and actions). No doubt the Shunammite woman regarded the visits of Elisha to her home as signs of Yahweh's steadfast love and faithfulness.

Reading I: Romans 6:3-4, 8-11.

This passage is used in full at the Easter vigil, and was commented on last year at that point. We remind the reader of what we said then, namely that while the references to the Christian's dying with Christ are all in the past tense, the references to resurrection are future and conditional. The new life in Christ is something that has to be constantly implemented. The Christian life means more than aspiring after an elusive ideal. What happened to us in baptism cannot be made to unhappen, however frequently we stumble and fall. The reality of baptism is always there. Luther, when he was tempted to despair of his faith, used to repeat *baptizatus sum.* That is something we too can always draw upon. So the Christian life is fitting oneself into that which we have already been made by baptism: *Werde das, was Du bist,* Become what you are!

Gospel: Matthew 10:37-42.

This is the last installment of the Matthean missionary charge to the Twelve. It embraces three complexes of material: 1. The warning that discipleship may involve the breaking of family ties. 2. The saying about taking up the cross. 3. A group of three sayings about the reception given to messengers.

The first two clearly go together. Both concern the cost of discipleship. They appear in various contexts in the gospel tradition, and only in this passage as part of a missionary charge. The first saying in the third group is found both in Matthew and Luke (in Luke in a different context); the second is peculiar to Matthew and the third is found also in Mark. The fact that the second saying (about receiving a prophet, v. 41) governs the choice of reading I suggests that this is the saying to which we should pay particular attention today. It is a challenge to those who hear the message of the envoys to receive them properly — not for the sake of their persons, but because they are the bearers of the divine message. What this passage has in mind may be illustrated from the words which St. Paul used when speaking of his reception by the Thessalonians: "When you received the word of God which you heard from us, you accepted it not as the word of man but as what it really is, the word of God, which is at work in you believers" (1 Thes 2:13).

The Homily.

The emphasis thrown upon the latter part of the gospel by the choice of the first reading suggests what the subject today should be: the proper reception of Christ's messengers. Priests and ministers have to be trained to preach — it involves particularly the study of biblical exegesis, so that the sermon may become, not the utterance of human opinions, but the authoritative declaration of the word of God enshrined in scripture. But there is also a responsibility laid upon the hearers. They, too, have to be trained what to look for in a sermon, to apply the right criteria, to look not for eloquent speech, but for a clear declaration of the word of God based upon a sound exegesis of the text. A homily on the responsibility of listening would be in order today.

As an alternative, the homilist might take up the Pauline teaching on baptism in reading II and stress the nature of the Christian life under the rubric of "become what you are."

✓FOURTEENTH SUNDAY OF THE YEAR

Reading I: Zechariah 9:9-10.

This passage is often associated with Palm Sunday for obvious reasons. Here it is used to complement the pericope called "The cry of jubilation," which forms today's gospel. When our Lord rode into Jerusalem on Palm Sunday his action was not a sudden inspiration, but something wholly in character with his previous ministry, his self-identification with the lowly.

Responsorial Psalm: 145:1-2, 8-9, 10-11, 13cd-14.

The same selection from Ps 145 was used on the thirty-first Sunday of the year, series C, and commented on there. If it is not chosen here as a general psalm of praise, it must have been selected as a response to the challenge in reading II, "Rejoice greatly, O daughter of Zion. Lo, your *king* comes to you," which is taken up in the words, "I will extol thee, O God and King." This would mean transferring to Christ what in the Old Testament is addressed to Yahweh, but there is ample New Testament precedent for such procedure.

Reading II: Romans 8:9, 11-13.

It is important to know what Paul means by "flesh and spirit." The New English Bible has perpetuated the misunderstanding of flesh as "lower nature." It is not lower nature (a Greek rather than biblical concept), but unredeemed nature, which includes what the Greeks would have called the higher nature (hence Paul can speak of the "mind of the flesh"). The whole man, his so-called higher nature as well as his lower, stands in need of redemption. Also, "body" does not mean body as opposed to soul, but the whole man, subject to sin and death, yet open to the possibility of redemption. "Lower nature" would suggest that there is a part of our nature which is beyond redemption, just as "higher nature" suggests there is a part of us which needs no redemption.

Gospel: Matthew 11:25-30.

The first half of this reading (through v. 27) is also found in Luke, and apparently comes from the common source which both evangelists share. It is therefore quite an early tradition, and sometimes called the "synoptic thunderbolt from the Johannine sky." It looks so different from most of the synoptic material and is highly reminiscent of the discourses and the prayers of the fourth gospel, especially the theme of the mutual knowledge of the Father and the Son. It is probably best understood as a liturgical fragment celebrating the knowledge of God which has come through Jesus Christ and is a half-way house toward the development of the Johannine discourses. But it is deeply rooted in our Lord's self-understanding, as registered by his use of the word Abba for his Father. This betokens a unique relationship, which he invites others to share through his word.

The second part of the pericope is peculiar to Matthew. It echoes the invitation of wisdom found in Sir 51:23-26 and is also found in a shorter (and perhaps earlier) form in the gospel of Thomas: "Jesus said: Come to me, for easy is my yoke and my Lordship is gentle and you shall find repose for yourselves." It is another liturgical fragment. In it Jesus is represented as the mouthpiece of the wisdom of God. This is quite an early type of church Christology, which again has its roots in the self-understanding of Jesus.

The Homily.

The combination of the Old Testament reading and the Matthean form of the cry of jubilation with the Saviour's invitation highlights the theme of Jesus' humbling of himself to bring the wisdom of God to men. A meditation on the humiliation of the incarnation would be in order, and perhaps an extension of this motif to the interpretation of the church as the bearer of the revelation of the truth of God in the world today. If the church is to follow the pattern of her divine Master, she must witness to the truth not by authoritarian demeanor but by humble testimony and suffering for the truth's sake.

An alternative for the homilist would be an exposition of Paul's doctrine of man. This should seek to correct the common misunderstanding of flesh as lower nature, and to emphasize that the whole man is both in need of redemption and redeemable.

Sundays 15 A to 24 A ✓

Reading I: Isaiah 55:10-11

It is a little surprising that the caption calls attention solely to the pictorial half of our pericope. This is not a piece of teaching about the natural order. Rather, the natural order is here used to provide an analogy for the supernatural: "*as* the rain . . . *so* my word." This lesson provides an Old Testament prototype for the parable of the sower, which likewise consists of the same pictorial and material sides: "as the seed . . . so the word."

Responsorial Psalm: 65:9abcd, 9e-10, 11-12, 13

This psalm, as the response indicates, forms a link between the Old Testament lesson and the gospel. It picks up the pictorial side of the analogy, and praises God for the gift of the rain. Commentators are divided over the original use of this psalm. Some have associated it with the autumn harvest festival (cf. the first line of stanza 3) — and indeed it is still so used in many churches. It is more likely, however, that it was intended for the beginning of the barley harvest: the rains are still falling (stanzas 1 and 2) and the grain is still standing in the fields (stanzas 3 and 4). It is certainly very fitting for use in this time of year. In the parched land of Judah the rain served as an obvious symbol of the grace of God.

Reading II: Romans 8:18-23

The present reading is familiar from its occurrence in the old lectionary at Pentecost IV (Roman Missal) or Trinity IV (Book of Common Prayer). Here Paul expounds his view of the created order. It is, as the Old Testament affirms, the creation (*ktisis*, v. 19), i.e., it owes its being to God and

223

was therefore good. But it became subject to futility (v. 20); it is in bondage to decay (v. 21) and "groans" (v. 22).

Paul is not a romantic nature worshiper but a realist who recognizes "nature red in tooth and claw." He attributes this lamentable state of affairs to Adam's fall. The basis for this assertion lies in Gn 3:17, where the ground is cursed because of Adam's sin. The creation, Paul says, was thus subjected not of its own will, but "because of him who brought it under subjection." Most commentators identify "him" here with God, but some refer it to Adam. In the latter case Adam through this fall dragged down the whole created universe with him. Some commentators would remove the colon after "hope" and translate the word for "because" (*hoti*) as "that." The whole sentence could then be paraphrased: "the creation was subjected to futility, not because of any wrong it had done itself but by the [disobedience] of Adam who thereby dragged it down into subjection. But there was still a hope of its ultimate liberation." Where did this hope come from? It must lie not in Gn 3 but in the apocalyptic expectation of a new heaven and a new earth. So the whole creation waits with eager longing. Just as its fall, its state of corruption and decay, was the consequence of man's fall, so the hope of its redemption is bound up with man's redemption. Its longing is therefore longing for the redemption of man, for the "revealing of the sons of God" (v. 19), for the redemption of their bodies (v. 23). Now this longing has been given substance — believers, as a result of Christ's finished work of redemption, have the first fruits of the Spirit. In them the process of redemption, for which the whole creation yearned, has already been initiated. But meanwhile they have to live in the tension between the "already" and the "not yet"; and therefore they, too, still share the groaning of the whole creation. (With some ancient manuscripts we omit "adoption as sons" in v. 23, for elsewhere (Rom 8:15; Gal 4:5) Paul regards adoption as a present reality. At the moment their sonship is hidden, and visible only to faith. But it will be revealed for what it is at the end, not brought into being only then for first time (cf. v. 19, also 1 Jn 3:2).

This picture of the unity between man's destiny and the destiny of the universe is magnificent, but is it tenable? Certainly there are mythological elements in it — e.g., it depends on a literal acceptance of the story of the fall and of the cursing of the ground as its consequence. Is the perishability and decay of the universe really a consequence of man's sin? And does man's redemption equally lead to the redemption of the universe from this decay? This much we may affirm. As result of the disturbance of man's relationship to God not only his relationship to his fellow men, but also his relationship to the whole created order is disturbed. Either man deifies nature (pantheism, romanticism) or he treats it with contempt (pollution!). When man's relationship to God is restored, then not only is his relation to his fellows rectified as in the sacramental community, but then too he recovers his harmony with the created order. This much of truth we can discern in Paul's daring picture. Western thought, especially since the Reformation, has tended to concentrate upon the salvation of the individual: our passage is a powerful reminder of the cosmic dimension of redemption.

Gospel: Matthew 13:1-23 (long form); 13:1-9 (short form)

The short form of the gospel substantially represents the parable as originally told by Jesus. The discussion about the purpose of parabolic teaching (vv. 13-17) and the allegorical interpretation of the sower (vv. 18-23) are later interpretive additions. Most, though not all, New Testament scholars would agree that this is so. The arguments for this position have been vindicated by the discovery of the Gospel of Thomas, which has the parable without any interpretation. That being the case, the short form offers an opportunity to deal with the original interpretation. To understand the shorter form we must entirely disabuse our minds of the allegorical interpretation, and look at the total impression the story creates. What we see is a tremendous harvest despite the loss of some of the seed. The climax comes at the end, and as so often in Jesus' parables contains an element of deliberate absurdity: a hundredfold yield is fantastic, the usual yield being in the neighborhood of seven-and-one-half, with ten as an outside possibility. The point of the parable is miraculous success in spite of apparent frustration. But this is not a general lesson. It bears quite concretely upon the situation of Jesus and his hearers.

There was much frustration in Jesus' ministry. Only a few followed him. He encountered much hostility from the authorities of his day. He was misunderstood by the crowds. Even some of his closest followers left when he deliberately broke with the crowds (Jn 6:66). Jesus is confident, nevertheless, that his ministry will result in the eventual triumph of God's kingdom.

The allegorical interpretation (vv. 18-23) adapts the parable to a missionary situation, most likely that of the Greek-speaking church prior to Mark. It warns new converts of the perils that beset the life of discipleship, and urges upon them the need for perseverance.

The central portion on the purpose of parabolic teaching appears to have been first inserted at this position by Mark, although it represents earlier tradition, and is possibly an authentic Jesus saying. It referred originally not to the teaching in parables, but quite generally to the kingdom of God mysteriously present in the words and works of Jesus. Mark constructs a theory of his own about parabolic teaching. He holds that parables were told deliberately to create misunderstanding and to mystify the hearers, producing hardness of heart and unfaith. The parables are riddles to the outsiders, and their meaning is entrusted to an inner group of disciples who will be able to make the meaning plain only after the resurrection. This is all part of the apparatus of Mark's messianic secret. Only after the cross and resurrection can the messiahship of Jesus be safely proclaimed. During the earthly life it remains a mystery. This was not a piece of abstract theologizing, but Mark's answer to a Christology which overemphasized the miracles of Jesus and minimized the cross.

Matthew has taken over the parable and its allegorical interpretation from Mark without any substantial changes. But he has introduced considerable changes into the central section, and this is obviously the most important part to study if we are following the longer gospel. Matthew makes the following major alterations:

1. V. 11. Instead of Mark's "to you is given the mystery of the kingdom of God" Matthew has: "To you it is given to *know the mysteries*. . . ." The fact that Luke has the same wording shows that both evangelists are following a second, non-Marcan source at this point.

2. V. 12. He adds this from Mk 4:25.

3. V. 13. He alters Mark's scandalous *hina* ("in order that") to *hoti* ("because").

4. Vv. 14-15. Our present text includes a citation from Is 6, which was already alluded to in v. 13. There is a growing opinion among scholars that this is a post-Matthew addition to the text.

5. Vv. 16-17. "Blessed are the eyes" from Q (par. Lk 10:23-24).

To get at Matthew's theology we will ignore point 4 and concentrate on the other points. Matthew has edited this section to bring out two antithetical points: (a) the disciples (i.e., the church) are the bearers of the new revelation, hoped for by the Old Testament worthies and now fulfilled (v. 17), and will be rewarded at the end; (b) the old Israel has rejected the new revelation, and will be rejected at the end. The motivation behind these redactional changes comes from Matthew's own situation. The mission to Israel has finally failed, and led to a debate between church and synagogue over which is the true people of God.

The Homily

Much will turn on whether the shorter or the longer form of the gospel is read. If the shorter, then attention is drawn to the parable as it was originally told by Jesus. It envisaged a situation of frustration, and sought to assure the disciples of the ultimate triumph of the kingdom. Such a message could be transferred quite easily to the church's situation today, where once more there are many frustrations and apparent failures. The assurance of abundant success despite these failures is the message for today, and one on thorough conformity with the gospel's *theologia crucis*. Allusions to the other readings may be drawn in the rain yielding fruit in the first reading and the psalm, and the groaning of the community with the whole created universe, in the second reading.

If the long form of the gospel is used, then it directs the preacher to an exposition of the great privileges of the Christian community as the bearers of God's truth in the world. One would not, in our changed situation, want to point to the synagogue as the community which had but rejected the truth, nor, hopefully, the Protestant communities. But the longer gospel could perhaps be used as an indictment of our secularized, once Christian civilization. The hope for the final vindication of Christianity in v. 12 could be related to the similar thought of the final cosmic vindication in the second reading: the revealing of the sons of God and the redemption of their bodies.

SIXTEENTH SUNDAY OF THE YEAR ✓

Reading I: Wisdom 12:13, 16-19

The caption highlights the idea of repentance. It appears however from the gospel, the parables of the tares (weeds), that the real reason for the choice of this lesson was to reinforce the notion of God's forbearance: "Thou who art sovereign in strength dost judge *with mildness*, and with *great forbearance* dost thou govern us" (v. 18). God's care, it says, is for all men, even for the tares among the wheat. "Thy sovereignty over all causes thee to spare all" (v. 16).

Responsorial Psalm: 86:5-6, 9-10, 15-16a

This psalm of individual lament is remarkable for its confidence in the faithfulness and steadfast love of Yahweh, a confidence unshaken by present distress. If God's forbearance is the main theme of this day, this is a highly suitable psalm to go with the Old Testament reading and the gospel.

Reading II: Romans 8:26-27

We note that two verses (24-25) have been omitted between the end of last week's reading from Romans and the beginning of today's selection. This is because v. 26 picks up from v. 23. The inward groaning of those who possess the first fruits of the Spirit are assisted by the Spirit who intercedes for us "with sighs too deep for words" (v. 26 — the word for "sighs" is akin to "groanings"). Herein lies the clue to Paul's meaning. It is not that speech of the Holy Spirit is in itself encompassed with infirmity and therefore itself groans or sighs in an unintelligible fashion (e.g., in glossolalia). Rather, Paul's thought is that the Spirit condescends to take up our infirm prayers and bear them up to God and present them before him in the form of intelligible speech. Here the Spirit acts as a Paraclete or advocate as in the Fourth Gospel, although Paul does not actually use the word.

We habitually think of prayer in terms of "me down here" speaking to "God up there." But when I pray as a believer it is not just "me down here." It is the Spirit of God within me praying to the "God up there." Thus immanence and transcendence are both acted out in the activity of prayer. Thus, too, prayer is an activity in which the believer participates in the mystery of the Holy Trinity.

Gospel: Matthew 13:24-43 (long form); 13:24-30 (short form)

We continue today with another of the parables from Mt 13. Like the sower, the parable of the tares has undergone allegorization, and once again the short form gives the nonallegorized version which is very probably close to the form in which Jesus originally spoke it. There is a further similarity: in the long form the parable and its allegorical interpretation are separated by other materials. In this case the intervening material consists of two parables found elsewhere in the gospel tradition, namely the parable of the mustard seed, which occurs in Mark and Q (Mk 4:30-32; Lk 13:18-19), and the leaven, which is found in Q (par. Lk 13-20-21). These little parables are followed by a shortened form of Mark's conclusion to the parables (Mt 13: 34-35, par. Mk 4:33-34) and a fulfillment from Ps 78:2, which is both unique to and typical of Matthew. We thus once more have three levels in the tradition: 1. The parable of the tares, substantially as told by Jesus. 2. The parable of the tares with its allegorical interpretation. 3. The insertion of the complex of other materials between the parable and its interpretation, and the shift of the latter from a public to private location. The meaning of each of these levels may be constructed as follows:

1. Jesus is criticized by his purist contemporaries for inviting the outcast to eat with him as an anticipation of God's salvation. He answers by saying that it is for God to make the separation and that he will do so only at the end. Then it will be clear who are the wheat and who the tares. Doubtless there will be some surprises in store.

2. The allegorical interpretation applies the parable to the Christian community. There are tares as well as wheat in the church now — the church is a *corpus permixtum*, and there need be no premature attempt to separate the wheat from the tares in the present life of the church.

3. By sandwiching the intervening material between the parable and the interpretation and especially by shifting the scene from public to private teaching just before the interpretation, Matthew has applied this complex of material to the situation of his own church. As we saw last week, that situation is marked by disappointment over the failure of the mission to Israel. Now the church is assured that when the gospel came to Israel it came as a *parabole*, a *mashal*, a riddle (Ps 78:1). Only the church comprehends the riddle. The tares are presently indistinguishable from the wheat but at the end God will separate them. The church must meanwhile be patient.

There is a remarkable amount of continuity between the three interpretations — more so than in the case of the sower. At each level the point remains the forbearance of God. What changes is the identity of the wheat and the tares. For Jesus it was the outcast and the authorities of his people. For the church tradition it was the good and the bad within the Christian community. For the evangelist it was nonbelieving Israel and the members of his church.

The Homily

The main point which is hammered home in today's readings is obviously the forbearance of God — the Old Testament reading, the psalm and above all the parable of the tares at its successive levels of interpretation all make this point. The preacher is free to identify those areas in which his people need to recognize this forbearance in action in their midst, what group it is tempted to treat as tares. Having made the identification he can use the scriptural materials to speak to that situation.

Alternatively he may find it more appropriate to take the epistle, with its teaching about the Holy Spirit as the power of God within the believers who takes their inarticulate prayers and renders them intelligible before the throne of God. If there are prayer groups in the parish or if there is a great concern with the problems of prayer this would be a fitting theme for a homily.

SEVENTEENTH SUNDAY OF THE YEAR

Reading I: 1 Kings 3:5, 7-12

In the Hellenistic tradition wisdom meant philosophical speculation. In the Old Testament tradition on the other hand wisdom had much more mundane significance. It included a practical know-how in various areas of life as well as the knowledge of God and of good and evil.

First Kings 3-11 demonstrates Solomon's wisdom in many different spheres: as practical psychologist in the case of the two prostitutes (3:16-28), as administrator (ch. 4), as builder (chs. 5-7), a merchant (ch. 9). Our pericope relates how Solomon acquired this wisdom in a dream in which he prays for wisdom rather than for riches or for length of days. Wisdom is thus the supreme value of human life.

This lesson is evidently chosen because of the parables of the treasure and the pearl, which represent the kingdom of God as the supreme value for which no sacrifice is too great.

Responsorial Psalm: 119:57 and 72, 76-77, 127-128, 129-130

The wise man (note the last two lines in the final stanza) is the man who knows and keeps the commandments of Yahweh. The psalm is thus linked to the first reading. For the wise man loves the commandments of God "above gold" (stanza 3), as Solomon chose wisdom rather than riches, and as Jesus in today's gospel urges the crowd to seek the kingdom of God as a man would do everything to get hold of treasure trove or a pearl of great price. Thus the psalm is also linked to the gospel reading.

Reading II: Romans 8:28-30

In the readings from Rom 8 which were selected for the previous weeks, Paul has been speaking primarily of the suffering, the transitoriness and the infirmities of human existence, including the Christian existence. But again and again the hope of ultimate transformation and vindication kept breaking through. This week's reading forms a transition from the shadow side of human and Christian existence to the glorious destiny which awaits the redeemed. Verse 28 states a proposition which was known to Paul's readers ("we know") and was apparently a religious maxim in Judaism. He then bases this maxim on the realities of Christian experience. It is not just pious make-believe to say that everything will turn out all right in the end. It is an assurance based upon what the believers have already experienced from God: he foreknew them, predestined them to be conformed to his Son's image, called them, justified them, and — surprisingly, for we should expect this to be reserved until the final fulfillment — glorified them. In other words, the Christian eschatological hope is not of something totally different from what we already have ("pie in the sky when we die"), but the ultimate fruition of our present life in Christ.

Gospel: Matthew 13:44-52 (long form); 13:44-46 (short form)

The long form contains the twin parables of the treasure and the pearl, followed by the parable of the dragnet and the concluding saying of the Christian scribe. The short form stops after the twin parables. It is a pity that it has also dropped the saying about the Christian scribe, as this saying is closely related to the twin parables (the kingdom of God as the supreme value, of which the Christian scribe is the custodian). It also provides an important clue to Matthew's self-understanding as an evangelist. The evangelist takes "things old," i.e., the gospel tradition as he has received it, and reapplies them to the new situation which confronts him and his church at his time. We have already seen him doing this in his treatment of the sower and the tares (his "redaction," as New Testament scholars call it). This process of reinterpreting the tradition of Jesus' words and works which was carried on between Jesus and the evangelists has continued ever since in the ongoing life of the church. The latest chapter in the history of exegesis — which is really what church history is all about — is accomplished when the preacher stands up on a Sunday and delivers his homily. The test of faithful exegesis is whether it enables the old to be said today in a new situation. This cannot be done simply by repeating the old as it stands but only by reproducing the old in a new way so that it can say what it said in past situations and not something different. In other words, the saying about the Christian scribe describes the task of hermeneutics.

Important as these considerations are for the self-understanding of the homilist and the self-understanding of the evangelist, they are not, however, the main point which today's readings propose for our consideration. As the first reading and the psalm show, the intention of this gospel is to speak of the kingdom of God as the supreme value to be preferred above all else, as a man would even cheat (by hiding the treasure) in order to acquire some treasure trove of the owners of the field in which he found it. Here we see an example of Jesus' propensity to use unattractive human behavior in his parables — as in the case of the Lucan parable of the unjust steward and unjust judge. This serves as a warning against treating the parables merely as moral lessons. Rather, they light up worldly behavior as worthy of imitating in quite a different context. The kingdom of God is of such great value that the most drastic action is worth taking to gain it.

The parable of the pearl is of a rather different type. It involves no discreditable conduct. But like the parable of the hidden treasure it holds up for our emulation in quite a different context the behavior of a man who was prepared to take drastic action to secure the object of his desire. Matthew of course relates these pictures to the life of the church in his day. It was a church threatened by antinomianism (disregard of the moral law), by false prophets, and by persecution. In that situation Christians must be prepared to take drastic action to be accepted among the righteous at the last day. Hence Matthew appends to the twin parables the further parable of the dragnet.

The Homily
The key note of today's passages is struck by the twin parables we have just discussed. To them, as we have seen, the picture of Solomon's choice and the psalmist's devotion to the Law are closely related. Persecution may not be a peril for the church in this country today as it was in Matthew's time, but doctrinal and moral laxity certainly are. The believer is urged to drastic action to remain faithful to God and to his kingdom.

THE TRANSFIGURATION: AUGUST 6[1]

The gospel has already been commented upon this year at Lent II, series A. There, as we pointed out, the transfiguration appeared as a

[1] Comments on Sunday 18 A will be found in the Appendix, below.

curtain raiser to the passion. On this day the accent is rather different. The transfiguration can now be considered for its own sake. It is related to Christology, to the understanding of the person of Jesus. The keynote is struck by the first reading (Dn 7:9-10, 13-14), the vision of the Son of man as he is presented before the ancient of days. Note that the scene is not of a coming of the Son of man to earth, but of his being brought before the presence of God. The analogue is the ascension rather than the second coming. The transfiguration as related in the gospel (Mt 17:1-9), in which Jesus' face shines like the sun and his garments are white as light, shows that it is he who is to be glorified like the Son of man. For although nothing is said in Daniel about the shining face or the white garments of the Son of man, similar features are combined with the picture of the ascended Christ as the Danielic Son of man in chapter one of the Apocalypse. The transfiguration reveals Jesus in his earthly existence as the one who is to be exalted as the Son of man after his suffering. It is an "anticipation of his eschatology" (R. Kittel).

The responsorial psalm (Ps 97:1-2, 5-6, 9) picks up the theme of kingship from the Danielic vision. The psalm of course concerns the kingship of Yahweh, but there is no difficulty for Christian interpretation in shifting the term Lord from Yahweh-Kurios to Christos-Kurios.

Reading II (2 Pt 1:16-19) contains an account of the transfiguration which, according to some scholars, is independent of, and in some respects more primitive than the accounts in the gospels. As it stands it serves two purposes: (1) it reinforces the pseudonymous claim of the letter to be by the Apostle Peter. We have to remember that the second century, when this letter was probably written, had very different ideas about pseudonymity from ours. It was a device to enable an authority, now dead, to continue to speak in the changed circumstances of the church subsequent to his death. By claiming to have been present at the transfiguration the author reinforces his claim to be speaking in the name of the Apostle Peter. (2) The transfiguration story is used to prove that the Christian gospel is not based upon a myth, but upon an event which actually happened, namely the earthly life of Jesus. Of course this historical event receives interpretation, albeit in mythological terms — for the Danielic Son of man is unquestionably mythological in its origin. But a myth *per se* is an entirely unhistorical speculation. The gospel involves the use of mythological concepts, but it uses them to interpret history, which is a very different thing.

The Homily

It is quite clear that the homily should draw out the christological significance of the transfiguration story. It unveils the glory of the ascended Christ in the midst of his incarnate life. We encounter the glory of Christ not in a transcendent sphere apart from his incarnate existence — that would be to follow a "cleverly devised myth" — but precisely in his historical existence as that is extended to us in the word and sacrament. Nor, on the other hand, can we regard him merely as a figure of the past, and make him an ideal for some cause we are keen on today — as in some contemporary theologies of revolution. Because of his ascended glory, unveiled in the transfiguration, he belongs not to the past as a mere human example, but to the present as the ever contemporary Lord. In this way we can seek to do justice to the traditional Chalcedonian definition of Christ as divine and human "without division or separation."

NINETEENTH SUNDAY OF THE YEAR

Reading I: *1 Kings 19:9a, 11-13a*

This lesson is obviously chosen to match the gospel story of the appearance of Jesus to the disciples on the lake. In each story an encounter with God/Christ takes place after the stilling of the storm.

Elijah has slain the prophets of Baal, and Jezebel has threatened his life in revenge. He retreats to Mount Horeb to commune with God as Moses had done before him (there are distinct parallels in the narrative, cf. the 40 days and the lodging in the cave). Yahweh is not in the storm, the earthquake or the fire, but in the gentle breeze after the storm. The place of encounter with God is not in the awesome events of nature, but in the word of revelation. At the same time, however, after the encounter of revelation has occurred, the storm, earthquake and fire can be seen as the harbingers of God's revelation.

Responsorial Psalm: *85:8ab, 10-11, 12-13*

The use of the psalm as a response to the Elijah passage is evidently suggested by the first two lines of the first stanza: "Let me hear what God the Lord will speak, for he will speak peace to his people."

The origin of this psalm is in dispute, and its original reference uncertain. Its affinities (cf. its soteriological vocabulary) seem to be with Deutero-Isaiah, and a reasonable assumption would be that it refers to the impending return from exile. In the Christian liturgy it is used most frequently at Advent and Christmas.

Reading II: Romans 9:1-5

In our readings in course from Romans we reach today the section (Rom 9-11) in which Paul wrestles with the problem of the place of Israel in salvation history. Their rejection of Jesus as Messiah has been a great shock for him, and he uses very strong language in praying for their salvation (Rom 9:3). From v. 4 on, Paul lists the great prerogatives of Israel in salvation history — eight of them, culminating in the Messiah himself, and ending in a doxology. The reading of the RSV margin is followed here. The RSV text inserts a period after "Christ" and relegates the doxology to a separate sentence, thus: "God who is over all be blessed for ever." Both renderings are possible renderings of the Greek, but it is unlikely that Paul would have called Christ God without qualifications as in the RSV margin. The whole subject has been well discussed by Rudolf Bultmann in his essay, "The Confession of the World Council of Churches."

In his attitude toward his fellow Jews Paul strikes a mean between two diametrically opposite attitudes which have characterized Christian thought at different periods — either anti-Semitism, or a complete "ecumenical" acceptance of Judaism as a valid religion and an abandonment of any hope for their conversion to faith in Jesus Christ. Both attitudes are seemingly a betrayal of the gospel as Paul understands it. Paul's attitude is in continuity with both Moses (Ex 32:32) and Elijah (see the sequel to reading I in 1 Kgs 19:14ff.).

Gospel: Matthew 14:22-33

Since Matthew has taken over the walking on the waters from Mark, we must pay special attention to Matthew's alterations. The two major changes may be noted:

1. The addition of the dialogue between Peter and Jesus and the walking of Peter on the water.

2. Instead of the ending of the disciples' misunderstanding of Jesus, the story now ends in a confession of faith: "Truly you are the Son of God."

It is reasonable to suppose, with G. D. Kilpatrick, that Matthew is drawing upon a special Petrine tradition, akin to the material he has added in 16:17-19. In that case the Peter episode may be another part of a story of Jesus' resurrection appearance to Peter.

The effect of these changes is to alter completely the thrust of the pericope. In Mark it was an element in the evangelist's theme of the disciples' misunderstanding, designed to play down the interpretation of Jesus' miracle as epiphanies in opposition to a "divine man" Christology. This is no longer an acute problem for Matthew. So he has altered the interpretation of the scene. It becomes a paradigm of discipleship. The boat represents the church, the storm the persecution through which Matthew's community is passing. Jesus appears and challenges Peter, the disciple *par excellence*, to trust him. Peter is afraid and cries out, "Lord save me." Jesus, half rebuking, half encouraging him, says: "O man of little faith, why did you doubt?" The Lord brings Peter to safety, and all the disciples make the adoring confession, "Truly you are the Son of God."

The Homily

Probably the most obvious choice would be to take Matthew's alterations to Mark's story of the walking on the water, and treat it as a paradigm of discipleship. To be the church is to be in a storm tossed bark. Christ comes and rebukes us for our little faith, and encourages us to trust in him. He stills the storm and brings us to safety. The realization of his present help in trouble should lead to adoration and confession of faith.

A relevant alternative might be to take the epistle as a basis for a discussion of the very tricky question of Christian–Jewish relations. There are centuries of anti-Semitism of which the church must repent, and she has probably lost the right today to seek to "convert" the Jews. The credibility gap is far too great and it is the church's own sin that this is so. But on the other hand, she cannot cease to pray with the apostle that the Jews may come to know Jesus as the Messiah — in their own way, perhaps, and not in ours.

TWENTIETH SUNDAY OF THE YEAR

Reading I: Isaiah 56:1, 6-7

This passage comes from Trito-Isaiah, the postexilic portion of that work. It is founded on the teaching of the Second Isaiah, as the opening verse of our pericope shows — it uses the same terms, justice and righteousness. On the other hand there is a new twist to these words: justice and righteousness are not exclusively Yahweh's mighty acts in bringing his people out of exile, but they are demands upon human conduct — Trito-Isaiah thus gives a moralistic slant to the teaching of his mentor.

Verses 6-7 deal with an acute practical problem arising after the return and the restoration of the temple.

Prior to the exile, foreigners had been allowed to perform certain functions in its precincts. Ezekiel had objected to uncircumcised foreigners around the place. Trito-Isaiah now stipulates the conditions under which they may serve: Sabbath observance and the keeping of the covenant as far as it was applicable to non-Israelites. This is not unqualified universalism. But at least in a symbolic way it is a prophecy foreshadowing the universalism of the gospel. It points to the time when the temple of God will be a house of prayer for all people. It thus points forward to the effects of Christ's redeeming work. Mark, or the tradition before him, puts these words on Jesus' lips as an interpretation of his cleaning of the temple. John further interprets that event by taking it as an act of prophetic symbolism, declaring the replacement of the old temple by the temple of his body. It is there that the text Is 56:7 comes to its final fulfillment.

This passage was chosen today because of the universalist implications of the episode of the Canaanitish woman.

Responsorial Psalm: 67:1-2, 4, 5 and 7

For comment on this psalm see the Sixth Sunday of Easter, series C above. Here the word "nations" in the antiphon underlines the universalist implications of the Old Testament reading and the gospel.

Reading II: Romans 11:13-15, 29-32

This occurs toward the end of the discussion of Israel's place in salvation history, the opening part of which we read last week. Paul believes that the pattern of salvation history will run like this: First, the gospel is proclaimed to Israel by the earliest apostles. But Israel rejects it, so Paul is called to proclaim it to the Gentiles. This step will provoke Israel to jealousy and Israel will then hurry to gain acceptance before the end.

Paul's view of salvation history will cause difficulties for us today. For one thing, he expected the end to come very soon. He did not think in terms of several millennia of history. Already Matthew was compelled to adjust the early Christian perspective on salvation history. He contemplated the failure and abandonment of the mission to Israel, and drew as a consequence the necessity of concentrating in future on the mission to the Gentiles. Matthew had no hope, as Paul had, that Israel would be provoked to jealousy and would want to come in. This adjustment of perspective need not surprise us. As Oscar Cullmann has shown, it is characteristic of the understanding of salvation history in both the Old and the New Testaments that it should constantly be adjusted in the light of later events.

For us, what is of permanent validity in this passage is not Paul's particular scheme of salvation history (which had to be corrected already by Matthew), but rather the great principle enunciated in v. 29 and highlighted in the caption: the gifts and calling of God are irrevocable. That must be the basic principle as we wrestle today with the place of Israel in salvation history.

Gospel: Matthew 15:21-28

Matthew took over the story of the Canaanitish woman from Mark, but with several important changes:

1. The woman is called a Canaanite instead of a Syro-Phoenician.
2. There is considerable expansion of the dialogue material in the body of the story (vv. 22-24).
3. Jesus praises the woman for her faith (v. 28).
4. Matthew removes Jesus' saying that the children (i.e., Israel) must be fed first.
5. The narrative of the woman's return home to discover that her daughter was cured of the demon is reduced to a brief statement that the girl was indeed healed — unlike Mark, Matthew was not interested in the fact that healing was performed from a distance.

It may well be that Matthew had access to an alternative version of the healing, perhaps a more primitive one (so Bultmann and Lohmeyer). But in any case Matthew's alterations have a theological rather than a historical motivation. Matthew shifts the interest away from the miracle to the woman's faith. As a Canaanite, she is (cf. the Old Testament conflicts between Israel and Canaan) a stranger to the covenants of Israel. Jesus takes the barrier very seriously. He first refuses to answer her, then announces that he was sent only to the lost sheep of Israel. It was the woman's faith that finally overcame the barrier. Mark and Matthew write for a different public at different periods. Mark writes for Gentile Christians, showing them that salvation is first for the Jews only and then for the Gentiles. Matthew writes for Jewish Christians, showing them that faith and faith alone breaks down the barrier between Jew and Gentile.

The Homily

On this Sunday a unitive theme runs through all the readings including the epistle. The homilist should wrestle today with the twin facts of the particularity and universalism of the gospel. Israel has a unique place in salvation history, and the gifts and call of God are irrevocable. Yet at the same time the temple of Christ's body is a house of prayer for *all* nations: all the nations will come and praise Yahweh, and faith, faith alone, opens up salvation to the Gentiles.

TWENTY-FIRST SUNDAY OF THE YEAR ✓

Reading I: Isaiah 22:19-23

In this passage Isaiah denounces one Shebna, the prime minister ("who is over the household," v. 19), and predicts his replacement by Eliakim (vv. 20ff.). The passage is notable for its use of the keys which is taken up in the gospel for this day, the *Tu es Petrus* saying.

Responsorial Psalm: 138:1-2a, 2bcd-3, 6 and 8bc

A slightly different selection from Ps 138 was used twice in series C on the Fifth and on the Seventeenth Sunday (for a comment on the latter see above).

Today's response ("Lord, your love is eternal") suggests that God's purposes are not defeated through the infidelity of his human instruments. God can replace a faithless agent by another who is faithful to him.

Reading II: Romans 11:33-36

This magnificent doxology comes at the end of the discussion of Israel's place in salvation history. Theology is an attempt to reflect on the ways of God in salvation history. This is what Paul has been doing in Rom 9–11. But the theologian must always confess the inadequacy of his work. The riches and wisdom of knowledge of God are always too deep for him to penetrate, his judgments and his ways are unsearchable. No theologian has ever known the mind of the Lord. No theology, however venerable, can claim to be absolute. There comes a time when the theologian must lay down his pen and confess the relativity of all his formulations. Theology is therefore always subject to change. And theology must be done in the context of liturgy. It must be doxological.

Gospel: Matthew 16:13-20

Matthew has introduced considerable alterations into his Marcan source.

The words "Son of the living God" are added to Peter's confession. In Mark Jesus almost ignores Peter's confession and enjoins the disciple to silence. He then proceeds at once to speak of the necessity of his passion. Peter protests and is met by the rebuke, "Get behind me, Satan." Matthew has placed the prediction of the passion, Peter's objection, and Jesus' rebuke in a separate pericope following the confession. Instead Jesus pronounces Peter blessed and gives him the name Peter, the Rock. Then come a series of promises: the building of the church on the foundation of Peter, the assurance that the powers of death shall not prevail against that church, the promise of the keys, and the saying of the binding and loosing.

There seems to be a growing consensus that the original situation of these words to Peter was not in the earthly life of Jesus, but in a post-resurrection setting, that the whole passage, vv. 17-19, enshrines very early material going back to the Aramaic-speaking church, and that the Rock on which the church is to be built is Peter himself, not his faith as some patristic and most Reformation exegesis has supposed.

But there is a division among exegetes along confessional lines over the question of the continuation of Peter's function in the church. Protestant exegesis sees the fulfillment of the Rock saying in the once-and-for-all role which played such a large part in the foundation of the church after the first Easter and resurrection appearances (Cullmann), and sees the power of the keys and of binding and loosing as continued in the church as a whole, though capable of being entrusted to particular officers by the community (Marxsen). Anglican exegetes tend to agree with the Orthodox that the power of the keys and of binding and loosing is shared by the whole episcopate, though many of them would be prepared to allow the Bishop of Rome a special place in this collegial office. Catholic scholars naturally maintain that the Petrine office is vested in the papacy. It is, however, significant that on all sides there is growing Christian awareness that one aspect of the Petrine office, witness to the resurrection, belongs to the events of the Christian beginnings and is therefore inalienable. At the same time its other aspects (keys, binding and loosing) continue in the church. This continuity is a sign of the faithfulness of God.

The Homily

We suggest two possibilities. Following the epistle, the homilist could speak of the nature of the theological task, drawing out the provisional, tentative and inadequate character of theology, its being subject to revision, and its doxological-liturgical character. True theology emerges from liturgy and returns to it. But the homilist will more likely wish to speak of the Petrine office in the church, distinguishing between its once-for-all and its continuing aspects.

TWENTY-SECOND SUNDAY OF THE YEAR ✓

Reading I: Jeremiah 20:7-9

Of all the Old Testament prophets, Jeremiah comes closest to the New Testament understanding of what is meant to be a bearer of the word of God. He foreshadows the truth, first emphasized in the New Testament by Paul, in opposition to the wandering preachers who set great store by their own miraculous powers and visionary experiences. This theme was then taken up by Mark (followed as we see in today's gospel by Matthew) in his redaction of the Jesus tradition. It is this aspect of the Jeremiah passage that the caption rightly emphasizes: "the word of the Lord has meant derision for me."

Responsorial Psalm: 63:1abc, 1d-3, 4-5, 7-8

For comment see series C, Twelfth Sunday, above.

Reading II: Romans 12:1-2

It is a pity that the text as printed omits a tiny, yet crucial word, the word "therefore" (Greek *oun*): "I appeal to you *therefore*, brethren." It is crucial because chapters 12–15 of Romans present Christian ethics as "*oun* ethics," "therefore ethics." That is to say, Christian ethics is a response to what God has done in Christ. My teacher Sir Edwyn Hoskyns used to say that Paul could not speak of Christian ethics until he had been through all the "theological turmoil" of Rom 1–11. Only after expounding the redemptive act of God in Christ and setting it in the context of salvation history, can Paul go on to discuss ethical problems. This ethic is seen as the true Christian worship. In a celebrated essay Käsemann has suggested that Paul is in some way anti-cultic, that for him true Christian worship is to be seen in ethical behavior, not in the cultus. This is the kind of either-or that appeals to the German mind, but does less than justice to the inclusiveness of the biblical material.

No one doubts that liturgy must penetrate life, but life must first find its focus in liturgy. We present our bodies as a living sacrifice in the liturgy (Cranmer included this phrase in the eucharistic prayer and it has remained a feature of Anglican liturgies ever since) precisely in order that we may go out into the world and present them in life.

Christian ethics is not primarily expressed in a code. Paul will give something that looks like a code in chapters 12–15 of Romans, with many single commandments. But these are meant as *illustrations* (Dodd) of what a renewed mind, not conformed to this world, will lead to. In an apt illustration, Bishop John A. T. Robinson has spoken of the Christian's antennae which should enable him to discern the will of God in a given situation, and which arises out of a transformed mind. Such transformation takes place through hearing the word of God and through his offering himself to God in union with Christ's offering. This takes place quite concretely in the liturgy.

Gospel: Matthew 16:21-27

As we noted in the comments for last week, Matthew has detached this section from Mark's Caesarea Philippi pericope and placed it by itself. As in the epistle, a tiny but significant word has been left out at the beginning, the word "then" (*tote*): "Then Jesus told his disciples." This word detaches this section, and yet links it as a sequel to the foregoing pericope. The other major alteration Matthew has made to the Marcan text is in the final verse (27), which he has converted into a parousia-last judgment scene: "The Son of man is to come with his holy angels, and then he will repay every man for what he has done." For Mark, the court of the Son of man will vindicate the church and pass judgment upon the believing world. For Matthew it is the church which will be judged — a theme which that evangelist hammers home again and again, right up to the parable of the sheep and the goats. The church will be judged according to the fidelity of its discipleship, even at the cost of taking up its cross and following Jesus, in its readiness to lose its life for his sake.

The Homily

Once again, the gospel determines the major message of today's readings. The challenge to the church to take up its cross and to lose its life for Christ's sake takes on a new form in every age. In Matthew's time it meant, quite literally, persecution, as the church could no longer come under the umbrella of Judaism as a *religio licita*. It is the same in many parts of the world today. The homilist must determine what form that challenge takes for the church in this country — maybe too in his parish —

today, and deliver the challenge of Jesus' words accordingly. Allusion can also be made to the fate of Jeremiah.

An alternative possibility is offered by reading II. Here the homilist has an opportunity to expound the distinctive characteristic of Christian ethics as "*oun* ethics," "therefore ethics," the ethics of response, involving not the meticulous observance of a detailed code, but the expression in each new situation of a mind renewed and not conformed to this world. Or the text could be treated from the perspective of cultus *versus* life.

TWENTY-THIRD SUNDAY OF THE YEAR

Reading I: Ezekiel 33:7-9

This passage comes from a chapter in which Ezekiel sets down the responsibilities of the prophet as he envisages them after the restoration from exile. One of the images under which he defines that role is that of the watchman, a familiar figure in the defense system of Palestine. Watchmen were posted on the hills to warn of the approach of a foreign invader. Verses 1-6 is a parable, vv. 7-9 (our reading) is its application to the prophetic role. It is characteristic of Ezekiel that he conceives the prophet's function as concerned with individuals. This was a result of the destruction of the nation as a corporate entity at the time of the exile. Henceforth all that the prophet can do is to speak to the individual.

If the prophet fails to deliver the warning, it is his own responsibility. If he does deliver it, on the other hand, and the individual refuses to pay heed, it is not the prophet's fault. He has discharged his responsibility.

Ezekiel's picture of the prophet as watchman is selected today to go with the gospel which speaks of fraternal concern in the eschatological community where all share the gift of the Spirit.

Responsorial Psalm: 95:1-2, 6-7abc, 7d-9

This psalm received comment on Sunday 18, series C, above. The response "If today you hear his voice, harden not your hearts" is singularly apt after Ezekiel's parable of the watchman.

Reading I: Romans 13:8-10

As we saw last week, the last three chapters of Romans (we assume that ch. 16 belonged to a different letter) consists largely of ethical exhortation. Here Paul presents the second table of the decalogue. Note the unusual order (Hellenistic-Jewish): 7, 6, 8, 10, according to the Reformed and Anglican enumeration; 6, 5, 7, and 9–10 in the Roman and Lutheran enumeration. Paul then summarizes its single injunctions in the all-embracing command of Lev 19:18: "You shall love your neighbor as yourself." Note the logical structure of this passage:

1. An imperative (v. 8).
2. The grounds for the imperative (v. 8).
3. A second table (v. 9).
4. A deduction from the imperative given in v. 8 (v. 10). Evidently Paul is drawing upon an established pattern of catechesis. This pattern was probably derived from Hellenistic Judaism as is shown not only by the order of the commandments, but also by the typically Hellenistic attempt to discover a single unifying principle behind the separate injunctions. The teaching of this passage is that there is really only one commandment which is universal and covers every situation, and to which we are always obligated, and that is the commandment of love. The separate commandments of the decalogue are no more than illustrations of what love may mean in particular situations.

Gospel: Matthew 18:15-20

This gospel reading is closely connected to last week's. These are the only passages in which the term "church" (ecclesia) occurs in Matthew (or for that matter, in all four gospels). Both passages include the promise about binding and loosing, in Mt 16, addressed to Peter only, in ch. 18 to the disciples generally. It would seem reasonable to suppose that Matthew has taken both passages from a common source which formed a commentary of church origins: (1) a community rule (vv. 15-17). This is paralleled at Qumran; (2) the promise about binding and loosing, which in our opinion comes from a resurrection story as is indicated by its combination with the *Tu es Petrus* saying in Mt 16 and by the parallel tradition in Jn 20:19-23.

In its original form this tradition was evidently a saying of the risen Lord empowering the Twelve to admit or exclude men and women from the kingdom according to whether they accepted or rejected the kerygma. By combining it with the saying about fraternal correction Matthew's source has converted it into a church rule. Binding and loosing now becomes the function of the whole community, and its character is changed to the administration of discipline within the community.

The Homily

As usual, the Old Testament reading, psalm and gospel go together. The homilist has the opportunity to speak of church discipline and the role of priest and community in discharging their joint responsibility. The widespread rejection of traditional forms of church discipline in post-conciliar Catholicism and the total breakdown of any kind of church discipline in Protestantism does not mean that there is no place for it in the church. The gospel text, which is part of canonical scripture, suggests that it is an essential aspect of church life. The Reformed tradition lists discipline along with word and sacraments as essential signs of the church. There is something for us all to learn from that.

The epistle reading suggests a consideration of the relation between the separate injunctions of the decalogue and the basic law of love.

TWENTY-FOURTH SUNDAY OF THE YEAR ✓

Reading I: Sirach 27:30–28:7

Sirach is one of the deutero-canonical or (in Reformation parlance) apocryphal books. Until recently it was known only in a Greek translation, although we knew from the prologue that it was originally written in Hebrew. The author was Jesus ben Sirach, who wrote it *ca.* 180 BC. It was translated into Greek by his grandson *ca.* 130 BC. It is therefore a late book, not too far removed from the New Testament period. The teaching of our excerpt reaches a height not far from the New Testament in what it says about forgiveness (cf. the Sermon of the Mount, the Lord's Prayer and today's gospel of the unforgiving servant).

Responsorial Psalm: 103:1-2, 3-4, 9-10, 11-12

Slightly different selections from this psalm were used in series C on Lent 3 and Sunday 7 of the year. The Lent 3 selection was commented on above. The reason for its choice today is that man's forgiveness of his fellows is meant to be patterned on the divine forgiveness, as both reading I and the gospel testify.

Reading II: Romans 14:7-9

The context of this passage is a discussion about the relation between the strong and the weak members of the church. Recent work on Romans suggests that this discussion was occasioned by recent tensions in Rome between Gentile Christians who were liberal in their attitude to the law, and Jewish Christians who were scrupulous about legal observances; these were the "strong" and the "weak" respectively. Paul urges mutual toleration. The strong in particular should respect the scruples of the weak. As so often, Paul moves from specific practical problems to the underlying theological principles. The fundamental principle here is that no Christian exists by himself, but only in relation to the Lord (the risen and exalted Kurios, i.e., Christ), and therefore in relation to his fellow church members, who are equally related to the Kurios.

The pericope looks very much like a baptismal hymn. This is indicated by the "we style" common in hymns, and by the way in which the hymn goes beyond the point immediately at issue, viz., the relation between weak and strong, to speak of the living and the dead. As the Lord of the living, Christ is the Lord of both groups within the church.

Gospel: Matthew 18:21-35

The parable of the unforgiving servant is found only in Matthew's gospel. We have not therefore to deal with Matthew's redaction of a known source like Mark or Q. Matthew's redactional contributions will be: (1) attaching the parable to the saying about forgiving seventy times seven, with the connecting link, "therefore"; (2) placing this whole complex at the conclusion of the community discourse, thus making the parable a moral exhortation for the community; (3) adding the final saying which draws the moral. Note the typically Matthean phrase, "my heavenly Father" (v. 35). Also note that the saying of v. 22 and the teaching of the parable don't really fit together. The parable does not inculcate repeated forgiveness, but rebukes refusal to show mercy on the part of those who have received mercy from God. There is no reason to doubt that this is an authentic Jesus parable. It fits in perfectly with the situation in his ministry. Jesus has offered God's eschatological forgiveness to his hearers already here and now. If they do not share this forgiveness with their fellows, God will revoke that forgiveness at the last judgment. This parable was told by Jesus not as a moral exhortation about life in the church but to shame the consciences of his hearers.

The Homily

On this occasion all four readings can be taken together. They deal with the necessity of forgiveness as the basis of relationships within the community. This of course necessitates taking the gospel at the redactional level. Perhaps the homilist could identify groups within the community which are in tension with one another, like the strong and the weak at

Rome. The necessity of forgiveness toward one's fellow church members is grounded upon the fact that all members live under the forgiveness of God — beginning with baptism and renewed in absolution and each reception of the holy communion, and in the fact that Christ died and rose again not only to achieve forgiveness of sin but also to be the Lord of all the living and the dead.

Sundays 25 A to 30 A

Reading I: Isaiah 55:6-9

The hymn, Is 55:1-11, was used at the Easter Vigil service, where it received comment. Here only the second of its three stanzas is used. The reason for its selection is indicated by the caption, which calls attention to the last two verses:

> "My thoughts are not your thoughts,
> and my ways are not your ways" (vv. 8, 9).

These words underline the teaching of the parable of the laborers in the vineyard, as we shall see.

Responsorial Psalm: 145:2-3, 8-9, 17-18

A somewhat different, though overlapping, selection from this psalm was commented on for Sundays 14 A and 31 C. The second and third stanzas, especially the latter, match both the Old Testament reading and the gospel today. Again, as we shall see, the difference between God's thoughts and man's, according to the parable of the laborers in the vineyard, is that God's justice is not a *quid pro quo* affair, but characterized by mercy and forgiveness.

Reading II: Philippians 1:20c-24, 27a

This week we turn from Romans, which we have been reading for the past several Sundays, to Philippians. Philippians was written some time while Paul was in prison. Traditionally this imprisonment was identified with that at Rome (see Acts 28:30-31). There is however a growing consensus among scholars today that the imprisonment in question must have occurred during Paul's stay at Ephesus (*ca.* 52–55, though the absolute chronology of Paul's life is somewhat conjectural). It was during this supposed imprisonment (of which there are hints in some of the letters, e.g., 1 Cor 15:32), that the great controversial letters were probably written: Galatians, 1 Corinthians, much of 2 Corinthians and also Philippians. The view is also gaining ground that Philippians, like 2 Corinthians, is a compilation from two or three short letters written by Paul to the community at Philippi over the space of several months. These fragments were subsequently put together when they were edited for the later use of the church. The letters may be identified as follows:

Letter A, 4:10-23. Paul's thank-you for the "care packet" sent by the Philippians to him in prison by a messenger from Philippi named Epaphroditus.

Letter B, 1:1–3:1, 4:4-7. This gives news about Paul's welfare and prospects in prison. Epaphroditus' recovery from illness while with Paul, Paul's desire to send Timothy to Philippi soon, and warnings against the possible arrival of false teachers.

Letter C, 3:2–4:3, 8-9. An attack on the false teachers after their arrival at Philippi.

Today's reading thus comes from Letter B. Paul faces the possibility of martyrdom. If we are right in placing the imprisonment at Ephesus in 52–55, we know his worst fears at this time did not come true: he was released, and able to visit his churches once more before he was arrested again, this time in Jerusalem, and transported to Rome. Our reading consists of the apostle's vivid meditation on the prospects of life and death. He is in a state of tension, pulled both ways. Whether he dies or lives, Paul is convinced that Christ will be honored in his body, that is either by his (Paul's) labors for the gospel (cf. the catalogues of sufferings in 2 Cor 12, etc. — that is what being an apostle meant for Paul) or by actual martyrdom. In either case it is not his own personal salvation that is at stake — he does not simply want to escape from his labors into personal bliss with Christ. Rather, he believes that his martyrdom will in some way contribute, perhaps even more effectively than his apostolic labors, to the fulfillment of God's purpose in salvation history. "To live is Christ" — the great Pauline saying highlighted in the caption does not mean simply the enjoyment of mystical communion between the believer and his Lord, but the execution of the apostolic mission.

Gospel: Matthew 20:1-16

As we have noted in previous discussions of our Lord's parables, there are three possible levels of exegesis:

1. The parable as taught by Jesus
2. The parable as modified in the oral tradition
3. The parable as presented by the evangelist in the context of his gospel.

At the level of Jesus' own teaching, the parable of the wicked husbandman must have concluded with the question, "Do you begrudge my generosity?" The context in which it was originally told must have been a complaint of Jesus' opponents that he was paying more attention to the outcast than to the respectable members of society. Jesus takes a situation as familiar in daily life then as now, long lines of unemployed waiting for a job. But he depicts the behavior of the employer in a quite surprising way. Out of pity for the unemployed and their families, the employer generously gives a full day's wages to everyone. That is what God is doing in Jesus' ministry — giving the tax collectors and prostitutes an equal share with the righteous in his kingdom. Obviously, the parable is not a moral lesson about labor relations!

At the level of the oral tradition, the proverbial phrase "the last shall be first and the first last" has been added. This looks like a reapplication of the parable to the situation of the post-Easter community. Israel has rejected the gospel, so Gentiles have been drawn in.

The evangelist shows his own understanding of the parable by appending it to the discourse, Mt 19:23-30. Here Peter, as the spokesman of the twelve, proudly claimed that they, unlike the rich whom Jesus was criticizing, had left everything to follow Jesus. They will indeed be rewarded, for they will sit on twelve thrones with Christ, receive a hundredfold and inherit eternal life. But then comes a warning: "many that are first shall be last and the last first." In Matthew this does not mean that the disciples are the last who will turn out to be the first, whereas the rich are the first who will turn out to be last. What Matthew means, or makes Jesus mean, is that those who forsake all and follow Jesus and who are therefore the first, may turn out to be the last. The parable of the laborers in the vineyard follows right on this, as a warning to the Christians in Matthew's church not to hanker after rewards. Rewards are not denied, but they are not the purpose of toil for Christ and his kingdom. They always come as a surprise. Paul in the second reading exhibited precisely the kind of attitude Jesus is enjoining in Matthew's presentation.

The Homily

The most obvious choice today would be to take the gospel at the Jesus level, emphasizing the generosity of God, and link it with the first reading ("my thoughts are not your thoughts") and with the responsorial psalm ("The Lord is good to all"). This should not be presented as a general religious lesson, but applied where possible to some quite concrete situation in the life of the community, for instance where pious people are grumbling because of the church's concern for the poor and the outcast, and thinking that more time should be spent on themselves.

Less obvious, and requiring very careful preparation, would be to link Paul's contemplation of martyrdom with the parable at the level of the evangelist's presentation. Like the disciples in Matthew, Paul has left all and followed Jesus, delivering his apostolic witness precisely through his sufferings. In such a situation, it would be tempting for the apostle to look for a reward when he departs through martyrdom. His longing to "be with Christ" could be regarded in such a light. But Paul resists that temptation. His martyrdom, like his continuing earthly life, is all part of his apostolic ministry — not a personal escape. The question is, which — martyrdom or continuing labor — is God's will for him.

TWENTY-SIXTH SUNDAY OF THE YEAR

Reading I: Ezekiel 18:25-28

Ezekiel is well known for his insistence upon individual responsibility for sin. In earlier days Israel had barely distinguished a man from his community — the overall picture was one of communal solidarity, with emphasis upon the corporate consequences of individual guilt (cf. "visiting the iniquity of the father upon the children to the third and fourth generation" in the decalogue). The destruction of Israel's national institutions during the exile accelerated a new emphasis on the individual, which was beginning to appear even earlier: "every man shall be put to death for his own sin," Dt 24:16; cf. 2 Kgs 14:6. The change must of course be understood precisely as one of emphasis, not as a denial of the older idea of solidarity but as a corrective. Both aspects — individual responsibility and corporate solidarity — have to be held together in tension, and it requires a finesse to know just when which has to be given priority.

These verses bring out another aspect of Ezekiel's doctrine of responsibility. This is that a person is free at any time to turn from wickedness to righteousness and *vice versa*. In each case, that person will be judged by the new life to which he has turned, not by his previous life. This is perhaps an oversimplification, but it fits in with the parable of the two sons in today's gospel reading.

Responsorial Psalm: 25:4-5, 6-7, 8-9
This psalm is an individual lament. The psalmist is oppressed by his enemies but equally aware of his own sin. He calls upon God to deliver him from his enemies by remembering not his sins but his own (God's) mercies, and to lead him (the psalmist) in the right way after his deliverance. It forms a suitable response to the reading from Ezekiel. Both passages view a man's life as bisected into past and future by the present moment. The past is characterized by sin, the future is filled with hope for righteousness. In the present moment man is thrown utterly upon the mercies of God — an aspect of the matter which Ezekiel in his emphasis on personal responsibility tends to overlook. The psalm corrects this.

The refrain, "Remember your mercies," calls attention to the very important biblical conception of remembrance. In modern parlance, to remember means simply to recall mentally an event of the past. In the Bible, when God remembers he does not merely recollect a past event in his mind, but brings it out of the past and makes it effective in the present. Thus the mercies of God, which he performed in the past, become renewed as present realities. This concept is very important for our understanding of the eucharist. "Do this in remembrance of me" means not only that we recall in our minds the messianic sacrifice, the supreme act of God's mercy. It means that in response to the church's action, God will make present that sacrifice. As was well said by the Anglican-Roman Catholic International Commission (1971):

"The notion of *memorial* as understood in the passover celebration at the time of Christ — i.e., the making effective in the present of an event in the past — has opened the way to a clearer understanding of the relationship between Christ's sacrifice and the eucharist. The eucharistic memorial is no mere calling to mind of a past event or of its significance, but the church's effectual proclamation of God's mighty acts. . . . In the eucharistic prayer the church continues to make a perpetual memorial of Christ's death; and his members, united with God and one another, give thanks for all his mercies, entreat the benefits of his passion on behalf of the whole church, participate in these benefits and enter into the movement of his self-offering."[1]

The repeated refrain, "Remember your mercies, O Lord," is thus a highly suitable chant for the eucharist.

Reading II: Philippians 2:1-11 (long form); 2:1-5 (short form)

The longer form of this epistle reading includes the great christological hymn which, following ancient tradition, was read on Passion (Palm) Sunday and received full comment last year. Whether we opt for the longer or the shorter form, it seems clear that today both comment and homiletical treatment should concentrate upon the ethical exhortation which it is the purpose of the hymn to reinforce.

But we cannot ignore the hymn entirely. Apart from the interpretation of the hymn itself there is a controversy among contemporary exegetes over its relation to the exhortation. Does the hymn merely present Christ as an example? In that case, the drift of thought is this: Let your relationship with your fellow Christians be marked by unity, love, humility, consideration for the interests of others. In so doing, you must display the same attitude to others that Christ showed when he humbled himself to become man and to die upon the cross. That is the way in which the passage has normally been taken. Karl Barth however, has popularized — at least among the Germans — another interpretation. It depends upon a different rendering of the final phrase in the short form of the reading: instead of "which was in Christ Jesus" this reads "which you have in Christ Jesus." Such a variant rendition is possible because there is no verb in the Greek for "was" or for "you have" — it simply reads "which in Christ Jesus," allowing the reader to understand either "was" or "you have." If we understand "you have," it gives a different meaning to "in Christ," viz. the characteristic Pauline sense of "in Christ," sometimes called (though Barth himself would have repudiated the term) mystical. On this interpretation the pattern of Christ's life, namely the pattern of humiliation-glorification, is not a model for Christians to imitate, but a pattern into conformity with which Christians are brought by their incorporation into Christ and their life in him.

It is difficult to decide which is the correct interpretation. The "Barth-

[1] *Worship* 46 (January 1972) 3-4.

ian" one at least has the advantage of giving to "in Christ" its normal Pauline sense of treating Christ not merely as an external example but as the source of redemptive life.

Gospel: Matthew 21:28-32

The second part of the saying, v. 32, is paralleled in Lk 7:29-30, and therefore it must have become attached at some stage in the tradition to the saying about the tax collectors and prostitutes (31b). It is clear that the latter phrase which occurs in both sayings attracted the saying about John the Baptist to the comment on the parable. Then coalescence of the two sayings must have taken place prior to Matthew because Matthew is responsible for placing the whole pericope in sequence with the question of authority (Mt 21:23-27), connecting them by the catchword John the Baptist (vv. 25, 32).

We thus have three levels of exegesis: (1) the Jesus level, consisting of the original parable of the two sons with Jesus' comment (21:28-31a); (2) the oral tradition: the parable with an extended comment, 21:28-32; (3) the evangelist's understanding indicated by his combination of the parable plus extended comment with the question of authority pericope (Mt 21:23-27 + 28-32). The exegete has to try and interpret the parable on all three levels.

Jesus evidently told this parable (N.B. some have thought that this was the original nucleus of the parable of the prodigal son) to vindicate his proclamation of the good news of the kingdom against his critics: "the tax collectors and prostitutes who receive me now will enter into the kingdom of God at the last judgment rather than you, who criticize me for consorting with them." The parable is a proclamation of God's mercy for sinners.

The addition of the saying about John the Baptist gives the parable a surprising and not altogether apt twist. Matthew however has straightened out this awkward state of affairs by sandwiching the pericope between the question of authority and the wicked husbandman. By doing so he makes it one of a series of three comments upon the Jewish authorities' response toward God's purpose throughout salvation history. This response was one of constant rejection, from the time of the prophets through John the Baptist to Jesus himself (and of course also in Matthew's own perspective, to the post-resurrection mission of the church). For Matthew it justifies his own church's abandonment of the mission to Israel and its concentration on preaching to the Gentiles (Mt 28:16-20, and see esp. Mt 21:43, added by Matthew to the third of his three pericopes in 21:23-45).

The Homily

There are several choices before the homilist today. The simplest one — though it involves fastening upon an incidental feature in today's readings — would be to take up the refrain of the psalm, expound the biblical conception of remembrance, and relate it to the eucharist. This would give an opportunity to transcend the Reformation/Counter-Reformation antithesis over the relation between the eucharist and Calvary, and would have an important ecumenical significance.

A second possibility, especially if one accepts Barth's interpretation of Phil 2:5, would be to speak of Christian ethics as formation (cf. Bonhoeffer's *Ethics*).

But the intention of the compilers of the lectionary was to highlight a theme derived from the gospel, the first reading and the responsorial psalm. Unfortunately this choice is complicated by the three levels at which the parables of the two sons may be interpreted. If we chose Matthew's salvation-historical level of interpretation, we would do best to drop all reference to the first reading and the psalm. We could however give it a highly relevant interpretation by relating the parable to the widespread rejection of Christianity in the Western world (the son who said he would go but did not), and the apparent eagerness, e.g., in Africa, for the gospel (the son who said he would not go but then went). This theme however could be left for the next week. The traditional level of interpreting the parable yields little contemporary meaning. The Jesus level, which can be readily combined with the first reading and the psalm, suggests an appeal to repentance addressed to backsliders and conventional Christians.

TWENTY-SEVENTH SUNDAY OF THE YEAR ✓

Reading 1: Isaiah 5:1-7

The song of the vineyard, it is thought, was composed by the prophet Isaiah during the early part of his ministry, and sung at vintage festivals. Only the last stanza equates the vineyard allegorically with Israel, thus turning a happy little song about country life into an expression of God's judgment upon his people. This represents a clever turn on the part of the singer, who has engaged the attention and approval of his hearers up to this point. The parables of Jesus are clearly in the same tradition.

The choice of this reading for today was obvious (see the gospel).

Responsorial Psalm: 80:8 and 11, 12-13, 14-15, 18-19

A different selection from this psalm is also used on Advent I, series B, and Advent IV, series C. Like Is 5 and other passages in the Old Testament, the vine appears in this psalm as a symbol for Israel. It is however not used for purposes of denunciation, but as a prayer for deliverance.

Reading II: Philippians 4:6-9

On the partition theory (see comments on Sunday 25) verses 6-7 form the conclusion of Letter B, verses 8-9 the conclusion of Letter C. This would explain the sudden shift from a blessing to a final exhortation (one would expect these to be in the reverse order at the end of a letter). It further eases the position of the word "finally" — some 15 verses before the actual end of the present "letter" (of course we all know preachers who go on for 15 minutes after saying "finally," but Paul was probably not of their number, at least not on this occasion!). It also explains why Paul should seemingly have repeated himself in vv. 7 and 9 ("peace of God," "God of peace").

The partition theory also enhances the understanding of the two paragraphs in our pericope. The first paragraph comes at the end of the thank-you note for the help Paul has received from the Philippians. The exhortation may be a reassurance in view of the possible arrival at Philippi of false teachers. Verse 7 will be the concluding blessing.

Verses 8-9 will have followed originally upon 4:3. Paul has been denouncing the false teachers who have by now arrived in Philippi (3:2-21). They were probably some kind of enthusiasts who believed they were already in heaven and had attained perfection, ignoring the not-yet-ness of Christian existence, and did not take seriously the place of the cross in the Christian life. They may, like the opponents in Galatia, have demanded the circumcision of Gentile Christian converts (cf. "whose glory is in their shame," 3:19). Paul seeks in a final exhortation to direct his readers to higher things. In order to do so he draws upon the ethical teaching of Stoicism: Things true, honorable, just, pure, gracious, excellence (virtue), worthy of praise — all these are categories of Stoic ethics; there is nothing about them distinctively Christian. But to Paul's thinking they are none the worse for that. Finally, the apostle reiterates what he said in 3:17, though in somewhat different words, holding up himself as an example for his converts to imitate. At first sight this idea looks rather embarrassing, even contrary to Paul's repudiation of justification by works. But Paul understands his life as an apostle (especially his sufferings) to be a manifestation of the cross of Christ. Therefore, in asking the Philippians to imitate him he is not asking them to copy his good works, but inviting them to pattern their lives on Christ as he is made manifest in his (Paul's) apostolic existence. This interpretation is borne out by what Paul says about himself in 3:12-16, where he disclaims any notion that he has already achieved ethical perfection.

Gospel: Matthew 21:33-43

In Matthew (and Mark, the source which Matthew follows here), the parable of the vineyard is heavily allegorized. Luke and the recently discovered Gospel of Thomas contain traces of an earlier form of this parable which is shorter and less allegorized. In this earlier form there are no echoes from Is 5 in the opening of the parable (v. 33). The emissaries prior to the son are reduced to two or three single ones, without any suggestion that they are identified with the Old Testament prophets. The christological upgrading of the son is missing, and the parable must have concluded with his murder. For the original meaning we have to ignore all the secondary allegorical features and consider the story by itself. As in the Lucan parables of the unjust steward and the unjust judge, Jesus draws a surprising lesson from an utterly discreditable piece of human behavior. See, he says, how these vinedressers stopped at nothing. They even murdered the heir to get hold of the vineyard. You must be just as resolute in laying hold of the kingdom of God!

It was all too easy for the later church to allegorize this parable. The vineyard became Israel, the vinedresser its religious leaders, the successive emissaries the Old Testament prophets, the son Jesus the Messiah, his murder the crucifixion. This interpretation was then clinched by combining with it the testimonium from Ps 118:22, so that the parable closes with Jesus' resurrection. Matthew goes further and adds v. 43, so that it closes with the prediction of the mission to the Gentiles following Israel's rejection of the gospel. All this is not wrong. It is simply the constant reapplication of the parable to new situations in the community's life.

The Homily

By combining the Matthew version of the parable of the wicked husbandmen with the reading from Is 5 and Ps 80, the liturgy intends us to hear the parable with its allegorical interpretation. The preacher's most obvious line would be to adapt this theme: the vineyard as God's people, the vine-dressers its religious leaders, the son as the gospel message of Jesus Christ, his murder the rejection of that message by the chosen people and their leaders, and the threat that the kingdom of God will be given to a nation bringing forth the fruits thereof as a threat to the church today — perhaps the church in the Western world, and a threat that the leadership of the Christian cause will pass, say, to Africans?

If this seems too much like dynamite, the homilist could fall back on the original form of this parable as told by Jesus, and preach a challenge to his hearers to seize hold of the gospel.

There remains the epistle reading. Here there are two possibilities: the conclusion of Letter B in Phil 4:6-7, which would lead to an exhortation against anxiety and an assurance of the peace of God which passes under-standing, or the conclusion of Letter C, which holds up the finest ethical ideals of pagan philosophy as worthy of Christian imitation. Should we take stoic ethics today, or should we by analogy hold up virtues, say of humanists or Marxists, for imitation?

TWENTY-EIGHTH SUNDAY OF THE YEAR

Reading I: Isaiah 25:6-10a
Just as the vineyard became, since the song in Is 5, an accepted symbol for Israel as the people of God in salvation history, so our present reading made the great banquet a classic symbol of the consummation of God's saving purpose in history. But this idea of the eschatological banquet was not created by Isaiah. Its roots can be traced back to earlier Canaanite literature. The Qumran community took up this symbolism in the insti-tution of their daily meal, and Jesus also put it to various uses: in his conduct in eating with outcasts, in his parable of the great banquet which forms the gospel for today, and above all in the saying at the Last Supper that he would no longer feast with his disciples until he could do so in the consummated kingdom of God.

Responsorial Psalm: 23:1-3a, 3b-4, 5, 6
It is instructive to compare the use of this psalm here with that on the Sunday 16, series B. There the emphasis is indicated by the refrain, which focuses on the image of the shepherd. Here, since it is in response

to the Isaiah reading on the messianic banquet, the emphasis lies upon the house or temple of the Lord, where he prepares the banquet table and invites his people to share the blessings of his kingdom. The third stanza marks a shift of imagery from God as shepherd to God as host at his banquet.

Reading II: Philippians 4:12-14, 19-20

On the partition theory, these excerpts from Philippians would be from Letter A, the thank-you note for the relief they had sent him while in prison, probably at Ephesus (see above).

Paul seems a trifle embarrassed to accept any gift at all. C. H. Dodd spoke of Paul's "sturdy bourgeois independence," which made him a little too proud to accept help readily in this way. Or was it just the stoic detachment (v. 12a)? Perhaps, however, it is more theologically based than that. Paul knows that the existence of an apostle is marked by the sign of the cross — in facing hunger and want as readily as plenty and abundance. There is a slight undertone suggesting that inadvertently the Philippians had deprived him of his boasting in his sufferings. But Paul is too gracious to say so, and although admitting that he could have gotten along very well without it, he nevertheless thanks them for their kindness. It is a pity that v. 18 has been omitted, for there Paul gives the Philippians' charitable act a theological meaning — it was a sacrifice acceptable and pleasing to God.

Gospel: Matthew 22:1-14 (long form); 22:1-10 (short form)

It is interesting to compare the long and the short form. The long form is really two parables spliced together, the parable of the great banquet and the parable of the man without a wedding garment. That the combination is secondary is shown by Luke (14:16-24) and by the Gospel of Thomas, where the great banquet occurs on its own without the addition of a wedding garment. The combination produces an unrealistic effect, for one inevitably asks, how could the poor man have been expected to have a wedding garment if he had been hauled unexpectedly from the streets? The answer is that in the original parable he had not just come off the streets. In its original form the parable stood on its own. The original opening of it was then lost when it was joined to the parable of the great banquet. Although it is difficult to be certain, it seems likely that the evangelist was responsible for the combination of the two parables. He interprets the gathering in of the ragtag and bobtail from the streets allegorically as Jesus' prediction of the subsequent Gentile mission, and adds the second parable as a warning against their admission on too easy terms. It is unlikely that the evangelist was requiring the circumcision of the Gentiles, since that issue had been settled long before at the apostolic conference (Gal 2; cf. Acts 15). Matthew may be inserting a bit of propaganda in favor of the apostolic decrees which, according to Acts 15, were promulgated at the council, but which in all probability were enacted at a later conference while Paul was away (cf. Acts 21:25). As an original parable of Jesus, the man with the wedding garment would be an exhortation to readiness in face of the coming kingdom of God, like many other parables. The invitation came sooner than the men had expected, and it caught him unprepared. Woe to the man in such a case!

The shorter form, as we have noted, consists of the parable of the great banquet by itself. A study of the parallels in Luke and in the Gospel of Thomas shows that the version in Matthew is highly allegorized. Again, the allegorization has produced some quite unrealistic features. It is most unlife-like — and Jesus' parables were life-like, even if they often end on a note of surprise. What invited guest would not merely spurn the invitation but actually kill the servants who brought it? And what host would send out his troops (!), not only to destroy those murderers but to burn down their *city* (!). Clearly, these details reflect the events of A.D. 66–70, the Jewish war and the destruction of Jerusalem. With these accretions, the parable is used by the post-A.D. 70 church as an interpretation of the debacle of those years: they were a punishment upon Israel for rejecting the gospel, for persecuting the Christian messengers and for putting them to death. But this is not the end of the allegorization. Comparison again with Luke and Thomas shows that in Matthew the parable has been transformed in other ways. In the other versions it is simply a great banquet given by a private individual. But in Matthew it is the story of a wedding feast made by a *king* for his *son*. The king is equated with God and the son with Jesus, the Messiah. This of course is an entirely natural post-Easter reinterpretation, but if we want to ask what Jesus meant when he told the parable we have to disregard these later elements. It is a judgment on Jesus' contemporaries, who rejected his invitation to the coming kingdom, and an assurance to the outcast with whom he celebrated in advance the great banquet.

The Homily

People are often puzzled by the longer form of today's gospel, and although the homily is not the place to air scholarly problems and solutions, experience has shown that it does help to introduce a little "higher criticism" to relieve the difficulties of this particular pericope. The accompanying first reading and the psalm however divert attention from the secondary allegorical features and accretions to the image of the great banquet. If we take the longer form, it would be convenient to take up the second parable, the man without the wedding garment, and speak of preparedness for the eucharistic banquet. An exhortation composed to be read before holy communion in the Book of Common Prayer at the time of the Reformation, though little used today, alludes to this little parable in the following words:

"Which [sc. the holy sacrament] being so divine and comfortable a thing to them who receive it worthily, and so dangerous to them that will presume to receive it unworthily; my duty is to exhort you in the mean season to consider the dignity of that holy Mystery, and the great peril of the unworthy receiving thereof; and so search and examine your own consciences . . . that ye may come holy and clean to such a heavenly Feast, in the marriage garment required by God in Holy Scripture, and be received as worthy partakers of that Holy Table."

The renewed emphasis on the banquet aspect of the holy eucharist would make this teaching singularly appropriate, when it often appears that the banquet emphasis has deprived the liturgy of the awesomeness it once had.

If the shorter version of the gospel is used, we would again recommend disregarding the allegorical additions, and concentrating on the image of the banquet, this time emphasizing that "everything is ready." "God fulfills his promises and comes forward out of his hiddenness. But if the 'children of the kingdom,' the theologians and pious circles, pay no heed to his call, the despised and the ungodly will take their place; the others will receive nothing but a 'Too late' from behind the closed doors of the banquet hall" (J. Jeremias). Can we discern something like this happening in our world today?

TWENTY-NINTH SUNDAY OF THE YEAR

Reading I: Isaiah 45:1, 4-6

In Deutero-Isaiah we find a remarkable treatment of the Persian emperor Cyrus. Although he is a pagan king, he is saluted as the anointed of Yahweh, his servant raised up to conquer Babylon and restore God's people to their homeland:

For the sake of my servant Jacob,
  and Israel my chosen,
I call you by name,
  I surname you, though you do not know me.

This inaugurates a line of Jewish teaching about the state, including the pagan state, which culminates in Jesus' pronouncement about the payment of tribute money (today's gospel) and Paul's teaching about the Roman state under the emperor Nero as the servant and minister of God.

Responsorial Psalm: 96:1 and 3, 4-5, 7-8, 9-10ac

Another selection from this psalm is used for the Second Sunday, series C. It is one of the enthronement psalms of which we had several examples before (see comment, for example, on Ascension Day last year). This psalm (which incidentally tends to be overworked in Anglicanism, I suspect because of the BCP's mistranslation of the first line of the third stanza as "worship the Lord in the beauty of holiness") has close affinities in theological outlook with the Second Isaiah. It emphasizes the sovereignty of Yahweh over all nations, and thus forms a fitting response to the proclamation of God's appointment of Cyrus.

Reading II: 1 Thessalonians 1:1-5b

First Thessalonians is interesting as the earliest written document in the New Testament — authored by Paul during his stay at Corinth in 50 A.D. Paul had founded the church at Thessalonica not very long before. He had had to leave it hurriedly, and in his anxiety over his recent converts, he sent Timothy to see how things were going along. The report Timothy brought back was largely favorable — hence the warm tone of the opening thanksgiving, which forms the main part of this epistle reading. But there were also a few problems, which we shall get on to on the 32nd and 33rd Sundays.

Gospel: Matthew 22:15-21

Apart from a few stylistic changes, Matthew has taken over this pericope substantially in the Marcan form. He also retains the Marcan context where it precedes the question of the Sadducees about the resurrection (Mk 12:18-27 / Mt 22:23-33), though Matthew has inserted the parable of the great banquet between the parable of the vineyard and the present pericope. Also, Matthew has rewritten the introduction so as to speak of a *plot* to entrap Jesus. The result of these changes is to emphasize that the episode of the tribute money was part of Jesus' conflict with his opponents. It thus is part of the material with which Matthew seeks to speak directly to the situation of the church in his day, locked as it was in mortal combat with the Jewish leaders of Jamnia over the question of what was true orthodoxy and who were the true people of God.

The Pharisees' question about the tribute money is a classic example of the so-called pronouncement story, with its threefold form of setting, action and pronouncement. Everything in this story is subordinated to the punchline: "Give to Caesar the things that belong to Caesar, and to God the things that are God's."

This pronouncement has been interpreted in many different ways in the course of Christian history. Often, like Romans 13, it has been construed in the interests of a conservative throne-and-altar theology as in Lutheran orthodoxy, which reached its tragic climax in the German Christian movement during the Nazi period. Exegesis in Germany has swung today to the other extreme: "only a penny for Caesar, everything else for God." A more reasonable interpretation would be that Caesar has his own legitimate sphere, but it is a limited one, and even that he holds under God, and is responsible to God for its proper governance. This does not necessarily mean — though in certain circumstances it has meant and could mean again — that the state itself has to profess Christianity. It means that the state must be what it is, and perform the proper functions of a state in maintaining law and order and promoting the welfare of its citizens. But when it oversteps the mark and puts itself in the place of God, the Christian is in the last resort absolved from obedience. He only had to give Caesar the things that are his, not the things that are God's. We must obey God rather than man.

The Homily

The obvious basis for today's homily is the gospel, supported by the first reading and the psalm. This would require a treatment of the proper biblical attitude to the state and what this entails today. Such a theme would provide a suitable occasion to discuss the Christian attitude to war in as concrete a way as possible, or the Christian's duty in an election year.

The opening of 1 Thessalonians offers several alternative possibilities. For example, one could give a meditation on the Christian greeting, "grace and peace," relating it to the Pax in the liturgy; or a meditation on faith, hope and love as the criteria by which the apostle measures Christian growth; or again, the gospel as coming not only by word, but in the power of the holy Spirit.

Reading I: Exodus 22:21-27

This reading is an excerpt from the book of the covenant (Ex 20:22–23:19). The materials in this book are akin to many legal codes of the Ancient Near East, the most famous of which is the Code of Hammurabi (toward the end of the first century B.C.). The biblical code was apparently crystallized in the ninth century. Today's reading comes from a section of the code dealing with laws of social conduct. They inculcate a social ethic based upon compassion. Abstract justice is not enough, especially for the underprivileged. This lesson was obviously chosen to go with the summary of the law, which forms today's gospel reading. The effect is to slant the summary in a social direction.

Responsorial Psalm: 18:1-2a, 2bc-3, 46 and 50ab

This is a royal psalm for thanksgiving for victory in battle, possibly written by David himself. The selected stanzas make an appropriate hymn of praise for any occasion, but it is difficult to discern any specific connections with the other readings here, except perhaps in the refrain, which takes up the thought of the love of God also found in the summary of the law.

Reading II: 1 Thessalonians 1:5c-10

This week we continue Paul's thanksgiving for the progress of the Thessalonians in the gospel. This passage is particularly important for the hints it gives of what Paul had preached at Thessalonica on his foundation visit: "you turned from idols to serve a living and true God, and to wait for his Son from heaven whom he raised from the dead, Jesus who delivers us from the wrath to come." From this it may be inferred that Paul's gospel to Gentile audiences would have comprised:

1. An apologetic for monotheism
2. A proclamation for the deliverance wrought by Jesus through his (death and) resurrection
3. The prospect of Jesus' impending return

In his evangelistic preaching to pagans Paul could take less for granted than when preaching to the Jews. He has to start with faith in the One

God. We shall see later how the promise of the parousia would lead to serious problems for the Thessalonians when some of their number died before it had occurred.

Gospel: Matthew 22:34-40

The summary of the law is not original with Jesus. Its two parts represent a combination of Dt 6:5 with Lv 19:18. Nor is the combination itself original to Jesus, for it is found in at least one earlier Jewish work, the Testimonies of the XII Patriarchs, an amalgam of wisdom and apocalyptic materials. Jesus' thought was similarly cast in both molds, wisdom and apocalyptic, and the summary of the law represents the wisdom facet of his teaching. Jesus undoubtedly appeared not only as the final apocalyptic preacher, but also as the authoritative declarer of God's wisdom.

In the Jewish parallels the two commandments stand side by side, as a convenient summary. Jesus understands the interlocking of the two commandments in a new and quite radical way. You cannot have one without the other. Without the love of neighbor the love of God remains a barren emotion, and without the love of God love of neighbor is but a refined form of self-love.

The Homily

Today the homilist's obvious choice would be to propound the summary of the law, pointing up the intimate connection between the love of God and the love of neighbor, and in the light of the Old Testament reading, giving love of neighbor a social slant, thus proclaiming a politics of compassion.

The epistle reading might give the homilist an opportunity to stress the importance of monotheism over against idolatry — which today can be demythologized as a false ultimate concern.

Last Sundays of Year A

Reading I: Malachi 1:14b–2:2b, 8-10

The caption provides a fair summary of the first paragraph of this denunciation, which is addressed to the priests of Israel. The prophetic book of "Malachi" (the name Malachi means "my messenger," and is taken from 3:1; the work is really anonymous) was written after the return of the exiles, and is directed against the abuses that marked the restoration of the sacrificial system. The priestly caste was particularly at fault. We generally think of the Old Testament priests as offerers of sacrifices. "Malachi" however lays greater stress on instruction, a priestly function no less important. The relationship between the Old Testament priesthood and ministerial priesthood as it is known in Catholic Christianity is not a direct one, for Christian priesthood can only be understood from the priesthood and sacrifice of Christ. Nevertheless, teaching is a function of both Old Testament and Christian priesthood. The Old Testament priests were guardians of the Torah, and just as sacrifice and instruction went on hand in hand in the old dispensation, so sacramental ministrations and teaching go hand in hand in the Christian ministry.

An old fashioned Anglican dogmatic theologian has written: "The priest's highest duty is to consecrate the Eucharist, and the next, to give absolution. But the Eucharist must be accompanied by preaching and teaching and the absolution must usually be accompanied by counsel. Therefore, the priest must be a man of holiness, of learning, with a knowledge[1] of human nature; he must know his Bible, and the art of teaching."

Despite the caption, however, it appears that this pericope was chosen because of the second paragraph and its opening question, "Have you

---

[1] C. B. Moss, *The Christian Faith* (1943), 394.

not all one Father?" This question is echoed by our Lord's statement in the gospel reading, "you have one Father."

One often hears it said in Christian circles that the teaching of the Fatherhood of God was new with Jesus and is unique to Christianity. This is not fair to the Old Testament, as our text from Malachi indicates, or to Judaism. There is some precedent for Jesus' teaching on the Fatherhood of God in the Old Testament, though it must be admitted that it is not the dominant aspect of its doctrine of God as it was for Jesus, nor does it have the unique features that it has in his teaching.

Responsorial Psalm: 131:1, 2, 3

This is one of the psalms expressing the individual's trust and confidence in Yahweh. It is a beautiful testimony to the piety of the "poor" in Israel.

Usually we have found that the responsorial psalm is what its name suggests, a response to the Old Testament reading. This time, however, it appears to introduce the epistle. The psalmist rests in Yahweh like a child on his mother's bosom, and in a similar image the apostle Paul speaks of himself in his pastoral ministry among the Thessalonians as like a nurse taking care of her children.

Reading II: 1 Thessalonians 2:7-9, 13

This passage comes from the part of 1 Thes where the apostle gives thanks to God and recalls his missionary preaching at Thessalonica and his converts' response to his preaching. This preaching was accompanied by a deep pastoral concern for the Thessalonians as people. His preaching of the gospel was not of a "take it or leave it" kind.

Part of this pastoral concern was shown in his refusal to be an economic burden on the infant community. He worked night and day, he says, to earn his living rather than make demands upon them. The Book of Acts explains that Paul worked as a tentmaker. This behavior of course is no universal prescription for the ministry, and Paul himself knew the dominical precept that the laborer was worthy of his hire. But he had special reasons not to avail himself of this privilege. Practice in this matter has varied during the history of the Christian church. In the western world we are mostly familiar with the "clergyman," a member of a paid profession. But circumstances are changing, and the idea of tentmaking priests is being seriously discussed again, and even beginning to be practised to some extent at least in Anglicanism. There was also the priest-worker experiment in France. Such a shift would in itself be contrary neither to scripture nor to ancient tradition. As for Paul, it must be a matter of expediency — whichever serves best the preaching of the gospel and continued pastoral care.

The third paragraph of this reading contains a whole theology of preaching. The Thessalonians received the proclamation of Paul and his colleagues not as the word of man, but for what it really was, the word of God. Preaching is the word of God given in and through the words of men. It requires on the part of the preacher fidelity to the apostolic witness to Jesus Christ (Paul as an apostle is a fountainhead of that witness) and prayer that God will take the feeble words of the preacher and make them vehicles of his word. On the part of the listeners it requires the discernment of faith, that they may hear the word of God given in and through the human words of the preacher, and prayer so that the word may bring forth fruit in their lives. Both preacher and congregation need to pray for the Holy Spirit.

Gospel: Matthew 23:1-12

Mt 23 is a lengthy denunciation of the Pharisees. It makes very painful reading, and we wonder today — especially since Pope John XXIII's laudable attempt to improve relations between the Christian church and the Jewish community — how Jesus could have indulged in such vitriolic condemnation of religious leaders who, as Jewish scholars are constantly reminding us, were for the most part good men.

Several considerations need to be borne in mind. Mt 23 as it stands has been composed by the evangelist himself: It is not a speech actually delivered by Jesus. The cumulative effect is created not by Jesus but by the evangelist himself. Second, Matthew was involved in the struggle between his own Jewish Christian church and the rabbis who after the fall of Jerusalem were consolidating their authority in Judaism. It is that struggle that is reflected here. Third, condemnation of one's opponents as hypocrites was not confined to the Christian side. The rabbis frequently retorted in kind. Fourth, in composing this speech Matthew drew on traditional material. He started with the quite short rebuke of the *scribes* (N.B. not the whole Pharisaic party!) in Mk 12:30-40. Some of the woes against the Pharisees come from the source common to Matthew and Luke (Mt 23:13 par., 23 par., 25-27 par.; 29-31 par.). But much of it comes from Matthew's special source, which reflects the views of a Jewish-Christian community rather than those of Jesus himself. There was certainly an element of anti-Pharisaic teaching in Jesus — he denounced *some* Pharisees, particularly the Pharisaic scribes, for hypocrisy. But, as Luke's special tradition also shows, he could take a quite favorable view of other Pharisees, and they were quite friendly toward him. We must keep the whole thing in proportion, and see this chapter in its historical context. An element which was present in Jesus' teaching has been exaggerated out of all proportions for historical reasons that no longer obtain.

In applying such material to the life of the church today, we have to remember that, to quote the title given to a course of sermons by Hoskyns, "*We* are the Pharisees." We must allow such denunciations to be addressed as warnings to us, especially to those of us who exercise a leadership role in the church — the clergy, and the bishops in particular. We, like the rabbis, are the guardians of tradition, only ours is the apostolic tradition, theirs a tradition going back to Moses. We also are in constant danger of not living up to our own teaching. We enjoy ostentation, flattery, special insignia and honorific titles. (The present attempt to reduce episcopal regalia in the Roman communion is a move in the right direction and to be applauded; it has hardly yet hit the Anglican episcopate, apart from the mild suggestion at the last Lambeth conference that English bishops should drop the title "My Lord".)

Non-Catholics are often puzzled by the seeming contradiction between Mt 23.9 and the practice of addressing priests as "father." We should not dismiss their puzzlement too lightly. If "father" is insisted upon as a personal distinction by the priest himself, or if the person using it does so without remembering that it means that the priest is the sacramental sign of the presence of God himself as Father, then such a usage would come under the condemnation of Matthew's injunction (it is hardly from Jesus himself). Anglicans should note that the Book of Common Prayer uses the ministerial title Father very sparingly — only in address to the bishop in a liturgical context, when he is clearly acting as the sacramental embodiment of the Fatherhood of God. Should it not therefore be used only in a functional context?

The Homily

Today's readings are joined together by the overarching theme of priesthood and ministry. The Old Testament reading emphasizes that teaching and instruction must accompany the performance of liturgical duties. The psalm and epistle reading highlights the notion of pastoral care. The pastor is like a nurse (note that feminine imagery is sometimes used of the ministry in scripture!). The gospel emphasizes the guardianship of apostolic tradition and the necessity of a life in conformity with the teaching, the warning against regarding the ministry as a ground for personal pride, rather than as a sacramental sign of the presence of God in the word and sacrament.

There is a second theme, shared by the Old Testament reading and the gospel, that of the Fatherhood of God. This could provide alternative material for meditation. Here it should be stressed that the Fatherhood of God is not a general, universal truth, but a covenant relationship.

✓ THIRTY-SECOND SUNDAY OF THE YEAR

As we approach the end of the church year and Advent draws near, the mood of the liturgy perceptibly changes [cf. our comments on the 31st Sunday, series C, above] and becomes eschatological. This is in accord with tradition, for anciently Advent started earlier and lasted longer.

Reading I: Wisdom 6:12-16

This excerpt comes from the conclusion of the first part of Wisdom. The theme of that part is that wisdom is the gateway to immortality. Hence the overall context — though it is hardly visible from our extract — is eschatological. The pericope itself is a concluding exhortation to seek wisdom, an assertion of her accessibility (cf. Proverb 8). Bearing in mind its eschatological context, we can relate this reading to other readings. Those who seek and find wisdom will have acquired something that will survive the last judgments which Paul describes in 1 Thes 4, while the gospel speaks of the "wise" virgins — those who sought after wisdom. Cf. also the emphasis on vigilance in v. 15 with Mt 25:13.

Responsorial Psalm: 63:1abc, 1d-3, 4-5, 6-7

The first part of this psalm (through v. 8) falls in the category of an individual lament. The soul expresses its thirst for communion with God in the temple and its delight when communion is established. We may link this with the search for the divine wisdom (first reading) and with the virgins' longing to meet the bridegroom (gospel).

Reading II: 1 Thessalonians 4:13-18 (long form); 4:13-14 (short form)

The short form is apparently permitted not merely on the grounds of brevity, but because it omits the highly bizarre eschatological imagery of the long form. Such imagery is certainly difficult for the modern

Christian and requires demythologizing if its message is to be rightly heard.

Paul's converts had received from him the impression that the second coming was imminent (cf. 1:9, also see 30th Sunday). Meanwhile some of them have died — before the parousia. First Paul urges them not to grieve and then states his grounds for not grieving: since Jesus died and rose again, the believers who die will likewise rise again. Then he seeks to prove this from a "word of the Lord." Scholars are divided as to whether this means a saying of the earthly Jesus (cf. perhaps Mk 9:1) or a saying received from the risen Christ through a Christian prophet like the sayings in the Book of Revelation.

How are we to demythologize, i.e., not eliminate the imagery but interpret it for faith? The clue lies in Paul's final word: "So shall we always be with the Lord." The ultimate hope of the believer is christological, and it is corporate. It is christological for it is not merely a hope of individual survival of death, but of being with the risen Christ in his transformed, resurrection existence. It is not attained through any intrinsic quality of one's own, such as an immortal soul, but solely because Jesus has entered into this existence before us and will enable us to enter into it, too. It is corporate, for again the Christian hope is not for individual salvation, but for the restoration in Christ of humanity, indeed of the whole cosmos. Paul was time-conditioned in his apocalyptic imagery and mistaken in his belief that the parousia was imminent, but he asserts an abiding truth. And because of that truth the Christian is enabled to transcend the grief of bereavement, unlike "the others who have no hope."

Gospel: Matthew 25:1-13

The parable of the ten virgins (R.S.V. "maidens") would appear to have a long history behind it. Like many other parables, it may be interpreted at three different levels of tradition — Jesus, the oral tradition of the early post-Easter church, and the evangelist's redaction.

It is often argued that this parable is an allegory and therefore could not have come from Jesus. But it is not a pure allegory even in Matthew. Any allegory concocted by the early church would have surely made the bride central to the story, for in the early church's ecclesiology the church was the bride of Christ. But the bride is never mentioned. If the parable comes from Jesus, it must be a story taken from real life. True, it contains several puzzling details — whose house was the groom entering, the bride's or his own, and in whose house did the marriage feast take place? What made the groom arrive so late? Would a wedding feast have taken place after midnight? Were the virgins bridesmaids, and if so, why did they have to escort the groom? The fact is, we know too little about contemporary marriage customs to answer all these questions and must assume that the whole story is true to life — though possibly with one element of surprise on which the whole meaning of the story turns, namely the astonishingly late arrival of the groom. In order to understand what the story could have meant on the lips of Jesus, we must forget all the allegorical equations (groom = the Son of man, his return = the parousia, the virgins = good and bad Christians or believers and unbelievers, the wedding feast = Messianic banquet) and let the parable make its own point as a story from life. The original parable was a comment on the situation in Jesus' ministry. Those who hear Jesus' message of the dawning kingdom and respond with repentance and faith will be accepted when it finally comes, while those who reject his message will find out their mistake too late.

The early church (cf. Lk 13:25) began to give allegorical interpretations to the individual elements in the story in order to adapt the parable to their own situation. The Jewish community by and large had rejected the church's preaching of Jesus as Messiah, while others had accepted it.

Finally Matthew places the parable in the framework of his gospel. The introductory word "then" in v. 1 (omitted in the incipit of the Lectionary) links the parable to the foregoing chapter, the so-called synoptic Apocalypse which culminates in the coming of the Son of man for the last judgment. At the end Matthew adds a floating saying in the Jesus tradition, "Watch therefore, for you know neither the day nor the hour." Viewed in the overall context of Matthew's gospel the parable now acquires a fresh meaning. The division between the wise and the foolish virgins becomes the division between those in Matthew's church who keep the commandments of Christ, the new lawgiver of the church, and those who hear his words but fail to do what he commands. Note also that Matthew follows the parable of the Ten Virgins with the parables of the Talents and of the Sheep and Goats. All three parables make pretty much the same point.

The Homily

Today's readings clearly invite the homilist to proclaim the eschatological message of the gospel. Three possible accentuations of this message are suggested, one by the Old Testament reading and psalm, one by the epistle and one by the gospel.

If he chooses to follow the Old Testament reading and psalm, the homilist will speak of the heavenly wisdom which alone can satisfy man's religious quest and which alone will stand him in good stead in the final judgment. The lives of Christians will be judged according to whether they have sought and found this wisdom or rejected it. Here an allusion to the wise and foolish virgins could also be introduced.

If he chooses to expound the epistle reading, the homilist will have an opportunity to demythologize Paul's picture of the parousia. This must be done in answer to the question of Paul's Thessalonians, also asked today, Where are our dead? What has become of them? Shall we see them again? The homilist will seek to express the Christian hope, which is both christological and corporate. If there are people in his congregation who hanker after "spiritism" the Christian hope as set forth by Paul should render that particular answer to a legitimate question unnecessary. For the ground of Christian hope is not that we can communicate with the dead but that Jesus died and rose again.

If the homilist chooses to preach on today's gospel reading, we would suggest that he follow Matthew's redactorial interpretation, and equate the wise and foolish virgins with two types of Christians, those who hear the word and keep it and those who hear the word but do not do it. But since the same point comes up in the following week in the parable of the talents, he may find it best to preach on one of the other readings for today's homily and plan next week to preach on the parable of the talents.

THIRTY-THIRD SUNDAY OF THE YEAR

Reading I: Proverbs 31:10-13, 19-20, 30-31

Proverbs' picture of the virtuous woman is a beautiful one, though it is hard to see its connection with today's other readings. Perhaps the caption helps us: "Give her a share in what she has worked" (v. 31), a thought which recurs in the parable of the talents, the profitable servants were given a share in their earnings. But to concentrate on this point detracts from the main thrust of both readings. The first reading is a picture of a gracious wife and mother who practises love for both God and man in that state of life into which God has pleased to call her. One can only hope that "women's lib" has not rendered this picture obsolete!

Responsorial Psalm: 128:1-2, 3, 4-5

Stanza II fits admirably with the Old Testament reading. It is also balancing the picture: the God-fearing wife (Prv 31:30) is matched by a God-fearing husband (Ps 128, v. 1 and 5). Note the typically Old Testament concern with the community. Its ideal is not just the happiness of an individual family — the welfare of the family enriches the life of the whole community. The same thought was present in the second stanza of Prv 31. The graces and virtues of the good housewife are not confined to the home but extended to the community at large by concern for the poor. The new marriage services emphasize that a Christian home should not be self-centered but reach out in blessing to the community around it.

Reading II: 1 Thessalonians 5:1-6

Paul is apparently replying to a question from his correspondents concerning "the times and seasons" — i.e., the precise date of the parousia, which Paul's original preaching had led them to expect imminently. Paul rejects the inference. There is one thing they need to know, the end will come suddenly (cf. Mk 13:32 and Acts 1:8). Despite these warnings of scripture, however, curiosity over the date of the end has continued to exercise the minds of Christians ever since, and ignorant and unscholarly fanatics claiming the date of the parousia can always win a ready hearing. But the Book of Revelation is about events in the first century, not in the twentieth or any other. The experience of history shows that announcements of the exact date of the end have invariably been proven wrong. And as fundamentalists such fanatics should take 1 Thes 5:1-6, Mk 13:32 and Acts 1:8 to heart!

Jesus' parable of the thief in the night (Mk 13:35 par.; Lk 12:39f.) is one which the Thessalonians apparently knew already (v. 2) — an interesting indication that Paul may have transmitted more Jesus tradition than the letters suggest. By citing this parable Paul elevates the parousia hope from one of curious speculation to one of existential attitude. The Christian must always live on tiptoe, as if the parousia were to come at any moment. But there is more to it than "as if." In a manner typical of his teaching (cf. Rom 13:11-14) Paul insists that the end has in some sense come already. Christian believers are already children of the light and the day. The imperative is based on an indicative: Be what you are, children of the light and the day. Here is the final answer to the fanaticism of parousia excitement. It is not a matter for idle curiosity but one of living here and now out of the power of the future which we have already begun to participate in through baptism.

Gospel: Matthew 25:14-30 (long form); 25:14-15, 19-20 (short form)

When I read the shorter form, I rubbed my eyes in astonishment. Is the reading meant to stop at v. 20? Surely, it should at least include v. 21. Otherwise the caption refers to nothing in the text. Hopefully, the longer form will be used for else the reading loses its whole point.

As with the parable of the ten virgins, we may distinguish three stages in the history of the tradition. At the Jesus level it was a story told from life.

The owner of an estate had to go on a long journey, so he left his money to three servants in trust lest it should remain idle during his absence. Two of them put it to wise use, made capital gains, and were commended by the master on his return. But a third servant carefully hoarded it, and on the master's return gave him back the exact sum he had been entrusted with. Instead of commending the third servant for his caution, the master rebuked him and handed over the money to the most enterprising of the three servants.

When Jesus first told this story, he must have applied it to something quite concrete in his ministry. Perhaps he was condemning the Jewish religious authorities. They were like the third servant, so carefully bent on preserving in its purity the tradition with which they had been entrusted that they lost their openness for new things and refused to accept Jesus' message.

In the early community the parable was moralized by the addition of the maxim, "To everyone who has, God will give: but from him who has not, he will take away even what he has." In addition, the parable was allegorized. The master was equated with Christ, his departure with the ascension, and his delayed return with the delay of the parousia. The words "enter into the joy of the Lord" are inserted so that the reward becomes participation in the messianic banquet.

Matthew places the parable in his sequence of parables following the synoptic apocalypse which culminates with the Son of man coming to judge the *church*. The profitable servant now stands for those Christians who hear the teaching of Christ and do it, the unprofitable servant the Christians who do not keep the new law enunciated by Jesus for the church.

The Homily

If the homilist is prepared to drop today's eschatological note, he could take the first reading and its responsorial psalm as the basis for an exposition of Christian marriage and family life. He should stick closely to the text, emphasizing particularly the responsibility of the family toward the community at large, and illustrating this from the new marriage rites. If, however, he wishes to preserve the eschatological aspect, three alternatives may be proposed. The choice between them will depend upon the pastor's knowledge of his congregation and its needs.

The second reading will provide an opportunity to damp down curiosity about the "times and seasons" and divert attention to the existential attitude of vigilance, living "as if" the Lord is to come at any moment, and the Christian's responsibility to be what he was made in baptism, a son of the day and a son of light.

The gospel reading suggests two possibilities, depending on whether we take it at the Jesus level or at the level of the evangelist. At the Jesus level there is a possible analogy between the servant who hid the treasure in a napkin and church people who oppose all change. Of course the genuine values of the past must be preserved, but clinging to past customs may indicate a desire for false security and a lack of adventurous obedience to the will of God here and now.

At the level of the evangelist's redaction the homilist could take the line suggested last week in connection with the parable of the ten virgins (see above), if he did not do it then.

CHRIST THE KING

Last year we noted how the liturgy now sets Christ's kingship in an eschatological context, as also does the Bible. "His enthronement at the Ascension is the opening act of his final eschatological reign, and his continued heavenly rule between the Ascension and his return marks the progressive defeat of the powers of evil. For he must reign until he has subjected all enemies under his feet." Today's readings, especially the epistle, confirm our point.

Reading I: Ezekiel 34:11-12, 15-17

As we noted last year, there is a close connection between the images of king and shepherd, a connection presumably going back to the figure of David.

Ezekiel prophesied during the Babylonian exile. In the earlier part of chapter 34 he delivers a strong indictment against the pre-exilic kings of Judah who had been false shepherds. Because of this, Yahweh himself will henceforth take over the shepherding of his people (v. 15). He will seek out the lost and bring back the strayed (vv. 12, 16) — an allusion to Israel's return from exile and resettlement in the Holy Land (cf. v. 13 omitted here). The verses suggest that Ezekiel envisaged a theocracy for the monarchy was not to be restored. Later on in chapter 34, however, Yahweh says that he will set over them David, who shall be a shepherd and prince among them. The apparent contradiction is resolved if the Davidic king is the agent and representative of Yahweh, a concept which carries over into the messianic hope. The same *prima facie* contradiction occurs in the gospels. In the synoptic parable of the lost sheep, which is undoubtedly authentic to Jesus himself, it is Yahweh who seeks out the lost sheep — though he does so implicitly through Jesus. But in the Johannine allegory of the Good Shepherd (Jn 10), Christ is the Good Shepherd not alongside of nor in addition to Yahweh, but as the representative of the Father. It is in Jesus Christ therefore that the prophecy of Ezekiel comes finally to rest.

The last verse, v. 17, introduces the note of judgment. The shepherd will distinguish between sheep and goats. This links the first reading with the gospels, cf. the caption.

Responsorial Psalm: 23:1-2a, 2b-3, 5-6
A slightly different arrangement of the same verses was used on Lent 4, series A. Here Ps 23 is much more suitable for it forms the obvious response to Ez 34.

Reading II: 1 Corinthians 15:20-26, 28
Many important problems are raised in this passage such as the concept of Christ as the first fruits, the Adam/Christ typology, the importance of "order" in the resurrection process and its relation to the Corinthians' gnostic view which held that Christians were already raised. But today's theme, the kingship of Christ, as well as the caption suggest that we should concentrate on v. 24.

One fact calls for comment and two problems for discussion. The fact in question is that according to Paul, Christ's reign is to be of limited duration. He reigns "until. . . ." It is destined to be replaced by the kingship of God himself when Christ delivers the kingdom to the Father.

The first of the problems is, what period is covered by Christ's reign? Verse 25 is one of the passages to which "chiliasm" or "millenarianism" appeals. Its chief basis is Rev (Apoc) 20. The Apocalypse speaks of a first and second resurrection. At the first resurrection only the faithful Christians rise, to reign 1000 years with Christ (the millennium). This is to be followed by a second or general resurrection. First Cor 15:26 is then interpreted by means of Rev 20. This interpretation is untenable for two reasons. First, it takes the events in the Apocalypse to be successive, rather than as varying description of the same event. Second, it allegorically harmonized Rev and 1 Cor.

It seems quite clear from 1 Cor that the reign of Christ is inaugurated with the resurrection/ascension (vv. 20, 27) and is destined to last until the second coming (vv. 23-24a). The kingdom of Christ is thus coterminous with the period of the church. "In chronological respect (not in spatial) the kingly rule of Christ and the Church completely coincide" (O. Cullmann). It is important to note that Christ's kingdom is a period of perpetual warfare with the "enemies" that will still be under his feet (v. 25). "The present kingdom of Christ is not a period of peace, but of glorious warfare" (H. L. Goudge).

The second problem is the idea of Christ's delivery of the kingdom to the Father and his subjection to him. What can this mean? It means that during the period of Christ's kingdom, the period of the church, God acts toward the world not directly, but through Christ. That is to say, every act that he does toward the world or the church is an extension of the act which accomplished once and for all the history of Jesus of Nazareth. But after the redemptive work of Christ has been completed at the consummation, God's relationship with the redeemed universe will become a direct one. "Now we see God and experience His action through the God-man who represents Him to us; then Christ will have brought us to the Father; we shall enjoy the Beatific Vision, and immediate union with God himself. . . . God will be all in all, not only in Christians but in the whole realm that Christ restored to him." [2]

[2] I have twice quoted from H. L. Goudge's commentary on 1 Cor (Westminster Commentaries, 1915, fourth ed. revised). I would call attention to this Anglican scriptural scholar whose work antedated biblical theology in Germany. Goudge was Regius Professor in the University of Oxford between the World Wars. His work has been much neglected even by Anglicans. Here is a subject for a master's thesis!

Gospel: Matthew 25:31-46

This pericope is often called the "parable" of the sheep and goats or of the last judgment. But such a designation is inaccurate. Except for the comparison in vv. 32-33, the whole story remains on the level of direct description. Its literary genre is that of an apocalyptic revelation. But there is a history behind the tradition. The parable is a combination of four elements:

1. Verses 32-33, the simile of the sheep and goats

2. A series of sayings about the reception accorded to Jesus' disciples, vv. 35-39, 40b, 41-45

3. the combinations (1) and (2) to provide an allegorical interpretation of the parable

4. Introduction, v. 31, and conclusion, v. 46, and the placement of the whole in its Matthean setting.

We will discuss each of these elements in turn.

1. The simile of the sheep and goats. Following J. A. T. Robinson we reconstruct this as follows:

It is with the kingdom of God as with a shepherd who separates the sheep from the goats. He will place the sheep on his right hand and the goats on his left.

There is no reason why this should not be an authentic parable of Jesus. There is nothing allegorical about it. The kingdom is compared not to a shepherd nor to the sheep and goats, but to the act of separation. It is similar to the parables of the wheat and tares and of the good and bad fish, both undoubtedly authentic parables of Jesus. The message is characteristic of Jesus' eschatology: acceptance or rejection at the end. It is a story taken from Palestinian life. During the daytime the sheep and goats are all mixed up. At night the shepherd separates them because the goats need shelter from the cold whereas the sheep are hardy enough to stay out all night (Jeremias). Since sheep are white and goats black, their separation can imply an act of judgment, enabling the parable to be applied to the kingdom of God in a way characteristic of Jesus. Acceptance or rejection of this message will determine which side one will be on at the last judgment, among the saved or the condemned. The final separation is being anticipated in Jesus' ministry.

2. The Sayings.

> I was hungry, and you gave me food,
> I was thirsty, and you gave me drink,

I was a stranger   and you welcomed me,
I was naked   and you clothed me,
I was sick   and you visited me,
I was in prison   and you came to me
When did we see you hungry and fed you
or thirsty and gave you drink?
When did we see you a stranger and welcomed you
or naked and clothed you?
When did we see you sick or in prison and visited you?
Amen, I say to you, as you did it to one of the least of these,
you did it to me.

Like other critics, T. W. Manson commented on the whole pericope that "It contains features of such startling originality that it is difficult to credit them to anyone but the Master himself." But as J. A. T. Robinson has rightly observed, when critics talk like that they are really speaking of these sayings, not the whole pericope. It is these that have the ring of the "Master himself." But what do they mean? They are commonly used by church preachers and by secular humanitarians as a piece of ethical teaching, inculcating concern for the victims of famine and oppression. God forbid that we should deny the necessity of such concern. But we must question whether this is the true exegesis of this passage, and whether therefore it should be so used homiletically It is closely akin to Mk 9:37 par.; Mk 9:41; and Lk 12:8f. par (Q), cf. Mk 8:38 par. Comparison with these sayings shows that the passage under examination, far from being a humanitarian lesson, is an assertion of the "shaliach" principle, according to which the acceptance or rejection of an accredited agent involves the acceptance or rejection of the sender, and the further assertion that acceptance or rejection of the accredited agent like acceptance or rejection of the sender will be validated at the last judgment. The life situation in which this passage would have been spoken by Jesus would therefore be when sending out his disciples on a mission.

That this is how Matthew himself understood these sayings is indicated by his addition of "my brothers" to the words "one of the least of these" (v. 40, not in 45). "Brothers" in Matthew always means disciples. Hunger, thirst, etc., symbolize the weakness and poverty of the disciples, the relief given to them the acceptance or rejection of them and their message exactly as in the saying about the cup of cold water in Mk 9:41. This interpretation will disappoint, perhaps even anger many, but we are responsible for a genuine exegesis of the text, not to make it say what we want to hear.

In the post-Easter church the shepherd is equated with a king (v. 40), i.e., God. Thus the parable became an allegory of the last judgment.

Finally, the evangelist takes up the allegorically interpreted parable and inserts the apocalyptic coloring, especially in v. 31 and 36. As a result the king of v. 40, somewhat unusually and awkwardly, became identified with the Son of man of v. 31. Matthew probably also inserted "all the nations" in v. 32, equating the judged with the nations to which the disciples will be sent to preach the gospel in all the world (Mt 28:16-20).

The Homily

The homilist will be very tempted to take the gospel in the popular humanitarian sense, linking it with today's theme of Christ the King. Unfortunately however as we have seen, a proper exegesis of this passage forbids him to do this. In preaching one must adhere to the exegesis of the text. Otherwise our preaching would be our own words, not the word of God.

If the preacher does want to give a humanitarian message he had better stick to the first reading, for Ez 34:16 will fit the bill. The caritative service of the Christian church can thus be expounded as an expression of the Christly care as king and shepherd. Ps 23 could also be related to this.

Other aspects of Christ's kingship expressed in today's readings are: Christ's kingship as the continued warfare with the powers of evil and the church as the agent of that warfare (second reading); Christ as judge over the nations of the world, who will be judged by the reception they have given to the church's proclamation of the gospel.

Advent to December 31 of Year B

In year B the gospel readings are taken from Mark, supplemented by John. This is necessary because since Mark's gospel is the shortest it requires supplementing. Also, in the three year cycle, John is otherwise only read at certain seasons (especially Lent and Eastertide) in years A and C.

Let us first remind ourselves of the new structure of the Advent season. The theme of future eschatology — the Christian hope for the final consummation of history — dominates the concluding Sundays of the year and reaches its climax in Advent I. On the following three Sundays, other themes, preparatory to the celebration of Christmas and the first coming of the Messiah, gradually take over. Thus each succeeding church season dovetails into its predecessor.

FIRST SUNDAY OF ADVENT

Reading I: Isaiah 63:16b-17, 64:1, 3b-8

This passage is a selection from the psalm of lament covering Is 63:7-64:11. It has been described as "one of the jewels of the Bible" (*Jerome Biblical Commentary*). The exiles had returned from Babylon with high hopes enkindled by Deutero-Isaiah's prophecies. But then nothing seemed to happen. The temple still lay in ruins:

> Our holy and beautiful house
>   where our fathers praised thee
> has been burned with fire,
>   and all our pleasant places have become ruins (64:11).

This is the historical context of the lament. The psalmist confesses his sins and the sins of his nation which he sees to be the cause of the delay in the restoration of Jerusalem: "our righteous deeds are like a polluted garment." He thus anticipates Paul's insight that every man's virtues are tainted with sin. The prophet cries out for God to intervene:

O that thou wouldst rend the heavens and come down,
    that the mountains might quake at thy presence!

These words were undoubtedly in the mind of the earliest evangelist when he recorded the story of Jesus' baptism. Mk 1:10 states that the heavens were "rent"—a word which the R.S.V. unfortunately obscures by translating it "were opened," thus assimilating it to the other synoptics and missing the point. This cry for divine intervention has long been associated with Advent. Many will remember that it provided the introit for the Fourth Sunday of Advent. *Rorate coeli desuper* was one of those Latin tags which everyone knew in the Middle Ages.

If with Mark we see the fulfillment of the psalmist's prayer in the Christ event, the church still looks for a final rending of the heavens when the Son of man shall come again. Indeed the church experiences a rending of the heavens in each liturgy, when Christ comes down in his sacrament to visit the people in their need.

Responsorial Psalm: 80:1ac and 2b, 14-15, 17-18
This psalm is a community lament, not dissimilar from the first reading, and thus a fitting response to it. As the refrain shows, it, too, is a cry for divine intervention. The same selection was used at Advent IV C.

In the last stanza, "man" and "Son of man" stand in synonymous parallelism, as often in Hebrew poetry. Both lines of the stanza are a petition for God to come and aid his creature, man. But the man in question is the king of Israel ("man of thy right hand"), for the king is the ideal embodiment and representative of humanity. Although there is no direct connection between this figure and the Davidic Son of man, it is possible to give the psalm verse a christological interpretation, since passages referring to the earthly king of Israel may be transferred to the messianic king. In that case, "man of thy right hand" and "Son of man" become references to Christ, and the stanza becomes a petition for God to intervene by sending his Messiah. That would make the psalm particularly appropriate for Advent.

Reading II: 1 Corinthians 1:3-9
This reading is the opening blessing and thanksgiving of 1 Corinthians (actually this was not the first letter Paul wrote to that community for

he tells us in 1 Cor 5:9 that he had written them a previous one). The thanksgiving is something of a *captatio benevolentiae*. Paul thanks God for the variety of charismatic gifts that have been manifested in the Corinthian community — their speech and knowledge (gnosis) — but later on he will have much to say in criticism of the way they are using these gifts, though never for a moment does Paul doubt that in themselves they are genuine gifts of God. Note how he immediately sets the charismatic gifts in an eschatological context. He reminds them that in spite of all their present knowledge, they are still waiting for the revealing of the Lord Jesus Christ. They need to be sustained by him to the end, and to be preserved guiltless in the day of our Lord Jesus Christ. Here are three reminders of the "not yet," which the Corinthian charismatics were so much in danger of forgetting in their intoxication with the gifts they already had. It is these reminders that make this lesson particularly appropriate for Advent. Paul's substantive criticism of the Corinthians' use or misuse of the charismatic gifts will be developed later in the letter, especially in chapters 12 and 14, which may be regarded as an unfolding of the implications of the eschatological pointers in the opening thanksgiving.

Gospel: Mark 13:33-37

As in the other years of the three year cycle, the requirements of Advent I (see above) make it necessary to begin the gospel readings not at the opening of each gospel but with the future-eschatological material in the synoptic apocalypse. This apocalypse in all three synoptics concludes with a series of eschatological parables. Today's reading is one of these, the parable of the doorkeeper.

This parable has a long and complicated history in the synoptic tradition, and as it stands in Mark has acquired secondary features, as comparison with the Lucan form (Lk 12:35-38) will show. These secondary features are: (1) "A man going on a journey" — a phrase taken from the parable of the talents: (2) "puts his servants in charge, each with his work," from the parable of the faithful and unfaithful servants (Mt 24:45/Lk 12:42). The insertion of (1) applies the parable clearly to the departure of Christ at his ascension, and identifies his return with the parousia. The second feature (2) applies the parable to the whole Christian community. It thus becomes a parable of the post-Easter church waiting for the delayed parousia. It is also likely that the fourfold division of the day (evening, midnight, cockcrow, morning) is an accommodation to Roman usage, replacing the Palestinian division of the first, second and third watches.

The original parable as told by Jesus will therefore be something like this: "A man goes out [for a dinner party] during the evening and commands the doorkeeper to be on the watch, so that when he comes back and knocks on the door he may open it at once and let him in." The parable concludes with an exhortation: "Watch then, for you do not know when the master of the house is coming, whether in the first or the second or even in the third watch."

We cannot be certain exactly what was the original application of the parable on the lips of Jesus. Joachim Jeremias thinks it was probably addressed to the religious leaders of Israel, the scribes. But it could just as well have been addressed to his disciples or to the crowd. In any case, it was originally a warning to be prepared for the final eschatological crisis which as Jesus saw it was soon to overtake his people as a result of his ministry. "It was not spoken to prepare the disciples for a long . . . period of waiting for the second coming, but to enforce the necessity for alertness in a crisis now upon them" (Dodd).

The church had to adapt this parable to the post-Easter situation. Now there was not one final crisis, but a phased out process: the ascension of Jesus, his waiting in heaven and his final return. The exhortation to watchfulness is now applied to the waiting church, and a series of fresh allegorical touches are added to the original parable in its various forms.

The Homily

The major emphasis today is on waiting for the divine intervention. This theme runs through all the readings. Nevertheless the context of this waiting varies. In the Old Testament reading and the psalm it is a context of disappointment and frustration. The history of the people of God has run into a bad patch. High hopes have remained unfulfilled. This perhaps could be directly related to the present situation of the church. The past years have seen great efforts at renewal and reform. Yet the drift away from the churches has been growing apace, despite their efforts to respond to the world's need. In this situation the church raises the advent cry "O that thou wouldst rend the heavens and come down!"

The charismatic movement has gripped the church in many places. As Paul did, so we must welcome it with thankfulness. Christian people are being enriched with all speech and knowledge, many are lacking in no spiritual gift. But those who have the gifts must be warned of the "not yet." They must still wait for the revealing of the Lord Jesus Christ. They still see through a glass darkly. They need to be sustained to the end and preserved guiltless to the day of the Lord Jesus Christ.

The gospel could be expounded either at the Jesus level, in which it is a warning to stay alert in the crisis caused by his coming, or at the church level, in which it is a warning to be alert for his return. The latter would be appropriate for this Sunday, and could be fitted well either to the first reading and the psalm or to the epistle reading.

SECOND SUNDAY OF ADVENT

Reading I: Isaiah 40:1-5, 9-11

This is the best known of the prophecies of Deutero-Isaiah. Indeed, it is one of the best known passages of the Old Testament, if for no other reason, because of its use by Handel in the three opening numbers of *The Messiah*.

Of course, the unknown prophet of the exile was not consciously thinking of the Christ event. He had in view the restoration of Israel from the Babylonian exile around 638 B.C. Cyrus of Persia had won his preliminary victories and the power of Babylon was waning. The prophet himself, then, is the voice that cries in the wilderness. He, according to the reading of the R.S.V. margin (anticipated by the English text of *The Messiah*) and certainly to be preferred, is the bearer of good tidings:

> Get you up to a high mountain,
>   O herald of good tidings to Zion;
> lift up your voice with strength,
>   O herald of good tidings to Jerusalem.

"Good tidings" — in the Hebrew original this is a verb which later gave us the noun "gospel" in its New Testament sense. The good tidings here is the good news of the impending divine intervention in history, bringing about the return from exile.

The prophet envisages this return as a second exodus, in which miracles similar to those of the first exodus will be repeated:

> Every valley shall be lifted up
>   and every mountain and hill be made low
> and the uneven ground shall become level,
>   and the rough places a plain.

One might call Deutero-Isaiah the father of typology. Henceforth the exodus event becomes the type of expected eschatological event, and is taken up into the New Testament as the type of Christ event itself. It was in this latter sense that this prophecy was applied in the text of *The Messiah*, and it is in the same sense that we read it today. Typology is based upon the conviction not that history repeats itself, but that God's mighty acts in history follow a consistent pattern because God is true to himself and his purpose.

The eschatological event is defined as the revealing of God's glory, a thought which will have a profound significance in New Testament theology (cf. e.g., Jn 1:14). "Glory" becomes a word of salvation history; it is an event, the event of the active, saving presence of Yahweh. Yahweh "comes with might."

If the expected event becomes in Christian interpretation the Christ event, so too, according to the New Testament, the prophet of the exile foreshadows John the Baptist. He is the "voice" (Jn 1:23, to be read next week) which cries: "in the wilderness prepare the way of the Lord" (cf. today's gospel). His preparatory work which will make a highway for the advent of the Messiah will be his preaching of repentance.

Responsorial Psalm: 85:8ab and 9, 10-11, 12-13

No one knows for certain when this lament was composed, or what concrete situation it had in view. It is not unlikely, however, that the psalm was more or less contemporaneous with Deutero-Isaiah. Like the Old Testament reading, the lament looks forward to the intervention of Yahweh in history. It picks up many of the themes in Deutero-Isaiah: "salvation is at hand," "glory may dwell in the land." Stanza II is a veritable compendium of theological terms for the eschatological event: steadfast love, faithfulness, righteousness, peace. Stanza III also speaks of the coming of Yahweh as being heralded in advance:

> Righteousness shall go before him,
> and make his footsteps a way,

reminding us how the exilic prophet described his mission, and how this terminology is taken up in the New Testament and applied to the Baptist.

Reading II: 2 Peter 3:8-14

Second Peter is commonly thought nowadays to be not only a pseudonymous work, but the latest document in the New Testament, written perhaps after A.D. 125. The unknown author appeals to the authority of Peter and to certain Petrine traditions in order to convey to his church a message which, he is convinced, is precisely what Peter would have said had he still been alive.

The author is faced with false teachers, perhaps of a gnostic character, who had no place for the belief in the second coming of Christ. As in I Corinthians these gnostics emphasize the "already" at the expense of the "not yet." They dismiss the church's traditional teaching about the second coming by pointing scornfully to its failure to occur, despite constant teaching that it was just round the corner.

In answer the author appeals to Ps 90 (91):

> A thousand years in thy sight
> are but as yesterday when it is past,
> or as a watch in the night.

God's time scheme is different from ours. But the author still seeks to retain the existential vitality of the parousia hope. The dominical parable of the thief in the night is cited to show that Christians must always expect the day of the Lord to come at any moment. This gives a motivation for holiness and godliness of living (v. 11). It is therefore not true to say, as some have said, that this letter like other early catholic writings in the New Testament, has relegated the parousia to the last chapter of dogmatics, and deprived it of significance for the Christian life.

The following points in this pericope seem still to speak to contemporary Christianity:

1. Christians must always live as though the end were to come at any moment. Watchfulness is a part of Christian living.

2. Rightly understood the imminent hope in Christianity is a motivation for the pursuit of holiness and godliness of life.

3. However much we demythologize the New Testament pictures of the end, the hope of a new heaven and a new earth as the final goal of history is something that can never be surrendered.

Gospel: Mark 1:1-8

Following the established pattern of Advent, John the Baptist occupies the forefront of our attention on the second and third Sundays. The Baptist marks the inauguration of the Christ event, and therefore the inauguration of the gospel. It is unclear whether Mark means "gospel of Jesus Christ" to be taken subjectively (the gospel preached by Jesus, the good news of the kingdom, as in Mk 1:14) or objectively (the gospel about Jesus). The subjective sense makes good history, for it is an incontestable fact that Jesus' mission grew out of the Baptist's. In some sense the one was a continuation of the other, in others a breakaway. John's accent was on judgment: Jesus' on salvation. This difference is expressed in the parable of the children in the market (Mt 11:16-19).

Mark (v. 3) picks up the Deutero-Isaianic prophecy of today's first reading and prefaces it with another prophecy of Malachi (3:1) which he alters significantly. "*My* face" becomes "*thy* face," so that it is addressed to Christ. Both techniques, the combination of two widely separated texts and the alteration of a text, are now familiar to us from the Dead Sea scrolls.

As reported by Mark, John's preaching consists of two aspects, first the preaching of repentance and baptism and the forgiveness of sins, second the announcement of the coming of the mightier One who will baptize with the Holy Spirit.

In recent years there has been something of a "quest of the historical Baptist" for similar reasons as those which motivated the quest of the historical Jesus. Both historical figures have been subject to reinterpretation in the light of post-Easter Christian faith. There can be no doubt that the "historical Baptist" did baptize — this is attested not only by the New Testament, but also by the Jewish historian Josephus. Josephus gives a non-sacramental interpretation to it. He regards it merely as a sign of a conversion from sin to righteousness which had already taken place. This we may suspect, however, as an attempt to de-biblicize the Baptist for the benefits of Josephus' pagan readers. But did John also speak of the stronger One who was to come after him? Josephus says nothing of this, but it is generally agreed that he did, although he was not consciously predicting the coming of Jesus. The stronger One whom the Baptist expected was either Yahweh himself or a very different kind of Messiah from what Jesus turned out to be — a Messiah whose accent, like John's own, would be on judgment rather than salvation (cf. "fire" in Mt 3:11/Lk 3:16). In that case "Holy Spirit" will be a Christian reinterpretation of "fire" from the perspective of Pentecost, but a wholly legitimate one.

The Homily

As we have seen, the dominant theme of today's readings is John the Baptist's work as the forerunner of Christ. As the *beginning* of the gospel of Jesus Christ, John could be regarded simply as a figure of the past, of historical interest only. But then he would not be the beginning of the *gospel*. John the Baptist is part of the good news, the beginning part, and therefore of permanent relevance in the life of the church. The church must allow John the Baptist still to perform his distinctive ministry of forerunner in her midst today. How is he to do this? By the preaching of repentance. Unless men are first convicted of sin, they cannot know the need of a Saviour. It is easy to quote Bonhoeffer against this (see his strictures on what he called "methodism" in *Letters and Papers from Prison* — "despair or Jesus"). No doubt this was a legitimate protest against many things, including Lutheran sermons which preached despair for 40 minutes and Christ as possible way out in the last five! But the New Testament, including John the Baptist, our Lord, St. Paul and the author of the Fourth Gospel, each in his own way, insists that repentance — the abandonment of any attempt to save ourselves — is the essential precondition for faith, which means allowing God to do for us what we cannot do for ourselves. The preaching of John the Baptist on this Sunday means the preaching of repentance as the indispensable *preparatio evangelica* and an indispensable preparation for the celebration of Christmas.

If the homilist is drawn rather to 2 Peter, this would give him an opportunity to drive home the existential vitality of the hope of an imminent parousia as the motif of the quest for holiness.

V THIRD SUNDAY OF ADVENT
Reading I: Isaiah 61:1-2, 10-11
Responsorial Psalm: Luke 1:46-48, 49-50, 53-54

This is one of the most familiar passages from Trito-Isaiah (56-66). It is akin to the servant psalms of Deutero-Isaiah (40-55), for although the prophet does not explicitly call himself the servant, he describes his mission in terms of servanthood. This passage appears to have profoundly influenced Jesus' understanding of his own mission. Even if (which however is by no means certain) the sermon at Nazareth (Lk 4:16-22) is a Lucan composition, Jesus himself alluded unmistakably to this text in his answer to John (Mt 11:2-6/Lk 7:18-23) whose authenticity is beyond reasonable doubt.

The christological interest of this text, however, would be more appropriate for the Epiphany season (a slightly different selection from Is 61 is used in the Episcopal Church's adaptation of the lectionary at 3 Epiphany C). Today's caption highlights the theme of *joy* in face of the impending advent of God's salvation, a theme which is reinforced by the responsorial psalm (the Magnificat and the refrain taken from its two opening words). This, it will be noted, is in accordance with the tradition of the Roman Missal, where this Sunday was known as *Gaudete* from the opening word of the introit. In the Book of Common Prayer this theme belonged, as generally in the medieval rites of Northern Europe, to Advent IV. We might note that the Magnificat is particularly associated with Advent, Bach's Magnificat for instance being frequently performed on one of the Advent Sundays.

Reading II: 1 Thessalonians 5:16-24

The opening of this reading continues the Gaudete theme. However the caption underlines the second paragraph with its references to the parousia. As we have already noted, the theme of the second coming is replaced after Advent I with that of the first coming, but there are occasional echoes of the earlier theme on later Sundays. Such is the genius of Advent. It refuses to contemplate the first coming apart from the second, or the second apart from the first.

Gospel: John 1:6-8, 19-28

This gospel lesson represents an ingenious combination of two separate passages. The first paragraph is a prose comment which the evangelist inserted into the Logos hymn. Bultmann thinks that the Johannine prologue was first composed as a hymn to John the Baptist by his followers who regarded him as the bearer of the eschatological revelation. Perhaps it is even earlier than that, a hymn to Wisdom, successively adapted for "baptist" and for Christian use. In any case the evangelist's prose insertion is clearly designed to counter a false estimate of the Baptist: He was not the light, but only a witness to the light.

The same tendency ostensibly to downgrade the Baptist continues in the second paragraph of our pericope. John is here presented as entirely repudiating all messianic or quasi messianic titles. He is neither the Christ, the prophet-Messiah, nor (*contra* the synoptics) Elijah, but only the "voice" of Is 40.

This disagreement with the synoptic interpretation should not worry us unduly. In the synoptists' environment it was perfectly safe to interpret John as an Elijah *redivivus*. But for the Fourth Gospel, in its different situation, Elijah could well be too high a title, suggesting that he was actually the Messiah, the immediate forerunner of Yahweh. Perhaps John reflects an earlier state of Christology than the synoptists, a stage when

Elijah was still pre-empted for Christ himself—the stage which Bishop John A. T. Robinson characterized as the view that Jesus was his own Elijah in the sense that he was the forerunner of the apocalyptic Son of man and was himself exalted to heaven to fulfill that role.

The Homily

The major theme today is again the mystery of John the Baptist as the forerunner. The reading from the Fourth Gospel emphasizes the self-effacing character of John's ministry. This self-effacing character reaches its climax in a later passage in the Fourth Gospel where the Baptist compares himself to the best man who must give way to the bridegroom when the task is done: "He must increase but I must decrease." Here John is the pattern for the church's ministry, a parallel which was suggested by the Book of Common Prayer collect for this Sunday (written by John Cosin in 1661 though unfortunately addressed to the second person of the Trinity):

"O Lord Jesus Christ, who at thy first coming didst send thy messenger to prepare thy way before thee; Grant that the ministers and stewards of thy mysteries may likewise so prepare and make ready thy way by turning the hearts of the disobedient to the wisdom of the just, that at thy second coming to judge the world we may be found an acceptable people in thy sight, who . . ."

Karl Barth was fond of illustrating the self-effacing character of the Baptist's ministry from the Isenheim altar piece, in which the Baptist is portrayed with a large index finger pointing to Christ on the cross, to the Lamb who takes away the sin of the world.

Two other possible ideas for a homily might be suggested. First, the Gaudete theme from the first reading, the Magnificat and the epistle reading. It is instructive to compare the three types of joy represented by Gaudete, Laetare and Jubilate; the joy of Advent, of mid-Lent and of Easter. Advent joy is the joy of anticipation, mid-Lent joy that of an oasis in the wilderness, and the joy of Easter that of sorrow which has been turned into joy.

FOURTH SUNDAY OF ADVENT

As we draw nearer to the Christmas festival the Advent lessons take us to the brink of the incarnation. The whole series of Old Testament prophecies, culminating in John the Baptist and his message, reach their fulfillment in the Christ event. The move from John the Baptist's ministry to the Blessed Virgin Mary and the annunciation looks at first sight like a step backward, chronologically. But theologically it is not, for John sums up the whole of Old Testament prophecy and announces the impending Christ event, and Mary was the appointed agent through whom the Christ entered into the world. She thus brings us to the fulfillment of the Advent hope in her role in the annunciation.

Reading I: 2 Samuel 7:1-5, 8b-11, 16

This passage gives classical expression to the Davidic-Messianic hope in the Old Testament. It is not the only type of the messianic hope but later became dominant in many circles, e.g., among the Pharisees, as we see from Ps Sol 17, among the covenanters of Qumran, who looked for both a Messiah of David and a Messiah of Levi, and the simple pious folk of Judea and Galilee as we see from the Lucan infancy narrative. In its original intention, however, 2 Sam 7 was an expression of royal ideology. The promise was that the Davidic dynasty would last forever. Note how David's original intention is reversed by the prophet's later word. David indicates his intention of building a house for Yahweh, i.e., a temple. At first Nathan approves of the king's proposal, but later corrects this in the light of a further word from the Lord received in the night. Instead of David's building a house (temple) for Yahweh, Yahweh covenants to maintain the "house" (dynasty) of David in perpetuity.

Strictly speaking, then, this is not a messianic prophecy in the later sense, for it does not speak of the coming of the ideal Davidic king. But after the destruction of the Davidic monarchy this promise could only take the form of the coming of a Davidic Messiah, and in Christian perspective the promise has been fulfilled in the coming of Jesus the Christ, whom the New Testament (as in the Lucan annunciation story which forms the gospel reading today) proclaims as the Son of David.

Responsorial Psalm: 89:1-2, 3-4, 26 and 28

This psalm makes a perfect response to the first reading for, as the Jerome Commentary points out, the two passages should be read in conjunction. Only stanzas II and III deal directly with the Davidic-Messianic hope. Stanza I comes from the opening of the psalm which is a general hymn of praise to Yahweh. But stanza I is not unrelated to the messianic hope, for the faithfulness of Yahweh is exhibited precisely in his faithfulness to his covenant with David. Note how stanza II refers back quite specifically to the covenant of 2 Samuel.

Reading II: Romans 16:25-27

In the manuscript tradition this doxology appears at three different places, after Rom 14:23, after 15:33 and in its canonical position here. Some have thought that it was a Marcionite gloss, for it seems to assume that the God who revealed himself in Jesus Christ had been silent through the Old Testament period, as Marcion taught. However, this is untenable for two reasons. First, Origen explicitly informs us that Marcion did not read these verses in his text. Secondly, Marcion would never have allowed that the writings of the Old Testament prophets were instruments through which the Christian revelation was proclaimed, even in the Christian era.

The doxology actually has close affinities with the style and thought of Colossians and Ephesians (cf. esp. Col 1:26-27; Eph 3:9-10) and is therefore probably the work of a Deutero-Pauline editor of Romans. Judging from the various places it appears in the manuscript tradition, it was probably added as a conclusion to Romans in the three different versions that were current in early times — ending respectively with chapters 14, 15, and 16.

The statement that the revelation was kept secret before Christ does not mean therefore that the Old Testament God is a different God from the God and Father of our Lord Jesus Christ, as Marcion thought, but that it is only with the coming of Christ that the Old Testament prophecies acquire their true meaning. The movement from silence to revelation is a good Advent theme.

Gospel: Luke 1:26-38

Annunciation stories are a regular literary form of scripture. There are a number of such stories in the Old Testament (cf. the births of Isaac, Sampson and Samuel), and of course Luke has already recorded the annunciation of John the Baptist. We should make full allowance for this literary form in assessing this narrative. The purpose of annunciation stories is to acquaint the *readers* with the role which the person about to be born is to play in salvation history. It is thus a device to effect this end, not a historical narration. At the same time, there are elements in the story of Jesus' annunciation which surpass the other annunciation stories. The usual situation is that of a miraculous birth granted to a barren couple, in the case of Isaac to parents who were even past the age of begetting and bearing children. In the case of Jesus it is an annunciation to a young woman without a husband. The emphasis rests on the creative act of the Holy Spirit, rather than on the virginal conception *per se,* which is its presupposition.

All that the historian can say with certainty is that the basic elements in this tradition are earlier than Matthew or Luke. For the name of Mary, her virginity and the function of the Holy Spirit are common both to Matthew and Luke, who are otherwise entirely independent of one another at this point. Many would also argue that these traditions can be traced back to the earliest Palestinian stratum of Christianity. Beyond that point, however, the historian *qua* historian cannot go. The exegete must deal rather with the meaning. What is the kerygmatic thrust of the annunciation? It is that the history of Jesus does not emerge out of the stream of ongoing history. As Adolf Schlatter put it, it expresses the transcendental origin of the history of Jesus. Or, as Edwyn Clement Hoskyns put it, the incarnation is a dagger thrust into the weft of human history. Our response to the annunciation story should be not to accept it as an entertaining story or even to insist merely on its historicity and leave it at that. As such, it would still be "flesh," which profiteth nothing. Our response should rather be the affirmation of faith in the transcendental origin of Jesus' history.

The role which the Child to be born is to play in salvation history is defined in terms of Davidic Messiahship. Thus the gospel reading is linked with the Old Testament reading. Christian faith sees the promise and covenant to David fulfilled in the coming of Jesus Christ.

The Homily

The most obvious subject for today's homily would be the annunciation. The homilist should be careful to remain within the framework provided by the liturgy and remember that this is still Advent and not yet Christmas. We stand on the verge of the fulfillment of the messianic hope, and the tension of waiting for it which is characteristic of the Advent season should not be relaxed today. Israel's hope could be related to the hopes of humanity in general and particularly of modern man, and Christ proclaimed as the One who comes to answer those hopes.

There are two other possibilities. One would be to draw out the kerygmatic sense of the dogma of the virginal conception, dealing with any difficulties that the congregation may feel about it (though of course refrain from putting into their minds difficulties they do not feel — the pastor must be the judge of what his people need). Thirdly, the homilist might speak of the mystery of the revelation of God (epistle reading), how it had been kept secret until the incarnation, and how it is only in the "preaching of Jesus Christ" in word and sacrament that this revelation can still be received.

Since the readings for each year are identical, we shall summarize what we wrote last year for the benefit of new subscribers.

The Christmas festival is not primarily a historical commemoration of the birth at Bethlehem, but the celebration of God's eschatological self-disclosure in the Christ event. The commercialization and sentimentalization of Christmas in the secular world, and their effects on the church make it advisable to de-emphasize the historical aspect of Christmas and stress its theological aspect.

MASS AT MIDNIGHT

Reading I: Isaiah 9:2-7

Originally this was a coronation anthem. Every new Davidic king was welcomed in that hope that he would be the ideal king. The joy of the occasion is expressed in two comparisons, the joy of harvest and the joy of victory on the field of battle (v. 3). The new reign ushers in the three freedoms, from want, from oppression and from war. In the original use of the anthem the birth of the child (v. 6) was the enthronement of the king, interpreted in the court theology as God's adoption of the monarch as his son (cf. Ps 2:7). The newly enthroned king is hailed by a series of honorific titles. He is even called "God." This bold ascription of divinity, common enough in the ancient near East, is rare in the Old Testament (cf. Ps 45:7) and should probably be interpreted in a biblical sense to mean the sovereignty of Yahweh.

In the perspective of Christian faith this hope for the ideal Davidic king comes to fulfillment in the coming of Jesus Christ. In him all the blessings of salvation — freedom from want and oppression and the realization of peace on earth — are given to man. We hail the birth of this child as the one who will be enthroned in his ascension. To him all the messianic titles will be rightly given, including that of God, though in the sense not of *Deus in se*, which in later dogmatic language would be the first person of the Trinity, but as *Deus pro nobis*, the second person of the Trinity, God turned toward us in his grace and salvation.

Responsorial Psalm: 96:1-3, 11-13

This is the greatest of the enthronement or Royal Psalms. The theme of the "new song" can be traced throughout the two Testaments. The original song was the song of Moses and Israel by the Red Sea (Ex 15). This song is continued in the liturgy of the tabernacle and the temple. Then the temple was destroyed, the song of the liturgy ceased and Israel cried out, How shall we sing the Lord's song in a strange land? The idea of a new song thus became part of Israel's eschatological expectation. In the New Testament, the Apocalypse tells us that the new song is sung by the redeemed in celebration of the victory of the Lamb. The angelic hymn at Bethlehem is the overture to this new song, and the church's liturgy its anticipation and partial realization.

Reading II: Titus 2:11-14

This reading speaks of the first (v. 11) and second (v. 13) comings of Christ. Thus the Advent theme of the second coming is carried right into Christmas. The first coming is an anticipation of the second, and it is celebrated at midnight because at midnight, according to New Testament imagery, the second coming will occur (cf. Mt 25:6).

Gospel: Luke 2:1-14

The infancy narratives both of Matthew and Luke raise a number of difficult historical problems. But in the words of the Jerome Commentary "the details of the narrative are symbolic and biblical; they communicate the mystery of redemption, not a diary of earthly events." It is as a communication of the mystery of redemption that we should listen to this gospel reading at the first mass of Christmas.

The shepherds in first century Palestine were members of a despised trade, like the tax collectors and prostitutes. They should not be romanticized.

The angelic announcements are a biblical device expressing the meaning of an event in salvation history. The first announcement, by a single angel, tells of the birth itself, the second, by the "multitude of the heavenly host," proclaims the blessings which will result from that birth: glory to God and peace—i.e., the messianic salvation—on earth. The words "among men in whom he is well pleased" translates a biblical idiom which means "among mankind, who are now made the objects of God's favor." It does not mean "men of good will" in the secular sense of the phrase.

The Homily

The homilist has a wealth of possibilities here. A combination of the Old Testament reading and angelic annunciation would suggest the message of peace—to which however he must be careful to give a biblical interpretation (shalom). Or he could take the theme of midnight as the time of Christ's first and second comings. Again, he could concentrate on the nativity story itself, either bringing out the fact that the shepherds were members of a despised trade, that the incarnation is especially intended for the poor, the despised and the oppressed, and therefore encourages Christian sensitivity to their needs. Yet again, he could contrast the words "men of good will"—who quickly become men of ill will when Christmas is over!—and the biblical notion of God's favor toward mankind in the incarnation.

MASS AT DAWN

Reading I: Isaiah 62:11-12

This passage from Deutero-Isaiah originally spoke of the joy which marked a Jewish festival—perhaps Tabernacles. In the present liturgical context, it speaks of the joy of the new Israel at the birth of its saviour, the advent of the messianic salvation.

Responsorial Psalm: 97:1 and 6, 11-12

This is another of the enthronement psalms. The second stanza and the refrain underline the dawn of the light—imagery which has passed into the lore of the season and is expressed in so many Christmas carols.

Reading II: Titus 3:4-7

A very similar passage to the second reading in the mass at midnight, but with the difference that it speaks only of the first appearance or coming of Christ. Also, instead of leading to an ethical exhortation, it speaks of the salvific consequences of the incarnation—our regeneration and renewal, or rebirth as sons of God. This is a traditional theme of Christmas: the Son of God became man that we might become sons of God.

Gospel: Luke 2:15-20

This is a continuation of the gospel for the midnight mass. Impelled by the angelic message, the shepherds go to Bethlehem and visit the new born babe with Mary and Joseph. The picture is familiar. What matters however is its inner significance. The shepherds make known, not only what they had seen, but what they had been told—i.e., the angelic message that this was the divine salvation come into the world.

The Homily

The Old Testament lesson has a pregnant phrase: the people of God are "sought out." The incarnation is God's search for man (Karl Barth). As such it is the answer to all human religion, which is man's search for God. The church is the outcome of this search, not merely as an institution for the cultivation of human religion. The church is the place where God's search for man continues.

Reading II suggests the theme of sonship. Only Christ is the Son of God by nature. Man's divine sonship is by adoption and grace. The Bible knows nothing of the modern humanistic idea that all human beings are by nature children of God. They are only so potentially until they are incorporated into Christ.

The gospel, with its interpretation of the nativity scene as a sign and its insistence on the thing signified—the coming of the messianic salvation into the world—is another protest against the sentimentalizing of Christmas.

MASS DURING THE DAY

Reading I: Isaiah 52:7-10

This passage from Deutero-Isaiah is similar in tone to the Old Testament reading for the mass at dawn and to the enthronement psalms which are read at all three masses this day. "Your God reigns" is an announcement of the return from exile, but these words were also used at the sovereign's enthronement. This proclamation is described in a verb, as bringing good tidings, the verb from which as we saw earlier the Christian word gospel (*euangelion*) is ultimately derived. Paul took up our present text and applied it to his own apostolic work of preaching the gospel, and it probably also influenced the formulation of Jesus' own message of the kingdom or reign of God.

In today's liturgy the good news can be referred specifically to the angelic proclamation at the nativity. In the incarnation the church discerns the return of Yahweh to Zion (v. 8) to comfort his people (v. 9). At Bethlehem Yahweh bares his arm and mankind sees the coming of his salvation (v. 10).

Responsorial Psalm: 98:1, 2-3ab, 3cd-4, 5-6

Selections of this psalm are used on Sunday 28 C and Sunday 33 C. It is very similar to Pss 96 and 97, used in the first and second masses of Christmas Day respectively. Its applicability to the nativity is obvious. Note the link between "arm" in the first stanza and "holy arm" in the Old Testament reading.

Reading II: Hebrews 1:1-6

The first part of Hebrews seeks to establish Christ's superiority over the angels — perhaps in a situation where a form of Jewish gnosticism was leading Jewish Christians to think of Christ as only one among other angelic mediators. The opening section of Hebrews is prefaced by a hymn to Christ similar to the Johannine prologue which is read in the gospel of this mass. The hymn in Hebrews seems to be based on an earlier Jewish hymn to the Wisdom of God and follows a regular pattern. Wisdom is described as preexistent with God from eternity. She is the agent of creation and preservation. She manifests herself to men on earth and returns to heaven.

This pattern was adapted by Christianity to express its own christological faith. Christ is identified with preexistent Wisdom. As such he is the agent of creation and preservation. He appears on earth and returns to heaven. Note that here the incarnation is presumed rather than expressed in the words "when he had made purification for our sins." This is an idea which is wholly Christian, and has nothing to do with the Wisdom hymn. Only in the series of scriptural quotations is the entry of Christ into the world explicitly stated. After his return to heaven Christ triumphs over the angels, here as elsewhere in early Christianity conceived as hostile powers.

One further point should be noted about the writer's treatment of this hymn. He sets it in the context of God's revelation throughout Israel's salvation history. In the Old Testament period God had spoken through the prophets "in many various ways" — a phrase which in the Greek expresses the fragmentary, partial character of his self-revelation in the Old Testament. The hymn, placed in this context, now expresses the finality of God's self-revelation in Christ.

Gospel: John: 1:1-18 (long form); 1:1-5, 9-14 (short form)

The shorter version of this gospel is arrived at by the omission of the prose comments inserted by the Evangelist into an already existing hymn (see above). The anti-John the Baptist polemic is hardly relevant to Christmas.

The function of the hymn in relation to the Fourth Gospel as a whole is to provide the eternal background of the ministry, life, and death of Jesus. This whole ministry was the revelation of the Word made flesh, the embodiment in the human life of the fullness of God's self-revelation to man. This self-revelation (Word, Logos) however did not begin with the Christ event, but with creation (cf. Heb 1:1-4). God created the universe in order to communicate himself to it in love (Jn 1:1-2). He communicated himself to man throughout human history (vv. 4, 9-10) especially, though not exclusively, in Israel's salvation history (v. 11). Wherever it is received, this revelation restores man to divine sonship.

It is often debated where precisely the prologue moves from the pre-existent Logos to the incarnate Christ. Clearly, it has done so by v. 14. Yet the parentheses have the effect of changing the earlier statements about the work of the Logos into statements also about the incarnate Christ. This makes the whole prologue a comment on the rest of the gospel. The entire life of Christ is the story of the Word becoming flesh.

The Homily

The homilist should look up what he preached on last year and choose another theme today. He may decide to take the epistle reading and gospel — the two christological hymns — together. Both speak of the Christ event as the culmination of God's revelation or self-communication to the world in creation to mankind in general and to Israel in particular. He will thus be able to relate the final revelation of God both to the Old Testament revelation and to human religions in general. All religions contain fragmentary and partial disclosures of God. But what was fragmentary and partial is now finally and fully disclosed in Christ.

HOLY FAMILY (SUNDAY AFTER CHRISTMAS)

The readings are the same as in series A, except for the gospel. Our comments here therefore summarize what we said last year, except for the gospel, where the comments are new.

Reading I: Sirach 3:2-6, 12-14

This passage forms a commentary on the fifth (fourth) commandment, "Honor thy father and thy mother." That the keeping of the commandments atones for sins is a typical idea of later Judaism, but we should not take this with full theological seriousness. For the New Testament, atonement for sin is through Christ alone. Sirach's statement should be taken merely as an incentive to obedience. In a loose, nontheological sense one could say that love of parents makes up for many other sins.

Responsorial Psalm: 128:1-5

This psalm presents piety as the true foundation of family and social life, and of economic prosperity, in a manner reminiscent of Deuteronomy. Naïve though it may seem, this should not be too lightly dismissed. Where there is a wholesome respect for God and his will, there is a better chance for man's relationships with his fellow men being well ordered and harmonious. The man who fears the Lord is not tempted to put himself in God's place, is therefore free to love his neighbor, and makes it easier for his neighbor to love him.

Reading II: Colossians 3:12-21

This reading is taken from the parenetic section or ethical exhortation of Colossians and, as is widely thought, reproduces the pattern of an early Christian catechism.

This catechesis begins with a list of virtues to be "put on"—an echo of the vesting of the candidate as he comes up out of the baptismal waters. Sometimes another imperative precedes it, a "put off," recalling the stripping of the candidate before baptism. Then comes a "household code," a list of the duties of the members of a family and of society in their several states. These codes were apparently already taken over by Hellenistic Judaism from Stoicism, and thence passed over into Christian usage. Their subordinationist tone is thus not distinctively Christian, but is derived ultimately from Stoicism. The distinctive Christian elements are to be found in the words "in the Lord," in the injunctions to husbands to *love* their wives, in the earlier definition of love as forgiveness, and in the motivation of that forgiveness in Christ's forgiveness of the sinner.

Gospel: Luke 2:22-40 (long form); 2:22, 39-40 (short form)

The caption at the head of both longer and shorter form, and the text of the shorter form itself throw the stress on the growth of the Christ child to maturity, and the fact that he was filled with wisdom. The presentation scene and the encounter between the Christ child and Simeon, the Nunc Dimittis, and the encounter with Anna are important kerygmatically, but they receive their proper due on the feast of the Presentation of the Lord

(February 2), when the same gospel is read. Our comment will therefore confine itself today to the growth of the Christ child.

Three points may be made here. The first is a dogmatic one. The Christ child is fully human, and as such he has to grow, not only physically, but also mentally and spiritually. If we are to understand the incarnation in scriptural terms, we must not think of it as entailing complete maturity from the outset. Rather, Christ is perfect man with the perfection that belongs to each stage of human growth. At each stage, too, he is the perfect manifestation of God in a manner appropriate for that stage.

The second point to notice is that this growth to maturity takes place in the context of a human family. Apart from the story of the visit to the temple when Jesus was twelve years old, this is the only verse in the New Testament which speaks of his life in the holy family. Scripture is very reserved about that life, unlike the later apocryphal gospels. But this verse is a priceless gem, for it contains all we really need to know about the holy family. First it was the divinely provided context in which the Christ was prepared for his saving mission. Second, the holy family is the paradigm for all Christian family life, for the Christian family is the divinely provided context in which the Christian child may grow to physical, mental and spiritual maturity.

The third point is typological. This verse points back through Lk 1:80 to 1 Sam 2:26. Jesus stands in the prophetic succession. He is the last and greatest of the prophets but transcends them all, for he is the eschatological prophet. But he is still a prophet.

The Homily

It is clearly the church's intention today that the life of the holy family should be held up as the pattern of Christian family life. The Old Testament and epistle readings, and the gospel provide different ways of doing this. The gospel suggests, as we have seen, the family as the divinely provided context for growth to physical, mental and spiritual maturity. The epistle reading suggests that the pattern of Christian family life is based on mutual forgiveness, while the Old Testament reading emphasizes the importance of the fifth (fourth) commandment — a tricky subject to tackle in the contemporary world!

January 1 to Sunday 4 B

Since the readings for this occasion are the same each year, we will here confine ourselves to summarizing our comments from the previous year.

The title of this solemnity is suggested by two sentences in today's reading. In the epistle we hear: "God sent forth his son . . . born of a woman," a sentence which has direct bearing on the title "mother of God." Then in the gospel we hear: "Mary kept all these things and pondered them in her heart." These words have no direct bearing on the title. Rather, they treat Mary as the paradigm of faith and therefore a paradigm both of the Christian believer and of the true Israel. Despite the title, the main thrust of today's reading is the birth of Christ in which the saving act of God is inaugurated.

Reading I: Numbers 6:22-27

The Aaronic blessing is a remarkable Old Testament anticipation of the church's trinitarian faith (cf. the threefold "holy" in Is 6).

The caption calls attention to the last verse, "They will call down my name . . . and I will bless them." In the Bible the "name," whether it be of God or of man, is very important. The name stands for the whole person, his character and personality. The name of God is his Being, as manifested in salvation history. Hence, to bless in God's name is to invoke upon the faithful all that God is and all that he has done for his people. In the act of blessing the name of God is passed on in the sense we have defined from age to age.

Responsorial Psalm: 67:1-2, 4, 5, and 7

As the refrain shows, this psalm picks up the theme of Yahweh's blessing of Israel.

304

Reading II: Galatians 4:4-7

Recent exegesis regards this passage as a pre-Pauline credal formula, expanded with the Pauline phrase "born under the law to redeem those who were under the law." Without the expansion the hymn would read:

> God sent forth his Son
> (born of a woman)
> that we might receive adoption as sons.

The purpose clause follows directly upon the sending clause, thus linking the incarnation with our existence. The coming of the Son of God into the world is not merely a fact of past history but an event of direct existential significance for believers today. The Son of God became man that men might become the sons of God (cf. second reading, Christmas, mass at dawn).

Paul's addition about the law points toward the event mentioned at the end of today's gospel reading, the circumcision of Jesus, in which he is shown to be born "under the law." The incarnation means that Christ entered into a human life with all its limitations, including the restrictions of human freedom which characterize human life. The law was one of these restrictions: it told men what to do, but left them powerless to do it. Only by such complete submission could Christ liberate man. For he only remained truly free and therefore able to pass on the "contagion" (Van Buren) of that freedom to others.

Gospel: Luke 2:16-21

See Christmas, mass at dawn. This selection, however, begins one verse later (v. 6) and continues through v. 21, to include the circumcision and naming of Jesus. Thus (cf. the second part of the caption) it is these two events that are highlighted today.

The Homily

We suggest three possibilities. Following the Old Testament reading and the psalm the homilist might deal with the biblical concept of blessing. Karl Barth's reflections on this subject in *Church Dogmatics* III/2, p. 587, are particularly helpful here. He says (p. 580), "Blessing is regarded in the Old Testament as the epitome of all the goods things which the father can pass on to the son and the son receive from the father. A blessing is the word which has divine power to pass on good things." The homilist might expound the biblical concept of blessing, then relate it to the priestly blessing in the liturgy, and finally apply it to the situation in which we stand this Sunday — at the threshold of a new (civil) year.

The second possibility would be to link the epistle reading ("born under the law") with the circumcision of Jesus and proclaim the liberation of man from the bondage of the law which results from Jesus' submission to it. In view of the present-day interest in liberation (which, it has been suggested, is the contemporary equivalent of salvation), this might be a relevant topic.

Thirdly, the homilist could take up the biblical concept of "name" from the Aaronic blessing in the first reading and the naming of Jesus in the gospel. In the case of the name Jesus (= Yahweh saves) this sets out in advance the whole program of his life. Each of us is given a baptismal name which sets before us a program and a goal for our lives — not in a Pelagian sense of having to do it in our own strength, but because of the name which Christ has already received and lived out for us. This again might be suitable for the New Year.

EPIPHANY

The feast of our Lord's baptism is omitted this year. The Epiphany readings are the same each year, hence we shall again summarize our comments from last year.

Epiphany originated in the Eastern Church, where it was primarily a celebration of our Lord's baptism. This was interpreted as the first of his epiphanies, or manifestations, of God in man. Other epiphanies such as the Cana miracle were added later. When this feast spread to the West it drew off some of the associations of the Western Christmas. Hence it became primarily a commemoration of the visit of the magi. Next, the magi came to be regarded as types of the Gentiles (cf. the collect and epistle of the Roman Missal and Book of Common Prayer). Finally especially in Lutheranism, the epiphany became associated with overseas missionary work. The new lections attempt to restore the original emphasis on the revelation of God in Christ and to subordinate all these secondary features to this primary theme.

Reading I: Isaiah 60:1-6

This reading falls into two halves: vv. 1-3, the fulfillment of Is 40ff in the return of the exiles from Babylon to Jerusalem; and vv. 4-6, a prediction of the eschatological pilgrimage of the Gentiles to Jerusalem after the rebuilding of the city.

In Christianity generally, and as it is used on this day especially, each half is reinterpreted. Verses 1-3, the Christ event, supersedes the return from Babylon as the salvation event ("light" and "glory"). Verses 4-6, the Gentiles respond to that revelation by coming to Christ, a response symbolized in the journey of the magi.

This passage (cf. "gold" and "frankincense" in v. 6) has clearly influenced the narrative of the magi in Mt 2:1-12, and has also contributed to its later legendary development (cf. the camels of v. 6).

Responsorial Psalm: 72:1-2, 7-8, 10-11, 12-13

Originally composed for the coronation of a Davidic monarch, this hymn has been applied by Christian faith to Jesus Christ. It emphasizes the milder, pastoral attributes of kingship — concern for justice and compassion for the poor.

The psalm further complements the Old Testament reading, adding what was missing there, namely the figure of the messianic king.

Christian faith again sees this picture, like the first reading, fulfilled in the mission of Christ and in the universality of the gospel. Again, too, this fulfillment is symbolically expressed in the visit of the magi (who "bring gifts" and "fall down before him"). And like the Old Testament reading, this psalm has contributed to the legendary development of the magi story in which they became the "three kings."

Reading II: Ephesians 3:2-3a, 5-6

This reading combines the same two themes as the Old Testament reading — viz., the revelation or epiphany of God (v. 3) and the Gentiles' participation in the messianic salvation (v. 6).

Ephesians was written (probably after the death of Paul by an unknown genius of the Pauline school) when the unity of Jew and Gentile in the church for which the apostle had striven was an accomplished fact. Matthew's story of the magi likewise takes for granted the success of the Gentile mission.

Gospel: Matthew 2:1-12

Many different traditions from early Christianity have provided the ingredients for the magi story. First there is the primitive kerygmatic assertion of Jesus' Davidic descent, which qualified him in Jewish eyes for the Messiahship (see Rom 1:3). This element in the kerygma explains the importance attached in the infancy narratives of Matthew and Luke to Jesus' birth at Bethlehem. Second, there is the dating of Jesus' birth, common to Matthew and Luke, toward the end of Herod the Great's reign (4 B.C.), a fact which is historically plausible. Third, there is the folk memory of Herod's general character and particularly his pathological fear of assassination and usurpation in his closing years, not unlike that of Queen Elizabeth I. Fourth, there is the use of the star as a messianic symbol (cf. Num 24:17, which surprisingly Matthew fails to cite, and the Dead Sea Scrolls). Fifth, there are the frankincense and myrrh, suggested by the first reading and the responsorial psalm, neither of which passage is cited by Matthew. The formula quotation from Micah (v. 6) was probably a redactional insertion by the evangelist himself, though it is unusual for such a quotation to be put in the mouth of a *dramatis persona*. The fact that the magi were Gentiles is not emphasized in the narrative, though it is present in the Old Testament scriptures which form the background of the story.

The Homily

It is important to note that the magi story does not stand alone but that its context is set by the first two readings and the responsorial psalm. The major themes of today's readings are the revelation of God in Christ and the universality of that revelation. The magi story is a symbolic expression of these kerygmatic truths. It may be taken as an expression of man's religious quest. Indeed, the magi were probably astrologists and magicians rather than astronomers and philosophers. Their gifts of gold, frankincense and myrrh may have been the tricks of their trade which they surrendered (see *Matthew*, Anchor Commentary, p. 13 *ad loc*). This interpretation would give the homilist an opportunity to relate the story to contemporary man's religious quest in some of its stranger manifestations.

SECOND SUNDAY OF THE YEAR ✓✓
Reading I: 1 Samuel 3:3b-10, 19

The call of Samuel serves as a type of the infancy narratives. Note particularly the echo of v. 19 in Lk 2:52. This Sunday, however, a rather different typology is suggested. Today's gospel, while not a direct narrative of Jesus' baptism (something that the Fourth Gospel studiously avoids), contains John the Baptist's witness to Jesus. This witness is probably based on the heavenly voice at the baptism of Jesus. In his baptism Jesus responded to his Father's call to take up the mission of the eschatological prophet. Thus the call of Samuel, which is a call to be a prophet, serves as a type of Christ's baptism. Like Jesus in his baptism, Samuel hears the call of God, and responds with the words, "Speak, Lord, for thy servant hears." So, too, the Fourth Gospel frequently speaks of the Son hearing the Father's words.

Responsorial Psalm: 40:1 and 3ab, 6-7a, 7b-8, 9

This psalm, commented on for Sunday 2 A of the year, is used today as response to the reading of Samuel's call, and this reinforces the typological interpretation we have offered above. For this psalm was applied by the author of Hebrews to our Lord. It is Christ who says the words of the refrain, "Here am I, Lord; I come to do your will." Hebrews pictures Christ as saying these words when he "came into the world." This "coming" need not be narrowly confined to the moment of his birth. His coming covers his baptism, in which he embarked upon his messianic mission, and indeed to every moment of the incarnate life, in which he responds constantly to the Father's call.

Reading II: 1 Corinthians 6:13c-15a, 17-20

The context of Paul's argument here is a discussion of immoral sexual behavior in the Corinthian community. Paul is not so much concerned with the guilty parties, (perhaps some kind of temple prostitution was involved; it was a question of a hangover from their previous pagan life) but with the failure of the Corinthians to discipline the offender. As "gnostics" they used the slogan "All things are lawful for me" — anything goes. They felt this way because as gnostics they believed that their Christian experience enabled them to transcend the realities of the material world.

Against this gnostic position Paul argues that so far from the soul's having been delivered from the body, the Christian experience brings the whole man, body and soul alike, under the lordship of Christ. Paul drives home his point with two figures. The first pictures the individual believers as members of Christ. Here we meet for the first time in Paul's letters the figure of the church as the body of Christ, which will be developed in chapter 12. Since sexual immorality involves the whole person, it deprives Christ of his rightful property. It is worth noting that Paul's first use of the concept of the ecclesial body of Christ is ethical.

The second figure is of the church as the temple of the Holy Spirit.

Sexual immorality desecrates the temple of the Lord. This last figure is particularly appropriate if temple prostitution was the point at issue.

Gospel: John 1:35-42

This is the Johannine version of the call of the first disciples. The Fourth Gospel connects that call very closely with the ministry of John the Baptist. The evangelist, interpreting his tradition of the baptism of Jesus (which as we have seen he suppresses because of his polemic against later members of the Baptist sect) has the Baptist point out to his disciples the presence of the "Lamb of God." The terminology (Lamb of God) may be a reflection of the heavenly voice, "Thou art my beloved son, the object of my favor." This voice in its synoptic form points to the figure of the servant of Yahweh, and it is not improbable that the title "lamb" is connected with the title servant, whether as a word-play in Aramaic, or as an echo of the comparison of the servant to the lamb led to the slaughter in Is 53.

Thus the message of this pericope will be: true followers of John the Baptist, those who really listen to their master, leave him and follow Jesus.

The true disciple of John therefore comes to Jesus with the question, "Where are you staying?" In the Fourth Gospel to "stay" means more than just to lodge in a house overnight. It is the same word as is used for "abide" in those christological passages which speak of the Son's abiding in the Father. This is what they really come and "see" — another theological word, meaning to perceive with the eye of faith the mystery of the Word in the flesh. In this encounter the new disciples make a christological confession, "We have found the Messiah." And because of this confession, Simon is renamed Cephas. Here the evangelist telescopes into a single scene a whole process of revelation and response which historically speaking covered a much longer period, extending from the baptism of Jesus through his exaltation and Easter appearances. The evangelist's concern is to present a theological interpretation of history, not a mere chronicle of historical events.

The Homily

A common thread seems to run through the first reading, the psalm and the gospel. This is the mystery of Christ's person, conceived in terms of his response to his Father's call. This mystery is something which we, like Andrew and Simon, can "see" if we, like them, come and follow him. In this post-Epiphany season it would be appropriate to offer an interpretation of the incarnation which replaces the traditional language of "divine and human natures" with the language of dynamic relationship between the Father and the Son, a relation of call and response. This pattern is prefigured in the call of Samuel, and, if we may coin a word, is meant to be "post-figured" in the life of the Christian believer.

The epistle reading offers the homilist another possibility — the Christian requirement of sexual purity, a highly relevant theme in this permissive age. Note that Paul does not simply issue a series of don'ts, but goes to the heart of the matter — the whole man in the totality of his being, including his bodily existence, belongs to Christ. He is a member of Christ's body and therefore must live responsibly in that relationship.

THIRD SUNDAY OF THE YEAR ✓

Reading I: Jonah 3:1-5, 10

The Book of Jonah is not a normal prophetic book, consisting of the prophet's oracles in poetic form. Ostensibly it is a prose narrative about the activity of the prophet himself. In reality, however, it is a kind of tract (almost a propagandist historical novel like those of Dickens or Kingsley), intended to put across the author's universalistic views as protest against the narrow nationalism of postexilic Judaism. The unknown author has used as the basis of his tale a saga which had grown up round the figure of the prophet Jonah mentioned in 2 Kgs 14:25. The first part of his work (chs. 1-2) concerns the prophet's unsuccessful attempts to escape from the task Yahweh has imposed upon him — viz., of preaching repentance to the Ninevites. The prophet thought that God could not possibly care for such Gentiles as they were! The story of Jonah in the belly of the great fish occurs in this part, and represents Yahweh's refusal to let the prophet run away from his mission. He was rescued at sea in order to preach. Our passage comes from the beginning of part two (chs. 3-4), where Jonah carries out his preaching of repentance to the Ninevites.

Jesus used Jonah's ministry as a type of his own, but claimed that with him something (*sic*: neuter) greater was present — namely, the presence of the kingdom (Lk 11:29-30). Matthew gave a different interpretation to this typology, taking Jonah's sojourn in the fish for three days and three nights as a type of Christ's resurrection. Since our lesson comes from the second part of Jonah, only the former typology is relevant to its interpretation. This is also indicated by the correspondence between this lesson and the gospel, which provides a summary of Jesus' eschatological preaching. Jonah is thus presented to us in today's liturgy as a type of Christ in his preaching of the kingdom of God.

Responsorial Psalm: 25:4-5ab, 6 and 7bc, 8-9
A different selection of this responsorial psalm was used for Sunday 26 A and received comment above. Both Jonah and Jesus figure today as preachers of repentance. But repentance must be followed by obedience to the will of God, a point not featured in the Jonah story (nothing about the Ninevites' subsequent behavior) but strongly emphasized in the gospel, where Jesus' preaching of repentance is followed by the call of the disciples.

Reading II: 1 Corinthians 7:29-31
In 1 Cor 7 Paul has been dealing with problems of sex and marriage which the Corinthians had raised in a letter they had written to him. He concludes the first part of his answer with a general discussion about the Christian attitude to the world, which for him is determined by his expectation of an imminent parousia. In view of this, he recommended living in the spirit of *hōs mē* ("as if not"), i.e., in a spirit of detachment from the world. It would be tempting to dismiss Paul's injunction of detachment as no longer relevant now that the expectation of an imminent parousia has been abandoned. But his injunction still has existential validity. For it is still true that the form of his world is passing away. All its structures and relationships are provisional, and must not be treated as if they were ultimates. They are only penultimate values. This is not because this world is unreal in a Platonic sense, but because as a result of the Christ event the kingdom of God has become a present reality awaiting its consummation. Our Lord taught the same eschatological detachment in the Sermon on the Mount when he enjoined his disciples to seek first the kingdom of heaven. It may sound a little brutal to apply this counsel even to marriage, but even the marriage relationship is only penultimate, for in the consummated kingdom of God "they neither marry nor are given in marriage" (Mt 22:30).

Gospel: Mark 1:14-20
The Matthean parallel to this pericope — the beginning of Jesus' preaching in Galilee and the call of the first disciples — was used on Sunday 3 A. Mark's version lacks the formula quotation from Is 9:1-2 ("The land of

Zebulun and . . . Naphtali . . ."), which was highlighted in the caption and the short form of the Matthean gospel. The absence of the quotation thus calls attention to Mark's summary of Jesus' preaching, a point which is further emphasized by the caption here and by the selection of the Jonah passage for the Old Testament reading.

As we have just noted, this summary is "redactional" — i.e., it is composed by Mark himself. To some extent Mark has picked the missionary language of the Hellenistic church ("believe in the gospel") and of the earliest post-Easter period ("the time is fulfilled"). But the central phrase ("the kingdom of God is at hand") undoubtedly reproduces Jesus' own message (cf. Q Mt 10:7 parallel, also Q Mt 12:28 par.). The exhortation to repent was part of Jesus' message, and taken over by him from John the Baptist, though with somewhat different overtones. John's message was that God was to act soon.

Jesus' message is that God is beginning to act eschatologically — with his own appearance — and will consummate that action in the not too distant future. This implies that "the time is fulfilled" — i.e., that the event to which the Old Testament looked forward is now beginning to happen. The challenge to repent therefore means much more than to be sorry for one's individual sins. The Greek word for repent is *meta-noiein,* which literally means to change one's mind. But Jesus must have used the Hebrew *shub,* or its Aramaic equivalent, which means to turn around 180 degrees, to reorient one's whole attitude to Yahweh in the face of his coming kingdom. It therefore includes within it the demand of faith. So Mark's addition of "believe in the good news," despite the later missionary origin of this particular language, brings out the force of Jesus' challenge to repent. This is how it differs from John the Baptist's use of the same word.

It is important to remember that Mark is not simply summarizing Jesus' preaching out of historical interest. He places this summary as a kind of title to his whole connected account of Jesus' ministry. "Gospel" is the characterization which Mark gives to his whole work (cf. Mk 1:1), which includes Jesus' way to the cross and beyond that, his resurrection. It is in this whole story that the kingdom or reign of God draws near and is inaugurated, and will surely be consummated.

The call of the disciples which follows serves to illustrate what it means to repent and believe in the gospel. It does not mean to accept certain timeless truths, but to be attached to the person of Jesus, to go along with him in his way — a way which will lead to the cross, as will become clear at Caesarea Philippi.

The Homily

The Jonah passage, the psalm, and the gospel taken together, suggest the theme of Jesus' preaching of repentance. The homilist could differentiate between the common moralistic understanding of repentance, and the New Testament notion of turning around, and reorienting one's whole attitude to God. This in turn results in a personal attachment to Jesus like that of the first disciples, and following him in his way (here the refrain of the psalm can be picked up) through the cross to the resurrection.

If the homilist is attracted to the epistle reading and to the theme of eschatological detachment he could also relate this theme to the call of the first disciples, whom Jesus detached from their earthly avocations in order to follow him. For some discipleship will mean literally this. For others it will mean remaining in the world and its structures, but living in the spirit of eschatological detachment from it.

✓ FOURTH SUNDAY OF THE YEAR

Reading I: Deuteronomy 18:15-20

In the original intention of the Deuteronomic author, the "prophet" whose coming Moses predicts stood for the prophetic office as such, exercised by a whole series of prophets in Israel. They were understood by the Deuteronomist as standing in a charismatic succession from Moses. Later on this text was interpreted eschatologically in certain circles of pre-Christian Judaism, as we see from the Dead Sea Scrolls (1 QS 7), and from the evidence of the Fourth Gospel (see Jn 1:21; 6:14 and 7:40). In these circles Dt 18:15 was interpreted as a prediction that God would send one final prophet (the eschatological prophet, as modern scholars call that figure) before the End. Jesus' own self-understanding, though perhaps not quite so explicit, was in line with this, for he understood his mission in terms of proclaiming the dawning of God's kingdom and himself as the last messenger before its consummation. It was apparently left to the earliest post-Easter community to work out an explicit christological interpretation of Jesus in terms of the eschatological prophet like Moses (see esp. Acts 3). As originally intended, this was a high Christology — emphasizing not only Jesus' authoritative teaching, but also his agency of redemption, just as Moses had led the forefathers out of Egypt as the agent of God's earlier act of redemption. When Christianity moved to the Hellenistic world, this early christological title seemed inadequate and was replaced by such titles as Kyrios, Son of God, and Logos.

The selection of Dt 18:15-20 for today seems to be determined by the allusion in the gospel reading to Jesus' teaching with authority.

Responsorial Psalm: 95:1-2, 6-7abc, 7d-9

The same selection of Ps 95 with the same refrain was used on Lent 3 A, and also on Sunday 18 C, where it received comment. Today the refrain serves to pick up the warning to give heed to the prophet like unto Moses (Dt 18:15, 19).

Reading II: 1 Corinthians 7:32-35

One can only speculate what motives led to the choice of the caption, which speaks of the advantage of the unmarried state to women, and unlike the text says nothing of men! Paul's views on marriage and celibacy cut right across the views commonly held by Christians today. He commends celibacy both for men and women, but regards marriage as perfectly lawful and proper for *any* Christian. At the same time, however, he has a distinct preference for celibacy. Both states have their advantages and their perils, but on balance, according to Paul, the celibate, whether man or woman, is less likely to be distracted from the service of the Lord.

At the same time, certain points of difference have to be noted about Paul's teaching on celibacy compared with that of the later times. Paul refuses to lay down a hard and fast rule (v. 35, "Not to lay any restraint upon you"). The celibate life requires a charisma which not every Christian has (see v. 7). Yet against much contemporary post-Freudian opinion, Paul clearly believes that celibacy is the higher state. This is seen from what he says in other parts of this chapter. (vv. 6, 8, 25, 38).

Gospel: Mark 1:21-28

This lesson follows immediately upon last week's gospel reading. After the call of the first disciples Mark has Jesus embark upon his public ministry in Galilee. The first item of material which Mark selects for inclusion from his material is an exorcism. Perhaps the miracles he includes from 1:20 to 3:12 are an earlier collection of miracle stories, which he edited and supplemented with other non-miracle material.

One special feature of this editorial work is the evangelist's emphasis on Jesus' teaching — though without indicating the content of that teaching. The effect of this is to play down the one-sided emphasis on the miracles which such a pre-Marcan collection of miracle stories might have created. The Marcan tradition saw the miracles as displays of Jesus' authority. The Greek word for authority in the "choric ending" of the exorcism story is *exousia*. This word also has the connotation of power, particularly in this context of miracle. Mark does not deny that Jesus displayed both authority and power in his miracles, but for him the miracles were only one aspect of his authority. The primary emphasis rests upon his teaching: "He taught as one having authority [*exousia* — the word is picked up by the Marcan redaction from the body of the exorcism story] and not as the scribes." The exorcism follows merely as an illustration of the power of Jesus' teaching with authority. "In Jesus' word heaven breaks in and hell is destroyed. His word is deed" (Eduard Schweizer).

The Homily

The first reading, responsorial psalm, and the gospel concentrate upon Jesus' teaching with authority. Jesus is the prophet of the end time, whose word is the very word of God himself. He is the "bearer of the word" (Rudolf Bultmann). Rightly understood, this description is not a minimizing Christology but a very high one. The prophets said, "Thus saith the Lord." The scribes quoted earlier rabbinic authorities. Jesus says, "I say unto you," and this puts himself in the place of God. Jesus is thus *aut Deus aut vir non bonus*, as the old quip has it. An exposition of the word-Christology might be in order today in this post-Epiphany season.

As an alternative, the epistle reading would offer an opportunity for a consideration of celibacy in the light of Paul's teaching. This teaching corrects a legalistic interpretation of celibacy, but at the same time offers a critique of the "muscular Christianity" common in many Protestant circles. Celibacy is a charisma, but where that charisma exists, it is a call to a life of less distracted devotion to the service of the Lord. Paul does not advocate celibacy because of a manichean dualism. Celibacy means the surrender not of a state which is evil, but one which is good, for a higher end, for a more completely devoted service of the Lord.

Sundays 5 B to 9 B

Reading I: Job 7:1-4, 6-7

The book of Job is rarely used in the eucharistic lectionary, so a word of introduction will be in order. Job belongs to the third group of Old Testament books, the group called the "Writings." It begins with a prose narrative in which Job, a hitherto prosperous paterfamilias, is suddenly overtaken by calamity, both domestic and economic. There follows a poetic dialogue between the unfortunate hero and his three friends, who seek to comfort him with platitudes. Job is thus led to wrestle with the problem of suffering. Suffering can no longer be interpreted as it was in Deuteronomy, viz., as a direct punishment for sin. For Job has been righteous and has maintained his integrity. What Job has to learn in the end is that man's righteousness gives him no claim upon God. The book closes with a prose epilogue in which the fortunes of Job are restored to him. The Book of Job can best be understood as a forerunner of the Pauline doctrine of justification by the grace of God alone.

Today's reading comes from the early part of the poetic dialogue. Job has just responded to the opening sally of his friends, and then trails off into a soliloquy on the miseries of human life.

It is not too easy to se why this reading was chosen for today. Since the Old Testament readings usually fit the gospel we may presume that Job's reflections on the miseries of human life are meant to provide a background for the healing work of Christ, of which the gospel speaks. It is from such miseries as Job speaks of that Christ comes to save us.

Responsorial Psalm: 147:1-2, 3-4, 5-6

The first stanza shows the original context for which this psalm was probably composed, namely the rebuilding of Jerusalem and the return of the exiles from Babylon. It is a hymn of praise. Our verses are derived from the first of the three sections of which this psalm is composed, and praises God for his mighty acts in the creation of the world and in Israel's salvation history. The refrain highlights the opening lines of stanza 2 and prepares the way for the gospel, thus supporting our interpretation of the relation between the Old Testament reading and the gospel.

Reading II: 1 Corinthians 9:16-19, 22-23

First Cor 9 looks like a digression from the concerns of the preceding chapters, the problems of community life raised by the Corinthians in their letter to Paul. Chapter 9 is not introduced by the formula "now concerning," which signalizes the questions the Corinthians have raised. For that reason some have thought that chapter 9 is part of another letter in which Paul was defending his apostleship against the attacks of his opponents, other parts of which are to be found in 2 Cor. There is perhaps more to be said for this view than is commonly thought. Compare however next week's reading which is linked to today's section by the idea of being all things to all men.

Paul has been criticized by his opponents for not letting his converts pay him for his preaching. They accuse him of lack of confidence in his authority as an apostle. Paul agrees that he has a perfect right to ask for payment. Although he does not say so here, he did actually accept money from the churches of Macedonia. But there were special reasons for his not doing so in Corinth. It was part of his becoming all things to all men in order that he might by all means save some. Why would it have hindered his goal to have received support? We know that very soon after this letter — perhaps already when these word were being written, if it is part of a slightly later letter — false teachers turned up at Corinth, sponged on the congregation, and nearly won over their allegiance. Paul does not want the Corinthians to take him for a wandering preacher like his opponents, for then the Corinthians would misunderstand his gospel. They would take it for the preaching of "another Christ" — maybe a miracle worker — not Christ crucified as Paul preached him. For Paul to preach the gospel means quite concretely and specifically to preach Christ crucified.

Gospel: Mark 1:29-39

Mark opens his account of Jesus' ministry in Galilee with a day of healing in Capernaum. After the first miracle of the Capernaum demoniac which we read last week comes the healing of Simon's mother-in-law, followed by a generalized summary of miracles at sundown, and Jesus' attempt to flee in order to carry on his mission elsewhere.

It is possible that these Capernaum miracles had already been combined together in a pre-Marcan miracle catena. Such catenae presented Jesus too exclusively as a miracle worker. It has been suggested that Paul's opponents at Corinth, of whom we spoke in the preceding comment on the epistle, used such miracle catenae in order to support their own claims and to propagate their own false Christology. Just as Paul countered their claims with the preaching of Christ crucified, and himself as a suffering rather than a wonder-working apostle (see gospel, Sunday 9 B), so by composing this Gospel Mark seeks to correct the false christological inferences that could easily be drawn from these collections of miracle stories. Here Mark makes his point by showing that Jesus got up very early in the morning, first to pray and then to move elsewhere. Jesus flees from the crowds, despite Simon's plea that he should continue in a campaign which had brought so much success, and insists that he must move on. The words "that is why I came out" may refer not to Jesus' departure from the house in Capernaum early that morning, but to the whole purpose of his mission in the world. In other words, Jesus regards his miracles as only a subordinate feature of his ministry. His main purpose is to preach (cf. Paul!) the good news of the coming kingdom. In this way Mark has corrected the pre-Marcan miracle catena, which presented the miracles as the principal feature of Jesus' ministry.

The silencing of the demons — a common motif in Mark — works in the same direction. The demons "knew him" — as in other stories they recognize him to be the "Holy One of God." But to call him by that title simply because he is a wonder-worker would be dangerously misleading. Hence the demons are enjoined to silence. Only the centurion at the foot of the cross can rightly confess Jesus as the Son of God, for the Jesus he sees is not the wonder-worker, but the crucified One.

What role then do the miracles play in Mark? They are now seen as prefigurations of the ultimate messianic miracle, which is the cross and resurrection. They are preliminary acts of healing which foreshadow the greatest act of healing.

This, then, provides the true context of meaning for today's responsorial psalm. It is not just that Jesus healed Simon's mother-in-law, or the concourse of patients at sundown. It is that by his death on the cross, in whose benefits we partake in every eucharist, he continues to heal the brokenhearted.

The Homily

Taken together, all the readings of this day are a proclamation of the healing power of Christ crucified. First, the preacher can picture the lesson from Job to depict the misery of human life, then he can connect this with the healing ministry of Jesus in the gospel reading, and show that according to Mark <u>these healing are foreshadowings of the supreme miracle in which the brokenhearted are healed, the miracle of the cross.</u> It was to preach Christ crucified that Paul, too, became all things to all men.

These readings might give the homilist an opportunity to help the people in the renewed understanding of unction as a sacrament of healing.

✓✓   SIXTH SUNDAY OF THE YEAR

Reading I: Leviticus 13:1-2, 45-46 (RSV)

The Book of Leviticus embodies much early legislation but in its final form it is the work of the priestly school (P) after the Babylonian exile. Today's reading is the beginning and the end of the section dealing with leprosy. This disease was not precisely what modern medicine classifies as leprosy, but included many other skin diseases which were temporary in character. Such diseases were serious not merely because of their contagious character, assumed or real, but because they were thought to make the patient spiritually unclean and therefore unfit to participate in the community's worship. Rules were set up for quarantine. The patient had to report to the priest, who diagnosed the malady not as a physician but as the minister of the Torah, and decided on the length of the quarantine, which involved a second visit to the priest — the one referred to in today's gospel. Obviously, this passage is selected as background reading for the gospel story.

Responsorial Psalm: 32:1-2, 5, 11

Psalm 32 is one of the traditional seven penitential psalms. Today it is regarded rather as a wisdom psalm (cf. the beatitudes of the first stanza) incorporating a thanksgiving. This psalm plays a key role in Paul's argument about justification, and was prominent in the controversies of the Reformation (cf. the word "imputed" in stanza 1). Evidently Ps 32 is used today because leprosy serves as a symbol for human sin. Just as the leper reports to the priest, so the sinner comes and confesses his sin to Yahweh (stanza 2) and receives forgiveness from him (stanza 1).

Reading II: 1 Corinthians 10:31-11:1

The context of these rather general-sounding remarks is a discussion of a further problem raised in the Corinthian letter, namely, the question of eating things sacrificed to idols. Christians at Corinth invited out to dinner were often offered meat which had been previously used in pagan sacrifices. The butchers would naturally stock such meat. Was it permissible to eat it? As instructed Christians they knew that the idols to which the meat had been sacrificed were nonexistent. Paul insists, however, that the Christians should not vaunt their knowledge over against their weaker Christian brethren who had scruples (Jewish Christians perhaps) or their pagan neighbors who took a malicious delight in making an issue out of the matter, to embarrass their Christian guests or fellow guests. So Paul lays down certain rules: it is not the food or drink in themselves that are holy, unholy or neutral, but the effect that the behavior of Christians will have on other persons. The scrupulous might be scandalized and an opportunity to bear witness before one's pagan neighbors might be lost. So the general rule is: do everything to the glory of God, and try to please all men (in the sense of not giving them offense). As a final rule of thumb Paul says, imitate my own behavior. He can ask them to do that without a trace of arrogance because he himself imitates the behavior of Christ. This must mean more than just following an external ethical example (Paul shows little knowledge of or interest in the earthly Jesus or the Jesus tradition). Rather, it must be something like what Paul hints at in Phil 2:6-11, an imitation of the path of Christ when he came down from heaven and humbled himself to the death on the cross. In his life as an apostle Paul reproduces the same pattern of self-emptying, humiliation, and suffering. His whole life as an apostle is thus an epiphany of Christ.

Gospel: Mark 1:40-45

This short miracle story follows the basic threefold pattern common to all such stories. 1. The diagnosis. This is quite briefly indicated with the simple statement that the man was a leper and his request for healing. 2. The cure: by word and touch. 3. The demonstration: the command to go and report to the high priest in accordance with the levitical law (see first reading).

The third point has been overloaded with the motif of the messianic secret, a fact which shows it to be Marcan redaction. The cured leper is told to say nothing to anyone, but he disobeys this command and his cure becomes the talk of the town. The result is that Jesus withdrew (unsuccessfully) to the country.

Mark adds this motif because of his polemic against the understanding of Jesus merely as a wonder-worker (see last week's comments on the gospel reading). We saw that Mark used commands to silence — there it is a command to the demon, here a command to the cured leper — in order to forestall the misunderstanding of Jesus and to point forward to the supreme miracle of the cross. A puzzling feature here is the fact that the command to secrecy is disobeyed. The man goes out and freely talks about his cure. (Cf. similar features in Mk 1:34; 3:13; 5:43; 7:36; 8:26.) Evidently we have here to do with a characteristic element in Mark's theory of the messianic secret. It is being repeatedly penetrated. Since we are dealing with a Marcan construction rather than with a historical fact, we have to ask not what was Jesus' purpose in giving an injunction he must have known would be broken, but what does Mark intend theologically by these injunctions to secrecy and their constant breach? The answer would seem to be that Mark wants to show that while the Messiahship of God is a mystery which must not be prematurely exposed, (because it is only rightly understood in the light of the cross), yet because it is the mystery of God's presence at work in Jesus' words and works, it can't be really suppressed but must come out. It comes out, for Mark, in the proclamation of the post-Easter church, which the irresponsible gossip of the healed leper is meant to foreshadow. The difficulties disappear when we realize that we are dealing not with history at this point, but with an artificial theological construction of the evangelist.

The Homily

The fact that leprosy symbolizes sin, like Mark's device of the messianic secret, compels us to take the first reading, the responsorial psalm and the gospel as a proclamation of the power of the cross to cleanse from sin. It is this cleansing power which is mediated in the sacrament of absolution and experienced in the eucharist. Here is the ultimate purpose of the epiphany of God in Jesus Christ. The homilist has thus an opportunity to deal with the sacrament of absolution.

The epistle provides material for ethical exhortation, dealing with the theme, "all things are lawful, but not everything is expedient," i.e., the right use of Christian freedom, and the need for respect for the scruples of the weaker brethren. The homilist might know some concrete situation in the congregation to which this teaching could apply.

Reading I: Isaiah 43:18-19, 21-22, 24b-25

To understand the very concrete meaning of this passage we need to re-call the situation in which Deutero-Isaiah uttered his prophecies. The exile by which God had punished his people for their sins was about to end and there would be a wonderful return to the holy land, conceived in terms of a second exodus.

"The former things" refers to the first exodus. Not that exodus, but a new one, the return, must henceforth be the focal point of the remem-brance (anamnesis) in Israel's liturgy. But Israel's new liturgy is reared on the foundation of the confession of sin (vv. 22, 24b). As Hoskyns remarked in respect to Johann Sebastian Bach's Mass in B Minor, the *Kyrie eleison* provides the ground base for the liturgy.

Nevertheless in the midst of the anamnesis and the confession of sin, there breaks through Yahweh's word of forgiveness: "I have blotted out your transgressions . . . and I will not remember your sins" (v. 25).

The reading is chosen to match the gospel reading, the story of the paralytic. This shifts the concrete application away from the original context of the Christian exodus, the church's experience of forgiveness of sin in Christ.

Responsorial Psalm: 41:1-2, 3-4, 12-13 (RSV)

This psalm is a thanksgiving for a recovery from sickness. It is not ob-viously suitable as a response to the theme of the new exodus return from Babylon, of which the first reading speaks. But when that reading is reinterpreted in the light of the healing of the paralytic it becomes more fitting. Stanza 1 consists of two beatitudes (cf. the psalm for last week). Stanza 2 recalls the prayer for forgiveness uttered by the patient during his illness. Stanza 3 returns to the theme of thanksgiving and closes with a doxology which however does not belong to this particular psalm but forms the conclusion of the first book of the psalter. The refrain has the effect of calling attention away from the thanksgiving to the man's prayer in his time of sickness. It thus prepares our minds to focus upon the plight of the paralytic, and therefore upon our own plight as sinners.

Reading II: 2 Corinthians 1:18-22

Second Corinthians is widely regarded today not as a single letter written by Paul on one occasion, but as a collection of various letters written in the course of a major crisis in Paul's relations with the Corinthian community. On this theory our present sections comes from the letter Paul wrote when the crisis was over and the relationship with the community had been happily restored. During the crisis Paul had twice changed his plans. First he had paid a lightning visit to the Corinthians, a visit which had ignominiously failed to bring them around. Then he had postponed visiting them again to give Titus time finally to straighten things out. This frequent change of plan gave rise to the charge that he was fickle and unstable. Paul defends himself (not, however, with the passion in which he had earlier defended his apostleship, but rather with a calm explanation) by arguing that his behavior has always been consistent. As usual, Paul goes back to first principles. His behavior was affirmative because it was an expression of the gospel which is itself affirmative. The gospel is God's affirmation of all his promises. This affirmative action of God comes to each Christian personally in the moment of his sacramental initiation, to which Paul now refers. In this God has established and commissioned us, put his seal upon us and given us his Spirit as a down-payment (*arrhabōn*, RSV guarantee) of our final salvation.

Gospel: Mark 2:1-12

The healing of the paralytic has a long history behind it. We need not doubt that Jesus did cure a paralytic at some time during his ministry, and that therefore the story rests ultimately on an authentic reminiscence. At first it was probably told as a straightforward miracle story, with a diagnosis (the helplessness of the man requiring the supreme effort of his friends to bring him to Jesus, vv. 1-4), the cure by Jesus' word (v. 11) and the demonstration (the cured paralytic takes up his bed and walks home under his own steam, and the "choric ending." At a later stage in the tradition, the saying about the man's faith and the declaration of the forgiveness of sins must have been added (vv. 5, 10). Thus the story is made edifying. Simultaneously an independent dialogue developed between Jesus and his critics about his authority to forgive sins, reflecting the debates between the Christian community and the Jewish authorities over the Christian claim to impart the forgiveness of sins through the sacraments. Finally, the evangelist combined the two traditions, inserting the conflict dialogue into the bosom of the miracle story, and thus making it serve his polemic against an interpretation of Jesus merely as a wonder-worker. To recap, Jesus heals the man as a sign of the ultimate messianic miracle, the forgiveness of sins through his death on the cross (Mark 10:45; 14:24).

The Homily

It is noticeable how clearly the readings in year B signalize the transition from the post-Epiphany season to Lent. First, we have had a series of lessons in which there is an unmistakable pointer to the cross. Now today we have readings which call particular attention to the forgiveness of sins. This theme should be dealt with not so much in a Lenten way, with emphasis on man's wretchedness, but rather as an extension of the Epiphany theme. The cross is the culmination of the supreme epiphany, of which the epiphanies in the life and ministry of Jesus are prefigurations. The purpose of Jesus' manifestation in his incarnation was precisely in order to take away our sins. The meaning of the incarnation does not lie in itself. It took place in order to make possible the atonement, which is the heart of the Christian message. This would seem to be the major theme for the homilist today.

The epistle suggests a different theme, and a somewhat intractable one, the affirmation of the divine promises in Christ. This theme can only come alive where the promises of God in the Old Testament are a vital issue for faith. Perhaps this notion could be translated today into the sense which modern man has of the "pull of the future" (Ernst Bloch). Man has hopes and aspirations for a better world, its humanization, and unless life is ultimately meaningless, these hopes will be ultimately fulfilled. The eschatology of the gospel proclaims that God has in fact in Jesus Christ given to man the assurance of the fulfillment of his hopes for redemption. Christ is the affirmation of God's "promises," he is the affirmation of the future which is the content of man's highest aspirations.

EIGHTH SUNDAY OF THE YEAR

Reading I: Hosea 2:14b, 15b, 19-20 (RSV)

The burden of Hosea's prophecy (precise date uncertain, somewhere between 750 and 721, the fall of Samaria) is that the northern kingdom has been faithless to Yahweh and has succumbed to Baal worship. Partly because the Baal cult focused on the idea of the sacred marriage between the deity and its worshipers, and partly because of his own marriage experience (he married Gomer, who was unfaithful to him), the prophet pictures the relationship of Yahweh and his people in terms of a marriage. Yahweh had married Israel in the desert, but Israel had subsequently been faithless, and gone a-whoring after Baal. Yahweh however will woo Israel back, renew his covenant with her in the wilderness, and remain betrothed to her forever. Such is the import of our pericope. Its selection is determined by the appearance of the same marriage metaphor in the gospel reading for today.

Responsorial Psalm: 103:1-2, 3-4, 8 and 10, 12-13

The same selection is used on Sunday 7 A and C, but it has not been commented on before in this series.

This is perhaps the best known of all the thanksgiving psalms of the whole psalter. The psalmist, speaking of his own individual experience of the purpose of God, transforms his own personal gratitude into a corporate hymn of praise. What precisely that personal experience was is difficult to say, but perhaps the reference to delivery from the pit (sheol) in stanza 2 suggests that he had been very ill and at the point of death. In his own personal experience he sees mirrored the experience of Israel throughout her salvation history (see v. 7, not used in this selection). The psalm praises God for his kindness and mercy manifested particularly in the forgiveness of sins. It therefore serves as a fitting response to the reading from Hosea.

Reading II: 2 Corinthians 3:1b-6

This part of 2 Cor comes from Paul's so-called "first apology." After Paul had sent off 1 Cor he got bad news from Corinth. False apostles had shown up there and his converts had succumbed to their blandishments. These interlopers sought to undermine the Corinthians' confidence in Paul, already strained by the factions of his congregation (cf. 1 Cor), by discrediting Paul's apostolic authority. He thus writes the first apology to defend himself against these attacks. One of the charges leveled against him by the false apostles was that on his first visit he had brought no letters of recommendation with him from the other churches, a sure sign that he was no true apostle. It was customary for itinerant preachers in the Hellenistic world to secure such letters from the communities they visited and carry them to their next port of call (cf. "to you and from you" in v. 1). These letters would record the miracles they had performed, the ecstasies and visions they had displayed, and their ability to speak in tongues. Paul admits that he has no letters of commendation like his opponents. He refuses to compete in that league. His true commendation, the true proof of his apostleship, is the converts produced by his preaching. Their faith is a "letter from Christ, written by the Spirit of the living God" on their hearts, not in pen and ink.

In the second paragraph Paul still has his eye on his opponents. They boasted of their miracles as personal achievements. They operated in a spirit of self-sufficiency. In his preaching of the word of the cross, however, Paul has no sufficiency of his own, but relies wholly on the enabling power of God. The final phrases of our reading introduce a new idea. The discussion shifts from the contrast between the letters of recommendation and the work of the Spirit in the hearts of the believers to a new contrast between the written code and the Spirit. Again, we must suppose that Paul's opponents made much of the "written code." This is probably a reference to their allegorical interpretation of the Mosaic law. To this Paul opposes the "Spirit" which for him must mean the proclamation of Christ crucified.

Gospel: Mark 2:18-22

This pericope consists of (a) a pronouncement story, (b) two little parables appended thereto, the patch and the wineskins. The pronouncement story has the usual threefold form: (1) the setting: John's disciples and the Pharisees are fasting; (2) the action: the people come and ask Jesus a question, Why don't your disciples fast like John's? (3) the pronouncement: you don't fast at weddings. This is undoubtedly an authentic incident in the life of Jesus. In his reply he expresses the complete newness of what has come in his ministry: the joy of the kingdom of God is already breaking through.

The appended parables may have belonged to the original pronouncement, but it is more likely that they circulated independently before being joined to it. In any case they fit their context perfectly, for both the pronouncement and the parables speak of the new bursting through the confines of the old.

The one saying that does not fit into the context is the assertion that the bridegroom will be taken away from them, and that then they will fast. Critics regard these words as a later addition. First, they identify the bridegroom allegorically with Jesus — an explicit post-Easter Christology. Second, they presume knowledge of Jesus' death. Third, they presuppose the reintroduction of the practice of fasting in the post-Easter community. "That day" may even refer quite specifically to the fast before the Christian passover, in which the church mourned for the giving up of their Saviour to death.

By inserting this pericope here, Mark intends that the cross should overshadow the gospel narrative almost from the very beginning of the ministry. In this way he converts the Jesus tradition from a miracle saga into the proclamation of the cross.

The Homily
The context of the Hosea passage (Gomer!) justifies the homilist in expounding human marriage as a parable of the relation between Yahweh and Israel in the Old Testament and Christ and the church. Remember, however, that in doing so we are treating the question of the fasting pericope at the level of the evangelist's redaction, not the level of the original Jesus tradition, and the homilist should be careful to expound the nuptial theology as the teaching not of the earthly Jesus but of the early community. This theme can then be related to the eucharist as the marriage supper of the Lamb.

The epistle provides many different lines of thought. The question of the false apostles is probably not immediately relevant to the contemporary life of the church, but there are two other themes which are always relevant for meditation. The first is the idea that the true commendation of a parish priest or minister is not in external success but is to be measured by the converts he has been instrumental in winning, the souls he has trained for the kingdom of heaven. The second is that the sufficiency of the Christian pastor comes not from himself, but from God, and what this means for each individual's prayer.

NINTH SUNDAY OF THE YEAR
Reading I: Deuteronomy 5:12-15
The fourth (third) commandment of the decalogue is read today in preparation for the gospel reading which consists of Jesus' conflicts with his opponents over his breaches of the sabbath.

It is to be noted that in Deuteronomy the fourth commandment is not merely a legal ordinance enacted as a ritual taboo. It is set in the context of remembrance (anamnesis). It is Israel's grateful response to the exodus, the foundation event of her salvation history. In the Judaism of New Testament times, as we can see both from our Lord's ministry and from Paul, this "evangelical" setting of the law was widely forgotten. Note that a different theological motivation for the observance of the sabbath is given in Ex 21, where it is interpreted as a memorial of Yahweh's rest after the six days of creation.

Responsorial Psalm: 81:2-3, 4-5ab, 5c-7a, 9-10ab (RSV)
This is a psalm designed for liturgical use at the feast of Tabernacles
(Passover is less likely). Like the weekly sabbath in Deuteronomy, the two
annual feasts of Passover and Tabernacles were memorials of the exodus.
Hence the appropriateness of this psalm as a response to the reading of
the fourth commandment in its deuteronomic version.

Reading II: 2 Corinthians 4:6-11
Like the previous week's epistle reading, this pasage comes from Paul's
defense of his apostolate, the so-called first apology. He has been attacked
for preaching a "veiled gospel" (4:3), probably because he does not prove
his authority by spectacular miraculous displays, like his opponents. Paul
concedes that sometimes his gospel is veiled, but in that case it is the
fault not of his gospel but of the hearers: if they receive his words in
faith, then his gospel is a manifestation of light, i.e., authentic revelation.
For the God who brought light out of darkness at the creation, has also
brought light in the new creation, the Christ event (v. 6). Paul is perhaps
recalling his own personal experience on the Damascus road: in it the
light of Christ shone in his heart to give him the knowledge of the saving
presence of God in the person of Jesus Christ.

But Paul is afraid he has conceded too much to his opponents in speaking like this of the revelation of light in his ministry. So he hastens at
once to qualify what he has just said. The treasure of God's revelation
is committed to earthen vessels — to the frail human personalities of his
apostles. How frail they are is shown by the catalogue of Paul's apostolic
sufferings, one of three such catalogues in 2 Cor (the others are in 6:4-10
and 11:22-33). Each of these catalogues has to be seen in contrast to the
boasting of Paul's opponents. As we have mentioned, they claim that
their miracles, their ecstasies and visions, their eloquence and brilliant
allegorical exegesis of the Old Testament were epiphanies of the divine
power. Paradoxically, Paul asserts the counter claim that it is his apostolic
sufferings that are the epiphanies of Christ. This is because for him the
center of the gospel is not Jesus the miracle worker, but Christ crucified.
Paul's apostolic sufferings are a manifestation of the crucified One. It is
in the cross that light shines in the darkness. This reading thus serves
as a suitable transition from the Epiphany to the Passion season.

Gospel: Mark 2:23-3:6 (long form); 2:23-28 (short form)
The two pericopes which make up the long form are linked by the common motif of our Lord's breach of the sabbath rule.

The first episode is a pronouncement story with the usual threefold structure: (1) the setting: the disciples are walking through the grainfields and plucking the ears of grain on the sabbath; (2) the action: the Pharisees object at this disregard of the sabbath regulations; (3) the pronouncement: Jesus defends his disciples' conduct by comparing it with David's eating of the showbread during his flight from Saul (note that in the Old Testament Abimelech, not Abiathar was the high priest: the other evangelists have understandably omitted the name). The renewed introduction "and he said to them" suggests that the two further sayings about the sabbath are independent logia which were added later.

Let us first take the original pronouncement. We regard this as authentic to Jesus because it asserts an implicit rather than an explicit Christology. Jesus does not say that he is the Son of God or Messiah, but draws an analogy between the situation in David's time and that in his own. Each situation, David's and Jesus', was one of emergency and crisis in which the normal rules were suspended. David was in flight from Saul; in Jesus' ministry the kingdom of God is breaking through. Therefore sabbath regulations must give way in both cases. Implicit is the thought that something (and therefore someone) greater than David is present. The saying "the sabbath was made for man, not man for the sabbath" we take to be an authentic Jesus saying (it differs so completely from anything possible in contemporary Judaism, and is perhaps also too radical for the early church, for both Matthew and Luke omit it), but originally independent of the story to which it has been attached. We infer this from the overloading of the pronouncement and the new beginning in v. 27, "and he said to them." Its radicality, however, must not be understood in a humanistic sense. It is not that all institutions, including religious institutions, are for man's use, and to be observed or broken as it best serves humanitarian interests. Rather, the saying is evangelical in its thrust. In contemporary Judaism the sabbath was regarded as a sign of the eschatological salvation intended by God for man, and now that the salvation is present in the ministry of Jesus, the sign which has pointed to that salvation must give way to the reality.

The last part of the saying is problematical. It uses Son of man as a self-designation of the earthly Jesus in a way which many modern scholars find difficult to accept as authentic. While Jesus spoke of the coming Son of man in judgment and glory, and implicitly identified himself with that figure, he probably did not use the title as a direct self-designation. We are therefore inclined to think that the Son of man saying is an explanatory note added by Mark. Mark wishes to guard precisely against a humanistic misunderstanding of the previous verse. It is only because Jesus dispenses his disciples with messianic authority from the sabbath regulations that they can break them and get away with it. They cannot take matters into their own hands.

The Homily

The Old Testament reading, the psalm and the gospel suggest the theme of the sabbath, its Old Testament institution as memorial of the exodus and its New Testament fulfillment by the coming of the messianic salvation. This raises the question of the Christian understanding of Sunday. Sunday is not itself the sabbath — a misconception which first filtered into Christianity after the Emperor Constantine made Sunday a weekly rest from toil, and which reached its apogee in the Puritan sabbatarianism of Britain and New England. Rather, Sunday is the *fulfillment* of the sabbath. It is a day not for legalistic prohibitions, but for joyous participation in the eschatological salvation to which the Old Testament sabbath looked forward. With the abandonment of the old legalistic sanctions for attendance at Sunday mass the Roman Catholic church has to face the challenge of thinking out anew the theology of Sunday. Today's lections should give the homilist an opportunity to tackle this problem.

For those who wish to use this Sunday to prepare the faithful for the keeping of Lent, the epistle reading provides suitable material for the transition from the Christmas-Epiphany to the Passion-Easter cycle. The coming of the light to shine in the darkness means the cross and passion, manifested in the lives of the apostles no less than in the life of the Lord.

Lent of Year B

As we have explained in previous years, the purpose of the Lenten readings is to prepare the people of God for participation in the paschal feast. The Old Testament lessons focus on Israel's salvation history, as the presupposition, preparation for and in some respects a prefiguration of the redemptive act of God in Christ. The epistle lessons are either expositions of the meaning of the cross, or of the believers' participation in salvation through baptism. The gospel readings of year B begin the Marcan temptation and transfiguration stories on the first two Sundays, which are traditionally associated with those events. Then follow a series of readings from the Fourth Gospel, which contain predictions of Christ's death on the cross and interpretations of its meaning. These gospels would form an admirable basis for a series of homilies on the cross.

FIRST SUNDAY OF LENT

Reading I: Genesis 9:8-15

This reading comes from the P (priestly) version of the flood story. The J story speaks of the divine promise, P of the divine covenant as the outcome of the flood. It is characteristic of P that it postulates a series of covenants, whereas J and E featured only the one basic covenant (J: Sinai; E: Horeb). The covenant with Noah is distinguished from other Old Testament covenants in that it is made not with Israel only but with the whole human race. In this covenant God undertakes never again to destroy the earth by a flood. This is a pictorial statement of the biblical faith in divine preservation. It is God's will ultimately not to destroy the earth but to redeem it. As usual in the Bible, the covenant is accompanied by a token or sign. In this case it is a God-given sign, the rainbow. The ancients of course were unaware of the laws of the refraction of light. Therefore this feature of the flood story is in part an "etiological myth" — a story designed to explain the origin of an enigmatic phenomenon.

These two features of the story — the universal covenant of preserva-

332

tion and its accompanying sign — are important theologically in their own right. However, the point of this reading today, as the epistle reading lesson shows, lies in the fact that Noah's flood is treated in Christian thought, and already in the New Testament, as a type of baptism.

Responsorial Psalm: 25:4-5ab, 6 and 7bc, 8-9

A slightly different arrangement of these verses with a different refrain was used on Sunday 26 A. Here the refrain suitably matches the flood story, with its reference to Yahweh's covenant and to his love and truth, of which the rainbow is a sign.

Reading II: 1 Peter 3:18-22

Behind this passage there probably lies an early christological hymn:

1 [Christ] suffered once for our sins
2   that he might bring us to God,
3 being put to death in the flesh
4   but made alive in the spirit,
5 in which also he preached to the spirits in prison
6   and having gone into heaven sat down
            at the right hand of God
7 angels and authorities and powers having been
            made subject to him.

The first two lines express the early Palestinian and Pauline doctrine of the atoning efficacy of Christ's death. It is "for our sins" and it "brings us to God." The third and fourth lines use Hellenistic language of the two spheres, the "flesh" (i.e., the earthly sphere) and the "spirit" (i.e., the heavenly sphere). (Cf. Rom 1:3-4. and 1 Tm 3:16.) Since by the end of line 4 we have already come to the resurrection, it follows that the preaching to the spirits in prison is performed by the already risen Christ. It has nothing to do with a *descensus ad inferos* between the death and resurrection, as in the Apostles' Creed. It expresses the early Christian interpretation of the death and exaltation of Christ as a triumph over the powers of evil.

This means further that the spirits in prison are not the dead, but cosmic powers of evil. Hence what Christ preaches to them is not the gospel of God's redeeming love, so that they may have a chance to repent, but the announcement of their final defeat. Line 6 speaks of the ascension, and line 7 is a résumé of the subjection of the powers first mentioned in line 5.

The first part of 1 Pt (to 4:11) consists of a baptismal homily. The author has taken the traditional hymn and adapted it to his baptismal purpose by a somewhat complex insertion. He understands the spirits in prison to refer not to the cosmic powers, as in the original hymn, but to the disobedient spirits at the time of Noah. This could mean either the wicked angels of Gn 6 or the wicked of Noah's generation who were destroyed in the flood. As a result, the "preaching" now becomes a preaching of salvation. The dead are given a chance to repent. By introducing the reference to Noah, the author acquires an opening for a typological treatment of Noah's flood with reference to Christian baptism.

This insertion, as noted, is complex, and not easy to interpret. "Saved through water" may mean either that Noah and his sons passed through the water and so escaped, the water being a hostile element which might have drowned them. Or it can mean that water was the means whereby the ark was brought to safety. In view of the analogy drawn between the waters of flood and the water of baptism the second meaning seems preferable. There is in fact a double typology here: the first between the flood and the waters of baptism, and the second between the eight persons in the ark and the Christian community. Many medieval fonts in England portray Noah's ark as a type of the church, and the notion may already be present here.

Finally, the author adds an interpretation of Christian baptism (v. 21b). The stress on water, he insists, must not be taken in a materialistic sense, as though the whole meaning of baptism resided in the physical washing. Baptism is not the removal of dirt from the body, but, literally, "the answer of a good conscience toward God." The RSV translation indicates that there is uncertainty over the meaning of this phrase. We would take it to mean an answer given to God and proceeding from a good conscience. At baptism there was scrutiny of the candidate, eliciting the fact that he came to baptism with a good conscience, i.e., with repentance of his sins and faith in Jesus as his Saviour. One may be surprised that the author does not replace the materialistic interpretation of baptism with a sacramental interpretation. He speaks not of what God does in and through baptism (though this is implied when he speaks of the type where, on our interpretation, the waters of the flood are a means of salvation) but on the candidate's part in baptism. The effect, however, is to give a comprehensive instruction on baptism which emphasizes both

God's part (in the type), and the response of the candidate (in the antitype).

Gospel: Mark 1:12-15

The Marcan form of the temptation narrative is extremely brief. Both Matthew (whose version we are more familiar with from the traditional pericopes) and Luke expand the story from their common source (the Q material). Mark lacks the threefold temptation and the statement that Jesus fasted. It is even possible that he intends to suggest that the angels fed (note that the Greek word for "ministered" is in the imperfect, suggesting an action over a prolonged period) Jesus during the 40 days. This in turn hints at a Moses/Elijah typology (the manna in the wilderness is called angel's food in Ps 78:25 and Elijah is sustained by the ravens during his 40 days fast). The mention of the wild beasts suggests a further piece of typology. In Ps 91:11-13 we are told that the righteous man of God will be protected by the angels and will be immune from the attacks of wild beasts. Even more striking is a passage from the Testament of Naphthali (from the intertestamental collection known as The Testaments of the Twelve Patriarchs). Here the patriarch Naphthali says to his sons:

> The devil shall flee from you
> And the wild beasts shall flee from you . . .
> And the angels shall cleave to you.

Here we get the same three features as in the temptation story — the devil, wild beasts and angels. Perhaps there is even the thought here that Christ is the second Adam, who restores the harmony of nature previously destroyed by Adam's fall. Satan put in his usual claim to a son of Adam, but this time he met his match.

Thus for all its brevity, the Marcan form of the temptation narrative is particularly rich in meaning. Mark is not interested in the psychological experience of Jesus, but in proclaiming him as the New Israel, the new Moses, the new Elijah, the righteous man of God, and the new Adam, through whom the powers of evil are defeated and the peace of paradise restored.

The Homily

Either the gospel or the Old Testament lesson can determine the homily. If we take the gospel, we can link it with the hymn enshrined in the epistle reading in its original form as reconstructed above. Taking both readings together, we can proclaim *Christus Victor* — Christ who is victorious over the powers of evil. This may be illustrated from pastoral experience, in which we can find examples of the continuing power of Christ to overcome the evil in human life. We can conclude by urging the faithful to seek the power of Christ to overcome evil in their own lives, especially the power of temptation.

If, however, we take our cue from the Old Testament lesson, the story of the flood can be linked to Christian baptism, as is done by the author of 1 Peter in his redaction of the early Christian hymn (see above). The two sides of baptism can be emphasized, what God does and what the candidate does. God saves "through water." Although, as Luther insisted, *Wasser tut's freilich nicht* — i.e., it is not the water in itself that effects salvation — God uses the water as the means of his saving action. The candidate for his part repents and makes his profession of faith. The whole purpose and climax of Lent is the renewal of our baptismal vows at the Easter Vigil. This treatment of today's readings can help prepare for that.

SECOND SUNDAY OF LENT

Reading I: Genesis 22:1-2, 9, 10-13, 15-18

The sacrifice of Isaac provided the early church with one of its types for the death of Christ. Indeed, it probably underlies Paul's statement in today's second reading, also highlighted in the accompanying caption: "God did not spare his own Son but gave him up for us all."

The interest of the Isaac story lies not so much in its primitive origins, which were connected with the abandonment of human sacrifice, nor with its meaning as it stands in the Pentateuch. It lies rather with its later development in Judaism,[1] The upshot of this development of interpretation was that whereas in the Old Testament interest was concentrated exclusively on the testing of Abraham's faith (cf. Heb 11:17), in later Judaism this interest was often combined with an emphasis on Isaac's voluntary surrender of his life. To this voluntary surrender was attributed atoning significance, and the sacrifice of Isaac was further connected with the passover lamb.

[1] See J. Massingberd Ford, *Wellsprings of Scripture* (New York: Sheed and Ward 1968) 25-35.

Responsorial Psalm: 116:10 and 15, 16-17, 18-19

A different selection from this psalm is used at the Mass of the Lord's Supper on Maundy Thursday. There its primary reference is naturally to the eucharist. Here the focus is upon the deliverance of the righteous man from his affliction, recalling the deliverance of Isaac. Note especially the phrase, "Thou hast loosed my bonds." In later Judaism the Isaac story was called the *Akedah* or "binding" of Isaac.

Reading II: Romans 8:31b-34

Last week we suggested that a possible theme for preaching might be the power of God in the lives of the believers to enable them to overcome evil and to surmount temptation. This is what Paul is speaking about here. He raises a series of rhetorical questions. The RSV text (see however RSV margin) takes the last of the sentences in our pericope also as a question. The sense must then be: "Is it (*sc.*, No, of course, it cannot be!) Christ Jesus who condemns us, Christ Jesus, who died, was raised, who is at the right hand of God and who intercedes for us?" Paul emphasizes the absurdity of the rhetorical questions by citing all that God in Christ has done and is doing for us — this in a series of traditional formulae derived from the kerygma and liturgy of the early community:

1. God did not spare his own Son, but gave him up for us all (cf. Rom 8:32).
2. Christ died (cf. 1 Cor 15:3).
3. He was raised from the dead (cf. 1 Cor. 15:4).
4. He is at the right hand of God (cf. Acts 2:33, etc.).
5. He intercedes for us.

Only the first part of (1) — the Isaac typology — and (5) — the statement about the heavenly intercession — are not otherwise directly paralleled in the kerygma. But their style (the relative "who" and the "we" style) and content (the basic assertions of salvation history) suggest that we have here also traditional formulae.

Gospel: Mark 9:2-10

We have commented on the other versions of the transfiguration narrative in previous years, and will confine ourselves here to the peculiarities of the Marcan version. These are as follows:

1. Mark says nothing about the change of Jesus' *face*.
2. He emphasizes the whiteness of Jesus' garments (v. 3b).

3. He places the name of Elijah *before* that of Moses (4a).

4. He emphasizes Peter's bewilderment and lack of understanding (6).

5. He states that the three disciples were also bewildered about his allusion to the resurrection of the dead (10) — this following the command to silence until after the resurrection, a command which Matthew also has, but which Luke omits.

The first four points are almost certainly taken by Mark from his tradition. Mark's redaction is to be found in points (4) and (5). Mark emphasizes the difficulty the disciples had in understanding Jesus, and the command to silence (here it is applied to the disciples, in the earlier chapters to the demons and those healed. What is the point of this command? The answer seems to be that Mark is trying to formulate a particular Christology, i.e., an understanding of the person of our Lord, over against another Christology which was current in his day, but which he rejects. This other Christology saw in Jesus a direct epiphany of divine power displayed in his miracles and culminating in the transfiguration. Against that Mark asserts his Christology of the suffering Son of man. Hence neither the true Christology nor the transfiguration can be disclosed until after the resurrection. Why do the disciples constantly misunderstand? They represent, I think, Mark's church, which is very attracted to the epiphany Christology of Mark's opppoents, but, like the blind man in chapter 8, they gradually come to see that Jesus is not merely the Christ, the epiphany of God, but the suffering Son of man, who attains to his glory only through the passion. This final disclosure of the true disciples comes only after the resurrection (14:28; 16:7) when they see the risen Lord in Galilee. If they disclosed the transfiguration before the death and resurrection, it would be an expression of a wrong Christology involving glory without the cross. The oblique message of Mark's version of the transfiguration is: No cross, no crown.

The Homily

In different ways, all of today's readings focus upon the cross. The cross can be treated in several ways: 1. As the act in which the Father gives up the Son to death for the benefit of sinners (Old Testament lesson, epistle). Here the homilist could emphasize the continuity of action between the Father and the Son. The cross is not the act of perfect man appeasing the wrath of an angry deity, as in some doctrines of the atonement, but an act of God himself to which the Son freely assents (both Isaac and Christ exhibit this). 2. The cross is not just an event of "30 A.D."

Its benefits are constantly being applied to us by the Lord's intercession in heaven (epistle) which finds its externalization on earth in the eucharist. 3. It is not in the miracles or even in the transfiguration of itself that we behold the glory of God in the face of Jesus Christ, but only in the crucified One. It is only when we have faced the cross with Jesus that we can proclaim the earthly life of Jesus to the world as the epiphany of the glory of God. The homilist must be determined in his choice of theme by the needs of his people.

THIRD SUNDAY OF LENT

Reading I: Exodus 20: 1-17 (long form); 20:1-3, 7-8, 12-17 (short form)
The short version of the decalogue is attained by the omission of those parts which have a rather narrow and temporary application — viz., the prohibition of idolatry in commandment 1 (according to the Latin-Lutheran enumeration, but, commandment 2 according to other traditions) and the abbreviation of commandment 3 (4). Anglicans are further accustomed to the abbreviation of commandments 9-10 (10) as "Thou shall not covet," a procedure which could have been followed here with advantage.

The decalogue appears in two places of scripture, here and at Dt 5 (part of the latter was read on Sunday 9 B): the two versions differ mainly over the grounds for the sabbath commandment. The content of the second table (duty to the neighbor) is paralleled in many primitive legal codes. The first table (duty to God) is unique to scripture. Both tables also differ from the other codes in form. They are apodictic: "Thou shalt." The other codes are conditional: if you do so and so, the consequences will be so and so. Thus the natural law is taken up and transformed by the insights of Yahwism.

It has been much debated whether, historically, the decalogue originates from Moses. Contemporary scholarship looks rather more favorably on the traditional ascription. If it is correct, then Moses probably reinterpreted earlier codes in the light of the ethical monotheism for which he stood. Obviously they have undergone at least two later recensions — the one Deuteronomic (Dt 5), the other priestly (Ex 20).

With the exception of commandment 3 (4) all of the ten words have a timeless validity. The New Testament quotes the second table at several places, and clearly regards it as valid for Christian believers. The decalogue was a constant element in medieval catechesis, and is expounded in the Reformation catechisms as the summary of Christian moral obligation. It has been frequently used as a form of self-examination before communion. In Christian use it has of course to be understood in the light of our Lord's teaching as given in the Sermon on the Mount.

Responsorial Psalm: 19:7, 8, 9, 10

Psalm 19 falls into two distinct halves. Part 1 through verse 6 is a nature psalm, celebrating the revelation of God in creation. Part 2 is a hymn of praise to the law of God similar to much of Psalm 119. It is from Part 2 that today's selection is taken. It forms an excellent response to the reading of the decalogue.

Reading II: 1 Corinthians 1:22-25

Paul had had a great deal of experience in preaching to both Jews and Gentiles. He had found again and again that the Jews wanted a sign, that is to say, a legitimating miracle (as in today's gospel reading, Jn 2:18) to authenticate his apostolicity and the truth of his message. The Greeks on the other hand looked for wisdom. That is to say, they were prepared to accept Christianity if it was presented as "wisdom" or "gnosis" — i.e., if it brought a convincing understanding of the universe and of man's place in it, so that a man could thereby be released from the trammels of earthly existence and reunited with his heavenly origin. It was wisdom rather than signs that the Corinthians — who were mainly Gentiles — desired at this time. Later on however, by the time of 2 Cor, they would be impressed by Jewish Christian preachers who came along offering signs. Paul does not altogether repudiate the religious quest either of the Jew or the Gentile, but he corrects it by the message of the cross. The cross is power (*dynamis*, the word frequently used for miracle, and corresponding to sign) and wisdom. But it is a paradoxical kind of power and wisdom — a foolishness (note the chiastic construction) in human eyes which is wiser than men, and a weakness which is stronger than men. Only believers can penetrate the wisdom behind the folly and the power behind the weakness. For all unbelievers the message of the cross remains a scandal (for Jews) and folly (for Greeks).

Gospel: John 2:13-25

The Fourth Gospel has a version of the cleansing of the temple which is parallel to but independent of the synoptic version. John's tradition combines two elements found separately in the synoptists: (1) the cleansing of the temple (Mk 11:11 par); (2) the prediction of the temple's destruction (Mk 14:58 par). There are other features not paralleled in the synoptists: (1) the whips: a greater degree of force used by Jesus (a feature which has been taken up in recent theologies of revolution); (2) the citation of Psalm 69:9: this was a psalm traditionally used in the early church's passion apologetics; (3) the interesting statement that the incident took place when the temple had been 46 years in building — pointing to the date 28 A.D. We take it that these features were already present in the Johannine tradition.

The evangelist himself seems responsible for the following features: (1) the shift of the cleansing from holy week to the beginning of the ministry (does that mean he is also responsible for the remark about the 46 years? Alternatively, following Fr. Raymond Brown, we may suppose that the saying about the destruction of the temple belonged already before John to this year, and John has shifted the cleansing to the earlier date and thus combined the originally separate traditions of the cleansing and the prophecy); (2) the statement that in the saying about the destruction of the temple Jesus was referring to his body.

We will concentrate on the meaning of these two redactional features. 1. The reason for the shift of the incident to the beginning of the ministry will be a programmatic one. John wishes to make Jesus lay out all his cards on the table right at the outset. The destruction of the temple — i.e., the end of the Jewish dispensation and its worship — is the ultimate purpose of his whole ministry. 2. Closely connected with this is the second redactional feature. This expresses the positive side of Jesus' program, as the destruction of the temple expresses its negative aspect. The old order of worship is to be replaced by a new one, an order focused no longer on the old temple, but on the body of Christ. In what sense is "body of Christ" here used? Does it mean the ecclesial body in the Pauline and Deutero-Pauline sense? Or is it the glorified humanity of Christ? The second sense seems closer to Johannine theology elsewhere (cf. Jn 1:14), but we cannot altogether rule out overtones of the Pauline meaning.

The Homily

If on the previous Sundays of Lent the homilist has taken the texts which expound the cross, he could well take the epistle and gospel together, and speak of the cross as a sign — not a legitimating sign, but the expression of the wisdom and power of God (the epistle) which inaugurates a new dispensation and a new worship (the gospel). The other possibility would be to deal with the interpretation of the ten commandments as a summary of duty to God and the neighbor, perhaps highlighting those commandments which he feels most relevant to the needs of his congregation.

Reading I: 2 Chronicles 36:14-16, 19-23

In his priestly rewriting of Israel's history the chronicler now reaches the exile and the return. He offers his explanation of the exile as a divine punishment along similar lines to 2 Kings, but significantly, from his standpoint, he stresses that it was a punishment of the pre-exilic *priests*, as well as the people, for not listening to the pre-exilic prophets. He compresses the burning of the temple and destruction of Jerusalem into a single verse, and interprets the 70 years exile as a sabbath for the land of Judah, during which it lay desolate. The last three verses, a verbatim reproduction of Ezra 1:1-3 were, it is generally agreed, added here by a later editor because 2 Chronicles was the last book in the Hebrew canon, and the editor did not want the Old Testament to end on a negative note!

This reading does not appear to relate directly to either the epistle or the gospel readings, and one wonders why it was chosen. Perhaps the idea is that the exile in Babylon is a type of the Christian Lent, as the return forms a type of the crucifixion and resurrection. That idea seems to be taken up in the responsory psalm (137:1-2, 3, 4-5, 6). Indeed, so effectively does this psalm, with its recalling of Israel in exile, suggest the situation of the people of God in mid-Lent, that one suspects that it was chosen first, and the lesson selected afterward to go with it! The theme of Jerusalem was a tradition on this Sunday, the old *Laetare*. The psalm presents Jerusalem to the exiles as a memory to be kept alive until better days when the people will be restored to their homeland.

Reading II: Ephesians 2:4-10

If, as is widely held today, Ephesians is a Deutero-Pauline composition (i.e., written by a disciple of Paul and a member of the Pauline school after the apostle's death) this passage certainly captures the spirit of the apostle himself. As in so many New Testament writings of the sub-apostolic period, we have here a citation from a hymn, evidently a baptismal hymn (note the relative "who," the concentration on the basic facts of the kerygma, and the liturgical "we" style) in verses 4-6. Note also the parenthetical insertion in verse 5, which changes from the we style to the second person plural. Note further the connection between this hymn and that in Colossians 2:12, as well as Paul's exposition of baptism in Romans 6. All of these passages associate baptism with the death and resurrection of Christ. But there is a difference. In Romans 6 the genuine Paul is careful to say that while we have died in Christ with baptism, nevertheless our rising with him lies in the eschatological future and is a challenge to ethical realization in the present. In Colossians both death and resurrection are experienced already in baptism. The hymn in Ephesians goes further: not only are we risen with Christ, we have already been translated into heaven with him. This approaches gnosticism (cf. 2 Tm 2:18). Probably Romans and Colossians are drawing upon the same hymn Ephesians also quotes. We thus have a trajectory: 1. Primitive Hellenistic-Christian baptismal hymn. 2. Romans 6. 3. Colossians 2:12. 4. Ephesians 2:4-10. 5. Second-century gnosticism.

Being in heaven with Christ is not a matter for self-congratulation or for a false sense of security. So the author inserts the parenthesis: by grace you have been saved. Christian initiation is not simply, as it was for the gnostics, an illumination about one's true, innermost nature. The author expands this Pauline affirmation very precisely in verse 8 (by grace through faith). He then introduces his second antignostic point: the Christian life is not an intoxication with being in heaven already, but a constant call for strenuous moral effort. It means to do the good works which God has prepared for us to walk in. This again is good Paulinism: Paul excludes works from any role in justification, but insists that they are its consequence.

Gospel: John 3:14-21

The conversation with Nicodemus is the first discourse in the Fourth Gospel. It is typical of this evangelist's procedure. He takes an incident from the life of our Lord from his tradition, here an encounter between Jesus and Nicodemus. There is good reason to think that as a historical occasion this encounter belonged to the later part of the ministry, shortly before the passion. He then has Nicodemus ask three questions (vv. 2, 4, and 9), each of which elicits a pronouncement from Jesus. Some of the material in these pronouncements, e.g., the saying about being born again in verse 3, comes from the sayings tradition and is paralleled in the synoptics. The rest is an elaboration of Johannine theology. The first part of the discourse enunciates the necessity for rebirth as the essential prerequisite for entry into kingdom of God. The second part, from which our section comes, explains that this rebirth can only come as a result of the "lifting up" of the Son of man, i.e., his death and glorification. As the quotation marks indicate, it is only the saying about the serpent and the Son of man which is represented as a saying of Jesus. Verses 16-21 are presented as a meditation of the evangelist. It looks back upon the coming of Christ and his saving work as an already accomplished event.

In the serpent-Son of man saying we have an interesting interpretation of the cross. There are several presentations of the atonement in the New Testament, but the one given here is frequently overlooked. It is almost an Abelardian interpretation. The very sight of Christ lifted up on the cross has power to bring men and women to faith and repentance, just as the contemplation of the serpent lifted up by Moses on the pole in Numbers 21:9ff was able to heal the Israelites who had been bitten by fiery serpents. Paul seems to envisage a similar interpretation of the power of the cross when he reminds the Galatians that Christ had been placarded before the eyes as the crucified One (Gal 3:1). This may not be a very satisfying doctrine of the atonement intellectually, but from a devotional point of view it has great power. It is saved from a purely exemplarist interpretation by the ensuing meditation, which asserts most emphatically that the cross is an act of the divine love: "God so loved the world that he gave his only Son." This also picks up the words at the opening of the epistle reading: "God who is rich in mercy, out of the great love with which he loved us."

The Homily

The most obvious choice of theme for today is that which comes to expression both in the epistle and in the gospel: the cross as the ultimate manifestation of God's love. The preacher should so try to hold up Christ crucified before his hearers as Paul placarded the crucified before the eyes of the Galatians, so that they realize the love of God for sinners and are led to repentance, faith, and devotion. The homilist might speak, too, of the devotional value of the crucifix — not the "triumph crucifix" so popular today, but the medieval crucifix which portrays the suffering Christ.

The Old Testament reading does not seem to yield very much appropriate material for the homilist, but he might like to depict the Jews in Babylon and their memory of the songs of Zion, comparing it with the liturgical situation of the new people of God in Lent, and reminding them of the joy of the festal liturgy in which they hope to share at Easter.

Reading I: Jeremiah 31:31-34

Jeremiah is prophesying to the Jews in Babylon. He interprets the un-
faithfulness for which the exile was a punishment as a breach of the old
covenant made at the exodus. The prophet looks forward to a new cove-
nent which Yahweh will make with his people. This time God will write
his law, no longer on tablets of stone, but in the hearts of his people. All
of them will then "know" him — i.e., live in obedience to his law. From
the time of Paul Christians have seen the fulfillment of this prophesy in
the covenant which was established by the blood of Christ and which
led to the outpouring of the Spirit into the hearts of the believers (2 Cor
3:6ff). As has often been pointed out, this is the one passage in the Old
Testament where the New Testament is expressly mentioned.

Responsorial Psalm: 51:1-2, 10-11, 12-13

An earlier comment on the Psalm *Miserere* will be found on Sunday 24
C. This is the most famous of the penitential psalms. It takes up and
turns into a prayer Jeremiah's prophecy that under the new covenant the
hearts of the believers will be inwardly transformed, so that their sins
will be forgiven and that they may walk in the law of the Lord.

Reading II: Hebrews 5:7-9

The Epistle to the Hebrews alternates between ethical exhortation
(*parenesis*) and theological exposition, the one reinforcing the other.
The theological exposition deals with Christ as the heavenly high priest.
The author does not really get down to his major theological theme until
chapter 7. Before that he prepares the ground for his treatment. He must
show that despite his lack of levitical descent our Lord was indeed a high
priest — a high priest after the order of Melchisedek. The author enunciates this theme several times before he develops it. Our present passage
is sandwiched in between two such enunciations (vv. 5-6, 10). In this
section the author wishes to prove that our Lord has the requisite qualifications for high priest. He does this by arguing that no high priest ap-
points himself to the office, but is chosen by God. He takes the Gethsemane scene as an illustration that this is true of Christ. At Gethsemane
Christ did not seek honors for himself, but dedicated himself unreservedly
to the will of God. But the Gethsemane prayer was heard. Not that
Jesus was saved from death, as he prayed ("Father, let this cup pass

from me"). Rather through death and resurrection he was made perfect — God brought him to "perfection." "Perfect" here means not moral perfection, but reaching a goal or destiny. His destiny was to become our high priest. To this office he was divinely appointed at the resurrection. He thus becomes the source of eternal salvation to all who accept the gospel.

Gospel: John 12:20-33

Like the Nicodemus passage we read last week, a traditional incident has been used as a springboard for a Johannine discourse. We are not told what happened to the Greeks — whether they really got to see Jesus. Doubtless in the earlier tradition the story came to a natural conclusion. Perhaps in a pronouncement of Jesus instead, the Johannine discourse develops the theme of the cross, with its two great pronouncements: 1. A grain of wheat must die if it is to bring forth fruit. 2. Only by being lifted up will Christ draw all men to himself. These pronouncements are not unconnected with the Greek's request. They cannot "see" Jesus — i.e., experience the Messianic salvation — until after Christ has been crucified. Historically this was so: the contacts of Jesus during his earthly ministry were almost exclusively confined to his own people (cf. Rom 15:8), and his contacts with Gentiles were strictly exceptional (the Greeks in this story, the Syro-Phoenician, a woman in Mark and the centurion in Q: each time there is a reluctance on the part of Jesus to break the barrier). It was only later that Hellenistic Christians began preaching to Gentiles (Acts 11). But there was also a theological reason. It was only after the middle wall of partition had been broken down — that is, the Jewish law as a barrier between Jew and Gentile — that the Gentile mission could begin. Thus the grain of wheat has to die before it can bring forth fruit (i.e., win Gentile converts) and the Son of man has to be lifted up (in Johannine language for the crucifixion-resurrection) before the Gentiles can be brought in. This discourse is followed by a prayer of Jesus, often called the Johannine Gethsemane.

The Homily

Today's readings are again focused upon the cross, and provide the homilist with various approaches to it. With the Old Testament lesson he can expound the cross as the means whereby a new covenant was established with man, a covenant in which God's law is written not on tablets of stone, but by the Spirit in the heart. In connection with this the responsorial psalm is a prayer for such a renewed heart. The epistle reading portrays the Gethsemane prayer of Jesus as the supreme renunciation of ambition for office, rewarded in the resurrection by his exaltation precisely to the supreme office. If the homily is based on this reading, the concluding part of the gospel (the Johannine Gethsemane) could be brought in too. The main part of the gospel speaks of the necessity of the death of Christ for universal salvation. Only by the surrender of his life in death could Christ bear fruit — i.e., bring all men to salvation.

Holy Week to Easter 3 B

Gospel for the Procession with Palms: Mark 11:1-10 or John 12:12-16

As we have pointed out in the two previous years, Jesus' entry into Jerusalem, while doubtless in popular estimation the major theme of this Sunday, is both historically and liturgically merely a subsidiary theme, serving only as a prelude to the passion. If the homilist chooses to deal with the entry, he should be careful to treat it as such.

As usual in the exegesis of the gospels, we have to distinguished between three levels of meaning in this pericope: the historical level — i.e., what actually happened in the life of the earthly Jesus and what he intended by it; the tradition, or the way the episode was shaped and interpreted in the early communities; and the redaction — the use to which the evangelists put the tradition.

1. The historical level. Jesus went up to Jerusalem to deliver his final eschatological challenge to Israel at the very heart of its corporate and religious life. His entry into Jerusalem to cleanse the temple was a symbolic expression of this eschatological challenge. The final salvation and judgment of God were breaking through. Israel must decide. If she accepted her salvation, all well and good. If not, then (as the cleansing of the temple indicates) the present order of things will be replaced by God's new, eschatological order. As Jesus approaches Jerusalem, he expresses this challenge by riding on a colt (a horse or an ass? Linguistically, "horse" would be possible and more expressive of the challenge, but asses were — and are — more common in Palestine). Two features suggest that the entry may have taken place at Tabernacles (or at the Dedication) rather than at Passover: the palms and the singing of Psalm 118:25. "Blessed is he who comes" in that case would not have originally had a messianic significance, but was merely a welcome to the pilgrims indiscriminately.

2. At the level of the tradition, Jesus' triumphal entry was messiani-

cally "overexposed" (Bornkamm). Jesus' work undoubtedly evoked messianic hopes and fears, and therefore he may even have been greeted as the prospective messiah in a politically Davidic sense at the entry. But it is hardly likely that he intended overtly to create this impression. The church, however, reinterprets the story in the light of the Easter faith. It makes Jesus act as sovereign "Lord" (v. 3), directing the whole proceeding. The miraculous discovery of the ass suggests to the earliest Palestinian community the supernatural foresight of the prophet-man of God, and in the Hellenistic church that of the "divine man." It is probable that the community further added to the original Hallel psalm the words of verse 10a as an expression of its faith. The term "our Father David" would be unusual in Judaism, and the whole phrase looks like a liturgical acclamation of the early community. At the level of tradition, then, the entry is an overt expression of Jesus' Messiahship conceived in terms of the Davidic Messiah, the eschatological prophet, the kyrios (Lord) and the divine man.

3. The redaction. Mark in turn attaches the story to his passion narrative. The effect is to say that the messianic images (son of David, eschatological prophet and man of God, Lord and divine man) are predicable of Jesus only because — and precisely because — he is the crucified one. Moreover, the divine man motif — namely, miraculous foresight displayed in the discovery of the ass, now serves to bring home to the reader that Jesus, as the Son of man who is to suffer, knows beforehand the whole saving plan of God, and sets the whole plan in motion by his own initiative.

We take John's version of the story to be not a fuller redactional modification of Mark or of the other synoptists, but an independent version derived ultimately from the same tradition used by Mark, but at a very early stage of its development. It lacks the miraculous discovery of the ass, showing that this motif had come into the pre-Marcan tradition somewhat later. In John, too, Jesus finds the ass *after* the acclamation of the crowd. It is difficult to decide whether this is the earliest tradition — which would make Jesus' decision to ride on an animal a response to the crowd's acclamation — or a later theological reinterpretation (Jesus wishing to correct expectation of the Davidic messiah with a suffering servant concept).

John has the crowd come out of the city to meet Jesus. John alone of the evangelists mentions that the branches were of palm. If the entry occurred at Tabernacles or Dedication this could be historical. The second half of the crowd's acclamation ("even the king of Israel") is worded differently, supporting our view that this second part is a later expansion. John, like Matthew (though in a different form, so that John is not using Matthew), but unlike Mark and Luke has the citation of Zechariah 9:9, thus indicating that the proof text came later into the tradition. Compare also John's explicit statement (v. 16) that the disciples did not realize the applicability of the Zechariah text until after the resurrection.

At the level of John's redaction the following points suggest themselves: 1. This was not Jesus' first visit to Jerusalem. Hence the crowd comes out to meet him because of his previous words and works at Jerusalem, especially the raising of Lazarus (v. 18). The entry in John introduces the episode of the Greeks at the feast (Jn 12:20-22). This makes Jesus the King of Israel not in a narrow, nationalistic sense, but in a universalistic sense (cf., in John, the title on the cross in three languages). It is in this sense that we must understand the revelation of Jesus in the raising of Lazarus as the resurrection and the life. He is that for all men.

John alone tells us that the true meaning of the entry did not dawn upon the community until after the resurrection, thus conforming to our contention that there was a development and reinterpretation of the incident in the post-Easter community.

Finally we must note that both Mark and John, by placing the story before the passion narrative, emphasize what the liturgy itself emphasizes, namely, that the entry is not an isolated episode, but introductory to and subordinate to the passion.

Reading I: Isaiah 50:4-7

This Isaianic reading occurs each year and was commented on the first year in series C. This is the third of the suffering servant songs. It presents the servant's sufferings as the outcome of his fidelity to the message or word he had received from God to proclaim to his people. So Jesus' death was the outcome of his proclamations of the kingdom of God.

Responsorial Psalm: 22:7-8, 16-17a, 18-19, 22-23ab

Again see series C for comments. This psalm is particularly appropriate to the Marcan passion, impregnated as it is with its language. We shall bring out in our discussion of the Marcan passion certain elements from this psalm.

Reading II: Philippians 2:6-11

Again see series C for comments. Scholars today generally regard Phil 2:6-11 as a pre-Pauline christological hymn with Pauline interpretations, particularly the words, "even death on a cross." This interpretation was meant as Paul's corrective of a christological trajectory which otherwise might have gone off course and developed into a gnostic-type myth: the redeemer from heaven who briefly sojourns on earth and returns to heaven again. Paul thus secures the truth that the incarnation and death of Jesus are not transient episodes, but abiding, living truths in the life of the believing community. We shall bring out in our discussion of the gospel reading certain features of the christology of this hymn which appear in Mark's passion.

Gospel: Mark 14:1-15:47 (long form); 15:1-39 (short form).

First, let us recall what we have said about the passions in previous years. These are the only parts of the gospel material which existed from the first in the form of continuous narratives. They were probably constructed as Christian Passover Haggadas or cult narratives for liturgical recital. Each passion has its particular timbre and theological emphasis.

The suggestion has sometimes been made that Mark's narrative combines together two earlier narratives of the crucifixion. Recently, a similar suggestion has gone further and proposed that the two pre-Marcan crucifixion stories which the evangelist combined in Mark 15:20b-41 express two different theologies of the passion. It will be helpful for our understanding of Mark if we follow up this suggestion.

The first and earlier narrative, it is suggested, consisted of 15:20b, 22, 24, 27. It would read as follows:

"And they led him away to crucify him. And they brought him to the place called Golgotha. And they crucified him, and divided his garments among themselves, casting lots for them, to decide what each should take. And with him they crucified two robbers, one on his right side and one on his left."

This crucifixion report, it is suggested, is very early. It is impregnated with echoes of Psalm 22 and Isaiah 53 (parting of the garments, numbering with the transgressors). This earlier crucifixion narrative represents the stage at which the passion story was formulated in apologetic terms. How could the righteous, innocent servant of God have suffered crucifixion, and execution reserved for the worst criminals? Answer: that is precisely the picture of the righteous servant of God in Psalm 22 and Isaiah 53.

The second and later tradition of the crucifixion has been found in Mark 15:25, 26 29a, 32b, 33, 34a, 37, 38. This tradition would read as follows:

"And it was the third hour when they crucified him. And the inscription of the charge against him read, 'The King of the Jews.' Those who passed by reviled him. Those who were crucified with him also reviled him. And when the sixth hour had come, there was darkness over the whole land until the ninth hour. And at the ninth hour Jesus cried with a loud voice (uttered a loud cry) and breathed his last. And the veil of the temple was torn in two, from top to bottom."

This narrative interprets Jesus' death not as that of an innocent, righteous suffering servant of God, but as an agonizing conflict between the powers of light and the powers of darkness. This is an apocalyptic interpretation. The loud cry of Jesus is an announcement of triumph of the power of light (and implicitly Jesus' exaltation), and the rending of the temple veil a symbolical expression of that victory. We have here an interpretation of the death of Jesus which recalls the hymn in Philippians 2:6-11. Jesus is the divine redeemer who has emptied himself of his divine glory and therefore it is concealed from the powers of darkness who are his enemies. They therefore crucify the lord of glory (1 Cor 2:8). His death leads to his exaltation and triumph over the powers.

Mark does not deny the validity of either interpretation, but combines them, allowing one to correct the other. Jesus' death is not just that of the righteous, innocent suffering servant, for that could be misunderstood as a mere ethical example (cf. 1 Pt 2:21-25). His death would then have had no cosmic significance as the triumph over the powers of darkness. On the other hand, the triumph over the powers of darkness could be misunderstood as mere mythology, unless it was insisted that this triumph was wrought out in a real, flesh and blood history, in an act of obedience cf. Paul's interpolation of "even death on a cross" in Phil 2:8).

It is this combination of the ethical and the cosmic-eschatological that creates the unique tone of the Marcan passion.

The Homily

The homilist has two major possibilities. Either he can take the entry into Jerusalem as the prelude to the cross or he can take the Marcan passion narrative by itself, using the other readings with it.

If he opts for the entry in its Marcan form, then he can speak of the messianic enthusiasm of the multitudes and the way Jesus corrects this by riding on an ass, thus foreshadowing the humiliation of the cross. It is only as the suffering servant that Jesus is the King.

If instead, the Johannine version of the entry is read, then the homilist has an opportunity to oppose the nationalist implications of the entry with its universalist understanding. Jesus is King not in a narrow, nationalistic sense, but because he is the resurrection and life of all men, and because in dying on the cross he is the light of the world, who will draw all men to himself.

If the homilist chooses to concentrate on the Marcan passion story, he has an opportunity to bring out Mark's distinctive understanding of the passion (cf. first reading and the responsory psalm) with the apocalyptic victory concept (cf. the pre-Pauline hymn in Phil 2:6-11). As the servant Jesus is not merely ethical example, but *Christus Victor*. But he is *Christus Victor* precisely in and through his obedient suffering on the cross. Mark superimposes the suffering crucifix on the triumph crucifix. Each of itself fails to comprehend the full meaning of the cross, and is in danger of imbalance.

Perhaps this is not so much the occasion to try and give a relevant message to the contemporary world as an occasion to assist the people as they begin "in the meditation of those mighty acts whereby God has brought" us salvation and life.

HOLY THURSDAY

All of the readings (Ex 12:1-8, 11-14; Ps 116:12-13, 15, 16-18; 1 Cor 11:23-26; Jn 13:1-15) are used each year, and were commented on in full the first year, in series C. We summarize our previous year's comments.

Three principal mysteries are celebrated in the mass of the Lord's Supper. The institution of the eucharist, the establishment of Christian priesthood, and the commandment to love one another.

1. The institution of the eucharist. Institution does not mean the enactment of a new rite, but a reinterpretation of Jewish custom, whether the last supper was an actual passover or an ordinary Jewish meal. The institution is the investment of an existing rite with new meaning. The variation between the eucharistic narratives in the gospels and in 1 Corinthians 11 shows that there was no fixed tradition of what Jesus said on that occasion. There was probably a liturgical expansion of an original nucleus, the precise contours of which, however, are hard to determine. The words "my body" said over the cup, and the words "covenant" and "blood" appear in all accounts and must belong to the earliest core. So, too, does some eschatological reference to the effect that the present meal looks forward to the eschatological banquet. There are thus backward and forward looking aspects to the eucharist.

2. *The establishment of Christian priesthood.* This theme requires great caution in handling. It is over-simplistic to say that Jesus by commanding the Twelve to celebrate the eucharist was consciously instituting the Christian priesthood, which later developed in succession from the apostles to the Christian priests, the bishops and presbyters of the church. The command "do this" is addressed to the whole community, and the eucharist is the focal act whereby the community expresses its priesthood (1 Pt 2:1-10). The eucharistic president performs a priestly role inasmuch as he expresses the priesthood of the whole community. It might also be said that in his actions the priesthood of Christ is exhibited to the community. But the priesthood of the church and the priesthood of the ministry derive their priestly character from the nature of the eucharist.

3. *The commandment to love the brethren.* This theme is given by the footwashing and the Lord's words which accompany that act in John. The theme of brotherly love emphasizes the horizontal as distinct from the vertical aspect of the eucharist — i.e., the relation expressed and cemented between the members of the community as distinct from the relation between the believer and his Lord. The exchange of peace by all members of the congregation is a current attempt to emphasize this horizontal aspect.

In choosing between these three suggested themes, the homilist will be guided by the concrete needs of the congregation as he knows them.

GOOD FRIDAY

The readings for Good Friday are always the same. Earlier comments will be found under series C and series A.

Reading I: Isaiah 52:13-53:12

The fourth servant song of Second Isaiah. This contributed three features to the primitive church's understanding of the crucifixion: Christ's suffering was innocent, vicarious and redemptive; it is for "the many," i.e., for all mankind; and the suffering servant will be vindicated (i.e., Isaiah 53 offered a way of understanding the resurrection in relation to the cross).

It is a matter of unresolved debate among New Testament scholars whether the earthly Jesus himself appropriated Isaiah 53 for the understanding of his mission. The sayings in which the references to Isaiah 53 occur are sparse and probably represent later additions (the ransom word, Mk 10:45; the addition of "for many" to the cup-word in Mk 14:24, absent from 1 Cor 11:25). Some of the passion predictions, esp. Mark 9:13, *may* echo Isaiah 53, but in their present form they have clearly been colored by the details of the passion narrative.

If Isaiah 53 was first used in the post-Easter church, that should not disturb us, for it relieves the passion from being a mechanical fulfillment of a preconceived dogmatic scheme. It is the culmination of the whole earthly mission of Jesus. In his ministry he had identified himself to the uttermost with sinners, thus breaking the barrier between man and God. He stood for God on the side of sinners. It was because the primitive church saw the cross in the light of this identification with sinners that Isaiah 53 was taken up as an almost perfect prediction of the passion and a quarry for theological affirmations about the cross. But these statements are not abstract theologoumena. They are an attempt to capture into words for the benefit of those who did not "see" the meaning of a real piece of history, wrought out in flesh and blood by God for us men and our salvation.

Responsorial Psalm: 31:1 and 5, 11-12, 14-15, 16 and 24 RSV
This psalm was used in the Jewish evening prayers as it is used at compline in the Christian church. Verse 5 provided Luke (or his special tradition) with an alternative "last word" from the cross. Luke evidently preferred it to Psalm 22:1, which he would have found in Mark. While lacking the profundity of the assertion of Jesus' God-forsakenness (the nadir of his self-identification with sinners), it conveys something of the Godward aspect of the cross. The cross is not only the act of God for the salvation of mankind, but it is also man's perfect offering of obedience to God. This idea is taken up in the second reading.

Reading II: Hebrews 4:14-16; 5:7-9
This passage is the third enunciation of the major theme in Hebrews, the high priesthood of Christ. That priesthood is characterized in three

ways: as sympathy for human weakness consequent upon Jesus' having shared our earthly experiences; as God's answer to the Gethsemane prayer; and as Jesus' learning of obedience through suffering.

As we suggested above, the doctrine of Christ's high priesthood expresses the Godward direction of Christ. The real sacrifice which God demands of man is the perfect offering of himself in obedience to the divine will. Since he is a sinner, man cannot offer that sacrifice, for all acts of man, even his righteous deeds, are still the deeds of a sinner. While they could not take away sin, the Levitical sacrifices acted as a constant reminder of the sacrifice God really wanted (cf. Pss 40 and 51). The Old Testament sacrifices were continued until God should undertake to do for man what man could not do for himself — i.e., offer the sacrifice of perfect obedience to God. This God did in sending his Son. But man is not thereby relieved of his obligations. He can now be taken up into Christ's own sacrifice, and be enabled to offer himself, soul and body, in union with that sacrifice, so that the imperfection of the believers' self-oblation is transformed by the perfection of his.

Gospel: John 18:1-19:42

John tends to pack his theological interpretation into the discourses, culminating in the farewell discourse and the high priestly prayer. When he reaches the passion narrative, he lets the facts speak for themselves. Only three overt "Johannine" theological points are made in the passion narrative. One is the definition of Christ's kingship in terms of witness to the truth (Jn 18:37-38). The second is the last Johannine word from the cross, It is finished (consummated, Jn 19:30), announcing the completion of the sacrifice of the Lamb of God which had been foreshadowed by the Baptist early in the gospel. The first two points indicate the two-way direction of the cross — God's saving act for man and man's offering to God. The final Johannine touch — perhaps added by a redactor — establishes the disciple at the cross as the witness for the Johannine tradition (Jn 19:35).

The Homily

The twofold direction of the cross — God's saving act for man, and man's perfect offering to God — corresponds to the twofold office of Christ, the *duplex munus* (as it was called in traditional dogmatics) of king and priest, which in turn follows the pattern of the yet older dogmatic formula of the two natures, human and divine. As king he comes from God, exercising his saving power among sinful men and women, identifying himself unreservedly with them. He stands where they are and in so doing brings to them the saving compassion of God. The cross is the nadir of Christ's kingly service of God toward man.

Christ is also priest. At his baptism Jesus accepted the call of the Father and at each moment of his ministry offers himself anew in perfect obedience. Thus the Father's words become his words and the Father's works his works. The cross is not a meaningless, tragic end to a life of surrender to the will of God.

On Good Friday the doctrine of the atonement should be proclaimed. This can be done at various levels. The cross can be interpreted as the culmination of God's search for man that took place in Jesus' identification of himself with sinners, in his baptism, in his eating with the outcast. It can at the same time be interpreted as the culmination of a life of perfect obedience to the Father. At the level of the tradition of the post-Easter church it can be interpreted as the fulfillment of the mission of the suffering servant vicariously dying for us and for our salvation. At the level of the evangelist's presentation the homilist can take the theme of kingship as witness to the truth, linking this with the title on the cross.

EASTER VIGIL

As we have pointed out in previous years, this is the archetypal liturgy of the church year. It has four parts: the kindling of the new light with the Easter proclamation; the nine scripture lessons (seven Old Testament readings and an epistle and gospel, the baptisms, and the Easter eucharist). The homily follows the gospel, and leads into the baptisms. In year C, above, we commented on readings I-III and the epistle and gospel (which varies each year; in year A, on readings V-VII. This year we shall comment on the gospel.

Gospel: Mark 16:1-8

The nucleus of historic fact behind this tradition is that Mary Magdalene (and other women? their names vary; only Mary Magdalene figures in all accounts) visited the grave of Jesus on the Sunday morning, and claimed to have discovered it empty. We cannot get back behind the women's testimony. All we can do is to take their report at their word, as the first disciples did. For the disciples and Peter welcomed their report as congruous with the conviction they had formed (in Galilee, as we should maintain) as a result of the appearances. The community then shaped the women's report into a vehicle for the proclamation of the Easter kerygma by means of an angelic message (Mark mentions a "young man," but his white clothing is generally understood to suggest an angelic figure). This of course is not historical description, but theological interpretation. "He has been raised [namely by God; thus the Greek], he is not here," said the young man. The women's response was a typical biblical reaction to an epiphany: fear, wonder, and silence.

To this traditional account Mark has added an element (16:7) which somewhat dislocates the story (cf. 14:28, a complementary addition from the evangelist), but serves to point to the appearances in Galilee, first to Peter and then to the Twelve. Why does Mark make these additions and yet does not relate the appearances? In my opinion Mark could not do so because he had no appearance stories available in his community. All he knew was the tradition that the risen One appeared first to Peter, then to the Twelve (cf. 1 Cor 15:5), and he indicated this by his addition to the angelic message of 16:7. Why did Mark do this? Because it is in the Easter revelation that all the misunderstanding of the disciples so emphasized by Mark is cleared up, their forsaking him, and in the case of Peter, denying him. The disciples are finally restored and commissioned to proclaim the gospel (Galilee in Mark's symbolism means the place where the proclamation of the message begins, cf. Mark 1:14-15).

The homilist thus has three levels at which he can treat this gospel: at the historical level of the tradition, and at the level of Mark's redaction. At the historical level it raises the place of the empty tomb in Christian faith. The belief in the resurrection of Christ does not rest primarily upon the empty tomb. The resurrection is not identical with the empty but the tomb does play an essential role in the New Testament witness. The empty grave is a symbol that the resurrection appearances are not spiritualist séances. Christ's resurrection is no mere survival. In the resurrection death has been overcome, man's destiny is opened up beyond the grave and death.

At the level of the tradition, the operative verse is 16:6, the angelic proclamation, "God has raised him; he is not here." "He" — the Jesus who lived and walked and taught and suffered and died on earth is not "here" — not to be sought in the past, in Palestine in A.D. 1-30. He is raised — his saving work is an ever-present reality in the community of the believers.

At the level of the redaction, Easter restores the disciples and commissions them as apostles to proclaim openly the saving act of God in Christ in his death and resurrection, a mission which the church continues today.

Once more we would remind the reader, especially the new reader, that the Easter Sunday mass is not itself the paschal liturgy, which has already been celebrated at the close of the Easter vigil. Rather, the Easter Sunday mass is the first of the great fifty days, the Easter season. For the new calendar has reverted to the older pattern, in which the Easter season is a single period of 50 days, rather than 40 days of Easter followed by 10 days of Ascensiontide as a distinct period. During these 50 days we are bidden to reflect upon the post-resurrectional appearances of the risen Lord, the consequences of the Easter event in the life of the church, the gift of the Spirit and the promise of eternal life.

The readings are the same for years A, B, and C. They received extended comment in year C, above. As last year, we confine ourselves here to a few pointers for the homilist.

Reading I: Acts 10:34a, 37-43

This passage comes from the kerygmatic speeches in the early part of Acts. Note the emphasis here on the importance of the apostolic witness (a word occurring no less than three times in the pericope). This witness covers both the earthly life of Jesus and the post-resurrectional appearances. The latter were — and are — problematic because, unlike the earthly life, the appearances were not public, verifiable events but confined to a few. This is the only "evidence" we have for the resurrection. No one else can see the risen Christ as the original witnesses saw him. Subsequent visions there have certainly been, but they are different in function if not in character as subjective experiences. Paul has both a post-resurrectional appearance and subsequent visions, but he distinguishes sharply between them (cf. 2 Cor 12:1-9 with 1 Cor 15:8). Psychologically, no doubt, both fall into the category of visions, but in meaning they are very different. The Easter appearances are revelatory encounters which founded the church and launched the Christian mission. As such they belong to the *eph hapax*, the once-for-all-ness of the original saving events and are unrepeatable. Our Easter faith depends in the first place solely upon the testimony of the first witnesses. We just have to take them at their word when they proclaim that God raised him from the dead and made him manifest. But this is not an irrational leap of faith. Once we accept the testimony of the original witnesses everything begins to fall into place. Our acceptance of the witness will find confirmation in our Christian experience.

Responsorial Psalm: 118:1-2, 15-16a, 17, 22-23
See the comments on Easter 2, below.

Reading II: Colossians 3:1-4 or 1 Corinthians 5:6b-8
Both of these alternative epistle readings emphasize the ethical consequences of Christ's resurrection and our participation in it. Although baptism effectively symbolizes and initiates our dying to sin and rising again to new life in him, our own resurrection has constantly to be implemented by obedience. Hence the imperatives: *seek* the things that are above, *set* your mind on them; *cleanse* out the old leaven: *celebrate* the festival with the unleavened bread of sincerity and truth.

Gospel: John 20:1-9
This story seems to consist of the two separate traditions: 1. The visit of Magdalene to the tomb and her subsequent report to the disciples; 2. Peter's visit of inspection to the tomb (cf. Lk 24:12). To this the evangelist has added his distinctive motif of the race between Peter and the beloved disciple. The beloved disciple functions here in a way similar to the angelic interpreter in the synoptic accounts (R. E. Brown). Since this is the distinctive element in the Johannine redaction, the homilist would do well to concentrate on this point. He could link it up with the emphasis on witness in the lesson from Acts.

The homilist thus has two major alternatives: 1. How do we come to Easter faith? Answer: through the report of the first witnesses, who themselves "saw and believed" (Acts and gospel reading); 2. The ethical consequences of Easter and baptism (the epistle).

SECOND SUNDAY OF EASTER

Reading I: Acts 4:32-35
In each of the series A, B, and C, readings from the Book of Acts replace Old Testament lessons during the Easter season. These readings show the continued work of the risen Christ in his church. This passage features two aspects of the life of the new community, first the sharing of all things in common, and secondly the apostles' preaching of the

resurrection with great power (*dynamis*, a word which calls attention to the charismatic nature of the early Christian preaching). This section anticipates to some extent the picture of the life of the earliest community which is given in Acts 2:42-47. Indeed, there is something to be said for the view that the author has combined two different accounts of the same thing from two different sources. As we pointed out last year, this so-called early Christian communism was not based on an economic doctrine but was a spontaneous expression of Christian *agape*, necessitated by the move from Galilee to Jerusalem. In New Testament times it was not treated as a law for all the churches. Paul gave the same principle a different expression in his collection for the Jerusalem church. Later Benedictine monasticism was yet another expression of *koinonia*. But whatever form it may take, in any given society, there must always be some expression of this principle in the life of the Christian community if it is to retain its integrity.

Responsorial Psalm: 118:2-4, 15c-16a and 17-18, 22-24

Similar, but not quite identical selections from Psalm 118 were used at the Easter vigil A, Easter Sunday A and Easter 2 A, also Easter 2 C. We repeat from *Worship* 45:4 (April 1971) 221, our comment when it first occurred. Psalm 118, with its reference to the rejection of the stone and and its subsequent elevation to be the chief corner stone, was perhaps the earliest Old Testament passage that the primitive community applied to the death and resurrection of Christ. It was the basic Old Testament passage for the "No-Yes" interpretation of the death and resurrection: the death of Jesus as Israel's (and all mankind's) "No" to Jesus, and the resurrection as God's vindication of him, his "Yes" to all that Jesus had said and done and suffered during his earthly life.

Reading II: 1 John 5:1-6

This reading overlaps with the traditional epistle for the old Easter 1, which was 1 John 5:4-10. By beginning at verse 1 the reading latches on to the paschal theme of baptism: "Jesus is Christ (Messiah)" was a primitive baptismal confession, and it is in baptism that believers become children of God. This carries with it the responsibility to love God and neighbor. Then in the typical "spiral" style of the Johannine school, the writer of the first epistle reverts to the theme of baptismal rebirth and adds a new point, viz., that through baptism we overcome the world. "World" in Johannine thought means unbelieving human society organized in opposition to God and subject to darkness, i.e., sin and death. The writer then makes the tremendous statement that Christian faith overcomes the world. As he at once makes clear, the faith he is talking about is not a dogmatic system, but an existential trust in Jesus Christ as the Son of God, the revelation of God's saving love. Such faith points beyond itself to its object — the saving act of God in Christ. That is the real victory that triumphs over unbelief.

This point is reinforced by the final paragraph, the perplexing passage about the three witnesses: the spirit, the water and the blood. A clue here is that the statement has a polemic thrust: it refutes those who say that Jesus Christ came by water only, not by water and the blood. "Came by water" is probably a reference to Jesus' baptism; "Came by blood" to his crucifixion. There were false teachers in the environment of the Johannine church who asserted that Christ was baptized but not crucified. This may refer to a gnostic teaching that Jesus was a mere man on whom the divine Christ descended at his baptism but left him before his crucifixion. A modern analogy would be those who base their whole theology on the incarnation, but ignore the atonement.

Gospel: John 20:19-31

The traditional Low Sunday gospel is used every year in the new lectionary on Easter 2 and was commented upon at length in the first year, on Easter 2 C. It contains two appearances. The first is that to the Twelve, a tradition which goes back to 1 Corinthians 15:5, and is developed in various forms in Matthew, Luke, and here in John 20. Perhaps the appearance to the seven disciples in John 21 is another variant of the same tradition. Luke and John 20 locate this appearance in Jerusalem, Matthew (cf. Mark 16:7) in Galilee, while in 1 Corinthians 15 no locality is given. Galilee seems to be the earliest tradition, though this is much disputed. The second appearance, resolving the doubt of Thomas, is peculiar to John and represents a manifest concern of the subapostolic age — how is it possible to believe in the risen Lord if one has not seen him? The answer is that even to see him is no guarantee of faith (cf. Thomas). Even the disciples had to make the leap of faith when they saw him. It is therefore possible for those who have not seen him to make that same leap. This does not mean that seeing the Lord was not necessary for the original witnesses. They had to see him precisely in order that they might become witnesses, and enable through their witness those who had not seen him to believe.

The Homily

This Sunday offers at least three possibilities for the homilist. Taking the reading from Acts he might expound the community life of the early Christians who had all things in common, and raise the question how this concern could be expressed appropriately in the life of the contemporary church.

The epistle reading suggests the theme of Christian faith as the power that overcomes the "world." This could be connected with two points in the gospel reading, the risen Christ's greeting of peace (shalom) which includes the notion of victory ("The Christian church cannot speak of peace save in the context of the death of Christ, in the context of victory over evil," Hoskyns). The epistle reading could also be related to the theme of doubting Thomas, and raise the question how in an age of widespread loss of faith and hope, doubt and despair can be replaced by the faith which overcomes the world.

THIRD SUNDAY AFTER EASTER ✓

Reading I: Acts 3:13-15, 17-19

Few scholars today would defend the speeches in Acts as representing what Peter or others said on any given occasion. As they stand, these speeches are the composition of the author of Luke-Acts, and represent his theology. At the same time, however, they very often enshrine very early christological materials. Here, for instance, Jesus is called by the very early title, the "Holy and Righteous One." This title describes Jesus in his earthly life as the righteous servant of Yahweh. The title "author of life" is probably very ancient. The Greek word for author is *archēgos*, captain or leader, and portrays Jesus as the new Moses. As the first Moses led God's people into the land of Canaan, so the new Moses leads the faithful into life, the kingdom of God, the new Canaan.

Note, too, the primitive picture of the death and resurrection as man's No and God's Yes (see the above comments on Sunday 2, responsorial psalm).

On the other hand, the second paragraph introduces some typically Lucan themes: the Christ must suffer as the scriptures foretell (cf. gospel).

Responsorial Psalm: 4:1, 3, 6b-7a, 8a

This psalm is an individual lament, in which a pious Israelite calls out for deliverance, and receives an answer to his prayers in the form of vindication from his enemies. Thus vindicated, he can lie down and sleep peacefully. Since Christ is the Holy and Righteous One, this psalm can be applied to his death and resurrection. He was in distress and called upon the Lord, who raised him from the dead and vindicated him. His work thus accomplished, he can sit down at the right hand of God.

Reading II: 1 John 2:1-5a

To apply to Christ the words, "I will lie down and sleep" does not imply that he is inactive. He is our "advocate" (paraclete, literally keeper) in heaven. Sin still occurs in the Christian life (the gnostics, when 1 John was written, were perfectionists who believed that proper Christians were sinless), but the exalted Christ still pleads our cause with the Father. He is the "expiation" for our sins, a better word than propitiation, which suggests that God was an angry deity who required appeasing. Rather, the exalted Christ acts as our advocate before God by applying the benefits of his death to our sins, cleansing and removing them, so that we can be restored to the right relationship with God. The gnostics, with their slogan "we know him," not only maintained that they no longer sinned and therefore required no continuing work of Christ to expiate their sin, but also believed that they were dispensed from the necessity of moral effort. The true test of our "knowing God" — i.e., of religious experience — however, is that we keep his commandments.

Gospel: Luke 24:35-48

This gospel reading represents a departure from the norm in year B, which is to follow a course of readings from Mark, supplemented by John during Lent and the Easter season. In Easter 3 A the Emmaus story was read, and this assignment completes the Lucan appearance stories by the account of the appearance to the disciples in the upper room. It is the counterpart of John 20:19-23, which we read last week. The location — in the upper room at Jerusalem — is the same; the risen Lord's greeting ("Peace to you") is identical. The emphasis on the physical is similar.

In John this emphasis takes the form of the invitation to touch the body of the risen One, while in Luke it takes the form of a demonstration by eating a piece of boiled fish. This detail is doubly interesting. The presence of fish suggests an original Galilean setting for this appearance story, while the meal context suggests the association of the original resurrection appearances with the eucharist. These primitive elements have been developed (probably by the pre-Lucan tradition) for apologetic purposes similar to those which were at work in John. Luke simply takes these elements over from his tradition. His real interest is to be found in the final paragraph — the instruction of the risen Lord to his disciples. This is again rooted in earliest tradition and has parallels in John and Matthew for it includes the command to mission (forgiveness of sins also includes the notion of baptism, cf. Mt 28:19). But in Luke there is a unique emphasis on the scriptures: "Everything written about me in the law of Moses and the prophets and the psalms must be fulfilled. Then he opened their minds to understand the scriptures. . . . Thus it is written." The same themes, as we have seen, recur in the final paragraph of the Acts reading. Clearly we have here a theological concern of Luke.

The Homily

The combination of the kerygmatic speech from Acts and the risen Lord's instruction to the apostles is like two searchlights focusing on the same target: the scriptures announce that Christ must suffer. Therefore, repent and receive forgiveness. Can we make something of this for today's homily? How do the scriptures foretell Christ's suffering? Not in a mechanical way, but in their insight into God's way with men. Those who fulfill God's mission, particularly as prophets, have to suffer at the hands of a godless world, viz., Moses, Jeremiah, the deutero-Isaianic servant. But God vindicates them, and their suffering proves to be an expiation of the sins of the people. We can link this with the theme of the epistle. We could then seek for contemporary analogies to the expiatory value of suffering, the death of Martin Luther King perhaps, or the deaths of those who died in Vietnam for a dubious cause. The themes of bloodshedding, expiation, victory, peace, belong to Easter, as they belong to the life of the body politic. They are "words which have been formulated out of the stuff of which human life is made" (Hoskyns).

Easter 4 to Pentecost of Year B

✓ **FOURTH SUNDAY OF EASTER**

Reading I: Acts 4:8-12

In the Book of Acts we can sometimes discern a pattern similar to that of the Fourth Gospel. A miracle takes place and is followed by a discourse expounding the theological significance of the miracle. Our present passage occurs after the healing of the crippled man in chapter 3. Peter moves from the immediate fact of the healing to a proclamation of the thing signified, namely, the power of the gospel of Jesus Christ, crucified and resurrected. The affinity between the sign and the thing signified is more obvious in the Greek than in the translation of the Revised Standard Version—"healed" in verse 9 and "salvation" in verse 12 come from the same Greek verb, *sōthenai,* to be saved or made whole. Note that Luke has once more incorporated into a speech of his own composition some very primitive material. This consists of (1) the No-Yes interpretation of the cross and resurrection (*you* crucified Jesus—*God* raised him); (2) the use of the stone passage from Psalm 118:22, one of the earliest pieces of Christian apologetic. The "name" of Jesus was probably used by early Christian exorcists as a formula to heal sick people. Luke takes up this formula of exorcism and applies it to "healing" in an ultimate salvific sense. It is in the "name" of Jesus that eschatological salvation is made available, and in that name alone. In other words, eschatological salvation comes solely as a consequence of the death and resurrection of Christ.

Responsorial Psalm: 118:1 and 8-9, 21-23, 26 and 28-29

Selections from Psalm 118, as we have seen before, are frequently used in the Easter season. This particular selection highlights the stone testimony quoted in Peter's apologia in the first reading. It has been suggested by Old Testament scholars that this psalm was originally used at the annual enthronement festival in Israel. As the king entered the temple in triumph and mounted the steps of the throne, "it was as if a new and highly decorative coping stone had been added to the cornice which the builders had failed to beautify completely" (Barnabas Linders). The exaltation of Jesus is the eschatological fulfillment of the enthronement festival in ancient Israel. He is the new coping stone of the eschatological community.

Reading II: 1 John 3:1-2

In his earthly life our Lord had admitted his disciples to the privilege of calling God "Abba, Father." This same privilege was made available to those who were baptized after the resurrection (Rom 8:15, Gal 4:6). The language used here (Father, children of God) is derived from the same background. The world — that is, human society organized in opposition to God — did not know "him," i.e., probably Christ, rather than God (so Dodd). This is reminiscent of Paul's statement that the rulers of this *world* did not know Christ, for otherwise they would not have crucified the Lord of glory (1 Cor 2:8). In Johannine thought the Jews who crucified Jesus similarly symbolize the unbelieving world which rejects the revelation of God in Christ. This links reading II with reading I with its assertion that "you" (i.e., Israel) crucified Jesus Christ of Nazareth. Next, another Johannine theme appears: as the world hated the Revealer, so it will hate the believer (cf. Jn 15:18). The world can see no more in the church than one religious organization among others. It can classify the church sociologically, and legitimately so on the world's own level. But it cannot perceive in the church the eschatological community which it is. For its true character is as yet hidden: it does not yet appear what we shall be. It is only when he, Christ, appears, only at the parousia, that we see him as he is — the Son of man exalted in his glory; only then shall we be like him, transformed into the same eschatological glory which has been his since his resurrection.

Gospel: John 10:11-18

In each of the years A, B, and C we read an excerpt from the good shepherd discourse (Jn 10) on the fourth Sunday of Easter which replaces the old Good Shepherd Sunday (Easter 2). The present passage forms the interpretation of the second of the two sheep parables (the first is Jn 10:1-3a; the second, that interpreted here, is 3b-5). Two applications of this second parable are given (11-13, 14-18), each headed with the same declaration, "I am the good shepherd" (vv. 11, 14). Each interpretation makes the basic point that the good shepherd lays down his life for the sheep (vv. 11b, 15b) and then proceeds to give this point a different actualization in the life of the church. The first application connects this with the defense of the sheep against "wolves," a traditional image for false teachers, which the evangelist probably applies to the gnostics. The second application speaks first of the inner life of the church — the shepherd knows his sheep by name — and then of the church's missionary outreach; the other sheep would be the Gentiles.

The Homily

A great wealth of themes is presented in today's reading. Indeed, the homilist suffers from an *embarras de richesses*. He can narrow down his possibilities if he bears in mind the liturgical season for which these readings are provided, that of Easter. Hence they all speak of the risen Lord, and his continued work within the church.

The Acts reading speaks of the risen Lord performing his saving work in the world, manifested symbolically by the healing of the impotent man. The "name" which saves is the name of the risen One. The church offers the world that which can be attained through Christ alone. The heart of the gospel lies in this little word "alone." Christian theology is going through a period when we would like to jettison this word, alone, and entering into dialogue with other religions in a spirit of broadmindedness, recognize that they too offer their devotees salvation. Against this we must place our text and the interpretation of it in Article XXVIII of the Church of England, entitled "Of obtaining salvation only by the Name of Christ." It reads: "They also are to be accursed that presume to say, That every man shall be saved by the Law or Sect which he professeth, so that he be diligent to frame his life according to that Law and in the light of Nature. For Holy Scripture doth set out unto us only the Name of Jesus Christ whereby man must be saved." In modern words, this article condemns the view that it is good to have a religion, but which one it is doesn't matter. The biblical exclusiveness which underlies the mission of the church can be linked with the second aspect of the interpretation to the parable of the sheep and the shepherd: "Other sheep I have, them also must I bring, and there shall be one fold and one shepherd." Perhaps, too, the "wolves" against which the good shepherd defends his flock are those broadminded Christians today who hold that salvation is through any religion, not through Christ alone. This exclusive claim is made because only Christ has been raised from the dead.

Only he has passed through death to man's final destiny, and therefore we can attain our final destiny only through him.

A somewhat different though not unrelated homily could be composed on the basis of the epistle reading. In that case we would emphasize the not-yet-ness which characterizes our present participation in the risen life of Christ: "It does not yet appear what we shall be." This is a major theme in the theology of hope.

√ FIFTH SUNDAY OF EASTER

Reading I: Acts 9:26-31

At first sight this passage seems to be a straightforward piece of historical narrative, creating no problems of interpretation, but yielding very little material for preaching. A comparison of this account of Paul's first visit to Jerusalem with his own account in Galatians 1:18-19 reveals however certain major discrepancies. Paul's own account emphasizes his entire independence of the Jerusalem apostles. On his first post-conversion visit he merely saw Cephas and accidentally ran into James the Lord's brother during his 15 days' stay. Luke gives a very different account: Paul was anxious to join up with the apostles, who in turn were reluctant to receive the ex-persecutor, and only when their scruples were overcome by Barnabas did they agree to accept him. Once introduced, however, Paul "went in and out with them"—a phrase which in Luke means intimate companionship. "By the very fact that he—known to many in Jerusalem as the Christian-baiter—allowed himself to be seen walking arm in arm, as it were, in the streets and lanes of the city with the leaders of the Nazarene sect . . . Saul made open confession of his faith in Jesus" (Zahn). We must certainly allow for some one-sidedness on Paul's part in Galatians 1:18-19. Obviously he *was* dependent up to a point on the tradition he had received from those who were Christians before him. His visit to Cephas may have been precisely for the purpose of obtaining information about Jesus, for in 1 Corinthians 15:3-7 Paul makes it clear that for certain Christian traditions about events that happened before his apostolic call he did depend on tradition.

But Luke's account must for the most part be regarded as an expression of Lucan theology rather than purely historical narration. For Luke, Paul is a model for the church in his own day, in the sub-apostolic age. It is only when the church remains in fellowship with the apostles—walking with them arm in arm as it were—that it remains apostolic, preaching the same gospel as the apostles preached. The final paragraph suggests that it was not the expansion of the church in itself that concerned Luke, but the fact that the apostolic message of the resurrection of Christ was spread so far and wide. It is not growth that matters, but what kind of growth.

Responsorial Psalm: 22:25b-26, 27 and 29, 30-31 (RSV)

Psalm 22, as we know, is the passion psalm *par excellence*. But it is really a passion-and-resurrection psalm. Verses 1-21 are about the suffering of the righteous servant of God, verses 22-31 about his vindication. Originally, when Christians' *pascha* was a unitary festival, the whole psalm could be sung at one go, with a highly dramatic change of key at verse 22. (The present writer had this burnt in upon him as a Church of England choir boy by the shift of the Anglican chant from a minor to a major key at this point.) The psalm expresses both the humiliation and the vindication of God's righteous servant. With the split up of passion week and Easter season, we now have to split the psalm. But we must remember that the Easter part which is sung today speaks of the vindication of the righteous man precisely in his suffering. The reference to the "afflicted" in the first stanza will help us to bear this in mind.

Reading II: 1 John 3:18-24

This passage is exceedingly difficult to summarize. C. H. Dodd suggests that the author has thrown together some notes he had never had time to develop. The same scholar discerns six different points here: 1. Only if we love the brethren are we assured of our standing as Christians. 2. If we are uncertain about this standing we may nevertheless trust that God knows us better than we know ourselves. 3. If our consciences are clear, we are free to live a life of prayer and of obedience to his commandments. 4. God's expectation from us can be summed up under two headings: faith in Jesus Christ and love for the brethren. 5. The external test of mystical union with God (mutual indwelling, as the text puts it), is whether or not we keep the commandments. 6. The internal test is the gift of the Spirit.

What impresses one in this passage is the way in which the Johannine author succeeds in holding together things which are often separated from one another in our thinking. Faith *and* works, belief *and* obedience, the prayer of union with God *and* the love for the brethren. It is not a matter of either/or, but of both/and.

Gospel: John 15:1-8

One is tempted to suppose that the earliest tradition behind the Johannine allegory of the vine was a genuine parable of Jesus, running something like this:

The vinedresser takes away from the vine every branch that bears no fruit and prunes every branch that does bear fruit, in order that it may bear more. The branches that are cut off wither. They are then gathered, thrown into the fire and burnt.

That would be a parable of judgment. Its Johannine allegorization is similar to that of the parables of the shepherd and the door in chapter 10. The vine is equated with Christ, the Father with the vinedressers, the disciples with the branches, the cutting away of the unfruitful branches is the excommunication of the unworthy. This cutting away of the unfruitful branch may earlier have been applied to Judas. For the evangelist, however, it means the gnostic heretics. The pruning of those who remain will mean the persecution of the disciples. The equation of Christ with the vine was doubtless suggested by the language of the eucharist, like "I am the bread of life," while the extension of the allegory to include the disciples as branches is reminiscent of the Pauline doctrine of the church as the body of Christ.

We should not argue for John's direct dependence on Paul: perhaps both concepts were Christian adaptations of a common gnostic theme. Added to this is the typical Johannine motif, already encountered in the epistle reading, of mutual indwelling.

The Homily

The fact that the epistle reading and gospel both feature the theme of mutual indwelling, constitutes a strong invitation to the homilist today. This mutual indwelling is not, as at first sight the epistle suggests, established by keeping God's commandments. Rather, we must first dwell in the vine, i.e., the risen Christ, partaking of the life that flows from him through the word and sacraments. Thus, believing in the name of the Son, living the life of prayer, and having the assurance of a forgiven conscience and the indwelling Spirit, we must proceed to show forth our Christian standing by loving not in word or speech, but in deed and truth, in loving one another, keeping his commandments, and bearing much fruit.

If the homilist should prefer to take the Acts lesson, he will have to be careful to treat it primarily not as an historical report, but as an expression of Lucan theology. Luke's concern is that the church in postapostolic times should remain in fellowship with the apostles, as Paul did. Some have tried glibly to contrast apostolic succession with apostolic success. If we understand apostolic succession to mean fidelity to the apostolic message of the resurrection of the crucified One as the event of redemption, then the only success which is apostolic is the success which follows upon that fidelity to the apostolic message. That is the relation between the two paragraphs in the first reading. Such a thought could be linked up with the second and third stanzas of the psalm, which speak of the worldwide acknowledgment of Yahweh consequent upon the vindication of his servant.

SIXTH SUNDAY OF EASTER
Reading I: Acts 10:25-26, 34-35, 44-48

For the believer the most important consequence of the resurrection is the gift of the Spirit. Although the day of Pentecost is the primary celebration of the outpouring of the Spirit, the whole period of the fifty days includes this as one of its motifs, just as the fifty days in Judaism were a celebration of the enjoyment of the fruits of the promised land. It is thus appropriate, especially in the latter part of the Easter season, that we should begin to think of the work of the Spirit in the church. The same shift of theme was still perceptible in the traditional lectionary.

Luke presents the Cornelius episode as the decisive step in the launching of the Gentile mission. Its decisiveness is emphasized by the length and detail of the narrative in chapter 10, of which today's reading forms the closing part, by the repetition of the story in full when Peter reports back to the Jerusalem church in chapter 11, and by Peter's reference to the episode at the apostolic council in chapter 15. This emphasis is a clue to Luke's theology. Historically, the mission to the Gentiles is more likely to have begun, almost in a fit of absence of mind, by anonymous Hellenistic Jewish Christian missionaries of the Stephen party (cf. Acts 11:19-20). Luke's interest is that every step forward in the Christian mission must have the sanction of the Jerusalem church (cf. his interpretation of Paul's first visit to Jerusalem in the first reading last week). Of course, Luke did not invent the Cornelius story — there is no need to doubt that Peter did convert a Gentile God-fearer. But this was not really the beginning of the Gentile mission, for Cornelius already had one foot in the Jewish camp. It is the significance of the event that Luke has blown up out of all recognition.

One striking feature of the story is that the Holy Spirit falls upon Cornelius and his companions *before* they are baptized. Usually, both in Acts and in the New Testament generally, the Spirit descends after baptism, with or without the laying on of hands. Luke's point is that the Spirit here takes a fresh initiative where the church was too timid to follow, going ahead and pointing the way. Hence this episode has been aptly called the Pentecost of the Gentiles. Why then would baptism still have to follow? What would have been the status of converts who had received the Spirit but who had not yet been baptized? The best answer to this question is that the Spirit has — in this unique instance — gone beyond the confines of the church and bestowed its blessing on outsiders. They are then brought into the circle of the people of God through baptism. Normally one is brought into the church and there receives the Spirit.

Responsorial Psalm: 98:1, 2-3ab, 3cd-4

Sunday 28 C had the identical selection from Psalm 98. It was one of the enthronement psalms, celebrating the victory of Yahweh as manifested in the enthronement of Israel's king. There we suggested that the primary emphasis should be the universal scope of Yahweh's victory. Here, in the Easter season, the emphasis is on the victory itself — the resurrection, in which God triumphed over the powers of sin and death.

Reading II: 1 John 4:7-10

The Johannine author has been insisting over against his gnostic opponents that the love of the brethren is the acid test of the claim to "know" God (*ginoskein*, from which we get *gnosis* and "gnostic"). After a digression the writer returns to this theme: only he who loves his brother "knows" God as the gnostics claimed to know him. Then comes the tremendous statement that the reason for this is because "God is love." This affirmation is frequently repeated out of context, as though it were a general, self-evident truth. Sir Edwyn Hoskyns was fond of saying in his lectures that the statement, God is love, occurs only in one passage in the New Testament, and only after the "whole turmoil of the Epistle to the Romans." That God is love is a confession of faith from those who have encountered the love of God in action in his Son Jesus Christ, not a philosophical presupposition. So here, in this very passage, the Johannine author goes on at once to say that we know God to be love only because he has sent his Son into the world, and sent him to be the expiation of our sins. Only on those grounds — because of the incarnation and atonement — do we affirm that God is love. It is not a general truth about the universe. Hence we cannot ask, why does a God of love allow this or that to happen. As Bultmann said of grace, God's love is an event.

Gospel: John 15:9-17

The gospel reading widens our understanding of the theme of love, already broached in the second reading. We encounter the love of God in Christ because first of all the Father has loved the Son and the Son has loved the Father. The word for "loved" in each case is in the aorist tense — that is to say, it refers to a single, concrete act. God loved the Son in calling him and sending him. The evangelist is not speculating about the timeless love of the Father and the Son, but is saying what happened. God called Jesus at his baptism and called him to a saving mission. The Son obeyed the Father and kept his commandments. That is to say, he concretely fulfilled the mission laid upon him; his obedience to the Father's commandment was consummated in his death on the cross.

By his death Jesus has constituted the disciples as a society of "friends." One might almost say that this is the Johannine doctrine of the church, opposed to the institutional, organizational understanding of the church which was gaining the upper hand in his day. The disciples are friends, not first of another, but of Jesus. Only because of that are they friends of one another. The life of this society is characterized by joy ("the delightful merriment of Christians," Hoskyns), bearing fruit, i.e., keeping the commandment of love. All these things are the outcome of the death and resurrection of Christ and characterize the life of the Christian community.

The Homily

Taken together, the epistle and gospel provide an opportunity for the homilist to wrestle with the theme of love. He could start with the great affirmation, God is love, and go on to point out how this is not a general truth but an event. Then he could characterize that event and draw out its effects. These are: abiding in the love of the Father and the Son, and manifesting this mutual indwelling by the keeping of his commandments, which in turn means love of the brethren. The homilist may speak of the church as a society of "friends," a truth to which the Quakers have born witness, and which is a judgment of much of our ecclesiasticism.

An alternative would be to take the Cornelius episode as the Pentecost of the Gentiles, speaking perhaps of how the Spirit sometimes takes a leap forward where timid churchmen are afraid to tread, and ask whether there are signs of something like this happening today in the church.

ASCENSION

Apart from the gospel the Ascension Day readings are the same every year, and were commented upon above. This year we will repeat our general remarks on Ascension Day and proceed to comment upon the gospel reading, on the assumption that the homilist will choose to preach on this.

Ascension Day, let us recall, is not to be thought of merely as a historical commemoration. In fact, there is no clear single event of the ascension in the New Testament. There was always a doctrine, or rather kerygma, of the ascension, from the earliest days. Christ was always proclaimed as resurrected and ascended. The pre-Pauline tradition in 1 Corinthians 15:3-8 and Philippians 2:6-11, Paul himself, and the first two earliest evangelists, Mark and Matthew, make no distinction between the resurrection and ascension as events, but regard the appearances as appearances of the resurrected and already ascended One. When the desire to portray the ascension as a separate event emerged in the later stages of the tradition, the dating of it varied. Luke 24:51 appears to place it on Easter Sunday evening. John 20 seems to suppose the ascension to have occurred on Easter Day between the appearance to Mary Magdalene and that to the disciples in the upper room. Only Acts 1 records the familiar story of an ascension forty days after Easter Day, and even there the 40 is probably to be taken symbolically as a holy period of revelation. The ascension story is the dramatization of a universal element in primitive Christian proclamation and faith. It is fitting, so long as we remember this, that particular concentration should be given to this facet of the Easter faith on one day in the Easter season. That is the rationale for the continued observance of Ascension Day.

Gospel: Mark 16:15-20

It is now universally acknowledged that the earliest texts of Mark end at 16:8, and that verses 9-20 are a later addition. But that is not to say that they are worthless. In any case they form a part of the canonical scriptures as the church has received them (hence the term, "canonical ending"). Also, the ending is a compilation of many traditions, some of them earlier than anything we have elsewhere in the Easter narratives. The older critical view that it was an artificial summary of the other gospel stories is now being increasingly abandoned. For instance, the command to preach the gospel and to baptize is presented in what is assuredly an earlier form than the more developed tradition at the end of Matthew. At the same time, the second paragraph of our reading is clearly a summary based on the end of Luke and the beginning of Acts (note the separation of the ascension from the resurrection and the location of the appearances between them). But unlike Luke and Acts it explicitly mentions the session at the right hand.

The homilist would naturally want to draw out what is distinctive about this canonical ending. If he follows the suggestion of the caption, he will speak about the session at the right hand. This of course is a figure of speech. To quote Calvin, it does not say that Jesus Christ is in a definite place, but that he has entered upon a particular function, which is to be prophet, priest and king.

Alternatively, the homilist may wish to expound the missionary command and the command to baptize, and to speak of the mission which the church has received from her ascending Lord and under the imperative of which she still stands today. He should relate this quite concretely to the mission of the church in the particular place where he and the people are.

✓ SEVENTH SUNDAY OF EASTER

Reading I: Acts 1:15-17, 20a, 20c-26

In the narrative of Acts the choice of Matthias occupies the 12 days interval between the Ascension and the day of Pentecost. It is therefore appropriately read on this Sunday, thus breaking the consecutive order in which the excerpts from Acts have been read hitherto in the rest of the Easter season.

This passage, like so many of the pericopes in Acts, combines earlier tradition with the author's redaction. There is no reason to doubt that the basic factual nucleus is historical. The number of the Twelve has to be made up after the defection of Judas by choosing one from among those who had received a resurrection appearance (one of the five hundred in 1 Cor 15:6?). Later tradition brought in the citation from Psalm 69 as an apologetic text for Judas' defection. Luke then wrote up the whole to express his own doctrine of apostleship. The original function of the Twelve was distinct from that of the apostolate (cf. 1 Cor 15:5 and 7). The Twelve had been appointed by the earthly Jesus as a *sign* of the eschatological community, the new Israel, which was to be the outcome of his work. As recipients of the second resurrection appearance after Peter they became the *foundation* of the eschatological community. The choice of the twelfth man would have preserved this eschatological significance. Later tradition tended more and more to make the Twelve as such apostles. The apostles on the other hand were originally missionaries, sent out to proclaim the gospel. The Twelve and the apostles formed overlapping circles. Luke carried further the later tendency, already discernible in Mark and Matthew, to make the Twelve as such apostles, by practically confining the apostolate to the Twelve. He also defines the function of the apostolate as witness to the original saving history of both the earthly ministry of Jesus and his resurrection. They thus serve as a bridge between the earthly Jesus and the ongoing life of the church, a paramount concern of Luke's.

Responsorial Psalm: 103:1-2, 11-12, 19-20ab
This psalm of thanksgiving is used on a number of occasions. Today the final stanza is highlighted by the response, "The Lord has set his throne in heaven," thus making the psalm one of thanksgiving for the ascension of Christ.

Reading II: 1 John 4:11-16
This reading follows immediately upon the second reading of the previous week, and in typical Johannine fashion it repeats the themes of the earlier passage with slight variation: the love of God, the duty of love among the brethren, the mutual indwelling of God in the faithful and of the faithful in God, the definition of God as love in the sense of the saving event. As usual in such Johannine repetition, a new point is made. That new point is that this mutual indwelling is exhibited in the confession of Jesus as the Son of God.

Gospel: John 17:11b-19
We have spoken in previous years of this chapter, the high priestly prayer or, as it has been called by some exegetes, the prayer of consecration. In a way it represents the Johannine equivalent to the words of institution, where Christ consecrates himself as the messianic sacrifice and offers the benefit of his sacrifice for the disciples to partake of in advance. In the Johannine prayer he consecrates himself that the disciples may be con-

secrated for their mission, to be preserved in unity and truth amid perse-cution.

At first sight, it might be thought that this reading is more appropriate for Maundy Thursday. It would certainly not be inappropriate there. But we have to recall that in Johannine parlance "I am coming to thee" refers to the whole process of the death, resurrection and ascension of Christ, and so it is just as meaningful today. As a result of Jesus' departure, the mission of the apostles is inaugurated. So the prayer looks forward to Pentecost and beyond, to the mission of the church.

The Homily

It is possible to link all three readings together under the rubric of apos-tolic mission. The ascended Christ sends out his apostles into the world to bear witness to the redemptive event. Thus Matthias is chosen to be with the rest of the Twelve as a witness of the whole Christ event. The first letter of John speaks of the confession as expressed focally in liturgy, but also implemented in the internal life of the community ("love one another") and in its unity (the high priestly prayer that all may be one) and in the confession of Jesus as Son of God to the outside world. The homilist may choose to emphasize the mission itself, the necessity of con-fession, or the need for unity in mission.

PENTECOST: SATURDAY EVENING

While the rubric states that the vigil services may be used in the afternoon on the Saturday, we understand that they will be widely used at the eve-ning mass. The corresponding set of propers in the trial use of the Episco-pal Church is the first of the two sets provided for the day of Pentecost itself.

Four alternative passages are provided for the Old Testament reading, in keeping with the concept of a vigil service. (It will be remembered that there were six prophecies in the Roman Missal.)

Reading I: Genesis 11:1-9 or Exodus 19:3-8a, 16-20b or Ezekiel 37:1-14 or Joel 2:28-32

The first alternative (Gen 11) forms a counterpart to the Pentecost story in Acts. The preaching in tongues, interpreted by the author of Luke-Acts as the gift of foreign languages rather than as ecstatic speech, as in Paul and elsewhere, symbolizes the overcoming of the divisions of mankind for which the building of the tower of Babel serves as an etiological legend.

The second alternative (Ex 19) is the theophany to Moses, which provides the Pentecost account with its imagery of the tongues of fire and the rushing wind. This establishes a Law-Gospel typology which Paul developed theologically.

The fourth alternative (Jl 2) provides the major text for Peter's sermon which follows the outpouring of the Spirit in the Lucan Pentecost story. The expected outpouring of the Spirit will include everyone, not only outstanding charismatic leaders as under the old covenant. And whereas "all flesh" meant for Joel the whole of Israel, in Peter's speech it means all of humanity.

The third reading (Ez 37), the vision of the dry bones, is the only one of the four alternatives which has no direct relation to the Pentecost story in Acts. It is surprising that it is never utilized in any of the New Testament texts on the Spirit. Indeed, nowhere in the New Testament is it explicitly asserted that the church is the old Israel renewed by the Spirit, an idea which Ezekiel 37 might have suggested. Yet the New Testament clearly understands the church as the eschatologically renewed people of God, and it would seem legitimate to use the Ezekiel passage as a parable of what happened at Pentecost.

Responsorial Psalm: 104:1-2a, 24 and 35c, 27-28, 29bc 30

This psalm has traditionally been associated with Pentecost. It speaks of the wisdom of God as the power which creates, sustains and renews the earth. The wisdom concept bifurcated in Christian tradition, providing materials both for the doctrine of the person of Christ and for the doctrine of the Spirit. Thus the psalm may be interpreted as a hymn to the work of the *Creator Spiritus*.

Reading II: Romans 8:22-27

Here Paul is drawing upon Jewish and early Christian apocalyptic traditions. Apocalyptic extended the earlier nationalistic eschatological hope of the Old Testament to include the whole of human history and the whole cosmos. God was bringing the cosmos, and in the center of it his covenant people, to a final goal, a goal described under various symbols — here the symbol of the redemption or adoption. Early Christian understanding of the Spirit was set in this framework of apocalyptic expectation. Indeed, Ernst Käsemann has called apocalyptic the matrix of early

Christian theology. The Spirit was an anticipation of the final apocalyptic goal: the Spirit is the first fruits (cf. the similar term, *arrhabōn*, used by Paul elsewhere, meaning down-payment), the first installment of the blessings of the final state of things.

In this passage Paul is careful to insist — against all false spiritual enthusiasm — on the element of not-yet-ness that characterizes the Spirit's activity. We have only the first fruits. We are still in travail with the rest of the cosmos. Our full adoption as sons, the redemption of our bodies, lies in the future. What the Spirit gives us can best be characterized as hope.

In this situation the Spirit impels us forward to the realization of that hope, helping the weakness of our prayers when, e.g., we pray, Thy Kingdom come. Our prayers are weak because we are still here, and have not yet reached the ultimate goal. We have to pray for a goal we cannot yet comprehend, since we have not yet seen it. But the Spirit knows what that goal is, since the Spirit is part and anticipation of that goal. So the Spirit can take up our weak prayers and present them effectively to the Father.

Gospel: John 7:37-39

Many commentators take this scene as an allusion to the ceremony of the drawing of water which was a feature of the last day of the feast of Tabernacles. The Johannine Christ invites men to come to him to partake of the water of life. "His heart" is best taken as the heart of Christ, and the scripture quoted as an allusion to Moses' striking of the rock in the wilderness so that water gushed out. This provides a type for what happened at Pentecost: The Spirit is poured forth from the heart of Jesus, i.e., as a result of his redemptive work.

The Homily

As we noted last year, there is an almost bewildering variety of themes for the homilist on this occasion. We mentioned the following:

1. The Babel story of which Pentecost is the reversal, suggesting the universality of the Spirit-filled community. Here is the only power that can transcend all the divisions which human history has thrown up between people and nations.

2. Sinai and Pentecost suggest the contrast between the law and the Spirit and raising in turn the question of the place of law in the Christian

life. Here the so-called third use of the law, the law as guidance for sanctification, is brought into consideration.

3. Ezekiel's vision of the dry bones and the refrain of the psalm suggest the Spirit as the power of renewal in the church.

4. The Joel passage suggests that all members of the community share the Spirit. It is not the monopoly of the ordained, any more than it is to be the monopoly of gifted charismatic leaders as it was under the old dispensation.

5. The psalm and the first paragraph of the epistle reading invite our consideration of the cosmic dimensions of the Spirit's work of renewal, a theme of which our Orthodox brethren have much to teach us.

6. (This is additional to our suggestions of last year.) The Spirit is the foundation of Christian hope. A helpful analogy is suggested by Prof. Rubem Alves in his *Theology of Christian Hope* — the Spirit is an aperitif, whetting our appetites for the ultimate fulfillment.

7. The second paragraph of the epistle reading invites the consideration of the Spirit as the organ of Christian prayer.

8. The Spirit flows from the heart of Jesus, that is, it is the outcome of his redemptive work.

The homilist should consider carefully the needs and situations of the local church, and decide which of these points speaks most to those needs and that situation.

PENTECOST: SUNDAY

Again, the readings are repeated each year. We summarize our suggestions of previous years. First, on the day in general, we recall that this is not merely the commemoration of a single, historical event. Indeed, while Acts locates the outpouring of the Spirit on the day of Pentecost, John places it on Easter Sunday evening, each for theological rather than for historical reasons. The important point is that the giving of the Spirit is the outcome of the work of the risen Christ. Nor should we think of the outpouring of the Spirit as a single event. Even the Book of Acts speaks of successive outpourings. We must avoid historicizing the Lucan presentation (reading I: Acts 2:1-11). The historical nucleus behind the Pentecost story is the beginning of the kerygma.

The responsorial psalm is a different and more appropriate selection of the psalm used at the vigil service (see stanza two, which is taken up by the refrain both here and at the vigil).

The second reading (1 Cor 12:3b-7, 12-13) deals with the specific gifts of the Spirit in the community (charismata). At Corinth there was great emphasis on the speaking in tongues. Paul will not suppress this activity (cf. 1 Thes 5:19) but would have the Corinthians be aware of its dangers by applying the criterion of true confession. If the person speaking by the Spirit acknowledges Jesus (the "Jesus" is emphatic: the incarnate, crucified One, over against the gnostic idea that the incarnation and crucifixion were at best transient episodes), then the charisma is genuine. Another point Paul makes is that there are other gifts beside speaking with tongues, and each has a necessary contribution to make. And this leads to his third point. The gifts of the Spirit must not produce individualism, but must be placed at the service of the whole body. In effect, there are three tests or criteria for the charismata: (1) right confession; (2) the renunciation of exclusive claims; (3) the placing of them at the service of the whole community.

The gospel reading (John 20:19-23) associates the gift of the Spirit with the apostolic mission, here defined not as the proclamation of the kerygma, but as the forgiving and retaining of sins. The primary reference here is probably to baptism rather than to the sacrament of penance. It can be extended to cover the latter only secondarily and derivatively. The forgiving and retaining will then be a reference to giving or withholding baptism on the ground of faith or its absence as a response to the hearing of the kerygma.

The Homily

The homilist might confront the Acts and the Johannine accounts of the giving of the Spirit with each other, pointing up the different theologies that underlie their different chronologies. By tying the gift of the Spirit to Easter the gospel emphasizes that the Spirit is the gift of the risen One, and as such conveys the benefits of his death and resurrection. The Pentecost story emphasizes the replacement of the law by the gift of the Spirit as the basis of the life of the new community.

The epistle reading deals with the problems of a local congregation in which there is a great deal of enthusiasm for the charismata or gifts of the Spirit. If this is the case in the homilist's own church, he has here an opportunity to echo the Pauline warnings and to speak of the Pauline criteria.

Trinity Sunday to Sunday 16 B

In previous years we have made the observation, which we now repeat, that the doctrine of the Trinity, contrasted with triadic formulas and the triple structure of the biblical experience of God, is implicit rather than explicit. By "triple structure" of biblical experience we mean that in both the Old Testament and the New, God is experienced as going forth out of himself (from his "aseity") in revelation and redemptive action, and also creating in the hearts of men a believing response to his revelatory and redemptive action.

Reading I: Deuteronomy 4:32-34, 39-40

We can discern this triple experience of God in the first reading. It speaks of God "in heaven above and on the earth beneath," that is of his aseity (he is Yahweh, God who is); of his transcendence (in heaven above) and his immanence (on earth beneath).

It speaks, too, of God going forth out of himself in his acts of revelation and redemption. The first revelatory act of God specified is the original act of creation ("the day that God created man upon earth"); and the second his speaking out of the fire in the giving of the law on Mount Sinai. The redemptive act it speaks of is the exodus, when God took a nation for himself by signs and wonders, which he did in Egypt before the eyes of his people. This redemptive act of course provides the supreme type for his eschatological redemption in Christ, in which God brought into being a new people for himself by the "signs and wonders" of the Christ event.

Finally, our passage speaks of the response which God creates in the hearts of his people: their faith in him who is, who reveals and redeems, and their obedience to his statutes and commandments.

Responsorial Psalm: 33:4-5, 6 and 9, 18-19, 20 and 22

Different selections of this psalm were used on Lent 2 A and the Easter Vigil, Easter 5 A, Sunday 19 A, and will be used again on Sunday 29 B.

Today's selection highlights the Old Testament concept of the "word of the Lord," which is one of the several concepts which contributed to the Johannine conception of the Logos.

In the priestly narrative of the creation (Gn 1) God brings the universe into existence by uttering his fiat: "Let there be light," etc. It is to this action that the psalmist is referring when he says that God created the heavens through his word. But with this formal affirmation the concept of the word is well on its way to becoming hypostatized, thus preparing the way for John 1:1 and forming part of the ingredients for the formulated doctrine of the Trinity.

Reading II: Romans 8:14-17

When the Letter to the Romans was read in course during the early summer of year A (1972/5), these verses were skipped. They are eminently appropriate today for they speak of God the Father (Abba), of the Christ with whom we are fellow heirs, and of the Spirit who leads us as sons of God. This supports our contention that the triadic formula is primarily a deposit of Christian experience. The Christian believer knows himself through Christ to have been adopted in baptism as a son of God, and in the eucharistic liturgy he is enabled by the Spirit to invoke the Father (for Abba is certainly a liturgical cry, derived from the ecstatic worship of the Aramaic-speaking church).

Here, as in Galatians 4:6-7, Paul assumes that the divine sonship is not a natural datum of human existence but an eschatological gift, made possible by the Christ event and conveyed to the believers through the operation of the Spirit (i.e., word and sacrament).

In his controversies with the Corinthians, Paul had never denied the ecstatic gifts of the Spirit, but always emphasized that the real test of the Spirit was not ecstasy but suffering in the way of the cross — hence the last point in this reading, the proviso that we must suffer with Christ now if we are finally to share his glory.

Gospel: Matthew 28:16-20

This was the gospel for Ascension Day of year A, where fuller comment can be found. Here of course the emphasis rests upon the baptismal command, the clearest instance of the New Testament triadic formula which gave the basis for the later doctrine of the Trinity.

In the earliest Palestinian church, baptism was administered in the name of Jesus (cf. Acts, Paul). The triple formula arose only toward the end of the first century and then outside of Palestine (cf. *Didache*). Yet from the earliest days baptism was understood to mean translation into the eschatological existence made possible by the Christ event and participation in the gifts of the Spirit. In a completely Jewish environment it would have gone without saying that if Jesus was the Messiah he was the one in whom God had acted eschatologically, and if God had inaugurated the messianic age in Jesus Christ, this involved also the gift of the Spirit. Thus baptism was always implicitly trinitarian.

The Homily

We need to guard against the notion that the Holy Trinity is a mysterious formula or still more a perplexing and complicated dogma, intelligible only to theologians. We must therefore interpret the experience of the believers, particularly their prayer and sacramental experiences, in such a way that they see that they are themselves constantly involved thereby in the life of the Blessed Trinity. "Thus the rudest man or woman who cannot reason about the Trinity may *know* the Trinity more perfectly than some acute theologian who has by heart all the writings of St. Athanasius or St. Augustine, and all the controversies of the first six centuries" (Thomas Hancock, 19th century Anglican divine).

TWELFTH SUNDAY OF THE YEAR/CORPUS CHRISTI

Thomas Hancock, whom we have just cited, expressed the reserve of many Anglicans (a reserve which the present writer shares), about the propriety of a Sunday devoted to Corpus Christi. Hancock wrote: "The feast of the Trinity . . . and not Corpus Christi (as some amongst us dream) ought to be the latest of the catholic feasts. Beyond God, what can there be to know? It is the completion of the order of festivals, for the Holy Spirit has led the church, ritually and liturgically, to the Father." At best, Corpus Christi should be regarded as a coda, rather than as a climax to the festivals. And for those who do not observe Corpus Christi on this Sunday, we will include this year comments on Sunday 12 B.

Reading I: Exodus 24:3-8

Two passages from the New Testament have made this section from Exodus central to the understanding of the Christian redemption and its re-presentation in the eucharist. The first is Mark 14:24: "This is *my* blood-of-the-covenant." Here the covenant blood of Christ is contrasted with the blood Moses sprinkled against the altar and over the people. The second New Testament passage is Hebrews 9:15-21, especially verse 20, which actually cites Exodus 24:8. (It is curious that the second reading stops short of this verse, and when the lectionary is reviewed the desirability of extending it accordingly should be considered.)

Why was it necessary in the Bible for a covenant to be ratified in blood? The idea seems to be that the death of the victim has a finality about it which makes it, and therefore the covenant which it ratifies, irrevocable. Sacrifice is expressive of the offerer's total commitment to carry out the terms of the covenant.

This passage suggests a way in which the eucharist can be interpreted into the atonement. Before the covenant is complete, the people have to become participants. In the Sinai covenant this is achieved when Moses sprinkles the people with half of the blood, after applying the other half to the altar, representing Yahweh himself. Similarly, in Christ's sacrifice on God's side the sacrificial death is completed when the Son presents himself ("blood" = his life surrendered in obedience unto death) to the Father. On man's side it is completed when the communicant receives the eucharistic cup in communion. The eucharist, understood thus, becomes an integral part of the once-for-all sacrifice of Calvary.

Responsorial Psalm: 116:12-13, 15 and 16bc, 17-18

The same selections of this psalm were used Holy Thursday, year A, the only difference being the refrain, which today is from verse 13 instead of from 1 Corinthians 10:16. This psalm is very appropriate after the Old Testament reading, for as we have suggested above, it is in our partaking of the eucharistic cup that the typology of Moses' sprinkling the people with the blood is fulfilled. It is the "cup of salvation" in the sense that by drinking of this cup we partake in the saving event.

Reading II: Hebrews 9:11-15

Although this passage is going to lead up to the quotation of Exodus 24:8, the background is not what Moses did there, but what the high priest did annually on the day of atonement. It may be said that the day of atonement provides a better analogy for Christ's role in his sacrifice, for it suggests the once-for-all event in which Christ entered into the presence of God at his exaltation, as the high priest entered the Holy of Holies on the day of atonement. On the other hand, the exodus analogy suggests more strongly the mode in which the *people* partake of this sacrifice, and therefore provides a closer type for the holy communion. By fulfilling the work of the high priest on the day of atonement, Christ puts himself in the position in which he can fulfill the work of Moses when he sprinkled the people at the ratification of the covenant. For this reason we would renew our plea for the extension of this reading through verse 20.

Note: in verse 11 the Revised Standard Version [RSV] translates "high priest of good things that *have come*." Other manuscripts have "of good things that *are to come*." The latter reading is preferable, not only on text-critical grounds, but also theologically. For it emphasizes that Christ's work is a piece of anticipated eschatology, thus leaving open (1) the idea of ultimate consummation; and (2) the continual anticipatory realization of this in the eucharist.

Gospel: Mark 14:12-16, 22-26

This passage combines two Marcan pericopes, the preparation for the passover and the institution of the eucharist. Two points may be noted from Mark 14:12-16: 1. It is here, not in the institution narrative that Mark identifies the Last Supper with the passover meal. As is well known, the Johannine account of the Supper dates it on the 14th of Nisan, a day before the passover, which began at sundown on the 15th. We are not called upon here to decide which dating is historically right, still less to try and harmonize the discrepancy. Rather, each account must be asked for its theological intent. Mark wishes to assert that the eucharist is the Christian passover meal. 2. Jesus is depicted in Mark 14:12-16 as the eschatological prophet (an early christological interpretation) by his supernatural foreknowledge indicated by the direction to the disciples to meet the man with the water jar. Similar powers were ascribed to Old Testament prophets, especially Elijah and Elisha.

The institution narrative is not a description of the passover meal, but is restricted to those aspects of the supper which were liturgically important to the early communities. What we really learn here is how Mark's church celebrated the eucharist, rather than precisely what Jesus did and said at the supper, though of course what Mark's church did is ultimately derived from what happened in the upper room.

Apparently in Mark's church the eucharist was celebrated at the conclusion of a common meal (in Paul's earlier account, 1 Corinthians 11, the bread precedes the meal and the cup follows it). Seven actions were performed:

1. Taking the bread
2. Blessing (of God for the bread; N.B. not of the bread: this accords with Jewish custom)
3. Breaking of the bread so that the congregation could share the one loaf in communion
4. The administration (note the words are words of administration rather than of consecration; consecration in accord with Jewish ideas was effected by thanksgiving)
5. Taking the cup
6. Giving thanks over the cup (a Hellenistic word for the Hebrew act of blessing, retained for the bread)
7. Administration

Three important words are spoken by Christ in Mark's account:

1. the bread word
2. the cup word
3. the eschatological saying

In the light of readings I and II exegesis today should concentrate upon the cup word: "This is my blood-of-the-covenant which is poured out for man." The trend in contemporary scholarship is to regard this version as a later rewording of the cup word in 1 Corinthians 11 due to liturgical development. Once the intervening meal had been brought forward to the beginning and the bread and cup consequently brought together at the end, the tendency was for the two sets of words to be assimilated. So we get: "This is my body. This is my blood." Mark's tradition interprets the blood as the blood of the covenant on the background of Exodus 24. Thus what the cup conveys is not a thing (blood), but participation in the event of salvation history.

The Homily

The obvious procedure for the homilist today would be to concentrate on the cup word at the eucharist in its Marcan form, relating it in turn to Exodus 24, the refrain of the psalm, and Hebrews 9:11ff. He should show how the cross and the eucharist are not to be detached from one another, but that the eucharist forms an integral part of the salvation event.

TWELFTH SUNDAY OF THE YEAR ✓

Reading I: Job 38:1, 8-11

Each of Job's comforters has had his say, and Job has responded to their arguments. None of them answered his basic problem: how could his suffering be explained in view of the fact that he had walked uprightly with God. Now Yahweh himself finally speaks to Job "out of the whirlwind"—a typical device to denote a theophany. Yahweh's answer is to assert his utter transcendence, and the inapplicability of all human criteria to judge his ways. Job was not present at creation! Our reading selects the creation of the sea, with its assertion of God's sovereignty over it (v. 11), thus preparing for the gospel reading, which is the stilling of the storm.

Responsorial Psalm: 107:23-24, 25-26, 28-29, 30-31

In this psalm four different groups of persons are invited to give thanks to God. The fourth group consists of those who have been rescued from a storm at sea. Thus it matches the first reading and the gospel. The key word linking the psalm with the gospel is of course verse 29: "he made the storm be still." In fact this verse is held by some to be part of the literary background for the gospel pericope.

Reading II: 2 Corinthians 5:14-17

We have to see this passage in the context of Paul's "first apology," discussed on Sunday 8 B, above. Paul is contrasting the motivation of his own ministry with that of the false teachers by whom the Corinthians are captivated. This impelling motivation is the love of Christ, concretely actualized in his death upon the cross. Hence it produces a pattern of apostolate which is itself marked by the cross: Paul, like all true Christians, but unlike the false teachers, lives no longer to himself, but for him who died and was raised.

The meaning of the second paragraph is much controverted. What does Paul mean when he speaks of regarding Christ from a human point of view? The fact that he acknowledges that he himself had once shared this point of view has led many to find the clue in Paul's pre-conversion conception of Christ. If "Christ" is here used as a proper name, the meaning would then be that Paul before his conversion had known Jesus in the flesh, but now knows him as the risen Lord. The trouble with this interpretation is that it makes Paul treat the earthly history of Jesus as an episode of the past in a way that was characteristic of the Corinthian gnostics in 1 Corinthians. It is no wonder that one critic (Schmithals) has recently suggested that it is a gnostic gloss added to the text.

An alternative view is to take "Christ" here not as a proper name, but as "Messiah." Paul is then saying that as Jew he accepted Jewish (political?) notions of Messiahship, but that when he became a Christian he rejected the view in favor of the message of the crucified and risen One. This interpretation has more to commend it, but it requires taking "from a human point of view" adjectively, as a modifier of Messiah. In Paul, however, this phrase when used pejoratively, as it clearly is, is used adverbially. If we keep in mind the concrete situation in which the first apology was written, everything seems to fall into place perfectly. Paul calls the christology of his opponents a way of knowing Christ from a human point of view. They view Christ as a "divine man" or wonder-worker, and claimed that this was to regard him from a super-human point of view. Paul however castigates this view of Christ as fleshly, sarkic (i.e., "a human point of view"). To regard Christ as merely a wonder-worker is precisely that. He is rather the crucified and risen One, and only as such has he opened the new age. The apparent contradiction between this realized eschatology of 2 Corinthians and the rejection of "realized eschatology" in 1 Corinthians (where the Corinthians asserted that in baptism they had been raised already) is explained once we realize that the situation in 2 Corinthians is completely different from that in 1 Corinthians. There the problem was the local gnostics, here the problem is with the wandering preachers who interpreted Jesus as an earthly divine man.

Paul's theology is thus intensely situational. In response to one situation he can make a point that is completely contradicted when he faces another situation. It shows how careful we have to be in trying to systematize Paul's theology — or indeed any New Testament theology, for that matter.

Gospel: Mark 4:35-41

First let us try and reconstruct the history of the tradition of this pericope. What historical nucleus underlies this story? Three things we can say for certain are historical facts: (1) the general scene — Jesus and his disciples crossing the lake in a boat and encountering a storm; (2) the impression of authority which Jesus gave in all that he said or did; (3) the data about Jesus' family.

The story has, however, been developed in the tradition along lines which were already familiar from the Old Testament, where Yahweh stills the raging sea and where prophets still storms (cf. Jonah 1:15). The story is now told to evoke an answer to the question, "Who is this?" The answer is that Jesus is the eschatological prophet in whom Yahweh (cf. reading I and the psalm) is epiphanously present.

Mark in turn has redacted this story. First, he has linked it to the parable collection in chapter 4 (note the opening words, "on that day . . . said to his disciples" — "that day" is the day of parabolic teaching when Jesus had promised the disciples that to them would be disclosed the mysteries of the kingdom of God). The stilling of the storm is part of the disclosure. But the disciples do not yet understand. Hence the insertion of the typically Marcan words, "Why are you afraid? Have you no faith?" This reproach to the disciples and the fact that they raise a question without answering it point the reader to Peter's confession in Mark 8, where an incomplete faith is expressed, and beyond that to the cross and resurrection, when finally the disciples will come to realize who Jesus truly is (Mk 16:7).

The Homily

The Old Testament reading, the psalm, and the gospel reading are linked together by the motif of the stilling of the storm. The homilist could relate this to the storms through which the church (which already in the New Testament is typified in the boat) is passing, and proclaim the power of Christ to still these storms today if truly we cling to him.

The epistle suggests that the homilist identify some contemporary ways of regarding Christ from a human point of view (e.g., superstar?)

and proclaim him as the one who died and was raised, through whom we too become a new creation.

SS. PETER AND PAUL: JUNE 29
The feast of SS. Peter and Paul is celebrated on Sunday in the 1975 Roman calendar. The commentary for Sunday 13 B will be found immediately after this June 29 entry.

There are very few critical historians today who would deny that both Peter and Paul suffered martyrdom in Rome. However, June 29 is not the date of their martyrdom. In fact it is unlikely that they were martyred on the same day. Some New Testament scholars would place the death of Paul at the conclusion of the two year imprisonment with which Acts closes (about 62), and Peter's death during the Neronian persecution in 64, a view which this commentator favors. Why then June 29? To quote P. Battifol, "The festival of the two apostles will be celebrated on the same day, June 29, not because this date is the anniversary of their martyrdom, but because it is the anniversary of the institution of a joint observance in their honor." Oscar Cullmann, the Swiss Protestant scholar, agrees, adding that the choice of June 29 was due to the earlier association of this day with the founder of the city of Rome, Romulus. This Christian observance in Rome began in 258.

Historically it is difficult to connect the foundation of the church in Rome directly with Peter or Paul. There must have been Jewish Christians in that city before Claudius expelled all the Jews from Rome in 48 (cf. Aquila and Priscilla, Acts 18:2). By the time Paul wrote Romans (c. 56) there were both Gentile and Jewish groups in Rome (the strong and the weak of Roman 15). Apparently the former had arrived between the expulsion of the Jews in 48 and the death of Claudius in 54, while the Jewish Christians would have drifted back after Nero's succession. This is what created tensions which are discussed in Romans 15. Galatians 2:7 states that Peter and Paul were recognized as the heads of the Jewish and Gentile missions respectively. In view of this it may be claimed that Peter and Paul indirectly were responsible for the foundation of the Roman church.

Reading I: Acts 3:1-10 [1]

It has been a dominant view among scholars that the author of Acts had no traditions to refer to when he wrote his work. Dibelius argued that this was because the apostles preached Jesus, not themselves. But we know from Paul that his opponents did preach themselves, boasting of their own marvelous exploits, while the news of Paul's apostolic successes and achievements were spread from church to church. It is not surprising, therefore, that this story has all the traits of a miracle story: diagnosis, cure and demonstration, and portrays the apostles rather in the image of the divine man. Like John's gospel, however, the author of Luke-Acts uses this and similar stories as a jumping off ground for a lengthy discourse. This discourse takes the form of a kerygmatic speech. Thus the author corrects his source's view that the apostles were merely figures of the divine man type. It is difficult to see how one could preach on this pericope without referring to its corrective in the kerygmatic speech that follows.

Responsorial Psalm: 19:1-2, 3-4ab

It is interesting how this psalm has undergone development in Christian usage. The first part speaks of the revelation of God in creation. "Their message" is the message of the created order, the heavens, the firmament, day and night, that "the head that made us is divine. . . ." But Paul identifies the "they" of verse 4 with the preachers of the gospel, specifically the Jewish Christian apostles whose labors he considers by c. 56 to have failed (Rom 10:18). In Christian liturgical usage Psalm 19 has accordingly been used on evangelists' and apostles' days. Paul thus gives full justification for its use today as a response to Acts 3.

Reading II: Galatians 1:11-20

This section from Galatians is an important piece of Pauline autobiography. The preacher to the Gentiles was notoriously reticent about his apostolic call. Only when misrepresented did he feel it incumbent upon him to set the record straight. The opponents in Galatia had accused him of (a) being entirely dependent on the Jerusalem apostles

---

[1] The following commentary is based on the readings assigned to the Vigil of SS. Peter and Paul. The Petrine text in Matthew 16, which is the gospel of the feast, was commented on for Sunday 21 A.

for his call, and (b) of falsifying the apostles' teaching by dropping the requirement of circumcision for Gentile converts. In answer to (a) Paul goes over what happened to him between the Damascus Road experience and his first visit to Jerusalem three years later (two by ancient reckoning). The apostle had embarked immediately on his mission after his call (that, and not retreat, was the probable purpose of the visit to Arabia, according to contemporary scholars), and when he went up to Jerusalem it was not to seek authorization from the apostles but to visit between equals.

This reading brings together the two apostles, Paul and Cephas, while being primarily concerned with Paul.

Gospel: John 21:15-19

This scene comes from the so-called appendix to John's Gospel. Although apparently added later by a member of the Johannine school, it enshrines far earlier material than the other resurrection traditions in John 20. Indeed, John 21 has its roots in the first appearance to Peter, reported in the early list of 1 Corinthians 15:5, alluded to in Luke 24:34, and narrated in a variant tradition (as many modern scholars, including Catholics, now think) in Matthew 16:17-19. In this call Peter was appointed the first of the apostles to witness the resurrection, and given the pastoral task of feeding the sheep. It is obvious that this latter function has to continue in Christ's church.

The last paragraph clearly reflects knowledge of Peter's martyrdom (? by crucifixion), and is in fact the earliest evidence we have of it.

The Homily

Today's double commemoration of Peter and Paul and its early history indicated that its real significance is the celebration of the foundation of the ancient church of Rome, which became the mother of the churches throughout the west. As such this feast is of ecumenical importance for all western Christians. It is perhaps even more significant that the church of Rome had a double foundation — the Petrine and the Pauline missions, the mission to Israel and that to the Gentiles, the apostolate to the circumcision and the free gospel apart from the law for the Gentiles, the institutional and the charismatic-evangelical. Those streams in Christianity and church life, which we normally take to be antithetical, Rome and the Reformation, are here held together in tension (cf. Rom 15!), but in what is hopefully a fruitful tension. Is that perhaps the mission of Rome today —

to be both Petrine and Pauline, Catholic and Evangelical? It would be exciting for the homilist to explore the contemporary ecumenical implications of this double foundation of the church of Rome.

✓ THIRTEENTH SUNDAY OF THE YEAR
Reading I: Wisdom 1:13-15; 2:23-24

The controlling reading, as usual the gospel, is the raising of Jairus' daughter, with its proclamation of Christ as Victor over death. The reading from Wisdom provides the Old Testament presuppositions for this victory (Protestants can be assured that although this reading comes from one of the "apocryphal" books, the doctrine it asserts is an interpretation of Genesis 1–3, consonant with Paul's teaching). The world as God created it was essentially good (1:14; cf. Gn 1). Man, in particular, was created to be immortal (Gn 3 contrariwise seems to assume that man was created mortal), but Wisdom deduces from the fact of man's creation in God's image (Gn 1:26) that man was created immortal, and Paul seems to share this assumption when he speaks of death, as does the last phrase in Wisdom 1:14 here, as an alien intruder into the world, consequent upon man's sin (Rom 5:12). Finally, Wisdom 2:24 equates the serpent in Genesis 3 with the devil. This is the first known instance of this identification, which is found elsewhere in the New Testament, including Paul (cf. 2 Cor 11:3), though not mentioned in Romans 5.

The doctrine of this passage appears at first sight to conflict with the self-evident truth that death is a biological fact. It is arguable, however, from the connection of immortality with righteousness (cf. Wis 1:15) that the author is speaking of moral and spiritual death, as Paul undoubtedly does in Romans 5. In that case, biological death has more than a merely physical meaning: it is the ultimate sign of man's alienation from God, the "sacrament of sin" (B. Althaus). It is death *in this sense* (not physical death *per se*, as Christians still have to die) that Christ overcomes by his death on the cross.

Responsorial Psalm: 30:1 and 3, 4-5, 10-11a and 12b

According to its title, this psalm was originally associated with the restoration of the temple in the time of the Maccabees in 164 B.C. In that case the original reference to "death" would be the catastrophes of the desecration of the temple by Antiochus Epiphanes and the Jewish war of independence. It thus becomes a psalm of national thanksgiving.

Here, however, it is a psalm for Christ's victory over death, as this is adumbrated in the gospel reading.

Reading II: 2 Corinthians 8:7, 9, 13-15

As usual, the epistle reading has no direct connection with the other readings, but simply appears in course. Chapter 8 of 2 Corinthians is concerned entirely with Paul's collection for the Jerusalem church. Paul had undertaken to raise this money several years previously at the apostolic conference (Gal 2), and had faithfully carried out his side of the agreement. Accordingly he had proposed to the Corinthian converts that they take part in the collection and suggested how it could be organized (1 Cor 16:1-4). Meanwhile, however, the great crisis in the relations of Paul with the Corinthians had supervened, the result of the appearance in that city of the false apostles. In the ensuing fray (involving a sudden and disastrous visit of Paul to Corinth), the severe letter, identified by many with 2 Corinthians 10-13, a visit by Titus, the Corinthian *volte-face* and the writing of the letter of thanksgiving (2 Cor 1:1-2:13; 7:5-16), the collection had been forgotten. Now that the crisis is over, Paul can return to the subject (2 Cor 8; 9, thought by some to be two separate communications on the subject). In the course of this correspondence Paul musters every argument he can think of to encourage the Corinthians to proceed with their fund-raising drive. The strongest motivation for Christian giving is in verse 9 — gratitude for the riches Christ has brought us through his self-emptying in the incarnation (for the doctrine cf Phil 2:6-11).

Gospel: Mark 5:21-43 (long form); 5:21-24, 35-43 (short form)

It is characteristic of Mark's gospel for one pericope to be inserted in the bosom of another. So here the story of the woman with the hemorrhage is inserted into the narrative of the raising of Jairus' daughter. It is disputed whether this insertion is due to the evangelist's redaction, or whether it came to him in this form from the tradition. The older form critics took the latter view, supposing it was a device to explain the delay between the arrival of the messenger from Jairus and Jesus' arrival at the house, a delay which meant that the little girl was dead by that time. Later redaction critics are inclined rather to see in the insertion an attempt by the evangelist to allow one miracle to interpret the other. The healing of the woman with the hemorrhage is interpreted as an act of salvation (vv. 28, 34). So also is the raising of Jairus' daughter. Each is therefore a prefigurement of Christ's salvation of man from death. The shorter reading simply omits the insert.

We first offer a reconstruction of the history of the tradition of the two stories. On the historical level we may suppose that Jesus *healed* the daughter of Jairus from a critical but not fatal illness (v. 23). In the tradition the narrative was then modeled on the raisings by Elijah and Elisha, and served to proclaim Jesus as the eschatological prophet. The background of this story seems to be thoroughly Palestinian.

The story of the woman with the hemorrhage, on the other hand, seems to be more Hellenistic. The woman's action in touching the healer's garments suggests that she thought of Jesus as a *theios anēr* (divine man). This aspect is enhanced by Luke, who adds that Jesus knew that power (*dynamis*) had gone out of him when the woman touched him. Mark seeks to correct this notion by transforming the woman's superstitious act into an expression of faith, and the whole episode into a personal encounter with the Saviour.

In addition, by combining the two episodes, Mark inserts at the end of the raising his motif of the messianic secret (v. 43a). From a historical point of view the command to keep the raising silent would be absurd. But as a theological device it makes sense. What Mark is saying is that the true significance of the act of raising is not yet apparent. It is only at the resurrection that the veil of secrecy over Jesus lifted (cf. Mk 9:9), and therefore it is only then that Jesus is seen as the Victor over death. The raising of the little girl is not itself Jesus' victory over death (in any case the girl had to die some time, and certainly did). It was only a parable or prefiguration of the act by which Jesus overcame death in its existential sense. The healing of the woman with the hemorrhage prefigures Christ's death as a cleansing from sin.

The Homily

The gospel, with the Old Testament reading and the psalm, has the strongest claim on the homilist's attention today. This would involve (1) an existential interpretation of physical death as the sign and seal and sacrament of sin; and (2) the proclamation of Christ as the one who by dying on the cross on our behalf has cleansed us from our sin and deprived death of its sting, thus restoring man to communion with God and to life which cannot be destroyed by physical death (cf. Rom 8:35-39).

Alternatively, the epistle would suggest a homily on the topic of

Christian stewardship and its motivation in the generosity of God in Christ, who became poor that we might be rich.

Reading I: Ezekiel 2:2-5

The choice of this reading is governed by the gospel which presents Jesus as a prophet rejected by his own countrymen. Ezekiel likewise was sent to his own countrymen and warned that they might reject him. This passage comes from the first of four different accounts of Ezekiel's call. He marks a new departure in Old Testament prophecy. Ever since the first prophet (Amos), the concept of the "Spirit" had been avoided by the prophets. It was originally too much associated with ecstatic prophecy and Baal worship. But by Ezekiel's time it could be brought safely out of cold storage and be used, for by now it had been purified from its older questionable associations. Henceforth endowment with the Spirit will be a characteristic of Yahweh's prophets. From this it passes into New Testament usage. "Son of man" simply means man; it is not a messianic title. It denotes a man in contrast to God, the human bearer of the divine message.

Responsorial Psalm: 123:1-2a, 2bc, 3-4

This is a community psalm. A representative of Israel pleads on behalf of the whole community for mercy. What concrete situation is envisaged is no longer determinable. It is a beautiful cry for help (note especially servant/master, maid/mistress as parables of Israel's relations to Yahweh). But it is not easy to see precisely what connection it has with the reading from Ezekiel. Perhaps the point lies in the final stanza, in which case it can be taken as a lament on the part of the prophet that his message is rejected and he receives nothing but contempt from his hearers.

Reading II: 2 Corinthians 12:7-10

This passage is from the so-called severe or tearful letter (2 Cor 10-13), written at the height of Paul's controversy over the false apostles who are undermining his influence among the Corinthians. It thus takes us back to an earlier stage in the story of Paul's relationship with the Corinthians than that envisaged in the previous week's readings. Paul had been contrasted unfavorably with the false apostles, who boasted of their ecstasies, visions, miracles, etc. The apostle replies that whenever he was tempted to preen himself like his opponents, he was pulled up short by the "thorn in the flesh," to keep him from being elated. There has been much discussion about the precise meaning of Paul's illness. Here he speaks of being "buffeted" (RSV, weakly, "harrassed"). This has often been taken to imply epilepsy, whose convulsions would throw him to the ground. Others have deduced from Galatians 4:14-15 that Paul had some ophthalmic affliction. The trouble is, as Lietzmann remarked, the patient has been dead 1900 years! This makes diagnosis difficult. The two references contradict each other, and should probably be taken metaphorically. The Galatians would have given Paul their most valuable physical organs, i.e., they would have done anything for him in his illness. The sickness did not literally throw him to the ground, but left him depressed. Karl Bonhoeffer, the father of Dietrich, and a medical authority, thought it might have been a chronic depression, a phenomenon often accompanied by spells of supranormal activity. The elder Bonhoeffer characterized it as the result of a "hyperrhythmic temperament." It seems safest to leave it at that. Paul does not complain about it, but used it positively. It brings home to him that the grace of God and only that is all he needs to carry out his apostolic labors. His life is thus an epiphany of the cross of Christ. That is what it means for him to be an apostle.

Gospel: Mark 6:1-6

Once again we must try to reconstruct the history of this pericope. It was claimed by the earlier form critics that the whole episode was constructed as a vehicle for the saying about the prophet being honored everywhere except in his own country. But other features of the story have a ring of historicity. Jesus was more than a prophet to the early Christian community and therefore it is unlikely that they would have constructed a scene for such a saying without modifying it in the light of their post-Easter christology. The family relationships of Jesus are surely based on historical reminiscences, too. Moreover, it is unlikely that the post-Easter church should have recorded that Jesus *could* do no mighty work in his home town unless this had been the case. So we may presume an authentic memory of an occasion when Jesus was rejected in his own native town. The memory was then cast into narrative form by the primitive community in order to reassure itself when the kerygma was rejected by their fellow countrymen. Their Master had suffered a like fate. Finally, Mark takes the story, adds verse 1 as an introductory link and 6b as a generalizing conclusion. The exceptive qualification in verse 5b has clearly been added to mitigate the offense of 5a, though whether this addition was made by Mark or by the pre-Marcan tradition is unclear. By inserting this pericope in its present position (Luke has another version of the same episode right at the beginning of the ministry), Mark introduces one of his reminders of the impending passion into the early part of his narrative (cf. 3:6, which, like this episode, also occurs at the end of a major structural section of the gospel). Mark is thus telling his readers that Jesus was not merely a successful wonder-worker. Even his miraculous deeds led to his rejection and to the cross.

The Homily

Reading I and the gospel give us the theme of rejection. If the church is true to its mission, it will inevitably encounter rejection. Of course we must not put unnecessary stumbling blocks (e.g., outmoded terminology, philosophical concepts, etc.) before modern man and prevent him from hearing the Christian message. But there are limits to which the gospel can be accommodated to modern man. The scandal of the cross must never be mitigated. The gospel must never be watered down so that "Jones can swallow it" (a memorable phrase coined by the late Mgr. Ronald Knox in his Anglican days). The basic responsibility of the church is not to win converts on any terms, but to proclaim the Christian message faithfully, "whether they hear or refuse to hear."

Reading II prompts a consideration of the way a Christian should face depression. Paul suggests that it can be used positively, driving the believer to rely solely on the grace of God and to find from him strength in his weakness.

FIFTEENTH SUNDAY OF THE YEAR

Reading I: Amos 7:12-15

This reading appears to have been chosen to go with the mission of the Twelve (see below). Amos is sent to God's people Israel (the northern kingdom) as the Twelve were sent to God's people in Galilee.

This passage places before us two contrasted conceptions of religion, one represented by Amaziah, priest of Bethel, and the other represented by the prophet Amos. Amaziah thought of religion in "civil" terms. It existed to promote loyalty to the status quo—the royal house and patriotism. Bethel was the king's sanctuary and the temple of the kingdom, a sort of national cathedral (or the White House on a Sunday morning?). Amaziah thought of his own role as that of a court chaplain (a preacher at the White House or at a political prayer breakfast?) — his job was to prophesy "smooth things." Amos, however, was not a card-carrying member of the prophetic guild (whose members had a similar view of their duties as the priest Amaziah), but an outsider whom God had called to denounce the government for its injustices and inhuman policies. We don't get the substance of Amos' message here, only his basic attitude. It is to deliver the word of the Lord, not to take the professional line of the court chaplains and spokesmen for an uncritical patriotism.

Responsorial Psalm: 85:8ab and 9, 10-11, 12-13
In commenting on the identical selection, Sunday 19 A, we pointed out that the original context of this psalm is uncertain, but that its theology reminds one of Deutero-Isaiah and its plausible context is the impending return from exile. While suitable for any occasion, it does not appear to have any particular connection with today's readings.

Reading II: Ephesians 1:3-14 (long form); 1:3-10 (short form)
The opening thanksgiving of Ephesians (which we regard as Deutero-Pauline) is suggested by Paul's thanksgiving in 2 Corinthians 1:3ff, and is today widely thought to be made up from a liturgical hymn. This liturgical material runs through verse 14. The shorter version is obtained simply by lopping off the latter portion, which is printed as a separate paragraph in RSV. In the Greek both parts consist of a simple sentence. Its contents suggest that it is a baptismal hymn. It speaks (1) of the election and predestination of the believer before the creation; (2) of the Christ event; (3) of the gnosis conveyed in Christian experience; (4) the definition of gnosis as the cosmic scope of salvation history; (5) the distinction between "we" (Jewish Christians) and "you" (Gentile Christians), and the sealing of the latter with the Holy Spirit in their initiation. It may be reasonably conjectured that in part 5 the distinction between Jewish and Gentile Christians has been introduced into the hymn by the author of Ephesians, thus adumbrating his major theme throughout the letter. That theme is the unity of both parties in the one church. Thus the hymn would have concluded with a celebration of the sealing of all the newly baptized. It will be seen that the shorter form omits an essential part of the hymn.

Gospel: Mark 6:7-13

It was claimed by some of the early form critics that the synoptic missions were creations of the post-Easter community. If this were so, one would have expected Jesus' charge to reflect the church's post-Easter christological kerygma, whereas in point of fact the terms of their mission in both Mark and Q are exactly those of the earthly Jesus. Mark does not specify, as Q does, that they were charged to proclaim as Jesus did the inbreaking of the kingdom of God, but implies it in (a) the eschatological haste (no bread, etc.); (b) the warning of possible rejection as Jesus' message was rejected; (c) the statement that they preached repentance (cf. Mk 1:14); (d) their performance of exorcisms and healings. "We must regard as authentic the commission to act like Jesus himself in proclaiming that God's kingdom has drawn near and is doing mighty works" (F. Hahn).

It is equally clear that the four forms of the charge (Mark, Q, Matthew, Luke) tended to expand or reduce the original nucleus in accordance with contemporary needs and practices. Thus in Mark, as we have seen, we find the reference to proclaiming the kingdom of God has been dropped (Mark knew only a christological kerygma in his church), and the reference to exorcism and healing is extended to include a specific mention of oil (cf. Jas 5:14 for this church practice).

What function does this charge play in Mark? Mark clearly is very interested in the Twelve. They are sometimes presented in a highly negative way, as blind and unperceptive to the mystery of Jesus and his mission. Here, however, they are presented in a positive light. They are entrusted with the same message and mission as the Master himself. Clearly, Mark wishes to hold before his church this twofold possibility. In Mark's church the successors of the apostles are simultaneously warned and encouraged. They may misunderstand Jesus, and in the supreme hour of persecution fail their Lord as the disciples forsook him and fled; or they may become true witnesses to the gospel message as the disciples did briefly in Jesus' earthly lifetime and as they did for good after the risen One had commissioned them in Galilee (Mk 16:7).

The Homily

The first reading and the gospel suggest a homily on the mission of the church. The following points can be brought out: 1. What matters supremely, more than apparent success or failure, is the church's fidelity to the gospel message. Amos failed at Bethel and the Twelve were warned that men might refuse to hear them. 2. Particularly, the word of God must be delivered in the teeth of opposition from the advocates of "civil religion." (A possible case in point: civil religion says that draft evaders must bear the full brunt of their punishment for life: the gospel proclaims forgiveness.) 3. There is an eschatological haste about the church's message. The church may be required to divest itself of much of its excess baggage accumulated over the centuries if the message is to be delivered in freedom.

Reading II, in either its short or longer forms, offers several possibilities for the homilist. One could speak about the ultimate purpose of God to unite all things in himself, drawing on the insights, perhaps, of Teilhard de Chardin, the theology of hope, and/or process theology. This ultimate hope of unity of all things must then be exhibited as the impelling motivation for present action in human society, and in Christendom toward a closer approximation to the ultimate goal. (See also *Faith and Order*, Louvain 1971.)

One might also speak on various aspects of the baptismal mystery — the initial redemption conveying "the forgiveness of our trespasses," or the wisdom and insight we presently have into God's ultimate purpose for the universe, or the relation between the gifts of the Holy Spirit and the final blessedness of the redeemed (longer form). If the homilist opts for the epistle reading he must, however, be careful not to be too abstract, but endeavor to relate the biblical message to the concrete situation of the congregation.

SIXTEENTH SUNDAY OF THE YEAR
Reading I: Jeremiah 23:1-6
The first reading is suggested by the observation in the day's gospel that Jesus had compassion on the multitude "because they were like sheep without a shepherd." In ancient Israel — as in other cultures of the ancient Near East — the figures of king and shepherd are very closely associated, viz., David the shepherd boy being taken from among the flock to be king over the united kingdoms of Judah and Israel. Although we should not sentimentalize the idea of shepherding (as talk of the "gentle Shepherd" might tempt us to do, although the Hebrew word for "to shepherd" also means "to rule"), it is still true that the image of shepherd contains within it the notion of feeding and providing for the flock, in fact much of what we associate with pastoral care.

Jeremiah, writing toward the end of the reign of Zedekiah just before the final captivity in 587, looks back over recent reigns and condemns the last kings of Judah as shepherds who have misgoverned their flock. The denunciation concludes with the promise of a righteous Branch ("the Lord our righteousness" is a play on the name "Zedekiah"). This scion of the house of David will be the Messiah, the ideal king. Jeremiah of course was thinking purely in historical terms — of the restoration of the Davidic monarchy after a period of exile. But his words kindled a hope in Israel which, in the perspective of Christian faith, find their ultimate fulfillment in Jesus the Christ.

Responsorial Psalm: 23:1-3a, 3b-4, 5, 6

The first two stanzas of this psalm, the most familiar in the psalter, pictures Yahweh as shepherd, the third and fourth stanzas as host at a banquet in the temple. The royal theology of Judah found no contradiction between the notion that both Yahweh and the king were Israel's shepherd, for the king was the sacramental embodiment of Yahweh's kingship and shepherdhood. Christian faith sees the same dual notion fulfilled in Jesus Christ. He is the One through whom God exercises his eschatological rule and shepherds his people. The second stanza suggests that it is particularly at the eucharist banquet that Christ exercises his shepherding function.

Reading II: Ephesians 2:13-18

This passage is the theological core of the letter to the Ephesians. Looking back over the career of Paul the Deutero-Pauline writer contemplates the results of the apostle's work. Jew and Gentile have been brought together into a single community, the body of Christ. Christ on the cross (i.e., by his death as the event of salvation) has fulfilled and abolished the law, not as moral demand, but as the way of salvation: Christians now keep the law *because* they have been saved by grace, not *in order* to earn salvation. Now both Jew and Gentile have access in one body to the Father. Access is a liturgical term, denoting the approach of God in worship. Note the trinitarian character of the final sentence: through Christ in one Spirit to the Father. Note, too, that verse 13 alludes to Isaiah 57:19, while verse 17 cites and provides its Christian application. This indicates the sermonic quality of Ephesians.

Gospel: Mark 6:30-34

This passage is highly composite. Verses 30-33 form a link between the mission of the disciples and the feeding of the multitude. They bear clear signs of Mark's editorial work. Verse 30 points back to the mission of the Twelve (here only in Mark are the Twelve called apostles, a term which was not originally a title, but functional). Verse 31 (often used in connection with retreats) points forward to the feeding. Verse 32 introduces a favorite theme of Mark—teaching given in secrecy to the Twelve, though the fulfillment of this intention is delayed until chapter 8 (Caesarea Philippi). Verse 34 is the beginning of a new pericope, the feeding of the multitude (cf. the variant in 8:2). The reference to the shepherd motif is probably pre-Marcan, and gives a special emphasis to the miraculous feeding. But the note about teaching looks redactional: Mark frequently emphasizes Jesus' teaching activity without giving the content of his teaching.

The Homily

It is the figure of the shepherd (reading I, the psalm and the gospel), that dominates today's reading and probably it is what the homilist will choose to expound. He could show how Christ still performs this function of shepherding in the liturgy. In the first part of the liturgy Christ teaches his flock through his word, a notion which Mark emphasizes as an essential function of the shepherd. In the second half of the liturgy he prepares a banquet for his flock (stanza three of the psalm). Thus the thought of Christ as shepherd can be shown to be the background of the church's understanding of the ministry as pastoral. The pastor is not a substitute for the absence of Christ, but the human vehicle through whose functions Christ renders himself present. The picture of Christ as the host at his table (stanza three of the psalm) provides a rationale for celebrating behind the altar.

Reading II presents an opportunity to speak of the church as transcending the distinction between Christian Jew and Gentile. The obvious contemporary application of this would be in the field of black-white relationships. But this theme must be tackled theologically, not sociologically or humanistically. Everything said must be based on the understanding of the cross of Christ as the abolition of the law. Only in those terms has a Christian preacher the right to talk in the pulpit about race relations.

Whatever happens in the secular world, it is clear that deliberate segregation in the church is a denial of the gospel — in other words, heresy.

Sundays 17 B to 26 B

Reading I: 2 Kings 4:42-44

This little story from the Elisha cycle is not widely known, but it has become quite important in recent New Testament scholarship. This is because it provides the literary prototype of the miraculous feedings in the gospels. The pattern of the feeding narratives is largely the same: (1) food is brought to the man of God; (2) the amount of the food is specified; (3) it is objected that the quantity is inadequate; (4) behaving as master of the situation the man of God ignores the objection and commands the food to be distributed; (5) the crowd not only have enough to eat, but there was some left.

Responsorial Psalm: 145:10-11, 15-16, 17-18

Psalm 145 is used quite frequently as a responsorial psalm, but this is the only time this particular selection is used on a Sunday. Stanza II obviously connects with the Old Testament reading and the gospel, and the common theme of both is further underlined in the refrain.

Reading II: Ephesians 4:1-6

In accordance with common critical opinion, we take Ephesians to be the work of a second generation Paulinist thoroughly steeped in the apostle's teaching. Ephesians follows a very clear division, chapters 1–3 being doctrinal and 4–6 parenetical (i.e., containing ethical exhortation), so that our reading is the beginning of the parenesis. But there is a close connection between the two parts of the document. The first part has set forth the unity of Jew and Gentile in the one body, providing a look back at the achievement of the apostle himself, while the parenesis begins with an exhortation to unity. But the exhortation to unity leads back into a further reminder of the theological ground for the appeal. The "ought" is based on an "is." There *is* one body, one Spirit, one hope, one Lord, one faith, one baptism, one God and Father of all Christians. And therefore the writer, speaking in the apostle's name, can exhort his readers to be what they are. As in Paul himself, the imperative rests upon an indicative. Unity is both a gift and a task (German: *Gabe* and *Aufgabe*). The imperative to unity is therefore like the imperative to individual sanctification, "become what you are."

Gospel: John 6:1-15

As we have seen, part of the background for this familiar story is provided in the less familiar story of Elisha. The same seven points we enumerated from the Elisha story reappear in the Johannine feeding and provide the basic framework for the narrative. But there are other motifs in John, such as the eucharist and the eschatological or messianic banquet. Note the acts of Jesus: took, gave thanks (the Hellenistic equivalent of "blessed," which Mark still preserves at one place), distributed. And when the text says that multitudes were *filled*, we have a word which is used elsewhere for the repletion of the messianic banquet. In the ensuing discourse in the synagogue at Capernaum (see next week's reading) the evangelist develops yet another aspect of the symbolism of this story, namely the Moses/manna typology. But this typology is scarcely evident in the story itself as John has received it from his tradition.

The concluding verse appears to enshrine a genuine historical reminiscence not recorded in the synoptists. It is impossible to ascertain what precisely happened in the feeding, but it is clear from all the gospels accounts that it represented a crisis in the Lord's ministry. We know that at some stage Jesus broke off his Galilean ministry and went to Jerusalem, and in all the gospels the feeding occupies a pivotal point in the narrative. This shows that its central position is due not merely to Mark's arrangement but goes back to earlier tradition. In Mark's first version of the feeding we are told that Jesus packed the disciples off in a boat while he dismissed the crowd. The reason for this becomes clear in John's note here: it was to prevent the disciples from being infected by the dangerous nationalistic-messianic enthusiasm of the crowd.

The Homily

As we have seen, the Johannine feeding admits of several theological interpretations (Jesus as the new Elijah, the messianic banquet, the miraculous meal as a type of the eucharist). It would seem appropriate on this

Sunday to take our cue from the responsorial psalm and its refrain: "The Lord feeds us; he answers all our needs." A consideration of this theme would lead to a treatment of the affluent nations' responsibility to provide for the impoverished peoples of the earth, and to conserve the bounties of nature. The United States is the most wasteful of all peoples on the earth. Not only is it depriving the poorer nations of a fair share in the world's goods, but it is consuming its own resources at such a rate that there will be insufficient left for our own descendants. A reflexion on these serious matters would be in order today.

If the subject of Christian unity did not come up in January, the epistle offers an opportunity to deal with it today. Here, as we have suggested, the gift of unity must be stressed first, and then the obligation it places upon us to exhibit this unity. The homilist should ask how concretely this has to be done on the local scene.

EIGHTEENTH SUNDAY OF THE YEAR

Reading I: Exodus 16:2-4, 12-15

There are two accounts of the manna and quails in the Pentateuch, the other one being in Numbers 11. There the manna was provided first, and after the people "murmured" (a constant motif in the exodus story) the quails were given. In this account greater emphasis is placed on the manna. Both are intelligible as phenomena in the Sinai desert, the manna being a sweet excretion from certain insects and the quails migratory fowl which often drop dead from exhaustion in their flight over the Sinai desert.

Note how the final remark of Moses highlights the manna at the expense of the quails, providing the phrase bread from heaven, which was destined to play an important role in later tradition. This phrase is taken up in the refrain of the responsorial psalm (78:3 and 4bcd, 23-24, 25 and 54-55ab). Psalm 78 is a long recitation of Israel's salvation history from Jacob to David. This section of it covers the Sinai period. The bread from heaven becomes the bread of angels, a further step on the road to its typological interpretation of the messianic banquet and the eucharist.

Reading II: Ephesians 4:17, 20-24

Today's reading from Ephesians continues the parenesis or ethical exhortation. The material is almost certainly derived from a primitive Christian catechism. Note first the reference to the teaching of Christ. Note secondly the pattern of renunciation and renewal. "Put off" and "put on" are suggested by the candidate's divesting himself of his garments to go down into the baptismal waters and his vesting again with the baptismal robe after emerging from them. We cannot be sure that this symbolism was already applied at this time, but it is not improbable. Running through this passage is the contrast between the old pagan life and the new Christian life. The word "likeness" in the Revised Standard Version is not in the Greek, and we have no reason to speculate that the author is here thinking of man as having lost the divine likeness (though retaining the image) at the fall. Also, the word "nature" translates the Greek word for "man." We might find it helpful here to use Tillich's term, the new being.

Gospel: John 6:24-35

This is the opening section of the discourse on the bread of life. Like so many of the Johannine discourses it is composed by the evangelist from traditional materials. The reference to "signs" recalls the discussion in Mark 8:11-13, and the figurative interpretation of bread the dialogue in Mark 8:14-21.

The evangelist himself is not averse to the term sign, but he polemicizes against a faith that does not penetrate beyond the sign to the thing signified. Hence the exhortation to labor not for earthly bread, but for the food that endures to eternal life. This introduces the theme of the bread from heaven. At the outset it is stated that the Son of man (i.e., he who came down from heaven and who will ascend thither again) will give this bread. The dialogue about the true work looks like a digression, but it serves to underline the nature of the bread from heaven. This bread has to be received in faith, that is the only way to labor for it. Having established the difference between the sign and the thing signified, the dialogue proceeds to draw a second distinction, that between the type and its fulfillment, between the manna and the "true" (i.e., eschatological) bread from heaven. Note how the evangelist draws both distinctions by means of the Johannine technique of misunderstanding. Each time the Jews misunderstand the Revealer, who then proceeds to give the correct interpretation. In the course of this dialogue a shift occurs. First, Jesus promises as Son of man to give the bread of eternal life. But later he says, "I *am* the bread of life."

There is a major dispute as to whether in this first part of the discourse the evangelist already has the eucharist in mind, or whether that theme does not really come to the fore until verses 51-58 (regarded by some as the addition of a redactor). Is Christ the bread of heaven already in the incarnation or only in the eucharist? Is this bread made presently available in the proclamation of the word only, or in the sacrament also? Are eating and drinking no more than metaphors for faith in the divine Revealer, or do they also include sacramental eating and drinking? The present commentator would hazard two opinions on this subject: First, it would be wrong to draw a sharp line between the historical and kerygmatic, and the sacramental. All are part of one single act of revelation and redemption, with the historical coming of Christ decisive, and the preaching of the word and partaking of the sacrament complementary as re-presentations of the once-for all revelatory and redemptive event. Therefore it is not either faith in the word or sacramental eating and drinking alone, but both, the one informing the other but the one incomplete without the other. Second — an even more hazardous opinion! — since verses 26-51b speak exclusively of the bread of life, and only verses 51c-58 of the flesh and blood of Jesus, the background of the earlier part is the fellowship meal and preaching of the word, the background of the later part the eucharist proper. If the later part is the addition of a redactor who is also of the Johannine school, it would mean that the evangelist had emphasized the agape meal and preaching, to the virtual exclusion of the eucharist proper. But his rather "way-out" view was seen within the Johannine school to require supplementation. It is in that supplemented form that John's gospel has been received by the church into the canon. As the text now stands it asserts that in the fellowship meal and in the word the incarnate Christ is present as the bread of life, and that in the eucharist proper the crucified one gives his flesh and blood to be the food of the faithful.

The Homily

If on the previous Sunday the homilist spoke of man's need for bread, and society's need for a just distribution and conservation of the earth's resources in order that the poor and the unborn man have enough to sustain life, he has an opportunity this week to move on to man's further need for the bread that comes down from heaven, for God's revelation in Jesus Christ.

If on the previous Sunday he spoke of the need of the church to strive to exhibit that unity which she already possesses as a gift, he may today go on to speak of individual sanctification under the rubric of "become what you are": grow into the new man which you put on once for all in your baptism.

Reading I: 1 Kings 19:4-8

This is one of the stories from the Elijah cycle. Elijah has reached a crisis in his career; the opposition of King Ahab had driven him to flight. In his despondency he requests that he might die, but is supernaturally provided with food to sustain him on the journey to Horeb, the mountain of God, where he will receive a theophany. In Christian usage this passage has a twofold interest: (1) it is a type of Jesus' fast in the wilderness and a type of the church's Lenten fast (this passage forms the Old Testament lesson for Friday in the first week of Lent in *Lesser Feasts and Fasts* of the Episcopal Church); (2) it forms a type of the holy communion considered as the food of the pilgrims on their way to the mountain of God (cf. its use as an Old Testament lesson among the votive for the holy eucharist #904, 5). On this Sunday it is obviously chosen to parallel the continuation of the discourse on the bread from heaven.

Responsorial Psalm: 34:1-2, 3-4, 5-6, 7-8 (RSV)

Selections from this psalm were used on Lent 4 C and Sunday 30 C, and comments on it will be found under the latter, in the first year. Chiefly because of verse 8a, which serves there as the refrain, this psalm was used in the early church during the time of communion. It goes suitably with the Old Testament reading and gospel today.

Reading II: Ephesians 4:30-5:2

This passage continues the parenesis of Ephesians. The baptismal references are again clear ("sealed with the Holy Spirit" and "put away"). Once again, the imperatives are grounded in indicatives. Christians are to forgive one another because Christ has forgiven them, and to walk in love because Christ loved us, a love which expresses itself in sacrificial terms.

Gospel: John 6:41-51

It is interesting to find the "Jews" (usually a symbol in the Fourth Gospel for the unbelieving world) "murmuring" at the discourse on the bread of life, just as the children of Israel did in the wilderness. The use of this same verb can hardly be accidental, and it calls further attention to the manna/eucharist typology. They murmur because of another typical Johannine misunderstanding. They knew where Jesus came from, they know his parentage (N.B. the reference to Jesus as "son of Joseph" has no relevance to the question of the virginal conception: it simply reflects the undoubted fact that Jesus passed for the son of Joseph, whether this evangelist knew of virginal conception or not). The evangelist has worked in a tradition from the story of Jesus' rejection in the synagogue at Nazareth as given in the synoptists. Jesus' reply to the misunderstanding asserts that a knowledge of his heavenly origin is only possible to those who are "drawn to him" in faith by the Father. To be drawn is further defined as hearing and learning from the Father. The earthly origins of Jesus are not denied, but faith sees beyond them to his heavenly origin, just as the creed asserts not only that Jesus was born of Mary, but also that he was conceived by the Holy Spirit. The one level is historical fact, the other a confession of faith. Faith is not, however, just abstract, notional insight; it involves participating in "eternal life." Faith, too, is paradoxical: on the one hand it is a free decision, but on the other hand it involves an element of predestination (the Father must draw the believers to the Son). The great "I am" is repeated here twice: "I am the bread of life" (as in v. 35) and "I am the living bread which came down from heaven." Once again there is a typical Johannine repetition of the manna typology (v. 49). The last clause of 51 (51c) introduces for the first time the theme of the flesh of Jesus, which as we saw last Sunday, may be the beginning of the passage added by the Johannine redactor.

The Homily

If the homilist elects to continue the exposition of the Johannine discourse on the bread of life, he is provided with a wealth of material from the gospel. First, there are the two levels of Jesus' being, the historical and the heavenly, a schema which will apply also to the sacrament. This would give an opportunity to speak of the mystery of the eucharistic presence under the signs of the bread and wine. There is also the paradox of faith and predestination. The Old Testament reading however suggests that the homilist should narrow down his treatment to the eucharist as viaticum, the food of the pilgrims on their way to the mountain of God.

If on the other hand he is following a course on the Ephesian parenesis, the homilist should first expound the indicative (Christ's life love for us in offering himself as sacrifice to the Father for our forgiveness), and then the imperatives that follow from it (forgiveness of others as we have been forgiven; cf. the Lord's prayer). He might point up some quite concrete instances where forgiveness is required in the life of the local community.

Reading I: Proverbs 9:1-6

This is one of several Old Testament and (for others than Roman Catholics) apocryphal passages which speak of wisdom's heavenly banquet. This concept forms part of the background of the bread discourse of John 6:35-51b (see R. E. Brown in the Anchor Bible Commentary, *The Gospel According to John* I, 272–273 on the "sapiential theme in vv. 35-50"). It is perhaps a little unfortunate that this reading should be paired off with verses 51-58, where the sapiential theme falls into the background somewhat (but see v. 58). On the whole it would pair off better with the gospel readings on the 18th Sunday, the reference to wisdom's wine preparing for the reference to "thirst" in John 6:35.

In the Book of Proverbs the present passage forms the close of the prologue on wisdom. Wisdom and folly each invite their prospective participants to a banquet and they are free to choose which to accept. Our present reading is wisdom's invitation.

Responsorial Psalm: 34:1-2, 9-10, 11-12, 13-14

This is a somewhat different selection from Psalm 34 compared with last week, but with the same refrain. As we noted in our comments on Sunday 30 C, above, this is a wisdom psalm. The last two stanzas of today's selection are strongly sapiential and fit beautifully with reading I (note especially the similarity between the invitations of the third stanza and of Proverbs 9:5).

Reading II: Ephesians 5:15-20

We reach now the second part of the parenesis of Ephesians. Here we have a section that (whether designedly or not) fits quite aptly the first reading and its context, viz., the contrast between wisdom and folly. Folly consists of *not* making the most of the time (literally "buying up the opportunity"), and of drunkenness and debauchery. This exhortation has an eschatological background: the days are evil and the present age is under the domination of the evil powers, but their time is short (cf. Rom 13:11-14). Thus again, though less explicitly, the imperative is rooted in an indicative: the powers of evil are being vanquished; therefore, live as children of the new age. The author is then led to contrast intoxication from wine with pentecostal ecstasy, which expresses itself here not in glossolalia, but in the more sober manner of "psalms and hymns and spiritual songs" — one of the earliest pieces of evidence we have of the use of hymns in the early community. This passage is thought by some to be part of the *Haustafel* (household code) that follows, for such catechetical patterns are sometimes prefaced by an exhortation to perform one's duty toward the gods (in the pagan *Haustafeln*) or to Yahweh (in the Jewish ones).

Gospel: John 6:51-58

Here at last we reach the definitely eucharistic part of the bread discourse; we move from bread as such to the flesh and blood of the Son of man. As already indicated above (on the 18th Sunday) we tend to regard these verses as an addition by a redactor who however is himself also a member of the Johannine school. We have suggested that the first part is a meditation on the agape-fellowship meal, and the added part a meditation on the eucharist proper. The thought moves from the revelation of the incarnate One as the heavenly wisdom to his sacrificial surrender in the death of the cross. The redactor seeks to balance the one-sidedness of the evangelist's eucharistic theology. For the evangelist appeared to emphasize the incarnation at the expense of the cross, and the agape-fellowship meal and the proclamation of the word at the expense of the eucharist. The redactor's additional material here is derived from the Supper tradition as it had circulated in the Johannine communities ("this is my flesh," "this is my blood," "eat," "drink," and the indication of the soteriological effects of sacramental eating and drinking).

The Homily

If we have been following the readings from the Johannine bread discourse we can move today from a consideration of the presence of Christ in the fellowship meal and the preached word to the sacramental presence of his flesh and blood in the eucharist proper. This is perhaps crude language, from which many modern Christians shrink. (Cf. the recent revision of the Anglican "prayer of humble access" in the first Trial Liturgy of the Episcopal Church, where the Johannine language about eating his flesh and drinking his blood is replaced by the slightly more refined language of "partaking in his body and blood"). Hoskyns however insisted flesh and blood in this context was language "by which Christianity stands or falls" (*Cambridge Sermons*, p. 137):

"By our Christian language, by the express doctrine of the Church and its worship, we are being thrust to the whole relativity of human life, into the life where men are not God, where their ideas and notions are not the absolute Truth of God, where at best men speak in parables, and where their actions are not the righteousness of God, where in fact life passes to death. . . . Into this realm of death the Lord passes with eyes wide open, with inexorable purpose, and into this realm He draws His disciples with Him."

It would be very congenial to have a form of Christian worship consisting of a fellowship meal celebrating Jesus as the bread of life and a proclamation of him as the incarnate wisdom. But our canonical John (whatever the evangelist originally may have planned) goes further than that, and insists that the Christian liturgy moves further to an eating and drinking of the flesh and blood of Jesus, that is, to participating in the sacrifice of Calvary. At a time when the eucharist is being stressed as a messianic banquet and the sacrificial aspect is being played down it is good to be reminded of this other aspect and seek to redress the balance.

TWENTY-FIRST SUNDAY OF THE YEAR

Reading I: Joshua 24:1-2a, 15-17, 18b

For the Old Testament scholar Joshua 24 is highly important in the history of Israelite traditions. It preserves remnants of an ancient liturgy for the renewal of the covenant at Shechem. This tradition stands in conflict with later Deuteronomic theology, and its doctrine of the central sanctuary at Jerusalem. It is believed to have originated from a covenant between the earlier inhabitants of Shechem and the Israelite invaders. The former had worshiped El-berith, the latter Yahweh. The ceremony recalls the choice then made by the two parties. Henceforth Yahweh, the God of the invaders, would be worshiped by both groups.

The appointment of this lesson for today is governed by the parallel between the choice made at Shechem and the choice confronting the disciples after the discourse in John 6. The challenge, "Choose this day whom you will serve," parallels "Will you also go away?", and the response, "We will serve Yahweh because he is our God," parallels Peter's response, "Lord, to whom shall we go? You have the words of eternal life."

Responsorial Psalm: 34:1-2, 15-16, 17-18, 19-20, 21-22

The refrain and stanza I are the same as in last week's responsorial psalm, while the rest of the stanzas are made up from verses not used last week. The new stanzas strike a different note, viz., God's vindication of the righteous sufferer. Some think that stanza 4 (vv. 19-20) rather than Exodus 12:46 is the source of the Old Testament quotation at John 19:36. If this view is correct, it would show that Psalm 34 was used in the early church's passion apologetic. The goodness of the Lord which we taste and see in the eucharist is the goodness manifested in the suffering and vindication of Jesus, the righteous servant of God.

Reading II: Ephesians 5:21-32

Verse 22 marks the beginning of the household code of Ephesians. This forms a major portion of the parenesis in the second half of the letter, and runs through 6:9.

Verse 21 serves as a heading for the household code. The primary principle of the household codes is that of subjection. Early Christianity seems to have taken over these codes from Hellenistic Judaism, which in turn adapted them from the Stoics. They set forth the duties of wives, husbands, parents, children, masters, and slaves. In the New Testament these codes have often been given a Christian veneer, generally by the addition of "in the Lord" to the injunctions. Occasionally, however, as in the present instance, the process of christianization goes much further. Ephesians provides a unique elaboration of marriage as a parable of the relation between Christ and his church. In this theological expansion of the code the author of Ephesians has brought together a remarkable variety of traditions. He takes the statement about the unity of man and wife in marriage from Genesis 2:24. He portrays the church in the language of Levitical purity. The command to love the neighbor in Leviticus 19 provides the basis of verse 27. An early Christian kerygmatic formula is reproduced in verse 25 and a baptismal-liturgical formula in verse 26. In verses 23 and 29 the Pauline figure of the church as the body of Christ reappears, but with Christ at the head of the body, a development which may be of gnostic origin. With these materials the author has skillfully interwoven two parallel themes, the duties of husband and wife and the ecclesiological theme of the relation between Christ and the church. We may sort out the two themes as follows:

22 Wives, be subject to your husbands	22 as to the Lord
23 The husband is the head of the wife	23 as Christ is the head of the church
24 [a repetition of v. 22]	24 the church is subject to Christ

25 Husbands, love your wives	25-27 as Christ loved the church . . . without blemish
28 Husbands should love their wives as their own bodies. He who loves his wife loves himself	
29 A man loves and cherishes his own flesh	29 as Christ does the church
	30 we are members of his body
31 Citation of Genesis 2:24	32 interpreted mystically of Christ and the church

By presenting this passage in two columns we get a clue to the author's procedure. He began with the duty of wife to husband as set forth in the household code with its slight christianization ("as to the Lord"). He then expanded the code by drawing upon a number of kerygmatic, liturgical, and ecclesiological traditions, and then supplemented the household code itself by drawing upon the tradition on the other side of the column. As a result the marriage relationship is transformed from one in which the wife is simply subjected to the husband without qualification into one in which the husband is to devote himself unreservedly to the love of his wife. Thus the household code is turned upside down — the emphasis rests no longer on the duty of the wife to the husband, but on the husband's love for his wife. Finally, the two columns are clinched together by the citation of Genesis 2:24. On the literal level this text speaks of the union of husband and wife. But this is a *mysterion*. It has another, higher level of meaning, portraying the unity between Christ and the church. The author's doctrine of the church is not built up from below, from a natural understanding of marriage. Rather, his understanding of marriage is built from above, from a theological understanding of the "mystical union betwixt Christ and his church."

Gospel: John 6:60-69

This pericope forms the conclusion to the discourse at Capernaum on the bread from heaven. Following as it does verses 51-59, it appears to contradict that section, especially in verse 63. Having insisted in 51c-59 that the believer must eat the flesh and drink the blood of the Son of man in order to have eternal life, Jesus now tells his hearers that the flesh is of no avail. But flesh here is not the eucharistic flesh of 51c-59. As in John 3:6, it means "the natural principle in man which cannot give eternal life" (R. E. Brown). Similarly, spirit here will mean what it means in 3:6, the life-giving Spirit which will be given as a result of the ascension of the Son of man to where he was before (v. 62). Our passage is therefore not speaking of the sacrament but of the reception of the revelation of Jesus as the heavenly wisdom, the bread from heaven. In other words, it refers back to verses 35-50, not to 51c-59, which as we have seen is best understood as a later redactional addition. It is Jesus' claim to be the revelation of God in 35-50 that many of the disciples find to be a hard saying, not the eucharistic teaching of 51c-59. Yet there are some who do accept his claim, namely the twelve. And in a scene parallel to the synoptic episode at Caesarea Philippi, the section concludes with a confession of Peter (68b-69). Thus, as throughout the Fourth Gospel, the division of the spirits is determined by the acceptance or rejection of Jesus as the life-giving revelation of God. The evangelist of course is thinking not only of what happened in Jesus' ministry but of a similar division of spirits in his own community. The many disciples who abandoned Jesus, and Judas Iscariot who was to betray him (v. 64; cf. also vv. 70-71), typify the gnostic docetists in the evangelist's own day.

The Homily

The captions over the Old Testament reading and the gospel rightly focus our attention on the theme of decision in the face of the divine revelation. Can we perhaps see parallels in the life of the church today as the evangelist saw in his? We could look to those who leave the church (or cancel their pledges!) because of the contemporary church's attempt to speak the word of God to the political and social realities of our day, or because the church is seeking to update itself to become a better instrument for the proclamation of the gospel in the modern world.

Alternatively, the epistle reading offers an occasion to speak of Christian marriage. It is important to bring out the chief purpose of the author. The Christian doctrine of marriage is acquired not merely by an empirical study of marriage as a human institution — valid as that is on its own level, like the original household code — but from an awareness of the relation between Christ and his church. Hence the church must preach to the married that the more they know of the relation between Christ and his church through their sacramental experience, the more they will understand the mystery of their own relationship.

TWENTY-SECOND SUNDAY OF THE YEAR ✓

Reading I: Deuteronomy 4:1-2, 6-8

This passage comes from the prologue to the Deuteronomic law. The prohibition to add or substract anything was a regular feature of ancient legal codes (cf. the Code of Hammurabi, where, however, the prohibition comes toward the end, not at the beginning as here). The second paragraph underlines the great privilege Israel enjoys through the possession of the law. The caption emphasizes the first paragraph, the prohibition to add to or subtract from the law, and makes it clear that this reading was chosen to underline the distinction between the commandment of God and the traditions of men which is the main point of the gospel reading.

Responsorial Psalm: 15:2, 3bc-4ab, 4c-5

Almost the same selection from this responsorial psalm was used in the first year at Sunday 16 C. As we noted then, this is one of the so-called entry psalms, sung by the pilgrims as they approached the temple. It describes the character of the pilgrim whom God will accept, a man of justice, sincerity and integrity. The only difference in today's selection is the addition of the first line in the third stanza, "Who swears to his own hurt and does not change." Why is this added today? Is it thought to have some special appropriateness in connection with the first reading? If so, then the idea must be that Israel must not change in its allegiance to the law. She must not change the law by adapting it to new needs. Of course in one sense this is precisely what has to be done. Fulfilling the legal code to the letter in a changed situation can result precisely in disobeying it. In that sense there must be change and adaptation. But it must be responsible change, change undertaken for the better observance of the law under changed conditions, not adaptation of the law to suit one's own interests.

Reading II: James 1:17-18, 21b-22, 27

For the next five weeks the epistle reading will be from the so-called Letter of James. Traditionally this work has been accepted as the work of James the brother of the Lord, though the author simply calls himself quite modestly a servant (slave) of God and of the Lord Jesus Christ. Critical opinion today is divided about the authorship and date. Although some reputable scholars would defend its traditional authenticity and early date, it is to be noted that there were considerable doubts about it even in the early church. Probably it was originally a Hellenistic Jewish document containing twelve exhortations based on the names of the twelve patriarchs in Genesis 49, and slightly christianized in the post-Pauline period by a Hellenistic Jewish Christian teacher. It enshrines a good deal of wisdom teaching and brings this to bear against the antinomians (gnostics?) who in a later generation were appealing to a (wrongly interpreted) Paul. We would date it toward the end of the first century.

The present excerpt is from the second exhortation supposedly based on the name Simeon (*shamah* — doers, not *hearers* only). The sentence beginning "Of his own will . . ." is a place where the author has christianized the exhortation by inserting a reference to baptism. It is then that the "word" — i.e., the gospel — was implanted, but it has to be constantly received anew and made the basis for Christian action. The word for "religion" is equivalent to cultus. The true cultus, James insists, consists in ethical obedience. James does not intend to give an exhaustive description of such obedience, but merely to illustrate it. He does not mean to decry the importance of liturgy (after all, he mentions baptism and the hearing of the word). But he insists that the performance of these must lead to a life of moral obedience, and cannot be a substitute for it (cf. the Old Testament prophets).

Gospel: Mark 7:1-8, 14-15, 21-23

Like so many passages in the gospel tradition, this pericope has a long and complicated history behind it. To begin with, the parenthesis in verses 3-4 is a note by the evangelist for the benefit of his Gentile readers, who were of course unfamiliar with Jewish customs. Other features in the passage point to the Hellenistic Jewish Christian community before Mark. The quotation of Isaiah 29:13 follows the Septuagint, not the Massoretic text used by our Lord and the earliest Palestinian community. The quotation does not altogether fit the situation, which is not a matter of honoring with the lips. Again, the distinction between the written law and the tradition does not adequately represent Jesus' teaching on the law, which is critical even of the law itself, when it is used as a cloak for disobedience. It represents the rationalistic approach of Hellenistic Judaism. The situation may well be an authentic memory about Jesus' earthly activity, but the Isaiah citation and the pronouncement of verse 8 are probably from the later Hellenistic Jewish community. The second pronouncement (vv. 14-16) which is addressed to the whole people, has, however, every mark of an authentic parable of Jesus. It could have been his response to precisely the type of situation indicated in the introduction to the pericope. The disciples are accused of not washing before dinner as the purity laws require. Jesus replies that it is not what a man eats that defiles him. It is man's inner purity, issuing in outward behavior that matters. Finally the catalogue of vices (vv. 21-23) was a common teaching device in the catechesis first of Hellenistic Jewish and then of Gentile Christianity.

The Homily

It is clear from the captions to the Old Testament and the gospel readings that the church recommends the homilist to deal with the antithesis between God's commandments and human ecclesiastical tradition.

Our critical analysis has shown that this antithesis comes from the Hellenistic Jewish church rather than from Jesus himself. This prevents us from assuming that the distinction between commandment and tradition is a complete answer to the question of radical obedience. It is, however, a distinction that has to be made where human traditions obscure the will of God, which is more clearly enunciated in the original commandments. The epistle reading suggests cultus and ritual as one area where this distinction between the commandment of God and the traditions of men may be usefully applied in the interests of radical obedience. Cultic and ritual traditions have constantly to be under review lest in course of time they actually impede the real end of cultus and ritual, which is to draw us to a more radical obedience to the will of God. The homilist might either (1) critically review inherited cultic or ritual observances at points where they no longer serve to the higher end of obedience to the will of God; or (2) interpret the abandonment of venerable cultic or ritual practices in recent years where they had become barriers to obedience and ends in themselves.

TWENTY-THIRD SUNDAY OF THE YEAR

Reading I: Isaiah 35:4-7a

Although this passage occurs in the first part of Isaiah, among the prophecies of the preexilic Isaiah of Jerusalem, it breathes the spirit of Deutero-Isaiah and, if not by him, must be contemporary with him and from the same school. Its life situation is the impending return from exile (cf. especially vv. 4b, 7b). This passage has been chosen today because of verses 5 and 6, which speak of the healing miracles that will accompany the return. When we remember that for Deutero-Isaiah the return was the final redemptive act of God, we can understand how early Christianity saw in this passage (like Is 29:18 and 61:1-3) predictions of Jesus' messianic healings. This was clearly in the mind of Mark (or of his tradition) when he chose the highly unusual word *mogilalon* (literally: "with difficulty of speech") to describe the deaf mute whose healing is recounted in today's gospel reading, for *mogilalon* is precisely the same Greek word which is used in the Septuagint for the word "dumb" in Isaiah 35:6. Thus this passage is eminently fitted for use with today's gospel reading.

Responsorial Psalm: 146:6c-7, 8-9a, 9bc-10

Selections of this psalm are used on other occasions in the lectionary, but particularly noteworthy is the use of the same selection on Advent 3 A (but with a refrain more suited to Advent) as a response to Isaiah 35:1-6a, 10, which is almost the same Old Testament reading as today's. It is a psalm of praise for the healing power of Yahweh, especially for his opening of the eyes of the blind. Unfortunately the psalm does not mention the opening of the ears of the deaf and the releasing of the tongues of the dumb, but that may be taken as implied.

Reading II: James 2:1-5

This is the exhortation said to be based on the name Judah (=Lord of glory, Gn 49:8-12). It is an exhortation to the right treatment of the poor. Because the early Christians for the most part belonged to the powerless classes of the Roman empire, the New Testament shows very little concern for social justice as compared with Old Testament prophets. But James' church consists of rich and poor members, and a concern for the proper respect of the poor as persons immediately surfaces. Yet there is no indication that the wealthy members of James' church had any political power, and therefore there is little suggestion of real social ethic. The utmost that this passage suggests is that the silence of the New Testament on such matters is no indication that the gospel has no social implications. It all depends on the conditions under which the church has to operate, which vary greatly between time and place.

Note further how James, who on the surface looks so moralistic, again bases his exhortation on the truths of the gospel: wealthier Christians should show concern for the poorer members because (in baptism) God has chosen the poor to inherit the kingdom.

Gospel: Mark 7:31-37

This is one of the two miracle stories peculiar to Mark (the other is the healing of the blind man of Bethsaida in Mark 8:22-23). Both stories represent our Lord as employing a physical healing technique, and perhaps for that reason did not appeal to the later evangelists, who preferred to depict him as healing solely through a word.

Like so many of the other gospel pericopes, this story seems to have passed through a number of successive stages:

1. An original exorcism by Jesus (its exorcistic character is suggested by the words, "his tongue was released").

2. The Palestinian church, which interpreted Jesus in terms of the eschatological prophet-servant, wrote up the story as a fulfillment of Isaiah 35.

3. The Hellenistic church, which interpreted Jesus in terms of the wonder-worker or divine man, preserved the foreign word, Ephatha, thus creating an impression of the wonder-worker's mysterious power, and emphasizing the physical means of healing (putting his fingers into his ears, spitting and touching his tongue).

4. The evangelist gives to the story a fresh meaning by the place where he locates it in his continuous narrative. It symbolizes what is happening to the disciples (cf. 8:22-26). They have been deaf to Jesus' word (7:18a), and were as yet unable to make any confession of faith in him. Eventually, however, at Caesarea Philippi, it will begin to dawn upon them who Jesus really is, and Peter will make his confession of faith. Thus the ears of the disciples will be opened, their tongues will be released and they will speak plainly, declaring through Peter their spokesman, "You are the Messiah" (see next week's gospel reading).

The Homily

The Old Testament reading, the psalm, and the gospel suggest the theme of the messianic miracle by which men come to hear the word of God and respond through confession of faith. This is what happens in the liturgy.

Today's gospel lesson used to occur in the Book of Common Prayer at Trinity 12, and in the Church of England that Sunday was popularly known as Ephatha Sunday, and dedicated to a special concern for the deaf and dumb. The meaning of the gospel miracles is not of course exhausted in humanitarian concern, for they proclaim the ultimate messianic healing, but as a parabolic expression of the meaning of the parable such humanitarian concern has a legitimate place.

The epistle reading provides an opportunity to speak of sensitivity to the poor as a continuing aspect of the Christian gospel. For God in Christ has chosen the poor to be heirs of God's kingdom. It would be appropriate to explore the mode in which that sensitivity should be expressed in a democracy where Christians have political power (as opposed to their situation in the Roman empire, in which the Letter of James was written).

TWENTY-FOURTH SUNDAY OF THE YEAR

Reading I: Isaiah 50:5-9a

The third servant song of Deutero-Isaiah is also used on Palm Sunday where it ends at verse 7, and was commented upon in the first year at that Sunday. The additional words included here run from "he who vindicates me is near" through "who will declare me guilty." These words tie in with the passion prediction in the gospel where Jesus confidently affirms his certainty of vindication ("after three days he will rise again").

Responsorial Psalm: 116:1-2, 3-4, 5-6, 8-9

On the other occasions when this psalm is used in the Sunday lectionary (Holy Thursday, Lent 2 B, Corpus Christi), the selections emphasize the theme of Yahweh's vindication of his servant. He was encompassed by the snares of death and the pangs of sheol (stanza 2) and cried to Yahweh, but God has heard him (stanzas 1, 3, 4). The psalm thus speaks of death and resurrection. The passion prediction in the gospel asserts that the Son of man "must" suffer. This "must" is equivalent to the early Christian formula, "according to the scriptures." It is not however immediately obvious what Old Testament scriptures speak of the death and resurrection of the Messiah. But the servant passages of Deutero-Isaiah, and the psalms about God's vindication of the righteous sufferer, of which this is one, provide a pattern of divine action which finds its fulfillment in Jesus Christ.

Reading II: James 2:14-18

This section on faith and works is said to correspond to Rachel, who here takes the place of Dan. Because of her barrenness (cf. Jas 2:17),

Rachel gave her maidservant to Jacob, and Dan was the fruit of this association. The kind of faith which James has in view is not the personal acceptance in God's saving act of which Paul generally speaks. With that kind of faith there could be no question of its dissociation from good works. Paul can speak of this kind of faith as naturally and inevitably working through love, and producing the firstfruits of the Spirit. James is thinking of a notional assent to orthodox formulae: see James 2:19. Such faith, if it be genuine, is bound to issue in good works, otherwise it is barren. Here James agrees with the best teaching of Judaism, with Jesus and with Paul and 1 John.

Gospel: Mark 8:27-35

The Matthean version of the confession of St. Peter is used on Sunday 21 A, and has been commented upon above. Mark's version is clearly more primitive. Nevertheless, it too is the result of a process of development.

To reconstruct the original historical event we start with the fact that it is inconceivable that the post-Easter church should have invented the Satan saying, given the fact that Peter was their most revered leader. Jesus must actually have called Peter Satan. But why did he do so? As the text stands, he does so in response to the prediction of the passion: Peter could accept the idea of Jesus as Messiah, but not as a suffering Messiah. But the prediction of the passion is clearly a post-Easter creation. It makes Jesus identify himself openly with the Son of man and shows a clear knowledge of the events of the passion and resurrection, reminiscent of the passion narratives in the gospels. We take it then to be a *vaticinium ex eventu*. The command to silence is a typical piece of Marcan redaction, reflecting his theme of the messianic secret. Remove these two elements, the charge to secrecy and the passion prediction, and the Satan saying follows directly upon Peter's "confession." Why then should Jesus reject it? He would do so if the term Messiah meant a political, nationalistic leader. Jesus consistently rejected that program as a diabolical attempt to divert him from his God-given mission. Given this meaning of Messiah — and this is the meaning which was current in Jesus' day, before it was appropriated for him after Easter — the Satan saying becomes intelligible. In the light of the post-Easter faith, however, Peter's confession became a positive confession, acceptable to Christ, and the Satan saying is therefore transferred to Peter's rejection of the idea of the suffering Messiah by means of the passion prediction. Finally, Mark introduces the motif of secrecy, to insure that the confession "You are the Messiah" can only be applied to the crucified and risen one, not to Jesus in his earthly ministry which would make him merely a divine miracle-worker. Such seems to be the history of the tradition.

A second scene follows, the saying about the cost of discipleship. Some have thought the saying about taking up one's cross must reflect a post-Easter situation, but the Greek word *stauros* probably meant originally not the gibbet but the taw (T) or Chi (X) — viz., the sign of ownership with which cattle were branded. As such it means here God's seal or sign. In this sense it means "surrender of self-assertion before God and surrender of the autonomous freedom which directs itself against God" (Erich Dinkler). It thus becomes intelligible as an authentic sayings of the earthly Jesus. After Good Friday, however, it acquires a new meaning: assuming one's cross, i.e., the life of suffering and martyrdom in union with the cross of Christ.

If it is the evangelist Mark who has combined the two traditions, the confession of Peter and the saying about cross-bearing, then the whole pericope as it now stands is directed against a wrong understanding of christological confession and apostleship, one which interprets Jesus as a miracle-working divine man, and conceives apostleship likewise in terms of the divine miracle-worker. In place of this Mark puts the confession of Jesus as Christ crucified and apostleship as following him in bearing the cross, manifesting the dying of Jesus in our mortal bodies, as Paul phrased it.

The Homily

The Old Testament reading, psalm, and gospel focus upon the christological confession of Jesus as crucified and vindicated, and the analogous understanding of apostleship. These are profound theological themes, but not easily translated into a homily for a contemporary congregation. Perhaps the simplest line would be to take Jesus' word about carrying the cross and bring out the understanding of Christian existence that it implies: surrender of self-assertion before God and surrender of that autonomous freedom which directs itself against God. This is the pattern of existence exemplified by the suffering servant, by Jesus, and by Peter. It is also meant to be the pattern for all Christian existence.

The epistle reading gives an opportunity to deal with the question of faith and works. The homilist should make clear that there is no ultimate contradiction between Paul and James on this point. (The subject of justification is a more difficult problem and one that has divided the churches of the Reformation from Rome, but fortunately that is not raised until the passage which follows today's selection.) The homilist should contrast the conception of faith which James has in view (*fides quae creditur*) with Paul's dominant understandiing (*fides qua creditur*) and make clear that where faith is interpreted in James' sense it can easily become a moribund orthodoxy which needs to be quickened into life by a devotion to good works.

TWENTY-FIFTH SUNDAY OF THE YEAR

Reading I: Wisdom 2:12, 17-20

This figure in the Book of Wisdom shows close affinities to the righteous man of the psalms, who is vindicated by God, and to the suffering servant of Deutero-Isaiah. In fact, one of the verses in this chapter not used in this selection (v. 13) actually calls the righteous sufferer God's *pais* (son, though it could mean servant). It is a picture of the true Israelite, the tenor of whose life is a standing protest against the lawlessness of the ungodly (probably the apostate Jews of Alexandria). They are irritated by the silent protest of his life and conspire to kill him. The parallels between this picture and Christ's passion (though cf. also Plato's Republic, which says something similar with Socrates in view) have led this passage to be regarded as a prediction of the passion. (In the Book of Common Prayer it is one of the lessons appointed for Morning Prayer on Good Friday.) It is perhaps a pity that the selection here stops short of the proclamation of God's vindication of his righteous servant (v. 22). It is obviously chosen to go with Mark's second passion prediction, which occurs in today's gospel reading. That prediction speaks of vindication as well as suffering.

Responsorial Psalm: 54:1-2, 3, 4 and 6

This psalm is also appointed for Good Friday in the Book of Common Prayer, and thus serves fittingly as a response to the Wisdom passage. The righteous man cries out to God for help against his enemies and expresses confidence in the divine vindication. For the Christian it speaks of the resurrection of Jesus Christ and of every Christian from his spiritual enemies.

Reading II: James 3:16-4:3

If we follow the division of James according to the twelve patriarchs (see Sunday 22 above) we should make a rather different division here, treating 3:13-18 as a single exhortation revolving around the distinction between the earthly and the heavenly wisdom (Leah corresponding to the earthly and Rachel to the heavenly wisdom) and 4:1-12 on the false and true warfare (Gad). So the first paragraph of today's reading will belong to the 7th exhortation and the second paragraph to the 8th. But the two exhortations are linked by 3:18: those who follow heavenly wisdom will sow in a spirit of peace and reap the harvest of righteousness. These words pave the way for the exhortation on the wrong warfare (the ensuing part about the true warfare comes in v. 7, "resist the devil and he will flee from you"), but it is unfortunately not included.

Gospel: Mark 9:30-37

The structure of this pericope is as remarkable as that of last week's gospel. First, we have a passion prediction (the second of three in Mark), followed by an exhortation to live out the cross in Christian life. Here this exhortation is expressed in terms of servanthood and humility. It is of course the evangelist himself, not historical reminiscence, which is responsible for the ordering of the material. Mark is again polemicizing against the false teachers of his time, who understood Christ as a divine miracle-worker and themselves as his successors. Against this false christology and false concept of ministry the evangelist sets the ideal of the suffering servant, of service and humility exemplified in the cross.

The Homily

The gospel suggests reflection today on the servanthood of the church and its ministry, based on the suffering servanthood of her Lord. Vatican II sought to replace the ideal of a triumphalist church with that of the servant church. How is this being implemented today in the pattern of ministry and in the life of the congregation?

The epistle reading would give an opportunity to make a plea for peace in the congregation if there is internal strife, to trace it to its roots in jealousy, selfish ambition, covetousness — which includes desire for power as well as money (Watergate!) — and passion. One can avoid being merely moralistic by rooting the exhortation to peace in the concept of the heavenly wisdom which is the gift of God.

Reading I: Numbers 11:25-29

This is a somewhat confused story. Moses has appointed the seventy elders to assist him in governing the people in the wilderness. They were given a share in some of the "spirit" of Moses to assist them. This resulted in a temporary manifestation of charismatic prophecy among the seventy. After it ceased, two men, Eldad and Medad, received a belated illapse of the spirit and likewise engaged in charismatic prophecy. (This is the confusing part.) It appears that Eldad and Medad were not members of the seventy, i.e., not in the legitimate succession. An overzealous young man urged Moses to stop them from exercising an unauthorized ministry, but Moses refused: The Spirit cannot be confined to the regularly appointed offices. Its freedom to blow where it listeth is a pointer to the day when the whole people of God will prophesy — an aspiration which Christian faith can see fulfilled at Pentecost. *N 13*

The caption does not adequately express the reason for the choice of this reading. The question is not "Who decrees that all men may prophesy," but, "Does God confine the gift of his Spirit to authorized channels?" It is the question raised in today's gospel.

Responsorial Psalm: 19:7, 9, 11-12, 13

Although selections from this psalm have been used on other occasions (Easter Vigil, Sunday 3 C), this is the only place in the Sunday series that the very fine prayer that we may be cleansed from our secret faults, especially the sin of pride, occurs. (The present writer remembers being told by the conductor of his pre-ordination retreat that this prayer should be constantly on the lips of a priest.) Its relation to the Old Testament reading is not immediately apparent, but perhaps if Moses had used his authority to stop unauthorized charismatics it would have been an expression of the sin of clerical pride and a misuse of clerical power!

Reading II: James 5:1-6

This exhortation, the tenth of the series in James, is allegedly based on the name of Asher (Gn 49:20). It is a warning to the rich against exploiting their employees. Like the selection for Sunday 23, this is one of the few New Testament passages which show concern for social justice (the reason for this comparative silence were indicated in our comments on Jas 2:1-5). Again, the author is careful to provide a theological basis for his social ethic: the cry of the exploited has reached the ears of the

Lord of Sabaoth. The divine title deliberately recalls the Old Testament prophets and their social teaching.

Gospel: Mark 9:38-43, 45, 47-48

[Note: the apparent omission of verses 44 and 46 is due to the fact that these verses are mere repetitions of verse 48, which do not appear in the earliest and best manuscripts.]

This passage combines two different traditions. The first is the pericope of the strange exorcist, the second, a series of warnings against offences, which appear in a different context in Q (Lk 17:1-2) and in yet another context in the Matthean redaction of Q (5:29-30). Mark's arrangement has the effect of making the sayings against offences a comment on the episode of the strange exorcist. To forbid the strange exorcist would be making one of these little ones to stumble, an effect to be avoided at all costs.

The Homily

The combination of the Old Testament reading, the psalm and the gospel offers exciting possibilities. We have here a warning against clerical arrogance which refuses to recognize the charisms possessed by members of the church (or indeed of people outside the church's fellowship, cf. the gospel) and to see in their activities a genuine witness to the work of the Spirit and the cause of Christ.

The epistle reading would provide the opportunity for a sermon on social justice. While in the U.S., as in most Western countries, the trade union movement provides adequate insurance against exploitation of the employees by employers, recent reports publicized in the *Manchester Guardian* have turned up evidence that there is serious underpayment (below subsistence level) of African labor in South Africa by British and American firms. The Christian churches in this country should speak out and act as shareholders against this, armed with the authority of James 5:1-6.

Sundays 27 B to 30 B

Reading I: Genesis 2:18-24

As the reader is doubtless aware, this passage comes from the J story of creation. It is an earlier tradition than the P creation story in Genesis 1. Whereas the P story pictures man as the culmination of creation, the J story makes the same theological point by picturing him as its center. Thus in the P story man is created *after* the animals, and in both male and female sexes. Here, however, man (male) is created first, the animals are then created to serve him (naming them indicates control over them) and finally woman is created from his "rib." The meaning of this word is uncertain, but it is intended to suggest the common humanity of man and woman (as the P story also does in a different way), as well as the derivative status of woman in relation to man. Thus it was the J story, rather than the P story, which provided the New Testament writers with materials to reinforce the then current view of woman's subordination to man (cf. 1 Cor 11:8-9; 1 Tm 2:13). However, the main thrust of Genesis is not the subordination of woman, but her complementariness to the man. Unlike the animals, she is a real consort — a help fit for him: the Authorized Version has "meet" for fit, giving rise to the popular nonword "help-meet." Verse 24 is a conclusion drawn from the story of woman's creation as just described.

The little word "therefore" in verse 24 is the linchpin of the whole pericope. The story of the "rib" is an aetiological myth designed to explain why it is that a man leaves his parents and marries a woman. It is because man and woman share a common humanity and are complementary to each other, and therefore neither is complete without the other. "One flesh" means more than merely physical union, though it includes that. "Flesh" in Hebrew means the whole human person in contrast to God, man in his humanness with all its historical limitations (Paul will

431

later add the notion of sinfulness to the word "flesh"). Flesh therefore includes the "spiritual" aspects of human nature as well as the physical.

Responsorial Psalm: 128:1-2, 3, 4-5, 6

This psalm portrays an idealized picture of family life in Israel. It also breathes the spirit of Deuteronomy, with its rather naive belief that devotion to the Torah ("fears the Lord . . . walks in his ways") is rewarded in this world with prosperity and happiness. But the idea that piety and virtue are the foundations of family life is not obsolete. As used today, this psalm follows suitably on the Genesis story of the institution of marriage with the gospel's reiteration of Genesis, followed in the longer form by the pericope about Jesus' blessing of the little children (see below).

Reading II: Hebrews 2:9-11

Today we begin a course of six readings from the Epistle to the Hebrews. A few words about our critical presuppositions in dealing with this document will therefore be in order. We would date it about 85 and regard it as written to Greek-speaking Jewish Christians in Italy (probably Rome). These addressees (1) form an esoteric group within the church; (2) have stagnated instead of growing to Christian maturity. The writer copes with this situation by an elaborate exposition of the theme of Christ's high priesthood, here used as the basis for a series of pep talks based on a typology of the church as the "wandering people of God" (Käsemann). Just as the Israelites wandered in the wilderness between Egypt and their entry into the promised land, so the Christian community exists "between the times," between the Christ event and the parousia. Israel stagnated in the wilderness and was punished. How much worse will it be for the Christian community if it neglects an even greater salvation, that effected through the priestly work of Christ.

In the first three readings the author is building up the case for Jesus' eschatological high priesthood. Although not of the tribe of Levi, he has all the qualifications for the job, including the sharing of our common humanity. He and we have a common origin, and he calls us brothers (v. 9).

This is of course only one side of Hebrews' Christology, for Christ has another origin, too. He was also the preexistent Son through whom the world was created (Heb 1:1-3). Christ was even made perfect (!) through suffering. But "perfect" here means not moral perfection, as though he were not morally perfect at the outset but had to become so. Rather, to become perfect means to achieve a goal or destiny. It was only by suffering that the Christ could perfectly achieve our salvation, and could become our high priest (which is a functional, not ontological category). In order to do his work effectively, i.e., to plead for us before the Father, the high priest must have an experimental knowledge of all human infirmities.

Gospel: Mark 10:2-16 (long form); 10:2-12 (short form)

The long form comprises two pericopes, the first on divorce, the second on the blessing of the children. A form-critical analysis would suggest that we have here part of an early catechism, built up of originally separate traditions about Jesus. A section on marriage would be followed immediately by a section on the family.

Jesus' prohibition of divorce is one of the most widely attested sayings in the tradition, being found in Paul (1 Cor 7:10), Mark-Matthew (the present passage and its parallel in Mt 19:3-9) and Q (Mt 5:31-32/Lk 16:18). The original Q form, best preserved by Luke, enunciates an absolute, unqualified prohibition. Paul, Mark, and Matthew modify the commandment in various ways. Paul introduces the "Pauline privilege" (making a Christian convert free to remarry if the non-Christian partner divorces him/her). By the device of secret teaching, Mark extends the prohibition of divorce on the part of the husband to divorce on the part of the wife, thus adapting Jesus' prohibition to Roman law, which, unlike Jewish law, allowed a wife to divorce her husband. Matthew in turn modifies the commandment by introducing into both his Marcan and Q sources the famous "Matthean exception," permitting divorce on the ground of the wife's unchastity (*porneiā*). It is clear that when the church came to treat Jesus eschatological enunciation of the absolute prohibition as a community law, it was compelled to adapt and even to modify its absolute character in various ways. The Marcan version recognizes that divorce was allowed in the Mosaic period because of the hardness of men's hearts, i.e., sin. Since sin is in principle done away with in Christ, a reversion to the prefall condition, where divorce is unknown, becomes feasible. But the New Testament church realized that despite the new life in Christ men were still open to temptation and sin, and if Christ's absolute prohibition was to be treated as a law, concessions would have to be made. The point is not that the particular concessions made in the New Testament are valid for all time, and these only, but that the New Testament grants

to the church the authority to make concessions that are pastorally necessary, while at the same time keeping Jesus' absolute prohibition before
men and women, making it clear that anything short of radical obedience
is sinful in the eyes of God, and therefore in need of forgiveness.

The pericope about the blessing of the children has its nucleus in the
saying about receiving the kingdom of God as a little child, a saying also
attested in a variant form by the Johannine tradition (Jn 3:3). The combination of this saying with the story of Jesus blessing the children may
have been taken as a justification for the early church's practice of baptizing the children of Christian converts (so J. Jeremias).

The Homily

The combination of the Old Testament lesson and the gospel permits a
treatment of marriage as a state of life created by God himself. Marriage,
in other words, is not a mere human ordinance which can be abolished
at will, as many seem to think today. True, marriage as God intended it
in creation can never be fully equated with the social institutionalization
of it in any given period of history. It is often the current institutionalized
form of marriage that young people are really rejecting, not marriage as
intended by God. The Bible, however, affirms that marriage is not a human option but a divine creation. Christian theology has expressed this in
various ways, e.g., in terms of natural law, as an ordinance of creation, or
more recently as a divine mandate (D. Bonhoeffer).

The reading from Hebrews offers an opportunity to grapple with the
full humanity of our Lord. Anyone who has read John A. T. Robinson's
The Human Face of God may be moved to do this. The New Testament
is emphatic that the humanity of Jesus was full and undiminished, and
that his divinity must never be taken as a presupposition into which our
understanding of Jesus' human history must be forced. But at the same
time, the divine which is manifested in Jesus is full and complete for its
purpose at every stage of his mission. Note how Hebrews can allow
1:1-4 and 2:10 to stand side by side, without letting the one compromise
the other: the heavenly origin of Jesus and his history must be asserted
along with their completely human origin.

√ TWENTY-EIGHTH SUNDAY OF THE YEAR

Reading I: Wisdom 7:7-11

The tradition of comparing wisdom and material wealth to the disad-
vantage of the latter goes back to Solomon's prayer in 1 Kings 3:6-9. The

comparison becomes a commonplace in wisdom literature (the price of wisdom is above rubies), and matches the gospel story of the Rich Young Man.

Responsorial Psalm: 90:12-13, 14-15, 16-17

Little is known about the origin of this psalm, familiar to many generations of Anglicans at funerals (but less used today). As the first stanza shows, it is influenced by the wisdom theology ("that we may get a heart of wisdom"). This is its link with the prayer of Solomon, and one might have expected the refrain to highlight this point.

Reading II: Hebrews 4:12-13

The New Testament teaching about the word of God takes for granted what is said about it in the Old Testament. There, God's word is an effective power which intervenes in the affairs of men, and particularly in Israel's salvation history. It effects what it says (Is 55:10-11). The present passage deepens the Old Testament teaching. The word's effects extend to the very heart of the individual believer. And whereas in the Old Testament the word of God was primarily his word announced by the prophets — a word which had in the first instance to do with Israel's contemporary history, interpreting it as judgment or salvation — the word of God in the New Testament is the gospel message. This gives us the context of our present passage. The addressees of Hebrews are drifting away from the gospel through boredom and stagnation (their behavior is typified by the murmuring of the Israelites in the wilderness). They are warned that the gospel is not something to be trifled with. Failure to persevere in faith and to develop towards maturity incur just as sharp a judgment as willful rejection of it in the first place.

Gospel: Mark 10:17-30 (long form); 17-27 (short form)

The long form of this reading represents a combination of three units of material: (1) the Rich Young Man (this is the usual name of the pericope, though only Matthew calls him a young man) (vv. 17-22); (2) the comparison of entry into the kingdom of God to a camel going through the eye of a needle (vv. 23-27); (3) the saying on the rewards of discipleship (vv. 28-31). The shorter form is obtained by omitting the third unit.

These somewhat disparate pieces of tradition have been combined to form a sort of catechesis on the Christian attitude to wealth. Of these items, the first is clearly the most important, and we shall concentrate upon it.

To begin with, we need to dispose of a preliminary problem. It has long been a difficulty for piety and orthodoxy that Jesus should have rejected the address, Good Teacher, with the reply that none is good save God alone. Was not Jesus good, and was he not God? Already Matthew felt something of this difficulty, for he substitutes, "Why do you ask me concerning that which is good?" Once more, however, we have to remind ourselves that we fall into difficulties if we approach the history of Jesus with the presuppositions of Christian piety or later dogmatics. We have to approach him first as a real human being, reacting as a real human being, especially as a devout Jew would, to flattery or insincerity, and as a prophet confronting men with the goodness of God alone. Later on, piety and dogmatics will discover the sinlessness of Jesus and his deity in that true humanity.

In seeking to understand this episode it is important to divest ourselves of unconscious memories of Matthew's version. There Jesus presents the renunciation of wealth and personal discipleship as counsels of perfection: "If you would be perfect . . ." (Mt 19:21). In other words, it is not necessary to salvation to renounce all wealth and follow Jesus in that particular way. Here, however, it is a challenge to radical decision in face of the coming of God's kingdom. This absolute challenge is far more in accord with Jesus' eschatological preaching. Note, however, that the renunciation of wealth is not an end in itself, but only a precondition for following Jesus. This particular man has to renounce what was an impediment for him in order to obey the command, Follow me. It is the life of discipleship, not the renunciation of wealth *per se*, that leads to eternal life. It is not enough to obey the Mosaic law in order to enter eternal life. Beyond all that it is necessary to accept Jesus' eschatological message and to follow him in the way of discipleship. This is one of the gospel episodes which show the high degree of continuity which exists between Jesus' proclamation of the kingdom of God and Paul's preaching of justification.

The Homily

Once again we have the choice between the Old Testament lesson and the gospel on the one hand and the epistle reading on the other. The first of these choices confronts us with the subject of riches as an obstacle to Christian discipleship. For some this can mean a complete renunciation (monasticism). But such renunciation is not an end in itself, but only a presupposition for life in discipleship. To most it will mean, not renunciation but stewardship of wealth. It is following Jesus that matters, and all Christians are called to that.

The epistle reading provides an opportunity to speak about the biblical understanding of the word of God. It would be all too easy here to speak in abstractions, and the only way to avoid this is by paying close attention to the concrete situation in which the author of Hebrews is writing (see commentary above). The situation of the church today has certain analogies with the situation of the church in Hebrews. We too are disillusioned. There is a certain loss of morale. Only by emphasizing the finality of Christ's claim and the dire consequences of backsliding can this state of affairs be overcome. Yet the author of Hebrews knew that a mere pep talk was not enough. It must be based on an exposition of the finality of the Christ event.

TWENTY-NINTH SUNDAY OF THE YEAR ✓

Reading I: Isaiah 53:10-11

We have commented in the past on the fourth servant song, especially in the Holy Week readings. This extract is chosen because it contains the key-word "many": by his knowledge shall the righteous one, my servant, make many to be accounted righteous. In later Judaism rabbinic comment interpreted "many" here to mean, not some, but all, i.e., the nations of the world, thus ascribing universal significance to the servant's work (the servant in rabbinic interpretation was not the Messiah, but Israel). In the Christian application of this prophecy to Christ, the universality of his redeeming work is expressed by the use of "many" from the servant song, as in the gospel reading for today (Mk 10:45).

Responsorial Psalm: 33:4-5, 18-19, 20, 22

Psalm 33 is a hymn of praise suitable for any occasion. The choice of selections from it for today does not appear to be motivated by anything in the accompanying readings, unless it be that we are meant to have in mind the servant of the Old Testament reading who waits for God's vindication of him from his unmerited sufferings.

Reading II: Hebrews 4:14-16

These verses take up the theme of Christ's full humanity, which was touched upon in reading II two weeks ago. They affirm that Christ is fully qualified to be high priest because he shares our common humanity, for this enables him to sympathize with our weakness. He knows what we are from his own personal experience. More than that. He has been tempted *in every respect* as we are, yet without sinning. How far are we meant to take "in every respect" literally? Several writers have recently seized upon this phrase and extended it to include sexual temptation. Now it is quite obvious that the writer of Hebrews did not arrive at this conviction by examining every phase of our Lord's inner life. The evidence was not at his disposal anyway, for the gospel tradition shows practically no interest in the psychological experience of Jesus. The case is similar to the ensuing phrase, "yet without sinning," a conviction shared by other New Testament writers and therefore part of the common early Christian tradition. No one ever examined every overt act our Lord did, and concluded that he was sinless. The clue to the meaning of his statements is to be found in the temptation stories of the gospels. Each of these temptations was concerned with the fulfillment of Jesus' role in salvation history — in post-Easter terms, with his messianic vocation. The temptations were temptations to abandon that role and follow a different line. Jesus' sinlessness, accordingly, means his total commitment to his Father's call to perform this unique function in salvation history. Speculations as to whether Jesus underwent any temptations unrelated to his messianic vocation, though prompted by this rhetorical statement of Hebrews, is for the New Testament kerygmatically irrelevant. If we ask, Was our Lord subject to sexual temptation? we are asking a question which the New Testament is not concerned to ask.

That may be disappointing to our post-Freudian world (and for Christians who want to be with it), but perhaps that is in itself a judgment upon our contemporary obsessions.

Gospel: Mark 10:35-45 (long form); 10:42-45 (short form)
This pericope consists of two units of material, the Zebedees' question and the saying about true greatness. The shorter form contains only the second of these units. Before Mark, the Zebedees' question was probably an independent piece of tradition, whose preservation in the church was due to a biographical interest in the fate of John; church tradition is ambiguous, part of it ascribing to John likewise an early martyrdom, the main stream identifying him with the author of the Johannine writings who allegedly lived to a very old age. Mark uses this traditional saying as an introduction to the saying on true greatness. It is part of Mark's use of the disciples throughout his gospel as symbols of the dangers to which the

church in his own day was exposed. These dangers were twofold: a fascination by the "divine man" Christology, and dismay at the prospect of persecution. These two concerns provide the background for Mark's use of the two elements of material at that point. This story forms the climax of Mark's central section (Mk 8:22–10:45) in which he counters the twin heresies afflicting his church with the proclamation of Jesus as the Son of man who is to be crucified (as opposed to Christ as the divine man or miracle-worker) and the Christian life as a challenge to take up one's cross and follow him.

The Homily

The Old Testament reading and gospel set before us the picture of Christ the suffering servant as the model for Christian existence. Mark saw this as a rebuke to the "heresy" that afflicted his church. It would be appropriate for the homilist to identify something in the life of the contemporary church which parallels the heresy of Mark's church (triumphalism? clericalism? or something on the local level?) and suggest ways in which the church must seek to become the servant church.

If the homilist is following the readings from Hebrews, he may wish to explore the implications of the statement that Christ was tempted in every respect as we are yet without sin, seeking to draw out first its christological implications and limitations and secondly its devotional value.

THIRTIETH SUNDAY OF THE YEAR ✓
Reading I: Jeremiah 31:7-9
This passage is part of the second of a series of four poems celebrating the return from the Babylonian exile. These poems are obviously akin to Deutero-Isaiah, though their exact literary relationship to that work is uncertain. Perhaps the four hymns are products of the Deutero-Isaianic school which somehow got attached to the prophecies of Jeremiah, as an attempt to relieve that prophet's preoccupation with the decline and fall of the southern kingdom, and the adjustment to life in exile. However, Jeremiah was certainly hopeful of the eventual restoration of his people as is indicated in the prophecy of the new covenant which comes later in this chapter. Like a similar hymn of the return in Isaiah 35, this hymn stresses the presence of the weak among the returning people, the blind and the lame, nursing and pregnant mothers. In pictorial language this underlines the *sola gratia* aspect of the return. It is the mention of

the blind here that has doubtless caused the selection of this passage to match the healing of the blind Bartimaeus.

Responsorial Psalm: 126:1-2ab, 2cd-3, 4-5, 6

It would be hard to find a more appropriate psalm to go with Jeremiah 31:7-9, for like that hymn it celebrates the return from Babylon, and indeed the contrast between sorrow and joy is the theme of both passages. Perhaps it is a pity that the psalm says nothing of the blind, though; for that would tie in with the gospel, too.

Reading II: Hebrews 5:1-6

Slowly, the author of Hebrews is preparing for the exposition of his great theological theme, the high priesthood of Christ. Except for the reading of Sunday 28, all our passages through today are concerned to establish Jesus' qualifications for high priesthood. Here the following qualifications are spelled out:

1. Due appointment by God.
2. His selection from among men to act as their representative before God in offering sacrifices for sins.
3. Sympathy with the ignorant and wayward (a repetition from our earlier readings).

The later part of our reading takes up point #1, the appointment by God. Jesus was appointed as Son and high priest at his resurrection (Pss 2:7; 110:4). Some may be surprised to see Psalm 2:7 applied to the resurrection. It suggests an adoptionist Christology (i.e., the heresy defined by a former colleague of mine as the view that Christ was a man who graduated in divinity with honors). But we are still moving within the orbit of Hebraic Christology which is functional rather than metaphysical. Psalm 2:7 originally celebrated the king's coronation. From that point he embarked upon the functions of kingship, i.e., the functions of the Son of God. So it is at his exaltation that Christ embarks upon his messianic functions, which include that of high priest. Incidentally this shows that Christ's high priestly work is performed in heaven, and that Calvary is only the preliminary to it.

Gospel: Mark 10:46-52

Normally the tendency of the synoptic tradition is for unnamed figures to acquire names — a process which continues in church tradition (e.g., the naming of the three wise men). Here, however, the process is reversed.

The earlier evangelist Mark names the blind man while Matthew and Luke drop the name. Bartimaeus must have been known later in the Christian community (at Jericho?) which first remembered and shaped the story. Probably he would have addressed Jesus simply as Rabbi (or Rabbouni, v. 51; RSV "Master"). The post-Easter community would have used this story as a vehicle for its Davidic Christology by inserting the address, Son of David (and is "have mercy on" liturgical?). Mark in turn received the story from the tradition, placed it here because of its geographical location (Jericho), and used it as a coda to his central section 8:22–10:45. That section thus ends as it has begun, with the healing of a blind man. This blind man follows Jesus in the "Way"— a technical term for Christian discipleship. All this is part of Mark's answer to the "heresy that necessitated his gospel" (the title of an important article by T. Weeden).

The true disciple is cured of his christological blindness (i.e., of seeing in Jesus only the miracle-worker, and not the suffering servant), and follows him in the Way of the cross.

The Homily

The homilist may like to take the gospel reading and feature the life of the contemporary Christian community which can be characterized as blindness (its refusal to abandon false securities from the past?) and show how the gospel of Christ crucified and the challenge to live a life following the way of the cross is the cure for that blindness.

The epistle offers an opportunity to examine the nature of priesthood: the representative nature of the priest's office ("taken from among men"), his appointment by God, the Godward direction of his function on behalf of man. It could then be shown how all this is fulfilled in Christ and made visible in the life of the church through the church's own priestly character and through the ministerial priesthood.

Last Sundays of Year B

Reading I: Deuteronomy 6:2-6

The first paragraph of this reading forms an introduction. Israel is entering the promised land, and her side of the covenant is to keep the law of God from generation to generation. The second paragraph consists of the She-mah, which became the daily Jewish prayer. God is to be loved in response to his prior revelation of himself as the one God. That divine unity was revealed through the Exodus event and, for the Deuteronomist, through the perpetual acessibility of his presence at the one central sanctuary. To love in this context means to trust solely in him and to reject the many Gods of the heathen. In Hebraic thought heart, soul and strength do not mean separate human faculties, but man in the totality of his being. Thus the radical nature of God's claim on the Israelite obedience is emphasized.

Responsorial Psalm: 18:1-2a, 2bc-3, 46 and 50ab (RSV)

Psalm 18 is one of the royal psalms (note stanza 3), possibly going back to David. It is a thanksgiving for victory in battle. The refrain, taken from the first verse, forms an admirable response to the Shemah.

Reading II: Hebrews 7:23-28

Having established the qualifications of Jesus to be high priest, the author at last embarks upon an exposition of his main theological theme. It consists of a point by point comparison of Jesus with the levitical priests of the old covenant, demonstrating that at each point Jesus and the effect of his work are superior to them and the effects of their work.

Here are the points of comparison in this excerpt:

Levitical Priest	Christ
many	only one
impermanent	eternal
subject to death	alive for ever
sinner — had to	sinless — no need to
offer for himself	offer for himself
repeated sacrifices	once-for-all sacrifice
appointed by law	appointed by oath
	superseding law

Gospel: Mark 12:28b-34

The double commandment of love had a triple attestation. In Mark it is presented in a Hellenized form. The Shemah is directed against pagan polytheism. The addition of mind/understanding to the list of faculties brings out the meaning of the Hebrew word for heart (*lebab*), which was the organ of intellectual activity, while the higher value placed on ethical obedience as contrasted with sacrificial cultus is typical of Hellenistic Judaism. Matthew's form lacks these features, and it is couched in a highly Semitic Greek. Hence it looks more primitive than Mark's. Luke's form, in our opinion, is an adaptation of the Marcan form and serves as an introduction to the parable of the Good Samaritan.

There has been much discussion about the originality of the double commandment to Jesus. Actually it is a combination of two different Old Testament passages, Deuteronomy 6 and Leviticus 19; so its contents cannot be regarded as original in themselves. But what of the combination of the two commandments, and what of their use as a summary of the whole Torah? The idea of summarizing the Torah under a single basic commandment was not unknown to rabbinic Judaism, which occasionally used the commandment to love the neighbor in this way. But the rabbis never combined this commandment with the other commandment to love God. However, the combination is found several times in the *Testaments of the Twelve Patriarchs* and there are other hints of it in the writings of Hellenistic Judaism. In fact, it seems characteristic of Jewish wisdom tradition, both Palestinian and Hellenistic. It must have been from that source that it came to Jesus. Is there then anything distinctive about his use of it? Yes, there is; for Jesus understands the interconnection between the two commandments in a quite radical sense. Love of God is illusory if it does not issue in love of neighbor, and love of neighbor is refined self-love if it does not proceed from the love of God.

The Homily

Most probably the homilist would wish to deal today with the double commandment of love as the summarization of Christian duty, and bring out the radical interconnection between the two commandments, illustrating it with examples from life. He should emphasize that this is not merely an external, legal requirement, but an existential response to God's revelation of himself as the one God (note the Shemah, which prefaces the commandment in its Marcan form as in the Deuteronomic source).

If on the other hand the homilist is giving a course on Hebrews, today's reading calls for an exposition of the nature of Christ's high priestly work — his offering of himself once for all and his pleading of that sacrifice eternally in heaven by making intercession for us. It is in the eucharistic that we find this heavenly intercession set before us as a concrete reality. In the words of the popular eucharistic hymn, composed by an Anglican hymn writer but sung ecumenically:

> Thou within the veil hast entered,
>   Robed in flesh, our great high priest;
> Thou on earth both priest and victim
>   In the eucharistic feast.
>   (W. Chatterton Dox)

It is in terms of this concrete realization at the eucharist that the homilist will find it most fitting to set forth the high priestly work of the ascended Christ.

✓ THIRTY-SECOND SUNDAY OF THE YEAR

Reading I: 1 Kings 17:10-16

Both the Elijah and the Elisha cycles contain miracles involving the multiplication of food, and as such exhibit the literary genre to which the stories of miraculous feedings in the gospels are conformed. This is their main importance for the New Testament.

The story of the widow's cruse, like the following story of the raising of her son, both emphasize the power of the word of God in the prophet's mouth. In this story the power of that word is seen in the fulfillment in verse 16 of the promise given in verse 14.

Neither of these points, however, has determined the selection of the episode of the widow's cruse. Rather, she is seen as a widow woman of the same character as the widow in the gospel story of the widow's two coins. Both the widows gave away all they possessed.

Responsorial Psalm: 146:6c-7, 8-9, 9bc-10

This is the first psalm in the final group of Hallel psalms. God is praised for his lovingkindness of the needy, including widows, hence its selection here.

Reading II: Hebrews 9:24-28

This reading continues the exposition of the high priestly work of Christ in terms of a series of contrasts with the levitical priesthood. Here are the points made this time, some of them repeated from the last excerpt, some of them new:

Levitical Priest	*Christ*
scene of his work: a material sanctuary	the heavenly sanctuary, the real presence of God
repeated offering (yearly)	once for all
offered blood of other creatures	offered his own blood

The last sentence of our reading seeks to elucidate the once-for-all character of Christ's offering by comparing it with the once-for-all character of human death. The reference to the parousia comes rather surprisingly here, but it is probable that all through this passage the author has in mind the ceremony of the day of atonement. After performing his priestly work in the Holy Place, the high priest came out of the temple again and showed himself to the people, indicating thereby that the work of atonement had been accomplished. The parousia likewise will mark the completion of Christ's high priestly work. Note that the last two weeks' passages from Hebrews feature the two phrases which most clearly indicate the nature of Christ's high priestly work in heaven: "he always lives to make intercession for" us (7:25) and "now to appear in the presence of God for us" (9:24).

Gospel: Mark 12:38-44 (long form); 12:41-44 (short form)

The longer form combines two quite distinct traditions, Jesus' denunciation of the scribes and the episode of the widow's two coins. The denunciation of the scribes forms the conclusion to the series of Jerusalem conflict stories, whose function is to show the widening gulf between Jesus and the Jerusalem authorities and so prepare the way for the Sanhedrin's decision to get rid of him. The episode of the widow is joined onto it by the *Stichwort* principle (the word "widow" occurs in each unit). Also, Mark has located the conflicts in the temple and the story of the widow is located there by its content.

Whether by design or not, however, the two stories taken together in this way, provide a foil for one another, for the behavior of the scribes is contrasted sharply with that of the widow. Perhaps the story of the widow was used in catechesis, for it would serve to indicate the duty of almsgiving.

The Homily

The lectionary invites the homilist to compare the behavior of the two widows, bringing out the similarities: each was prepared to give up all that she had. Both therefore are examples of service and almsgiving.

If the homilist is giving a series on Hebrews, he will want today to expound the work of Christ in appearing before the presence of God for us, again relating this to the eucharist as he related his heavenly intercession to the eucharist last week.

THIRTY-THIRD SUNDAY OF THE YEAR

This Sunday marks the shift in the post-Pentecost season to the great themes of the End. This theme will be in the forefront from now through Advent I.

Reading I: Daniel 12:1-3

Apocalypses follow a regular pattern. The apocalyptist first recounts under the guise of future prediction a selected series of historical events up to the moment of writing, then indicates future historical events rather vaguely, and finally becoming airborne as it were, foretells the cosmic events of the End: resurrection, and the last judgment, the cosmic consummation. Our present passage comes precisely at this last transition. "Trouble" is vaguely historical, but the deliverance which follows is the point at which history yields to cosmic eschatology. The deliverance takes the form of resurrection. Daniel 12 is notable as one of the earliest passages in the Old Testament which speak of resurrection. Then follows the final judgment in which the righteous and the wicked are separated, the former passing to eternal life, the rest to eternal "shame and contempt." Note that the resurrection life involves a radical transformation: the redeemed shall shine like the brightness of the firmament and like stars. This apocalyptic concept of radical transformation is taken up in the New Testament, where the synoptic Jesus speaks of it as a life like that of the angels in heaven (Mk 12:25 par.) and where Paul speaks of the spiritual body (1 Cor 15; Phil 3:21). Thus it is important to note that the resurrection is understood not as a resuscitation to the same mode of existence as in the present life, but a complete transformation. What that life is like can only be described in poetic terms, as here, or in Paul's more abstract but question-begging phrase, a spiritual body. It means entrance into a totally transcendental mode of existence.

Responsorial Psalm: 16:5 and 8, 9-10, 11

This psalm expresses a devout individual's trust and hope in Yahweh to deliver him from Sheol and the Pit. It can hardly have meant resurrection from the dead in the apocalyptic sense, but, as so often in the Old Testament psalms, deliverance at death's door. Later, this passage will be taken up into early Christian apologetic and applied to the death and resurrection of Christ (see the kerygmatic speeches in Acts 2 and 13). This is not a falsification of the psalm's original meaning, but a deepening of it. It is in this latter sense that we are invited to understand the psalm as a response to Daniel 12 — though further extended to cover the hope of the general resurrection, not only to Christ himself.

Reading II: Hebrews 10:11-14, 18

This passage marks the conclusion of the theological core of Hebrews, the contrast of the high priesthood of Christ with the levitical priesthood. The author reiterates once more his point about the repetition of the levitical sacrifice. Last week's reading, in making the same point, had spoken of the yearly offering on the day of atonement. Here the writer turns to the daily sacrifices offered not by the high priest, but by the ordinary levitical priests.

"He sat down" must not be pressed to mean that Christ has no further priestly work in heaven, as has been suggested by some commentators. The heavenly session is only an image conveying one aspect of the truth; not an exclusive definition. In relation to his death, resurrection, and ascension, Christ's work is completed — hence he can sit, waiting for the full effects of his victory to be gathered in at the parousia ("until his enemies shall be made a stool for his feet"). But in relation to the ongoing life of the Christian community his priestly work continues. He still makes intercession for us and still appears before the presence of God. That could be expressed by the image of standing (cf. Acts 7:56), which does not contradict the other image of his sitting. "Perfected" does not denote moral perfection. It means rather that the beneficiaries of Christ's sacrifice have been completely initiated. They are privileged through Christ to enter the heavenly sanctuary while here on earth in liturgical worship, and thus to attain already here by anticipation the goal and destiny of human life. "Here is no longer any offering for sin" — Christ's sacrifice can never be repeated. But this does not rule out its constant application through his heavenly intercession and his appearing in the presence of God for us.

Gospel: Mark 13:24-32

This excerpt from Mark's "Little Apocalypse" starts at exactly the same place in the apocalyptic as the reading from Daniel — at the point where the apocalypse moves from future historical events vaguely conceived (cf. Mark's "tribulation" with Daniel's "time of trouble") to a series of cosmic events. Here the latter are expanded with imagery drawn from other parts of the Old Testament: the failure of sun, moon and stars. Then comes the last judgment, where however Mark differs from Daniel in the role given to the Son of man (this figure has appeared earlier in Daniel, in chapter 7, a passage which will be read next week). The portrait of the Son of man is, however, more precise than that in Daniel. In Daniel he appears as a symbol and personification of the people of God at the end, whereas in Mark he is an individual figure who performs the eschatological judgment. Some seek to assimilate Mark's Son of man to Daniel's by harmonizing the two figures. They argue that the Son of man in Mark 13 does not descend from heaven to earth, but, as in Daniel 7, is manifested in heaven: in other words, it is not a parousia but an exaltation scene. In view, however, of firmly established Christian tradition, discernible as early as 1 Thessalonians 4:16, this seems most unlikely, and we are on surer ground if we take it to refer to the parousia. The Son of man comes from heaven to earth on the clouds with power and great glory and sends out his angels, who accompany him to gather the elect and escort them to heaven. Clearly there has been a development of the Son of man myth between the Book of Daniel (165 B.C.) and the New Testament. Such a development is attested in Enoch 37–71, though it is not certain whether that part of Enoch predates the New Testament.

That Jesus himself spoke of the Son of man in this developed sense as the eschatological judge and saviour is most probable, but that he painted elaborate apocalyptic pictures as in Mark 13 is improbable. Jesus proclaimed that the Son of man would judge men according as they accepted or rejected his own eschatological message. He thus reduced the Son of man to the status of a rubber stamp for his own word and work. After the resurrection Jesus was manifested as himself, the heavenly Son of man — in other words, as his own rubber stamp, ratifying his own word and work. The early church then expanded the apocalyptic imagery to express its faith that the Son of man would come again as Jesus.

In the synoptic apocalypses there is a tendency for eschatological parables to be collected at the end, and so here we have the parable of the fig tree — undoubtedly a genuine parable of Jesus, which in its original setting spoke of his ministry as the dawning of the shortly-to-be-consummated kingdom. It is placed here to assure Mark's readers that the apocalyptic events just described are near at hand. Mark's gospel was written in the 60's, before the hope of the imminent end had begun to fade, with a consequent deferral of the parousia.

After the parable come three sayings. The first (v. 30) could well be an authentic saying of Jesus in which "these things" referred to something other than the apocalyptic denouement — perhaps to the vindication of his own word and work. The second saying (v. 31), also probably authentic, expresses similarly Jesus' certainty about the validity of his eschatological message. Placed here by Mark, "my words" again refer to the apocalyptic events. The final word (v. 32) has caused much debate, centering around two questions: (1) the saying's authenticity; (2) Jesus' disclaimer of knowledge of the date of the final consummation. On (1) many would agree with Schmiedel, for whom this was one of the "pillar passages," i.e., indubitably authentic precisely because of its frank admission of the Son's ignorance. But did Jesus explicitly call himself the Son (that he has a unique filial consciousness is beyond doubt; cf. his use of Abba)? This verse seems to lie somewhere along the trajectory leading from the cry of jubilation (Mt 11:25-26 par.) to the Johannine sayings about the Father and the Son. (2) Whether this saying goes back to Jesus or to the early post-Easter community, neither party shared the perspectives of Chalcedonian Christology.

Therefore we should not approach this text with the assumption of later Christology. Historically, Jesus' knowledge comprised what was sufficient for the performance of his eschatological mission, no more.

As we look back over the Little Apocalypse of Mark 13, we see that it was developed by combining authentic eschatological sayings and parables of Jesus with traditional apocalyptic material (e.g., the saying about the coming of the Son of man). Thus a very different impression is created from Jesus' own proclamation which spoke of the inbreaking of the kingdom and the certainty of the speedy vindication of his message. We may believe that this apocalyptic elaboration spoke meaningfully to Mark's church, beset as it was by temptations of a divine man Christology and by persecution.

The Homily

Apocalyptic material such as our first reading and the gospel passage creates a delicate problem for the homilist. Traditionally, the church has ignored the biblical sense of imminence and has taken this material as a prediction of a remote consummation of history, appealing sometimes to Mark 13:32 with its admission that only the Father knows the date of the end. Apocalyptic thus became the last chapter of a dogmatic system, lacking any existential relevance for the present life of the church. In the modern period, apocalyptic has more often than not been dismissed as "Jewish old clothes," representing the mistaken and eventually falsified ideas of early Christian days. Is there a third way in which we can find a relevant word of God for the contemporary Christian community without falling into the trap of literal imminent expectation? Such an interpretation would have to recognize (1) the essentially mythological character of the apocalyptic material; (2) the cruciality of the imminent expectation. Imminent expectation is a mode of expressing certainty of conviction. Out of the troubles (Daniel) and tribulation (Mark) that beset the church at present we have the certainty of Jesus' promise that there will come vindication and the final achievement of God's saving purpose. It is this conviction that the homilist must seek to put across to his people.

The epistle reading forms the conclusion of a course of readings on Hebrews. Probably the homilist would want to relate Hebrews' insistence on the once-for-all, nonrepeatable character of Christ's sacrifice, with the church's theology that the eucharist is a sacrifice, though in the sense that in and through its due performance the once-for-all sacrifice becomes a present reality for our participation. If we do not do this, the theology of Hebrews remains a remote transaction speaking of Calvary or the ascension, with no relevance to the life of the church today.

CHRIST THE KING

We remind the reader what we have noted in previous years, namely that the feast of Christ the King, coming as it does at the end of the church year, has acquired thereby an eschatological significance.

Reading I: Daniel 7:13-14

As we noted last week, the Son of man in Daniel stands for the people of the Lord, the saints of the most high. We have noted, too, that a development of this concept took place in Jewish apocalyptic, so that by the time of the New Testament it had become an individual, heavenly figure, the agent of the final judgment and salvation.

It has been argued recently by a number of scholars that the New Testament, especially the gospels (e.g., Mk 14:62), find the fulfillment of this prophecy in the *ascension* of our Lord. In other words, the coming is interpreted as a coming *to* the Ancient of Days and not *from* heaven. We reject this interpretation so far as the New Testament is concerned. Christian faith must read Daniel 7 not as a prediction of what had already happened — that would be to ignore the not-yet character of the Christ event and make this passage more suitable for Ascension Day than for the last day of the Christian year. Rather, we must read it as a proclamation (in mythological terms) of the final establishment of Christ's kingly rule. For we do not yet see all things subdued under his feet. Not yet do all peoples, nations and languages serve him. That they will do so at the End is an inalienable aspect of the Christian hope.

Responsorial Psalm: 93:1ab, 1c-2, 5

This, as we have previously had occasion to observe, is one of the enthronement psalms. Two points need to be observed today. (1) Psalm 93 originally spoke of Yahweh's kingship, not predicting the kingly rule of Christ. (2) The kingdom of which it speaks is an eternal reality. But for Christian interpretation, many Yahweh texts in the Old Testament can be applied to Christ. It is through Christ, from the time of his ascension on, that the Father exercises his kingdom. Indeed, following the precedent of Paul's interpretation of the Old Testament (that the rock was Christ), we may say that already in the Old Testament, in the perspective of Christian faith, God was exercising his kingly rule through Christ, if by Christ we here mean not Jesus of Nazareth, but God going out toward the world and toward man in his revelatory and redemptive work.

Reading II: Revelation 1:5-8

By starting at v. 5 instead of at the beginning of the sentence, our reading obscures the fact that this passage comes from the epistolary address of the Apocalypse. It is a greeting *from* Jesus Christ as well as from the Father and the seven spirits. Then follows a triple doxology: Point 1: he loves us — note the present tense: Christ's love is perpetual and goes beyond the historical event of the redemption (*Jerome Biblical Commentary*). Point 2: the historical event of the atonement, couched in a traditional credal formula. Point 3: the effect of the redemption is to set up a community which shares Christ's kingly and priestly functions.

After the doxology there follows a proclamation of the imminent parousia which is to be the theme of the whole apocalypse. This proclamation draws upon a combination of Old Testament *testimonia* used elsewhere in the New Testament, from Daniel 7:13-14 (our first reading) and Zechariah 12:10. The reading ends with a self-proclamation of Yahweh under three titles: Alpha and Omega, a hellenized expression of the Old Testament's "first and last"; a second title asserting that God's being comprises present, past and future (a reflection on the meaning of Yahweh?); and the third title (*pantocrator*), a Greek rendering of Sabaoth (hosts). Combined together, all three look like a meditation on the meaning of *kyrios ho theos, Yahweh 'elohe sebaoth.*

Gospel: John 18:33b-37

It is beyond all doubt that Jesus was crucified on the charge of being a messianic pretender. This is established by the *titulus* on the cross, handed down in various forms but always agreeing on the essential core: the King of the Jews (king being the Roman equivalent of Messiah). It is not certain precisely what attitude Jesus took toward this charge at the investigation before the Sanhedrin and at his trial before Pilate. Some traditions present him as preserving a stony silence (pleading the fifth amendment, as it were), while others represent him not as rejecting it, but as being at pains to correct it (the answer, "you say so," will be equivalent to, "It's your word, not mine"). In the Johannine version of the trial before Pilate Jesus explicitly corrects the charge by offering a reinterpretation of what kingship means for him. This is done by his answers to three questions put to him by Pilate.

First, Pilate asks him if he is a king. Jesus, in a reply which may be traditional, for it is devoid of Johannine theology, asks where Pilate got his idea from. This is to establish the terms of the debate: are we debating a charge trumped up by the Jewish authorities, that Jesus was a messianic pretender? Pilate indicates that the charge originates from the Jewish authorities and asks the defendant what basis there is for his behavior. Jesus' second reply is negative. He says what his kingship is not — it is not political in character ("of the world" is Johannine; "world" means human society organized on the basis of its unbelief). But Jesus insists that in a certain sense — not as yet defined — he is a king. Pilate therefore repeats the first question, thus giving Jesus the chance to state his own definition of kingship. He has come into the world to be the bearer of the divine revelation. Here, then, we have a complete redefinition of messiahship or kingship in terms of Johannine theology. "Truth" in Johannine thought means the reality of God as seen through his revelatory and redemptive action.

The Homily

There are several possible lines for the homilist to take today. He might concentrate on the second coming, drawing from the first reading and the proclamation in Revelation 1:7. If he does so we would suggest that he treat the second coming not as the last chapter of Christian dogmatics, but as an immediate, relevant concern of Christian existence. Christian faith always lives "as if" the second coming were just around the corner, for it is so certain of its vindication.

The second reading also suggests an exposition of the way in which the Christian community already here and now shares Christ's kingship and priesthood. We might point to the liturgy as the focal point where its priesthood is expressed and to secular life as the place where its kingship is exercised through service. But then it becomes necessary to insist that Christ's kingship is "not of this world" — suggesting a consideration of the relationship between the church and political power.

Thirdly, the homilist could concentrate upon the Johannine Christ's redefinition of kingship in terms of witness to the truth. Perhaps it is particularly relevant just now to refute recent attempts to portray Jesus as the paradigm of a political revolutionary.

Advent to December 31 of Year C

Reading I: Jeremiah 33:14-16

These verses are an almost verbatim repetition of Jeremiah 23:5-6 (see Sunday 16B). In the precritical age readers would have had no difficulty in supposing that Jeremiah spoke the same oracle on two separate occasions. The common opinion today among scholars is that Jeremiah 23 contains the prophet's original oracle and that Jeremiah 33 is a revival of this oracle in a later situation by one of his disciples. Jeremiah had predicted that the Davidic dynasty would be restored shortly after the fall of Jerusalem in 586. But the years of exile were prolonged and the promise went unfulfilled. The exiles were tempted to abandon their ancestral religion and adopt the religion of the surrounding nations. In this situation a later writer repeats Jeremiah's prophecy. No doubt its partial fulfillment was discerned in the return from exile. But Christian faith has seen in it a promise that was not fulfilled until the coming of Jesus, the real Messiah. While we should not read into the phrase "The Lord is our righteousness" the full Pauline meaning of "righteousness," the use of the word here provides a background for Paul. "Righteousness" is not an ethical or moral quality, but the saving act of Yahweh. The restoration of the Davidic monarchy after the exile will be seen as Yahweh's mighty act of salvation. Christian faith will see the advent of Christ as God's final act of salvation.

Responsorial Psalm: 25:4-5ab, 8-9, 10 and 14

Other selections of this psalm are used on Sunday 26A, Lent 1B, Sunday 3B. The idea of Yahweh's righteousness is picked up in the words "truth" (i.e., God's fidelity to his promise) and "salvation" in the first stanza, and "steadfast love," faithfulness, and covenant in stanza 3. The psalm, accordingly, should not be interpreted moralistically. It speaks of patient waiting for the advent of Yahweh's "righteousness."

Reading II: 1 Thessalonians 3:12–4:2

This reading straddles two halves of 1 Thessalonians. In the first half the apostle reviews his relations with the Thessalonians to date. He is led to thanksgiving and an expression of his loving concern. This section concludes with a blessing or intercession. Paul prays that his converts may continue to grow in holiness until the parousia, the "coming" of Christ, which of course he expects will happen very soon. This is the first paragraph of our reading.

The second paragraph marks the beginning of part 2 of the letter. This contains specific ethical exhortations and a discussion of several theological problems of concern to the young community. Before embarking on specifics, Paul reminds his readers in general terms of the catechetical instructions which he had given them during his foundation visit. Paul's original instruction was given "through our Lord Jesus." What precisely does this mean? Paul generally chooses his christological titles carefully, with an eye on context. The catechesis of the church rests upon the words of the historical *Jesus* perpetuated by the living *Lord* in his church. Tradition is not something left behind by a Jesus now dead, but a process inaugurated by Jesus in his earthly life and constantly reenacted as a living word by the exalted *Kyrios*.

Gospel: Luke 21:25-28, 34-36

It will be recalled that in year C we are reading the Gospel of Luke in course. Today's selection, however, is out of course in order to present Luke's future-apocalyptic teaching on Advent 1, where it is particularly seasonable.

Although Luke follows Mark in his location of the apocalyptic discourse (just before the passion narrative), he draws much of its content from his special material. Only in verses 25, 26b and 27 does he follow Mark closely. The synoptic apocalypse was constantly adjusted so that it could speak to the ever-changing situation of the early Christian community. Luke's version, unlike Mark's, regards the church as here to stay. This lengthy period is marked by distress of nations and by human fear and foreboding. And in the Christian community slackness is setting in. There is dissipation, drunkenness, and "cares of this life" (cf. the interpretation of the parable of the sower). In such a situation Luke calls upon his contemporaries to watch and pray.

The Homily

There is a remarkable similarity between the situation of the redactor in the Jeremiah reading and that of the evangelist Luke. Both inherit traditions — the one from Jeremiah, the other from Mark (and ultimately, no doubt, from the historical Jesus himself), traditions which have apparently not been fulfilled. Both feel impelled to reiterate these traditions and to assure their readers that the promises of the oracles will be fulfilled despite the long haul. The homilist ought to be able to find analogies in the contemporary situation of the Christian community and to reassure it of God's faithfulness to his promises, summoning the faithful to watch and pray (the gospel) and to grow in holiness (the epistle).

IMMACULATE CONCEPTION: DECEMBER 8

This is not a feast in the calendar of the Episcopal Church (although in the calendar of the Church of England December 8 is marked as the Conception of the Blessed Virgin Mary, and in 1928 it was provided with a collect but no readings). To Anglicans it appears that this doctrine (a) is not in scripture, (b) was unheard of until the middle ages, and (c) even then was not universally accepted (Aquinas, as is well known, did not hold it). They would feel that it is contrary to Paul's statement on the universality of human sin (Rom 3:9, 23) and to the statement of Article XV that Christ alone is without sin. Nevertheless, we must try to understand how and in what sense Roman Catholics hold to it. The dogma of 1854 was careful to make the Immaculate Conception entirely dependent in advance on the redemptive act of God in Christ: "The Virgin Mary at the moment of conception was preserved in advance from all defilement of original sin by a unique privilege of grace in view of the merits of Jesus Christ." But why should such a claim be asserted? What biblical considerations led to a desire to affirm it? Perhaps we may understand it as *the way* in which Roman Catholics seek to affirm something which the Bible affirms and which other Christians also would want to affirm without the dogma — namely, that it was the total surrender of Mary to the divine will that, humanly speaking, made the incarnation possible.

The rest of us would, for biblical and historical reasons, want to dissociate ourselves from this particular way of affirming that total obedience of Mary, so crucial for the incarnation. Yet we can respect the reasons for the Roman Catholic acceptance of the dogma, and share with them that biblical truth which the dogma is a way of affirming, i.e., the total surrender of Mary to the divine will.

Reading I: Genesis 3:9-15, 20

The story of the fall is generally regarded today as an aetiological myth — that is, it expressed how faith understands the origin of evil. Eden cannot be located on a map nor can the eating of the forbidden fruit be dated. The story of Adam and Eve is the expression of profound truths about man; e.g., it asserts that the woes of human life are largely brought about by man's rejection of his divine destiny. Yet that evil is something greater than man's sin. It is a transsubjective reality, symbolized by the serpent. Verse 15 is traditionally known as the *protevangelium*, the earliest promise of man's final conquest of evil.

It should be noted, however, that the text actually speaks only of the perpetual antagonism between man and the serpent. It is clearly because of the *protevangelium* that this pericope is chosen for today. The seed of the woman who achieved the final triumph over evil was born through Mary. The early church fathers drew a contrast between Eve and Mary similar to Paul's contrast between Adam and Christ. As Eve by her disobedience let evil into the world, so Mary by her obedience made it possible for the Victor over evil to enter the world.

Responsorial Psalm: 98:1, 2-3ab, 3cd-4

An almost identical selection (but with a different refrain and a fourth stanza) is employed at the third mass of Christmas in year A. If we take the *protevangelium* as the promise of man's victory over evil, this psalm thanks God for that victory, a victory achieved through the Christ, which Mary's obedience made possible.

Reading II: Ephesians 1:3-6, 11-12

Ephesians is probably a circular letter in which a faithful disciple sums up Paul's achievement and elucidates its significance for the Pauline churches after the apostle's death. The opening thanksgiving sets the salvation effected by God in Christ in the context of the whole sweep of salvation history, beginning with God's purpose "before the foundation of the world." It is appropriate for today, because the "us" who are chosen includes the Blessed Virgin Mary, the first of those who believed (Luke 1:45). This reading strongly affirms that Mary was what she was solely through the salvation effected by God in Christ (cf. the papal decree of 1854).

Gospel: Luke 1:26-38

This reading occurred at Advent 4 B and was commented upon fully there. Today, we note that there is no gospel passage which relates or affirms the

Immaculate Conception but that this is the passage which most emphatically affirms the obedience of Mary which made the incarnation possible. Its use here supports our interpretation of the dogma of the Immaculate Conception as a way of affirming this fact about Mary which is so important for all of us.

The Homily

The scriptures chosen for this feast suggest that the emphasis of the homily should be twofold: (1) the dogma of the Immaculate Conception, properly understood, does not compromise the essential truth that all men, the BVM included, belong to a fallen humanity (reading I) and that their salvation depends on Christ alone — again, the BVM included (reading II); (2) that the affirmation of her Immaculate Conception is *a way* of affirming the biblical truth of Mary's total commitment in faith and obedience to God's will for her (gospel).

SECOND SUNDAY OF ADVENT

Reading I: Baruch 5:1-9

Baruch is one of the deuterocanonical and pseudonymous Old Testament writings which are not found in the Hebrew Bible and have been termed, in Reformation tradition, the Apocrypha. Like the Book of Daniel, it is attributed to a figure of the past: Baruch was Jeremiah's secretary. The book presupposes for its situation the Babylonian exile (586-538), but it consists of various materials written later. Our reading comes from the last part, comprising two prophetic poems modeled on Deutero-Isaiah, and forms the concluding section of the second poem. The fictitious situation it assumes is that of Israel waiting to return from exile. It is difficult to be precise about the real situation, but it was evidently written for Jews who later were living in the diaspora. The miracle of the return is pictured in a series of supernatural events reminiscent of Isaiah 40 and, earlier still, of the exodus itself.

This reading is a magnificent choice for Advent 2. It matches the quotation of Isaiah 40 in the gospel, and it captures the church's Advent stance in the thrilling words: "Arise, O Jerusalem! Stand upon the height and look toward the east." The symbolism of salvation coming from the east like the dawn is deeply embedded in the church's Advent lore.

Responsorial Psalm: 126:1-2ab, 2cd-3, 4-5, 6

The identical arrangement of this psalm was used on Sunday 30 B, and as we have noted there, it celebrates the return from Babylon. It is equally appropriate as a response to the reading from Baruch, since the author of that poem pictures the deliverance of the diaspora in terms of the return from Babylon as foretold by Deutero-Isaiah.

Reading II: Philippians 1:4-6, 8-11

This passage comes from the opening thanksgiving (par. 1) and intercession (par. 2) of Philippians. If we accept the recently suggested theory that Philippians is a compilation of three different letters sent by Paul to that community within a short period of time, this passage will come from the second letter. Paul is in prison at Ephesus (?). The Philippians' envoy, Epaphroditus, who has brought along a "care parcel" for the incarcerated apostle, had fallen sick but has now recovered. Paul has also heard rumors that false teachers had either arrived or were about to descend to stir up trouble in this faithful community, and so he is somewhat anxious about them. He sends his second letter (1:1–3:1, 4:47) to tell them the news about himself and Epaphroditus and to exhort them to unity. These concerns are reflected in the thanksgiving and intercession.

As in 1 Thessalonians (see last week's reading II), Paul regards the "day of Jesus Christ" (i.e., the parousia) as the terminal point of Christian maturation. Of course he thought that he and his readers, the majority anyhow, would still be alive on that day and that therefore all spiritual growth would take place entirely within their earthly existence. Yet by this time he had already written 1 Thessalonians and had faced the problem of Christians who died before the parousia. It is therefore a reasonable extension of his meaning to suppose that the parousia remains the term of spiritual growth for all believers, including those now dead.

It is interesting that Paul characterizes Christian growth in the ethical terminology of Stoicism: "knowledge," "discernment," "approve what is excellent." Most interesting is the word for discernment (*aisthēsis*). Knowing that the will of God in concrete situations requires a kind of aesthetic sensibility, John A. T. Robinson once spoke of the Christian as having a set of built-in antennae to tell him what love required in a particular situation. This is of course not the whole truth about Christian ethics, but it is an important factor and one to which the apostle here gives countenance.

Gospel: Luke 3:1-6

On Advent 2 and 3 the gospels each year focus upon John the Baptist. In an elaborate dating (pointing probably to the year 27) Luke connects the appearance of the Baptist both to secular history and to salvation history as he brings the Baptist on stage in wording reminiscent of the appearance of the Old Testament prophets. Luke has a view of John the Baptist different from Mark's. Mark thought of the Baptist as the *archē tou euangeliou*, the beginning of the gospel, the point at which the salvation event began. Luke, by contrast, places John *before* the beginning of the salvation event. The Baptist in his own person sums up the whole salvation history of the Old Testament, stands at the head of the Old Testament prophets and points as they did to the coming Christ. The one difference is that John is the last of the prophets, who announces Jesus' impending arrival. Luke operates with two periods of salvation history, the Old Testament period culminating in John, and the Jesus period, which is divided into two parts: the earthly history of Jesus (what he "began to do" [Acts 1:1]), and what he continues to do in the church. This scheme is preferable to Conzelmann's three periods: the Old Testament, Jesus, and the church. John's baptism of repentance for the forgiveness of sins is, as the ensuing quotation of Isaiah 40 shows, essentially preparatory for the coming of the Messiah. Mark had already cited Isaiah 40, but Luke lengthens the quotation to include "all flesh shall see the salvation of God," which gives it a typically universalistic accent. This, incidentally, also shows that John foretells what is essentially a single period, for the universal mission of the church is included in the salvation event. That event embraces the content both of Luke's Gospel and the Book of Acts.

The Homily

The homilist's purpose today must be to awaken in his people a sense of tingling expectation, such as is characteristic of Advent. The Baruch lesson and the citation from Isaiah 40 in the gospel will help him to do this. Expectation for what? In Advent we focus on two events: we put ourselves in the time of preparation for the first coming, and we kindle anew our expectation of the second coming. As we have noted before, the second coming is in the forefront of our attention in the last few Sundays of the church year and especially on Advent 1. Then from Advent 2 the first coming moves to the front of the stage — yet the second coming is not dropped altogether, as the epistle reading shows.

The importance of the Advent expectation for God to act lies in the fact that man cannot produce his own salvation. The resources for man's salvation do not lie within the possibilities of human history. They can only come from outside. Neither the incarnation nor the parousia can be thought of as products of human evolution. The process theology currently in vogue sometimes seems to forget that. A few years ago man's possibilities seemed limitless. Recent events, e.g., the ecological and energy crises (with the very real possibility that man will have exhausted all his sources of energy in the next decades, without discovering any substitutes), should make us more receptive to the Advent message than we were in the 60's.

THIRD SUNDAY OF ADVENT ✓

Reading I: Zephaniah 3:14-18a

Since this is the only occasion in the three-year Sunday cycle when a passage from Zephaniah is read, a few words about this minor prophet would be in order. Zephaniah's prophetic activity coincided with the earlier part of the reign of Josiah, c. 640-630. He was probably located at Jerusalem. His prophecies are almost exclusively predictions of judgment. His message is that of Amos: "The day of Yahweh will be darkness and not light." Our present passage is from the only positive section. It consists of a psalm inviting Zion to rejoice because her salvation is at hand. The passage is so out of tune with the general tenor of Zephaniah's work that it has been thought to be an addition by a later editor.

Like last week's lesson from Baruch, this reading engenders an attitude of excited expectation for the intervention of Yahweh and is therefore fitting for the Advent season.

Responsorial Psalm: Isaiah 12:2-3, 4bcde, 5-6

This week we depart from the usual practice of drawing upon the psalter for the responsive reading and instead have an arrangement of the first song of Isaiah. It is uncertain whether this canticle is the work of Isaiah of Jerusalem. In fact its tone rather suggests a situation at the return from exile.

In *Services for Trial Use* of the Episcopal Church this song is provided as a canticle between the Old and the New Testament readings at the daily office. The song gives thanks for the divine salvation which had been promised in the Old Testament and is now on the brink of fulfillment. This makes it equally suitable for Advent. Note particularly the emphasis on the presence of God in Israel (stanza 3 and the refrain). The incarnation is the supreme realization of the coming of God to be present among his people.

Reading II: Philippians 4:4-7

If we accept the partition theory of Philippians, this passage will again come from Paul's *second* letter to the Christians of Philippi (see last week's notes). This reading was the traditional one for Advent 3 and gave it the name *Gaudete*. (In the Book of Common Prayer the reading was shifted to the last Sunday of Advent.) As the caption ("The Lord is near") shows, its focal point is the statement that the Lord (i.e., the exalted Christ) is at hand. Advent is not a gloomy season (it does of course have a penitent aspect — cf. John the Baptist's message of repentance) despite the traditional use of the same liturgical color as for Lent. Rather, Advent is marked by a crescendo of joy. As the Lord comes nearer and nearer, so we become more excited. The rhythm of Advent is well captured by the Advent wreath, which starts with one lighted candle and ends with four.

Gospel: Luke 3:10-18

This reading consists of two pericopes (in the form-critical rather than the liturgical sense of the word). The first, Luke 3:10-14, is called by the Germans (who always seem to have neat names for pericopes) the *Standespredigt* of the Baptist, i.e., his preaching to various classes of people: the crowds in general, the tax collectors, and the soldiers. The second part is the Baptist's messianic preaching. He disclaims any suggestion that he is the Messiah (cf. the interpolations in the Johannine prologue). Both Luke and John may reflect the claims of continuing followers of the Baptist: their man, rather than Jesus, was the Messiah. In point of fact, the Baptist had pointed forward to the coming of another, the strong one ("he who is mightier than I"). Unlike the Baptist, who administers a water baptism, the strong one will baptize with Spirit and fire. John's baptism is preparatory. The strong one's baptism will actually mediate the eschatological judgment, or salvation.

Mark had simply "Spirit," while Matthew and Luke add "fire." Probably "fire" alone is original and Spirit is a Christian addition, reflecting the Pentecost event. Yet the coming of the Spirit was part of Jewish eschatological expectation and therefore implicit in the Baptist's words. Nor can we suppose that in speaking of the strong one the Baptist himself consciously had Jesus in mind. It is more likely that his conception of the Messiah was of one whose function would be more judgmental than salvific. It has been suggested that this is why later on in prison John asked whether

Christ was the coming one or whether people were looking for another. Jesus turned out to be a very different kind of Messiah from what John had expected.

The Homily

This week again John the Baptist is the obvious theme for the preacher. One might concentrate today on his disclaimer: he is not the Christ but only the one sent to prepare his way by preaching repentance (the *Standespredigt* shows what repentance concretely means). In the gospels, especially here in Luke and in the Fourth Gospel, there is great emphasis on the self-effacing attitude of John. He points away from himself to the other (cf. the Isenheim altarpiece by Grünewald in which John the Baptist is portrayed pointing to Jesus Christ hanging on the cross). The old collect of this day in the Book of Common Prayer drew an analogy between this self-effacing work of the Baptist and the work of the "ministers and stewards," whose function is to point men and women away from themselves to Christ and so prepare them for his coming (both at Christmas and at the last day) by preaching repentance. These considerations might lead the homilist to speak of confession and amendment of life in preparation for Christmas.

FOURTH SUNDAY OF ADVENT ✓

Reading 1: Micah 5:2-5a

As with Zephaniah last week, this is the only use of Micah in the Sunday lectionary, so we will again provide some introductory information. Micah prophesied in the southern kingdom of Judah at the end of the eighth century, in the reigns of Ahaz and Hezekiah. Although he lived through a series of intense international crises (including the destruction of the northern kingdom of Israel and the invasion of Judah by Assyria), he took little note of these events (contrast Isaiah of Jerusalem) but concentrated rather on the denunciation of Judah for its social injustices (cf. Amos). Micah, like Zephaniah, was later edited, and more positive promises were added. The oracle about the birth of the messianic king at Ephrathah ("Bethlehem" is thought to be an explanatory gloss) is probably one such addition. The situation it presupposes seems to be that prevailing at the end of the exile, when hopes ran high for the restoration of the Davidic monarchy. Christian faith has, since Matthew 2:6, seen the final fulfillment of this oracle in the birth of Jesus.

Responsorial Psalm: 80:1ac and 2b, 14-15, 17-18

The same selection from this responsorial psalm was used at Advent 1 B. Notice particularly the last two lines of stanza 1 ("Stir up your might, and come and save us"). It is hard to imagine a more appropriate Advent prayer. Its words are echoed in the ancient Advent collects which begin with *Excita*. As we pointed out at Advent 1 B, the third stanza is a prayer for God's blessing on the Davidic king. Coupled today with reading I, this may be referred appropriately to Jesus Christ. Thus we put ourselves in the position of old Israel waiting for the coming of the Messiah, and so wait for the celebration of his coming at Christmas.

Reading II: Hebrews 10:5-10

This reading (beginning at v. 4) is also used on the Annunciation (March 25), a day with which this Sunday has much in common. It is one of the most important passages in Hebrews. For it defines Christ's sacrifice as the offering of his body (i.e., the instrument of his will) in obedience to his Father. This, says the author of Hebrews, building upon Psalm 40, is the whole *raison d'être* of the incarnation. Christ took a body so as to have an instrument by which to offer this perfect obedience to the will of God. The choice of this reading today is a salutary reminder, needed perhaps particularly at this time of year, not to dissociate the incarnation from its supreme goal, the atonement. Bethlehem was the prelude to Golgotha.

Gospel: Luke 1:39-45

Since there are only two annunciation stories in the gospels (see Advent 4 A and B), year C switches to the visitation (cf. May 31). Today's reading in the Episcopalian lectionary runs through verse 49, thus including the first four verses of the Magnificat, which has traditional associations with Advent 4.

Three times in this pericope Mary is pronounced "blessed" (cf. also the second verse of the Magnificat; this is the scriptural ground for our calling her the "Blessed" Virgin). And two closely connected reasons are given for Elizabeth's calling her this: Mary's faith (v. 45), which is the same as her obedience (Lk 1:38, the introductory alleluia versicle), and her bearing of the Christ child (v. 42). So Mary is blessed not for what she was or is in herself but only in relation to the incarnation. The Mariology of scripture is grounded in Christology.

In order to follow the evangelist's understanding of the annunciation, the conception of the Christ child, and the dialogue between Mary and Elizabeth at the visitation, we should avoid prematurely harmonizing Luke's presentation with the Johannine prologue. Luke does not operate with a preexistent Logos-Christology like the fourth evangelist, any more than the fourth evangelist operates with a conception and birth narrative. The virginal conception, for Luke, is not the way in which the preexistent divine Son assumes humanity, for he does not think in those terms. Rather, the miraculous conception is to Luke the supreme example of those Old Testament conceptions in which God raises up a man to perform a specific function of salvation history (cf. Isaac, Moses [?], Sampson, and Samuel). Thus Mary's miraculous conception of Jesus marks the birth of one who is to perform the eschatologically unique role in salvation history (Lk 1:32, 33 — note the future tenses, which speak of this child's future role, not of his "divine nature"). In Luke (and the same is doubtless true of Matthew) the infancy narratives are strictly *Vorgeschichte*, a historical prelude to a unique salvation history which begins with the baptism of Jesus and continues through his exaltation (cf. the qualifications for apostolic witness in Acts 1:22). We shall discuss how this exegetical interpretation of Luke is to be squared with the church's later ontological interpretation of the incarnation, and propose a contemporary interpretation of it in our comments on the Johannine prologue at the third mass of Christmas Day.

The Homily

Since the figure of Mary is central today, the homilist will probably wish to explain why we call her blessed, emphasizing that Mary's importance to Christian faith depends upon her faith and obedience as the preconditions which made the incarnation humanly possible, and upon the fact that she bore the Christ child. The homilist thus has an opportunity to propound a true and, it is to be hoped, ecumenically acceptable Mariology, one that is grounded solely in Christology.

The lesson from Hebrews suggests a different line of thought: that the final purpose of the incarnation was the atonement. This would give the homilist the occasion to relate Bethlehem to Golgotha.

CHRISTMAS: DECEMBER 25

Year C has the same readings as A and B. We shall summarize what we have said before and offer some fresh comments on the Johannine prologue (for the mass during the day), as promised above.

We should disabuse ourselves and our congregations of the notion that the primary thrust of Christmas is the historical occasion of Jesus' birth. (I have heard of Episcopalian clergy getting their church school children to sing "Happy birthday, dear Jesus," a fatuous misunderstanding of what Christmas is really about.) It is the celebration of God's eschatological self-disclosure in the Christ event.

MASS AT MIDNIGHT

Reading I: Isaiah 9:2-7

Originally this was a coronation anthem sung at the enthronement of the kings of the Davidic dynasty. Each new king, it was hoped, would prove the ideal king (cf. British hopes for a new Elizabethan age at the accession of Queen Elizabeth II in 1952). Christian faith finds this hope fulfilled in Jesus Christ. In him all the blessings looked for at each royal accession in Judah's history — freedom from poverty and oppression, the realization of peace — are given to Christian faith. The Davidic king was even hailed as God — i.e., as the sacramental embodiment and representative of the divine presence. How much more is this true of Jesus Christ! He is God in the sense not of *Deus in se*, but as *Deus pro nobis* or, in Gogarten's words, "God turned to us" in his grace and salvation.

Responsorial Psalm: 96:1-2a, 2b-3, 11-12, 13

The "new song" is the celebration of messianic redemption, replacing the old song of Moses which celebrated the exodus. The hymn of the angels at Bethlehem is the choral prelude to this new song. The church's liturgy is its partial anticipation. Its final realization awaits the heavenly liturgy described in the Apocalypse.

Reading II: Titus 2:11-14

Note how the Advent theme of the two comings of Christ is kept right to Christmas. The first coming anticipates the second. The midnight mass of Christmas has symbolic significance, for the New Testament looks for Christ to come again at midnight (e.g., Mt 25:6). Note, too, the traditional collect for Christmas: "Grant that as we joyfully receive him for our Redeemer, so we may with sure confidence behold him when he shall come to be our judge" (Book of Common Prayer; in the Roman Missal, Vigil of Christmas).

Gospel: Luke 2:1-14

We are not meant to take the birth stories as exact transcripts of historical events. It is vital to Christian faith that Jesus really was born into this world. And it is equally vital that his birth was "for us men and for our salvation." But "the details of the narrative are symbolic and biblical; they communicate the mystery of the redemption, not a diary of earthly events" (*The Jerome Biblical Commentary* [1968]).

The shepherds were members of a despised class, like tax collectors and prostitutes, in the gospel story. The evangelist is telling us that Christ came especially to the outcasts, an emphasis that will characterize Luke's Gospel throughout.

Appearances of angels bringing messages to accompany events are the biblical way of expressing the meaning of salvation events as the acts of God (cf. the angel[s] at the empty tomb). There are two such accounts in the birth story. The first, by a single angel, announces the messianic birth; the second, by "a multitude of the heavenly host," interprets the saving significance of the birth: "Glory to God in heaven, and peace to his people on earth." "Men of his good pleasure" does not mean men of good will in the popular sense of civil religion. It is a Hebraism, meaning mankind, who are now made the objects of divine favor.

The Homily

Several possibilities suggest themselves: (1) the birth of the Christ as a message of peace in the rich sense of *shalom* (Old Testament reading and angelic hymn); (2) midnight, the symbolic hour of the first and second comings of the Christ; (3) the first Christmas came to shepherds, and so the incarnation is a message of hope for the poor and oppressed and a challenge to the Christian church to become more sensitive to their needs; (4) the contrast between the civil notion of men of good will and the biblical concept of mankind on whom God's favor rests. No Pelagian do-it-yourself recipe but only the intervention of God's grace can cope with man's fundamental predicament of sin.

MASS AT DAWN

Reading I: Isaiah 62:11-12

A passage from Trito-Isaiah, originally referring to one of the Jewish festivals (Tabernacles ?). Read today, it speaks of the new Israel's joy at the advent of the messianic salvation.

Responsorial Psalm: 97:1 and 6, 11-12

This is another of the enthronement psalms. The second stanza and the refrain underline the dawn of the light — imagery which has passed into the lore of the season and is expressed in so many Christmas carols.

Reading II: Titus 3:4-7

Compare reading II of the midnight mass. But this passage speaks only of the first appearance or coming of Christ. And it does not lead, as the earlier reading did, to an ethical exhortation but to an affirmation of the saving consequences of the Christ event — regeneration and renewal, the rebirth of men and women as children of God. A traditional Christmas theme: the Son of God became man to make us sons of God..

Gospel: Luke 2:15-20

A continuation of the gospel reading at the midnight mass. The shepherds go to Bethlehem to visit the Christ child. The familiarity of the picture should not blind us to its theological significance. Here the divine salvation is disclosed to the outcast. The shepherds tell what they have seen (the Christ child) and heard (the angelic proclamation that this is God's salvation entered into the world). That is, they declare both fact and interpretation.

The Homily

The Old Testament reading speaks of the people of God as "sought out." This idea is fundamental to an understanding of the incarnation, which, as Karl Barth used to say, is God's *search* for man. The church is the place, not merely where men search for God but where, through the word and sacraments and witness to the world, God searches for men.

Reading II suggests a consideration of what it means to be a child of God. Christ alone is Son of God "by nature." Christian believers become sons of God only by "adoption and grace." The Bible, however, teaches that all men are by nature sons of God. They are such only potentially until they are reborn in Christ.

MASS DURING THE DAY

Reading I: Isaiah 52:7-10

Cf. reading I of the mass at dawn and the enthronement psalms of all three masses this day. The prophet proclaims the reign of God now being actualized by his mighty act. In his case this act was the return from exile; for us it is the birth of the Christ child announced by the angelic hymn. In that event Yahweh is returning to Zion (v. 8) to comfort his people (v. 9). He bares his arm and all mankind sees the event of salvation (v. 10).

Responsorial Psalm: 98:1, 2-3ab, 3cd-4, 5-6

Other selections from this psalm are used on Sundays 28C and 33C. Compare also the enthronement psalms used at the earlier masses this day. They all praise God for his saving intervention and are thus applicable to the birth of Christ.

Reading II: Hebrews 1:1-6

Hebrews opens with a christological hymn. This hymn was evidently drawn from an earlier tradition and was perhaps derived originally from a Jewish hymn in praise of the divine wisdom. In any case it reflects Jewish teaching. Wisdom is a hypostatized, or personified, entity pre-existent with God from eternity, the agent of creation at the beginning of the world and its sustainer ever since. She is also the agent of divine revelation through all of Israel's salvation history. In the Jewish tradition she seeks to dwell with men and, when rejected, returns to heaven.

This wisdom myth was adapted in early Christianity as a vehicle to express its own faith in Christ. As early as 1 Corinthians (cf. 1:21, 23-24, 30; 2:6-7) he is identified with wisdom: he was the preexisting agent of creation and preservation, and of revelation in Israel's salvation history. He appears on earth and then returns to heaven. The mythical pattern rarely appears in its entirety when applied to Christ. In Hebrews, for example, there is no mention of his descent in the incarnation or of his incarnate life. These are presumed in the mention of his having made purification for sins, an idea which of course is unparalleled in the Jewish wisdom myth.

Particularly noteworthy is the contrast between the partial and fragmentary revelations in Israel's salvation history ("in many various ways") and the eschatological finality of God's self-revelation in Christ.

Gospel: John 1:1-18 (long form); 1:1-5, 9-14 (short form)

The shorter form omits the remarks about the Baptist, which are often regarded today as prose insertions into an earlier hymn to the Logos.

The evangelist intends the prologue to serve as a theological commentary on his gospel as a whole. The gospel relates the history of Jesus from his baptism until his glorification. The word "flesh" signifies the whole of human history, not just the humanity of Jesus considered in the abstract. This history, however, is the manifestation of the Logos, the self-communication of God. Now this self-communication did not begin with the Christ event. In eternity God was already a self-communicating God. Creation (1:1-3), general revelation (man's natural knowledge of God: cf. vv. 4, 9), and the special revelation to Israel (cf. v. 11) were all activities of God in which he went forth from his being-in-himself, in self-communication. Finally this self-communication culminates in the whole visible history of Jesus of Nazareth.

John is not thinking in terms of the ontological christological dogma of Nicaea (325) and Constantinople (381). He does not combine the concept of incarnation with a birth narrative, though he is aware of birth traditions (cf. 7:41-42). No doubt he would have regarded these as *Vorgeschichte*, historical prelude, as did Matthew and Luke. He prefers to interpret the baptism of Jesus (which he does not directly narrate, but which he clearly knows) as the point where the Word's becoming flesh was initiated as a dynamic process which occurs continually throughout the ministry. In this ministry Jesus is in constant communion with the Father, surrenders himself so completely to the Father's will that his words become the Father's words and his works the Father's works, so that in his history the Word continually becomes flesh. His coming into the world, or coming down from heaven, is to be seen as the visible side of this dynamic process.

John does not think of the incarnation as a combination of two abstract entities, humanity and divinity, in a divine-human person. This is not to say that John's Christology was adoptionistic in the later heretical sense. For historical adoptionism thinks in far more precise ontological categories than John does. Nor is it to say that the later ontological Christology was a mistaken development, for it was a translation of the New Testament proclamation into the Hellenistic categories of the fourth and fifth centuries. Exegesis, however, requires that we should not read back these categories into John but let him speak for himself. Incidentally, this more dynamic understanding of the incarnation can probably speak more intelligibly to our day than later ontological categories. We need to interpret the latter by means of the former.

The Homily

Perhaps the homilist would like to take the opportunity of exploring the Fourth Gospel's dynamic understanding of the incarnation, so as to help his hearers grasp something of how God could communicate himself in a fully human life. The homilist may find some useful hints in John A. T. Robinson's *The Human Face of God* (1973), although this work should not be read uncritically.

If this is too demanding, the homilist might at least point up the significance of the fact that we read Hebrews 1 and John 1 on Christmas Day. This shows we are not just celebrating the birth of a human baby but the mystery of God's self-disclosure in the whole history of Jesus.

HOLY FAMILY [ALTERNATIVE BELOW]

The readings remain constant except for the gospel. We shall, accordingly, summarize our previous comments on the other readings and offer fresh comments on the gospel.

Reading I: Sirach 3:2-6, 12-14

The text offers a commentary on the (fifth/fourth) commandment to honor father and mother. The assertion that love of parents will make atonement for sins must be taken rhetorically as an incentive to obey the commandment, not as a serious theological statement. In the New Testament, atonement for sin is through Christ alone.

Responsorial Psalm: 128:1-2, 3, 4-5

Piety is the foundation of family and social life and even of economic prosperity (cf. Deuteronomy). Perhaps we should not want to take this too naively today. Yet it remains true that where man seeks to fear God and do his will, his relations with his fellow man stand a better chance of being on a sound footing. One who fears God is less inclined to put himself in God's place. That frees him for the love of neighbor and helps the neighbor to love him in return.

Reading II: Colossians 3:12-21

This passage is taken from the parenesis or ethical exhortation of Colossians, reproducing (according to a widely accepted view) material from an early Christian catechesis.

It begins with a list of virtues. These are to be "put on," an idea suggested by the vesting of the candidate with his new white robe as he emerges from the baptismal waters. This section of the catechism is sometimes preceded by another list, a list of vices which are to be put off or renounced, an idea suggested by the disrobing of the candidate before his descent into the baptismal waters. Following these two general exhortations, the later New Testament letters often provide a *Haustafel* or household code, listing various members of the household and stating their duties. It is thought that such forms were derived ultimately from Stoicism *via* Hellenistic Jewish catechesis. That will explain the subordinationist ethic characterizing them, which is Stoic rather than Christian. The distinctive Christian element is the addition of "in the Lord," and the emphasis on love and forgiveness.

Gospel: Luke 2:41-52

The form critics classify this pericope as a "legend." This does not necessarily mean that the incident is wholly unhistorical — as indeed Dibelius was careful to point out. To call it a legend means that its purpose is not historical. There are many similar stories of the precocious childhood of a great man whose boyhood showed signs of his coming greatness (e.g., in the life of the Buddha or Josephus).

We recognize certain redactional concerns of Luke: the legal piety of Jesus' home (cf. Lk 2:21, 22), shown in their devout observance of passover customs, Luke's interest in the effect of these remarkable incidents on Jesus' mother (cf. Lk 2:19), and the emphasis on the human growth of Jesus (cf. 2:40), though the last point may be modeled on the childhood of Samuel and be designed to portray Jesus as the eschatological prophet. In that case it may even have been a feature of Luke's source. That the core of the narrative is pre-Lucan is shown by the absence of any hint of the virginal conception ("his parents," "your father"). The answer of the boy Jesus in verse 49 with its reference to God as "my Father" seems to reflect the church's Christology. The basic incident, however, is not only pre-Lucan but may well rest upon an authentic memory. And even the allusion to "my Father" may be prechristological, reflecting Jesus' growing historical awareness of his unique filial relation with God. This awareness will then be the basis and presupposition for his later submission to the Father's call and acceptance of the unique eschatological role in salvation history. Thus one hesitates to dismiss this story as entirely without historical worth even if in the form-critical sense it should be characterized as a "legend."

Our real concern must be with the evangelist's purpose in including this story in his gospel. It is evidently part of his picture of the family of Jesus and its devout adherence to the Jewish law, which provided the environment in which he developed, as Samuel had developed, so that he could later fulfill his role as the eschatological prophet and the bringer of redemption to Israel.

The Homily

The Old Testament and epistle reading together with the gospel provide different ways of treating the importance of family life in Christian nurture. The Old Testament reading emphasizes the importance of the fifth/fourth commandment, and the epistle, if we concentrate on its specifically Christian elements, as opposed to the Stoic emphasis on subordinationism, sets a pattern of Christian family life based upon mutual forgiveness, while the gospel suggests that the family is the context for growth to physical, mental, and spiritual maturity.

FIRST SUNDAY AFTER CHRISTMAS DAY

(As appointed in *Services for Trial Use* of the Episcopal Church.) The provisions for this day continue the theme of the incarnation from Christmas Day, in lieu of the theme of the Holy Family in the new Roman lectionary.

Reading I: Isaiah 60:13-21

This reading forms part of Trito-Isaiah's description of the new Jerusalem as it was being rebuilt after the exile. Just as foreign enemies had destroyed the old Jerusalem, so foreigners will build the new city. This reading forms a suitable lesson for any Christian festival, for Christian faith finds the fulfillment of this picture of the new Jerusalem in the establishment of the Christian church through God's redemptive act in Christ, and its ultimate fulfillment at the end (cf. the picture of the new Jerusalem in the Apocalypse, which draws on some of the imagery in this passage).

Reading II: Galatians 4:4-7

This passage is the same as the second reading for the Solemnity of Mary the Mother of God (Jan. 1) in the Roman lectionary and has already been commented upon. Here is a résumé of our comments.

The pericope is an expansion of a pre-Pauline hymn which, according to recent scholarly investigation, reads as follows:

> God sent forth his Son
> (born of a woman)
> that we might receive adoption as sons.

This hymn makes the important point that the birth of the Christ is not just a story of something that happened long ago and which, however beautiful, has no relevance to our own lives. The purpose of the incarnation for us was that we might become sons of God by adoption and grace.

Paul probably added the words "born under the law, to redeem those under the law," for they reflect his theological concerns. In his incarnation and earthly life the Son of God submitted to the limitations of human life, including man's bondage to the law. The law, for Paul, told man what to do but left him powerless to do it. The Son of God, however, broke this bondage by submitting to it while still remaining absolutely free, so that he could pass the "contagion" (Van Buren) of that freedom to others.

Gospel: John 1:1-18

This is the gospel for the third mass of Christmas Day, lengthened to include verses 6–8 and 15–18. The prologue properly ends at verse 18. Verse 16 is actually the concluding line of the pre-Johannine hymn, while verses 15 and 17–18 are prose additions of the evangelist (so Bultmann). In verse 15 the congregation concludes its confessional hymn to the Logos by acknowledging him as the source of grace. Verse 15 is another of the evangelist's polemical insertions against an overestimate of John the Baptist (cf. vv. 6–8), while verses 17–18 are also polemical, in this case against an overestimate of Moses, who gave the law, not grace, and who did not, despite Jewish claims, see God (cf. Ex 33:17-22, where Moses sees only the "back" of God).

The Homily

The Pauline addition to the traditional hymn in the epistle reading and the Johannine addition to the prologue in 1:17-18 both focus upon the contrast between law and grace. The combination of these two texts offers the homilist an excellent opportunity to expound the true nature of Christian freedom. God in Christ liberates us from the bondage of the law — of having to work for our own salvation — by giving us salvation as a gift and so freeing us for the love of God and neighbor.

January 1 to Sunday 3 C

SOLEMNITY OF MARY, MOTHER OF GOD: JANUARY I
In year C the readings of year A are repeated for this day. They were commented upon above.

Reading II and the gospel are traditional to the Christmas season. In *Services for Trial Use* of the Episcopal Church, reading II is appointed for Christmas I, and while today's gospel is the same, the day is entitled "The Holy Name of Our Lord Jesus Christ." The new Roman title of the day is suggested by two verses in reading II and the gospel — viz., Galatians 4:4c and Luke 2:19. These verses, however, emphasize Mary not as Theotokos but as the paradigm of faith and therefore of the Christian believer and the true Israel. But the main thrust of today's reading is the birth of Christ as the inauguration of the saving act of God.

Reading I: Numbers 6:22-27
Note the threefold structure of the Aaronic blessing, which in a remarkable way anticipates the Trinitarian structure of Christian faith (see below).

The last verse is also important (cf. the caption: "They will call down my name on the sons of Israel and I will bless them"). The concept of the name is highly important in biblical theology. The "name" of a man means his whole person, what we mean when we speak of character and personality. The name of God means his being as this is disclosed in the salvation history of the Old and New Testaments. By invoking God's name upon the people, the priestly blessing confers upon them all that God is and all that he has done for Israel. For the Christian church the name of God further includes all that he has done in Jesus Christ. This is not an addition to the Aaronic blessing, but, as its Trinitarian structure shows, its full explication. In the act of blessing, all that God is and has done is passed on from age to age.

Responsorial Psalm: 67:1-2, 4, 5 and 7
The refrain "May God bless us in his mercy" shows how this psalm picks up the theme of reading I. The mercy (*hesedh*) of God embraces all that he has done in his mighty acts toward Israel and for us also in Jesus Christ.

Reading II: Galatians 4:4-7
This reading was commented upon immediately above in the alternatives for the trial lectionary of the Episcopal Church. It emphasizes that the purpose of the incarnation was man's *liberation* from the law to the status of sonship: "no longer a slave but a son."

Gospel: Luke 2:16-21
This reading is repeated from the dawn mass of Christmas. But today it continues through verse 21 to relate the circumcision and naming of Jesus. The circumcision ties in with the epistle reading ("born under the law"), and the naming of Jesus with the threefold name of the Aaronic blessing.

The Homily
The scripture readings suggest three possible choices for the homilist. Reading I and the psalm suggest a meditation on the theme of blessing. Valuable material on this will be found in Karl Barth, *Church Dogmatics* III/2, pages 578–587. On page 580 Barth sums up his exegesis in these words: "Blessing is regarded in the Old Testament as the epitome of all the good things which the father can pass on to the son and son receive from the father. A blessing is the word which has divine power to pass on good things." This biblical concept of blessing could be related to the priestly blessing in the liturgy, while the idea of passing on good things, i.e., our Christian heritage, from generation to generation is an appropriate thought for New Year's Day.

Second, there is the theme of liberation, suggested by Paul's explanation of the purpose of the incarnation and the connection between "born under the law" in reading II and the circumcision of Christ in the gospel. Today there is much talk of liberation as a meaningful equivalent of the biblical word "salvation." The homilist might confront contemporary understanding of liberation with that of the Bible.

A third possibility would be to take up the theme of the divine name in the Aaronic blessing and its connection with the naming of Jesus [= Yahweh saves]. Jesus' name is a programmatic definition of the whole purpose of the incarnation. Similarly our own baptismal names are programmatic for us. They give us identity, meaning and purpose in life. Such a reflection, however, needs to be guarded against a Pelagian misinterpretation. For our baptismal name is given "in the name of Jesus." His name — what he is and has done for us — alone makes it possible for us to realize the program denoted by our name. This, too, could be an appropriate reflection for New Year's Day.

EPIPHANY

The Epiphany readings being the same each year, our previous comments will be summarized here.

It will be remembered that in the Eastern Church, where today's feast originated, Epiphany was primarily a celebration of the baptism of Christ as the first of the "epiphanies" or manifestations of God in man. Other epiphanies in Jesus' earthly life were also associated with this day, especially the changing of the water into wine at Cana of Galilee. When east and west exchanged the feasts of Christmas and Epiphany, January 6 in the west drew some of the associations previously attached to Christmas, especially the story of the magi. Since the magi were presumed to be gentiles (a point not emphasized, however, in the Matthean pericope), the feast acquired a new emphasis as the manifestation of Christ to the gentiles (the Anglican subtitle for this day). This finally led, especially among the Lutherans, to an association of the day with the mission of the church in foreign lands.

Reading I: Isaiah 60:1-6
This reading is from Trito-Isaiah. Part I (vv. 1-3) announces the return of the exiles in language taken up from Deutero-Isaiah (chs. 40-55). Part II (4-6) foretells the eschatological pilgrimage of the gentiles to the restored city of Jerusalem. Part I is typological of the birth of Christ, part II of the visit of the magi.

Although the evangelist (curiously, in view of his special interest in quoting Old Testament prophecies) does not cite this passage, it has clearly influenced the magi narrative as the reference to gold and frankincense (v. 6) shows. Later legend added other features from this passage to the story of the magi that were not noted by Matthew — namely, the fact that the magi were gentiles, to say nothing of the camels of v. 6!

Responsorial Psalm: 72:1-2, 7-8, 10-11, 12-13

This psalm was originally a coronation hymn composed for kings of the Davidic dynasty. Christian faith sees its fulfillment in Christ, for it emphasizes the "pastoral" aspects of kingship, such as the establishment of justice and compassion for the poor. The psalm also brings out a feature absent from reading I — namely, the figure of the messianic king.

We may suspect that this psalm, like reading I, has also influenced the Matthean narrative of the magi. Once more we note lack of any explicit quotation, yet the psalm speaks of the pilgrims bringing gifts and falling down before the messianic king. Like Isaiah 60, this psalm has also contributed something to the legend of the magi, viz., their identification as kings. That they were *three* kings was an inference from the three gifts specified by Matthew.

Christian faith sees Psalm 72 appropriately fulfilled in the coming of Christ as the messianic king who brings justice and compassion for the poor (stanza 4), and in the universality of the acknowledgment accorded to the messianic king ("all nations" in stanza 3, echoed in the refrain).

Reading II: Ephesians 3:2-3a, 5-6

This reading is an explicit theological statement of the two themes adumbrated in reading I: viz., the revelation or epiphany of God in Christ (v. 3) and the universality of the messianic salvation (v. 6).

Many modern scholars regard Ephesians as the work not of Paul himself but of a member of the Pauline school looking back after the apostle's death upon his achievement in maintaining the unity of Jew and gentile in the one church.

Gospel: Matthew 2:1-12

This pericope gathers together early Christian traditions from different sources. First, the primitive kerygma had affirmed Jesus' Davidic descent (Rom 1:3). According to Jewish expectation this qualified him for the messiahship. As a christological affirmation, Jesus' Davidic descent explains the importance attached in the infancy narratives to his birth at Bethlehem. A tradition common to Matthew and Luke dates the birth of Jesus in the reign of Herod (d. 4 B.C.). This dating is plausible and may well rest on fact.

Third, there is the folk memory of Herod's cruelty and especially the pathological fear of assassination and usurpation which marked the closing years of his reign. A fourth element is the star as a messianic symbol. The star originates in Numbers 24:17 and was given a messianic interpretation as early as the Testaments of the Twelve Patriarchs. Matthew's failure to quote Numbers 24:17 is again surprising. Fifth, the gifts presented to the Christ child were suggested by our reading I and responsory psalm, although again the Matthean text does not cite them.

Sixth, there is the *testimonium* from Micah 5:2 cited in verse 6. This passage was already interpreted messianically in Judaism (cf. Jn 7:42 and the fact that, unusually for Matthew, it is placed here on the lips of the scribes). It seems likely therefore that it was used as a *testimonium* before Matthew, though the structure of the pericope suggests it was first inserted into the story by the evangelist. Finally, although Matthew does not emphasize it, there is the tradition of *gentiles* coming to see the messianic salvation, from reading I and Psalm 72.

All these factors have contributed to the shaping of the magi story. The only certain historical facts behind the narrative are the names Jesus, Joseph and Mary, the dating of the birth, and perhaps also its location at Bethlehem, though that tradition may have originated from Micah 5:2 and Jewish expectation about the Messiah. The significance of the story is almost entirely symbolical.

The Homily

The magi story is set in the context of readings I and II and the responsorial psalm. This brings out the kerygmatic truths the story symbolizes: the revelation of God in the messianic event and the universality of that revelation. It may be taken as an expression of the truth that the Christ event provides the answer to man's religious quest, especially if the magi were astrologists and magicians rather than astronomers and philosophers. Gold, frankincense and myrrh may have been the tools of their dubious trade, offered not as tokens of homage but "as a declaration of dissociation from former practices" (Anchor Bible commentary, *ad loc.*). This interpretation, if accepted, would provide the homilist with an opportunity to relate the story to some of the more bizarre manifestations of man's contemporary religious quest. The gospel is the answer to man's search for God, as well as its corrective.

BAPTISM OF THE LORD ✓

The readings for today are the same every year, with the exception of the gospel, which follows the account of the baptism from the synoptic gospel read in course each year. Hence this year it is read from Luke's version.

The comments that were given previously on reading I, the responsorial psalm and reading II will be summarized. The commentary on the gospel will be new.

As mentioned earlier, the baptism of the Lord was the primary mystery celebrated in the east on this day. The whole life of Christ was understood as a series of epiphanies, or manifestations, of which the baptism was the first and constitutive. In the west, the baptism was relegated to a subordinate place in the Epiphany season. It has now been restored to something of its former prominence by being assigned to the first Sunday after the Epiphany. This arrangement helps to restore emphasis to the theological aspect of the Christmas mystery, as opposed to its historical aspect, most of which now seems to us to be legendary.

Reading I: Isaiah 42:1-4, 6-7

This first of the servant psalms has clearly been a major influence in the shaping of the synoptic baptismal narratives. The words "with whom I am well pleased" in the heavenly voice is almost certainly a rendering of "in whom my soul delights" (Is 42:1b), and although the more obvious source of "thou art my son" would seem to be Psalm 2:7, it is possible, as some hold, that "son" is a translation of an ambiguous word in Aramaic for "servant." Although in Deutero-Isaiah the term "servant" has some other meaning (Israel, a faithful remnant of Israel, or an individual figure), for the New Testament and Christian faith the servant's role is fulfilled in Jesus, and it is as the servant, at least in part, that the baptismal story in the gospels proclaims him.

Verses 2-3 describe the character of the servant, verses 6-7 his work. Both descriptions apply fittingly to Jesus and are useful introductions to the series of readings on the earthly ministry of Jesus which will occupy us from now until Lent.

Responsorial Psalm: 29:1-4, 9b-10

In part this is an enthronement psalm of the familiar type (cf. stanza 3). Stanza 2, however, may have been connected originally with Baal Hadad, the storm god of Canaan. The psalm is written in a meter reminiscent of Canaanite poetry as found in the Ugaritic texts. Whatever its origin, the psalmist has transferred it to Yahweh. The storm becomes an epiphany of his presence as the Creator God.

Like reading I, stanza 2 points to the heavenly voice at the baptism.

Reading II: Acts 10:34-38

This is part of the kerygmatic speech attributed to Peter in the Cornelius episode. Like Mark and John, the kerygma here begins the earthly life of Jesus with his baptism. In this rite he is anointed with the Holy Spirit and so prepared for a ministry of charismatic healing. Note that in summarizing the story of Jesus' ministry, the kerygmatic speech emphasizes what God did in Jesus.

It has often been observed that whereas Jesus preached the kingdom, the church preached Jesus — with the suggestion that the church was wrong. However, in preaching the kingdom and performing his exorcisms and healings, Jesus was proclaiming that God was acting eschatologically in his words and works. And in preaching Jesus, the church proclaimed that in the earthly ministry of Jesus God had been decisively at work. So despite the formal change, there is material continuity between Jesus and the church's kerygma.

Gospel: Luke 3:15-16, 21-22

Luke has made four major alterations in his Marcan source. First, he has prefaced his account of John's messianic preaching with the remark that the people were wondering whether *he* were the Messiah. The second alteration is obscured by the lectionary's omission of verses 19-20. Here, between the Baptist's messianic preaching and the baptism of Jesus, Luke has inserted the account of John's imprisonment, which Mark and Matthew placed after the temptation and just before the beginning of the Galilean ministry (Mk 1:14a par.).

Third, Luke has suppressed the statement that it was John who baptized Jesus and has thrown the mention of Jesus' baptism into a subordinate clause (a genitive absolute in Greek, a temporal clause in the Revised Standard Version: "when Jesus . . . had been baptized and was praying"). Fourth, Luke omits the statement that Jesus saw "the heavens opened." Fifth, Luke has added that the Spirit descended upon Jesus "in bodily form."

What is the point of these alterations? It could be that Luke prefers here to follow an alternative version of the baptism narrative (Q? Special tradition?). In favor of Q is the fact of Matthew's and Luke's agreement against Mark in the word they use for the "opening," verse 21, and "upon him," verse 22. At the same time it is clear that Luke is seeking to play down John's role in the baptism of Jesus, for he, not his non-Marcan source, must have been responsible for placing the imprisonment of John before Jesus' baptism. Why did Luke do this? Perhaps for polemical reasons similar to those which operated in the Fourth Gospel. But Luke may have had weightier theological motives for suppressing any reference to John's role in Jesus' baptism. The Baptist, for Luke, is not the "beginning of the gospel," as he is for Mark. Rather, the Baptist is the last of the Old Testament prophets, standing at the head of the old age and pointing to the coming one. Hence the line between the old age and the new runs between the first and second paragraphs of our reading as printed in the lectionary.

As we saw at Christmas, Luke presents the birth of Jesus as *Vorgeschichte*, preparatory history, the bringing into the world and the marking out of the one who was destined to be the epiphany and redemptive act of God. Thus the angel at the annunciation promises that he shall [future] be called the Son of God. This means that for Luke sonship is not an ontological status but a function Jesus will embark upon later. The descent of the Spirit and the heavenly voice now inaugurate that function. He will now embark on a life of obedience to his eschatological mission, the function which the annunciation narrative had foretold.

The Homily

How do we preach about an event, the baptism of Jesus, which the gospel of the day hurried over with a genitive absolute? Clearly, we must emphasize, not the role of the Baptist, but the meaning of the descent of the Spirit and the heavenly voice. Decisive for what Jesus was and did is not the part played in his life by his human contemporaries, but the act of God initiated in Jesus' history. The Lucan account of the baptism emphasizes this divine initiative. Is this just a *theologoumenon*, or does it have something to say to us today? We tend to think of Christianity as a cause which somehow we must support. And if it does not prosper, we become anxious about it. The Bible, however, is not concerned about Christianity but with the mighty acts of God, culminating in Jesus Christ. Our task is to respond to these mighty acts in faith and obedience, not to defend a human religious cause.

SECOND SUNDAY OF THE YEAR

Reading I: Isaiah 62:1-5

This passage comes from a section of Trito-Isaiah which consists of songs celebrating the return from exile. The subject of the present song is the restored city of Jerusalem. God is now rejoicing over the city as a bride-groom rejoices over his bride.

While this reading comes from a section appropriate for any festival season, it is clearly intended to match the gospel, the marriage at Cana in Galilee, for it uses nuptial imagery — a familiar tradition established since Hosea — to depict the relation between Yahweh and Israel.

The speaker in verse 1 is the prophet. His style and vocabulary suggest that he was a pupil of Deutero-Isaiah. His master had prophesied the return. That return had doubtless now taken place, but Jerusalem has not yet been rebuilt (cf. Haggai and Nehemiah). The prophet is, however, undaunted and still convinced that his master's predictions will be completely fulfilled. So he refuses to keep silent or to rest (in intercession for the city) until God vindicates her.

The writer then expresses the restoration of Jerusalem in three pictures: (1) She will be a crown and a diadem in the hand of Yahweh. It has been suggested that this image derives from the ancient near eastern practice of depicting the god of a city wearing a crown patterned after the city walls. (2) The city will be given a new name, "My delight is in her" = Hephziba, a girl's name in Hebrew. (3) The nuptial imagery already noted. Note the bold mixture of images: your sons will marry you (!), then Yahweh will rejoice over Jerusalem as a bride. We should not press this imagery too closely. The general idea is clear enough.

Responsorial Psalm: 96:1-2a, 2b-3, 7-8a, 9-10ac

Stanzas 1 and 2 of this psalm are used each year at Christmas midnight mass, and practically the same selection in a slightly different arrangement on Sunday 29 A. As well as being a psalm generally suitable for festivals, it has a strong missionary note, brought out here by the refrain "Proclaim his marvelous deeds to all the nations."

Reading II: 1 Corinthians 12:4-11

This reading overlaps with reading II on Pentecost Sunday which received comment above, in cycle C. The selection for that day comprised three sections: (1) confession of Jesus as Lord; (2) the varieties of gifts [abbreviated]; (3) diversity and unity within the body. Today (1) is dropped, (2) given in full, specifying the varieties of gifts, and (3) will form the beginning of next week's epistle.

Note first the artless triadic structure of verses 4-6:

charismata — the Spirit
service [*diakoniai*] — the Lord [= Christ]
workings [*energemata* = functions] — God.

Paul's intention here is in part polemical, directed against the Corinthian gnostics, who overemphasized the importance of some of the gifts, especially speaking in tongues. The apostle prefers the term *charismata* to the term *pneumatika* [spiritual things], for it emphasizes that the gifts are gifts of grace [*charis*], not natural endowments to be proud of. The word "service" [*diakonia*] strikes a polemical note to be taken up later in the development of the image of the body. The Corinthians thought the gifts existed for their own glory rather than for the service of the community. Since it is the same triune God who is at work in all of them, no gift can be exalted above any other.

Verse 7 then sums up verses 4-6 and serves as heading for verses 8-10: every spiritual phenomenon is given for the common good. Verses 8-10 spell out the *charismata*, listing nine in all: (1) wisdom, (2) knowledge [*gnosis*], (3) faith, (4) healing, (5) miracle-working, (6) prophecy, (7) distinguishing of spirits, (8) tongues, (9) interpretation of tongues.

The gifts fall into three groups: Group I: (1), (2); Group II: (3), (4), (5); Group III: (7), (8) and (9). I. Elsewhere in the epistle there is hardly any perceptible difference between wisdom and knowledge. Both refer to gifts which the Corinthian gnostics claimed to possess and criticized Paul for not having. II. Faith here does not mean the faith by which all Christians respond to the gospel and so are justified, but a special gift confined to some. It is connected with miracle-working. III. Prophecy does not require interpretation, for it is not unintelligible speech, but the discerning of spirits — to see whether it is genuine or false prophesy. In verse 1 Paul has already set up the criterion: whether the prophecy confesses Jesus as Lord or says *anathēma Iēsous*.

Verse 11 rounds off the list by repeating the substance of verse 7 and prepares for the ensuing section on the churches as the body of Christ: *one* Spirit — *one* body.

Gospel: John 2:1-12

The view is gaining ground that the Fourth Gospel used a source consisting mainly of miracle stories, i.e., an "aretalogy" (for the name see Sirach 36:14: "wondrous deeds" in RSV). Its purpose was to use a series of stupendous miracles to convince potential converts that Jesus was the Messiah (cf. Jn 20:30, probably the conclusion of the aretalogy). It was therefore a missionary writing. Its basic conception was that Jesus was the messianic prophet, recalling Moses, Elijah and Elisha, as these were interpreted in later Judaism — i.e., as "divine men." In short, it was designed as a missionary tract to convert Greek-speaking Jews to Christianity.

The evangelist, as distinct from the aretalogist, wrote at a later time when Christians had been expelled from the Jewish synagogue. His purpose was not to convert but to force a decision upon Jewish Christians who were concealing their faith in order to avoid expulsion from the synagogue. So he incorporates the earlier aretalogy into his gospel, adding glosses to the miracle stories, expanding them with dialogues and discourses, and combining the whole with a passion and resurrection narrative. In this way he sets before his readers the purpose of Christ's coming into the world — to bring about a *krisis*, a decision between light and darkness, truth and falsehood, life and death.

Unlike most of the other signs in the Fourth Gospel, the Cana marriage story has no dialogue or discourse attached to it by the evangelist. Rather, he has contented himself here with a few extra touches. These may be identified as follows: verse 4 (especially "My hour has not yet come"); verse 6b ("for the Jewish rites of purification"); verse 11c ("and manifested his glory"). Each of these additions serves to link up the Cana miracle with the passion story: the hour, for the evangelist, is the hour of the passion; the Jewish rites of purification are replaced by the messianic purification accomplished on the cross (cf. 1 Jn 1:7, "the blood of Jesus his Son cleanses us from all sin"); the cross is the supreme moment of Jesus' glorification.

In effect, what the evangelist is saying is that we are not to take the Cana miracle as a direct and complete epiphany of Christ's glory. Though the evangelist accepts the reality of the miracle, it has for him a further, symbolic significance, pointing toward what Jesus is to accomplish on the cross. There the old order will be replaced by the new. This is what the changing of the water symbolizes. The real, final, epiphany is the cross.

The Homily

It is usually possible to take the Old Testament reading and the gospel together. Today, however, the only possible connecting link we have discerned is the nuptial theme. But this is not central to the gospel story, only its incidental setting. Hence the homilist will find it difficult to take these two readings together, and it would be better not to try.

If the homilist wishes to preach on the Old Testament lesson, he had better take the nuptial theme from there and treat it on its own. It would provide an opportunity to interpret the eucharist as the marriage between Christ and his church. Here the church knows herself to be Hephziba, the one in whom the Lord delights.

Reading II provides the homilist with an opportunity to inculcate a balanced view of charismatic gifts in the community. This would be a fitting choice where the charismatic movement is creating problems and tensions. It is necessary to remind ourselves that there are many gifts of the Spirit and that there is a fundamental unity between them all, for they are all equally the work of the one Spirit.

It is ironical that much homiletic exposition of the Cana wonder at the Epiphany season (it was read on Epiphany 2 in the Roman Missal and in the Book of Common Prayer of the Church of England, and on Epiphany 3 in the American Book of Common Prayer) has been done on the level of the aretalogy. The changing of the water into wine has been taken as a direct epiphany of the glory of God in Christ. Compare Christopher Wordworth's hymn:

> And at Cana, wedding guest,
> In thy godhead manifest.

But it is doubtful whether miracles carry the same convincing power today as they did in the ancient world or even in the eighteenth century (cf. Paley's *Evidences*). We are much more likely to be impressed by the symbolical significance which the evangelist has given to the story. Perhaps it would be appropriate to preach Christ today as the agent of change: as he replaced the old Jewish purifactory rites with the messianic purification wrought out on the cross, so he is the agent of change in renewal of the church and in the world today; yet Christians are often so frightened of change and opposed to it.

THIRD SUNDAY OF THE YEAR
Reading I: Nehemiah 8:1-4a, 5-6, 8-10

The reason for the choice of this passage today is not clear. Probably a parallel is intended between Ezra's reading of the Law and Jesus' reading of the prophecy of Isaiah 61 in the synagogue (see the gospel).

There is no reason to dispute the historicity of this narrative. But there has been much discussion among scholars about the identity of the book of the law. Wellhausen propounded the attractive theory that it was the completed Pentateuch brought back from Babylon. Internal evidence, however, indicates that the prescriptions for the celebration of the Feast of Tabernacles follow D, not P. This passage offers a model of synagogue worship: the reading of the Torah, with the people standing, and the "giving of the sense" of it (i.e., its exposition), so that the people will understand clearly, and finally the response of worship. A similar liturgical order may be glimpsed in the synagogue at Nazareth and survives today in the Christian liturgy of the word, including the standing at the reading of the gospel, as the Jews stood for the Torah.

Responsorial Psalm: 19:7, 8, 9, 14

Selections from this psalm were used twice last year (Lent 3 B and 26 B). Today's selection differs from Lent 3 B only in the final stanza. The first three stanzas praise God for the perfection (stanza 1), truth (stanza 2), and purity (stanza 3) of the Torah, while stanza 4 contains the fine prayer that God's law may be the subject of our constant meditation, so that both our thoughts and our words may be acceptable in his sight.

It should be remembered that "Law," Torah, had a wider meaning than commandments, precepts and ordinances, though of course it included these. This wider meaning embraced the whole range of God's revelation. For the Christian the word or law of God is even more extensive. It embraces the revelation of the Word made flesh. Note that the refrain from John 6:63b refers to the teachings of Jesus, specifically to his discourse on the bread of life. Hence the psalm is not only a response to God's self-revelation in the law as proclaimed by Ezra, but also a response to Jesus' sermon in the synagogue of Nazareth, which will be read in the gospel.

Reading II: 1 Corinthians 12:12-30 (long form); 1 Corinthians 12:12-14, 27 (short form)

There has been much discussion among exegetes and biblical theologians over the sense of the Pauline image for the church, the "body of Christ." Is it a metaphor, a simile, or an ontological reality? In this passage — briefly in the shortened form, at length in the long form — the term clearly stands for simile and for ontological reality. Paul starts with the simile: "*Just as* the body . . . *so*. . . ." But then one would expect him to say, "so it is with the Christian community." No wonder Calvin was surprised at this apparent equation of Christ and the church. But Paul probably is expressing himself a bit loosely. What he really means by it is: as is the case with the human body, so it is with the body of Christ. This clearly shows that for Paul the body of Christ, though a simile, is more than that. It is an ontological reality. The point is clinched at verse 27 after the exposition of the simile: "you *are* the body of Christ," not "you as a community are like a body."

So Paul uses body in an ecclesial context *both* as an ontological reality *and* as a simile. Why does he do this? The answer lies in the probability that Paul did not himself coin the term "body of Christ" nor did he receive it from pre-Pauline tradition (in the New Testament it occurs only in the Pauline literature). Where, then, did he get it? Probably from the Corinthian gnostics, who used it to express the solidarity between Christ and the baptized, as pre-Christian *gnosis* may have used the concept to express the solidarity between the gnostic revealer-redeemer and the redeemed. For the Corinthians, "body of Christ" expressed a substantial identity between Christ and the believers. They shared a common *pneuma*-substance.

Paul accepts the truth behind this insight but tones it down. To affirm the ontological identity between Christ and the believers without qualification is to overlook the christological distinction between Christ and the believers. He is risen but the believers are not yet risen. Therefore their salvation is not an assured possession. They have to work at it through obedience to the *Kyrios*. Paul's corrected use of the body of Christ means just this. To be the body of Christ means to be dependent upon him and subject to his lordship. Hence Paul picks up the Stoic comparison of human communities to a body, in which each member has its function to fulfill and in which each function is indispensable (vv. 14-26). Paul thus emphasizes the ethical implications of the term body.

We may say, then, that for Paul, as for the Corinthian gnostics, the term body of Christ was an ontological reality. But whereas for the Corinthians this ontological reality was a substantial one (of identity of substance, a *pneuma*-reality), for Paul it was a reality denoting christological dependence: the lives of the believers shared a common determination by the saving act of God in Christ and were under the lordship of Christ. Consequently they had to exhibit what they were in ethical obedience. It is significant that when Paul was not in dialogue with the Corinthians, and therefore not restricted to use their term, he substitutes the more satisfactory expression "one body in Christ" (Rom 12:5), which plays down the aspect of identity and conveys a stronger suggestion of sharing a common dependence on the Christ event.

The long form of the epistle goes on to elaborate the simile of the body.

Like a human body, the church has members, each with its special function:

1. apostles
2. prophets
3. teachers

---

miracles
healings
helps
administrations
tongues

We confine ourselves to three observations about this list. First, it is the clearest evidence that we have about the shape of ministry in Corinth and probably in the other Pauline communities too. It was charismatic, not institutional. Second, in this setup apostles, prophets and teachers were preeminent. They alone are enumerated (first, second, third). They are designated by personal titles, whereas the others are designated impersonally as gifts, a fact obscured in the RSV translation. Third, this ministerial setup is not prescriptive for all time. Later the free charismatic ministries developed into ordained institutionalized ministries. But one element remained permanent, the element of apostolic control. Paul exercised this control in the very act of writing 1 Corinthians, and in the canon of the New Testament a similar control was exercised by the episcopate in the second century.

Gospel: Luke 1:1-4; 4:14-21

Luke 1:1-4 is the preface to the two-volume work of Luke-Acts. It is curious to place this preface immediately before the sermon in the synagogue at Nazareth. Only here in the synoptic gospels does an evangelist address the reader in his own name. The preface discloses a number of significant things about Luke's work as an evangelist. Luke is not the first in the field. "Many" have written before him. This probably should not be pressed too much; all Luke is saying is that he has predecessors. We know that Mark, the author of the Q material, and the author or authors of the special Lucan material preceded him. Luke understands his work as a "narrative" rather than as a gospel (contrast Mk 1:1) — i.e., it is intended as a historical work, a description of the beginnings of Christianity.

It is commonplace nowadays to say that the gospels are not biographies. But this is only partly true of Luke, for his gospel aims at being a *vita Jesu* rather than a proclamation of the Christ event, as Mark's is. "The things which have been accomplished among us" will include not only the life of Jesus but also the history of the early church which is covered in the Acts of the Apostles. "Us" means the Christian community from its inception. The Jesus tradition and the traditions about the early history of the church have been handed down from eyewitnesses and ministers of the word, i.e., the apostles and evangelists. Luke does not include himself among the eyewitnesses: he is a member of the second or even perhaps the third generation, dependent upon secondhand or thirdhand traditions for both the life of Jesus and the history of the early church.

His work rests upon his researches, not upon immediate inspiration: "having followed all things closely for some time past." His account is intended to be orderly, a criticism perhaps of the work of some of his predecessors: "to write an orderly account." As we see from his actual work, however, his idea of being orderly is to follow one source at a time. His work is addressed to an individual, Theophilus, not designed like the other synoptic gospels for liturgical use in a community. Its purpose is the instruction of catechumens.

The second paragraph of our reading (Lk 4:14-15) is an editorial link with the temptation story — note the phrase in square brackets inserted in the lectionary: "After forty days in the wilderness." The wording is based on Mark 1:14-15 but with two significant alterations. Luke emphasizes that Jesus' ongoing ministry was performed "in the power of the Spirit" — an idea taken up by the citation of Isaiah 61 in the sermon at Nazareth. Luke wants us to bear in mind that the whole of Jesus' ministry was inspired by the Spirit. Second, Luke suppresses Mark's summary of Jesus' eschatological preaching (Mk 1:15) and substitutes the statement that Jesus *taught* in the synagogues. This prepares for the next scene too.

Luke has shifted the sermon in the synagogue from its later position in Mark (Mk 6:1-6) to the beginning of the ministry. He has done so for programmatic reasons. In the synagogue of his home town Jesus lays his cards on the table and interprets his role as that of the Isaianic servant. The servant's work will consist of preaching, the deliverance of the oppressed and the performance of healings. All this has an eschatological significance: it is the fulfillment of scripture. It is not certain whether Luke himself composed this material, which is absent from Mark, or whether it came from his special source. Probably the latter.

The Homily

Some will doubtless be tempted to apply Ezra's sermon in the square before the Water Gate (!) to recent national events. If so, they should avoid treating Ezra's account as a direct prophecy, as the sects treat the Book of Revelation. Instead they should concentrate on the call to the nation to hearken to the word of God and obey his laws. For the contemporary Watergate crisis is the symbol of a moral rot in the nation as a whole, the consequence of its increasing secularization.

Reading II would provide an opportunity to talk about the church as the body of Christ. That means the local community as well as the universal church, for the local meaning was what Paul had primarily in mind. Particular stress should be laid on the obligations of each member to the others, for that is Paul's major concern in consenting to use the image at all.

The sermon in the synagogue is coming to be regarded as a magna charta of the theology of liberation. The homilist could prepare to preach on this by reading one or more of the works of James Cone. But he should not be uncritical of this theology and should ask himself how far it really squares with the text.

Sundays 4 C to 7 C

Reading I: Jeremiah 1:4-5, 17-19

Today's Old Testament reading consists of the first and last portions of the account of Jeremiah's call to be a prophet. The call properly speaking covers verses 4-10, 17-19, and it would have been more consistent with the structure of the text to divide the material thus, omitting only the two visions which interrupt the narrative of the call (11-16). The call is related in the form of a dialogue between Yahweh and the prophet. Jeremiah was predestined from the womb to be a prophet — a characteristically biblical emphasis on the initiative of Yahweh in Israel's salvation history. "Consecrated" refers to the separation of the prophet for a distinctive role in salvation history. Jeremiah's call played an important role in Paul's understanding of his apostolic call (Gal 1:15). The liturgical selection today, however, treats Jeremiah's call as a type of Jesus' messianic call, for this passage is chosen to match the second half of the sermon in the synagogue at Nazareth.

Jeremiah's mission is not merely to Israel but to "the nations." Since Amos, the prophets had a strong sense of God as the sovereign Lord of all history, not just that of his people. This lordship was expressed more in his judgments than in his acts of mercy. The caption "I have appointed you as prophet to the nations" calls especial attention to this universality of Jeremiah's mission because of the epiphany season and also because of the gospel reading, which invokes the stories of Elijah and Elisha as types of Christ's universal ministry. In these two types, however, the emphasis is on the salvation of Yahweh reaching out beyond Israel rather than on his judgment. In the second paragraph of our reading, Jeremiah is warned of the opposition he will incur in Israel — which again links this reading with Jesus' rejection at Nazareth. There is a consistency both in God's dealings with his people and in his people's reaction to his word, a consistency running through both the Old Testament and the New.

Responsorial Psalm: 71:1-2, 3-4a, 5-6ab, 15ab and 17

This psalm is an individual lament, sung by an aged man in a time of sickness (stanza 3). He flees to God and prays for deliverance (stanzas 1 and 2) and concludes with a vow to praise God henceforth (presumably in thanksgiving for delivery from his sickness). This hymn would be suitable at any time for Christian devotion, as the Christian's fundamental sickness is sin, and the delivery is forgiveness through the atoning work of Christ. However, the reason for its choice today seems to be that Jeremiah frequently fled for refuge to God in face of the hostility of the kings, princes, priests and people of Judah (reading I).

Reading II: 1 Corinthians 12:31–13:13 (long form); 13:4-13 (short form)

Paul's hymn to charity falls into four parts: (1) verses 1-3; (2) 4-7; (3) 8-12; (4) 13: conclusion. The shorter reading consists of parts 2 and 3 plus the conclusion. The longer reading reproduces the whole hymn plus 12:31 which indicates its context in the letter — namely, Paul's discussion of the charismata. Parts 1 and 3 refer to the charismata, part 2 is more abstract and general in its characterization of *agapē*. The hymn's place in the letter is problematical. Verse 14:1 would follow directly on 12:31a. Whereas 12:31b in the Revised Standard Version [= 13:1 in the New American Bible] promises one "more excellent way," the hymn gives us the three virtues of faith, hope and love, although love is acknowledged to be the greatest. These problems have led some to suppose that the hymn is a post-Pauline interpolation, but parts 1 and 3 are too specifically related to the context, the discussion of charismata, for that.

Striking, too, is the lack of any specific christological reference in the hymn. But the triad of faith, hope and love belongs to Christian tradition and occurs elsewhere in the Pauline epistles, especially in the opening thanksgivings. Otherwise the hymn is akin in style to hymns in praise of wisdom and other virtues found in Hellenistic Jewish wisdom literature. It might be suggested that part 2 of the hymn was preformed in Hellenistic Jewish Christianity or even in Hellenistic Judaism, and that Paul himself has adapted it to the context by adding parts 1 and 3. Note the difference of style: parts 1 and 3 are written in an "I" style. This is not Paul's own ego speaking but refers to anyone or everyone. This use of the I-style is characteristic of Hellenistic rhetoric (cf. Rom 7:7-25).

If the central paragraph originally stood on its own, before Paul used it here, and was modeled on Hellenistic Jewish material, we can see why *agapē* is treated simply as a human virtue without any reference to Christology and why there is no clarification about its object — whether it is God's love for man, or man's love for God or for his fellows. It is simply the description of an abstract virtue, like the praise of wisdom in the wisdom literature.

Gospel: Luke 4:21-30

As we have already noted, this is the second part of the sermon in the synagogue at Nazareth. The first part, read last week, consisted of the sermon's text (Is 61) and the brief declaration in verse 21, which today's reading also opens.

The synagogue congregation expresses its astonishment at Jesus' teaching and is perplexed because it knows his human origins. This material is similar to Mark 6, though the reference to Jesus' family is different, recalling John 7:41-42 and therefore suggesting a second source. Then comes the proverb "Physician, heal thyself" (not found elsewhere in the synoptics) and the awkward reference to works already done in Capernaum, awkward because in Luke's Gospel Jesus has not yet worked there. This would suit the Marcan context better, but the reference to Capernaum is absent from Mark. Therefore the proverb and the reference to Capernaum must be a fragment of a non-Marcan version of the rejection which Luke has inserted here. Then comes the saying from Mark about the prophet's not being honored in his own country.

After this we have more material peculiar to Luke — viz., the references to the miracles performed for gentiles by Elijah and Elisha. The style and vocabulary of this section are definitely Lucan, as noted by A. R. C. Leaney in his commentary on Luke. The interest in turning to the gentiles after the rejection by Israel is also a characteristic Lucan theme. It is impossible to say for certain whether the whole of this section of the sermon is Lucan composition. (Leaney leaves the question open.) There is of course the possibility that the examples of Elijah and Elisha had already been used in Christian preaching before Luke and that he has worked these traditional features into his composition, just as he formed the kerygmatic speeches in Acts out of earlier christological formulae and Old Testament testimonia.

The story closes with a hostile attempt on Jesus' life. At first sight this looks like a Lucan expansion of Mark's statement (6:3) that the people of Nazareth were offended at Jesus because of his teaching. But the miraculous escape from a hostile crowd is paralleled in John 10:39, so it is hardly likely to be a Lucan creation. It seems therefore that Luke has a special source containing a version of the Nazareth episode differing from Mark's. This alternative tradition will include: 1. the citation of Isaiah 61; 2. the proverb about the physician and the reference to earlier works in Capernaum; 3. the attempt to stone Jesus. Luke will then have combined this narrative with Mark's, expanding it by his own composition and embodying the references to Elijah and Elisha. The effect of this Lucan redaction is to make the story programmatic to his two-volume work. Luke will repeatedly stress the fact that because of Israel's rejection of the Messiah the gospel goes forth to the gentile world.

The Homily

The more obvious choice for the homilist today would be to start from the Lucan redaction of his two sources (Mark and special Luke) in the Nazareth episode. The homilist should follow Luke's understanding of salvation history. Those originally called reject the gospel, with the consequence that it goes to others. The homilist must be careful, however, not to introduce an anti-Semitic note into a contemporary application. The more obvious application today is that while the church is losing ground in America and Europe, it is making phenomenal gains in Africa, according to all reports.

An alternative possibility would be to speak of Paul's hymn to *agapē*. If the longer form is read, this would suggest relating it quite concretely to the situation in Corinth (an excessive attachment to the charismata). There may be a parallel situation in the homilist's own congregation. Alternatively, if the shorter reading is used, it might be best to concentrate on part 2 of the hymn (the first paragraph of the shorter reading) and give a general meditation on the virtue of Christian love or charity.

FIFTH SUNDAY OF THE YEAR

Reading I: Isaiah 6:1-2a, 3-8

The vision and call of Isaiah form one of the most familiar parts of the Old Testament. Isaiah describes his vision of Yahweh in heaven in imagery derived from the earthly temple at Jerusalem, in which his experience takes place — the underlying conviction is that the Jerusalem temple is an external expression of the heavenly temple. One is led to suppose that the Sanctus was likewise part of the liturgy of the earthly temple, just as it in turn passed into the Christian liturgy. [This passage is also read on Trinity Sunday in the Episcopal trial lectionary; it has long been associated in Anglicanism with this feast, the threefold Sanctus suggesting an Old Testament adumbration of the Trinity.]

The primary emphasis today, however, is not on the vision but on the call, which parallels the call of Peter in today's gospel. The vision of God's holiness, the *mysterium tremendum*, leads Isaiah first to confess his sense of utter unworthiness. His call thus comes to him as a sheer miracle of grace. The prophet first receives forgiveness for his sin, is then called to "go for us" and responds by accepting the call. Note the contrast between his initial diffidence in reaction to the vision and the confidence with which he finally accepts the call.

Responsorial Psalm: 138:1-2a, 2bcd-3, 4-5, 7d-8

This is a psalm of praise and thanksgiving, following appropriately upon Isaiah's vision. It should be noted that whereas the combination of the Old Testament reading with the gospel highlights the call, the psalm highlights Isaiah's vision, as indicated by the refrain and the third line of stanza 1.

Reading II: 1 Corinthians 15:1-11 (long form); 15:3-8, 11 (short form)

This is one of the most important passages in the New Testament. Paul has to deal with the Corinthians' uncertainty and doubt about the resurrection of the dead. The older view was that they held the Greek belief in the immortality of the soul as opposed to the Jewish-Christian belief in the resurrection of the body. More recently it has been supposed that as gnostics they believed that through the sacraments they were raised already and therefore did not require a further resurrection of the body.

In order to correct the Corinthians, Paul recalls the gospel that he had preached to them (c. A.D. 50; 1 Corinthians was written a few years later). This gospel was encapsulated in a traditional formula or more likely a series of formulae, which, Paul claims, he had received from those who were Christians before him. Since he mentions Cephas (Peter) and James (the brother of the Lord) by name, and since he met these two men at Jerusalem on his first postconversion visit there about the year 35, a substantial part of these formulae must be very ancient, taking us back to within five years or so of the events alluded to. The formulae embrace: 1. the death of Christ as a saving event; 2. his burial; 3. his resurrection as a saving event; 4. a list of appearances, including the appearance to Paul himself in which he received his apostolic call (which, following Acts, we usually refer to as his conversion). The longer reading emphasizes the grace-character of Paul's apostolic call. The shorter reading follows the summary of the traditions with Paul's claim that his own kerygma and that of his predecessors was identical.

Gospel: Luke 5:1-11

The history of the tradition here is very similar to that of the gospel readings of the previous two weeks. Luke again shifts the position of the Marcan pericope. This time the call of the first disciple is moved to a later point in the narrative. Again, too, Luke combines it with another tradition from his special material. This special tradition consists of the miraculous draft of fishes, a story found in a postresurrection setting in John 21. It is much disputed whether this was originally a postresurrection story later retrojected into the earthly life of Jesus or *vice versa*, and the weight of the arguments on both sides is about equal.

By combining this tradition with his Marcan source, Luke psychologizes the call of Simon Peter (the other disciples are only background survivals from the Marcan source). The call does not come as a bolt out of the blue, as in Mark. Simon had already witnessed the healing of his mother-in-law and now he experiences the miraculous fish-catch. This creates in him a feeling of utter unworthiness: "Depart from me, for I am a sinful man, O Lord." Those who think that the postresurrection setting was original can explain this as a reaction to the Lord's appearance after Peter's threefold denial. In Luke's narrative, however, it is a reaction to the *mysterium tremendum* of the miracle (cf. Isaiah's vision). The call comes in the metaphorical words about catching men, as in Mark, but the wording is different, thus suggesting that it comes not from Mark but from Luke's special material.

The Homily

If the long form of the gospel is read, the homilist has the rare opportunity to take all three readings together, the calls of Isaiah, Paul and Simon (Peter). In each case there is a sense of utter unworthiness which is later overcome in an act of grace and forgiveness, leading to a commissioning for a unique role in salvation history and an immediate response. This seems to be a constant biblical pattern, and it would give the homilist an opportunity to speak of vocation to Christian service in its various forms, whether ordained or unordained.

If the shorter version of the epistle is read, the emphasis rests upon the identity of Paul's teaching with that of his predecessors. The homilist could discuss what is basic to the Christian tradition (the proclamation of the central saving events of the cross and the resurrection of Christ) and the importance of agreement and unity in these basic traditions.

Reading I: Jeremiah 17:5-8

This poem of two stanzas consists of a woe pronounced upon those who trust in man and a beatitude upon those who trust in Yahweh. The woe and the beatitude are accompanied by two corresponding comparisons (a shrub in the desert and a tree by the waterside). The poem differs from the usual prophecies of Jeremiah because of its wisdom character and its corresponding lack of direct connection with Israel's salvation history. Whether Jeremiah wrote it or not is disputed by Old Testament scholars precisely because of its unique character in this respect, but there seems nothing in it contrary to Jeremiah's teaching elsewhere. Some scholars have tried to give the poem a concrete situation in Jeremiah's ministry but without success.

The choice of this reading for today seems to be governed by considerations of form rather than of content, for the gospel reading consists of our Lord's beatitudes and woes from the Great Sermon (though note that they occur in reverse order). The people designated for blessing and woe, however, are not exactly the same as those in the Jeremiah reading (but see below).

Responsorial Psalm: 1:1-2, 3, 4 and 6

This psalm is an obvious choice to go with the poem from Jeremiah because it uses precisely the same comparison as stanza 2 of the poem: the man who hopes in the Lord is like a tree planted by streams of water. In stanza 3 of the psalm, however, the wicked are compared to chaff, not to a shrub in the desert as in the poem.

But there is a far more significant difference between the psalm and the poem from Jeremiah. The psalm (stanza 1) emphasizes the Torah (law) as the ground of man's trust in Yahweh, about which the poem says nothing at all. This shows that the psalm was written from a later, postexilic perspective than the wisdom poem.

Reading II: 1 Corinthians 15:12, 16-20

Having stated the kerygma, Paul first turns upon the Corinthians and reproaches them for their inconsistency. If they accepted the proclamation, or kerygma, of Christ's resurrection, how then can they deny the resurrection of the dead? What the Corinthians meant by denying the resurrection of the dead was discussed last week (see above). The bodily resurrection of Christ and that of the departed believers (this is what is meant by "the dead": Paul is not expounding a generally valid anthropology) depend on one another. On the one hand, surprisingly, Christ's resurrection depends upon the validity of the Jewish apocalyptic hope, for to say that Christ has been raised from the dead makes sense only if you grant the validity of that hope (v.16). For Christ's resurrection is not an episode in his own individual biography, but the first of the resurrections from the dead for which the apocalyptists had hoped and the one which determines all other resurrections. He is the firstfruits of those who have fallen asleep (v. 20). And conversely, since he is the firstfruits, the others shall also be raised because of his resurrection.

Verses 17-20 merit particular attention. Here Paul is arguing existentially. To deny the resurrection of the dead is not to hold an incorrect theoretical philosophy of life. Rather, it is to undercut the reality of our own present Christian existence: "your faith is futile and you are yet in your sins" (v. 17). The Christian hope of resurrection is not a philosophical opinion but an inference from present Christian experience. We are forgiven sinners. We have been brought into a new relationship with God through Christ, a relationship which, if it is real, must issue in an ultimate consummation beyond this present existence. Faith in our resurrection cannot be argued on theoretical grounds; it depends on the reality of the present Christian experience of forgiveness. It is not just that we hope to go to heaven when we die or that we believe that the souls of all men are intrinsically immortal. These things may or may not be true; they lie outside of Paul's perspective. It is rather that God has forgiven us in Christ, and nothing, not even death itself, can deprive us of that new life.

Gospel: Luke 6:17, 20-26

In Luke (unlike Matthew) the Great Sermon is delivered on a "level place." If you go to the Holy Land they will show you the "mount of the beatitudes." This mountain, however, exists only in Matthew's redaction and is symbolical: the new law is given on a new Sinai. Luke probably follows his Q source in placing it on a plain. The Sermon on the Plain is delivered "where cross the crowded ways of life" — where crowds are seeking to hear Jesus and be healed of their diseases. Thus verse 17 gives the Lucan setting for the sermon.

The sermon is addressed not to the crowds but to the disciples in the presence of the crowds (v. 20). This means that the ethics of the Great Sermon are not meant for the world in general but for those who have already decided to follow Christ. They presuppose grace. This is not a general law but the demands upon those who have already been enabled by grace to fulfill them. Hence Jesus' lack of concern for whether his disciples will be able to fulfill such a demanding ethic. Only insofar as men are "in Christ" (to use the Pauline equivalent of the synoptic "follow me") will they reproduce this kind of life in their own lives.

In both Matthew and Luke the Great Sermon opens with a series of beatitudes. There are nine in Matthew. But in Luke there are four beatitudes followed by four woes. Each beatitude has its corresponding woe:

Beatitude	Woe
poor	rich
hungry	full
weeping	laughing
hated	spoken well of
(like prophets)	(like false prophets)

There is a sociological aspect to the beatitudes and woes in Luke, but we should not interpret them exclusively in sociological terms. The poor, hungry, etc., include the underprivileged of society, but not them only. In the last analysis Matthew is correct when he glosses "poor" by "in spirit" and "hungry" with "for righteousness." For ultimately it is a question of man's relationship with God. The poor, hungry, etc., are those who know that they have nothing in and of themselves to entitle them to a right relationship with God. They know themselves to be the have-nots.

The Homily

We might combine the Old Testament reading and gospel by taking our cue from the opening words of the two stanzas of the wisdom poem in reading I: "Cursed is the man who trusts in man," and "Blessed is the man who trusts in the Lord." These words interpret what the Lucan beatitudes and woes are about. Trust in man is the attitude of the rich, of those who are full, who laugh and of whom men speak well. Trust in the Lord is the attitude of those who are poor, hungry, who weep and are hated, ostracized and reviled. It appears that this curse and this blessing are being spoken dramatically by God over our affluent industrial society, now threatened with chaos and dissolution.

Reading II would provide an opportunity to distinguish between the Christian hope for a life beyond the present life and general notions of immortality and survival. The Christian hope is characterized by: (1) its roots in Christology: only because of Christ can we be raised from the dead; (2) its existential character: only because of what we already are in Christ do we know that this existence is indestructible by death.

SEVENTH SUNDAY OF THE YEAR ✓

Reading I: 1 Samuel 26:2, 7-9, 12-13, 22-23

First Samuel contains two versions of this episode in which David spares King Saul after being hunted down by the king. The other version is in 1 Samuel 24:1-22. The two versions differ considerably in detail, but both reflect one of the most attractive features of David's character, his magnanimity. Both versions, however, express something more — viz., the royal ideology according to which David is reluctant to put forth his hand against the Lord's anointed. This reading matches the gospel, an extract from the Great Sermon which inculcates Jesus' demand for forgiveness toward others, as God has forgiven us.

Responsorial Psalm: 103:1-2, 3-4, 8 and 10, 12-13

As would be expected, portions of this psalm are frequently used, and the same selection has already occurred at Sunday 7A and 8B and was commented on above (Sunday 8 B). It was there pointed out that Psalm 103 is an individual's thanksgiving after some personal trial (sickness? see stanza 2). It emphasizes the kindness and mercy of Yahweh (note especially the refrain "The Lord is kind and merciful"). Today it seems to be intended as a response to verses 22-23 of reading I, though 1 Samuel 26 speaks of God's *rewarding* human righteousness and faithfulness. We shall discover the same quality of grace and reward in today's gospel reading.

Reading II: 1 Corinthians 15:45-49

Let us first remind ourselves of what we have frequently observed before — namely, that Paul's letters are not abstract theologizings but responses to highly concrete situations in his churches. Exegetes have long agreed that in this passage Paul is polemicizing against some other view. He asserts emphatically that the physical Adam was first, and the spiritual second (v. 46). Commentators have contrasted this statement with Philo's exegesis of the two stories of man's creation in Genesis 1 and 2. Philo took the man created in Genesis 1:26 to be the heavenly, archetypal man, and the Adam of Genesis 2-3 to be empirical, fallen man, and built up a dualistic anthropology of a Platonic kind.

More recently Philo's exegesis has been regarded as one form of a widespread gnostic anthropology. This is what Paul is polemicizing against — in the form in which it was held by the Corinthian gnostics. According to this view, the souls of the gnostic elite consisted of divine sparks emanating from the heavenly man. These sparks had tragically become incarnated in the physical bodies of the earthly Adam. On this view the Christian gospel becomes a means of recovering one's heavenly origin, one's authentic selfhood. This recovery, the Corinthians believe, has already taken place for them through the communication of the Christian *gnōsis* or divinely revealed knowledge, and through the sacraments.

Paul reverses the order of the two Adams. The attainment of authentic existence is not the recovery of something innate but an eschatological possibility opened up by the death and resurrection of Jesus. Although to some extent we begin even here on earth to participate through the sacraments in the new being (a point Paul makes elsewhere, but not here), we do not completely do so until the end. Hence Paul writes this passage to emphasize the eschatological reserve, the "not yet" that marks Christian existence. Only at the end "shall" we bear the image of the heavenly. Here some MSS read, ". . . let us bear the image of the heavenly," but this would push Paul somewhat in the direction of his gnostic opponents, something that, in the exigencies of controversy, he is at pains to avoid.

Gospel: Luke 6:27-38

The first two paragraphs of this reading correspond to the sixth and last of the antitheses in Matthew's presentation of the Great Sermon: "You have heard. . . . But I say to you" (Mt 5:43-44). Such an antithesis is implicit in the Lucan form, since the love of one's enemy was not current Jewish teaching. (Here "enemy" means the non-Israelite; cf. the attitude of the Qumran community to outsiders.) Note the golden rule, at the end of the first paragraph, a saying which Matthew places later in the sermon (7:12).

Of especial interest is the saying which concludes the second paragraph: "Be merciful, even as your Father is merciful." Matthew places this saying in the same context, just after the saying about loving one's enemy. But his version reads: "You therefore must be *perfect*, as your heavenly Father is *perfect*." Matthew of course has a special interest in the idea of perfection, as his treatment of the rich young man indicates (19:16-22). Hence it is likely that Luke's form represents the earlier reading. This point is thoroughly biblical: man's behavior toward his fellows is to be the reflection of the treatment he receives from God. The biblical ethic is essentially one of response to God's treatment of his people — this is true both in the Old Testament and in the New. For in the Old Testament the decalogue is given in the context of response to God's act of deliverance in bringing Israel out of Egypt.

The third paragraph, again judging, which comes later in Matthew's version (7:1-2), uses a series of "reverential periphrases" — i.e., roundabout ways of speaking about God and his action. Thus, "you will not be judged . . . condemned . . . forgiven," means that God will not judge you, etc. This paragraph seems to reverse the order of God's action and man's action. In the previous paragraph the emphasis was upon imitating God's treatment of us. Here it is upon God's responding in kind to our behavior. This apparent contradiction seems to run through much of the teaching of Jesus, especially on forgiveness. The point must be that while God in Christ has initiated forgiveness toward man, man must continue to show forgiveness to his fellows if he is to remain in that forgiveness. We should avoid any suggestion of a *quid pro quo* relationship between ethics and rewards.

In closing this passage on judging, Luke has strengthened the exhortation to generosity and forbearance by the addition of verse 38a; 38b is found also in Matthew.

The Homily

As usual, the homilist is faced with two main alternatives. Taking his cue from the caption to the gospel, "Be merciful as your Father is merciful," he may expound the Christian ethic as an ethic of response. We are to behave to others as God in Christ has treated us. The story of David and Saul can be used as an illustration. And to give this teaching concrete application, reference could be made to the problem of amnesty for those whose consciences impelled them to avoid military service in Vietnam. That this is a vital subject for Christians to face is indicated by the fact that whereas the bishops and other clergy voted for amnesty at the General Convention of the Episcopal Church in Louisville in October 1973, the lay delegates turned it down. How would they answer the commands "Love your enemies" and "Be merciful as your Father is merciful"? One wonders what these laity will think when they hear this passage read in church. Maybe they will cancel their pledges!

Any homilist who feels this too hot a subject to tackle could of course take refuge in the epistle reading and expound Paul's concept of the first and second Adams. If we are true to Paul in this text, we should emphasize as he does that our participation in the "new being" is marked by the eschatological reserve, the not yet. At present we bear the image of the man of dust, and only at our resurrection shall we bear the image of the heavenly man, even if the outlines of that image have been traced over us in our baptism. Perhaps we should want to amplify the negative implication of Paul's rather one-sided polemic by insisting that we have in principle already begun to participate to some degree in the new being and that it is the task of the Christian to seek to grow in that image (cf. Ephesians).

Lent of Year C

Over the centuries the scripture readings of Lent, like those of other seasons, had accumulated a good deal of debris. Many of the selections reflected concerns which had become obsolete. Among these concerns were the final preparation of catechumens for the Easter baptisms, the papal station masses in the city of Rome, and the public restoration of penitents. The new lectionary has swept away much of this material, replacing it with a course of readings designed to prepare the faithful to celebrate the paschal feast. The Old Testament readings set forth Israel's salvation history as types or shadows of the Easter event. The readings from the epistles tell of our participation in the paschal mystery. This participation with Christ, initiated through baptism, is to be progressively realized in Christian living and will be consummated at the end. Finally, the gospel readings present stories from Jesus' earthly ministry. They feature episodes which foreshadow the ultimate messianic event of the death and resurrection which will be celebrated at the paschal feast.

FIRST SUNDAY OF LENT

Reading I: Deuteronomy 26:4-10

This reading is normally associated, at least for Anglicans, with the Harvest Festival or, in this country, with Thanksgiving Day. When read at the beginning of Lent, its emphasis shifts from the offering of the first-fruits to the confession of faith which accompanies the offering (vv. 5-9). For contemporary exegetes this is perhaps the most important passage of the whole Old Testament, or at least of the Pentateuch, occupying a position similar to that of 1 Corinthians 15:3-8 in the New Testament as the early Christian kerygma. What Christ's death and resurrection are to the New Testament, the exodus is to the Old. These are the basic messages of the two canons. In each case the mighty acts of God lead to a confession of faith, a recital of those mighty acts.

Responsorial Psalm 91:1-2, 10-11, 14-15

Psalm 91 is traditional to this Sunday, the old Introit having given the day its name of *Invocavit*. It was this psalm that the devil quoted in the temptation story — at the third temptation in Luke. The devil misapplied the promise of angelic assistance, and verses 14-15 correct it. Only those who set their love upon God can expect him to deliver them. For that reason Christ was delivered; he more than all others set his love upon his Father. He was delivered from the cross to the resurrection.

Reading II: Romans 10:8-13

Here we have a New Testament confession of faith (v. 9) corresponding to the Old Testament confession in reading I. This confession represents the subject matter for catechetical instruction and the profession of faith the candidate made for himself at his baptism. Such simple confessions as we find them in the New Testament are the nucleus out of which grew first the baptismal creed (e.g., the Apostles' Creed) and later conciliar creeds (e.g., that of Nicea). The same confession, too, forms the basic content of the great eucharistic prayer. The unity of the church despite the pluralism of its members (Jew and Greek), the unity of the New Testament despite the variety of its expressions of the Christian message, the unity of the liturgy despite the existence of different eucharistic prayers or canons, lies in this common, basic confession: God has raised Jesus from the dead and made him Lord.

Gospel: Luke 4:1-13

The Lucan version of the temptation differs very little in wording from the more familiar Matthean form. The only notable differences are: the rearrangement of the second and third temptations, and the statement that the devil left Jesus "until an opportune time" (v. 13). Hans Conzelmann saw in this a major clue to Luke's theology. The ministry of Jesus is the "satan-free" period; the devil returns to assail Jesus in the passion (22:3). Thus Luke deliberately links the temptation story with the passion.

There is an even more suitable link with the passion in the replies of Jesus to the three temptations:

> "Man shall not live by bread alone."
> "You shall worship the Lord your God
>   and him only shall you serve."
> "You shall not put the Lord your God to the test."

For this threefold confession plots the future course of Jesus' ministry, culminating in the confession which he made before Pontius Pilate. It was this confession, this single-minded commitment to God's will for him (which is what the dogma of Christ's sinlessness really meant) that characterized the whole course of Jesus' ministry, and finally led him to the cross.

The Homily

Today's reading are linked by the idea of confession. The homilist could develop the place of confession in the life of the Christian community. Our readings suggest three types of confession: eucharistic confession, baptismal confession, and Jesus' own confession in his temptations and on the cross. Some churches pride themselves on being "confessional" churches, meaning that they have their own confession of faith, usually from the sixteenth century. Other churches pride themselves on not being confessional churches at all. Such differences are the products of different histories. Whether a church is "confessional" or not, it belongs to the essence of the church that it should be a *confessing* church. If the church is to be the church, it must boldly confess its faith before the world in the face of persecution and when tempted to abandon its faith for the sake of accommodation to the spirit of the age.

At baptism we commit ourselves to this confession ("in token that hereafter he shall not be ashamed to *confess* the faith of Christ cruci- fied" — Book of Common Prayer, baptismal office). In the liturgy we set forth this confession at every eucharist, and in life this confession must be lived out day by day. The 1967 *Liturgy of the Lord's Supper* of the Episcopal Church contained the noble petition, unfortunately dropped in the revised rites of 1970: "and grant that with boldness we may confess thy Name in constancy of faith." It is to this that the homilist will want to exhort his congregation today.

Reading I: Genesis 15:5-12, 17-18

This reading combines three different themes: Yahweh's promise of an abundant posterity to Abraham, his promise of the land to Israel, and the sealing of that promise with a covenant ceremony. Genesis contains several stories of God's establishment of his covenant with Abraham, all of them variants of the same tradition. In Abraham God decisively intervened in human history to create a people for himself. God's choice is, on his side, a sheer act of grace; and faith is set, be it noted, not in the context of individual salvation but of a people's history. This is the context in which the Old Testament views *sola gratia, sola fide*. The apostle Paul discerned the fulfillment of God's promise to Abraham in the Christ event and in the emergence of the New Israel, the church (Gal 3; Rom 4).

Responsorial Psalm 27:1, 7-8a, 8bc-9abc, 13-14

This psalm serves as a link between readings I and II. Stanza 4 begins with the words: "I believe that I shall see the goodness of the Lord in the land of the living." For Abraham this land was *eretz Israel*, the territory which his descendents were destined to occupy. For Christian believers this land is the kingdom of God, the "commonwealth of heaven" of which the epistle reading speaks.

Reading II: Philippians 3:17-4:1 (long form); 3:20-4:1 (short form)

Both the epistle reading and the gospel speak of a "change." The epistle speaks of the change of our earthly existence in the final consummation. The gospel speaks of the change of Jesus as he prayed on the holy mountain. The term "glorious body" like the other term, "spiritual body," which Paul uses in 1 Corinthians 15, reflects the apocalyptic hope. According to this hope, the life of the age to come will not be merely a prolongation of this present life but an entirely new, transformed mode of existence. It was into this mode of existence that Christ entered at his resurrection. But his resurrection is not merely an incident in his own personal biography, as it were. He entered into that existence as the "firstfruits" (1 Cor 15:20) — i.e., as the one who made it possible for believers also to enter into that new mode of existence after him. That is the Christian hope.

Gospel: Luke 9:28-36

The use of the transfiguration story in the new Roman lectionary on the Second Sunday of Lent follows the tradition of the *Missale Romanum*. The Book of Common Prayer and the Lutheran orders followed a different tradition. Hence both the Episcopal and Lutheran trial lectionaries have departed from the new lectionary here and have followed each other in reading the transfiguration story on the last Sunday after Epiphany. On that day it forms an admirable transition from the contemplation of the earthly ministry of Jesus as the manifestation of God in the Epiphany season to a contemplation of the passion as the ultimate epiphany. In the new Roman lectionary the transfiguration story serves the theme: Behold we go up to Jerusalem (see below, The Homily).

That Jesus and his disciples ascended a mountain for solitude after his abrupt conclusion of his Galilean ministry and that he communicated to them his change of plan — which was to go up to Jerusalem and challenge the religious authorities in the nation's capital — is historically plausible.

This original nucleus of historical fact was then rewritten by the post-Easter community in the light of its Easter faith. There is some indication in the gospels of an awareness that the events of Jesus' earthly life appeared in a different perspective after the first Easter (cf. Jn 2:22; 12:16). Thus what happened on the mountain was rewritten with the use of Old Testament materials. The change in the appearance of Jesus' face is reminiscent of Moses on Mount Sinai (Ex 34:29). Moses and Elijah, both of whom figured in first-century Jewish apocalyptic as returning at the end, talk with Jesus about his "departure" (Greek *exodos*), i.e., Jesus' death and exaltation. The disciples were ready enough to accept Jesus as *one* of the end time figures along with Moses and Elijah but not yet as a unique figure of the end time. So a voice from heaven proclaims the finality of Jesus: "This is my Son; listen to *him*" (note the allusion to Dt 18:15). Then we are told that after this "Jesus was found alone." The story as retold is rich in symbolism, proclaiming that Jesus is the Son of God, his final emissary, and the second Moses who accomplishes the new exodus.

The addition of the words "at Jerusalem" in verse 31 looks like a redactional addition, for it is one of Luke's major themes that the holy city is the focal point to which the ministry of Jesus moves. It is there that the saving event is accomplished, and it is from there that in Acts the proclamation of that saving event goes forth to the ends of the earth. The point of all this is that the gospel proclaims not a timeless myth (cf. 2 Pt 1:16, also about the transfiguration) but something which actually happened at a particular time and place in history.

Episcopal Lectionary Gospel: Mark 10:32-45

The Episcopal lectionary curiously departs from the normal sequence of Lucan readings in year C and offers instead the third of the Marcan passion predictions, the question of Zebedee's sons and the ransom saying — the last of these three items is omitted in the Lucan parallel. Mark has carefully constructed the whole section 8:27–10:45 to put across his conception of the suffering Son of man. There he corrects the earlier Christology of a mere wonderworker and braces the church of his day to endure similar persecution.

Lutheran Lectionary Gospel: Luke 13:31-35

This pericope has the merit of following the Lucan sequence, and functions in much the same way as the transfiguration story and the complex pericope of the Episcopal lectionary in that it points up the transition from Galilee to Jerusalem. It is probably the most historical of all three choices, for verse 33 has high claim to be an authentic saying of the historical Jesus. It indicates something of Jesus' historical intention in going up to Jerusalem, in the kind of terms he would himself have used. Thus he speaks of himself as a prophet, whose purpose was to lay down his prophetic challenge at the heart of Judaism and to face the consequences. He does not use a messianic title or speak of his death as a ransom or a second exodus. These were later, post-Easter interpretations of the meaning of Jesus' person and death, though of course true interpretations.

The Homily

Probably the most obvious theme today would be: "Behold we go up to Jerusalem" (Mk 10:33 in today's Episcopal gospel). Many Christians nowadays are fortunate enough to make this pilgrimage physically at least once in a lifetime. Each year the church in her liturgy invites us to go on the same pilgrimage "in heart and mind." Today the homilist has the opportunity of preparing his people to embark on that pilgrimage and explaining the importance of Jerusalem as the center of salvation history.

Other possibilities would be: Abraham as the paradigm of faith and grace alone; or, taking up the common theme of the epistle reading and the transfiguration story, the concept of eschatological transformation, the Lord's and ours, his transformation being foreshadowed in the transfiguration ("an anticipation of his eschatology" — R. Kittel) and ours being symbolized at baptism and finalized at the consummation.

THIRD SUNDAY OF LENT

Reading I: Exodus 3:1-8a, 13-15

A single thread runs through today's readings. It is indicated by the name of God as revealed to Moses: "I am who I am," or, as many contemporary exegetes interpret it: "He causes to be what comes into existence." Our God is the God of Abraham, Isaac and Jacob, not the God of the philosophers (Pascal); that is to say, not an abstract, impersonal reality, but the transcendent one who intervenes powerfully in human history. He calls Moses and sends him to lead his people out of Egypt through the wilderness (reading II), refreshing them with water from the rock and bringing them into the promised land. Then finally he sends his Son, offering his people one last chance to repent and accept his salvation (the gospel reading).

Once again the exodus story functions in the liturgy as a type of the saving act of God in Christ. God sees the affliction of his people. He "comes down" — i.e., intervenes in history out of his transcendence — to deliver them from the slavery of sin and to bring them into the land "flowing with milk and honey," the kingdom of God.

Responsorial Psalm 103:1-2, 3-4, 6-7, 8 and 11

In this psalm we praise God for showing his ways to Moses and his works to the people of Israel as these ways and works are spoken of in reading I. A psalm sung by Israel about the exodus becomes a hymn of the Christian community which celebrates the death and resurrection of Christ.

Reading II: 1 Corinthians 10:1-6, 10-12

The situation confronting Paul at Corinth is that the Christians there are supposing that the sacraments automatically confer the fullness of salvation even here and now. Probably they were under the influence of early gnostic enthusiasm. Paul therefore has to stress the "not yet" aspect of the sacraments. They anticipate symbolically the fullness of salvation, but effectively they initiate and foster a process which looks to its final completion at the end. To illustrate his point Paul draws an analogy with Israel in the wilderness and finds in the exodus story types of the two major Christian sacraments of baptism and the eucharist: the children of Israel were baptized when they passed through the cloud and through the Red Sea, and they were nourished with spiritual food and drink by the manna and the water from the rock in the wilderness.

It is probable that Paul did not invent this typology but took it over from earliest Christianity. It may well have had its origin in Jewish speculation about the messianic banquet and have been taken up in pre-Pauline Christianity to interpret the eschatological banquets of the early community, such as those alluded to in Acts 2:42 and 46. Certainly there is rabbinic influence present in the idea that the Rock *followed* the Israelites, an inference from the fact that it is mentioned *twice* in the Pentateuch (Ex 17 and Num 20 — a modern commentator would regard these as doublets of the same tradition). More extraordinary is Paul's claim that "that Rock was Christ." Probably the basis for this identification is the equation of Christ with the divine "wisdom," the personified agent both of creation and of all God's acts in salvation history. "Wisdom" stands for God going out of himself in self-communication and activity. For Paul, as for the New Testament as a whole, God's going out of himself culminates in his redemptive act in Jesus.

Gospel: Luke 13:1-9

Jesus here refers to two recent disasters, otherwise unknown to historians. One was the outrage of a tyrant, the other an accident involving construction workers. He draws from both events a warning for Israel. Unless the nation repents, it too will perish. Repentance means, for Jesus, accepting his message of the kingdom of God. The parable of the fig tree reinforces the challenge to repent. This provides a link with the epistle reading: "Let anyone who thinks he stands take heed lest he fall." Neither the old Israel nor the new dare presume upon a false sense of security.

The Homily

We tend to think of Lent as a time to step up acts of personal devotion and piety. Reading II and the gospel suggest that Lent addresses itself just as much to the church as an established institution. Like all institutions it is often threatened by a false sense of security. We have the warning example of Israel. In the wilderness the old people of God were lulled into a false sense of security when Yahweh, fulfilling his promise to Moses in the burning bush, brought his people out of Egypt through the cloud and the sea, fed them with the manna and quenched their thirst with water from the rock. We also have the warning example of the New Israel. The Corinthians were lulled into a false sense of security by their possession of the two sacraments of the gospel. The homilist should not find it difficult to apply these warnings to the contemporary church as an institution today. "Unless you repent, you will likewise perish."

FOURTH SUNDAY OF LENT

Reading I: Joshua 5:9a, 10-12

Last Sunday's epistle reading interpreted the manna as a type of the eucharist. Today's Old Testament reading tells us that the manna ceased when the first Passover was celebrated in the promised land. So too the eucharist will cease when it finds its fulfillment in the messianic banquet of the kingdom of God.

Reading II: 2 Corinthians 5:17-21

It is remarkable that Paul should appeal to the very people he calls a new creation to be reconciled to Christ. This is because the community's status as the new creation is not an assured possession but something that must constantly be worked at. To renew that status is the work of the apostolic ministry, the ministry of reconciliation, as Paul calls it. God's saving act in Christ and the ongoing work of the apostolic ministry are not to be separated. The second is an extension of the first, part of the same salvation history.

This salvation history is inaugurated by an event in which "For our sake he made him to be sin who knew no sin." This bold affirmation can best be understood in the light of the Marcan-Matthean word from the cross: "My God, my God, why hast thou forsaken me?" Here Jesus enters the deepest consequences of man's sin — his alienation from God. He takes his stand where we are as sinners, under the wrath of God, alienated from him, so that we may become what he, Jesus, is — the righteousness of God. The Greek fathers were really saying the same thing when they asserted that Christ partook of our human nature in order that we might become partakers of his divine nature.

Lent of Year C 513

Gospel: Luke 15:1-3, 11-32

Reading II provides the right context for the interpretation of the parable of the prodigal son. This parable is often understood as a simple illustration of God's readiness to forgive in response to man's repentance, without the necessity of Christ's atoning death on the cross. "There is no place for Jesus in the parable of the prodigal son," it has been said. But the Jesus of the parables is never promulgating timeless truths of religion and ethics. He is always commenting on what is happening concretely in his own ministry.

The Pharisees were grumbling because he was eating with outcasts (vv. 1-3: the Roman and Lutheran lectionaries wisely start with this setting, the Episcopal lectionary unwisely omits it). The parable is a comment on Jesus' action in eating with the outcast. He is not left out of the parable for the simple reason that the parable presupposes and interprets his action. When Jesus eats with outcasts, it is not just humanitarian broadmindedness, as though the laws of God or the Pharisaic regulations didn't matter. It is *God* breaking through the condemnation of his own law in order to reach out and save the lost.

The Homily

The homilist today has a rare opportunity to preach the atonement. He can link the Pauline statement, "For our sake he made him to be sin who knew no sin," on one side with the cross as interpreted in the Marcan-Matthean word and on the other with Jesus' action in eating with outcasts. In this way the cross will not seem an isolated event but the culmination of a whole life of self-identification with sinners, and the Pauline doctrine of the atonement not an abstract piece of theologizing but a fitting interpretation of Jesus' intention. The father in the parable, too, came out to meet the son, to stand where *he* was in order to bring him back home. So God in Christ came out to meet man as sinner.

FIFTH SUNDAY OF LENT

Reading I: Isaiah 43:16-21

In Deutero-Isaiah the impending return from exile in Babylon is depicted as a new exodus. "The former things" and "the things of old" refer to the first exodus. This is now replaced by a "new thing," the return. In this new event the events of the first exodus repeat themselves: I will make a way even in the wilderness"; "I will provide rivers in the barren desert." In Christian biblical theology the proclamation of God's act of salvation in Christ picks up the same imagery. The "new things" are now the death and resurrection of the Messiah, and the "drink" God provides his people the sacraments of the new covenant.

Responsorial Psalm 126:1-2ab, 2cd-3, 4-5, 6

Stanza 4 entitles us to apply the restoration of which stanzas 1 and 3 speak and the "great" things of stanza 2 to the death and resurrection of Christ:

> "He that goes forth weeping,
>   bearing the seed for sowing,
> shall come home with shouts of joy,
>   bringing his sheaves with him."

"The metaphor of sowing in the Old Testament almost demanded a Messianic application" (Hoskyns).

Reading II: Philippians 3:8-14

Philippians 3 is a polemic against Paul's opponents. Whether they were Judaizers, i.e., advocates of imposing the Jewish law on Gentile converts, or some kind of syncretists or "enthusiasts," is not certain, but current exegesis is inclining toward the latter (so not only the German Lutheran Schmithals but also the German Catholic Gnilka). As enthusiasts these opponents would fondly imagine that through baptism they had "already attained" and were already perfect. Against their position Paul holds out his *theologia crucis*, not simply as an abstract doctrine but as a reality to which his whole life as an apostle is conformed. Only by becoming like Christ in his death, only by sharing his suffering and living under the "not yet," can the apostle know the power of Christ's resurrection now and eventually attain the resurrection when Christ returns.

Gospel: John 8:1-11

The pericope *de adultera*, it is now agreed by most scholars, is not part of the original text of John, though of course it is part of the canonical text and as such rightly restored from the margin in the new edition of the Revised Standard Version (The Common Bible). The earliest manuscripts either omit it or place it elsewhere. Some place it after Luke 21:38, which is interesting, for the story has a definitely Lucan ring. Despite its late attestation it is certainly a very early and good tradition. Professor Bruce Metzger's verdict in his textual commentary is that it "has all the earmarks of historical veracity."

The Swedish New Testament scholar Harald Riesenfeld has offered an interesting explanation why this story went under ground, so to speak, for such a long time. It happened, he thinks, during the period when church authorities were trying to enforce a strict discipline over Christian marriages. The story of the adulteress seemed at that time to encourage laxity in marriage standards. Actually this is a false impression. After all, Jesus did say to the woman, "Go and do not sin again." He recognized sin as sin. And in saying, "Neither do I condemn you," he was not condoning the sin but pronouncing the forgiveness of God. The scribes and Pharisees, however, come in for sharper condemnation and are put to shame. None of them could claim to be without sin. Here is a pictorial illustration of Jesus' saying, "Judge not, that you may not be judged" (Mt 7:1).

The Homily

The pericope of the adulteress would provide the homilist with the opportunity to treat a very hot subject — Jesus' attitude toward sex and marriage and particularly toward adultery. The homilist could contrast it with (a) modern secular attitudes, and (b) the tendency of the church in the past to regard sexual sins as the deadliest of all sins. As Dorothy Sayers and others have remarked, the deadliest of sins in the biblical-Christian ethic is the sin of pride.

An alternative possibility would be to explore Paul's conception of apostolate as involving conformity to the cross. This is not an ethic for apostles only, but something which the church proposes through her liturgy for all Christians, especially during Lent. The last stanza of the responsorial psalm could also be drawn into the presentation.

Appendix of Missing Sundays

NINTH SUNDAY OF THE YEAR [A][1]

Reading I: Deuteronomy 11:18, 26-28

The introductory verse 18 (cf. 6:8, where the same instruction is given) was later taken literally and gave rise to the practice of wearing phylacteries, mentioned in the sayings of Jesus (Mt 23:5). Whether it was taken literally in Deuteronomic times we do not know. This verse provides a setting for verses 26-28, the choice between blessing and curse. Such blessings and curses were customarily attached to covenants as sanctions for their enforcement. From these primitive origins the idea passed into the "Two Ways" of Jewish ethical teaching (*Manual of Discipline*, 1 QS 4) and was taken over in the catechesis of the early church (cf. *Didache* 1:1). The same idea appears in the parable of the two houses at the conclusion of the Sermon on the Mount, which forms the gospel reading for this day.

Responsorial Psalm: 31:1-2ab, 2cd-3, 16 and 24

Psalm 31 is an individual thanksgiving, praising God in the temple for deliverance from sickness and trouble. Today's selection combines several verses which speak of God as the source of man's security and refuge. In Christian usage (cf. Luther's *Commentary on the Psalms*) such psalms are to be read as thanksgivings of the sinner who has been justified by the grace of God — interpreted otherwise, they are sentimentalized and trivialized. This suggests that we treat the curse in reading I to mean specifically the curse of the law (Gal 3:10), under which all men live apart from Christ and from which Christ by his redeeming work has saved us (cf. the epistle).

Reading II: Romans 3:21-25a, 28

The word "now" represents a major turning point both in the argument of Romans and in the history of salvation. In Romans 1:18–3:20

[1] The five commentaries which follow cover readings that did not occur in the Roman calendar from Lent 1971 to Lent 1974.

Paul has established that "all" — whether Jew or Greek, godly or impious — "have sinned." Now, however (*nyn de*), the situation has been dramatically changed by God's intervention in Christ. First, Paul repeats in the same terms as in Romans 1:16 his definition of the gospel as the revelation of God's righteousness, and into this he weaves his conclusion, drawn from the preceding analysis of man's situation before God — namely, that all, whether Jews or Gentiles, have sinned.

Next, Paul cites what is widely recognized today to be a pre-Pauline formula, with glosses of his own that express his distinctive emphasis on the role of faith (as opposed to the works of the law) in the process of man's justification. Here is the formula, or rather the part of it included in this reading, with the gloss in parentheses:

> through the redemption which is in Christ Jesus,
> whom God put forward as an expiation by his blood,
> (to be received by faith)

The reading ends with a summary conclusion of Paul's understanding of the gospel: "For we hold that a man is justified by faith apart from the works of the law." The pre-Pauline fragment is concerned with the Christ event in itself. Paul himself is concerned with our appropriation of it by faith.

The meaning of the passage may be best grasped by a study of the key words:

"Righteousness" here is not a moral quality, as in Matthew or James, but God's saving act, as in Deutero-Isaiah (e.g., Is 51:5, where it occurs in synonymous parallelism with "salvation"). The law and the prophets (i.e., the Old Testament canon) bear witness to the coming of this salvation, for the Old Testament is an incomplete book pointing forward through type and prophecy toward its fulfillment. That God should act to save mankind through Christ is therefore not something unheard of, but the key to the true meaning of the Old Testament.

"Apart from the law" and "through faith" go together. A righteousness dependent upon the law would be one which sought to secure God's favor by fulfilling the law — which Romans 1–3:20 demonstrated to be beyond the capacity of sinful, fallen man. Instead, it comes through faith — that is, it can only be attained by receiving it "as a gift" (v. 24a).

"Justified," aptly rendered by the old English word "rightwised," means being put right with God. This is the quest, conscious or unconscious, of all human religion.

"Redemption," a word which comes from the pre-Pauline formula, is an Old Testament term, there used of God's saving act in bringing Israel out of Egypt. Later in the Old Testament it signified the looked-for deliverance at the end (Dn 4:30c [LXX ed. Swete [4] 1912/1930] = Dn 4:34 [LXX ed. Rahlfs [7] 1935/1962], "At the end of the seven years the time of my deliverance came. . .."). In early Christianity it refers specifically to the deliverance from sin and death which Christ's death has accomplished.

"Expiation" (Greek: *hilastērion*) is one of the most controverted words in the New Testament. Three meanings have been held: 1. The traditional interpretation: propitiation. Here the actor is man, the object God, and the presupposition is that man must do something to satisfy God and appease his wrath. Man being unable to do this by himself, God undertook to do it in Christ, and so Christ propitiated the Father. 2. A modern view: expiation. Here God is the subject and the object sin. God in Christ undertook to wipe away man's sin. 3. The mercy seat — that is, the place where atonement is wrought. The first interpretation is supported by the use of the Greek word *hilastērion*; the second has the support of the Old Testament verb which underlies the Greek words derived from the root *hila-*; the third is linguistically possible.

Perhaps we should opt for "expiate" without excluding all notions of propitiation. "We can hardly doubt (since Paul says that God set forth Christ in this capacity) that expiation rather than propitiation is in his mind; though it would be wrong to neglect the fact that expiation has, as it were, the effect of propitiation: the sin that might justly have excited God's wrath is expiated (at God's will), and therefore no longer does so" (C. K. Barrett).

"Blood" is a term derived from the cup word in the Supper tradition. It means not the physical stuff as such but the saving event of Christ's death considered as a sacrifice. Probably the pre-Pauline hymn which Paul cites was designed for use in connection with the eucharist (at the Christian passover?).

Gospel: Matthew 7:21-27

Matthew's Sermon on the Mount ends with a series of sayings directly by the evangelist against the charismatic prophets and healers (divine men) who were troubling the church in his day. The test at the End will be not their charismatic achievements but their obedience to the new righteousness set forth in the great sermon. It is realized today that Matthew was fighting on a double front. On the one hand there was strict Pharisaic

Jewish orthodoxy, consolidating itself after the fall of Jerusalem, and on the other hand there were the charismatic enthusiasts.

Against both groups and in different ways Matthew sets forth an understanding of Christianity which, while not denying God's redemptive act in Christ (cf. his interest in Christology and in prophecy fulfillment), emphasizes that after the Christ event has been appropriated, its effects must be shown forth — not in charismatic achievements and not in observance of the minutiae of the rabbinic law — but in works of love and mercy. So the Christian, like the wise man who built upon rock, is the one who "hears my words and does them." This is a very different presentation of Christianity from that which we find in Paul, and much closer to James, but both are valid and there is a right time for each.

The Homily

Which does the congregation today need most to hear? Is it Paul's message that "we are justified by faith [Luther added "alone"; it wasn't there in the Greek and he probably should not have done so, though it can be held that he captured Paul's true intention] apart from the law," or Matthew's version, which insists that the Christian must not only hear Christ's words but do them? Could we preach both Paul's version, that we are justified by faith (only), and also the Matthew-James version, that we are justified by works and not by faith only, and see that both are true — each at its own time?

EIGHTEENTH SUNDAY OF THE YEAR [A]

Reading I: Isaiah 55:1-3

Having announced the return of God's people to their homeland as the culminating event of Israel's salvation history, Deutero-Isaiah concludes his prophecies with an invitation to the eschatological banquet. This banquet imagery continues to develop along a trajectory both in the wisdom literature and in Jewish apocalyptic. It is taken up in the New Testament and underlies the accounts of the feedings, one of which forms the gospel of the day.

Responsorial Psalm: 145:8-9, 15-16, 17-18

This psalm received comment at Sunday 31 of year C. Stanza 2 of today's selection, linking as it does with both the Old Testament lesson and the gospel, explains the psalm's presence here. Note particularly the verb "satisfy" both in verse 16 and in the gospel (Mt 14:20). The Greek word is not, however, the same in these passages. The psalm has "filled," the gospel passage a rather coarse word meaning "stuffed full." But the notion of repletion, however expressed, figures frequently in descriptions of the eschatological banquet.

Reading II: Romans 8:35, 37-39

In this concluding selection of Romans 8, Paul rises to great heights of eloquence. It is almost a hymn of triumph. In both paragraphs, as arranged in the lectionary, the word "separate" occurs. The first paragraph is a question: "Who [not "What"] shall separate us. . . ?" Paul regards the seven forms of suffering which he is about to enumerate as quasi-personal powers, perhaps because they are earthly manifestations of the cosmic-demonic powers enumerated in the second paragraph, which is in the form of a statement, not a question. Here Paul names ten cosmic powers that cannot separate us from "the love of God in Christ." This last phrase corresponds to "the love of Christ" in the first paragraph. The two are essentially the same thing, the same love.

For Paul, this love is not an abstract quality but an event that happened — namely, the cross. The cross was the obedience of the Son (cf. Phil 2:8) and at the same time the redemptive act of the Father (2 Cor 5:19). In this passage, then, Paul is interpreting the death of Jesus as a victory over the demonic powers, who can do no ultimate damage to the believers. Paul does not say that believers are already immune from the onslaughts of these powers, but he is sure that amid all demonic onslaughts the believers are "superconquerors."

Gospel: Matthew 14:13-21

The feeding of the multitude occurs more frequently than any other episode in the four gospels, six times in all. This testifies to its importance for the early community, an importance due to its connection with the eucharist. Whereas we tend to see the origin of the eucharist exclusively in the Last Supper, the early church laid at least as much stress on Jesus' eating with his disciples in Galilee, to say nothing of the postresurrection meals. The telling of the story has been shaped by the eucharisic customs of the community: "taking the . . . loaves," "blessed," "broke," "gave," "ate." The words "he looked up to heaven" may also be eucharistic, though not attested elsewhere in New Testament eucharistic texts.

Note, however, the complete absence of any reference to passover, covenant or sacrificial motifs. There is no mention of the "words of institution." There is no cup; instead of wine, fish figure twice in the early part of the narrative, though later on they disappear. Clearly the account has in mind the early Christian rite of breaking of the bread, celebrated daily (Acts 2), rather than the covenant-sacrifice meal, which was probably in the earliest days a single, annual Christian passover celebration. This daily breaking of the bread would have eschatological associations: it was an anticipation of the messianic banquet. The church's eucharist today combines or should combine both of these associations, the eschatological and the sacrificial. In the recent past, emphasis has been placed more on the sacrificial than on the eschatological aspect, but the imbalance is now being redressed.

All this applies to the meaning of Jesus' feeding of the multitude in the oral tradition. What of the evangelist's redaction? As we compare Matthew's account with its parallel in Mark 6:30-44, not only do we find Matthew's account abbreviated, but we see too that the role of the disciples in the episode differs considerably, and this must in fact be Matthew's chief redactional concern. In the opening dialogue between Jesus and the disciples (vv. 15-18 of our reading) Mark portrays the disciples as lacking in understanding, whereas in Matthew they understand well enough but are deficient in faith (H. J. Held).

In the actual feeding — the final paragraph of our reading — the disciples' role is more prominent, and what happens to the multitude is deemphasized. The disciples bring the bread to Jesus at his command (v. 18). Matthew explicitly states that the disciples "gave" the bread to the crowd. The evangelist seems concerned to underline the functions of the ministry as they are developing in his church.

The Homily
The Old Testament reading and the psalm slant our attention to the gospel reading toward the level of the oral tradition rather than toward Matthew's redaction. This suggests that the most obvious line for the homilist to take would be to expound the eucharist in terms of the eschatological banquet. He may, of course, if he sees fit, also emphasize with Matthew the role of the church's ministry in providing the food of the banquet. The ministers have an important role to perform, but it is Christ who really acts in the meal, giving through their ministry the bread of life.

The epistle reading provides an opportunity to deal with a perennial pastoral problem, that of suffering. People often expect Christian faith to serve as an insurance policy against suffering. The words of Jesus about taking up one's cross and the words of Paul in reading II show that there is no justification for this view. Both Jesus and Paul hold out to Christians a power that will enable them to cope with suffering and triumph over it. The Christian "solution" to the problem of suffering is not an intellectual argument but practical help in facing it.

Among the various kinds of suffering the Christian has to face is death itself. The New Testament pictures of what is to happen to the Christian after death are derived for the most part from Jewish apocalyptic and are therefore mythological in their imagery. They cannot, therefore, as such be the objects of Christian faith, for Christian faith cannot consist of holding extraneous mythological ideas. Rather, these ideas are used to express Christian faith. What that faith is, Paul expresses in nonmythological terms when he says that no one — not even death itself — can separate us from the love of God which we have experienced in Christ. That is the Christian "answer" to the problem of death. Is the love of God in Christ so real to us that when faced with death, we ask only his assurance?

BAPTISM OF THE LORD [B]

Gospel: Mark 1:7-11

Except for the gospel lesson, the readings today are the same as those already commented upon in series A above. Here the first paragraph of the Marcan lesson consists of John the Baptist's messianic preaching; the second is Mark's version of the baptism of Jesus.

The content of John's messianic preaching can be discussed at two levels: at the level of the "historical Baptist" and at the level of post-Easter Christian interpretation. That John, historically speaking, pointed to the coming of a stronger one (Yahweh himself, or a distinct messianic figure? — the answer is not clear) and that he spoke of this stronger one as a judge (baptism with fire in Q; Mark's "Holy Spirit" is clearly a Christianization, but "Spirit" could mean "wind," another image for judgment). It is historically unlikely that John recognized Jesus as the coming one — see the Baptist's question in Matthew 11:3 and parallels, and note also the modern critical view that Jesus' earthly life was only implicitly messianic, the expressly messianic interpretation of his person having arisen only after Easter.

Similarly we can discuss the significance of Jesus' baptism on the historical level. That Jesus was baptized by John is a fact beyond all reasonable doubt (although it has occasionally been questioned), for it caused much embarrassment to the early Christian community, especially in controversies with the continuing followers of the Baptist. The clue to its interpretation lies in Jesus' subsequent conduct. After his baptism he broke away from John and embarked upon a career of eschatological preaching and a healing ministry distinct from John's mission. Historically, therefore, Jesus' baptism must have meant for him a call to this mission. In various ways Jesus alludes to the decisive significance of his baptism (cf., e.g., the question of authority in Mk 11:27-33 par.).

In Mark these two traditions, John's messianic preaching and Jesus' baptism, have been Christianized. First, the two traditions have been tied closely together. This shows that for Christian faith Jesus in his baptism is marked out precisely as the stronger one whose coming the Baptist had predicted. Second, the stronger one becomes even in John's preaching a saviour rather than purely a judge; he baptizes with the Holy Spirit rather than with fire. Third, the baptism of Jesus is interpreted in an explicitly messianic sense by two narrative devices: the descent of the Spirit like a dove, and the voice from heaven. Here many Old Testament passages have contributed to the narration: the rending of the heavens, Isaiah 63:11; the descent of the Spirit on the Messiah, Isaiah 11:2; the voice from heaven, Psalm 2:7 and Isaiah 42:1. The Christology of the voice from heaven combines the motifs of the messianic Son of God and the suffering servant.

Mark, unlike Matthew and Luke, still describes the descent of the Spirit and the voice from heaven as inner experiences of Jesus rather than as objective events. Yet he intends his readers to overhear the voice and share the vision. It is therefore improbable, though many have interpreted the passage this way, that Mark thought in adoptionist terms. The voice *declares* rather what Jesus *is* in his ensuing history. In all that Mark proceeds to narrate about him Jesus shows himself to be the Son and the servant of God. Thus Mark means us to read the baptism of Jesus as the first in a series of secret epiphanies, revealing to us, though not yet to Jesus' contemporaries, the significance of the whole story which is to follow. That story is the account of God's eschatological act in Jesus, in his ministry and his death.

The Homily

In preaching on the baptism of Jesus in year B it would be appropriate to stress that Mark relates this event as an inner experience of Jesus — his call to a unique eschatological ministry — but that at the same time Mark, by recording it in his gospel, makes it for his readers an epiphany of who Jesus was. In the coming weeks we shall read of Jesus' words and deeds, culminating first in his transfiguration and then, after the move to Jerusalem, in his passion. The baptism of Jesus puts us in the right frame of mind to hear these stories, the whole story of our redemption. This liturgical pilgrimage with Jesus from Galilee to Jerusalem is a paradigm of our whole Christian life of discipleship, which was inaugurated for us at our baptism.

ELEVENTH SUNDAY OF THE YEAR [c] ✓
Reading I: 2 Samuel 12:7-10, 13

This lesson fits in neatly not only with the gospel but also with the epistle. All three readings proclaim the forgiveness of sin. The prophet Nathan acts as a father confessor to David. Nathan had previously stabbed David's conscience wide awake with the parable of the ewe lamb, confronting him with the brutal truth: "You are the man." David confesses, "I have sinned against the Lord," and Nathan declares that God has put away his sin. This is the classic Old Testament statement of the pattern of self-examination in the light of God's law, followed by confession of the sin as an offence against God and not merely against a fellow man (cf. Ps 51:4, "Against thee, thee only, have I sinned") and concluding with the confessor's declaration that God *has* put away the sin.

Two thoughts suggest themselves. First, a better and more scriptural name for the sacrament of penance, a juridical concept, would be the "sacrament of absolution." It is an evangelical sacrament, a declaration of the gospel of God's forgiveness in a concrete situation. Second, the tremendous authority conferred upon Old Testament prophet and Christian priest, not merely to *pray* that the sinner be forgiven but to pronounce him forgiven on God's behalf. He cannot presume to do this because of some innate personal authority of his own but because of his office and commission.

Responsorial Psalm: 32:1-2, 5, 7, 11

Instead of using the psalm which according to picturesque tradition David sang after the Bathsheba episode (Ps 51), we respond with another of the seven traditional penitential psalms. This is one which Paul used (Rom 4:7-8), preceded by the comment: "So also David pronounces a blessing upon the man to whom God reckons righteousness apart from works." Sacramental absolution is, like baptism and the eucharist, a sacrament of man's justification through the grace of Christ alone, apart from the works of the law.

Reading II: Galatians 2:16, 19-21

This is one of the classic Pauline statements about justification. To be justified means to be in the right with God. The basic quest of religion —
here Paul, Luther and Trent are at one — is to be in the right with God.
Paul had tried to get himself right with God by keeping the Mosaic law.
In his encounter with Christ he learned that this justification is something
not to be earned but to be received as a gift — through the Christ event.
It is not faith that is the primary cause of justification but the act of God
in Christ, an act described by Paul as "grace," sheer unmerited forgiveness
of the sinner. Faith is the subjective condition on the human side for receiving God's forgiveness. "Justification by faith alone" is shorthand for
"Justification by the grace-full act of God in Christ apprehended by man
through faith alone."

That we are justified by faith and not by the works of the law does not
mean that works have no place in the Christian life, for they are the fruit
of faith. The justified sinner now "lives with God." This new life is a
paradox. The Christian puts forth the utmost moral effort, and yet he
knows that it is not he, but "Christ who lives in me" (cf. the similar paradox in Phil 2:12-13). This paradoxical understanding of the relation between faith and works should help us to transcend the antitheses of the
Reformation.

But is the message of justification relevant today? Does contemporary
man, like Luther, seek a gracious God? Is not modern man's question, as
Martin Marty suggests, rather the question whether there is a God at all?
Was Bonhoeffer right in rejecting the notion that man first has to be
made a sinner — which he does feel himself to be — before he can hear
the gospel? Do we transcend the dichotomy between the Council of Trent
and the Reformation by saying that both sides were concerned about an
obsolete issue? Or is the question of justification not merely *one* approach
to the Christian message but rather its central concern? Do we answer
that question from an analysis of modern man or from a confrontation
with the message of the New Testament? These are basic issues for contemporary theology, exegesis and preaching.

Gospel: Luke 7:36–8:3 (long form); 7:36-50 (short form)

The crucial problem of this gospel is highlighted in the title: "Her many
sins were forgiven her, because she has shown great love." Taken at face
value, they suggest that the woman has earned forgiveness by her act of
devotion and so was justified by works and not by faith. But a closer

examination of the pericope shows that if this be the correct interpretation, it contains a glaring contradiction. The parable of the two debtors, which precedes our saying, makes love the *outcome* of forgiveness. To the question, Which of the two debtors will love more?, the answer comes: "The one, I suppose, to whom he forgave more." Later on it is stated that he who is forgiven little, loves little. This means that we can only understand the woman's action in one way. Her extravagant act of devotion is a sign that her sins, "which were many," have already been forgiven. How were they forgiven? By Jesus' acceptance of her, sinner though she was.

The longer form of the gospel, with its list of the women who also accompanied Jesus, might encourage the long-standing but erroneous tradition that Mary Magdalene was the woman whose many sins were forgiven and who therefore performed the extravagant act of devotion. There is nothing in the New Testament to warrant this identification. Moreover, our pericope may be a combination of two different incidents, that of a woman who anointed Jesus and that of a woman who washed his feet with her tears and dried them with her hair. The latter action is much more a sign of penitence than the former.

TWENTIETH SUNDAY OF THE YEAR [C] ✓

Reading I: Jeremiah 38:4-6, 8-10

This is the episode of Jeremiah in the miry cistern. Jeremiah has been predicting the impending destruction of Jerusalem as a judgment from Yahweh. Quite naturally the government regards this kind of talk as defeatist and treasonable. So they seek to silence Jeremiah by lowering him into a miry cistern. But on this occasion his life is spared through the good offices of Ebed-melech the Ethiopian.

The caption, "You bore me to be a man of strife for the whole world," which comes, not from this reading, but from Jeremiah's prayer (Jer 15:10, though the meaning there is probably "the whole land," i.e., Judah, rather than the whole world), indicates that our interpretation of this reading today should concentrate, not upon Jeremiah's deliverance, but upon the fact that his proclamation of the word of Yahweh brought him rejection and suffering. Thus the passion of Jeremiah foreshadows the passion of Jesus, adumbrated in the gospel reading.

Responsorial Psalm: 40:1, 2, 3, 17

A different selection from this psalm was used at Sunday 2 A and commented upon there. The reference to the miry bog in stanza 2 links today's selection with the preceding Old Testament reading. However, the main point today is the deliverance of the psalmist, whereas the main point of the Old Testament reading, as we saw from the caption and the gospel lesson, lies in the rejection that results from being a bearer of the word of God.

Reading II: Hebrews 12:1-4

This is the exhortation concluding the roll call of Old Testament heroes of the faith. They were "witnesses" to the power of faith to endure against every temptation to apostasy. The author of Hebrews pictures the Old Testament worthies as a host ("cloud" — a good classical Greek term) of spectators standing by a race track and cheering on those who are now running the same race as they did in their day. The race we have to run is "set before us" — i.e., we have been entered for it (cf. New English Bible) at our baptism. Like athletes stripping for the contest, we must strip ourselves of the constriction (this is the connotation of the adjective translated "which clings so closely") of sin.

But there is one who is even greater than the heroes of the Old Testament — Jesus, here described as the "pioneer and perfecter of our faith." Jesus in his earthly life was the pioneer because he initiated the way of faith — the way through suffering to glory (v. 2b) — and its perfecter because he completed it, thus enabling the believers to run the same race, through suffering to glory.

In the second paragraph of our reading, which begins a new section of Hebrews, the writer returns, as so often throughout his work, from christological exposition to ethical exhortation bearing directly on the situation in the church he is writing to. These believers were subject to hostility from their neighbors (pagan? Jewish?), but none of them have yet had to suffer martyrdom.

Gospel: Luke 12:49-53

This reading falls into two parts. The first (vv. 49-50) speaks of Christ's divine destiny to endure suffering. This first block of material is peculiar to Luke. The second part (vv. 51-53) speaks of the breakup of families caused by Christ and his message. This second block of material is paralleled in Matthew 10:34-35. We will first consider the two parts separately and then discuss the implications for Luke's theology of his procedure in bringing them together.

The first part consists of two "I-sayings" in which Jesus speaks of his mission as an accomplished fact. The first I-saying may well be authentic to Jesus, expressing his consciousness of prophetic mission, whereas the second I-saying, which refers to his martyrdom as a baptism (cf. Mk 10:38), looks like a *vaticinium ex eventu*, reflecting Christian baptismal theology (cf. Rom 6). This second saying is probably an amplification of the first, authentic I-saying by the early church. The "fire" (a symbol of eschatological judgment) which Jesus came to cast upon the earth will be his call to decision in face of his eschatological message. The church's additional I-saying, with its explicit reference to Jesus' death, will mean that after Easter Jesus' eschatological message was replaced by the church's kerygma of the cross. This, too, calls for a decision.

The second (Q) saying about the breakup of family ties reflects an apocalyptic tradition going back to Micah 7:6. "Social disruption has always been associated in the oriental mind with the reign of terror which will precede the age of salvation, and it is not surprising that it figures in Jewish apocalyptic as one of the signs of the end" (J. Jeremias). It is difficult to be sure whether this saying goes back to Jesus himself or only to the post-Easter community. The situation, however, was found both in Jesus' ministry as a result of his call to decision, and in the post-Easter community as a result of its kerygma of the cross.

By putting together these two traditions, the two I-sayings and the saying about family divisions, Luke shows that the breakup of families is a consequence precisely of the kerygma of the cross. Luke has recently been criticized and downgraded for having no theology of the cross. It is true that he does not, like Paul and Mark, speak of the cross as an atoning death — but see Luke 22:19b-20 [" 'which is given for you. Do this in remembrance of me.' And likewise the cup after supper, saying, 'This cup which is poured out for you is the new covenant in my blood.' "], which is now generally regarded as authentically Lucan and not a textual addition, and which shows that Luke was familiar with the idea of atonement in liturgy.

But even though Luke does not appropriate the language of atonement for his own theology, he does have his own theology of the cross. It is that the cross is for Christ the divinely willed pathway to glory (cf. 24:26). The believers in turn are drawn into the same pathway of suffering (see the second part of our reading). This suffering may take various forms: rejection, ostracism from family and society, and — though this is not specified here — martyrdom.

The Homily

This is one of the few Sundays when a common theme runs through all the readings, the epistle included. The message of today's readings may be summed up in the familiar saying: No cross, no crown. This was true of Jeremiah; of the cloud of witnesses; of Jesus, the pioneer and perfecter of our faith, who came to bring fire and to be baptized with a baptism of martyrdom; of the early Christians, who, as a consequence, experienced the breakup of families; and of many Christians today. It should not be hard for the homilist to identify the precise form the cross takes in the lives of contemporary believers and to encourage them to run with endurance the race for which they have been entered.

Index

	SUNDAYS AND HOLY DAYS		
	A	B	C
NUMBERS			
6:22-27	126	304	475
11:25-29		429	
DEUTERONOMY			
4:1-2, 6-8		419	
32-34, 39-40		383	
5:12-15		328	
6:2-6		442	
8:2-3, 14b-16a	207		
11:18, 26-28	517		
18:15-20		314	
26:4-10			1, 505
30:10-14			50
JOSHUA			
5:9a, 10-12			7, 513
24:1-2a, 15-17, 18b		415	
1 SAMUEL			
3:3b-10, 19		308	
16:1b, 6-7, 10-13a	157		
26:2, 7-9, 12-13, 22-23			501
2 SAMUEL			
5:1-3			97
7:1-5, 8b-11, 16		293	
12:7-10, 13			525
1 KINGS			
3:5, 7-12	230		
17:10-16		444	
19:9a, 11-13a	234		
4-8		411	
16b, 19-21			46
2 KINGS			
4:8-11, 14-16a	219		
42-44		406	
5:14-17			74
2 CHRONICLES			
36:14-16, 19-23		342	

	SUNDAYS AND HOLY DAYS		
	A	B	C
40:1-9	134	309	
1-17			527
41:1-13		323	
42:2-4	173		
45:9-15			62
47:1-8			34
50:1-15	211		
51:1-13		345	
1-15	149		
1-17			68
10-17	174		
54:1-6		427	
63:1-7	270		
1-8	241		44
65:9-13	223		
66:1-20	190		48
67:1-7	126, 237	304	32, 476
68:3-10			65
69:7-34	216		
13-36			50
71:1-17			493
72:1-13	128	307	478
1-17	105		
80:1-18		283	464
8-19	256		
81:2-10		329	
85:8-13	234	287, 401	
86:5-16	227		
89:1-18	219		
1-28		293	
90:3-17			66
12-17		435	
91:1-15			2, 506
93:1-5		451	
95:1-9	155, 243	315	57, 72
96:1-10	262		483
1-13	115	297	466
97:1-9			36
1-12	118	298	468
98:1-4		373	75, 457
1-6	120	300	469
5-9			95

	SUNDAYS AND HOLY DAYS		
	A	B	C
100:1-5			28
103:1-11			6, 511
1-12	245		
1-13		326	501
1-20		377	
104:1-30	200	379	
1-34			38
107:23-31		389	
110:1-4			42
112:4-9	142		
113:1-8			69
116:1-9		424	
10-19		337	
12-18		386	17
117			63
118:1-23		360	24
1-29		366	
2-24	178	361	
2-27			25
119:1-34	145		
57-130	230		
121:1-8			77
122:1-5			98
1-9	102		
123:1-4		398	
126			9
1-6		440	458, 515
128:1-5	123, 274	302	471
1-6		432	
130:1-8	160		
131:1-3	267		
138			54
1-8	239		496
145:1-14	221		83
2-18	248		
8-13			30
8-18	520		
10-18		406	
146:6-7	107		
6-10	139	422, 445	70
147:1-6		317	
12-20	207		

	SUNDAYS AND HOLY DAYS		
	A	B	C
PROVERBS			
8:22-31			40
9:1-6		413	
31:10-13, 19-20, 30-31	273		
ECCLESIASTES			
1:2; 2:21-23			56
WISDOM			
1:13-15; 2:23-24		395	
2:12, 17-20		427	
6:12-16	270		
7:7-11		434	
9:13-18			66
11:22–12:2			82
12:13, 16-19	227		
18:6-9			58
SIRACH			
3:2-6, 12-14	123	301	471
17-18, 20, 28-29			64
15:15-20	144		
27:30–28:7	245		
35:12c-14, 16-18b			79
ISAIAH			
2:1-5	101		
5:1-7	255		
6:1-2a, 3-8			495
7:10-14	110		
8:23–9:3	137		
9:2-7	114	296	466
11:1-10	104		
12:2-3, 4bcde, 5-6	172		461
22:19-23	239		
25:6-10a	258		
35:1-6a, 10	107		
4-7a		421	
40:1-5, 9-11		286	
42:1-4, 6-7	131		480
43:16-21			9, 514
18-19, 21-22, 14b-25		323	

	SUNDAYS AND HOLY DAYS		
	A	B	C
45:1, 4-6	261		
49:3, 5-6	134		
50:4-7	164	350	12
5-9a		424	
52:7-10	119	299	468
13–53:12	168	354	18
53:10-11		437	
54:5-14	171		
55:1-3	520		
1-11	171		
6-9	248		
10-11	223		
56:1, 6-7	236		
58:7-10	142		
60:1-6	128	306	477
13-21			473
61:1-2, 10-11		290	
62:1-5			482
11-12	117	298	467
63:16b-17; 64:1, 3b-8		282	
66:10-14c			48
18-21			63

JEREMIAH

1:4-5, 17-19			492
17:5-8			498
20:7-9	241		
10-13	216		
23:1-6		403	
31:7-9		439	
31-34		345	
33:14-16			454
38:4-6, 8-10			527

BARUCH

3:9-15, 32–4:4	172		
5:1-9			458

EZEKIEL

2:2-5		398	
18:25-28	251		
33:7-9	243		

	SUNDAYS AND HOLY DAYS		
	A	B	C
34:11-12, 15-17	276		
36:16-28	173		
37:1-14		378	
12-14	159		
DANIEL			
3:29-30, 31, 33, 32, 34	204		
7:13-14		450	
12:1-3		446	
HOSEA			
2:14b, 15b, 19-20			325
6:3-6	211		
JOEL			
2:28-32		378	
AMOS			
6:1a, 4-7			70
7:12-15		400	
8:4-7			69
JONAH			
3:1-5, 10		311	
MICAH			
5:2-5a			463
HABAKKUK			
1:2-3; 2:2-4			71
ZEPHANIAH			
2:3; 3:12-13	139		
3:14-18a			461
ZECHARIAH			
9:9-10	221		
12:10-11			44
MALACHI			
1:14b–2:2b, 8-10	266		
4:1-2a			94

	SUNDAYS AND HOLY DAYS		
	A	B	C
14-30	275		
31-46	279		
26:14–27:66	164		
28:16-20		385	
MARK			
1:1-18		288	
7-11		523	
12-15		335	
14-20		312	
21-28		315	
29-39		318	
40-45		321	
2:1-12		324	
18-22		327	
23–3:6		329	
4:35-41		391	
5:21-43		396	
6:1-6		399	
7-13		402	
30-34		404	
7:1-8, 14-15, 21-23		420	
31-37		423	
8:27-35		425	
9:2-10		337	
30-37		428	
38-43, 45, 47-48		430	
10:2-16		433	
17-30		435	
32-45			510
35-45		438	
46-52		440	
11:1-10		348	
12:28b-34		443	
38-44		445	
13:24-32		448	
33-37		284	
14:1–15:47		351	
12-16, 22-26		387	
16:1-8		357	
15-20		375	

	SUNDAYS AND HOLY DAYS		
	A	B	C
11-19			76
18:1-8			79
9-14			81
19:1-10			85
28-40			12
20:27-38			92
21:5-19			96
25-28			455
22:14–23:56			15
23:35-43			100
24:1-12			22
13-35	181		
35-48		364	
46-53			35

JOHN

1:1-18	121	300	469, 474
6-8, 19-28		291	
29-34	136		
35-42		310	
2:1-12			484
13-25		340	
3:14-21		343	
16-18	205		
4:5-42	156		
6:1-15		407	
24-35		409	
41-51		411	
51-58	209	414	
60-69		417	
7:37-39	201	380	
8-1-11			10, 515
9:1-41	158		
10:1-10	183		
11-18		367	
27-30			28
11:1-45	161		
12:12-16		348	
20-33		346	
13:1-15			17
31-33a, 34-35			30

	SUNDAYS AND HOLY DAYS		
	A	B	C
ROMANS			
1:1-7	111		
3:21-25a, 28	517		
4:18-25	211		
5:1-2, 5-8	155		
1-5			41
6-11	213		
12-15	216		
12-19	149		
6:3-4, 8-11	219		
3-11			21
8:8-11	160		
9,11-13	221		
14-17		384	
18-23	223		
22-27	200	379	
26-27	228		
28-30	230		
31b-34		337	
35, 37-39	521		
9:1-5	235		
10:8-13			2, 506
11:13-15, 29-32	237		
33-36	239		
12:1-2	241		
13:8-10	243		
11-14	102		
14:7-9	245		
15:4-9	105		
16:25-27		294	
1 CORINTHIANS			
1:1-3	135		
3-9		283	
10-13, 17	138		
22-25		340	
26-31	140		
2:1-5	143		
6-10	145		
5:6b-8	175	360	24
6:13c-15a, 17-20		309	
7:29-31		312	

	SUNDAYS AND HOLY DAYS		
	A	B	C
32-35		315	
9:16-19, 22-23		318	
10:1-6, 10-12			6, 511
16-17	208		
31–11:1		321	
11:23-26			17, 43
12:3b-7, 12-13			38
4-11			483
12-30			487
31–13:13			493
15:1-11			496
12, 16-20			498
20-26, 28	277		
20-27			62
45-49			501
2 CORINTHIANS			
1:18-22		323	
3:1b-6		326	
4:6-11		329	
5:14-17		389	
17-21			7, 513
8:7, 9, 13-15		396	
12:7-10		398	
13:11-13	205		
GALATIANS			
1:11-20		393	
2:16, 19-21			526
3:26-29			45
4:4-7	126	305	173, 476
5:1, 13-18			46
6:14-18			49
EPHESIANS			
1:3-6, 11-12			457
3-14		401	
17-23			35
2:4-10		342	
13-18		404	
3:2-3a, 5-6	129	307	478
4:1-6		406	

| | SUNDAYS AND HOLY DAYS | | |
	A	B	C
17, 20-24		408	
30–5:2		411	
5:8-14	158		
15-20		413	
21-32		416	
PHILIPPIANS			
1:4-6, 8-11			459
20c-24, 27a	248		
2:1-11	253		
6-11	164	351	13
3:8-14			9, 515
17–4:1			4, 508
4:4-7			462
6-9	256		
12-14, 19-20	259		
COLOSSIANS			
1:12-20			99
15-20			51
24-28			53
2:12-14			54
3:1-4	175	360	24
1-5, 9-11			57
12-21	124	302	471
1 THESSALONIANS			
1:1-5b	262		
5c-10	264		
2:7-9, 13	267		
3:12–4:2			455
4:13-18	270		
5:1-6	274		
16-24		291	
2 THESSALONIANS			
1:11–2:2			84
2:16–3:5			92
3:7-12			95
1 TIMOTHY			
1:12-17			68
2:1-8			69
6:11-16			71

	SUNDAYS AND HOLY DAYS		
	A	B	C
2 TIMOTHY			
1:6-8, 13-14			72
8b-10	153		
2:8-13			75
3:14–4:2			78
4:6-8, 16-18			80
TITUS			
2:11-14	115	297	466
3:4-7	118	298	468
PHILEMON			
9b-10, 12-17			67
HEBREWS			
1:1-6	120	300	469
2:9-11		432	
4:12-13		435	
14-16		437	
14-16; 5:7-9	169	355	19
5:1-6		440	
7-9		345	
7:23-28		442	
9:11-15		387	
24-28		445	
10:5-10			464
11-14, 18		447	
11:1-2, 8-19			59
12:1-4			528
5-7, 11-13			64
18-19, 22-24a			65
JAMES			
1:17-18, 21b-22, 27		419	
2:1-5		422	
14-18		424	
3:16–4:3		428	
5:1-6		429	
7-10	108		
1 PETER			
1:3-9	178		
17-21	180		

	SUNDAYS AND HOLY DAYS		
	A	B	C
2:4-9	186		
20b-25	183		
3:15-18	190		
18-22		333	
4:13-16	197		
2 PETER			
3:8-14		287	
1 JOHN			
2:1-5a		364	
3:1-2		367	
1-3			89
18-24		370	
4:7-10		373	
11-16		377	
5:1-6		361	
REVELATION			
1:5-8		451	
9-11a, 12-13, 17-19			25
5:11-14			27
7:2-4, 9-12			88
9, 14b-17			28
11:19a; 12:1-6a, 10ab			61
21:1-5a			30
10-14, 22-23			32
22:12-14, 16-17, 20			36